This book argues that there is no one best institutional arrangement for organizing modern societies. Therefore, the market should not be considered the ideal and universal arrangement for coordinating economic activity. Instead, the editors argue, the economic institutions of capitalism exhibit a large variety of objectives and tools that complement each other and cannot work in isolation. The various chapters of the book explore challenging issues in the analysis of differing institutional arrangements for coordinating economic activity, asking what logics and functions they follow, and why they emerge, mature, and persist in the forms they do. They conclude that any institutional arrangement has its strengths and weaknesses and that such institutions evolve according to a logic specific to each society. They also note that institutions continuously respond to changing circumstances and are not static entities.

D0880047

CONTEMPORARY CAPITALISM

CAMBRIDGE STUDIES IN COMPARATIVE POLITICS

General Editor
PETER LANGE Duke University

Associate Editors
ELLEN COMISSO   University of California, San Diego
PETER HALL   Harvard University
JOEL MIGDAL   University of Washington
HELEN MILNER   Columbia University
RONALD ROGOWSKI   University of California, Los Angeles
SIDNEY TARROW   Cornell University

OTHER BOOKS IN THE SERIES

CONTEMPORARY CAPITALISM

The Embeddedness of Institutions

Edited by

J. ROGERS HOLLINGSWORTH

University of Wisconsin, Madison

ROBERT BOYER

CEPREMAP, Paris

CAMBRIDGE
UNIVERSITY PRESS

AD G—3336

PUBLISHED BY THE PRESS SYNDICATE OF THE UNIVERSITY OF CAMBRIDGE
The Pitt Building, Trumpington Street, Cambridge CB2 1RP, United Kingdom

CAMBRIDGE UNIVERSITY PRESS
The Edinburgh Building, Cambridge CB2 2RU, UK   http: //www.cup.cam.ac.uk
40 West 20th Street, New York, NY 10011-4211, USA   http: //www.cup.org
10 Stamford Road, Oakleigh, Melbourne 3166, Australia

HB
501
C7257
1997

First published 1997
First paperback edition 1998

Printed in the United States of America

Typeset in Garamond #3

A catalogue record for this book is available from the British Library

Library of Congress Cataloguing-in-Publication Data is available

ISBN 0-521-56165-5 hardback
ISBN 0-521-65806-3 paperback

To Karl Polanyi, for teaching us about the dynamics of capitalism

CONTENTS

ACKNOWLEDGMENTS

The preparation of this book was facilitated by support from the American Institute for Contemporary German Studies, Washington, D.C.; the Center for Urban Affairs and Policy Research, Northwestern University; the Council for European Studies; the Ford Foundation; the Global Studies Program, University of Wisconsin (Madison); the Maison des Sciences de l'Homme, Paris; the Rockefeller Foundation; the Social Science Research Council; and the Swedish Collegium for Advanced Study in Social Sciences. The Bigorio Convento Santa Maria dei Frati Cappuccini (Switzerland) generously made its facilities available for a conference as the project neared completion, with funding from Delegato alli Problemi Universitario dei Ticino, departimento della Instruzzione e della Cultura, Switzerland.

Many scholars provided helpful criticism and input into all or parts of this project, and we gratefully acknowledge their assistance. In particular, we wish to thank Larry Dickey, University of Wisconsin; Hal Hansen, University of Wisconsin; Gary Herrigel, University of Chicago; Gerhard Lehmbruch, University of Konstanz; Yoshitaka Okada, Sophia University of Tokyo; Woody Powell, University of Arizona; Joel Rogers, University of Wisconsin; Marc Schneiberg, University of Arizona; David Soskice, Wissenschaftszentrum, Berlin; Burton Weisbrod, Northwestern University; and Richard Whitley, University of Manchester. As Ellen Jane Hollingsworth offered vigorous criticism and editorial assistance on each draft of the manuscript, the participants very much appreciated her generosity and excellent sense of what makes for a good book.

LIST OF CONTRIBUTORS

Catherine Alter is Dean and Professor at the University of Denver Graduate School of Social Work and Codirector of the Center for Evaluation and Assessment. She has researched a wide variety of service delivery systems and networks, and has used network analytic methodologies to do program and system evaluation. Her publications include articles, books, and technical monographs on networks as structures for the delivery of human services, with special regard for social welfare programs.

Robert Boyer is Senior Researcher in Economics at CEPREMAP, a research center related to Commissariat General du Plan and the national center for research (CNRS). He is a Professor at Ecole des Hautes Etudes en Sciences Sociales (EHESS). His research has investigated French and American long run economic history, with a special concern with growth, productivity, and inflation. He is a major contributor to the well-known *régulation* approach, which focuses on the impact of institutions and organizations upon cyclical economic patterns, long term growth, and external competitiveness. His publications include *The Regulation School: A Critical Introduction* (1990), *The Search for Labour Market Flexibility* (1988), and *The Return of Income Policy?* (with Ronald Dore and Zoe Mars, 1994).

William D. Coleman is Professor of Political Science at McMaster University, Hamilton, Ontario, Canada. Educated at Carleton University and the University of Chicago, he is the author of *The Independence Movement in Quebec, 1945–1980* (1984), *Business and Politics: A Study in Collective Action* (1988), and *The State, Business and Industrial Change in Canada* (with Michael M. Atkinson, 1989). The latter book was awarded the Charles H. Levin Prize for the best book in the fields of public administration and public policy by the International Political Science Association. His most recent book is *Financial Services, Globalization and Domestic Policy Change: A Comparison of*

North America and the European Union (1996). In addition to these books, he has written articles published in Australian, Canadian, American, and European journals dealing with Quebec politics, business–government relations, and the making of economic policy.

Benjamin Coriat is Professor of Economics at the University of Paris XIII University and is head of the Center for Research on Industrial Economics (CREI). He is a well-known scholar in the area of industrial relations, and has recurrently investigated the impact of new technologies on firms' organization and macroeconomic regimes. His recent books include *Made in France* (1993) and *Europe's Next Step: Organizational Innovation, Competition and Employment* (1995). He is a prominent member of the so-called French *régulation* school.

Lorraine Eden is an Economist and Associate Professor of Management, Texas A&M University, and Adjunct Research Professor, the Norman Paterson School of International Affairs, Carleton University. Her research specialization is multinational enterprises, focusing on the areas of regional integration, transfer pricing, and international taxation, and the North American auto industry. Recent awards include a 1991–92 Pew Faculty Fellowship, a 1992–93 U.S.–Canada Fulbright Research Fellowship at Harvard University, and a 1994–95 Carleton University Faculty Research Achievement Award. She has published four edited books: *Multinationals and Transfer Pricing* (with Alan Rugman, 1985), *Retrospectives on Public Finance* (1991), *Multinationals in the Global Political Economy* (with Evan Potter, 1993), and *Multinationals in North America* (1994).

Wyn Grant is Chair of the Department of Politics and International Studies at the University of Warwick, where he is also Chair of the Social Studies Faculty Graduate Committee and serves on a number of other University committees. His recent books include *Dairy Industry: An International Comparison* (1991), *Politics of Economic Policy* (1993), and *Business and Politics in Britain* (2nd ed., 1993).

Jerald Hage, Professor of Sociology at the University of Maryland and Director of the Center for Study of Innovations, has written numerous books in the area of organizations, his most recent being *Organizations Working Together* (with Catherine Alter, 1993). His other recent books include *Formal Theory in Sociology: Opportunity or Pitfall* (ed., 1994) and *Post-Industrial Lives: Roles and Relationships in the 21st Century* (with Charles Powers, 1992).

Fen Osler Hampson is Professor of InternationalAffairs at the Norman Paterson School of International Affairs, Carleton University, Ottawa, Canada.

He is the author of *Multilateral Negotiations: Lessons from Arms Control, Trade, and the Environment* (1995), *Unguided Missiles: How America Buys Its Weapons* (1989), and *Forming Economic Policy: The Case of Energy in Canada and Mexico* (1986). In addition, he is the coeditor of seven books on international affairs and Canadian foreign policy. In 1993–94 he was a Jennings Randolph Peace Fellow at the United States Institute of Peace. He is also the recipient of a Research and Writing Award from the John T. and Catherine D. MacArthur Foundation.

Paul Hirst is a Professor of Social Theory, Birkbeck College, University of London. He is author of *Associative Democracy* (1994), *Representative Democracy and Its Limits* (1990), *After Thatcher* (1989), *The Pluralism Theory of the State* (1989), and other works. He is a member of the editorial board of *Political Quarterly* and the editorial advisory boards of *Renewal* and *The Journal of Industry Studies*. He is the author, with Grahame Thompson, of a forthcoming book on globalization, *Globalization in Question* (1996) and of a major article on globalization in *Economy and Society* (21 [4] 1992).

J. Rogers Hollingsworth is Professor of Sociology and History and Chairperson of the Program in Comparative History at the University of Wisconsin. Recently awarded an honorary degree by the University of Uppsala (Sweden) and a Humboldt Research Prize, he is the author or editor of numerous books and articles on comparative political economy. His recent publications include *Governing Capitalist Economies* (with Philippe C. Schmitter and Wolfgang Streeck, 1994) and *Governance of the American Economy* (with John Campbell and Leon Lindberg, 1991). He is currently president of the Society for the Advancement of Socio-Economics.

Charles F. Sabel (B.A. and Ph.D., Harvard University) is a Professor at Columbia Law School. Author of *Work and Politics* (1982) and *The Second Industrial Divide* (with Michael Piore, 1984), he has published many essays in various journals. He was previously in the Department of Political Science at the Massachusetts Institute of Technology.

Philippe C. Schmitter has been on the Stanford faculty since the fall of 1986. He taught for many years at the University of Chicago (1967–82) and held visiting appointments at many universities in Europe, South America, and the United States. Before going to Stanford, he spent the previous four years as a professor at the European University Institute in Florence. Schmitter has conducted research on comparative politics and regional integration in both Latin America and Western Europe, with special emphasis on the politics of organized interests. He is the coauthor of *Transitions from Authoritarian Rules* (4 vols., 1986). He has been the recipient of numerous professional awards and followships, including a Guggenheim in 1978, and has been vice president of the American Political Science Association.

Wolfgang Streeck is Director of the Max-Planck-Institut for Social Research in Köln, Germany. He is the author or editor of the following books: *Social Institutions and Economic Performance: Studies in Industrial Relations in Advanced Capitalist Economies* (1992), *Beyond Keynesianism: The Socio-Economics of Production and Employment* (with Egon Matzner, 1991), *Industrial Relations in West Germany: The Case of the Car Industry* (1984), *Private Interest Government: Beyond Market and State* (with Philippe C. Schmitter, 1985).

Grahame Thompson is Senior Lecturer in Economics at the Open University. He is a member of the editorial board of *Economy and Society*. His latest books include *The Political Economy of the New Right* (1990), *Markets, Hierarchies and Networks* (ed., 1992), *The Economic Emergence of a New Europe? The Political Economy of Cooperation and Competition in the 1990s* (1993), *Managing the UK: An Introduction to Its Political Economy and Public Policy* (ed., 1993), and *America in the Twentieth Century: Markets* (ed., 1994).

Jonathan Zeitlin is Professor of History, Sociology, and Industrial Relations at the University of Wisconsin–Madison. He has written widely on flexible specialization and industrial districts in both contemporary and historical settings. Among his publications are *Reversing Industrial Decline? Industrial Structure and Policy in Britain and Her Competitors* (coedited with Paul Hirst, 1989), *Between Fordism and Flexibility: The Automobile Industry and Its Workers* (coedited with Steven Tolliday, 1992), and *World of Possibilities: Flexibility and Mass Production in Western Industrialization* (coedited with Charles F. Sabel, 1996).

COORDINATION OF ECONOMIC ACTORS AND SOCIAL SYSTEMS OF PRODUCTION

J. Rogers Hollingsworth and Robert Boyer

This volume addresses several distinctive but interrelated problems. First, it is very much concerned with identifying the various institutional mechanisms by which economic activity is coordinated, with understanding the circumstances under which these various mechanisms are chosen, and with comprehending the logic inherent in different coordinating mechanisms. Throughout Eastern and Western Europe as well as in North America during the 1980s, there was a dramatic shift toward a popular belief in the efficacy of self-adjusting market mechanisms. Indeed, the apparent failure of Keynesian economic policies, the strains faced by the Swedish social democratic model, and the collapse of Eastern block economies led many journalistic observers to argue that capitalism is a system of free markets that has finally triumphed. Some added that the more pervasive the market could become, the more impressively national economies would perform.

Paradoxically, during the same period, there was a rapidly accumulating theoretical literature that demonstrated that markets were not ideal mechanisms for coordinating transactions among actors when either the quality of products is uncertain, increasing returns to scale prevail, most future contingencies are uncertain, or there is a multitude of repetitive transactions within a truly decentralized monetary economy. Moreover, there has been increasing evidence that the market as a coordinating mechanism does not lead to the best economic performances in industries whose products have technologies that are very complex and change very rapidly (Campbell, Hollingsworth, and Lindberg, 1991; Chandler, 1977; Hollingsworth, 1991a; Hollingsworth, Schmitter, and Streeck, 1994; Piore and Sabel, 1984; Sabel and Zeitlin, 1985, 1996; Williamson, 1975, 1985). In short, the basic features of most modern economic activity point to the importance of coordinating mechanisms alternative to markets. Indeed, the history of twentieth-century capitalism demonstrates that nation-states have different trajectories of capitalist development, in which there is considerable variation in the role of markets and other institutional arrangements as coordinating mechanisms (Crouch and Streeck, 1996), and this volume focuses on several of these trajectories.

Second, the volume develops the argument that markets and other coordinating mechanisms are shaped by and are shapers of social systems of production. By a social system of production, we mean the way that the following institutions or structures of a country or a region are integrated into a social configuration: the industrial relations system; the system of training of workers and managers; the internal structure of corporate firms; the structured relationships among firms in the same industry on the one hand, and on the other firms' relationships with their suppliers and customers; the financial markets of a society; the conceptions of fairness and justice held by capital and labor; the structure of the state and its policies; and a society's idiosyncratic customs and traditions as well as norms, moral principles, rules, laws, and recipes for action. All these institutions, organizations, and social values tend to cohere with each other, although they vary in the degree to which they are tightly coupled with each other into a full-fledged system. While each of these components has some autonomy and may have some goals that are contradictory to the goals of other institutions with which it is integrated, an institutional logic in each society leads institutions to coalesce into a complex social configuration. This occurs because the institutions are embedded in a culture in which their logics are symbolically grounded, organizationally structured, technically and materially constrained, and politically defended. The institutional configuration usually exhibits some degree of adaptability to new challenges, but continues to evolve within an existing style. But under new circumstances or unprecedented disturbances, these institutional configurations might be exposed to sharp historical limits as to what they may or may not do (Friedland and Alford, 1991). Why these configurations occur within a particular place and time is a complex theoretical problem which has yet to be solved. In this volume, we tend to confine most of our attention to mapping the coordinating mechanisms that are important in various types of social systems of production.

Why do all of these different institutions coalesce into a complex social configuration which we label a social system of production? The literature suggests two contrasting interpretations. Part of the answer – indeed a controversial one – is that these institutions are functionally determined by the requirements of the practice of capitalism in each time and place (Habermas, 1975; Parsons, 1951, 1967). Another part of the explanation emphasizes the genesis of the actual configuration, via a trial and error process, according to which the survival of firms, regions, or countries is the outcome of complex evolutionary mechanisms (Maynard-Smith, 1982; Nelson and Winter, 1982). However, the problem is even more complex. Markets and other mechanisms for coordinating relationships among economic actors place constraints on the means and ends of economic activity to be achieved in any society. The other coordinating mechanisms include different kinds of hierarchies, various types of networks and associations (e.g., trade unions, employers, and business artisan associations; see Campbell, Hollingsworth, and Lindberg, 1991). These various coordinating mechanisms provide actors with vocabularies and logics for pursuing their goals, for defining what is valued, and for shaping the norms and rules by which they are to abide (Friedland and Alford, 1991). In short, in contrast to the logic of the neoclassical paradigm, we argue that economic coordinating mechanisms place severe constraints on the definition of needs, preferences, and choices of economic actors. Whereas the neoclassical paradigm assumes that individuals are sovereign, we argue that individual action is influenced by the hold that institutions have on individual decision making (Campbell, Hollingsworth, and Lindberg, 1991; Etzioni, 1988; also see the essays in Streeck and Schmitter, 1985; Hollingsworth, Schmitter, and Streeck, 1994).

That is the basic and common inspiration of the various authors whose work is presented in this volume, but this does not mean that they agree on every detail concerning their conceptions about institutions. Some authors come from industrial sociology and tend to emphasize the importance of labor institutions and their impact on the organization of firms and economic specialization. Others have studied the governance mode of national economies by a close investigation of sectoral differences across nations (Hollingsworth, Schmitter, and Streeck, 1994). Still others have tried to work out an economic theory that does justice to the impact of the wage labor nexus, forms of competition, and monetary regimes on long-term growth (Boyer, 1990). There is a political science perspective which argues that the architecture of economic institutions cannot be understood independently from a given constitutional order (see the paper by Sabel in this volume). Some authors try to extend transaction cost economics to the issue of networks, and in the process they develop the concept of adaptive costs

(Hage and Jing, 1996). Some are concerned with the economic rationale behind international regimes, whereas those with a background in political
science prefer to consider the issue of power in the building of supranational economic rules of the game, as well as in European institutions (see the
chapters in Part III).

Despite the different backgrounds of these authors, they share a common set of concerns about complementary institutions that constitute a
social system of production. Given their diversity of backgrounds, it is
remarkable how much they share in common. Their commonality suggests that the study of institutions and how they configure in a social system of production has the potential to facilitate a great deal of integration among the social sciences. This book aims at presenting a set of
common definitions in order to analyze the complementarity of institutions that may borrow their legitimacy and efficacy from quite different
sources. We do not argue that a process of homogenization among authors, approaches, and theories is fully achieved within this text. Nevertheless, the issue of the coherence of social systems of production is a unifying theme, which has already been discussed in previous publications
by several of the authors (Hollingsworth, 1991a, 1991b; Hollingsworth,
Schmitter, and Streeck, 1994; Hollingsworth and Streeck, 1994) and is
being pushed a step forward again in another study (Hollingsworth,
Whitley, and Hage, 1996).

The third problem the volume confronts is whether specific forms of
economic coordination are more likely to be used at some levels of society
than at others. There are four levels of society at which there may be variation in the dominant forms of economic coordination:

1. The regional level within a country.
2. The level of the nation-state.
3. Transnational regions, such as the European Community.
4. The global level.

Thus far, social scientists have made little effort to specify how institutions
for coordinating economic actors vary at these four levels of society. We believe we make some advance in the social science literature by confronting
these issues.

Basically, the post–World War II order has been built upon a rather stable international regime, which has allowed significant differences in economic institutions across rather independent nation-states. There has been
a blending of interdependence among nation-states, along with a significant

autonomy for national preferences, both of which are now being challenged by two shifts away from the national level. On the one hand, internationalization puts severe constraints upon some national economic arrangements, both through more competition among interdependent markets and through the building of supranational rules of the game. Both shifts constrain national governments, even though they participate in the development of organizations that undermine the autonomy of nation-states (World Trade Association, European Union, NAFTA, etc.). On the other hand, some sources for competitiveness exist at a lower level – e.g., the regional or even local levels where under some circumstances trust and tacit knowledge are better nurtured within communities and networks than within large firms and hierarchies.

This volume therefore surveys how each institutional arrangement for coordinating economic actors may evolve according to these two trends. Will an anonymous market mechanism replace previous coordination by the state? Or will alternative devices emerge, such as coordination by communities at the local level or various types of associations at the transnational level? Is there an ideal mix of institutional arrangements for coordinating economic actors for each broad system of production? Should we attempt to contemplate a future with the emergence of the different coordinating mechanisms that are associated with or complementary to a supranational state?

These questions are too complex and underresearched for us to reach definitive answers at this time. The reader may note a few different assumptions among the following authors, but this is not a weakness of the volume. Rather, it is a reflection of variation in knowledge at the frontiers of research on social institutions. Some of the authors think that the nation-state is bound to remain an important actor and level for the coordination of economic activity, and they argue that social systems of production will continue to have a strong national flavor (see chapters by Boyer, Hollingsworth, Streeck). Others suggest the importance of regional economies, especially for such emerging social systems of production as flexible specialization (Sabel, Zeitlin). Still others believe that the absence of any recognized polity at the international level provides a premium to market mechanisms (Schmitter). Clearly, the jury is still out, but readers will find new elements to feed their curiosity. Nevertheless, the book suggests that we are living in an epochal shift, from one mix of international-national-regional institutions to another configuration with different weights and feedbacks. At no single level are institutions able to triumph, nor will they vanish completely from any level.

A fourth issue the volume raises is whether forms of economic coordination and social systems of production are converging at the level of sector, region, nation-state, or global economy. The convergence thesis tends to assume that there is one best solution for organizing labor, raw materials, and capital in order to manufacture and distribute goods. The authors herein tend to express scepticism about such arguments of convergence.

FORMS OF ECONOMIC COORDINATION

All capitalist economies involve a matrix of interdependent exchange relationships, or transactions that occur among individual actors and organizations, either individually or collectively, in order to develop, produce, and distribute goods or services. Transactions occur among a wide range of interdependent actors, including producers and suppliers of raw materials, researchers, manufacturers, labor, and many others, who must routinely solve various problems such as raising capital, determining the quantity of output, setting wages and other conditions of employment, standardizing products, establishing prices, and communicating information about product quality to consumers. At a rather general level, economic coordination or governance is the process by which these problems are managed among various actors.

In many countries there has in recent years been a widely shared belief that the market is the most efficient institutional arrangement for coordinating economic activity, and that most alternative forms of collective activity and state intervention generally do more harm than benefit. In the eyes of many, there is considerable evidence to support such a view. Have not the various forms of Keynesian compromises led to stagflation, budget and external trade deficits, and capital flights? Have not the "socialist" regimes of Eastern Europe collapsed?

Under these circumstances, the market as an ideology has made an impressive comeback in the design of economic policies, at odds with the previous Keynesian orthodoxy. Similarly, within academic research in the social sciences, the neoclassical paradigm has become very pervasive and conquered new territories: The interactions and bargaining processes among conflicting actors have increasingly been modeled according to the concepts of economic rationality and market equilibria (Etzioni, 1988). The micro analytic neoclassical paradigm is individualistic, rationalistic, and utilitarian, and shapes not only much economic analysis but also public choice scholarship (Coleman, 1992) in political science (Ostrom, 1986), sociology (Hechter, 1987), history (North, 1981, 1990), and law (Posner, 1977).

The following essays do not deny the importance and utility of the market as a coordinating mechanism. However, the achievements of the market as a dominant mode of coordinating an economy rest less on the grounds of static efficiency, as argued by many who rely on the neoclassical paradigm, than on terms of dynamic efficiency (Leibenstein, 1966, 1976). In fact, the major achievement of the market has not been so much the invisible hand as formalized by modern equilibrium theory, but the stimulus to innovation which markets as coordinating mechanisms bring about, a neglected theme first put forward by Adam Smith.

In the following essays, we use a more restricted definition of market than that which exists in much of the contemporary literature. For us, the classic market occurs when transacting actors engage in decentralized, arm's-length bargaining, the parties are generally informally organized and remain autonomous, each actor presses his/her own interests vigorously, and contracting is relatively comprehensive. Actors then specify preferences and prices through contracts that, when completed, are self-liquidating and require no further interaction among the transacting parties. Moreover, the identities of the parties do not influence the terms of the exchange (Lindberg, Campbell, and Hollingsworth, 1991; Williamson, 1975, 1985). Basically, no durable relation is observed among economic actors, and the only purpose of the market adjustments is to make on-the-spot, coherent instantaneous transactions, without any concern about future strategies. Within this restrictive definition for markets, however, there are a lot of variants, for example, the African market for craft art, Christies' auction market for antiques, the Wall Street stock market, or the Chicago market for futures. These transactions can become embedded in, or shade off into, various types of networks (see the chapter by Hage and Alter on networks). Obviously this characterization of markets as a coordinating mechanism encompasses only a fraction of the transactions that occur in a capitalist economy.

Many scholars who operate within a neoclassical paradigm recognize that markets are not always the most efficient institutional form for economic coordination. Thus, according to Williamson (1975, 1985), economic actors often carry out their transactions within a firm or a hierarchy, in order to enhance efficiency, reduce transaction costs, and minimize the opportunism inherent in exchange relations. Alternatively, Alfred Chandler (1977, 1990) argues that it is the incentive to achieve lower production costs and greater economies of scale that encourages economic actors to do within firms – i.e., hierarchies – what might otherwise be done outside the firm – i.e., in a market. Thus, for Chandler, the modern corporation has been a functional response to the demands of large-scale markets and capital intensive but relatively stable technologies. Instead of conducting transactions among actors outside firms, the modern corporation has internalized the process. And for Chandler, this process has provided firms with the capability of overcoming risk and uncertainty and of achieving lower costs and higher levels of productivity through administrative coordination. While Chandler has little to say about industrial relations, Williamson (1985) and others (Marglin, 1974, 1991) argue that capitalists adopted the modern factory system in order to restrain opportunism and to economize on costly bargaining with labor. As human asset skills become more firm-specific and idiosyncratic, firms develop elaborate internal labor markets in order to promote training, discipline, promotions, and layoffs (also see Coase, 1960, 1981).

Also using the neoclassical paradigm, a number of scholars have identified and theorized forms of coordination that are neither markets, coordination within a corporate hierarchy, nor coordination by the state. This literature clearly acknowledges the limits of what organizations can do in coordinating economic actors (Arrow, 1974; Stinchcombe and Heimer, 1985). For example, Eccles (1981) has analyzed the quasifirm, Williamson (1985), Macneil (1978), and Powell (1990) have discussed long-term contractual relations among actors who are neither in a market nor within a firm, while others have elaborated on the concepts of coordination by network (Alter and Hage, 1993; Campbell, Hollingsworth, and Lindberg, 1991; Chisholm, 1989; Scharpf, 1993). In all of this, actors are neither integrated into a formal organization nor do they act autonomously within a market. Rather, actors are loosely joined to each other in long-term relationships that ensure their capacity to cooperate and collaborate with each other through repeated exchanges.

Much of the literature on economic coordination remains fragmented and unintegrated. However, by reflecting on these various forms of coordination, we might array them in a complex two-dimensional taxonomy, as in Figure 1-1:

- Along the vertical dimension, the economists' vision of a self-interested agent is contrasted with a more sociological perspective, according to which obligation and compliance with social rules are the guiding principles shaping human actions.
- Along the horizontal dimension, we display a continuum of modes of coordination. At one extreme, horizontal coordination takes place when many and relatively equal agents interact (e.g., in a well organized spot market). At the other extreme, inequality in power results in a hierarchical form of coordination whereby either a private or public hierarchy structures the interaction between a principal and an agent or between a leader and a follower.

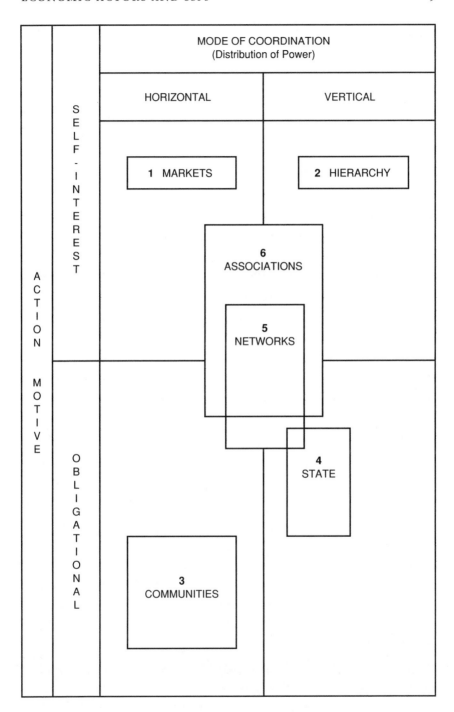

Figure 1-1. A General Taxonomy of Institutional Arrangements

Thus, institutional arrangements can be disentangled from this combination of the two dimensions: the nature of action motive on the one hand, and the distribution of power on the other. Markets (cell 1) combine self-interest with horizontal coordination transactors, and they reflect sensitivity to concerns about supply and demand, thus providing ex post an unintended equilibrium. Paradoxically, the more pure and perfect the market competition, the greater the need for codified rules of the games for coordinating economic transactions. Thus, collective associations (cell 6) and various forms of state intervention (cell 4) are required to enforce rules for transacting partners (Schneiberg and Hollingsworth, 1990; Schmitter and Streeck, 1981; Garcia, 1986). There are also networks (cell 5) which exhibit various mixes of self-interest and social obligation, with actors being formally independent and equal, even if some networks (the large firms and their subcontractors) partially rely upon unequal power and initiative. Networks may constitute all kinds of actors, ranging from those consisting only of firms to those that also include associations and the state.

Along the horizontal axis, actors are linked together in a high degree of integration, being joined within an organization or a firm: "hierarchy" is the generic term for this institutional arrangement (cell 2). Along the horizontal line, one recognizes the choice between market transactions and their integration within the firm. The work of Coase (1960, 1981) and Williamson (1975, 1985) uses the role of transaction costs in explaining the emergence of corporate hierarchies. But we must also turn to the vertical axis. The vertical axis deals with action motives. Toward the upper part of Figure 1.1, actors are engaged in individualistically oriented behavior, whereas toward the lower part, actors are more engaged in collective behavior and strive to cope with problems of common interest. Cell 3 – communities – consists of institutional arrangements that are based on trust, reciprocity, or obligation, and thus are not derived from the pure selfish computation of pleasures and pains. This is an unconventional perspective for most economists (however, see Arrow, 1974), but not for many anthropologists, political scientists, and sociologists (Streeck and Schmitter, 1985; Polanyi, 1946; Gambetta, 1988; Fukuyama, 1995; Sabel, 1992; Putnam, 1993). In the neoclassical paradigm, theorists argue that actors engage in those forms of exchanges that best promote their individual interest. If some structural conditions are fulfilled (absence of increasing returns to scale, the reversibility of transactions, absence of uncertainty, and complete contingent markets, with no collusion between actors), then the invisible hand theorem applies, and markets function quite well and also provide the optimum for society, therefore combining efficiency, harmony, and order. However, our view is that transacting exchanges may well lead to ruinous competition and excessive conflict. Indeed, there is variation in the extent to which ruinous competition occurs, depending on the social context within which individual transactions take place. Thus, it is important that we be sensitive to the social context in which transactions are embedded and that we understand the degree to which social bonds exist among transacting actors. Strong social bonds sustain relationships of trust and limit conflict. As Etzioni (1988) reminds us, social bonds exist at both the micro and macro levels of analysis. Micro bonds facilitate exchanges in a society, but at the societal level social bonds exist at the level of the collective – in the community or region, and among members of racial, religious, and ethnic groups. All other things being equal, the more powerful the social bonds among transacting partners, the more economic competition is likely to be restrained. Thus, most transactions occur not simply in an impersonal, calculative system of autonomous actors unrestrained by social ties – as implied by the neoclassical paradigm – but in the context of social bonds, variation in the strength of which leads to variation in levels of trust and transaction costs (Elam, 1992; Etzioni, 1988: 211; Granovetter, 1985; Streeck and Schmitter, 1985).

In short, the choices of coordinating mechanisms in Figure 1-1 are constrained by the social context within which they are embedded. And depending on the nature of that embeddedness, there is variation in the collective forms of governance, some of which are specified in the lower part of the figure. Because some obligational forms of coordination tend to exist simultaneously with those on the upper side of the typology, the forms of behavior in which actors are involved invariably influence the degree to which actors engage in market, networks, or hierarchy. Figure 1-2 provides many more varieties of coordination than does Figure 1-1. For example, Figure 1-2 accounts for the existence of various kinds of regimes at the global level. And at the subnational level, it includes such institutional arrangements as clans and clubs as well as communities. Moreover, it suggests that many forms of networks coordinate economic activity. There are forms of coordination by which actors collectively monitor one another. Examples are extensive corporate interlocks for information sharing, dominant firm pricing systems, and the *zaibatsu* and *keiretsu* systems in Japan. There are also collective forms of networks, sometimes called promotional networks (Campbell, Hollingsworth, and Lindberg, 1991, Chapter 1). These usually involve long-term relational contracting among various parties. Examples of promotional networks are the United States government's bringing together during the 1950s and 1960s a number of commercial firms and university-based scientists to work collectively to develop certain technologies and/or products in advance of commercial markets – e.g., semiconductors, integrated circuits, and computers (Hollingsworth, 1991a).

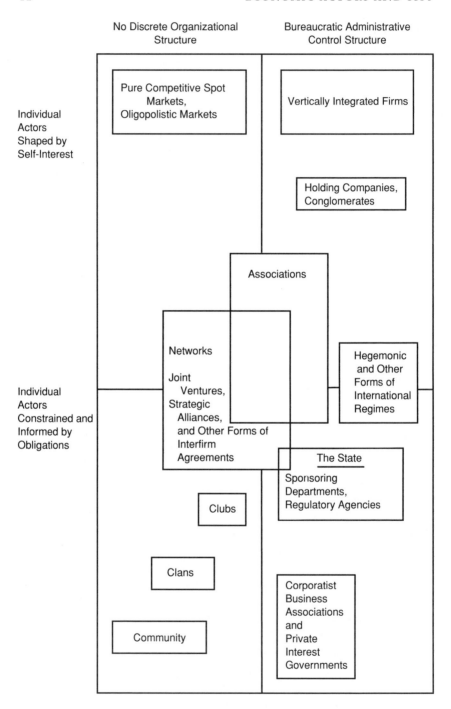

Figure 1-2. Modes of Coordination or Governance

Without the multilateral relations involving university research facilities, various agencies and departments of the United States government, and numerous business firms, it is unlikely that these technologies and products could have emerged in the United States at the time they did (Landau and Rosenberg, 1986; Nelson, 1982, 1991a). Other forms of promotional networking are the German system of apprenticeship training – a collective form of training in which unions, business associations, schools, the state, and students are all collectively involved (Streeck, 1989; Streeck et al., 1987); or the cooperative activities in which various firms engage in the Jutland region of Denmark, or in the central and northeastern regions of Italy – the so-called *terza Italia* (Brusco, 1982, 1986; Pyke, Becattini, and Sengenberger, 1990; Pyke and Sengenberger, 1992; Sabel, 1992).

While the Lindberg, Campbell, and Hollingsworth (1991) typology was a useful beginning for thinking about types of networks, it was somewhat oversimplified. Hence, in this volume Jerald Hage and Catherine Alter – drawing on a vast literature that has emerged about many kinds of networks in Europe, Asia, and North America – develop a more extensive typology of networks. However, they make a distinction between dyadic and multilateral relations among actors.

Another form of multilateral coordination consists of various types of associations. Unlike networks, clans, and communities, associations are formal organizations. Whereas markets, corporate hierarchies, and obligational networks tend to coordinate economic activity among different types of actors (e.g., producers with suppliers, capital with labor, producers with customers), associations typically coordinate actors engaged in the same or similar kinds of activities. Business associations and labor unions are some of the most common forms of associations for coordinating economic activity in capitalist economies (Schneiberg and Hollingsworth, 1990; Schmitter and Streeck, 1981).

Finally, there is the state, which is a coordinating mechanism quite unlike any of the others. It is the state that sanctions and regulates the various nonstate coordinating mechanisms, that is the ultimate enforcer of rules of the various mechanisms, that defines and enforces property rights, and that manipulates fiscal and monetary policy. At the same time, the state may also be an economic actor by engaging directly in production and exchange relations.

On both sides of the Atlantic, confidence is at an all-time low in the ability of states to enhance the performance of advanced capitalist economies. Neoliberal theorists believe that nonstate institutional arrangements are supposed to govern a capitalist economy. For them, the proper role of the state in economic affairs should be limited to securing the prerequi-

sites of conducting contracts (specifying property rights, using civil authority to enforce contracts, and providing national defense). One may argue
that the voluntaristic assumptions of neoliberal thinking are misplaced and
that, without much more substantial exercise of public authority by the
state, advanced industrial societies will be unable to develop their potential
for economic prosperity. The new growth theory has pointed out that, when
one considers the spillover effects of innovations, educations, and various
types of infrastructure, some supply-oriented interventions by the state may
promote efficiency and long run growth (Romer, 1986, 1990, 1994).

A perspective that emerges in several of the papers in this volume is
that neocorporatist theories of organized interest intermediation between
state and civil society offer the possibility for the assertion of public authority, but under limited state sovereignty. In short, neocorporatist state-
society interfaces enable economic actors to cooperate in developing long-
term obligations for themselves and others, thus preventing excessively
rational individuals from pursuing goals that are in conflict with their own
longer-term interests. And it is the state, interacting with the organized interests, that permits neocorporatist institutional regimes to outperform liberal ones in a variety of areas.

Each of these various coordinating mechanisms has its own logic – its
own rules, its own procedures for enforcing compliance, its own norms and
ideologies which help to reduce the costs of enforcement. These are sum-
marized in Table 1-1. Tables 1-1 and 1-2 provide further elaboration about
the various coordinating mechanisms one finds in almost every capitalist society. Table 1-1 lists the organizational structures, the rules of exchange, and
means of enforcing compliance associated with each type of coordinating
mechanism. While each type of coordinating mechanism has various positive features – or else it would be strongly opposed by various economic actors – nevertheless each mechanism does have particular failures, and these
are featured in Table 1-2. It is the contest between those who support and
those who oppose these various coordinating mechanisms that tends to lead
to transformations in coordinating mechanisms over time (Campbell,
Hollingsworth, and Lindberg, 1991).

The reader is urged to reflect on these two figures, which encapsulate a
number of arguments presented in this volume. The limitation of space pro-
hibits a full elaboration here about how these coordinating mechanisms relate to each other, but we do wish to summarize a few key findings of the
following chapters.

Let us consider the conventional and overdone polarization between
markets and state. It is striking that they cannot really compete since one is
built upon voluntary exchange and the other upon coercion and power. The

Table 1-1. Governance Modes: Rules of Exchange and Compliance

Governance mechanisms	Organizational structure	Rules of exchange	Individual means of compliance	Collective means of compliance
Markets	Free entry and exit Bilateral exchange or market place (Wall Street)	Voluntary spot exchange	Legal enforcement of control Regulations to maintain a public market	Norm of private property Legitimacy of free market
Communities	Informal membership evolves over long period of time	Voluntary exchange based on social solidarity and high degree of trust	Social norms and moral principles impose obligations Knowledge of others and reciprocity over time	Highly institutionalized norms and rules require members to accept "corporate" obligations
Networks	Semiformal membership Bilateral or multilateral exchange	Voluntary exchange over a time period	Contractual bonds Resource dependence	Personal relations Trust built outside the economic arena
Associations	Formal membership Multilateral exchange	Restricted to members Opposition insider/ outsider	Self-interest Reputation effect	Some degree of compulsion Partially private administration

Table 1-1. (*cont.*)

Governance mechanisms	Organizational structure	Rules of exchange	Individual means of compliance	Collective means of compliance
Private hierarchies	Complex organizations which tend to become bureaucratic	Restricted to members, exchange based on asymmetric power, bureaucratic rules	Rewards to individuals Asymmetric power, threat of sanctions	Highly institutionalized rules Members socialized into corporate culture, use of sanctions
State	Public hierarchy De jure and imposed membership	Unilateral action Indirect and global political and economic exchange	Exit (tax evasion, migration) Voice (vote, lobbying)	Coercion Social rules or norms

Table 1-2. Each Coordinating Mechanism Has Its Own Specific Failures

| Type of failure | Coordinating mechanisms | | |
	Market	Communities	Networks
Enforcement	Needs an internal enforcement authority	Needs trust and loyalty, often coming from outside (family, religion, ethnicity)	Need an external enforcement authority
	Facilitates collusion and imperfect competition	Compatible with various types of competition	May facilitate cartelization and monopoly
Public good and externality	Cannot provide collective goods or deal with externalities	Can internalize some collective goods (quality, training) but not others (welfare, general public goods)	Useful for enhancing quality and training but not very good in providing for societal general welfare
	Inadequate monitoring of technical change and innovation	Members tightly integrated into community, have limited capacity for innovations	Weak in the provision of collective goods
Efficiency	Some basic social relations cannot be provided by pure market mechanisms	Some goods cannot be delivered at sufficiently low costs	Slow to enhance efficiency and speed of adaptiveness, except in industries where technology is complex and rapidly changing
Equity	Facilitates inequality in income and wealth	Might lead to retarded development	When widely developed into industrial districts, networks may facilitate greater equality and income distribution. When weakly developed, networks tend to increase societal inequality

Table 1-2. (cont.)

Type of failure	Coordinating mechanisms		
	Associations	Private hierarchies	State
Enforcement	Usually relies on the state as an enforcer Resembles enforcement mechanism of cartels	Might enhance opportunistic behavior The ideal of internal markets might hurt incumbent workers	Needs controls external to state bureaucracy (judges, parliament, market) to correct state abuses Lobbies can capture public interest goals
Public good and externality	Useful for establishing standards and quality, for setting rules of competition in the industry Useful for providing many goods collectively that individual members cannot provide for themselves	Governance costs might exceed the benefits of internal division of labor Slow to react to changes in the environment	Can provide public goods but has difficulties in providing them in precise amounts Might fail in inducing technical change
Efficiency	Facilitates cooperation and X-efficiency but not allocative efficiency	Deficient in cooperation and X-efficiency	Can be highly bureaucratic and cannot easily deliver goods at low cost
Equity	Narrow encompassing associational structures lead to income inequality	Excessive multiplication of controllers (frustration and inequality)	Might enhance inequality (power and privilege)

market needs a minimal legal enforcement (implemented by the state) whereas taxation by the state assumes a sufficient level of wealth derived from the incentives brought by a market economy. The efficiency of markets is strong for private and divisible goods, but quite weak for the supply of major public goods (education, research and innovation, transport, infra-structures, etc.). The issue is not to select *one* coordinating mechanism but to combine *both* according to the nature of the objectives, the resource, and the characteristics of the goods.

The same conclusion can be derived for the relative merits of markets and firms (here private hierarchies). Again, it is difficult to conceive of pure forms – either exclusively markets or exclusively hierarchies – since it has been well known since Adam Smith's *Wealth of Nations* that the division of labor within the firm cannot be disentangled from the existence and extent of the market. Both forms have their efficiency (good static efficiency for the market, dynamic efficiency for firms) and inefficiency, often leading to con-siderable inequality. Neither networks nor communities are panaceas for eco-nomic coordination, without being configured with other forms of coordina-tion. Networks and communities may solve certain issues, but they raise other, no less severe problems. It is extremely important to recognize the im-perfection of any single coordinating mechanism if one is to comprehend the origin of the evolution and transformation of any institutional arrangement.

SOCIAL SYSTEMS OF PRODUCTION

Standard neoclassical economic theory tends to downplay the role of pro-duction and consequently of firms. Even the transaction cost theorists (Coase, 1960, 1981; Williamson, 1975, 1985), who tend to be concerned with analyzing the firm as a coordinating mechanism, are relatively uncon-cerned with the various components of a social system of production. In-deed, as long as there was widespread optimism about the efficacy of Key-nesian economics, there was relatively little concern among neoclassical economists with the supply side of the economy. Even in the opinion of most Keynesians, a group of experts ideally should be able to shape the size of aggregate demand while the supply side of the economy would be left to the two minimalist institutions of neoclassical economics – the markets and managerial hierarchies. In recent years, however, it has become increasingly obvious that some of the most competitive and successful patterns of indus-trial output and industrial production in capitalist economies do not derive from the neoclassical prescription of unregulated markets and corporate hi-erarchies complemented by a neoliberal democratic state. Indeed, empirical evidence has been growing for some years that certain highly successful production patterns require for their emergence and survival institutional arrangements the very opposite of the prescriptions found in the neoclassical paradigm (see especially Streeck, 1991, but also Aoki, 1988; Boyer, 1991; Hollingsworth and Streeck, 1994; Katzenstein, 1989; Piore and Sabel, 1984; Zeitlin, 1992). Thus, if we are to understand the behavior and performance of contemporary economies, concerns about production must be brought into the picture. But production involves more than technology. It is for this reason that a major concern of this volume is the social systems of production. The same equipment is frequently operated quite differently in the same sectors in different countries, even when firms are competing in the same market (Hollingsworth, Schmitter, and Streeck, 1994; Maurice, Sorge, and Warner, 1980; Sorge, 1989; Sorge and Streeck, 1988). Variations in production and process technologies are influenced, partly, by variations in the social environments in which they are embedded. In other words, firms are embedded into complex environments, which, among other things, place constraints on their behavior. Thus, a social system of production is of major importance in understanding the behavior and performance of an economy. How the state and the various coordinating mechanisms (see Figures 1-1 and 1-2) are related to particular social systems of production is an important concern of this volume.

During the past sixty or seventy years there have been several broad types of production systems in the histories of Western Europe, North America, and Japan. One system, labeled in the literature as a Fordist pattern of production, tended to produce highly standardized goods on a large scale with highly specialized equipment, operated by semiskilled workers. In contrast to Fordist production systems, there have been various types of flexible systems of production, each tending to produce a wide array of products in response to different consumer demands, supported by a skilled workforce with the capability of shifting from one job to another within a firm (Boyer, 1991; Piore and Sabel, 1984; Hage, 1980; Pollert, 1991; Sabel and Zeitlin, 1985, 1996; Streeck, 1991; Zeitlin, 1992, 1994).

Because both standardized and flexible systems of production are ideal types, it is important to emphasize that, for analytical purposes, each is subject to the usual strengths and weaknesses of ideal types. They are not meant to be descriptive statements about specific firms, industrial sectors, or individual firms at specific periods of time. Rather, they are heuristic devices to sensitize us to possible interrelationships that might exist among a broad set of variables or social categories. Neither type ever existed alone in space or time. Even where standardized mass production was the dominant technological paradigm, there were always firms – or even entire industries – that were organized on opposite principles. The two organizing principles were complementary one with another: Mass production tended to respond to the stable component of demand, while batch or medium-size production systems tended to cope with the variable part of the same demand. So the coexisting forms of production broadly shared the same short-run flexibility and long-run performance (Boyer and Durand, 1993). It is not uncommon for different components of varying social systems of production to exist simultaneously in a particular country (Herrigel, 1989, 1995; Pyke, Becattini, and Sengenberger, 1990). For example, standardized systems of production have always required customized machines or some form of flexible production. And flexible production processes have required standardized equipment and therefore some standardized production processes. In other words, the customization of products has long been based on the standardized production of component parts and equipment. Hirst and Zeitlin in this volume and others (see the special issue of *Economy and Society*, 1989, XVIII; Hirst and Zeitlin, 1990; Pollert, 1991; Sabel, 1991; Zeitlin, 1996) have made the important point that firms frequently engage in hybrid forms of production – producing both long and short runs of particular products, sometimes engaging in both flexible and standardized production – but that these hybrid type firms are usually embedded in a dominant type of social system of production.

Of course, flexible systems of production predate Fordist systems of production. Sabel and Zeitlin (1985), as well as others (Hounshell, 1984; Zeitlin, 1996), have demonstrated that flexible social systems of production existed in a number of nineteenth-century industrial districts of Europe and Great Britain, from Lyon to Sheffield, as well as in parts of the United States. Though flexible systems of production both pre- and postdate Fordist systems of production, we must recognize that in recent years flexible systems of production have become further differentiated into various subtypes. One system we label as flexible specialization production (FSP) and another we label diversified quality mass production (DQMP) (Aoki, 1988; Boyer and Coriat, 1986; Streeck, 1991). Originally, these models emerged from an analysis of local structural conditions; they mainly concerned coordination among actors and were less concerned with technology or innovation. For example, industrial districts with flexible systems of production existed long before the development of recent information technologies (Sabel and Zeitlin, 1985, 1996). On the other hand, the adoption of new, microelectronic production technology has increased the number of areas of the world that have social systems of flexible production (e.g., either flexible specialization or diversified quality mass production). Therefore, the existing institutions are filtering the emergence and diffusion of

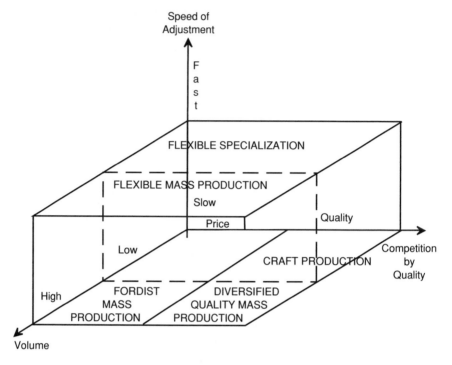

Figure 1-3. A Typology of Social Systems of Production

new technologies, and conversely, over the long run, some radical technological innovations seem to call for epochal changes in institutions, but the
success of those changes is not always guaranteed (Freeman, 1986).

In any case, the high flexibility of microelectronic equipment and the
speed with which it can be shifted to a variety of products have permitted
previous mass producers to engage in customized quality production and
producers with only small batches of specific items to shift to larger batches
of production. Thus, there has been a restructuring of two different trajectories of production: Craft producers have been able to extend their production
volume without sacrificing their high quality standards and customization,
and many mass producers have had the capacity to upgrade their product design and quality and thus to reduce the pressures of price competition and
shrinking mass markets (Sorge and Streeck, 1988). The multidimensional
classification portrayed in Figure 1-3 is a useful starting point for understanding these distinctions. Note in the figure that there has been some
blending of the characteristics from the standardized mass production with
the flexible specialization system to produce the system of diversified quality mass production. Forms of flexible specialization existed during the nine-

teenth century, for example in the American textile industry (Scranton, 1984). As dominant forms of production, however, they were defeated by standardized mass production, at least in the United States but not everywhere else, especially in Germany and Italy (Herrigel, 1995; Piore and Sabel, 1984; Sabel and Zeitlin, 1985, 1996). There was no single and unique pattern of industrialization. Rather, it was possible in various countries for contrasting social systems of production to coexist and this remains true today.

There are certain similarities between the systems of flexible specialization (FSP) and diversified quality mass production (DQMP). Rather than viewing these two perspectives as competing or conflictual, it is best to see them as complementary (Elam, 1992; Sorge, 1989; Sorge and Streeck, 1988). In contrast with social systems of standardized mass production, both FSP and DQMP require workforces with broad levels of skills, i.e., employees who have "learned to learn" about new technologies and who can work closely and cooperatively with other employees and management. Moreover, these systems tend to require that firms develop long-term stable relations with their suppliers and customers.

Social systems of mass production have performed best when firms serve large and stable product markets, and have products and process technologies that are relatively stable or have a low level of technological innovation (Chandler, 1962, 1977, 1990). However, technological complexity and the speed of technical change are not to be confused. For example, the car industry used to implement rather simple components but nevertheless exhibited complex coordination problems (Tolliday and Zeitlin, 1992). Markets, corporate hierarchies, and inegalitarian and short-lived networks are the dominant forms of coordination in social systems of mass production. On the other hand, social systems of flexible specialization and diversified quality mass production tend to function more effectively when firms are responding to small market niches with product markets that are unstable and volatile (the Italian garment industry) or whose product and process technologies change rapidly (microelectronics, biotechnologies) and are quite complex (aircraft industry, luxury cars). For firms to perform well under these circumstances, they require different forms of coordination from those that are most effective for social systems of mass standardized production.

Markets and hierarchies as coordinating mechanisms can work effectively in mass standardized systems of production even if the transacting actors are embedded in an impoverished institutional environment – one in which such collective forms of coordination as associations and promotional networks (cells 5 and 6 in Figure 1-1) are poorly developed (Hollingsworth, 1991a, 1991b). But social systems of flexible specialization and diversified quality mass production work best when transacting actors are embedded in an institutional environment in which collective forms of coordination are highly developed. Broadly speaking, both of these social systems of production are basically incompatible with neoliberal regimes of unregulated economies (Pyke and Sengenberger, 1992; Streeck, 1991). Nevertheless, the relative success of the Japanese transplants in the United States and the United Kingdom does challenge the view that these alternatives to typical Fordism cannot be implemented in countries with weakly developed collective forms of coordination (Boyer, 1991; Florida and Kenney, 1991; Kenney and Florida, 1993; Oliver and Wilkinson, 1988). The long-term success of flexible specialization and diversified quality mass social systems of production requires a high degree of trust and cooperation among economic actors – between workers and managers within firms and between firms on the one hand and their suppliers and customers on the other (Boyer and Orlean 1991; Hollingsworth, 1991a, 1991b). This can be organized in some localities with a strong tradition of providing the collective goods of trust and cooperation (examples are the German cooperative partnership between labor and management and the Italian industrial districts). Firms operating in isolation from such collective goods may provide local examples of flexible production or diversified quality mass production, at least in the short run (e.g., Japanese transplants in the United States and the United Kingdom). But in the long run, successful firms that are involved in flexible social systems of production must engage in cooperative behavior with suppliers, competitors, and employees far in excess of what is needed for markets and hierarchies to function effectively and in excess of what single firms can develop for themselves (Streeck, 1991; Hollingsworth and Streeck, 1994).

Sabel's essay in this volume and his writings elsewhere (1991, 1992) are insightful discussions of the relationship between collective behavior and trust. Trust is an important lubricant in a capitalist economy, and it enhances efficiency in transactions (Arrow, 1973; Etzioni, 1988; Fukuyama, 1995). As consumer demand becomes more diversified, technology more complex, and the economy more decentralized, there is potentially more uncertainty among actors and therefore trust may erode. Yet only with high degrees of trust among actors can flexible systems of production be sustained (Elam, 1992; Luhman, 1979).

ALTERNATIVE LEVELS OF COORDINATION

SUBNATIONAL REGIONS AND NATION-STATES

In this as in our previous work (Hollingsworth, Schmitter, and Streeck 1994), we focus on economic coordination as occurring along two axes: one spatial-territorial and the other economic-sectoral. In previous work, we were primarily concerned with economic coordination at the sectoral level, both within and across countries. In this volume, we are also concerned with variations in forms of coordination and social systems of production within particular spatial-territorial areas. Specifically, we are interested in understanding the interaction of spatially-based forms of coordination with social systems of production. Economic coordination varies by territory, for social institutions are rooted in local, regional, national, or even transnational political communities with their shared beliefs, experiences, and traditions.

By *region,* we mean a territorial area with little or no state sovereignty over its borders. It is in particular regions within countries where the social systems of flexible specialization have been located. Obviously, the development of regional economies does not necessarily lead to social systems of flexible specialization. The heavy concentration before World War II of the automobile industry in and around Detroit and the textile industry in parts of South Carolina are examples of how mass standardized producers were often spatially concentrated, and this is a subject about which geographers have written very widely. But the concern here is with the existence of regional economies having a high concentration of small firms that are integrated into a social system of flexible production, a subject about which Sabel and Zeitlin have written both insightfully and extensively (Sabel and Zeitlin, 1985; Zeitlin, 1992). Historically, when the demand for products was differentiated and diverse, different forms of production have existed from those in use when demand has been more stable and homogeneous. In general, the more stable the demand and the less frequent the change in technology, the more firms have found it advantageous to organize production in large vertically-integrated firms and to reap economies of scale by producing standardized products and extending the market. Historically, such a process tended to justify the large investment in single-purpose machines operated by relatively low-skilled workers (Chandler, 1962, 1977, 1990; Sabel and Zeitlin, 1996). But when demand has been differentiated, markets have been volatile, and/or technology has changed rapidly, then firms have chosen flexible strategies – flexible machines, labor, and/or marketing. More specialized firms must constantly innovate. Being relatively small, however, they require a host of common services that individual firms lack the capacity to provide: sophisticated training facilities in order to develop a highly skilled labor force, a continuing supply of credit, and complex marketing capacity. In response to these needs, producers in some areas have engaged with other firms – sometimes competitors, sometimes firms in complementary industries – to produce collective goods. The collective activities have historically varied, but the most common have been cooper-

ative training institutes and cooperative marketing facilities (e.g., to forecast fashion trends, to monitor foreign technical standards, to establish cooperative sales facilities, cooperative finance and credit programs, cooperative sales initiatives, local trademarks). Over time and across industries, the
cooperative mechanisms for this kind of coordination have varied, but without artisan, employer, and/or worker associations, this form of collaboration
and cooperation has failed. In sum, for a social system of flexible production
to survive, firms must be integrated into collective institutions which can
balance cooperation and competition (Zeitlin, 1992, 1994).

Where social systems of flexible production are more developed, the
boundaries between firms and their environment are extremely blurred – so
much so that such firms are very reluctant to move from one region to another. Thus, local governments in Sardinia and Sicily have a limited capacity to attract firms from Prato even by offering free land, cheap labor, and
low taxes because the Prato firms are embedded in all kinds of collective
institutions that provide a variety of world-class inputs. The underlying social conditions that facilitate the development of such a social system of
production vary. Sometimes that development has emerged from a population viewing itself as a religious minority, while elsewhere it has emerged
from a common ethnic base, common craft pride, common forms of pro-
fessionalization, or common political affiliation. Without some forms of
common social bonds, it has historically been difficult to develop the collective institutions which are prerequisites for social systems of flexible
production, though as Sabel (1992) has argued, common social bonds are
not a necessary condition for an emergence of such a system (also see
Zeitlin, 1992).

Examples in the contemporary world of regions with social systems of
flexible production include Jutland in western Denmark, the Smaland region in southern Sweden, and areas in the central and northeastern parts
of Italy. Each of these districts produces highly specialized products. For
example, Bologna produces machine tools and small appliances, while
Tuscan and Venetian towns manufacture textiles and footwear. Whether
in the contemporary world or in the nineteenth century, social systems of
flexibly specialized production involved an integration of petty entrepreneurship, family-based small scale artisan firms, and/or municipalism.
While flexibly specialized systems of production are pursued in a variety
of institutionalized forms, there are limits to their ranges of variation
(Grabher, 1993; Pollert, 1991; Sabel, 1992). Clearly, unregulated markets
do not provide adequate incentives for the survival of flexible social systems of production. Cooperation among competing producers, a minimum of conflict between employers and their employees, and long-term

stable relations with suppliers and customers are prerequisites for the survival of flexible production systems.

Occasionally, the national state has been a modest actor in facilitating the emergence and persistence of flexible specialized production systems, but more frequently regional and local governmental authorities have promoted this form of social system, as with various German *länder* or Italian local authorities (Herrigel, 1989; Sabel, 1992; Sabel and Zeitlin, 1996; Zeitlin, 1992). For example, the state has often facilitated the development of training institutes for labor, and provided low cost loans as well as market and export information. However, the state alone has rarely been capable of promoting and developing the institutions necessary for the emergence of a flexible social production system. Of course, public procurement for defense and specific research programs have generally benefited large firms and conglomerates in developing plants with flexible production capacities (e.g., the aviation industry), and various governmental policies can be effective in promoting a high density of medium-sized and innovative firms in some industrial sectors. But the socioeconomic environment within which firms are embedded is the key to whether a social system of flexible production can emerge in a region.

Thus far, countries such as the United States and the United Kingdom have been deficient in the communitarian infrastructure necessary for the emergence of institutions with the capability of generating the high levels of trust among competing economic actors that are essential for successful social systems of production (Brusco, 1982; Kristensen, 1986; Sabel and Zeitlin, 1985, 1994b; Storper, 1989; Zeitlin, 1994). Nevertheless, this is not absolutely fatal, since public authorities can use existing institutions to mimic or help in implementing flexible systems of production. In France, for example, the Ministry of Telecommunications helped to launch Minitel during the 1980s. This is a network, the infrastructure of which was provided by public funding, but the content of which was defined by a myriad of private software firms. The outcome was finally equivalent if not superior to that of a completely private, flexible form of production (Phan, 1991). But for flexible forms of production to become widespread, firms must be embedded in a social environment very different from that which exists in most of France.

In a few environments, the Americans have also developed small regions of social systems of flexible production with the kind of cooperation among competitors described above. The dairy industry in the upper middle west is such an example (Young, Lindberg, Hollingsworth, 1989), as is Silicon Valley (Saxenian, 1994). But such districts have been rare in twentieth-century America.

Social systems of diversified quality mass production have certain similarities with those of flexible specialization. Both social systems of production are embedded in distinctive environments and are not easily imitated by other societies. But whereas firms with a high degree of flexible specialization tend to be small artisanal firms located in modest-sized regions – though there are exceptions – the key to understanding diversified quality mass production is the increased flexibility of large firms. New technology has enabled large firms to make their production functions more flexible and to reduce the batch size of specialized products inside large systems of production. Whereas social systems of flexible specialization engage in diversified low-volume production and emphasize economies of scope, diversified quality mass production combines economies of both scope and scale and is thus able to emphasize quality differentiated mass production. In other words, scale is one of the major variables differentiating diversified quality mass production from flexible specialized production systems. Significantly, the territorial space in which firms are embedded also differs. In contrast to flexible specialization social systems of production, diversified quality mass social production systems are generally either embedded in much larger regions or are more coterminous with an entire nation-state (Mueller and Loveridge, 1995). Nevertheless, wherever flexible social systems of production survive – whether they are systems with small firms engaged in flexible production or systems with larger firms engaged in diversified quality mass production – they are tightly integrated with the society's business associations and labor unions, the industrial relations system, the capital markets, and the systems of training for both labor and management of an industrial district.

It is difficult to disentangle what differences between flexible specialization systems of production and diversified quality mass of production are related to their inner and theoretical properties and what parts of their systems derive from the fact that they have evolved in distinctive regions or nations with idiosyncratic institutional configurations. A priori, mass production presupposes institutions that transcend a region in a particular nation-state: a vast transportation system and other kinds of infrastructure, large quantities of capital, macroeconomic stabilization in order to prevent large and unexpected economic fluctuations, etc. These factors suggest the need for a host of *national* institutions. Historical analyses and international comparisons demonstrate that diversified quality mass production systems are *actually* embedded in national sociopolitical structures, while flexible specialization systems can be embedded in subnational sociopolitical structures.

Diversified quality mass social systems of production are unlikely to exist unless they are embedded in national sociopolitical structures that are democratic corporatist in nature. Examples of contemporary societies with relatively strong neocorporatist institutional arrangements – and hence strong diversified quality mass forms of social production – were Germany and Sweden of the 1980s. Both were highly developed systems of trade unions and business associations that were embedded in an ideology of partnership, that mitigated against intense class conflict, and that emphasized a careful balancing of conflict with cooperation among competing firms. For students of democratic corporatism, Japan poses a problematic case. Japan, like most democratic corporatist societies, has both peak associations of business, and, at the level of the firm, a strong ideology of social partnership between labor and capital. But there is an absence of well-organized labor unions at the level of the nation-state. Nevertheless, the strong emphasis on social partnerships that exists in Japan leads many scholars to classify it as a democratic corporatist society. Therefore, it is understandable that Japan also has a social system of diversified quality mass production (Katzenstein, 1985; Pempel and Tsunekawa, 1979; Schmitter and Lehmbruch, 1979). But whereas the system of strong labor unions and business associations in various European countries has led to a social system of production complemented by a well-developed social democratic neocorporatist welfare state, the weakness of national unions in Japan means that the dominant Japanese social system of production is embedded in a somewhat different type of corporatist political economy. This has been labeled as microcorporatism (Boyer, 1991), in opposition to conventional macro- or even mesocorporatism, typical of social democratic countries.

How do we explain the absence of a diversified quality production system in the United States? Indeed, why did its opposite – a system of mass standardized production – excel there and in many respects persist? In general, the larger the spatial-territorial area in which a social system of production is embedded, the larger the number of parties and interests that must be involved in efforts to develop national forms of collective coordination – e.g., labor unions, business associations, etc. Thus, a country as large as the United States – in contrast with smaller democracies – has a very complex economy (e.g., large numbers of industrial sectors), as well as regions with uneven levels of development and racial, religious, and ethnic diversity. With so much heterogeneity of interests, it has historically been more difficult to develop highly institutionalized collective forms of economic coordination. When these societywide collective forms of coordination are either absent or weak, markets and corporate hierarchies are more prominent as forms of coordination, and as a result Fordist systems of production are more likely to occur (Hollingsworth, 1991a, 1991b). Nevertheless, as Hage and Alter argue in their chapter on networks in this volume, a variety of cooperative ventures may exist among firms even in an environment that is weak in highly institutionalized forms of collective behavior. Hence, in the United States there are among business firms numerous joint ventures, cross-licensing agreements, franchises, and various forms of strategic alliances (Porter, 1986, 1990). Thus in the film, biotechnology, publishing, microelectronics, or software industries, there is a great deal of networking as a form of economic coordination (Powell, 1990). To some observers, this kind of collaboration resembles the type of industrial districts in which flexible forms of social production flourish, but most of these forms of networking are not embedded in the same kind of rich institutional environment which Sabel, Zeitlin, and others have discussed in their analyses of industrial districts. In most societies, geographical concentrations of related industries facilitate some degree of cooperation and trust, but these are generally developed quite modestly unless they are accompanied by an environment in which firms have membership in highly developed organizations of a collective nature. Again, the success of Japanese transplants to North America and Britain suggests that it may be possible for quasi-diversified quality mass production to emerge in a few industries, even within the more unfriendly institutional environments of these countries (Florida and Kenney, 1991; Kenney and Florida, 1988; Oliver and Wilkinson, 1988). In all these examples, firms succeed in building long-term relationships and trust, either by carefully selecting the workers to be hired, by training the subcontractors (Japanese transplants), by benefiting from personal links developed within universities (the biotech industry), or by developing business contacts over a long period of time (the movie and publishing industries). However, these are a very few industries in a very large national economy. And Hollingsworth argues in this volume that a flexible social system form of production is not likely to become pervasive in the American economy unless the national system of training, the industrial relations system, financial markets, state structure and policies, and political culture are fundamentally transformed.

COORDINATION AT THE TRANSNATIONAL REGION AND GLOBAL LEVELS

At the level beyond the nation-state, whether at the global level or at the multinational regional level such as the European Union, collective forms of coordination, such as associations and unions, are either weakly developed or nonexistent. Moreover, the power of states as coordinating actors is weak at the transnational level. However, regardless of the spatial-territorial location, whether at the subnational region, the nation-state, or the transnational level, there is a need for some institutional arrangement to coordinate relations among economic actors. Indeed, irrespective of the territorial level at which economic coordination is to occur, economic actors confront many of the same problems: the issues of promoting efficiency among transacting partners, reducing macroeconomic instabilities, minimizing distributional conflicts, reducing conflicts and resolving disputes, and monitoring compliance in regard to domestic and/or international norms and rules.

Economic coordination at the international level may occur in many forms (Risse-Kappen, 1995). Just as economic coordination in domestic economies is carried out by different types of institutional arrangements (see Figure 1-1), this is also true at the transnational level. At the lowest level of control, the market is the most prominent form of coordinating transactions among unrelated firms. At a higher level of control, there may be coordination through hierarchies such as transnational corporations or collective forms of coordination such as international trade associations or international cartels. Industries that are generally coordinated by markets – irrespective of the level – are securities, banking, textiles, apparel, shoes, and hotels, while industries coordinated by corporate hierarchies are highly capital intensive ones, such as chemicals, bauxite, oil, aircraft, and automobiles (Chandler, 1962, 1977, 1990; Hollingsworth and Lindberg, 1985; Porter, 1990). Some industries are highly cartelized, e.g., illegal drugs and from time to time oil, coffee, cocoa, and bauxite. Of course, coordination at the global level may also involve actions by nation-states, and their form of coordination may also vary from low control (e.g., bilateral agreements) to high control structures (supranational government, colonial empires). International regimes are a form of middle-level control among states, somewhat analogous to international cartels or trade associations among unrelated firms (Keohane, 1984; Krasner, 1983; Rosenau and Czempiel, 1992; Young, 1986, 1989).

How do international regimes emerge and persist over several decades? For some authors (Kennedy, 1987), the historical record suggests that a hegemonic power has been necessary for either the establishment or the persistence of international regimes. But when a hegemonic power is decaying without any evident successor, the stability of the international system is at stake. The 1920s provide a suggestive example of such a collapse (Kindleberger, 1978). Other authors argue that because international regimes provide public goods and lower transaction costs among their members, it is in the rational self-interest of states to abide by the rules and norms of regimes even if there is no hegemony to enforce them (see Eden and Hampson in this volume; also Keohane, 1984; Snidal, 1985, 1991). Of course, this argument assumes a "pure" coordination problem and the absence of any conflict of in-

terests. If, on the contrary, the configuration of the system is close to a prisoner dilemma problem, the rational strategy of each nation will not lead to
the emergence of cooperation. Conflict among international actors might
then become severe, since a great deal of economic coordination takes place
by markets and hierarchies at the global level.

Ultimately, it is the existence of international regimes that institutionalize the norms and rules that allows economic actors to carry out most effectively their transactions at a global level. Eden and Hampson (in this volume) provide a discussion of a few prominent international regimes in the
contemporary world and the kinds of problems that they attempt to confront. Just as a number of the following papers argue that there are institutional arrangements that attempt to reduce transaction costs within the
nation-states, Eden and Hampson argue that, at the global level, there are
international regimes, a major goal of whose is to reduce transaction costs.
For example, the World International Patent Organization registers domestic patents and copyrights internationally and attempts to protect these
forms of property rights at the international level, an activity which greatly reduces transaction costs in international trading. Regimes that provide
specialized trading privileges for members also have the effect of reducing
transaction costs. Examples include GATT, the European Union structure,
and the emerging North American Free Trade Agreement which is designed
to oversee the gradual reduction of trade and tariff barriers among Canada,
Mexico, and the United States.

Other types of regimes have other goals. For example, some states have
organized international cartels in order to strengthen their domestic
economies. This has been common in the oil, uranium, bauxite, and coffee
producing countries. Meanwhile, other regimes have been established to
cushion and to control the effects of autonomous macroeconomic policies by
individual states. Some of the institutional arrangements created to bring
this about include the International Monetary Fund, the World Bank, the
Bank of International Settlements, the Group of Seven, and the European
Monetary System (EMS). Finally, states attempt to minimize distributional
conflicts with the following regimes: GATT with its preferences to less developed countries, the World Bank, and the IMF (Gilpin, 1987; Keohane,
1984; Krasner, 1983; Young, 1989).

Obviously the effectiveness of these regimes in lowering transaction
costs, promoting macroeconomic stability, and minimizing distributional
conflicts varies from time to time and from one institutional arrangement
to another. However, as regimes acquire greater effectiveness in coordinating economic activity at the supranational level, there will be some alter-
ation of coordinating mechanisms at the level of the nation-state. Hence,

the emergence of a common European internal market is expected to lead to some kind of deregulation of various European economies, providing for "regime shopping" by mobile capital and to a lesser extent by labor as national borders are weakened or abolished. Throughout the European Union there may well emerge political institutional arrangements with greater pluralism, institutional fragmentation, deregulation, and voluntarism – in short, socioeconomic-political forms of coordination that have many similarities to the neoliberal type of institutions that characterize the political economy of the United States. There is increasing concern that, as the various European societies become integrated into the European Union, there will be an undermining of the essential institutional prerequisites of the type of bargained, cooperative political economy which has facilitated the development of such social systems of production as diversified quality mass production in Germany or flexible specialization in Italy. Of course, it remains to be seen how much the emergence of a stable regime at the level of the European Union can erode local cultures, traditions, and power structures on which flexible social systems of production are built. But even to pose the problem is to suggest that changes in coordination at one spatial-territorial location may alter the forms of coordination and social systems of production in place at other spatial-territorial locations. These are a few of the issues that the papers in Parts II and IIII of this volume confront.

CONVERGENCE OR DIVERGENCE AMONG SOCIAL SYSTEMS OF PRODUCTION

During the 1960s, there was a widely held view that the diffusion of common production technologies and divisions of labor at the societal level would eventually lead to convergence both in the institutional arrangements employed by societies for coordinating economic activity and in their economic performance. This prognosis was made for Europe and Japan, which were expected to converge toward the American model. Even the East European socialist countries were seen as part of this global process, and it was believed that they would eventually evolve toward a variant of a mixed economy, combining both market mechanisms and state interventions.

If one restricts the concern about convergence to social systems of production, discussions about convergence and divergence are still very much alive in the social science community. For example, some of the industrial organizational literature argues that firms competing in the same product markets tend to become similar in their structure and behavior, else they disappear. In other words, the convergence thesis assumes that there is one

best solution to organizing labor, raw materials, and capital in order to manufacture and distribute goods. Producers, processors, and distributors must
at least emulate if not surpass their most efficient competitors in order to
survive. Every time a group of innovators discovers a new, but highly efficient method of increasing output, their competitors are likely to follow.
Thus, competition and survival involve discovering and implementing the
best techniques and strategies (Chandler, 1962, 1977; Chandler and Daems,
1980). But industrial censuses persistently demonstrate that a whole spectrum of different vintages of firms and technologies coexist in most countries over long periods of time. In a world in which innovation is permanent, there will exist simultaneously innovators and imitators, leading and
lagging firms (Nelson and Winter, 1982). For neo-Schumpeterians, this diversity of technology and organizations plays a positive role in providing
flexibility and adaptability, whereas a country with a single or unique social
system of production would face the danger of long-term instability in its
economy (Eliasson, 1989). Some losses in static efficiency (the average firm
is far from the best practice) might be overcome by the gain in dynamic efficiency, due to the variety of alternative technologies and organizations that
could be developed as firms constantly face new environments (Herrigel,
1989; Hyman and Streeck, 1988).

In the field of sociology, organizational analysts have confronted the divergence – convergence debate by focusing on the way that environmental
constraints shape organizational behavior. Several scholars (DiMaggio and
Powell, 1983; Hollingsworth and Hollingsworth, 1987; Pfeffer and Salancik, 1978) have argued that organizations in similar environments will converge in their behavior as they respond to like pressures. In short, this is a
variant on the industrial organization literature: Organizations competing
in the same environment begin to resemble one another because they are
subject to the same resource constraints and to similar regulatory and normative pressures.

Transaction cost economics also speaks to a similar set of concerns. It argues that there will be differences in governance forms depending on the
variability in organizational environments (Schneiberg and Hollingsworth,
1990; Williamson, 1975, 1985). Thus, transaction cost economics allows for
the possibility that firms in the same industry may have different governance
forms because they may encounter different kinds of transaction costs. On
the other hand, most transaction cost theorists argue that there is one best organizational form for firms that have similar or identical transaction costs.
All these conceptions share the same concern for a static optimization of
transaction or production costs, with the implicit hypothesis of the unique-
ness of the adequate productive organization. Again, evolutionary models

provide diverse answers: Biologists observe that various species have solved differently many of the same problems, although the ecological system may be stable due to the dynamic complementarities of the different species. When refined and extended to social sciences, these models usually reveal a multiplicity of institutions fulfilling the same coordination purposes (Lesourne, 1991). Of course, such a transposition of biological analyses has been severely criticized, but the same results are obtained concerning the diffusion of technologies with increasing returns to scale (Arthur, 1988). In these theories, history matters (David, 1988), since, once implemented, an institution can persist, even if it would be rational for the society to replace it with one better suited to the new environment (Boyer and Orlean, 1991).

Finally, a group of economists has recently addressed the issue of convergence, focusing on the extent to which nations converge over time in their levels of productivity, income, and technology (Abramowitz, 1986; Baumol, 1986; Baumol, Blackman, and Wolff, 1989; Baumol and Wolff, 1989; Maddison, 1982; Nelson, 1991b). In much of this literature, the argument for convergence relies heavily on the concept of technological transfer: The greater the technological and productivity gap between leading and following nations, the greater the follower's potential of productivity advances. "In short, the follower, *ceteris paribus,* tends to catch up to the leader" (Williamson, 1991: 56). The argument is complemented by models of accumulation: Diminishing returns to capital assume that productivity growth will be slower for the lead country that starts with high initial levels of labor productivity. Followers are especially likely to exhibit higher rates of productivity growth if they invest heavily in human capital relative to physical capital (Barro, 1989; Williamson, 1991).

However, the argument for such a convergence is far from convincing, as numerous exceptions can be found. First, the catching up has taken place for a limited number of countries, with a number of counter examples such as Argentina or even Great Britain, not to speak of most African countries. Second, this type of convergence has been quite specific to the last three decades and has not occurred over the long run (Amable, 1991). Third, what is missing in much of this literature is the social dimension. An important exception in the economic literature is the work of Abramovitz (1986; also see Veblen, 1916: 70), who argues that a country's potential to catch up is not strong simply because it is backward. Rather, its potential depends on its social capabilities (for a discussion of this concept, see Abramowitz, 1986; Ohkawa and Rosovsky, 1973: Chapter 9). The problem with incorporating social capability into the convergence argument is that thus far scholars have been rather vague as to what it means, and we have not learned how to measure it, though Ohkawa, Rosovsky, and Abramowitz have recognized that it must take into consideration the nature of the skills of labor and management, a country's industrial relations system, as well as its financial markets, industrial structure, and political system. In short, what Abramowitz means by a nation's social capabilities is remarkably similar to what we in this volume mean by a nation's social system of production.

For us, the key to understanding the degree to which the economic performance of countries will converge is influenced very much by the extent to which they have similar social systems of production. Because the social systems of production of modern societies are complex configurations of numerous institutional sectors, however, it is problematic that they can diffuse across countries – except over an extraordinarily long period of time. In fact, given the strong complementarities and syncretic flavor of any national system of innovation (Nelson, 1993), it would be surprising to observe an easy catching up by followers: The structural advantage taken by a leading country or industry initially prevents an easy imitation. Still more, followers, while trying to imitate, usually encounter unexpected problems, which trigger a series of induced adaptations or even innovations that may finally deliver a different model, building on their own national specificities. When France and Germany tried to follow the first British industrial revolution, both countries moved toward quite different new models (Gerschenkron, 1962). Similarly, after World War II, many Japanese manufacturers wanted to follow American mass production practices but got, quite unintentionally, diversified quality mass production (Ohno, 1989).

The following chapters suggest not only that different coordinating mechanisms are associated with different social systems of production, but also that different coordinating mechanisms and different social systems of production result in different types of economic performance. Hence, as long as countries vary in the type of coordinating mechanisms and social systems of production that are dominant in their economies, there are serious constraints on the degree to which they can converge in their economic performance. Different social systems of production tend to maximize in a more or less explicit manner different performance criteria, usually mixed considerations about static and dynamic efficiency, profit, security, social peace, and economic and/or political power. In short, in contrast to the implications of neoclassical economic theory, in real world economies there are no universal standards which all economically rational actors attempt to maximize. Economic history provides numerous examples of how the variety of principles of rationality are implemented in different societies (Boyer, 1990; Gustafsson, 1990; Hollingsworth and Streeck, 1994; North, 1981, 1990; Tolliday and Zeitlin, 1991: 1–31).

Performance standards or goals are socially selected, and they vary greatly in space and time. Of course, profitability is a goal of firms in all capitalist economies, but depending on the social system of production within which firms are embedded, returns on investments may be sought in the short or long term. Moreover, different social systems of production vary in the norms dictating the level of profits that are acceptable at different stages in various product life cycles. In other words, how long and under what conditions profitability can be neglected in product development depends on what other economic performances a particular social system of production attempts to maximize.

The following chapters suggest that social systems of production vary not only in the ways firms approach profits, but also in the degree to which they attempt to maximize (a) the criteria of allocative efficiency or X-efficiency considerations, (b) social peace and egalitarian distribution considerations, (c) quantity versus quality aspects of production, and (d) innovation in developing new products versus innovation in improving upon existing products (Hage, 1980).

Perhaps in the world arena, where different social systems of production confront one another, we can best learn about the efficacy of specific standards of competitiveness. In the international arena, where there is competition over different social systems of production involving firms in the same industrial sectors, there is some potential to adjudicate heretical claims that a diversified quality mass production system (DQMP) – with its low wage spread, high wages, high employment stability, and highly institutionalized collective forms of coordination – may perform better than a social system of production coordinated primarily by markets and hierarchies (Hollingsworth and Streeck, 1994). In a DQMP system, slower adjustments to unexpected disturbances might deliver some losses in the short run on productivity and profit criteria, but in the long run the internal mobility of labor and its permanent upgrading within existing organizational structures are likely to provide a strong incentive to process innovations and productivity increases (Buechtemann, 1991). In contrast, when markets and hierarchies are the two major coordinating mechanisms in a social system of production, their industrial relations system with its emphasis on short-term decision-making processes is likely over time to result in more labor market segmentation, more productivity slowdown, and a cumulative deficiency in training (Streeck, 1991).

On the other hand, the following chapters as well as our previous volume *Governing Capitalist Economies: Performance and Control of Economic Sectors* (Hollingsworth, Schmitter, and Streeck, 1994) suggest that not all of a country's sectors compete and perform equally well. Some social systems of production perform better in some product markets than in others. Most countries succeed in a few industrial sectors but not very well in most. National success tends to occur when there exist clusters of sectors that are complementary to one another. Most industrialized countries rarely have sectors that are not part of clusters of sectors performing well at the global level. Moreover, firms within globally successful sectors are often concentrated within specific regions or districts of countries where they are part of similar social systems of production (Hollingsworth, Schmitter, and Streeck, 1994; Porter, 1990; Sabel and Zeitlin, 1985).

As the social sciences increasingly recognize that noneconomic domestic institutions are important determinants of success in world markets, economic competition is increasingly becoming competition over different forms of social systems of production, and competitive pressures for better economic performance are more and more often translated into pressures for broad societal change. During the 1950s, the United States was widely perceived as the world's most competitive economy, and its social system of mass standardized production was widely admired. But in our own age, as the American economy tends to perform poorly in an increasing number of industrial sectors, there are mounting pressures to change many of its social institutions – its systems of education and training, industrial relations, financial institutions, the internal structure of firms, etc. In other words, countries whose social systems of production tend to compete poorly in the international arena are subject to pressures to deindustrialize and/or to rebuild institutions in order to enhance economic performance. Thus, international competition among national social systems of production may cut deeply into a country's social and political fabric (Streeck, 1991; Hollingsworth and Streeck, 1994).

On the other hand, the competitiveness of a country's dominant social system of production depends, in part, on the international rules of the game. Within certain limits, powerful countries can create international regimes that favor their firms and sectors and that encourage competitor nations to alter their productive systems in the image of those in the hegemonic country. To understand the coordination and performance of capitalist economies, we must be sensitive to how economic coordination is linked at all spatial-territorial areas – the level of regions within countries, the level of the nation-state, and levels beyond the nation-state. This volume attempts to shed light not only on economic coordination, social systems of production, and economic performance at each of these levels, but also on how coordination and performance are linked in these various spatial-territorial arenas.

REFERENCES

Abramowitz, Moses. 1986. "Catching Up, Forging Ahead, and Falling Behind." *Journal of Economic History.* 46 (June): 385–406.

Alter, Catherine and Jerald Hage. 1993. *Organizations Working Together: Coordination in Interorganizational Networks.* San Francisco: Jossey Bass.

Amable, B. 1991. "Changement Technique endogene en economie ouverte, institutions et trajectoires nationales de croissance." Ph.D. thesis, E.H.E.S.S. Paris.

Aoki, Masahiko. 1988. *Information, Incentives and Bargaining in the Japanese Economy.* Cambridge: Cambridge University Press.

Arrow, Kenneth J. 1973. "Social Responsibility and Economic Efficiency." *Public Policy.* 21: 303–17.

———. 1974. *The Limits of Organization.* New York: Norton.

Arthur, W. B. 1988. "Competing Technologies: An Overview." In R. Dosi et al., eds. *Technical Change and Economic Theory.* London and New York: Printer Publishers. Pp. 590–607.

Barro, Robert J. 1989. "A Cross-Country Study of Growth, Saving, and Government." National Bureau of Economic Research Working Paper No. 2855.

Baumol, William J. 1986. "Productivity Growth, Convergence, and Welfare: What the Long-Run Data Show." *American Economic Review.* 76(5): 1072–85.

Baumol, William J., Sue Anne Batey Blackman, and Edward N. Wolff. 1989. *Productivity and American Leadership: The Long View.* Cambridge and London: MIT Press.

Baumol, William J. and Edward N. Wolff. 1989. "Three Fundamental Productivity Concepts: Principles and Measurement." In George R. Feiwel, ed. *Joan Robinson and Modern Economic Theory.* London: Macmillan. Pp. 638–59.

Becattini, Giacomo. 1990. "The Marshallian Industrial District as a Socio-Economic Notion." In Frank Pyke, Giacomo Becattini, and Werner Sengenberger, eds. *Industrial Districts and Inter-firm Cooperation in Italy.* Geneva: International Institute for Labor Studies. Pp. 37–51.

Benson, J. "The Interorganizational Network as a Political Economy." *Administrative Science Quarterly.* 20: 229–49.

Boyer, Robert. 1990. "Economie et histoire: Vers de nouvelles alliances?" *Annales ESC.* November–December: 1397–1426.

———. 1991. "New Directions in Management Practices and Work Organization: General Principles and National Trajectories." Revised draft of paper presented at the OECD Conference on Technological Change as a Social Process, Helsinki, December 11–13, 1989.

Boyer, Robert and Benjamin Coriat. 1986. "Technical Flexibility and Macro Stabilization." *Ricerche Economiche.* XL (October–December): 771–835.

Boyer, Robert and Jean-Pierre Durand. 1993. *L'apres-Fordisme.* Paris: Syros.

Boyer, R. and A. Orlean. 1991. "Why Are Institutional Transitions So Difficult?" Mimeograph CREA, prepared for the Conference "L'Economie des Conventions." Paris.

Bradach, Jeffrey L. and Robert G. Eccles. "Price, Authority, and Trust: From Ideal Types of Plural Forms." *Annual Review of Sociology.* 15: 97–118.

Brusco, Sebastiano. 1982. "The Emilian Model: Productive Decentralization and Social Integration." *Cambridge Journal of Economics.* 6: 167–184.

1986. "Small Firms and Industrial Districts: The Experience of Italy." In D. Keeble and E. Weaver, eds. *New Firms and Regional Development in Europe.* London: Croom Helm.

Buechtemann, C. F. 1991. "Does (De-)Regulation Matter? Employment Protection in West Germany." In E. Matzner and W. Streeck, eds. *Beyond Keynesianism, the Socio-Economics of Production and Full Employment.* Hants, UK: Edward Elgar Publishing.

Campbell, John L., J. Rogers Hollingsworth, and Leon Lindberg, eds. 1991. *The Governance of the American Economy.* Cambridge and New York: Cambridge University Press.

Chandler, Alfred D. 1962. *Strategy and Structure.* Cambridge: MIT Press.

1977. *The Visible Hand: The Managerial Revolution in American Business.* Cambridge: Harvard University Press.

1990. *Scale and Scope: The Dynamics of Industrial Capitalism.* Cambridge: Harvard University Press.

Chandler, Alfred D. and Herman Daems, eds. 1980. *Managerial Hierarchies: Comparative Perspectives on the Rise of the Modern Industrial Enterprise.* Cambridge: Harvard University Press.

Chisholm, Donald. 1989. *Coordination Without Hierarchy: Informal Structures in Multiorganizational Systems.* Berkeley: University of California Press.

Coase, Ronald H. 1981. "The Coase Theorem and the Empty Core. A Comment." *Journal of Law and Economics.* 24: 183–7.

1960. "The Problem of Social Cost." *Journal of Law and Economics.* 3: 1–44.

Coleman, James S. 1992. *Foundations of Social Theory.* Cambridge: Harvard University Press.

Coriat, Benjamin. 1991. *Penser.* Paris: C. Bourgeois.

Crouch, Colin and Wolfgang Streeck. 1996. *Varieties of Capitalism.* London and Paris: Pinter.

David, Paul A. 1988. "Path-Dependence: Putting the Past in the Future of Economics." *IMSSS Technical Report.* No. 533 Stanford University.

DiMaggio, Paul and Walter W. Powell. 1983. "The Iron Cage Revisited: Institutional Isomorphism and Collective Rationality in Organizational Fields." *American Sociological Review.* 48: 147–160.

Eccles, Robert. 1981. "The Quasifirm in the Construction Industry." *Journal of Economic Behavior and Organization.* 2 (December), 335–58.

Elam, Mark. 1992. "Markets, Morals, and Powers of Innovation." Unpublished paper presented before the School for Workers, University of Wisconsin, Madison. April 6, 1992.

Eliasson, G. 1989. "Modelling Long-Term Macro-Economic Growth as a Based, Path-Dependent, Experimentally Organised Economic Process: The Swedish Micro-to-Macro Model." Mimeograph paper prepared for the International OECD Seminar on Science, Technology and Economic Growth.

Etzioni, Amitai. 1988. *The Moral Dimension: Towards a New Economics.* New York: The Free Press.

Florida, Richard and Martin Kenney. 1991. "Transplanted Organizations: The Transfer of Japanese Industrial Organization to the U.S." *American Sociological Review.* 56: 381–98.

Freeman, Christopher, ed. 1986. *Design, Innovation and Long Cycles in Economic Development.* New York: St. Martin's Press.

Friedland, Roger and Robert R. Alford. 1991. "Bringing Society Back in: Symbols, Practices, and Institutional Contradictions." In Walter W. Powell and Paul J. DiMaggio, eds. *The New Institutionalism in Organizational Analysis.* Chicago: University of Chicago Press. Pp. 232–63.

Fukuyama, Francis. 1995. *Trust: Social Virtues and the Creation of Prosperity.* New York: Free Press.

Gambetta, Diego. 1988. *Trust: Making and Breaking Cooperative Relations.* New York: Basil Blackwell.

Garcia, A. 1986. "La Construction Sociale d'un marche parfait: le Marche au Cadran de Fontaine en sologne." *Actes de la Recherche en Sciences Sociales.* 65.

Gerschenkron, Alexander. 1962. *Economic Backwardness in Historical Perspective.* Cambridge: Harvard University Press.

Gilpin, Robert. 1987. *The Political Economy of International Relations.* Princeton: Princeton University Press.

Ginsburger, F. 1982. "Le Role du travail Precaire Dans Les Transformations de la Relation Salariale." Thesis, University of Paris, VIII.

Grabher, G., ed. 1993. *The Embedded Firm: On the Socioeconomics of Industrial Networks.* London: Routledge.

Granovetter, Mark. 1985. "Economic Action and Social Structure: The Problem of Embeddedness." *American Journal of Sociology.* 91: 481–510.

Gustafsson, Bo, ed. 1990. *Power and Economic Institutions: Reinterpretations in Economic History.* Aldershot: Edward Elgar.

Habermas, Jurgen. 1975. *Legitimation Crisis.* Boston: Beacon Press.

Hage, Jerald. 1980. *Theories of Organizations: Form, Process, and Transformation.* New York: John Wiley.

Hage, Jerald and Zhongren, Jing. 1996, forthcoming. "Adaptive Costs: A New Paradigm for the Choice of Organizational Form." In J. Rogers Hollingsworth, ed. *Social Actors and the Embeddedness of Institutions.* M. E. Sharpe.

Hechter, Michael. 1987. *Principles of Group Solidarity.* Berkeley and London: University of California Press.

Hechter, Michael, Karl-Dieter Opp, and Reinhard Wippler, eds. 1990. *Social Institutions: Their Emergence, Maintenance, and Effects.* New York: Aldine de Gruyter.

Herrigel, Gary. 1989. "Industrial Order and the Politics of Industrial Change: Mechanical Engineering." In Peter Katzenstein, ed. *Industry and Political Change in West Germany: Towards the Third Republic.* Ithaca: Cornell University Press. Pp. 185–221.

———. 1995. *Industrial Constructions: The Sources of German Industrial Power.* New York: Cambridge University Press.

Hirst, Paul and Jonathan Zeitlin. 1990. "Flexible Specialization Versus Post-Fordism: Theory, Evidence, and Policy Implications." Working paper, Birkbeck Centre for Public Policy.

Hirst, Paul and Jonathan Zeitlin, eds. 1989. *Reversing Industrial Decline? Industrial Structure and Policy in Britain and her Competitors.* Oxford: Berg.

Hollingsworth, J. Rogers. 1991a. "The Logic of Coordinating American Manufacturing Sectors." In John L. Campbell, J. Rogers Hollingsworth, and Leon

Lindberg, eds. *The Governance of the American Economy.* Cambridge and New York: Cambridge University Press. Pp. 35–73.

1991b. "Die Logik der Koordination des verarbeitenden Gewerbs in Amerika." *Kolner Zeitschrift fur Sociologie und Socialpsychologie.* 43: 18–43.

Hollingsworth, J. Rogers and Ellen Jane Hollingsworth. 1987. *Controversy about American Hospitals: Funding, Ownership, and Performance.* Washington: American Enterprise Institute.

Hollingsworth, J. Rogers and Leon Lindberg. 1985. "The Governance of the American Economy: The Role of Markets, Clans, Hierarchies, and Associative Behavior." In Wolfgang Streeck and Philippe C. Schmitter, eds. *Private Interest Government: Beyond Market and State.* London and Beverly Hills: Sage Publications. Pp. 221–54.

Hollingsworth, J. Rogers, Philippe Schmitter, and Wolfgang Streeck, eds. 1994. *Governing Capitalist Economies: Performance and Control of Economic Sectors.* New York: Oxford University Press.

Hollingsworth, J. Rogers and Wolfgang Streeck. 1994. "Countries and Sectors: Performance, Convergence and Competitiveness." In J. Rogers Hollingsworth, Philippe Schmitter, and Wolfgang Streeck, eds. *Governing Capitalist Economies: Performance and Control of Economic Sectors.* New York: Oxford University Press. Pp. 270–300.

Hollingsworth, J. Rogers, Richard Whitley, and Jerald Hage, eds. 1996, forthcoming. *Firms, Markets, and Production Systems in Comparative Perspective.*

Hounshell, David A. 1984. *From the American System to Mass Production, 1800–1932.* Baltimore: John Hopkins University Press.

Hyman, Richard and Wolfgang Streeck. 1988. *New Technology and Industrial Relations.* Oxford and New York: Basil Blackwell.

Katzenstein, Peter J. 1985. *Small States in World Markets: Industrial Policy in Europe:* Ithaca: Cornell University Press.

1989. *Industry and Politics in West Germany: Toward the Third Republic.* Ithaca: Cornell University Press.

Kennedy, Paul. 1987. "The Relative Decline of America." *The Atlantic.* 260: 29–38.

Kenney, Martin and Richard Florida. 1988. "Beyond Mass Production and the Labor Process in Japan." *Politics and Society.* 16: 121–58.

1993. *Beyond Mass Production: The Japanese System and Its Transfer to the U.S.* New York: Oxford University Press.

Keohane, Robert. 1984. *After Hegemony: Cooperation and Discord in the World Political Economy.* Princeton: Princeton University Press.

Kindleberger, Charles P. 1978. *Manias, Panics, and Crashes: A History of Financial Crises.* New York: Basic Books.

Krasner, Stephen D. 1983. *International Regimes.* Ithaca: Cornell University Press.

Kristensen, Peer Hull. 1986. *Industrial Models in the Melting Pot of History and Technological Projects and Organizational Changes.* Roskilde, Denmark: Institut for Samfun Dsokonomi.

Landau, Ralph and Nathan Rosenberg, eds. 1986. *The Positive Sum Strategy: Harnessing Technology for Economic Growth.* Washington, D.C.: National Academy Press.

Lazarson, Mark H. 1988. "Organizational Growth of Small Firms: An Outcome of Markets and Hierarchies." *American Sociological Review.* 53: 330–42.

Leibenstein, Harvey. 1966. "Allocative Efficiency versus X-Efficiency." *American Economic Review.* 66: 392–415.

——— 1976. *Beyond Economic Man: A New Foundation in Microeconomics.* Cambridge: Harvard University Press.

Lesourne, J. 1991. *Economie de L'ordre et du Desordre.* Paris: Economica.

Lindberg, Leon, John L. Campbell, and J. Rogers Hollingsworth. 1991. "Economic Governance and the Analysis of Structural Change in the American Economy." In John L. Campbell and J. Rogers Hollingsworth, eds. *Governance of the American Economy.* New York: Cambridge University Press. Pp. 3–34.

Luhmann, Niklas. 1979. *Trust and Power.* Chichester: Wiley & Sons.

MacNeil, I. R. 1978. "Contracts: Adjustments of Long-Term Economic Relations Under Classical, Neoclassical, and Relational Contract Law." *Northwestern University Law Review.* 72: 854–906.

Maddison, Angus. 1982. *Phases of Capitalist Development.* Oxford: Oxford University Press.

Marglin, S. 1974. "What Do Bosses Do? The Origins and Functions of Hierarchy in Capitalist Production." *Review of Radical Political Economics.* 1(6): 60–112.

——— 1991. "Understanding Capitalism: Control versus Efficiency." In Bo Gustafsson, ed. *Power and Economic Institutions: Reinterpretations in Economic History.* Aldershot: Edward Elgar Publishing. Pp. 225–52.

Maurice, M., F. Sellier, and J. J. Silvestre. 1982. *Politique D'education et Organisation Industrielle en France et en Allemagne.* Paris: Presses Universitaires de France.

Maurice, M., A. Sorge, and M. Warner. 1980. "Societal Differences in Organizing Manufacturing Units. A Comparison of France, West Germany, and Great Britain." *Organization Studies.* I: 59–86.

Maynard-Smith, J. 1982. *Evolution and the Theory of Games.* Cambridge and New York: Cambridge University Press.

Mueller, Frank and Ray Loveridge. 1995. "The 'Second Industrial Divide'? The Role of the Large Firm in the Baden-Württemberg Model." *Industrial and Corporate Change.* 4 (3): 555–82.

Nelson, Richard R., ed. 1982. *Government and Technical Progress. A Cross Industry Analysis.* New York: Pergamon Press.

——— 1993. *National Innovation Systems: A Comparative Analysis.* New York: Oxford University Press.

Nelson, Richard R. 1991a. "The Role of Firm Differences in an Evolutionary Theory of Technical Advance." *Science and Public Policy* 18 (6): 347–52.

——— 1991b. "Research on Productivity Growth and Productivity Differences: Dead Ends and New Departures." *Journal of Economic Literature.* 19(3): 1029–64.

Nelson, Richard R. and Sidney Winter. 1982. *An Evolutionary Theory of Economic Change.* Cambridge: Harvard University Press.

North, Douglass. 1981. *Structure and Change in Economic History.* New York: Norton.

——— 1990. *Institutions, Institutional Change and Economic Performance.* Cambridge and New York: Cambridge University Press.

Ohkawa, Kazushi and Henry Rosovsky. 1973. *Japanese Economic Growth: Trend Acceleration in the Twentieth Century.* Stanford: Stanford University Press.

Ohno, T. 1989. *L'esprit Toyota.* Paris: Masson.

Oliver, Nick and Barry Wilkinson. 1988 *The Japanization of British Industry.* Oxford: Basil Blackwell.

Ostrom, Elinor. 1986. "An Agenda for the Study of Institutions." *Public Choice*. 48: 3–25.

    1990. *Governing the Commons: The Evolution of Institutions for Collective Action.* New York: Cambridge University Press.

Parsons, Talcott. 1951. *The Social System.* New York: Free Press.

    1966. *Societies: Comparative and Evolutionary Perspectives.* Englewood Cliffs, N.J.: Prentice Hall.

    1967. *Sociological Theory and Modern Society.* New York: Free Press.

Pempel, T. J. and Keiichi Tsunekawa. 1979. "Corporatism Without Labor? The Japanese Anomaly." In Philippe Schmitter and Gerhard Lehmbruch, eds. *Trends toward Corporatist Intermediation.* Beverly Hills: Sage Publications. Pp. 231–70.

Pfeffer, J. and G. R. Salancik. 1978. *The External Control of Organizations: A Resource Dependence Perspective.* New York: Harper and Row.

Phan, D. 1991. "Structures de marche et diffusion de services a valeur ajoutee sur un reseau de telecommunication." Roneotype, Ecole Nationale Superieure des P&T.

Piore, Michael J. and Charles F. Sabel. 1984. *The Second Industrial Divide: Possibilities for Prosperity.* New York: Basic Books.

Polanyi, Karl. 1957. *The Great Transformation: The Political and Economic Origins of Our Time.* Boston: Beacon Press (originally published in 1944).

Pollert, Anna, ed. 1991. *Farwell to Flexibility?* Oxford: Blackell.

Porter, Michael. 1986. *Competition in Global Industries.* Boston: Harvard Business School.

    1990. *The Comparative Advantage of Nations.* New York: Free Press.

Posner, R. A. 1977. *Economic Analysis of Law.* Boston: Little, Brown.

Powell, W. W. 1990. "Neither Market nor Hierarchy: The Limits of Organization." In Barry Staw and L. L. Cummings, eds. *Research in Organizational Behavior.* Greenwich, CT: JAI Press. Vol. 12, Pp. 295–336.

Putnam, Robert D. 1993. *Making Democracy Work.* Princeton: Princeton University Press.

Pyke, F., G. Becattini, and W. Sengenberger, eds. 1990. *Industrial Districts and Inter-firm Co-operation in Italy.* Geneva: International Institute for Labour Studies.

Pyke, F. and W. Sengenberger, eds. 1992. *Industrial Districts and Local Regeneration.* Geneva: International Institute for Labour Studies.

Risse-Kappen, Thomas, ed. 1995. *Bringing Transnationalism Back In: Non State Actors, Domestic Structures, and International Institutions.* Cambridge and New York: Cambridge University Press.

Romer, P. 1986. "Increasing Returns and Long-run Growth." *Journal of Political Economy.* 94: 1002–1037.

    1990. "Endogenous Technological Changes." *Journal of Political Economy.* 98(5), part 2, S71–S102.

    1994. "The Origins of Endogenous Growth." *Journal of Economic Perspectives.* 8 (1): 3–22.

Rosenau, James N. and Ernst Otto Czempiel, eds. 1992. *Governance Without Government: Order and Change in World Politics.* Cambridge and New York: Cambridge University Press.

Sabel, Charles F. 1991. "Moebius-Strip Organizations and Open Labor Markets: Some Consequences of the Reintegration of Conception and Execution in a Volatile Economy." In Pierre Bourdieu and James S. Coleman, eds. *Social Theory for a Changing Society.* Boulder: Westview Press. Pp. 23–63.

1992. "Studied Trust: Building New Forms of Co-operation in a Volatile Economy." In Frank Pyke and Werner Sengenberger, eds. *Industrial Districts and Local Economic Regeneration.* Geneva: International Institute for Labor Studies. Pp. 215–50.

Sabel, Charles F. and Jonathan Zeitlin. 1985. "Historical Alternatives to Mass Production: Politics, Markets, and Technology in Nineteenth Century Industrialization." *Past and Present.* 108 (August): 133–76.

1996, forthcoming. "Stories, Strategies, Structures: Rethinking Historical Alternatives to Mass Production." To appear in Charles F. Sabel and Jonathan Zeitlin, eds. *World of Possibilities: Flexibility and Mass Production in Western Industrialization.* New York: Cambridge University Press.

Saxenian, Annalee. 1994. *Regional Advantage: Culture and Competition in Silicon Valley and Route 128.* Cambridge: Harvard University Press.

Scharpf, Fritz W. 1993. "Games in Hierarchies and Networks." In Fritz W. Scharpf, ed. *Games in Hierarchies and Networks: Analytical and Empirical Approaches to the Study of Governance Institutions.* Boulder: Westview Press, 1993. Pp. 7–23.

Schmitter, Philippe C. and G. Lehmbruch, eds. 1979. *Trends Towards Corporatist Intermediation.* New York: Sage Publications.

Schmitter, Philippe and Wolfgang Streeck. 1981. "The Organization of Business Interests: A Research Design to Study the Associative Action of Business in the Advanced Industrial Societies of Western Europe." Berlin: Wissenschaftszentrum, II M/LMP Discussion paper 81-3.

Schneiberg, Marc and J. Rogers Hollingsworth. 1990. "Can Transaction Cost Economics Explain Trade Associations?" In Masahiko Aoki, Bo Gustafsson, and Oliver E. Williamson, eds. *The Firm As A Nexus of Treaties.* London and Beverly Hills: Sage Publications. Pp. 320–46.

Scranton, Philip. 1984. *Proprietary Capitalism: The Textile Manufacture at Philadelphia, 1800–1885.* Cambridge and New York: Cambridge University Press.

Snidal, Duncan. 1985. "The Limits of Hegemonic Stability Theory." *International Organization* 39(4): 579–615.

1991. "Relative Gains and the Pattern of International Cooperation." *American Political Science Review.* 85: 701–26.

Sorge, Arndt. 1989. "An Essay on Technical Change: Its Dimensions and Social and Strategic Context." *Organization Studies.* 10(1): 23–44.

Sorge, Arndt and Wolfgang Streeck. 1988. "Industrial Relations and Technical Change: The Case for an Extended Perspective." In Richard Hyman and Wolfgang Streeck, eds. *New Technology and Industrial Relations.* New York and Oxford: Basil Blackwell. P. 19–47.

Stinchcombe, Arthur L. and Carol A. Heimer, eds. 1985. *Organization Theory and Project Management.* Oslo: Norwegian University Press.

Storper, Michael. 1989. "The Transition to Flexible Specialization in the U.S. Film Industry: The Division of Labour, External Economies and the Crossing of Industrial Divides." *Cambridge Journal of Economics,* 13(2): 273–305.

1993. "Regional 'Worlds' of Production: Learning and Innovation in the Technology Districts of France, Italy, and the U.S.A." *Regional Studies.* 27: 4334–55.

Streeck, Wolfgang. 1987a. "Industrial Relations and Industrial Change: The Restructuring of the World Automobile Industry in the 1970s and 1980s." *Economic and Industrial Democracy.* 8(4): 437–62.

1987b. "The Uncertainties of Management in the Management of Uncertainty: Employers, Labour Relations and Industrial Adjustment in the 1980s." *Work, Employment, and Society.* 1(3): 281–308.

1988. "Coments on Ronald Dore, 'Rigidities in the Labour Market': The Andrew Schonfield Lectures (III)." *Goverment and Opposition.* 23(4): 413–23.

1989. "Skills and the Limits of Neo-Liberalism: The Enterprise of the Future as a Place of Learning." *Work, Employment, and Society.* 3(1): 89–104.

1991. "On the Institutional Conditions of Diversified Quality Production." In Egon Matzner and Wolfgang Streeck, eds. *Beyond Keynesianism: The Socio-Economics of Production and Full Employment.* Aldershot, Hants, England: Edward Elgar. Pp. 21–61.

Streeck, Wolfgang, et al. 1987. *The Role of Social Partners in Vocational Training and Further Training in the Federal Republic of Germany.* Berlin: European Centre for the Development of Vocational Training.

Streeck, Wolfgang and Philippe C. Schmitter. 1985a. "Community, Market, State, and Associations? The Prospective Contribution of Interest Governance to Social Order." In Wolfgang Streeck and Philippe C. Schmitter, eds. *Private Interest Government: Beyond Market and State.* Beverly Hills: Sage Publications. Pp. 1–29.

Streeck, Wolfgang and Philippe C. Schmitter, eds. 1985b. *Private Interest Government: Beyond Market and State.* London and Beverly Hills: Sage Publications.

Tolliday, Steven and Jonathan Zeitlin, eds. 1991. *The Power to Manage: Employers and Industrial Relations in Comparative Historical Perspective.* London and New York: Routledge.

1992. *Between Fordism and Flexibility: The Automobile Industry and Its Workers.* Oxford and New York: Berg.

Veblen, Thorstein. 1916. [1966]. *Imperial Germany and the Industrial Revolution.* Ann Arbor: University of Michigan Press.

Williamson, Jeffrey G. 1991. "Productivity and American Leadership: A Review Article." *Journal of Economic Literature.* 29: 51–68.

Williamson, Oliver. 1975. *Markets and Hierarchies: Analysis and Antitrust Implications.* New York: Free Press.

1985. *The Economic Institutions of Capitalism.* New York: Free Press.

Young, Brigitte, Leon N. Lindberg, and J. Rogers Hollingsworth. 1989. "The Governance of the American Daily Industry: From Regional Dominance to Regional Cleavage." In William D. Coleman and Henry J. Jacek, eds. *Regionalism, Business Interests and Public Policy.* London: Sage. Pp. 127–52.

Young, Oran R. 1986. "International Regimes: Toward a New Theory of Institutions." *World Politics* 39(1): 104–22.

1989. "Politics of International Regime Formation: Managing Natural Resources and the Environment." *International Organization.* 43(3): 349–76.

Zeitlin, Jonathan. 1992. "Industrial Districts and Local Economic Regeneration: Overview and Comment." In F. Pyke and W. Sengenberger, eds. *Industrial Districts and Local Economic Regeneration*. Geneva: International Institute for Labour Studies. Pp. 279–94.

———. 1994. "Why Are There No Industrial Districts in the United Kingdom?" In Arnaldo Bagnasco and Charles Sabel, eds. *Ce que petit peut faire: Les petites et moyennes enteprises en Europe*. Poiters: Observatoire du Changement Social en Europe Occidentale.

———. 1996, forthcoming. "Between Flexibility and Mass Production: Strategic Ambiguity and Selective Adaptation in the British Engineering Industry, 1840–1914." In Charles Sabel and Jonathan Zeitlin, eds. *World of Possibilities: Flexibility and Mass Production in Western Industrialization*. New York: Cambridge University Press.

PART I

THE VARIETY OF INSTITUTIONAL ARRANGEMENTS AND THEIR COMPLEMENTARITY IN MODERN ECONOMIES

Robert Boyer and J. Rogers Hollingsworth

For many years, social scientists have had a division of labor in studying the key institutions constituting a modern economy. Political scientists have given privileged attention to power and have focused major attention on the state as the key institution for coordinating or coercing individual behavior. For them and for many other social scientists, the market was the basic coordinating mechanism of an economy and should be investigated by an economist. In the case of market failure, some public intervention was supposed to occur in order to restore the optimality of an equilibrium, and ideally this should be one of the functions of the state, along with the enforcement of property rights. This issue too drew the attention of political scientists. However, the concerns of political scientists and the economists were generally quite different. In contrast with both, many sociologists argued that the nature, role, and emergence of social norms was the starting point of any investigation about the viability of any political and/or economic system.

In recent years, however, social scientists have begun to challenge this division of labor (Coleman, 1991). First, a few theoreticians have applied rational choice axioms to some basic issues in political science, thus developing some of the same methods as have many economists. Other political scientists, using different theoretical tools and methods, have argued that variation in the mobilization of interest groups explains divergences in macroeconomic performances among industrialized countries (Hollingsworth and Hanneman, 1982). Clearly, economists no longer have a monopoly on the study of macroeconomic issues. Second, the discipline of economics in the Anglo-American world is no longer so preoccupied with the study of markets. Some economists now recognize that organizations such as firms are more efficient than contracts and markets, and that labor and credit markets behave differently from typical product markets of standardized manufactured goods, due to fairness issues or moral hazard (Coase, 1988). The challenge then is to understand the institutional forms that deliver viable, if not necessarily the best, economic performances. Third, a number of sociologists have investigated how such core social relations as family, religious, and ethnic ties contribute to the development of the most essential but volatile ingredient in market relationships: trust and cooperation (Granovetter, 1993; Hamilton and Kao, 1991; Hamilton, Orrù, and Biggart, 1987). Furthermore, the coexistence of alternative types of coordinating mechanisms in the same product market area has rejuvenated the old issue of industrial diversity and its persistence through time (Campbell, Hollingsworth, and Lindberg, 1991)

This concern with economic issues in most of the social sciences has implications for understanding changes in institutions that have been taking place during the last two decades. Has the nation-state been losing its autonomy as it confronts the forces of globalization? How is the social science community to explain the phenomenon that more market-oriented societies have frequently had less desirable economic performance in terms of growth, innovation, employment, and competitiveness than some less market-oriented societies? What is the rationale and significance of the surge in networking, joint ventures, and strategic alliances across the globe? More particularly, how is the social science community to interpret the shift taking place in various institutional arrangements which coordinate relations among economic actors: Are they mainly governed by market selection – as some economic theory would suggest – or is this to be explained in sociological and political terms?

This section of this book attempts to shed light on these issues. Here, it is important to understand how various institutional arrangements are related to one another and their common principles, if any. Let us recall the basic typology proposed in Chapter 1: All institutional arrangements are classified in terms of how they relate to the pursuit of individual self-interest with the principle of coordination. The concerns of economics and sociology provide strategies for the study of a whole spectrum of actors who are driven either by the pursuit of individual self-interests or moral sentiments, and this delineates a first axis along which institutional arrangements can be analyzed. But institutions organize their interactions among individuals along a second axis which describes their behavior as taking place at a decentralized level according to horizontal relations among equals or, on the contrary, according to relations in which a principal has the power to structure the behavior of agents.

Consequently, the first and central message of the following chapters is clear: There is more than a single optimal institutional arrangement for organizing modern societies. Indeed, there is a large array of institutional arrangements for effectively organizing modern societies, depending on the larger environment in which economic activity is embedded and the problem to be solved. Thus, the market should not be considered as the ideal and universal institutional arrangement for coordinating economic activity in most circumstances. Numerous problems result when efforts are made to organize the world exclusively in terms of markets (e.g., the problem of public goods, spillover effects, uncertainty about quality, indivisibilities, etc.), and a confrontation with these problems usually requires some form of external intervention in order to restore a minimal efficiency. For example, professional associations or public authorities frequently have to devise, implement, and enforce new rules of the game. Thus markets are embedded in a nexus of obligational rules and/or public interventions, in the absence of which they could not properly function (see Chapter 2).

Thus, this book provides a complex vision about the economic institutions of capitalism: Not only do they exhibit a large variety of objectives and tools which are not at all minor variants of a single cardinal mechanism, but they complement one another and cannot generally operate in isolation from one another. The pursuit of individual self-interest in order not to be destructive requires a minimal set of obligations, i.e., an alternative institutional order. The same demonstration holds for private hierarchies, such as firms. From Adam Smith to Ronald Coase, scholars have learned that the division of labor within and among firms is linked to the size and the stability of the market. More recently, Alfred Chandler (1962, 1977, 1990) has provided considerable evidence about the importance of the relationship between the size and organizational structure of firms and the size of markets. In the 1980s and 1990s, firms have become increasingly interdependent. Firms seem less motivated to develop vertically integrated relationships, conglomerates, or holding companies but more concerned with pursuing strategic alliances and joint ventures for specific and delimited purposes. Thus the viability of private hierarchies increasingly depends on their ability to enter into such horizontal relations as networks, which blend self-interest and social obligation in order to deliver individual and collective outcomes that overcome some of the limits of private hierarchies (slow reaction to technical change) and of spot markets (the inability to internalize the spillover effects associated with innovation). This framework enlightens one of the most impressive transformations in contemporary manufacturing: When uncertainty is large and information is strategic, and if radical innovations are expected, networking and trust building with competitors and suppliers are preferred to both vertical integration and outsourcing (see Chapter 3).

The theory of public goods assumes that the function of the state is to overcome market failures. Public choice theorists warn that bureaucrats tend to use the power delegated to them to pursue their own interests and to make public interventions inefficient. However, the dichotomy between the market and the state is spurious, and the notion that all, or even most, public interventions are inefficient is very simplistic (Hollingsworth, Hage, and Hanneman, 1991). As Figure 1-2 in Chapter 1 reveals, the state consists of a variety of institutional arrangements — regulatory agencies, sponsoring departments, and legislative bodies, just to mention a few — and there is great variation in their goals, processes, and consequences. Moreover, there are important interdependencies between some forms of state intervention and associational governance. For example, the state delegates many of its functions to the regulation and monitoring of stock exchanges, occupations, and professions, etc. The way that government delegates its functions to private interest groups is a very important consideration in shaping economic performance (see Chapter 4).

The reappraisal of the role of polity, even in a highly internationalized world, is pushed a step further if one considers one major issue in the theory of economic institutions: How could individuals behave in conformity with any given institutional order, if they were perpetually pursuing their self-interest and disregarding social obligations, which are the cement of any stable economic and social order? In a world devoid of any deliberative body, opportunism and defection would be the rule, cooperation the exception. Modern neoclassical theory asserts that only exit is available to individuals when they are unhappy with a system, whereas political economists suggest that voice is a necessary ingredient for the cohesiveness and viability of any institution. In this respect, the notion of a constitutional order can be usefully applied to a vast array of coordinating mechanisms, both of a public and private nature. Of course, modern states are governed by constitutions which reflect certain principles in order to solve possible conflicts among various objectives of governments and/or departments and public agencies. And the principle of deliberation and reflexive analysis about the malfunctioning of a system is an efficient means of searching for alternative rules of the game, when the previous ones fail to deliver expected or desired outcomes. The access of constituents to deliberations about the amendment or transformation of a constitutional order is necessary if there is to be the trust needed for the successful functioning of a social system. Even markets express a similar logic, since they too are embedded in a set of rules, which are not natural, but are derived from previous interactions and deliberations. Thus, private and public constitutional orders are worthwhile, especially when changes have to be engineered due to emerging internal disequilibria or a rapidly evolving environment (see Chapter 5).

In spite of their diversity, the chapters in Part I explore the same vast and challenging issues in the analysis of different institutional arrangements for coordinating economic activity. What are their logics and functions? Why do they emerge, mature, and persist? As a result of these chapters, several conclusions emerge:

- The old but pervasive dichotomy between states and markets has to be discarded, to be replaced by a broader array of institutional arrangements, which mix in varying degree the pursuit of individual self-interest and social obligation, relations among equals, and power asymmetries.
- Because each type of institutional arrangement simultaneously exhibits strengths and weaknesses, its performance and viability depends on the precise context and configuration of interests within which it is embedded. No single institution can pretend to have universal or eternal superiority – even such a celebrated institutional arrangement as the invisible hand of the market.
- In the real world, as distinct from abstract mathematical models, any economy consists of a combination of institutional arrangements, all of which complement one another and thus acquire some efficiency. No institutional configuration can simply be borrowed and implemented

in any given social setting. Institutional arrangements evolve according to a distinct logic in each society.

- Institutions are not static entities defined once for all, but they continuously respond to changing contexts and emerging structural crises. This is of special importance, given the present transformations occurring in social systems of production and the changing status of subnational regions, nation-states, and the world economy.

REFERENCES

Campbell, John, J. Rogers Hollingsworth, and Leon Lindberg. 1991. *The Governance of the American Economy.* New York and Cambridge: Cambridge University Press.

Chandler, Alfred D. 1962. *Strategy and Structure.* Cambridge: MIT Press.

___ 1977. *The Visible Hand: The Managerial Revolution in American Business.* Cambridge: Harvard University Press.

___ 1990. *Scale and Scope: The Dynamics of Industrial Capitalism.* Cambridge: Harvard University Press.

Coase, R. H. 1988. *The Firm, the Market and the Law.* Chicago: University of Chicago Press.

Coleman, James S. 1992. *Foundations of Social Theory.* Cambridge: Harvard University Press.

Granovetter, Mark. 1993. "Coase Revisited: Business Groups in the Modern Economy." Paper presented for ASSI Conference on Hierarchies, Markets, Power in the Economy: Theories and Lessons from History. December 15–17. Milan, Italy.

Hamilton, Gary and Cheng-Shu Kao. 1991. "The Institutional Foundations of Chinese Business: The Family Firm in Taiwan." In Craig Calhoun, ed. *Comparative Social Research (Vol. 12): Business Institutions.* Greenwich, Connecticut: JAI Press. Pp. 135–51.

Hamilton, Gary, Marco Orrù, and Nicole Biggart. 1987. "Enterprise Groups in East Asia: An Organizational Analysis." *Shoken Keizai* (Financial Economic Review). September.

Hollingsworth, J. Rogers, Jerald Hage, and Robert Hanneman. 1991. *State Intervention in Medical Care: Consequences for Britain, France, Sweden, and the United States, 1890–1970.* Ithaca: Cornell University Press.

Hollingsworth, J. Rogers and Robert Hanneman. 1982. "Working-Class Power and the Political Economy of Western Capitalist Societies." *Comparative Social Research,* 5: 61–80.

2

THE VARIETY AND UNEQUAL PERFORMANCE OF REALLY EXISTING MARKETS: FAREWELL TO DOCTOR PANGLOSS?

Robert Boyer

A RETURN TO FREE MARKET CONCEPTIONS: WHY?

The conceptions about the self-regulating mechanisms associated with markets have undergone the equivalent of a long wave. During the Great Depression of the 1930s, a majority of economists were critical of the institutional impediments to the free functioning of markets. Only a minority argued that it was in the very nature of free markets to trigger large instabilities and/or stagnation (Weir and Skocpol, 1985). After World War II, the Keynesian heterodoxy became the core of significant revolution concerning the respective roles that the state and market should play in the long run social and economic reproduction of capitalism: Adequate public regulation and fine tuning of monetary and fiscal policies could promote quasifull employment, along a steady growth path. Basically market mechanisms had to be tamed by a series of legislation, regulation, and collective agreements, as well as built-in stabilizers in the tax system and/or in the reaction functions of central banks. As Joan Robinson recurrently pointed out, markets were efficient for allocating scarce resources between alternative goals via the formation of relative prices. But one major drawback resulted from the fact that pure market mechanisms were generally unable to provide full employment and macroeconomic stability. In fact during the fifties and sixties this view was widely shared by almost all governments, including the most conservative ones. Did not Richard Nixon declare, "Now we are all Keynesians"?

A REVERSAL OF THE KEYNESIAN REVOLUTION

In the seventies and still more in the eighties, there was a drastic move away from this Keynesian conception. And in the nineties, there has emerged a common ideology that markets are basically the most efficient methods for coordinating the economies of modern societies and that public interventions tend to do more harm than benefit, given the intrinsic limitations of public bureaucracies. In some respects, this change in ideology has been justified by a large amount of empirical evidence. First, the Keynesian compromise, when extended through the last two decades, did not deliver the same results as during the 1950s. For example, most national reflations – at least outside the United States – had led to serious inflation, external deficits, capital flight, and finally austerity policies. Second, these resulting problems seem closely related to a deepening in the internationalization process regarding trade, investment, finance, and, of course, money. Consequently, each firm, region, or nation must now compete in the international arena and can no longer be protected by stabilized oligopolistic national markets, which tended to be the case during the fifties and the sixties. Competition within the world economy is now perceived as a strong constraint on national compromises and distinctive forms of organized national institutions. In some extreme cases, the troubles, or even the quasibankruptcy, of some national champions have clearly exhibited the important role attributed to market mechanisms, which are currently identifying the world's more efficient firms and productive organizations. Thus, most governments have deregulated their national financial and labor markets, precisely in order to respond more efficiently to the changing patterns and recurrent disturbances associated with the globalization of most economic activities. The third factor in explaining the revival of faith in the market is the adoption of free market recipes by many governments and policy makers. The dynamism of financial innovations (Aglietta, 1991), and the progressive transition from one productive regime to another (Coriat, 1991) have highlighted the references to free market mechanisms: Some regulators, having lost many of their objectives and instruments, are now embracing the most extremist "laissez-faire" strategies.

Moreover, two major structural changes have strengthened the omnipotence attributed to market mechanisms. The movement toward European integration, associated with the single market that has been implemented by the end of 1994, and the free trade agreement between United States and Canada have clearly made competition in the product and financial markets a cornerstone in the building of a quasicontinental integration. Again, each firm, region, or nation has to compete over a larger economic space than previously, in such a way that markets seem to lead political and institutional transformations, at odds with what was observed in the Bretton-Woods system during the Keynesian era (Kuttner, 1991). Consequently, the market appears to be triumphing all across developed capitalist economies. Such an unexpected success would have been much less widespread, had not the Eastern bloc economies totally collapsed at the end of the eighties. In conventional terminology market economies correspond to a complex institutional setting in which markets are supposed to be the leading force, contrary to what was observed in the so-called socialist or controlled economies. The eagerness of the new democratic governments in Europe to embrace the project of a fast transition toward market mechanisms has made the triumph of free marketers overwhelming in the early nineties.

THE EIGHTIES: THE MARKET AS A PHOENIX

The market is now considered by a majority of managers and politicians as the coordinating mechanism "par excellence." Some economists, more cautious, might recognize minor or significant limits to markets but still consider that it is, along with democracy for political life the least imperfect coordinating mechanism for economic activity in societies featuring a high degree of complexity and decentralization.

The promarket arguments belong to four broad categories:

1. The invisible hand argument is again fashionable, in the very sense that Adam Smith discussed it in the eighteenth century. Markets are the only known mechanisms for making compatible initially independent and possibly conflicting strategies of a large number of individual agents, pursuing their own selfish interests. This process unintentionally delivers an efficient use of existing resources and talents, i.e., a Pareto optimum: the satisfaction of one agent cannot be improved without impairing that of another. By contrast, even the most sophisticated central planning routines would be less efficient, more costly in information management and statistics (Heal, 1971), and less alert in responding to changing consumers' needs or desires. This argument has

been recurrently used in interpreting the structural crisis of the Soviet model and its collapse (Bourguignon, 1990). The demonstration of the possibility of general equilibrium is fairly complex (see "Toward a Typology of Contrasted Market Mechanisms," page 66), but policy debates do not need to incorporate a high degree of technicalities, which can be reserved to academics or to candidates campaigning for the Nobel Prize!

2. Socializing and combining scattered and partial information is another major attribute of market economies. In the Austrian conception that follows (e.g., the ideas of Ludwig von Mises and Friedrich von Hayek), the main merit of markets is not so much to organize transactions and to set prices and incomes. Rather, it is the more efficient method for taking into account the scattered and specific knowledge owned by each household or firm and transmitted to the rest of society via supply and demand and ultimately price formation. Contrary to the hope for a socialist market economy (Brus, 1987), no central planner will ever be able to collect the relevant information about consumers' tastes and firms' production functions. In socialist economies, managers have vested interests in hiding their true productive capabilities, whereas planners have no effective method for revealing the changing preference of consumers or for enhancing organizational and technological innovations.

3. Stimulating technical change and innovations identify an additional feature for economic systems, with the diffusion of markets as the main coordinating mechanism. The argument here does not relate to the role of the market in converging towards the so-called "natural prices," i.e., the only legacy taken into account by the Marshallian or Walrasian theories. To take the example of the Soviet Union, its socialist model collapsed not only due to problems revolving around static efficiency (e.g., failure to make an equal number of right and left shoes), but also due to its failure in delivering the transition towards mass consumption. In other words, the major shortcoming of the socialist system was due to its inhibition in promoting effective technical change and innovations. Consequently one of the best arguments for market capitalism is that competition enhances a division of labor, invention of machinery, learning by doing, and thus a cumulative decline in some relative prices, opening yet new markets in a cumulative causation model (Boyer and Schmeder, 1990). In other words, markets might be inefficient in the short run, by inducing oversupply, unemployment, and possibly some transitory instabilities. Nevertheless, they are the necessary ingredients for reaping dynamic increasing returns to scale associated with competition and its stimulus of innovations.

4. Selecting among alternative organizations and institutions is another task rather well fulfilled by markets. If the model of development were clear enough for everyone, the role of markets would simply be to coordinate decentralized behaviors along such a path of growth. Unfortunately, the visible hand implemented by the large firm and conglomerates (Chandler, 1977) or the invisible handshake between capital and labor (Okun, 1981) have somehow vanished into contrasted and competing models for the internal organization of firms, subcontracting, and the wage labor nexus (Boyer, 1988, 1990a). How do economic agents make decisions among different alternatives, since most agents do not have the relevant information for making decisions on purely rational criteria? It is very tempting to assume that markets are Darwinian mechanisms for selecting among numerous and complex strategies. One recognizes the evolutionary process put forward by Joseph Schumpeter and his modern followers. Let the market decide among options about which individual actors are unable to screen out and to make rational choices. For example, if some successful and innovative industrial policies could be implemented during the golden years of the Fordist years, the eighties underwent a drastic revision of the possibility that governments or public agencies could efficiently influence most strategic choices. It is now widely believed that governments lack the ability to "pick the winners!" Thus, it is now widely believed that the process of diffusion of new technologies and organizations should accelerate once market forces identify the good ones.

In fact, the multiple meanings of the word "market" helps in explaining the extraordinary comeback in legitimacy of the market during the last fifteen years. The basic message of the present paper is to challenge the omnipotency of the market as a coordinating mechanism within contemporary societies. These societies exhibit a whole spectrum of alternative mechanisms for coordinating economic activity. The apology for a return to the free market might derive from a misperception or an erroneous interpretation of the structural changes that have been taking place during recent years. But the bulk of the paper develops a more formal argument.

MODERN ECONOMIC THEORY CHALLENGES THE FREE MARKET IDEOLOGY

To argue in favor of this seemingly unconventional view, the paper will capitalize upon the most recent advances in modern microeconomic theory: Market failures are frequent and require adequate monitoring (Akerlof, 1984; Benassy, 1982; Stiglitz, 1987; Stiglitz and Mathewson, 1986).

On the other hand, a careful reading of the theory of markets reveals how numerous and precise are the hypotheses necessary to guarantee that any market equilibrium is an optimum. If the quality of the good is uncertain and information asymmetric, if the technology derives from a learning by doing and using process or from network externalities, if the auctioneer is replaced by a complete decentralization of transactions in a monetary economy, if only few contingent markets or insurance mechanisms can be implemented, and/or when the commitment of workers is related to the fulfillment of a fairness criterion (i.e., if the equity principle partially explains static and dynamic efficiency), then the superiority of the market may totally collapse (Wolf, 1990). There might be no equilibria or too many or unstable ones, and, more generally, the market can be Pareto-inferior to alternative organizations provided by networks, associations, or even vertically integrated firms. Modern theoreticians therefore strongly disagree with the rather optimistic views propagated by the more vocal advocates of free markets: When the economy becomes complex, the reliance on pure market mechanisms raises as many problems as it solves.

During the thirties and forties, large numbers of market failures resulted in widespread calls for public intervention. As a result there emerged extensive regulation by the state and the monitoring of macroeconomic activity. Nowadays, economists and political scientists have converged toward a much more balanced view: Government failures tend to be as preoccupying as market failures. The comparison is no more between an optimum reached by the free functioning of markets and the existing equilibrium, but the task is to compare the pros and cons of alternative second-best arrangements. Here, it is useful to emphasize one original aspect of the present book: An elegant solution of the dilemma between inefficient bureaucrats on the one hand and unstable or unfair markets on the other is to recognize the existence of a quasicontinuum of coordinating mechanisms. They can be selected at the microlevel – given the structural and institutional external conditions – but may be combined at the economywide level.

Consequently, beneath the seemingly powerful return to free market mechanisms, most developed countries experience the complex and uncertain transition from one regime of a mixed economy towards another one, more adapted to the new configuration of the international arena, the specificity of organizational and technological innovations, and, of course, the new balance between various social groups. Perhaps here much can be learned from Karl Polanyi's prophetic work (Polanyi, 1946). By anthropological and historical analyses, he has convincingly demonstrated that most markets for commodities call for highly sophisticated institutional arrangements for their coordination, if their efficiency and self-adjusting property are to be obtained in really existing economies. Moreover, some key fictitious commodities such as money, labor, and nature will never be regulated by pure market mechanisms, since their supply is not set according to a maximization principle in response to changing relative prices. In fact, money is the prerequisite for any decentralized economy, not the unintended result of a free banking principle. Similarly, labor cannot be disentangled from human activity and life itself, so that labor markets will never exhibit typical self-clearing properties. Since nature is not an economic actor, certainly not a maximizing one with rational expectations, no market will ever solve the long-run biological survival of mankind and the ecological reproduction of health.

Mutatis mutandis, it is most likely that contemporary societies are experiencing a similar but much more complex transition to that observed during the interwar period. The majority of the analysts, policy makers, and journalists expect (and work for!) the triumph of the market. Yet the real issue is the institutional transition and organizational innovations that will provide a significant but ancillary role to markets, provided they are embedded in a set of social relations providing trust, loyalty, and commitment, i.e., the basic ingredients under which markets might be self-equilibrating and efficient.

THE MARKETS BETWEEN TAXONOMY AND GENERAL EQUILIBRIUM THEORY

For the average person in the street, the Keynesian "paradox of saving" is not so easy to understand. During depressions, the more eagerly people want to save in order to restore investment, the lower the employment level and ultimately the less optimistic the views about the future, and finally the lower the investment level. By contrast, the notion of market equilibrium is so intuitive and widely observed in everyday life, that most of the arguments of free marketers find an immediate impact upon public opinion. For instance, in order to induce a recovery in investment, it is not sufficient to save more? Similarly even the most ignorant economic agent would generally recognize that in many instances the replacement of an administrative or bureaucratic organization by a free market would improve the welfare of both suppliers and demanders. These two supplementary arguments call for a closer investigation.

FROM LOOSE AND CONTRADICTORY DEFINITIONS FOR MARKET

At one level, almost everyone in our society speaks about markets, and by everyday experience and behavior, most everyone has a seemingly clear definition or view. Unfortunately, the rhetoric about markets exhibits so many meanings that the success of the reference to markets might be attributed to their loose and partially contradictory definitions. They probably vary from one culture and language to another. The reading of newspapers, financial articles, applied research, and, of course, grand economic theories suggests at least six different meanings of markets (see Table 2-1).

In French, the term *marché,* which is usually translated as market, is generally defined as the equivalent of a contract, i.e., a bilateral agreement for delivering at a future date a given quantity of a specified good for a fixed price, eventually revised according to some explicit formula. For example, building companies have been competing to get the contract for the Paris la Défense Arch new tower. The bid and the related and sophisticated public legislation and private routines for organizing this competition is named *un marché.* In English, public or private procurement would be the more proximate equivalent to this selection device. In this case, the market does not coordinate ex post independent strategies but organizes the screening of the various offers and helps in selecting the best, i.e., generally the least costly or the second least costly, project. Let us stress that the final contract, actually negotiated, is bilateral and is enforced by the general legal system provided by the commercial laws prevailing in the area considered. This meaning is at odds with the conventional definition of the market as the locus where anonymous supplies and demands interact, with weak or no legal enforcement. Nevertheless, this conception is less marginal than it might seem, since this is a common routine in capitalist economies, if not in socialist countries. This absence contributes to block the transition toward market mechanisms, the commercial contracts being an elementary but basic ingredient of markets.

In the emergence of modern capitalist economies, the market is clearly associated with a precise localization and time schedule. A marketplace is "an authorized public concourse of buyers and sellers of commodities, meeting at a place more or less strictly delimited or defined, at an appointed time." This is the definition provided by the British Royal Commission on Market Rights and Tools in 1891 (Hill, 1987). In contemporary economies, only few markets are organized accordingly, with the exception of itinerant and periodic markets for food, agricultural products, flowers, and antiques (i.e., very limited scope in the whole set of transactions). Nevertheless,

Table 2-1. From a Micro Adjustment Process to a Complete Economic System: Too Many Meanings for the Single Word "Market"

Time horizon \ Space	Local	Intermediate	Global
Low periodicity	The market place		
Rather permanent		A market for a commodity	
Intertemporal		Financial markets	(Money)
		(Labor)	
Long-run dynamics			Market economy
Secular Trends			(Land/nature)

Note: The circles are used to label fictitious commodities in the sense of Karl Polanyi's work.

Polanyi (1946) and Braudel (1979) have carefully investigated how the market mechanisms have emerged from a highly regulated and institutionalized economic life. Consequently, contemporary global markets are the last followers of this embryonic form of market, which has been conquering a larger and larger fraction of commodities and ultimately some factor markets, such as labor (Rothenberg, 1992).

By extension, classical or neoclassical economists have given a wider definition for markets: "In the literal sense, a place in which things are bought and sold. In a modern industrial system it has expanded to include the whole geographical area in which sellers compete which each other for consumers" (Marshall, 1890). For example, one can read in the financial press that during the Spring of 1996 the market for beef underwent a severe recession in Europe due to the threat of and uncertainty about the "crazy cows" episode and that the price of beef has declined. This third concept proposes a kind of aggregation over a given geographical area and/or for one product or close substitutes. Note that the market is therefore losing its intuitive contents – it is no more the marketplace – but is gaining some analytical relevance, at least for economists or people engaged in marketing. In some extreme cases, the market could mean the demand addressed to a given sector or even at the economywide level, implying the equivalent of effective aggregate demand. This second definition is not at all equivalent to the first one.

According to a fourth conception, the market is basically a mechanism for making compatible a series of individual supplies and demands. Consequently, the theoreticians insist upon the fact that the market is clearing when the equilibrium price is obtained, and this tradition goes back to Adam Smith and has been prolonged until now by neoclassical economics. To quote Marshall again (1890), "Economists understand by the term of market, not only particular market places in which things are bought and sold, but the whole of any region in which buyers and sellers are in such a free intercourse with one another that the price of the same goods tends to equality, easily and quickly." A new and rather abstract property is therefore added to the definition of a market: It should adjust and converge toward a unique price. Subtly, the concreteness of the marketplace is contrasted with the theoretical and abstract properties of a self-equilibrating mechanism. The shift from a positive conception to another one, much more normative, is very clear in Marshall (1890): "The more nearly perfect the market is the stronger is the tendency for the same price to be paid for the same thing at the same time in all parts of the market." Here comes the ideal type of pure and perfect market mechanisms. Again this is not an evident property since, for example, the presentation by *Encyclopedia Britannica* (1980) immediately puts emphasis upon the variety of truly existing markets. On some of them, the producers offer their goods, whatever the price set by the market. On others, the producers set their own price and the demand is adjusted accordingly. One could recognize the distinction between buyers' and sellers' markets which are far away from the ideal of purely atomistic competition among economic agents taking for given the current relative prices.

A fifth conception generalizes the previous one to a whole set of inter-dependent markets. When, for example, economists and politicians consider the transition of socialist economies toward markets, they in fact character-ize an economic system, in which market competition is dominant or exclu-sive. For example, the intermediate products can be distributed according to an indicative or imperative planning (consider the surprising success of early French planning after World War II), but markets still prevail for consumer durables and final goods, land, labor, and capital. Therefore, there exists a complete spectrum of so-called market economies according to the extension of this coordinating mechanism. Implicitly, and explicitly for some authors (Braudel, 1979), a market economy is an alternative labeling for capitalism, private property, and competition, i.e., terms that are not logically equiva-lent. As far as economic theory is concerned, the conception of Walras (1988) is extended in modern equilibrium theory (Arrow and Hahn, 1971). In this very extreme vision, all economic agents are interacting *via* the equilibration of a complete system of interdependent demands expressed on every com-modity market but also for capital goods and the services of labor. Only money is not supplied and offered, since it is the simple numeraire in which all the nominal prices are expressed. In this vision, any macroeconomic mechanism is abolished; for example, sixty million French people are sup-posed to express their joint demand upon thousands of commodity markets. Again, one is struck by the large discrepancy between the empirical defini-tion of a market economy and its more sophisticated formalization. The truly existing institutions are implicitly compared with the ideal of a society co-ordinated by a series of pure and perfect markets upon which not any single individual has any influence but among which individuals are free to choose (Friedman, 1962; Friedman and Friedman, 1981).

In a metaphoric view, a market is assumed to exist when and where so-cial actors compete one with each other in order to get scarce resources or some restricted positions or status. When individuals with conflicting ob-jectives interact and finally converge toward an agreement or transaction, some economists and/or sociologists might conclude that there is the exis-tence of a quasimarket. For example, the Chicago school of economics has extended the concepts of rationality, equilibrium, and market to a large di-versity of social issues: the market for marriage, the economics of crime, the supply and demand of justice, and the market for donations to churches and or beliefs in eternal life (Becker, 1964, 1981). Such an extensive – even im-perialist – use of the concept of market is not without interest and simulta-neously exhibits very severe limits. On one side, Karl Marx and his follow-ers – including an American institutionalist school à la Veblen – have quite rightly pointed out that under capitalism everything (e.g., social respect, love, promise of eternal life, and political influence) becomes a commodity. In a sense, the Chicago theoreticians have taken seriously this Marxist prognosis. But on the other side, the use of the concept of market becomes so loose that it is more mystifying than enlightening: For instance, even if some private firms specialize in matching offers and demands for marriage, is it really serious to consider that the market is the allocating process by which spouses are chosen? Similarly, the market of political ideas and programs probably exists but does not provide any deep insight into the underlying issues of political debates. In fact, the interactions between markets and politics are far more complex (Alesina and Carliner, 1991; Hibbs, 1987). In this last conception, the market becomes so wide in its scope that it does not mean anything any more.

Nevertheless, no doubt that the polysemy of such a rich notion has played some role in the impressive comeback of free market ideas: Most people have long encountered one form or another of market, which therefore acquires a rather intuitive meaning, at the possible cost of major misunderstandings. Is there any relation between the marketplace for antiques and the call for a transition of Eastern European economies toward a market system? Between a contract or public procurement and the enchanted world of the Marshallian partial equilibrium or Walrasian general equilibrium?

TOWARD A TYPOLOGY OF CONTRASTED MARKET MECHANISMS

For our own purpose, it is important to propose a clear definition for the term "market," however imperfect and provisional, in order to bring some clarity into the following analyses. Basically, four different levels have to be disentangled and recombined in a second step.

At the level of a single commodity, a market is an institution that coordinates ex post the strategies of multiple traders, competing one with each other, therefore initially independent, but finally interacting via price formation. A full-fledged market supposes furthermore a well-defined commodity, with respect to quality and quantity, and repetitive transactions that are regularly organized and somehow centralized or at least made compatible by joint adjustments. Implicitly, any single market is inserted into a whole set of other markets, organizations, and institutions, at least in existing economies. For example, the existence of a monetary system is a prerequisite for the functioning of any commodity market, as nominal prices must be expressed in some unit. How are transactions paid? What are the methods for balancing the agents with deficit and surplus, i.e., how is the credit market structured? Similarly, a minimum legal environment is needed in order to assure the economic agents with respect to their buying and selling orders, which means either the existence of a business association in charge of the functioning of the market or a public authority with the capacity to enforce private contracts. In the absence of these two series of institutions or rules of the game, any market would collapse, due to the spreading of opportunistic behaviors among the traders. For instance, insider trading upon the stock market can destroy the confidence of outsiders and stop or reduce transactions. In other words, even if pure and perfect markets can be self-equilibrating, they are not self-enforcing, for they need an external foundation in the legal system, business ethics, and/or agreed rules of the game (Shand, 1990).

No single type of regime but a multiplicity of regimes may provide support for the functioning of markets. Contrary to the ideal of markets with pure and perfect competition put forward by Adam Smith, then elaborated by Alfred Marshall and ultimately generalized by Leon Walras, the interactions among a limited number of traders, with unequal wealth and market power, might deliver contrasting market structures. For example, a market may emerge as a structure of roles with a differentiated niche for each firm (White, 1981). The joint competition over quality and price does not necessarily lead to a sustainable market configuration since several market failures are theoretically observed. Thus a large variety of markets (White, 1988), are structurally embedded in a series of constraints (Leifer and White, 1988). Still more, the very precise institutionalization of a market may have important consequences upon its functioning and its macroeconomic outcome (Lesourne, 1991). Modern industrial economics, as well as the microformalizations about technical change and innovations, exhibit a complete spectrum of market configurations: complete or partial monopoly, cartel, and collusion, oligopoly, contestable market, perfectly contestable market, pure and perfect competition, complete or partial monopsony, etc. This is only a partial listing of different forms of competition (Stiglitz and Mathewson, 1986; Tirole, 1988). As far as the efficiency and welfare properties of a market are concerned, they cannot be assessed independently from a precise description. This is a major contribution of the abundant literature about a renewed microeconomic theory. It should inform any decision about deregulation and privatization. If, for example, Eastern European firms in a position of monopoly or oligopoly are privatized in the absence of any foreign competition, then few of the expected benefits of a pure and perfect competition will be reaped. The same remark could be addressed to the privatization program launched by the British and French governments in the mid-1980s: Changing the forms of property does not mechanically imply any strengthening of competition.

The extent and the scope of the market can itself vary from a totally marginal role (for instance, the long-distance trade in the Middle Ages) to an overwhelming mechanism percolating within the whole society and transforming even subtle social relations into mere commodities transacted upon specific pseudomarkets. Therefore, the notion of a market economy is often misleading since it implies that there is one unique configuration for the market mechanisms. This is largely contradicted by any international comparison between North and South or East and West (Esping-Andersen, 1990; Freeman, 1989) and by long-run historical studies showing the very slow process of the emergence of markets (Braudel, 1979; Galenson, 1989; Lindblom, 1977; Polanyi, 1946). Basically it is important for us to investigate whether market mechanisms are limited to the exchange of intermediate products between firms, or whether they concern final goods, directed to the domestic or the international markets. Similarly, property can be priced upon specific markets such as the stock exchange, whereas various financial assets may or may not be traded on specific markets. After the gale of financial innovations of the last two decades, still more sophisticated markets have been implemented in which traders are exchanging forecasts about the evolution of key macroeconomic variables, i.e., the so-called market for futures. This kind of market, based upon the photography game imagined by John Maynard Keynes, consists in finding the equivalent of the prettier face according to that which is expected to be the feeling of the majority. This clearly has few relations with the marketplace for antiques in Foire Saint Germain, which takes place each year near Paris! Finally, the market might become a major coordinating mechanism when a lot of fictitious commodities are turned into effective trading upon rather specific markets: labor, if this very genuine social relation can be regulated by pure supply and demand mechanisms; money, if various banks can issue their own currency, the value of which would be assessed upon an interbank currency market evaluating what is every day the exchange rate between one dollar deposited in one bank with respect to other banks; polluting rights, when they can be exchanged between firms. Remember that in this case it is not an exchange between economic agents and nature, but between individuals buying and selling rights granted by a local or national public authority. In fact it is not a private good but a public good with strong externalities and, consequently, possible failures of pure market adjustments.

Consequently, market economies exhibit a whole spectrum of configurations, not only as frequently implied by the discussions about the so-called return to free markets. Thus, an economic system with a leading role attributed to market competition should be characterized by the cross definition of the following features (see Table 2-2):

Table 2-2. What is a Market Economy? A Quasicontinuum of Configurations

Definition: A configuration for a market economy is any viable matrix such as …

The Prerequisites to any Market
- Private contracts
- Commercial Laws
- Monetary Regime
- Self-enforcing mechanisms/external referee

	Commodities	Fictitious	Extended
Monopoly			X
Oligopoly	X X		
Imperfect competition	X X		
Contestable market			
Perfect contestability	X		
Pure and perfect competition			

Extent of the market	Commodities				Fictitious commodities			Extended commodities		
Degree of perfection	Raw material	Intermediate	Equipment	Consumer good	Labor	Money	Land/nature	Finance	Futures	Pollution
• Monopoly (/monopsony)	Emerging merchant capitalism									
• Oligopoly		Early	industrial	market	economy					
• Imperfect competition			The Fordist regime							
			Mature industrial market economy		Interwar period					
• Contestable market		The		trends		for		the		
• Perfectly contestable market			contemporary			economies				
• Pure and perfect competition	advanced	as	the	The ideal of	neoclassical					
					theory			of a capitalist economy		

big market

- The list of institutions, organizations, legislation, or associations that are organizing the functioning of the various markets, with a detailed description of their responsibilities, objectives, tools, and enforcement tools or incentives.
- The series of commodities, the supply and demand of which is regulated by market institutions, with their possible interactions with alternative coordinating mechanisms (hierarchies, networks, state regulation).
- A characterization of the forms of competition, according to the number of traders, the distribution of ownership, the distribution of market power, and the possible explicit or implicit coordinating mechanisms, in order to solve overcapacity problems or to respond to uncertainty and/or structural changes.

This three-dimensional matrix defines rigorously as many market economic systems as there are combinations of cells in this matrix. The proportion of markets among the alternative mechanisms could define a measure for the proximity to a pure, perfect, and complete market economy. For instance, it can be argued that in modern economies the coordination within the large firms is as important as market adjustments (Coase, 1937, 1988) and that quasiplanned coordination has largely replaced market coordination (Lazonick, 1991). Then the most interesting problem for the social sciences, especially political economy and economic analysis, would be to assess the viability of these various configurations and compare them with respect to their welfare properties.

More generally, each form of market is completed by or embedded in a series of other coordinating mechanisms, which are based either on obligation (and not only self-interest) and/or vertical coordination, alliances, hierarchies, communities, networks, or public authorities (Campbell, Hollingsworth, and Lindberg, 1991; Coleman, 1990; Schmitter, 1990). The task for social scientists would then be to assess the viability – and not so much the efficiency – of such a complex hierarchy of constitutional principles, institutions, incentive schemes, and organizations (North, 1990). Thus, the product, labor, and credit markets organize a competition among alternative organizations (Favereau, 1989), not only among old and new technologies (Nelson and Winter, 1982). This is the huge but stimulating agenda proposed by recent analyses (Hollingsworth, Schmitter, and Streeck, 1994).

AN ARGUMENT OF LAST RESORT: THE RIGOR AND THE ELEGANCE OF TWO WELFARE THEOREMS

In everyday life, managers, unionists, households, bankers, bureaucrats, and, even more so, politicians have to rely on simpler ideas than those suggested by the previous typology. Given the structural crisis of Fordism, should national economies evolve toward more market competition or toward more public interventions and different forms of institutionalization? When the world is complex and uncertain, clear and crisp conceptions, perhaps grossly or partially erroneous, usually win over more tricky but difficult to capture alternative representations. Here the ideal of pure and perfect markets has very good arguments.

Market prices are better than administered prices: On any single market, most economic agents usually consider this property as intuitive and convincing. Basically, when suppliers and demanders are free to make offers and counteroffers, the final outcome is considered as defining the equivalent of an optimum since all the economic agents have exhausted the opportunity for mutually advantageous exchanges (Eggertsson, 1990). Of course, this is the case if unfettered competition has pushed the price toward its pure and perfect competition level, which in some sense is an optimum. But the same superiority of market will be recognized by agents even if competition is imperfect, at least to some degree (for a strong objection, see "Modern Micro Theories against the Omnipotence of Pure Market Mechanisms, page 75). Striking examples are available:

On labor markets, the eighties and the nineties have frequently exhibited the following argument: Minimum wages are to be discarded since they price out young and inexperienced workers with low marginal productivities. If wages were free to move downward, then firms with production processes intensive in labor would have an interest in hiring these workers. Symmetrically, some wage earners, especially outsiders, would prefer being employed at lower market wages over being unemployed (Lindbeck and Snower, 1986). The welfare system itself, as well as the state, would be better off, since they would recover higher contributions to collective insurance and larger taxes. In other words, any regulation imposing minimum – or maximum – wages would not be Pareto optimal. In the absence of any general equilibrium effect operating in the opposite direction, the reasoning seems convincing to a large fraction of public opinion. A Keynesian argument about the nonexistence of any true labor market and the absence of a clear equilibrating role for wages would be discarded as counterintuitive and paradoxical. Fairness should be totally disconnected from efficiency (OECD, 1993), whatever the empirical findings about the importance of fairness upon the functioning of labor markets (Kahneman, Knetsch, and Thaler, 1986).

For agricultural products and especially policies of administered prices, the same reasoning can be extended to show the nonoptimality of any fixed prices. Of course, prices higher than the world levels benefit the income maintenance of farmers, as they do in Europe, Japan, and the United States. But the cost is paid by consumers, who are spending more for food and thus are worse off. If the national economies were allowed to buy at the world prices, the supplement of welfare for consumers could be partially used to compensate the loss of farmers' income due to their declining production. Sophisticated simulations derived from an applied general equilibrium model seem to demonstrate that the potential welfare gains are significant if not very large (Martin et al., 1990). If politically the related transfers could be implemented, the whole society would be better off. Basically, let market forces provide an efficient allocation of scarce resources and, if governments disagree about the associated income distribution, adequate transfers can be organized to provide the desired new equilibrium, which will deliver another Pareto optimum.

This is a wonderful example of more general results, known as the two welfare theorems, which will now be presented. In a Walrasian world, any equilibrium is a Pareto optimum. According to this First Fundamental Theorem of Welfare Economics, a society that would be organized entirely through market mechanisms would reach an efficient allocation of scarce resources and productive factors. This means that the situation of any economic agent could not be improved without the welfare of another one deteriorating. More precisely, this theorem deserves the following conditions. If there are enough markets, if all consumers and producers behave competitively, and if an equilibrium exists, then the allocation of resources in that equilibrium will be Pareto optimal, i.e., the satisfaction of any consumer or producer cannot be improved without impairing that of others (Arrow and Hahn, 1971; Debreu, 1959; and the survey by Ledyard, 1987). This theorem is important since it shows under which conditions a pure market economy can deliver an efficient equilibrium. Note that these conditions are numerous and not so easy to fulfill in actual economies: An auctioneer is coordinating ex ante all the exchanges after an initial trial and error process during which he finds out the vector of equilibrium prices clearing all the markets simultaneously. In a sense, such an economy is managed as the equivalent of Wall Street or a centrally planned economy (Heal, 1973).

Atomistic competition prevails, i.e., the traders are so numerous that none of them can exert any monopoly power, and consequently they adjust passively their supply and demand according to the system of relative prices, without any strategic behavior. Ideally some very abstract models show that, if the number of agents tends toward infinity, pure and perfect equilibrium will then be asymptotically reached.

The number of goods is finite and their quality is common knowledge. In the simplest models, each good is supposed to be given by its physical characteristics and eventually its localization. In more sophisticated formalizations, the goods are indexed according to the various states of nature, and intertemporal transactions can be organized due to the existence of a complete set of future contingent markets (Debreu, 1959). No existing economy exhibits such a characteristic even though the financial markets for futures have developed tremendously. It is not possible, however, to place a contingent order for December 31, 2002 for a black Saturn automobile, with the provisions that I will not be unemployed and the price of the oil barrel will be below $15!

All the goods are privately appropriated, i.e., no public good or external effect is present in this market economy. If such a good exists, no rational agent will agree to finance it due to a free rider dilemma: Why not benefit from public goods paid for by others? Consequently, in the absence of a collective authority, no public good will be provided in this economy. Of course, the concept of equilibrium can be extended to such public goods (e.g., general education, security, trust, loyalty, research and development, transport infrastructures). Yet there might exist a multiplicity of equilibria, each of them associated with various tax or incentive systems: The market is no longer able to provide an adequate supply of such goods. Since such public goods are more and more important in modern economies, this is a serious challenge to pure market competition.

Returns to scale are constant, which is a condition for any equilibrium of private property to exist. If these returns were increasing, then only one monopoly firm could provide the market and would eventually push the equilibrium to an infinite production! Again, if such increasing returns to scale are observed, pure market forces are unable to provide either any satisfactory equilibrium or any Pareto optimum.

A complete set of contingent markets exists in order to solve all the problems associated with intertemporal choices of consumers and producers. Consequently, any loss associated with uncertainty is removed and the historical path does not matter at all, since all the transactions in the future are already organized at the initial period. No irreversibility is allowed by such a model, quite at odds with a fundamental feature of industrial capitalism (Boyer, Chavance, and Godard, 1991).

By hypothesis, all equity problems can be separated from the objective of efficiency. Such a distinction allows one to disconnect value judgments completely from economic criteria about static efficiency. This is an elegant method for escaping some crucial issues in contemporary economies, as will be developed more extensively in the following section.

Whatever the restrictive character of these seven hypotheses, a free marketer can use this first welfare theorem to push the argument in favor of more and more market mechanisms. Of course, in present societies some markets are missing, some monopolies or oligopolies are inducing unsatisfactory equilibria, and information about the quality of goods is asymmetric. But let one extend the scope of the markets, and these imperfections will be removed and a Pareto optimum will be reached. If politically and socially pure and perfect competition could be implemented, then most contemporary problems about inflation, unemployment, and financial instability would vanish.

Conversely, in the second welfare theorem any Pareto optimum can be obtained as a market equilibrium, under certain conditions quite similar to those of the first welfare theorem. Both the preference set of consumers and the production set of producers have to be convex, i.e., marginal utility of any good has to be decreasing along with marginal productivity of any factor. Of course, all economic agents have to behave competitively, i.e., maximize satisfaction or profit for any given system of prices (Debreu, 1959). Of course, this result is very abstract, and one imagines that only trained professional economists know it and can use it during the discussion about the design of alternative economic systems (Brus, 1987; Bourguigon, 1990). Nevertheless it has some relevance for this paper.

First, this second welfare theorem reinforces the disconnection between social values and economic efficiency. Basically, imagine a socialist planner who would like to maximize any collective objective function, including the satisfactions of each individual agent (Lesourne, 1964). He could, under certain conditions, converge toward the collective optimum by totally relying upon market forces. He would have only to organize the transfers in initial resources which will sustain the corresponding market equilibrium. Second, and consequently, it is not necessary to build brand new coordinating mechanisms to fulfill a socialist objective: The idea of market socialism (Lange, 1937) is comforted by such a theorem. Third, for authors such as Lerner (1934) and Taylor (1929), an ideal socialist economy would look like a perfect Walrasian economy, in which a benevolent planner would play the role of a general auctioneer. Fourth, the present transition of Eastern European countries puts a strong emphasis upon the possible relevance of such a conception of market and democratic socialism: Instead of breeding a large and oppressing bureaucracy, why not use the market as a tool to stimulate entrepreneurship, workers' commitments, and more generally the concern for efficiency?

So far, so good: The market seems the most wonderful mechanism ever invented to coordinate individual strategies and enhance global efficiency. This was the core conclusion of mathematical neoclassical economists during the early seventies. Since then, the intellectual climate and the economic problems have drastically changed. To paraphrase one of the leading mathematical economists, these findings have been challenged by the very success of the methodology which consists of applying intensively deductive reasoning and mathematical formalization to economic issues (Hahn, 1992: 47). The deepening of the theory has recently led to provocative conclusions, which totally contradict the generality of self-equilibrating market mechanisms. Furthermore, these new results deliver interesting insights as regard the most pressing contemporary macroeconomic problems: the hysteresis of employment (at least in Europe), and financial instability in spite of the sophistication of market for futures.

MODERN MICRO THEORIES AGAINST THE OMNIPOTENCE OF PURE MARKET MECHANISMS

For Adam Smith, the invisible hand argument was intuitively very strong. Unfortunately, the mathematical investigation of the conditions for the existence of one equilibrium, its stability, and its equivalence with a Pareto optimum has shown that such a miraculous harmonization of interests was exceptional. Given the core features of modern economies, the market mechanisms — if they were exclusive and ruling the totality of society — would do as much harm as good to welfare. In a sense, the very success of the general equilibrium research program has unwound into an unprecedented crisis in economic theory (Ingrao and Israel, 1990). Neoclassical tools now contradict rather critically the optimism of Doctor Pangloss and consequently the claims of free market ideologies. In real economies, the market is too clumsy to be given major responsibility for monitoring monetary creation, quality, evaluation, or worker loyalty.

For a decade, academic reviews have abounded in papers exhibiting an incredible number of market failures and arguing for alternative coordinating mechanisms. A brief synthesis will be provided here and will be organized according to the seven hypotheses that are necessary to warrant the two fundamental welfare theorems (Table 2-3).

THE DECENTRALIZATION OF MONETARY ECONOMIES AGAINST THE COMPLETE CENTRALIZATION OF GENERAL EQUILIBRIUM THEORY

In a decentralized monetary economy, no equilibrium may exist or, if one exists, the equilibrium may not be a Pareto optimum. The paradox of the Walrasian model has long been unnoticed: In fact, this corresponds to a rather strange economy in which all the supplies and demands are centralized and transmitted to an auctioneer. This is a beginning and acceptable hypothesis

Table 2-3. A Typology for Market Failures and Their Consequences

The hypotheses of the two welfare theorems	Stylized features of contemporary economies	Consequences upon market functioning
1. De facto, complete centralization of transactions, no need for money	1. Largely decentralized exchanges are allowed by money and credit.	1. Multiplicity ... or absence of any equilibrium. Efficiency is no more warranted.
2. Atomistic competition among very numerous agents.	2. Imperfect competition via product differentiation is the rule.	2. Market equilibria are no more efficient.
3. Finite list of goods, their quality known.	3. Producers are better informed than consumers; product innovation is crucial.	3. Markets do not clear: unemployment and overcapacities.
4. Purely private goods, without any external effect.	4. Existence of many public goods and external effects (security, education, R&D, etc.).	4. Competitive markets imply an underinvestment in collective goods.
5. Constant returns to scale and fixed technologies.	5. Learning by doing, by using and increasing dynamic returns to scale are significant.	5. Imperfect competition is the rule; inefficient techniques can persist, with multiplicity of path-dependent equilibria.
6. All contingent future markets exist.	6. Only few financial markets allow intertemporal transactions.	6. Existing markets cannot deliver an adequate intertemporal coordination: inefficient equilibria are the rule.
7. Equity principles have not any influence upon efficiency.	7. Workers' loyalty and commitment are linked to a fair treatment.	7. Markets do not clear; unemployment can persist.

for a very specific and highly organized market, such as the stock market, but not at all for the bulk of transactions on the products and factors markets, where such a centralization does not occur. It is precisely the strength of really existing economies that transactions take place in a sequential manner in a vast number of segmented markets. On the contrary, the pure theory of general equilibrium finally assumes a quasicentralized economy in which all the transactions are simultaneously fulfilled through the equivalent of a planning agency. Still more, money only plays the role of numeraire, but does not intervene in the transactions or in the holding of reserves.

If totally decentralized transactions are introduced and, of course, if money balances are the only method for expressing effective demand, then a totally different kind of theory has to be elaborated: The so-called disequilibrium theory deals with such generalization, which exhibits a multiplicity of regimes, the Walrasian equilibrium being only a specific one, very unlikely to be reached by pure market mechanisms. Still more, it can be shown that, in the absence of a single and accepted money or numeraire, the equilibrium may not exist or, if it exists, it is far from any optimum for the society. Consequently, in a totally decentralized monetary economy, pure and perfect competition in product and labor markets does not lead to a satisfactory equilibrium (Benassy, 1982). Even a casual observation of post-Communist transitions to markets in Eastern Europe shows that a series of free markets in the context of uncertainty and multiple currency may lead to quite unsatisfactory outcomes in terms of growth, employment, and welfare.

STRATEGIC BEHAVIOR VERSUS PRICE TAKING: THE POSSIBLE INSTABILITY OF MARKET ECONOMIES

If agents behave strategically (i.e., if they do not take as given the prices they observe), then competition is no longer atomistic, and economic agents can collude in order to coordinate their supply and demand. They can form cartels and oligopoly, and, in some extreme cases, increasing returns to scale or natural scarcity can create a pure monopoly. In all these cases production is not a social optimum – in comparison with a pure and perfect competition case in which everybody is acting parametrically and takes as given the price and the strategies of other suppliers or demanders. No general results can be obtained under imperfect competition, and the property of the equilibrium will depend drastically upon the distribution of monopoly rents (D'Aspremont, Dos Santos Ferreira, and Gerard-Varet, 1989).

The unequal power of economic agents has an impact on the level of production and employment and the distribution of income – as well as wealth – when the transactions are repeated through time. Contrary to the idealistic Walrasian model, no optimum distribution is obtained, and cumulative inequalities tend to be generated. Again, the transition toward a market economy – for example, in Russia – clearly shows that markets can be associated with collusion, speculation, and even corruption and do not necessarily correspond to the ideal of economics textbooks. Some agents have more resources, power, and information than others, and they can capture oligopolistic rents without providing any significant increase in the supply of the more required basic goods.

WHEN QUALITY IS UNCERTAIN, MARKETS MIGHT BE INEFFICIENT

When information is asymmetric about the nature and the quality of goods, markets have a difficult task to perform: The price is then usually considered as indirect evidence for the underlying quality (the higher the price posted, the better the expected quality). Consequently, the price is to fulfill two potentially conflicting objectives. First, it is to allocate scarce resources by revealing marginal cost and/or marginal utility. Second, it is to transmit a signal about the level of quality. Of course, Akerlof (1984) has demonstrated with very simple models that no equilibrium can exist in such markets for lemons. This is not a curiosity limited to exotic or used goods, but this can explain why firms might be unwilling to hire workers demanding too low wages, since this will be interpreted as the result of a poor productivity or quality. Consequently, the wage will no longer fulfill its task for equilibrating labor markets. Similarly, firms proposing to pay excessively high interest rates upon their loans will be rejected by any rational banker in fear of a very risky business and probably bankruptcy (Stiglitz and Weiss, 1981).

Once more, the nice symmetry and smoothness of pure market mechanisms vanish and turn into unequal market power. Usually, the producers know better than the buyers the basic quality of the goods they supply, and consequently they can fool them, especially if the related transaction is infrequent. Of course, if such a situation is repeated, the consumer may counterattack and refuse to buy any more the highly priced but low quality goods, by a so-called reputation effect. Again, durable good markets, as well as labor and credit ones, will no longer be at their full equilibrium and the two welfare theorems are no longer true: The market does not any longer automatically provide an optimum for the society. It might well be more efficient than a centralized planning of the Soviet type, but its efficiency will depend upon the precise institutional setting in which each market is operating: Some might be very efficient, whereas others might deliver catastrophic results. It is sufficient to consider the supply of agri-

cultural products in the former Soviet Union republics in order to realize
that the dissolution of the central planning agency (Gosplan) and its replacement by a series of rather anarchic markets has not enhanced the supply of farmers. A very bad market can be inferior to moderately imperfect
planning.

MARKET MECHANISMS ARE UNABLE TO COPE WITH EXTERNALITIES AND PUBLIC GOODS

Even if one supposes that quality is well defined and that a large number
of economic agents are pushing toward a competitive equilibrium, the result might be far away from a Pareto optimum if the services derived from
the use of a product cannot be totally appropriated by the buyer. A well-
known example relates to public goods such as security, law enforcement,
defense, and clean air: The benefits from such goods cannot be appropriated privately, and conversely it is difficult to rely on pure market mechanisms in order to organize the equilibrium between supply and demand
(Coase, 1960). For example, everybody would like such collective goods
to be available but nobody will be ready to pay for them. When asked if
they should be implemented by a public agency, agents would refuse to
reveal their private utility: One recognizes the free rider problem inherent in public goods (Schotter, 1990) and collective action (Olson, 1965:
Sandler, 1992). Consequently, the market mechanism has to be replaced
by another coordination device, such as regulations, compulsory requirements, delegation to an agency, provision of a typical public good by the
state, etc. A special field of economic theory exists in order to enlighten
public choices. It recurrently shows that it is quite difficult to design optimal devices that would be as efficient as markets for purely private
goods. Consequently, the market failure related to their inability to deal
with public goods finally leads to intervention by the state or associations'
interventions, which in turn tend to encounter other forms of failures
(Wolf, 1979, 1990).

But the existence of externalities is far more general than the diffusion
of pure public goods. Some of them can be partially appropriated but nevertheless have positive or negative external effects. For instance, it has been
recurrently shown that education exerts considerable spillover on innovation, health, and consequently growth and productivity at a society-wide
level. If individuals freely decide both to consume and invest in education,
the level of aggregate investment will be inferior to the optimal level for the
whole economy. Again, the pure market mechanism has to be mitigated or
complemented by collective intervention in order to restore more efficient

results: subsidies to schools or students, public funding of the educational system, etc. *Mutatis mutandis,* the same arguments could be put forward for health care: In the absence of adequate insurance or welfare, individuals will tend to underinvest in prevention and health maintenance, since the general level of health is the equivalent of a public good.

The same inefficiency of markets prevails when these externalities can be negative: If clean air and water are considered as free goods, then firms and individuals will prefer to save costly resources instead of preserving the environment. Again, some public intervention is needed: either standards for limiting pollution levels or implementation of allocating polluting rights. This seems to mimic a quasimarket mechanism. Yet it is not at all the equivalent of a conventional supply and demand adjustment, since nature does not react in accordance with economic objectives, nor is its behavior easy to forecast, given such basic uncertainties about the underlying physical and chemical mechanisms as weather warming, ozone layer, urban pollution, etc.

In all these instances, a pure market economy would underinvest in health, education, infrastructures, i.e., every time positive externalities are observed, and conversely would over-invest in polluting or hazardous equipment. Given the importance of these issues in contemporary societies, there is a clear limit to the omnipotence of markets.

INCREASING RETURNS TO SCALE CANNOT BE MONITORED BY PURE AND PERFECT MARKETS

A special configuration for positive externalities relates to the increasing returns to scale associated with the most powerful engine of growth for capitalist economies, i.e., division of labor. This idea has to be traced back to Adam Smith, when he put forward the basic hypothesis that labor division allows specialization and consequently large productivity increases, which are positively related to the size of the product market. *The Wealth of Nations* consequently delivers a paradox: The stability of a monetary order induces the diffusion of markets, which in turn allows labor division and increasing returns to scale. But this hypothesis is disruptive for General Equilibrium Theory: If the returns to scale are superior to one, then no pure and perfect competition equilibrium can be sustained (Debreu, 1959). In existing economies, one large monopoly firm would capture the whole market and then charge a monopolistic price: This would deplete the level of demand and the output below the optimum level for the society. In old-fashioned terms, in the presence of increasing returns to scale, competition leads to oligopolistic or even monopolistic configurations – which will be far from the optimum toward which market mechanisms were supposed to converge according to the two welfare theorems.

This argument has been rejuvenated by recent researches about the sources of capitalist growth. It has been shown that, in the absence of increasing returns to scale or positive externalities, the growth of any national economy would exhaust itself (Amable and Guellec, 1992; Romer, 1986). This was precisely the Schumpeterian argument concerning the viability of capitalism: The competitive process induces the search for innovation, that in turn delivers monopoly rents which can be invested. Yet followers usually copy the path breaking innovation, and the diffusion process progressively erodes profit and ultimately puts an end to the long boom triggered by the initial innovation. Endogenous innovation and technical change are at the core of two basic features of capitalism, both development (i.e., a long-term trend toward rising productivity and standard of living) and the inescapable recurrence of booms and depressions. This vision is far from the smooth process postulated by conventional economic theory.

Another paradox of contemporary economic theory emerges. If the emphasis is shifted from a static adjustment process to the sources of innovation and endogenous growth, then increasing returns to scale have to be taken into account as a prerequisite for any cumulative and sustained growth. Provided that firms take for granted the external effects exerted by their own decisions, a series of static equilibria can be obtained by a totally decentralized market economy (Lucas, 1988; Romer, 1990). But the related equilibria will no more correspond to Pareto optima, since everybody will generally underinvest in research and development, which exhibits positive external effects. Thus, alternative coordinating mechanisms have to be designed in order to fight market failures: subsidies to innovating firms, public laboratories, and credit incentives. In some extreme cases, the rivalry about innovations may induce a duplication of R&D expenditures and consequently an innovation rate that is too rapid. Then comes the possibility of structural unemployment: More old jobs are destroyed by innovation than created by its implementation (Aghion and Howitt, 1993).

In other words, markets are good for triggering innovation but might be very bad at monitoring the optimum pace for technical change. Too many market mechanisms might hurt growth, i.e., the inner mechanisms for capitalism, dynamism, and survival. Modern economic theories have definitely discarded the Panglossian optimism of old conventional neoclassical theory: There exists an optimum degree for market competition, which is not necessarily the maximum one.

WHEN IT IS COSTLY TO IMPLEMENT CONTINGENT FUTURE MARKETS, SPECULATION AND INSTABILITY ARE LIKELY

Basically the previous limits of market mechanisms derive from the difficulty of coordinating behaviors in case of external effects within a given geographic space. *Mutatis mutandis,* the same difficulties emerge when time is concerned, i.e., every time a decision exerts a possibly irreversible impact upon the outcome and decisions taking place tomorrow. One has to remember that in General Equilibrium Theory the auctioneer is in charge of centralizing all the supply and demand for all the subsequent periods according to contingent markets upon all the states of nature that may occur from now until the most remote future. This elegant device is actually abstracting from the most pressing problems addressed by markets – when the future is basically uncertain and every economic agent has to make an irreversible decision in the absence of any contingent market (Newberry, 1989).

Actually, only a few future markets are operating in contemporary economies and they basically concern raw materials, stocks and bonds, and quite recently financial future markets. Consequently, firms and traders cannot fully insure themselves against uncertainty in product and labor markets: Too few intertemporal markets are in charge of equilibrating supply and demand over the long run (Hahn, 1989). Thus, agents have to use any available information in order to work out expectations for all the subsequent periods and make their decisions about investment and commitments via future contracts. But now, contrary to the totally deterministic Walrasian economy, these expectations and plans can turn out to be erroneous, inflicting severe losses both to individuals and even to the national economy given the possible externalities created by inflation, hyperinflation, deflation, and cumulative depression (Bryant, 1983).

As a matter of consequence, macroeconomic dynamics might exhibit large instability, due to the very efficiency of market mechanisms. The relative price of goods will tend to reflect both consumer preferences and marginal costs, but the cybernetic process of inventory, production, and employment adjustments might lead to overshooting, especially on financial markets, which diffuse themselves to labor and product markets. For some critical values of the speed of reaction to market disequilibria, the economy may fall into a low employment trap (Duménil and Lévy, 1989). This might reflect the process that took place in the United States from 1929 to 1932: Such a free marketer but smart economist as Fisher (1933) was thus obliged to discard his pet hypothesis about the self-equilibration of markets and to work out an innovative model anticipatory of Keynes' General Theory.

Once observing a debt deflation, all firms and consumers will have an interest in restructuring their debts by distressed sales, therefore exacerbating the fall in production and employment. Clearly, markets are not always and everywhere delivering full employment and efficiency.

Facing these disturbing results, a free marketer economist usually puts forward two propositions. First, all these disturbances are seemingly emerging from inaccurate expectations, i.e., an ad hoc hypothesis about the irrationality of economic agents. As time elapses, most of them will learn about the real functioning of the economy and consequently will converge toward fully rational expectations, thus a more satisfactory configuration for the economy. Unfortunately, this conventional argument, coined and illustrated by Lucas (1984), has not proven sufficient to restore the stability of a market economy with no contingent market but rational expectations. A multiplicity of equilibria, basic instability, and very frequently no Pareto efficient property are frequent features of such a configuration. The rational expectation hypothesis does not help in preventing the existence of exogenous arrangements and conventions (Chiappori, 1991).

But a second strategy in the defense of markets has been proposed. Since all these disappointments come from an insufficient number of future and contingent markets, why not create new ones and restore the basic efficiency of a complete market economy? Incidentally, this was the rationale for some financial innovations during the eighties and led to the creation of still more sophisticated markets. But this has not been a general trend for product markets or labor markets, and this is easy to explain. One of the core hypotheses about market efficiency is that the transaction costs to design contracts, to organize marketplaces, and to synchronize a complete set of supplies and demands are nil or very small indeed. Nevertheless, this is not necessarily so: "The operation of the market costs something and ... forming an organization and allowing some authority [an entrepreneur] to direct the resources, certain marketing costs are saved" (Coase, 1937). Even if until now few studies have been devoted to measuring these transaction costs (Coase, 1992), this argument is strong enough to relativize completely the inner superiority of the market. Networks, associations, quasivertical integration, clubs, and in some instances state regulations might be superior to the market (Williamson, 1985).

Thus, future markets will likely be limited to a very restricted set of goods unless technical change, concerning specialty communications and computer science, deliver a sharp reduction in transaction costs. If so, the financial markets are bounded to focus all the expectations about the future configuration of the national and international economies. But then another threat challenges the stability of such financial instruments by opposition to the self-equilibration of typical market goods: Self-fulfilling prophecies might occur (Kreps, 1977) and induce financial bubbles far from the equilibrium price that would be rationally deduced from a careful analysis of the underlying fundamentals (Orléan, 1990). Consequently, any disturbance might trigger the bursting of such bubbles, a defect which recurrently affects all financial markets since their creation (Kindleberger, 1978). Instabilities are still exacerbated when strong horizontal interaction occurs in the formation of traders' opinions about the future of the market and more generally the prospects of the economy (Orléan, 1990).

This dynamic inefficiency of markets is far from being restricted to finance and credit, since it may apply even to new technologies. If, for instance, the rate of return of a technological device (or social convention) is not only related to the inner payback for each individual but is positively linked to the number of adopters, then a series of seemingly efficient choices through market mechanisms might ultimately prove to deliver unsatisfactory results (Arthur, 1988). Let us think, for example, about AZERTY and QWERTY keyboards, software standards, electrical norms, physical units, and so on (David, 1988). All these examples demonstrate that a minimal public intervention, if not indicative planning, would deliver a more efficient configuration than does a sequence of spot markets. Again, time and externalities basically challenge the assumptions about the omnipotence of market.

FOR SOME MARKETS, EFFICIENCY AND EQUITY CANNOT BE DISENTANGLED

For conventional economic theory, distributional equity issues are totally separable from efficiency in a Pareto vision. Any competitive equilibrium delivers outcomes in which the well-being of any agent cannot be improved without impairing the situation of another one. While economic theory has only to consider efficiency, the philosopher and political scientist will take into account the equity issue. If, for example, the distribution of income and wealth is not accepted by public opinion and citizens, an optimal redistribution scheme can be implemented in order to shift the economy from one Pareto equilibrium to another that is more satisfactory from a social justice point of view (Wolf, 1990). From this standpoint, the market would be neutral with respect to social justice.

This vision has been challenged by many analysts. For societies, social justice is as essential as truth for scientific theories, whereas efficiency comes after such a basic requirement has been fulfilled (Boltanski and Thevenot, 1992). So inefficient economy configurations could be accepted, provided they fit with the prevailing conception about fairness and social justice.

Thus, existing democratic regimes and market economies are facing a dilemma between economic efficiency and social justice. The conventional answer is well-known: Let the economist depict the related trade-off and give the politician the task of selecting the optimal mix between efficiency and equity (Samuelson and Nordhaus, 1992).

More recent research totally challenges this clearcut distinction, but implements contrasted strategies. On one side, experimental economics suggests that initially, even if the outcomes of market mechanisms are perceived as unfair, when the game is played again and again, progressively agents consider that the outcome is finally fair (Kahneman, Knetsch, and Thaler, 1986). Thus economic efficiency would shape the prevailing conceptions about social justice. Similarly, some theoreticians argue that law and jurisprudence are finally aiming at increasing the surplus or welfare of the economy (Posner, 1981). The institutions devoted to the implementation of justice would therefore enhance efficiency.

On the other side, it is clear that some extreme inequalities that are delivered by the strengthening of market allocation might finally hurt the acceptance of the principles of a market economy, especially if citizens can vote and express their dissent with the prevailing configuration of income and wealth distribution. According to this vision, too extreme inequalities would finally do more harm than good to market efficiency, fostering poor commitment and loyalty, insecurity, and threat to private property and personal security. All these factors finally call for more public interventions and spending, which induces the allocation of too many resources to unproductive uses. These ideas specially apply to contemporary labor markets. If unfairly treated, wage earners will reply with poor productivity, low quality, high absenteeism, and a multiplication of social conflict. Thus, a more equitable income distribution can enhance private and global efficiency (Akerlof, 1984). Similarly, labor markets are not self-adjusting as typical good markets, because workers have definite feelings about the unfairness of wage cuts which would destroy group solidarity (Solow, 1990). This has definite consequences upon the existence of a stable unemployment equilibrium, contrary to that postulates the new classical macroeconomic theory (Hahn and Solow, 1995).

Historical analyses suggest that one last market failure is the possible inability of this mechanism to cope with the prevailing conceptions about social justice. For example, the widening of inequalities early during the industrial revolution was responsible for a great deal of political and social flux, which eventually undermined economic efficiency. *Mutatis mutandis,* the current transition of Eastern European countries toward a market economy has put forward the possible contradiction between the implementation of the market and the preservation of a minimum degree of solidarity and equity. Finally, this experience reminds us that the social acceptance of markets is not automatic but assumes a voluntary adhesion to their values and consequences, i.e., a definite social fabric (Douglas, 1986).

Thus, the advances of research in microeconomic theory have weakened most of the conventional reasons for believing in the absolute efficiency of markets. They are self-equilibrating and deliver Pareto optima only under very restricted conditions (Fleurbaey, 1990). It is a question of empirical analysis for each issue, not of grand theory. This opens a much more modest approach: Markets may be the least unsatisfactory form of private information, given the inability of agents to draw a complete picture of a myriad of interdependent decisions in a very uncertain environment. This is the argument first expressed by Hayek in his 1945 essay "The Use of Knowledge in Society" (Hayek, 1980), and recently rediscovered by the economic profession, outside the neo-Austrian school (Lavoie, 1986).

Paradoxically, in the nineties the reliance on markets has become more a question of informed or naive belief than the outcome of mathematical demonstration. In this respect, East European governments may rightfully prefer the dynamism (and possible disorder) of markets to the stagnation that ended the centralized planning era (Kornai, 1980, 1992). Markets may deliver an acceptable mix between short-run efficiency, long-run innovation, and a minimal degree of social justice (Kregel, Matzner, and Grabher, 1992). However, Eastern Europe also must develop new rules of the game and institutions in order to have a well-functioning economy, and this is more and more recognized by experts (Clague and Rausser, 1992).

THE FREE MARKET IDEOLOGY AGAINST A RATIONAL USE OF MARKETS?

The present analysis leads to an impressive paradox. At the very moment when the post–World War II institutions are reconsidered and partially reformed under the pressures of deregulation, foreign competition, and anti-Keynesian political programs, the sophistication of modern economic theory warns about the numerous market failures that affect societies devoid of any complementary or alternative coordinating mechanisms. Persisting unemployment, recurring financial crises, rising inequalities, underinvestment in productive activities such as education or research, and cumulative asymmetry of information and power are some of the possible outcomes of a complete reliance on pure market functioning (Table 2-4).

Of course, the motto "Let's return to free market economies" has played some role in disciplining and restructuring most of the institutional forms inherited from the Fordist era. Similarly, in most Eastern European countries, the market has been used as a dissolving device for most communist

Table 2-4. The Promises and the Deliveries of the Free Marketers

	Promise	Outcome
1. Capital labor relation	Deregulation allowing full employment	No clear impact
2. Forms of competition	Deregulation, more welfare by competition	Re-regulation, fewer producers; from one oligopolistic form of competition to another
3. Monetary regime	Possible control of monetary base	Monetary innovation preventing this control
	No cost for price stability	Price stability, but mass unemployment
4. State	Minimal state to enhance growth and productivity	Lack of public investment
		Poor private productivity due to the lack of education and infrastructures
5. International regime	Smooth currency adjustments	Large ups and downs in exchange rates
	Vanishing external disequilibria	Unprecedented and stable polarization of deficit and surplus countries
	Complete autonomy of national economic policies	Stronger constraints upon national room for maneuver

political organizations and centrally planned mechanisms. But it is now realized that the market per se cannot create the requisites which would warrant its long-term efficiency: clear rule of the games, a stable monetary regime, adequate property rights, minimal solidarity through a welfare state, emergence of Schumpeterian innovators, and not only lucky speculators. It took nearly one or two centuries for old capitalist countries to make familiar and acceptable the harsh logic of typical market mechanisms. It is wise to expect that the great transformation currently taking place in Eastern Europe is not a matter of years but of decades (Boyer, 1993).

Even Western financial markets, in order to be efficient, have to be constantly reformed and adequately regulated by a large amount of institutional or technological devices. For example, the Wall Street crash in October 1987 was not the repetition of the 1929 crash and the following Great Depression, since many equilibrating mechanisms have been implemented by institutional design. Consequently, these mechanisms prevented the repetition of such a catastrophic episode. Similarly, the reforms undertaken after October 1987 have so far prevented a dramatic collapse of world stock markets and the triggering of a collapse in economic activity of the 1929–32 type. Even markets have to be constantly redesigned in order to be self-equilibrating. This basic teaching from economic history is too frequently neglected.

Our knowledge about market implementation, functioning, and efficiency will probably be totally transformed by the difficult and potentially dangerous experiments that will take place during the nineties, not only in old industrialized countries, but also in the previously "socialist" countries of Eastern Europe – and in China. In the meantime, it would be wise for economists not to confuse the ideology of free marketers with the actual – and real but limited – capabilities of contemporary market mechanisms, which are embedded in a complex mix of alternative and largely complementary governance modes.

REFERENCES

Aghion, Philippe and Peter Howitt. 1993. "A Model of Growth through Creative Destruction." In Dominque Foray and Christopher Freeman, eds. *Technology and the Wealth of Nations*. London and New York: Pinter Publishers. Pp. 145–72.

Aglietta, Michel. 1982. *Regulation and Crisis of Capitalism*. New York: Monthly Review Press.

    1991. "Ordre monétaire et banques centrales." *Colloque L'Economie des conventions,* Paris, 27–28.

Aglietta, Michel, Anton Brender, and Virginie Coudert. 1990. *Globalisation financière: l'aventure obligée*. Paris: Economica.

Akerlof, Georges A. 1984. *Economic Theorist's Book of Tales*. Cambridge: Cambridge University Press.

Alesina, Alberto and Geoffrey Carliner, eds. 1991. *Politics and Economies in the Eighties*. Chicago and London: University of Chicago Press.

Amable, Bruno and Dominique Guellec. 1992. "Les Théories de la croissance endogène." *Revue d'Economie Politique* 102(3), 313-377.

Arrow, Kenneth and Frank Hahn. 1971. *General Competitive Analysis*. San Francisco: Holden Day.

Arthur, Brian W. 1988. "Competing Technologies: An Overview." In Giovanni Dosi et al., eds. *Technical Change and Economic Theory*. London and New York: Pinter Publishers. Pp. 590–607.

Becker, Gary S. 1964. *Human Capital*. New York: Columbia University Press.

    1981. *A Treatise on the Family*. Cambridge: Harvard University Press.

Benassy, Jean-Pascal. 1982. *The Economics of Market Disequilibrium.* Boston: Academic Press.

Boltanski, L. and L. Thevenot. 1992. *Les économies de la grandeur,* Paris: Gallimard.

Bourguignon, François. 1990. "L'après communisme: une troisième voie?" *Le Débat* 59: 11–14.

Boyer, Robert. 1987. "Labour flexibilities: many forms, uncertain effects." *Labour and Society* 12(1) 107–29.

1988. *The Search for Labour Market Flexibility.* Oxford: Clarendon Press.

1990a. *The Regulation School: A Critical Introduction.* New York: Columbia University Press.

1990b. "The Capital Labor Relations in OECD Countries: From the 'Golden Age' to the Uncertain Nineties." Couverture Orange CEPREMAP 9020 (September).

1991a. "Capital Labor Relation and Wage Formation: Continuities and Changes of National Trajectories among OECD Countries." In Toshiyuki Mizogushi, ed. *Making Economies More Efficient and Equitable: Factors Determining Income Distribution.* Tokyo: Kinokuniya Company Ltd. and Oxford: Oxford University Press. Pp. 297–340.

1991b. "Justice Sociale et performances économiques: De l'alliance cachée au conflit ouvert?" Couverture Orange CEPREMAP 9135.

1993. "La grande transformation de l'Europe de l'Est: Une lecture régulationniste." Mimeograph CEPREMAP.

Boyer, Robert, Bernard Chavance, and Ollivier Godard, eds. 1991. *Les figures de l'irréversibilité en économie.* Paris: Editions de l'E.H.E.S.S.

Boyer, Robert, and Geneviève Schmeder. 1990. "Un retour à Adam Smith." *Revue Française d'Economie* V(1) (Hiver): 125–94.

Braudel, Fernand, 1979. *Civilisation matérielle, économie et capitalisme XV-XVIIIe siècles,* 3 Tomes. Paris: Armand Colin.

Brus, W. 1987. "Market Socialism." In J. Eatwell, Murray Milgate, and Peter Newman, eds. *The New Palgrave: A Dictionary of Economics,* Tome III. London: Macmillan Press. Pp. 337–42.

Bryant, J. 1983. "A Simple Rational-Expectations Keynes-Type Model." *Quarterly Journal of Economics* 98: 525–28.

Campbell, Colin D. and William R. Dougan. 1986. *Alternative Monetary Regimes.* Baltimore and London: Johns Hopkins University Press.

Campbell, John L., J. Rogers Hollingsworth, and Leon N. Lindberg. 1991. *Governance of the American Economy.* Cambridge, New York, Melbourne: Cambridge University Press.

Chandler, Alfred D. 1977. *The Visible Hand: The Managerial Revolution in American Business.* Cambridge: The Belknap Press of Harvard University Press.

Chiappori, P. A. 1991. "Anticipations rationnelles et conventions." *Colloque L'Economie des conventions.* Paris, 27–28.

Clague, C. And G. C. Rausser. 1992. *The Emergence of Market Economies in Eastern Europe.* Cambridge: Blackwell.

Coase, Ronald. 1937. "The Nature of the Firm." *Economica.* n.s., 4 (November). Reprinted in Ronald Coase. 1988. *The Firm, The Market and the Law.* Chicago and London: University of Chicago Press. Pp. 33-56.

1960. "The Problem of Social Cost." *Journal of Law and Economics.* 3: 1–44.

1988. *The Firm, The Market and the Law.* Chicago and London: The University Press of Chicago.

1992. "The Institutional Structure of Production." *American Economic Review.* 82(4): 713–19.

Coleman, William D. 1990. "State Traditions and Comprehensive Business Associations: A Comparative Structural Analysis." *Political Studies.* 38(2): 231–52.

Coriat, Benjamin. 1991. *Penser à l'envers. Travail et organisation dans l'entreprise japonaise.* Paris: C. Bourgois Editeur.

D'Aspremont, Cl., R. Dos Santos Ferreira, and Louis André Gérard-Varet. 1989. "Pricing-Schemes and Cournotian Monopolistic Competition." Mimeograph CORE, Louvain la Neuve.

David, Paul A. 1988. "Path-Dependence: Putting the Past in the Future of Economics." IMSS Technical Report. No. 533. Stanford University.

Debreu, Gérard. 1959. *Theory and Value: An Axiomatic Analysis of Economic Equilibrium.* Cowles Foundations Monograph No. 17. New York: John Wiley.

Douglas, M. 1986. *Les institutions parlent.* Paris: Editions de Minuit.

Dumenil, Gérard and Dominique Lévy. 1989. "Micro Adjustment Behavior and Macro Stability." *Seoul Journal of Economics.* 2(1): 1–37.

Eggertsson, T. 1990. *Economic Behavior and Institutions.* Cambridge: Cambridge University Press.

Esping-Andersen, G. 1990. *The Three Worlds of Welfare Capitalism.* Princeton: Princeton University Press.

Favereau, Olivier. 1989. "Marchés internes, marchés externes." *Revue Economique.* 40(2): 273–328.

Fisher, Irving. 1933. "The Debt Deflation Theory of Great Depressions." *Econometrica.* 1(4): 337–57.

Fleurbaey, Marc. 1990. "Le marché: Horizon indepassable?" Mimeograph INSEE. Paris (Juin).

Freeman, J. R. 1989. *Democracy and Markets. The Politics of Mixed Economies.* Ithaca: Cornell University Press.

Friedman, Milton. 1962. *Capitalism and Freedom.* Chicago: University of Chicago Press.

Friedman, Milton and Rose Friedman. 1981. *Free to Choose.* New York: Aron.

Galenson, D. W., ed. 1989. *Markets in History: Economic Studies of the Past.* New York: Cambridge University Press.

Hahn, Frank. 1989. *The Economics of Missing Markets Information and Games.* Oxford: Clarendon Press.

1992. "The Next Hundred Years." In John D. Hey, ed. *The Future of Economics.* Oxford, U.K. and Cambridge, Mass.: Blackwell. Pp. 47–50.

Hayek, von Fredrich. 1976–82. *Law, Legislation and Liberty,* 3 vols. Chicago: University of Chicago Press and London: Routledge and Paul Kegan.

1980. *Individualism and Economic Order.* Chicago and London: University of Chicago Press.

Heal, G. M. 1971. "Planning, Prices and Increasing Returns." *Review of Economic Studies.* 38: 281–94.

1973. *The Theory of Economic Planning.* Amsterdam: North-Holland.

Hibbs, Douglas A. 1987. *The Political Economy of Industrial Democracies.* Cambridge, Mass. and London, U.K.: Harvard University Press.

Hill, P. 1987. "Market Places." In John Eatwell and Alii, eds. *The New Palgrave: A Dictionary of Economics,* Tome III. London: The Macmillan Press. Pp. 332–34.

Hollingsworth, J. Rogers, Philippe Schmitter, and Wolfgang Streeck, eds. 1994. *Governing Capitalist Economies: Performance and Control of Economic Sectors.* New York: Oxford University Press.

Ingrao, B. and G. Israel. 1990. *The Invisible Hand: Economic Equilibrium in the History of Science.* Cambridge: MIT Press.

Kaldor, Nicholas. 1939. "Speculation and Economic Stability." *Review of Economic Studies* (October). Reprinted in *Essays on Economic Stability and Growth.* 1960. London: Duckworth.

Kahneman, Daniel, Jack L. Knetsch, and Richard H. Thaler. 1986. "Fairness as a Constraint on Profit Seeking: Entitlements in the Market." *American Economic Review.* 76(4): 728–41. Reprinted in Richard H. Thaler. 1991. *Quasi Rational Economics.* New York: Russell Sage Foundation. Pp. 199–219.

Keohane, Robert. 1984. *After Hegemony: Cooperation and Discord in the World Political Economy.* Princeton: Princeton University Press.

Kindleberger, Charles P. 1978. *Manias, Panics, and Crashes: A History of Financial Crises.* New York: Basic Books.

Kornai, Janos. 1980. *The Economics of Shortage.* Amsterdam: North Holland.

1992. *The Socialist System: The Political Economy of Communism.* Oxford: Clarendon Press.

Krasner, Stephen D., ed. 1983. *International Regime.* Ithaca: Cornell University Press.

Kregel, Jan, Egon Matzner, and G. Grabher, eds. 1992. *The Market Shock: An Agenda for the Economic and Social Reconstruction of Central and Eastern Europe.* Ann Arbor: The Austrian Academy of Sciences and University of Michigan Press.

Kreps, D. 1977. "A Note on 'Fulfilled Expectations.'" *Journal of Economic Theory.* 14: 32–43.

Kuttner, Robert. 1991. *The End of Laissez-Faire.* New York: Alfred A. Knopf.

Lange, O. 1937. "On the Economic Theory of Socialism." In O. Lange and F. Taylor, eds. 1948. *On the Economic Theory of Socialism.* Minneapolis: B. Lippincott, University of Minnesota Press. Pp. 53–143.

Lavoie, D. 1986. "The Market as a Procedure for Discovery and Conveyance of Inarticulate Knowledge." *Comparative Economic Studies.* 28(1), 1-14.

Lazonick, William. 1991. *Business Organization and the Myth of the Market Economy.* Cambridge, New York, Melbourne: Cambridge University Press.

Ledyard, J. O. 1987. "Market Failure." In J. Eatwell and Alii, eds. *The New Palgrave: A Dictionary of Economics,* Vol. 3. London: The Macmillan Press. Pp. 326–28.

Leifer, Eric M. And Harrison C. White. 1988. "A Structural Approach to Markets." In Mark Mizruchi and Michael Schwartz, eds. *Intercorporate Relations.* Cambridge, New York, Melbourne: Cambridge University Press. Pp. 85–108.

Lerner, A. 1934. "Economic Theory and Socialist Economy." *Review of Economic Studies.* 2: 51–61.

Lesourne, Jacques. 1964. *Le calcul économique.* Paris: Dunod.

1991. *L'économie de l'ordre et du désordre.* Paris: Economica.

Lindbeck, A. and D. J. Snower. 1986. "Wage Setting Unemployment, and Insider-outsider Relations." *American Economic Review.* 76: 235–9.

Lindblom, Charles. 1977. *Politics and Markets. The World's Political Economic Systems.* New York: Basic Books.

Lucas, Robert E. Jr. 1984. *Studies in Business-Cycle Theory.* Cambridge: MIT Press.

Lucas, Robert. 1988. "On the Mechanisms of Economic Development." *Journal of Monetary Economics.* 72: 3–42.

Martin, John, Jean-Marc Burniaux, François Delorme, Ian Lienert. 1990. "Walras. Un modèle international multisectoriel d'équilibre général appliqué à l'évaluation des politiques agricoles." *Revue Economique de l'OECD.* 13: 73–109.

Marshall, Alfred. 1890. *Principles of Economics,* reprinted. London: MacMillan.

Nelson, Richard R. And Sidney Winter. 1982. *An Evolutionary Theory of Economic Change.* Cambridge: Harvard University Press.

Newberry, D. M. 1989. "Missing Markets: Consequences and Remedies." In Frank Hahn, ed. *The Economics of Missing Markets Information and Games.* Oxford: Clarendon Press. P. 211–42.

North, Douglass. 1990. *Institutions, Institutional Change and Economic Performance.* Cambridge and New York: Cambridge University Press.

OECD 1985. Perspectives de l'Emploi, Septembre.

OECD 1993. Economic Outlook (July). Paris: OECD.

Okun, Arthur M. 1981. *Price and Quantities: A Macroeconomic Analysis.* Washington: Brookings Institution.

Olson, Mancur. 1965. *The Logic of Collective Action.* New Haven: Yale University Press.

Orléan, André. 1990. "Le rôle des influences interpersonnelles dans la détermination des cours boursiers." *Revue Economique.* 41(5): 839–68 (Septembre).

———. 1992. "Decentralized Collective Learning and Imitation: A Quantitative Approach." Mimeograph CREA presented at the Second Workshop on the Emergence and Stability of Institutions. Louvain-LaNeuve (December).

Polanyi, Karl. 1946. *The Great Transformation.* Traduction française. 1983. Paris: Gallimard.

Posner, R. A. 1981. *The Economics of Justice.* Cambridge: Harvard University Press.

Romer, Paul. 1986. "Increasing Returns and Long-run Growth." *Journal of Political Economy* 94: 1002–38.

———. 1990. "Endogenous Technological Change." *Journal of Political Economy.* 98(5): 71–102 (2nd part).

Rosenan, James N. and Ernst-Otto Czempiel, eds. 1992. *Governance without Government: Order and Change in World Politics.* Cambridge, New York, Melbourne: Cambridge University Press.

Rothenberg, Winifred B. 1992. *From Market-Places to a Market Economy: The Transformation of Rural Massachusetts 1759–1850.* Chicago and London: University of Chicago Press.

Samuelson, Paul A. and William D. Nordhaus. 1992. *Economics.* New York: McGraw-Hill. Chapter 3: 35–47.

Sandler, Todd. 1992. *Collective Action. Theory and Applications.* Ann Arbor: The University of Michigan Press.

Schmitter, Philippe C. 1990. "Sectors in Modern Capitalism: Models of Governance and Variations in Performance." In Renato Brunetta and Carlo Dell'

Aringa, eds. *Labour Relations and Economic Performance.* London: Macmillan and International Economic Association. Pp. 3–39.

Schotter, A. 1990. *Free Market Economics,* 2nd ed. Cambridge: Basil Blackwell.

Shand, Alexander D. 1990. *Free Market Morality: The Political Economy of the Austrian School.* London and New York: Routledge.

Smith, Adam. 1776. "An Inquiry into the Nature and Causes of the Wealth of Nations." Edited by R. H. Cambell, A. S. Skinner, and W. B. Todd. 1976. London: Croom Helm.

Solow, Robert M. 1990. *The Labor Market as a Social Institution.* Cambridge: Basil Blackwell.

Stiglitz, Joseph. 1987. "Dependence of Quality on Price." *Journal of Economic Literature* 25: 1–48.

Stiglitz, Joseph E. And Frank G. Mathewson, eds. 1986. *New Developments in the Analysis of Market Structure.* Cambridge: MIT Press.

Stiglitz, J., and A. Weiss. 1981. "Credit Rationing in Markets with Imperfect Competition." *American Economic Review.* 71.

Taylor, F. 1929. "The Guidance of Production in a Socialist State." In O. Lane and F. Taylor, eds. 1948. *On the Economic Theory of Socialism.* Minneapolis: University of Minnesota Press, B. Lippincott. Pp. 39–54.

Triole, Jean. 1988. *The Theory of Industrial Organization.* Cambridge: MIT Press.

Walras, Léon. 1988. *Elements d'économie politique pure ou théorie de la richesse sociale,* 8 vols. Paris: Economica.

Weir, Margaret, and Theda Skocpol. 1985. "State Structures and the Possibilities for 'Keynesian' Responses to the Great Depression in Sweden, Britain, and the United States." In Peter B. Evans, Dietrich Rueschemeyer, and Theda Skocpol, *Bringing the State Back in.* Cambridge: Cambridge University Press. Pp. 107–63.

Weitzman, Martin L. 1982. "Increasing Returns and the Foundations of Unemployment Theory." *Economic Journal.* 92: 787–804.

——— 1985. "Steady State Unemployment Under Profit Sharing." Working Paper 399. Cambridge: Department of Economics, MIT.

White, Harrison C. 1981. "Where Do Markets Come From?" *American Journal of Sociology.* 87(3): 517–47.

——— 1988. "Varieties of Markets." In Davvy Wellman-Berkowitz, eds. *Social Structures: A Network Approach.* Cambridge, New York, Melbourne: Cambridge University Press. Pp. 226–60.

Williamson, Oliver. 1985. *The Economic Institutions of Capitalism.* New York: Free Press.

Wolf, Charles Jr. 1979. "A Theory of Nonmarket Failure." *Journal of Law and Economics.* 22.

——— 1990. *Markets or Governments: Choosing between Imperfect Alternatives.* Cambridge, Mass. and London: MIT Press.

3

A TYPOLOGY OF INTERORGANIZATIONAL RELATIONSHIPS AND NETWORKS

Jerald Hage and Catherine Alter

AN EVOLUTIONARY TYPOLOGY OF INTERORGANIZATIONAL RELATIONSHIPS AND NETWORKS

Interorganizational networks have been one method of coordinating prices, wages, and purchases for some time. The most common examples were agricultural cooperatives, cottage industries, and cartels – types of coordination commonly found in Europe and Asia. These associations of organizations, frequently called *obligational linkages* (Williamson, 1985), were found even in the industrial age, which saw the emergence of large corporations and the vertically integrated firm in the United States (Aldrich, 1979; Chandler, 1962, 1977; Williams, 1975). Large companies were created in a number of countries through mergers as managers attempted to drive down costs, eliminate competition, and achieve large economies of scale by means of stable and large production runs. The dominant concern of vertically integrated hierarchies was to increase productivity by reducing transaction costs vis-à-vis their suppliers or customers (Williamson, 1975), thus earning a competitive advantage in the marketplace. Now many small firms can survive in specialized niches, but they frequently join in joint ventures with large companies that produce and/or market their products (Powell and Brantley, 1992). Even more complex alliances involving large numbers of organizations are being formed to accomplish tasks and objectives that no single firm could achieve on its own, such as establishing industrial standards, developing complex products such as automobiles, semiconductors, and aircraft, and expanding the pool of industrial knowledge (Alter and Hage, 1993; Wikström and Normann, 1994).

In the last two decades, there has been an acceleration in the number and variety of joint ventures and interorganizational alliances (Jarillo, 1993; (Kraar, 1989; Pollack, 1992; Wikström and Normann, 1994; Work, 1988). The new forms differ from the older, more traditional, types of interorganizational relationships in the following ways:

1. The nature of coordination has changed from relatively simple tasks to complex ones, from coordinating prices and pooling financial resources to joint research and production of products or services (Alter and Hage, 1993; Gomes-Casseres, 1994).
2. The span of networks has broadened, crossing industrial sectors rather than being contained within them.
3. The same firm is involved in a number of networks, both joint ventures to produce products and strategic alliances to set national standards, which are competing with other joint ventures and alliances (Gomes-Casseres, 1994).
4. Their membership has become more diverse, even when they are in the same industry, frequently involving a third party to ensure the enforcement of agreements.

All of these factors make the structures of the networks more difficult.

The more traditional forms of network cooperation were certainly not without variation. They differed in regard to their purpose; they pooled resources for marketing or distribution, provided ecological contexts in which simple subcontracting could occur, and were designed to restrict supply and/or divide the marketplace. Similarly, the aim of trade associations varied enormously, from simple information management and lobbying in the United States to the regulation of wages and industrial activities in Europe (Schneiberg and Hollingsworth, 1990).[1] Nevertheless, the four trends just listed have produced new forms that are distinctively different from the more traditional forms and are themselves highly diverse. Their most distinctive features are their complex coordination in particularistic relationships that cross market niches, industrial sectors, and/or national boundaries as opposed to being linkages among many firms within the same industry and/or locality. These are groups of organizations competing against other groups of organizations (Gomes-Casseres, 1994).

Networks, whether joint ventures or alliances, are not some halfway point between the coordination of the market and the hierarchy (Hollingsworth, 1991; Powell, 1990; Williamson, 1985), but represent a new stage in organizational forms (Alter and Hage, 1993; Grandori and Soda, 1995). Networks differ from hierarchical coordination because of the autonomy of each member. Indeed, if one organizational member is dominant, it is no longer a network. Networks differ from market coordination because there is an attempt to coordinate through elaborate decision-making committees at multiple levels, that is, not as if there is a visible hand, but rather visible hands. For both reasons, interorganizational relationships are not bureaucratic and are more complex organizational forms. The problems of coordination are much more difficult because of member autonomy and the complex decision-making process.

The formation of these new joint ventures and alliances has been so rapid that it has been difficult to obtain accurate counts. Furthermore, there has been a tendency to emphasize international networks because they are reported in the leading newspapers (Hergert and Morris, 1988). By the late 1980s, U.S. corporations had 2,000 joint ventures or alliances in Europe alone (Kraar, 1989) and 12,000 worldwide (Work, 1988). A study at Columbia University found that the number of partnerships grew by 20 percent per annum in the late 1980s rather than the 5 percent found in the first part of the decade (Wikström and Normann, 1994: 41). More recently it was estimated that over one-half of the fastest growing American firms were involved in an average of three interorganizational relationships (*Wall Street Journal,* April 20th, 1995).

A better sense of the growth rate is obtained from a study reported by Pollack (1992) on the number of international joint ventures in several high-tech industries during the 1980s. The number doubled in biotech and material sciences, increased by about 30 percent in information technology and chemicals, and trebled in the automobile industry. But since this only counts international joint ventures, it is a serious underrepresentation. For example, a detailed count in human biotech firms of ten employees or more found 765 interorganizational agreements (Powell and Brantley, 1992) among 126 firms, most of them within the United States.

Also it would be incorrect to assume that this is only an American phenomenon. Hkänsson (1990) found that two-thirds of the small Swedish firms that did product development worked jointly. Furthermore, each week there are new reports of joint ventures and alliances in Europe and/or Asia, many of which are cited as examples here (see the index of the *Wall Street Journal*).

The objective of this paper is to describe a new typology of networks that captures these many evolutionary changes. In its development, we started with existing typologies (Astley and Fombrun, 1983; Grandori and Soda, 1995; Hollingsworth, 1991), built on our own (Alter and Hage, 1993), and combined their most useful features. Each of these typologies was created for a different purpose. Astley and Fombrun's (1983) was concerned with defining alternative collective strategies, and thus they emphasized trade associations, social movements, and the like. Grandori and Soda's (1995) approach centered on the forms of coordination in the network and distinguished between interpersonal networks, bureaucratic authority relationships, and proprietary contracts. Hollingsworth's (1991) formulation combined markets, hierarchies, and networks. Finally, our own previous effort (Alter and Hage, 1993) placed more emphasis on the extent of cooperation rather than the complexity of the activities that need to be coordinated.[2] All of these efforts are descriptive classifications, rather than predictive theories.

Our typology is predictive in two senses. On the one hand, we are concerned with connecting the dimensions of the typology – complexity, differentiation of members, and particularism of members – with some of the basic causal forces, in particular the expansion of knowledge and its rapid rate of change. On the other hand, we want to employ these same dimensions to predict levels of conflict and difficulties of coordination within specific types of networks (Alter, 1990; Alter and Hage, 1993). Our proposed typology, presented below, centers on the structural evolution of firms towards more complex forms of collaboration and coordination, and is designed to highlight both the direction of change and the nature of the difficulties that are generated by these changes.

ANALYTICAL PROBLEMS

DEFINING INTERORGANIZATIONAL NETWORKS

A number of writers have observed that the term "network" is much used and abused (Alter and Hage, 1993; Grandori and Soda, 1995). Furthermore, in this paper we have already employed several cognates – relationships, joint ventures, linkages, and alliances. In general, the term "network" or "relationship" is the generic term, while "linkages" and "joint ventures" reflect two to four organizations and "alliances" usually many more than this. Finally, we find that firms are involved in a large number of joint ventures and strategic alliances.

For example, Siemens' Medical Corporation is doing joint research with Imatron, Inc. to improve the former's tomography heart scanning equipment (*Wall Street Journal,* April 6, 1995) outside of a formally constituted joint venture. But Siemens is also involved in a alliance with MIPS, the RISC chip designer, as well as a number of other firms, attempting to impose a standard (Gomes-Casseres, 1994). Another example is Swissair buying 49.5 percent of Sabena Airlines, making this a joint venture, as part of a strategy of developing a competitive alliance of the small European airlines to compete against the alliances created by Lufthansa, British Airways, and Air France (DuBois, 1995).

The definition of an interorganizational network, whether a joint venture or an alliance, needs to be made as precise as possible. Grandori and Soda (1995) stress two characteristics:

1. An interfirm network is a mode of regulating interdependence between firms which is different from the aggregation of these units within a single firm and from coordination through market signals based on a cooperative game with partner-specific communication.
2. The attributes of a network – i.e., coordination processes and structures an interfirm coalition may employ – are not necessarily "intermediate" with respect to those of firms and markets but they need not be unique with different mixes and intensities also in firms and in markets...

To these we add a third: that no organization in the network has absolute authority and all have some autonomy. In other words, the network cannot be dominated by a single organization that has absolute hierarchical power, but rather it must be governed by the collective which operates through joint decision making, problem solving, and sharing of profits or prestige. Only when there is a true collaboration do the full benefits appear (Kanter, 1994). It is the characteristic of sharing that makes the new forms of interorganizational coordination so interesting, since the standard assumption in organizational theory has always been that organizations strive to maintain their autonomy at any cost (Gouldner, 1959). Indeed, the popular transaction costs (Williamson, 1975) perspective is a strong version of this idea.

Within this generic category of network or interorganizational relationships, we distinguish between joint ventures or linkages when only a few organizations (two to four) are involved and alliances when larger numbers of organizations are involved. Some joint ventures have more than four organizations and some alliances have less. There is some overlap, but usually it is useful to distinguish between these kinds of networks because, as the alliance grows larger and larger, the problems of coordination become more difficult. Although it is not always the case, joint ventures are more likely to be covered by formal arrangements such as detailed contracts whereas alliances are likely to have a considerable variety of coordination modes, formal contracts being only one of many (Gomes-Casseres, 1994). But since not all joint ventures are necessarily contractual (Hkänsson and Johanson, 1988), we also employ the term "linkages" to represent those relationships of several organizations that are not contractual at all.[3]

When does a network cease to be a network and become an organization? The boundaries are not always clear because there are a variety of ways in which one organization can dominate the actions of others, preventing the joint decision making that is so crucial to the postindustrial form of network. One way is through contracts that are excessively detailed. The more specific a contract, the farther the relationship has moved from being a network. This is, of course, a variation on resource dependency theory (Pfeffer and Salancik, 1978; also see Alter and Hage, 1993). Likewise, if a single organization purchasing goods or services (e.g., the federal government) purchases all the output, then monopoly control exists because the producer has little autonomy.

Another common form that is usually not a network is the franchise. A franchise may contain entrepreneurs who own their franchises, but this does not necessarily mean that they have operational independence. As soon as there is effective control over prices, wages, decor, quality, and the like from the franchiser, then there is an implicit authority structure or hierarchy. There is enormous variation, of course, ranging from the total control that McDonalds exerts through its extensive socialization techniques in Burger University and continual evaluations, to others where there is much less control (Jarillo, 1993: 6–7). Indeed, McDonalds is moving to the next logical step in control, namely joint ownership; within a decade the number of joint ventures between McDonalds and the franchise's central firm has increased from 48 to 400 (Gibson, 1995). Each situation has to be evaluated individually to determine if the franchise is a network.

Still a third pattern that should not be classified as a network is the vertical filière of firms across the production chain where the coordination is done in the final stage by one commercial firm. Beneton is an example because it totally controls the production process, buying the fabric, dying the materials, and then giving specific orders to its large number of subcontractors (Jarillo, 1993: 97–103). Again, the critical test is whether or not there is joint decision making across the chain of production.

WHAT KIND OF TYPOLOGY?

In addition to clarifying the definition of interorganizational networks, another analytical problem is the nature of the typology that is developed to describe the wide variety of interorganizational relationships. As we have already suggested, our aim is to develop a predictive typology that helps explain the evolution of organizations in two ways. First, we are concerned with the trajectory of the evolution of interorganizational networks (toward more complexity and greater differentiation), and what is driving this evolution (the need for innovation, the reduction in adaptive costs, and the continual need for economies of scale).[4] Second, we are concerned with how these same typological dimensions – complexity, differentiation, and number of organizational partners – are related to the problems of coordination (conflict, ineffectiveness, failures).

Most of the typologies that describe modes of coordination and interorganizational relationships suffer from placing too much emphasis on categorical concepts such as interpersonal networks and bureaucratic structures (Grandori and Soda, 1995) or on variables such as self-interest vs. obligation (see Chapter 1) that have few evolutionary implications. It is not immediately obvious whether there would be an increase or decrease in bureaucratic structures or the degree of self-interest. In contrast, we believe that, given a careful definition of what is meant by the degree of complexity in the interorganizational network, one might more easily comprehend how the need to compete over innovation and the reduction in adaptive costs leads to more complex forms of interorganizational coordination. In particular, this dimension is especially helpful in distinguishing among the many kinds of joint ventures and alliance types that range across a wide variety of modes of coordination, number of organizational partners, etc. For example, our typology contrasts the kinds of trade associations found in Europe with those in the United States (Schneiberg and Hollingsworth, 1990), and does the same with the research consortia in Japan, which are unlike those in the United States (Aldrich and Sasaki, 1995). The many examples we provide make apparent the usefulness of the number of organizational partners as a dimension and imply the importance of their differentiation.

Our central argument is that, as knowledge becomes more complex and changes more rapidly, organizational forms are forced to evolve in more complex forms (Alter and Hage, 1993; Hage and Powers, 1992). Specifically, this means the *dis*vertical integration of large firms, their downsizing, the creation of profit centers, and, for the purposes of this paper, their engagement in interorganizational joint ventures and alliances that have more complex forms of coordination – the number of activities coordinated, the complexity of some of these activities, the variety of coordination modes, the complexity of some of these modes, the presence of some third party or alternative kind of organization (trade association, government), etc. In addition, we suggest that in their search for organizational partners to develop innovative products, there are incentives to form these joint ventures and alliances with firms in disparate market niches or industrial sectors and with firms that have complementary skills, expertise, and tacit knowledge (Hage and Yang, 1995). Implied in this argument are three distinct dimensions:

1. The degree of complexity of coordination (Alter and Hage, 1993; Killing, 1988).
2. The number of organizational partners involved in the interorganizational relationship (Hollingsworth, 1991).
3. The extent of the distance between the partners or the degree of symbiosis (Astley and Fombrun, 1983).

THE EVOLUTION TOWARD MORE COMPLEX, SYMBIOTIC, AND PARTICULARISTIC ORGANIZATIONAL NETWORKS

North (1990) suggested that institutional change occurs with new incentive structures. Two new competitive factors are driving organizations into interorganizational collaborations:

1. Innovation is becoming a more pivotal competitive factor than are productivity or cost cutting.
2. Adaptive costs – the costs of monitoring the environment for technological and product change, of developing and implementing competitive responses, and of doing so fast enough to protect market share – have replaced transaction costs as the more critical concern (Hage and Jing, 1995).

The increasing need for industries to do research and product development, as well as consumers' desire for novelty and technology, means that in many sectors the firm with the first and most innovative product enjoys first mover advantages and collects a premium price until there is a competitive response. Examples are Michelin and radial tires, Miller and light beer, Intel and its series of computer chips. If firms do not respond quickly with competitive products, then they may lose large market share, as did the American tire companies, other American breweries, and Japanese, European, and other American computer chip companies.

The shift in competition to innovation has made the concept of adaptive costs (Hage and Jing, 1995) highly useful because in one sense adaptive costs might be understood as the costs associated with being innovative. These costs are defined as:

1. Monitoring the environment for signs of technological change, product innovation, and competitor moves in these areas.
2. The research and product development needed to respond to the competitive challenges.
3. The implementation of the competitive solution.
4. The loss of market share due to delays in response to competitive challenges.

In some respects this last is the most critical. The American automobile industry failed to respond to the Japanese cars of higher quality for some time and lost about 25 percent of their market. Likewise, IBM lost market share by being slow to develop a personal computer.

As companies struggle to be innovative and reduce adaptive costs, they often find it advantageous to form joint ventures or alliances in order to gain access to expertise, share the costs of research and product development, and to be able to respond more quickly to competitive moves. The thesis of adaptive costs is the reverse of transaction cost analysis, which argues that being small means being vulnerable. Williamson (1975) suggested that with costs sunk in equipment, customers might shift their allegiances. In a customer–seller relationship, this is possible. But small numbers have quite different consequences when the objectives are to be innovative and to reduce adaptive costs by being quicker to respond to competitive pressures. One partner can withdraw but immediately loses the benefits because one gains the product only at the end of a long research effort. Furthermore, it requires time to learn the tacit knowledge of the organizational partner and, as this unfolds, there is a building of trust (Hage and Yang, 1995).

Joint research and development is a win/win situation precisely because participants can remain small (or downsize to become small), yet realize a reduction in adaptive costs and at the same time benefit from the joint profits generated by the new products developed with their organizational partners. Quicker responses to competitive moves mean they can protect market share. Increases in tacit knowledge gained from cooperating in research and product development mean that the most important asset in contemporary competition, human capital, is increased (Hage and Jing, 1995). Furthermore, the growth in tacit knowledge can lead to more innovative products down the road. Collaboration also leads to experience in adapting to other companies' cultures and increases the likelihood that the organization will be more adaptive, flexible, and creative in the future as the nature of the market shifts. Thus, the logic of competing over innovation and reducing adaptive costs is quite different from the logic of competing over productivity and reducing transaction costs.

Research projects often generate many new ideas, but they move in peculiar ways, often beyond the intellectual capacities of the firm. To amortize the costs of research, a firm will benefit if it enters into joint ventures with firms that have the needed expertise relative to each of the required knowledge areas. For example, Smith Kline and Takeda Chemical Industries, Ltd. are collaborating in the discovery, development, and marketing of novel pharmaceuticals based on genomic technology (*Wall Street Journal,* Journal 26, 1995). A particularly interesting example of the attempt to amortize the costs of research are the research consortia within the same industry that have been created in Japan, Europe, and more recently the United States (Aldrich and Sasaki, 1995). How this can then affect the competitiveness of an entire industry is demonstrated by Sematech and the semiconductor industry (Browning, Beyer, and Shetler, 1995).

In addition to the demand for research and product innovation, there are other processes pushing organizations away from autonomy. Many new markets or specialized niches have developed, generating symbiotic opportunities. While this is happening in traditional product markets, it is most striking in the high technology sectors where research and development provide many new opportunities for small companies – one reason this is the fastest growing segment of most advanced industrialized economies. Small companies frequently lack expertise in large scale production or distribution, thus they form joint ventures with large high-tech companies to gain access to expertise in these areas (Powell and Brantley, 1992).

As the amount of knowledge grows, it forces many companies to concentrate on a few areas, rather than manage the expertise required by the entire production chain (Gomes-Casseres, 1994). In other words, rather than General Motors attempting to make all the parts of its cars, increasingly the components are subcontracted. And in turn General Motors is making the engines for Toyota's forklift trucks (Henderson, 1995)

There are two important facets to this observation. First, the Toyota-General Motors partnership has evolved from their strategic alliance created a decade earlier. This is a movement away from vertical integration and concerns about transaction costs (Williamson, 1975). It is common today to observe breadth of knowledge sacrificed for depth of knowledge, which then creates a need to reintegrate across the production chain. Second, the growth in knowledge also means more elaborate production chains, which again forces firms to form joint ventures. The most obvious example is the addition of microcomputers to the production chain of many products. Equally important, but less obvious, is the explosion in the variety of new and exotic materials that are being used in the manufacturing of products. As more and more new kinds of materials are added – gortex, fiberglass, plastic compounds, etc. – new kinds of expertise are required for the production processes.

Consistent, then, with the general evolutionary force of the growth in knowledge, organizations are divesting themselves of various units at distinct stages in the production chain. They are devolving vertically, and reintegrating horizontally, using joint ventures and alliances of various kinds. These relationships are most easily formed across market niches or sectors where complementarity is most compelling. But as commodity chains of production become increasingly complex and markets become more and more specialized, firms find themselves in a highly differentiated world.

Finally, while firms are foregoing vertical integration to gain the expertise to develop innovative process and products, they are still faced with the economic imperative of maintaining increasing productivity (Sydow and Windeler, 1995). Although we suggest that innovation is currently more critical than productivity, the latter cannot be ignored. This problem, containing costs, is handled in three ways. *First,* many small organizations work together to achieve economies of scale. The best examples are the networks of subcontract arrangements in Italy (Lazeron, 1988; Piore and Sabel, 1986), but, as we have seen, these may not be networks if controlled by a single firm such as Beneton. And even large firms are merging their production plants in market niches that are felt to be declining; Germany's Hoechst and Bayer companies merged their textile dye business in a new joint venture that is 50 percent owned by each (*Wall Street Journal,* June 30, 1995). *Second,* more and more joint ventures are created precisely to spread the cost of product development and particularly to improve the effectiveness of the product in the marketplace. Here the best examples are the automobile, aircraft, and semiconductor industries. *Third,* joint ventures are created with companies in other countries so as to more effectively adapt the product to the cultural tastes of the other country and yet maintain economies of scale and scope. This is a common practice across a wide variety of distinct product niches. For example, L'Oreal S.A. of France and Kose Corp. of Japan formed a new company to market L'Oreal's products in Japan (*Wall Street Journal,* June 8, 1995).

KEY DIMENSIONS OF THE TYPOLOGY

COMPLEXITY OF COORDINATION: THE BASIC PROBLEM

As we have already suggested, the theoretical problem in the construction of typologies is which dimensions to use and for what purpose. Given our belief that interorganizational networks are evolving toward increased complexity, it is not surprising we select as our key dimension the degree of complexity. The growth in knowledge is the basis of the prediction that all forms of collaboration are moving toward more complex forms, of which strategic alliances are a prime example (Gomes-Casseres, 1994; Hage and Powers, 1992). At one level this is why interorganizational networks are neither markets nor hierarchies, but rather halfway in between, and as such they represent a much more complex organizational form. But at another level, the theoretical question that informs much of this discussion is the question of coordination modes (Alter and Hage, 1993, Chapters 3 and 7; Grandori and Soda, 1995; Hollingsworth, 1991). Inherent in complexity is the dilemma of coordination, the need to control many discrete activities. It is not just a problem of coordinating prices (as in a cartel) or wages and industrial disputes (as in some European trade associations), but rather many processes simultaneously including ongoing research projects, production activities, and marketing. One simple test for assessing the extent of the complexity involved in the coordination of activities is to count the number of activities being coordinated. If the joint venture involves only marketing, then it has a relatively simple coordination problem. Likewise, licensing to manufacture relatively simple products does not involve complex coordination issues. But as the product becomes more intricate – variety of component parts, sophistication of materials, and including of elaborate computer and information system technologies – then it is logical to assume that the type of coordination also becomes more complex. Automobiles and airplanes are complex products, whose production requires the coordination of large numbers of distinct technologies, parts, and people. Because of this, one finds both joint ventures between two competitors (e.g., Diamond Corporation, which was formed by Chrysler and Mitsubishi to spread the costs of automobile product development in specialized market niches) and elaborate alliances across the product chain itself – what Kanter (1994) calls the value added chain partnerships as reflected in the vertical *keiretsu* in Japan (Womack, Jones, and Roos, 1990) and now increasingly emulated in the automobile industry of the United States.

Another way of thinking about complexity of coordination is to acknowledge that interorganizational relationships increasingly employ a variety of coordination modes (Grandori and Soda, 1995), that is, the particular mechanisms used to ensure control or compliance, which range from contracts to interpersonal relationships to teams to normative appeals, etc. (see Alter and Hage, 1993; Etzioni, 1975; Hage, 1974; Lawrence and Lorsch, 1967).[5] As more modes are involved, the greater the degree of complexity (Alter and Hage, 1993). As Gomes-Casseres (1994) observes in his analysis of the alliances built around the RISC chips, a variety of different kinds of coordination modes occurred within the same alliance. While our own research (Alter and Hage, 1993; Chapter 3) is on service delivery systems for clients with complex needs, we found that networks used a variety of coordination modes and that few networks used a single mode.[6]

Our insistence that the definition of an interorganizational network should include joint decision making, for example, is based on the fact that this coordination mode is itself a more complex form than either the invisible hand or the contract (Kanter, 1994). When decision makers come from different organizational and national cultures, and expand the cooperative domain, a variety of committees and other communication techniques will have to increase, or poor performance will result (Alter, 1990; Alter and Hage, 1993). This is a far more complex situation than decentralization in a multiple-unit firm.

The complexity of interdependent activities has been shown to be a predictor of the complexity of coordination in several interorganizational analyses (Alter and Hage, 1993; Killing, 1988).[7] For example, these studies showed that multiple coordination modes and decentralized decision making lead to a complex system of committees and consultations. The case history of SEMATECH (Browning, Beyer, and Shelter, 1995) makes this quite apparent.

DIFFERENTIATION AMONG THE ORGANIZATIONAL PARTNERS: COMPETITIVE VS. SYMBIOTIC COORDINATION

The second dimension, borrowed from Astley and Fombrun (1983), categorizes interorganizational forms into those used for competitive cooperation by organizations in the same sector and those used for symbiotic cooperation by organizations in different industrial or service sectors. Competitors are organizations of the same kind (producing the same product or service), while symbiotic relationships occur among organizations that have some similarities but operate in different sectors. As Astley and Fombrun (1983) observed, this distinction, an old one in the human ecology literature, allows us to predict when interorganizational cooperative behavior is more easily achieved. Understandably, if organizations are not direct competitors, cooperative behavior is more possible because interaction is more likely and easier. In contrast, when competitors form joint ventures, frequently an attempt is made to specify all contingencies in long detailed contracts, itself a measure of conflict. The variable we use is the degree of symbiosis or complementarity.

But, as Grandori and Soda (1995) indicate in their recent review of interorganizational network forms, the competitive vs. symbiotic distinction is insufficient to capture the distinctions among partners in the joint venture or network. There is the problem of "psychological distance" and cultural differences at both an organizational and national level. Firms can also be too close – hence competitive pressures pull them apart and create conflict in coordination – as well as too far apart – hence tendencies to disassociate. The right balance is hard to achieve, and becomes harder as chains of production become longer and more complex. Under these circumstances, the problem of distance applies even to same-sector organizations. Consider the case of General Motors' purchase of Hughes Electronics to gain access to expertise involving computers, which are used in cars; the former's organizational culture was bureaucratic and the latter's was not.

NUMBER OF ORGANIZATIONAL PARTNERS: PARTICULARIZATION OF NETWORKS

The particularism of joint ventures and alliances is easily illustrated in Gomes-Casseres' (1994) examples of the implicit alliance between General Motors and Toyota, Isuzu, Suzuki, and Saab as partners in various joint ventures and Ford's partners in Nissan, Mazda, Kia, and Jaguar. More complex alliances are illustrated by the structures of the various RISC groups. Sun designed a RISC chip and licensed semiconductor companies to produce the chips, who in turn sold them on an OEM basis to resellers and system manufacturers (Gomes-Casseres, 1994: 64). Furthermore, some companies cross-invested as well. The Sun alliance included Texas Instruments, Cypress, Unisyx, LSI Logic, Fujutsu, I.C.L., Phillips, Mentor, Tandon, CompuAdd, Prime, Goldstar, Hyundai, Matsusita, Solbourne, AT&T, Seiko, Nippon Steel, C-Itoh, and Toshiba. Other alliances were built on the MIPS-designed chip and the ones designed by IBM and Hewlett-Packard.

The particularism reflects the interpersonal relationships and need for specific kinds of expertise. In contrast, the traditional cooperatives, trade associations (or federations), and cottage industries involved all organizations of similar kinds. These new alliances are particularistic in their objectives. Some attempt to set a specific standard, others to share the costs of a specific product development, still others to gain some tacit knowledge for future product development. The interwar cartels in the sugar, rubber, nitrogen, steel, aluminum, magnesium, incandescent lamp, and chemical industries banded together to allocate world markets, while cooperatives and cottage industries forged associations to buy or sell common products. In other words, their objectives were general and membership included all.

It is extremely difficult to discern how the growth of knowledge and the speed of change – specifically the need for product innovation and reduction of adaptive costs – leads to more or less members in a specific network. Thus, the emphasis is on the particularism of the relationship: There is a tendency for firms to be involved in more and more networks of various kinds.

Three variables – the degree of complexity in the coordination, the degree of differentiation of the organizational partners, and the particularism of organizational partners – form the basis of a typology that can be used to predict the direction of evolution in the nature of interorganizational relationships. The growth in knowledge and the speed with which it changes has forced organizations toward more complex modes of coordination, greater differentiation of partners, and increased involvement in multiple interorganizational networks.

AN EVOLUTIONARY TYPOLOGY OF INTERORGANIZATIONAL RELATIONSHIPS

SYMBIOTIC COORDINATION AMONG DIFFERENT ORGANIZATIONAL PARTNERS

Since our principal focus is on the most common forms of interorganizational relationships, those among organizations from different marketplaces and/or different countries, our discussion of the typology starts with the symbiotic or highly differentiated relationships. Each of the increasing levels of complexity and of cooperation produces two types of interorganizational collaboration, depending on the number of organizational partners. First, we discuss each level of complexity, and then, within each level, we describe linkages/joint ventures (few organizations) and alliances (many organizations). Given our focus on the evolutionary tendency towards even more complex forms (Aldrich and Mueller, 1982), our analysis concentrates on highly complex particularistic linkages – joint ventures in product development and production being the proto-typical illustration – and highly complex alliances, exemplified by the vertical *keiretsu* in Japan. At low and moderate levels of complexity, we highlight alliances rather than linkages because they are more perplexing and thus more interesting.

LIMITED COMPLEXITY AND SIMPLE COORDINATION

Limited complexity reflects the coordination of only a single activity. The most common example would be subcontracting but to be a true network, the subcontractor must have at least some minimal say in the design of the component that is being subcontracted. There are many examples involving only a few organizations and each would have to be examined to determine whether or not it was a minimal level or coordination or domination by a single organization

More interesting are the subcontracting arrangements across large numbers of organizations. Good examples of this are the preferred physician provider alliances (Hollingsworth and Hollingsworth, 1987; Kaluzny, Zuckerman, and Ricketss, 1995) in health care. These systems are complex subcontracting alliances that include multiple hospitals, physicians, specialized diagnostic centers, long term care facilities, and home health care associations – all with capitated rates. But the providers of the service have a great deal to say about the service provided. This same kind of arrangement exists with the suppliers of component parts in the automobile industry in Germany, who are encouraged to work with all the automotive companies so that they become more innovative and flexible.

Simple coordination is also involved in any joint ventures in marketing, which represents about one-third of the joint ventures that have been studied (Herget and Morris, 1988). Some contemporary examples are Ticketmaster Corp. and Viacom MTV Networks, Inc., who have created a joint marketing venture to sell concert tickets and merchandise directly to viewers of the popular music TV channel (*Wall Street Journal,* April 14, 1995). Another simple form of coordination is found in joint ventures to distribute goods and services such as the one between Davidson & Associates, Inc. and Mattel, Inc. to distribute software (*Wall Street Journal,* April 14b, 1995).

Simple coordination can also occur with other than component parts in subcontracting relationships or with joint ventures involving either mar-

Table 3-1. Symbiotic Linkages and Alliances

Mode of coordination	Few organizations/sectors	Many organizations/sectors
Limited complexity	Obligational linkages	Obligational alliances
	Subcontracts	Subcontracts in health care in U.S.
	Overlapping board memberships	Interlocking directorates in U.S.
	Joint ventures in marketing	Cross-investments in Japan
	Joint ventures in distribution	Grand corps in France
Moderate complexity	Promotional linkages	Promotional alliances
		Campaign against universal health insurance in U.S.
		Programs to develop jobs in U.S.
		Job protection in horizontal *keiretsu*
High complexity	Product development and production linkages	Product development and production alliances
	Joint ventures in biotech	Japanese auto *keiretsu*
	Joint ventures in Sweden	Research consortia for Apollo and supercomputers
	Joint ventures across telecommunication and computers	Commercial aircraft design and production in Europe, Japan, U.S.

keting or distribution. A very common pattern and one much discussed in the literature is the pattern of board memberships such as interlocking directorates. More interesting are the various ways in which money is cross-invested, in particular when it involves a large number of organizations. The horizontal *keiretsu* (Gerlach, 1992), sometimes called *gurupu* or corporate groups (Wolferen, 1990: 46–7) found in Japan, involve many partners such as a bank, an insurance company, a trading company, a steel manufacturer, an automobile company, and a ship building company. *Gurupu* are different from conglomerates, because they do not have a central headquarters and their coordination involves investments rather than bureaucratic control; indeed there is no one single person in control. These obligational networks of financing had their origins in the latter part of the nineteenth century in the *zaibatsu* (Gerlach, 1992), or trading companies, built around powerful families and then gradually evolved into large family alliances. A similar pattern of cross-investment across firms can be found in France, where there are groups of companies connected through banks (Le Point, 14 Avril, 1994).

Human capital networks are typically ignored but frequently they form the interpersonal cement that provides security for the cross-investments. In Japan most of the top economic elites come from the University of Tokyo law school (*Todai*) (Wolferen, 1990: 45), which also supplies the top political elite. In France, rather than one school faculty being dominant as in Japan, different *grandes écoles* control distinct sectors of the society. The students from *École des Mines* go into industry, while those from *Écoles des Ponts et Chausses* enter construction. Then there are the *grand corps* associated with the *École Nationale d'Administration* that dominate the major political positions (Suleiman, 1976). In contrast to Japan, there is much more movement in France back and forth between the public and the private sector, which is also reinforced in the pattern of *pantouflage,* that is, the appointment of government officials to the boards of key businesses (Suleiman, 1976).

MODERATE COMPLEXITY OF COORDINATION

When obligational linkages and alliances are maintained over a long time and a level of interorganizational trust is established, then interorganizational structures may take on additional functions (Johanson and Mattsson, 1987). For example, the horizontal *keiretsu* or *gurupu* in Japan can evolve from a simple level of coordination of investment to more complex levels when plants are closed and the workers are shifted to other companies within the same corporate group. This is a more complex problem of coordination than the migration of senior personnel as in the French case. We label this moderate level of complexity a promotional network.

An interesting example of a promotional network that crosses public and private sectors is in Chicago, Illinois: the Jane Addams Resource Corporation (JARC) (Alter et al., 1992). JARC conducted an economic analysis of its declining neighborhood on Chicago's south side and found that there were over 60 marginally profitable small metalworking firms that employed over 2,000 workers. JARC organized these companies, their suppliers, and their distributors into a consortium that gave them a scale of operation that enabled them to adjust to market conditions. JARC now serves as staff to the consortium which provides cooperative purchasing, collective marketing, and staff training and creates opportunities for below-market-rate financing and venture capital options. The consortium also serves as an advocate for members regarding industrial land use issues, offers relocation and expansion assistance, and links members with city and state economic development programs. Several years after the creation of the consortium, JARC bought an abandoned industrial property in the neighborhood and renovated it for use as incubation space (Alter et al., 1992).

Some of the best examples of promotional networks in the United States are federations of employers or unions which form across sectors, mobilized for political action to achieve policy or legislative objectives. During 1994, we observed the relative power of particular promotional networks in the battle over health care. The Business Roundtable, the National Association of Manufacturers, Chambers of Commerce, and the Independent Association of Small Businesses formed an implicit alliance against health care reform, with both the AFL-CIO and the majority of the people favoring it. The former alliance won.

HIGH COMPLEXITY OF COORDINATION

Having described symbiotic interorganizational forms requiring limited and moderate levels of cooperation, we turn to the complex levels of coordination which are the most important in postindustrial society: namely, systemic production linkages, joint ventures, and alliances necessary for basic research, product development, and the production of complex products and services. We have already provided a number of examples of joint ventures either for product development and/or production:

1. Siemens' Medical Corporation's joint research with Imatron, Inc. to improve the former's tomography heart scanning equipment (*Wall Street Journal,* April 6, 1995).
2. Most of the Swedish examples cited by Häkansson and Johanson (1988).
3. Most of the biotech joint ventures studied by Powell and Brantley (1992).
4. Smith Kline and Takeda Chemicals (*Wall Street Journal,* June 26, 1995) and the pharmaceutical industry more generally.

To this list, we add a number of others including the following joint ventures between:

1. Silicon Graphics and Dreamworks to create a $50 million digital animation studio (Rigdon and King, 1995).
2. IBM and TelePort Corp. to build virtual dining rooms for business executives (*Wall Street Journal,* June 28, 1995).
3. Envirogen, Inc. and Netherlands-based NVVam to treat odors, toxic materials, and the like (*Wall Street Journal,* February 14, 1995).
4. Campbell Soup Co.'s Pace Foods and Phillip Morris Co.'s Kraft Foods unit to meld Pace's salsa with Kraft's Velveeta products (*Wall Street Journal,* June 14, 1995).
5. ASEH, the leading Swedish supplier of heavy electrical equipment and almost all of the Swedish steel companies, producing major innovations such as inductive stirring in electric arc furnaces and the ASEHSTORH power metallurgy process (Laage-Hellman, 1989).
6. Corning Glass, Sony, and Asahi to produce glass for TV screens.
7. Intel Corp., Oracle Corp., and Sequent Computer Systems, Inc. to develop and sell computers and software for interactive TV (*Wall Street Journal,* April 13, 1995).
8. Waste Management, International and Wheelabrator Technologies, Inc. to develop trash-to-energy projects in Italy and Germany (*Wall Street Journal,* June 8, 1995).

One could go on with many more examples, but these indicate the enormous variety of product development/production efforts and how each of them reflects the uniting of distinct sets of skills.

An interesting example of an alliance is when a group of organizations attempt to impose a global standard. We have already mentioned the distinctive alliances around the RISC chips (Gomes-Casseres, 1994), but this is not the only example. Matsushita Electric Industrial Co. and Pioneer Electronic Corp., both of Japan, and Thomson S.A. of France, have decided to support a rival videodisk play format to the one proposed by Toshiba Corp. and Time Warner, Inc. (*Wall Street Journal,* January 23, 1995). Another, called the SD alliance, involving 17 electronics and entertainment companies – including Matsushita Electric Industrial Co., MCA, Inc., Time Warner, Inc., and Hitachi, Ltd. – adopted a format for rewritable laser disks (*Wall Street Journal,* May 19, 1995).

But organizational networks, compared with production and product development joint ventures or linkages, are best illustrated by the Japanese automobile industry (Womack et al., 1990: 148–82). Rather than manufacture the whole car through extensive vertical integration, Toyota and other Japanese car manufacturers design and produce cars with their suppliers who seldom change across time. Suppliers, who provide particular components, also have suppliers who, in turn, also have suppliers. What makes these first, second, and third source suppliers a network, as distinct from a production chain, is that they engage in joint design and problem solving. The Japanese call these vertical *keiretsu* or system lines. Japanese auto production networks might be thought of as same-sector competitor networks, but in reality they more closely resemble symbiotic networks.

The car assembler targets a total price, a price that allows a reasonable profit for both the assembler and the suppliers. To achieve this profit, the assembler and supplier work together to lower the cost of each part. For this system to be effective, both the primary supplier and the assembler must share a great deal of information about production costs and profits, participate in designing the component parts, and work with the engineers of the secondary suppliers. Joint design of a car and its components is a complex coordination issue. But it is not the only one. The production of cars requires engaging in a great deal of joint problem solving relative to quality and the movement towards customization of automobiles. Here we observe how complicated coordination can become.

Supercomputers are another example of cooperation across industrial sectors when different technical expertise was needed to achieve innovation. A new consortium was formed with AT&T, IBM, Massachusetts Institute of Technology (MIT), and Lincoln Laboratories, a separate government-funded lab at MIT. The consortium was founded on the recommendation of the White House Science Council which predicted that, without such collaboration, dominance would be lost to other countries, as it has in the laser and videotape technologies. Ralph E. Gomory, IBM senior vice president for science and technology, says that "the notion is the absolute sharing of information ... and the companies will give up control of the work to the consortium." (Hilts, 1989: A1). The participants each contribute the equivalent of 25 full-time professionals and facilities estimated at a value of $10 million to the work effort, and they relinquish control over them to managers named by the governing board of the consortium. Management of the consortium directs all the researchers as a team and is responsible for producing new electronic devices, circuits, and interconnections, and new materials to make them with. In return for their investments, the companies get help from university researchers in developing commercial products, and the universities and government labs get additional funds to add staff and students. They all share in any profits that derive from successful product development (Hilts, 1989). In other words, although it is a research consortium, it does have production implications.

Still another example of systemic production and product development networks is found in the aircraft industry, where complex products require many components from different sectors. There is Airbus Industrie, a consortium involving four governments – France, West Germany, the United Kingdom, and Spain – and their respective companies, Aerospatiale, Deutsche Airbus, British Aerospace, and CASA. Yet another is Boeing-Japan, which includes the American firm Boeing with two Japanese consortia – Japan Aircraft Development Corporation and Japan Aircraft Corporation – as well as three Japanese heavy industry companies – Mitsubishi, Kawasaki, and Fuji Heavy Industries. In aircraft engine manufacturing there are also two joint ventures: CFM International, which combines General Electric with Snecma, a French company, and International Aero Engines which combines Pratt and Whitney (a U.S. firm), Rolls Royce (a U.K. firm), Japan Aero Engines, Motoren-und-Turbinen-Union (a German firm), and Fiat (an Italian firm) (Moxon, Roehl, and Truitt, 1988).

COMPETITIVE COORDINATION AMONG SIMILAR ORGANIZATIONAL PARTNERS

As with symbiotic coordination, our major emphasis is on the more complex forms, particularly joint ventures or linkages to develop and produce complex products and services. At this level the most critical types are research consortia because they create public goods for all firms within an industry or market niche. Furthermore, they allow for the acceleration of economic growth and are thus an important element in the endogenous theories of economic growth (Roemer, 1985). But, as with trade associations and federations and other forms, research consortia vary in their level of complexity (Aldrich and Sasaki, 1995), as shown in Table 3-2.

LIMITED COMPLEXITY AND SIMPLE COORDINATION

A very common international form for coordination and cooperation is a joint venture for marketing. A good example is L'Oreal S.A. of France and Kose Corp. of Japan (*Wall Street Journal,* June 8, 1995), already mentioned. Subcontracts across two or three organizations within the same production chain are increasingly common. California Steel now buys basic steel from a joint venture which is owned by Brazilian, Japanese, and Italian interests and which is located in Brazil. California Steel no longer produces steel itself, but finishes steel products. Each firm gains in efficiency (Nielsen, 1988: 482), illustrating how depth in expertise is a prerequisite to replacing the vertically integrated firm.

Table 3-2. Competitive Linkages and Alliances

Mode of coordination	Few organizations/sectors	Many organizations/sectors
Limited complexity	Obligational linkages	Obligational alliances
	Joint venture for marketing	Cartels
	Subcontracting in the shoe industry	Cottage industries
		Information networks
		Trade associations in the U.S.
		Airline alliances
Moderate complexity	Promotional linkages	Promotional alliances
		Research consortia in Japan
		CCOPs network
		Trade associations in Germany
High complexity	Product development and production linkages	Product development and production alliances
	Joint ventures in automobiles	Research consortia in the U.S.
		Electronics *keiretsu* in Japan

Other striking examples are found in the U.S. footwear industry, which has essentially become an importer. Nike, Reebok, and L.A. Gear do research to create more sophisticated shoe technologies, design diverse varieties of customized athletic shoes, have them manufactured in Asia, import them into the United States, and market them worldwide. Many of the older, traditional shoe companies such as Brown Shoe, Melville, and U.S. Shoe are closing their factories and becoming importers as well.

Consistent with our argument about the evolution of coordination between firms, competitive alliances with limited coordination among large numbers of firms (farms) have been present for many decades. Examples of some of the more common types are shown in Table 3-2. A surprising entry in our typology is that of cartels, which represent a limited form of coordination. Several previous typologies, including our own, have placed cartels in cells representing a high degree of cooperation. But on reflection, and adding the dimension of the complexity of coordination, it seems to us that cartels, while requiring a certain degree of cooperation, are generally not complex because they usually coordinate only one activity, namely prices. If everyone agrees on a price, usually above the costs of the least inefficient producer, then there is little problem. The next level of coordination is to agree on quotas. This is more complicated and difficult, as has been illustrated many times in the history of OPEC, where the interests of member nations are at odds. Even so, setting prices and quotas requires much less complexity of coordination than does the development of complex products.

Cottage industries typically band together to purchase common distributional and marketing services. Small numbers of wine growers in France, Italy, Germany, Spain, and Chile frequently take advantage of economies of scale by jointly bottling and selling their products, as have the much larger prune and cranberry cooperatives in the United States (Nielsen, 1988).

Similarly, trade associations in the United States usually are information-gathering operations for the mutual benefit of their members; e.g., the Automotive News publishes extensive data on production and sales, as do many other trade associations. Sometimes American trade associations are also involved in setting standards, but this is a limited form of coordination (Schneiberg and Hollingsworth, 1990). Trade associations also engage in lobbying activities, but this entails little coordination unless there is a major campaign; then it would evolve to the next level of complexity.

More interesting are the competitive alliances in the airline industry; the objective is to have a critical mass of routes around the world and to gain access to passengers. We have already mentioned SwissAir (DuBois 1995), but there are also the alliance between Air France and United, between British Airways and U.S. Air and that between KLM and Northwestern. In each instance, other airlines have joined these alliances as well in various parts of the world. Another example of an alliance offering comparable services is the one forged between the Blue Cross and Blue Shield organizations in six New England states to provide a unified managed health care plan to multistate employers (*Wall Street Journal,* June 16, 1995).

Universities in the United States provide a large number of examples of cooperation in the exchange of information, including bitnet and internet, interlibrary loans, special programs to recruit minority students, and other formal exchanges of research findings and information. Sports programs have been organized within intercollegiate associations in all regions of the United States, such as the Ivy League and the Big Ten. Increasingly there are various kinds of particularistic exchange programs of students and faculty with specific universities in various parts of the world. Again, these are simple coordination problems (visas, money, program content, policing of infractions in sports, etc.).

MODERATE COMPLEXITY OF COORDINATION

To find examples of moderate complexity of coordination, we can locate trade associations that have evolved toward higher levels of complex coordination. Trade associations in Germany, for instance, regulate wages and industrial disputes and act as mediators within their industries (Schneiberg and Hollingsworth, 1990). The historical origins of these functions date back to the guilds, many of which survive in the modern era. The presence of a strong civic society in certain regions of Italy (Putman, 1993) has allowed cottage industries in these regions to develop forms of district coordination which settle problems such as wage disputes and negotiate the partitioning of the market among firms (Lazeron, 1988). Local government, trade associations, and other tertiary bodies ensure cooperative behavior and account for the ability of these competitors to cooperate.

Research consortia vary in the degree of complexity needed for coordinating. An example of a moderately complex one is a medical research network. In the 1980s the National Cancer Institute (NCI) in the United States created Community Clinical Oncology Programs (CCOPs) to support and coordinate clinical trials in the search for a cure for cancer. Each CCOP consists of a cluster of hospitals, physicians, and support staff, and can range in size from a few physicians and one hospital to as many as 50 physicians and multiple hospitals. The objective of these networks is to link the development and evolution of protocols for cancer treatment and control with ongoing service organizations. NCI provides overall direction, program management, and funding. CCOPs find patients willing to accept experimental treatments and feed research outcome information to regional research bases. Currently there are 51 operating CCOPs in 31 states, and 15 research bases. Together they involve 253 hospitals, 103 group practices, and 2,000 practicing physicians (Kaluzny, Morrissey, and McKinney, 1990). The coordination problems are relatively simple and in some respects reflect the evolution of an information network for cancer patients. A fascinating comparison (Aldrich and Sasaki, 1995) of industrial research consortia in Japan and the United States suggests that in Japan they are much less complex in the nature of their coordination than are their American counterparts. Japanese consortia typically consist of highly focused projects, conducted mostly within individual industrial research laboratories, rarely coordinating research projects across companies.

Furthermore, the variety of technical activities is also less, reducing the complexity further. However, the government is involved in the coordination that does exist, illustrating that a third party is one important component of postindustrial networks, especially when they involve firms in the same sector.

HIGHLY COMPLEX COORDINATION AND COOPERATION

In some sectors, such as the automobile and aircraft industries, the costs and risks of product development are so high that competitors are forced to cooperate in market niches that have small demand or where the risks are extraordinarily high (Berg and Hoekman, 1988; Hladik, 1988; Moxon, Roehl, and Truitt, 1988). These joint ventures should not be confused with the previously described production networks, which cross the production chain and are usually contained within a single country. Instead, we are concerned here with joint ventures between competitors for the development of products in highly specialized niches.

The most dramatic developments in the creation of joint ventures between competitive organizations are in the automobile industry, where the number of joint ventures jumped from 26 to 79 between the first half and the second half of the 1980s (Pollack, 1992). Where there were formerly bitter rivalries, now there are working relationships. For example, Ford currently builds minivans with Nissan at a Ford plant in Ohio, assembles Mazda's Mercury Tracers in Mexico, has a working agreement with Mazda to build Ford Probes in Michigan, and merged its operations in Brazil and Argentina with Volkswagen (Kraar, 1989).

Although the usual objective is to amortize the cost of product development in small markets such as minivans, convertibles, and subcompact cars, sometimes the explanation is highly particularistic and very pragmatic. For example, there is NUMMI, the joint venture between General Motors and Toyota, formed because Toyota needed General Motors to lobby Congress and the administration to block import quotas and General Motors needed Toyota's lean production technologies. This is a mixed political and technological exchange, one that Kanter (1989) called opportunistic.

As the costs of production development soar in other sectors, we will see more of these joint ventures between competitors, such as in the semiconductor industry, where the costs of building factories for the next generation are skyrocketing. There is now a joint venture between Texas Instruments and Hitachi (Zuckerman and Kaluzny, 1990) and more can be expected in the future. Unfortunately, the large number of studies on joint ventures does not make a distinction between joint ventures in the same industry/market niche and those that span industries/markets, nor do they analyze the niches in which joint ventures are created.

If we think that the automobile and commercial aircraft industries are in the same sector, then we would put their production networks in this cell of the typology. Perhaps the best examples, however, are the *keiretsu* in electronics in Japan (Sako, 1994). Their products are less complex and they do not span sectors. Equally exemplary are the basic research and product development consortia in the United States. While some span sectors, most are within sectors. Examples with their dates of creation include Micro Electronic and Computer Technology Corporation (1983), a software productivity consortium (1985), the National Center for Manufacturing Science (1986), and Sematech for semiconductors (1987) (Richards, 1989). The objective of these efforts is to assist a specialized niche or industry to improve the scope and quality of its research.

Although Sematech has been in operation for only five years, it has had a positive impact on the competitive position of American industry in this key sector, significantly increasing America's share of the world market. U.S. research consortia like Sematech are larger than those in Japan, are primarily involved in idea generation and the measuring of technical feasibility, and are housed in a joint facility, a university, or an independent laboratory (Aldrich and Sasaki, 1995). Furthermore, organizational members of American consortia tend to generate the majority of their own operating funds. All of these characteristics make coordination far more difficult than in Japan, as is illustrated in the history of Sematech (Browning, Beyer, and Shetler, 1995). On the other hand, U.S. consortia have fewer resource dependency problems and more organizational autonomy. Regardless of the differences, our prediction is that all countries will increasingly compete with each other through the research programs carried out by their consortia.

CONCLUSION AND DISCUSSION

The value of a typology lies in its ability to integrate isolated ideas and present them within a coherent framework. Our typology asserts that the direction of interorganizational evolution is toward more complex linkages and alliances both within sectors and between them, a further stage in the evolution of organizational forms (Aldrich and Mueller, 1982) and away from vertical integration (Williamson, 1975). The reason for the movement toward more complex forms of coordination is the appearance of new economic incentives (North, 1990), the increasing importance of innovation, and the reduction of adaptive costs (as measured by average product age and amount of industrial research investment, respectively). As productivity becomes less crucial and transaction costs decrease, both innovation and adaptive costs become the mechanisms by which firms are selected for survival.

We have, at various points in this chapter, suggested some specific directions that linkages and alliances will take:

1. The movement from vertical integration toward joint ventures and production networks will continue.
2. So will the creation of joint ventures between small and large high-tech companies.
3. So will the movement of semiconductors toward joint ventures because of the high cost of building plants.
4. So will the increasing use of research consortia as ways for governments to join business in international competition.

The predictive capacity of this typology can thus be tested as the future unfolds, providing feedback on the quality of the ideas.

The degree of differentiation and the number of organizational partners will continue to be affected by the continued growth in knowledge. The search for specific kinds of expertise leads to more particular relationships, while paradoxically, the complexity of the components in the product chain leads to a growth in the number of organizations and movement toward alliances, as distinct from joint ventures. All of these trends imply an evolution toward greater particularism, both horizontally and vertically.

By emphasizing these interorganizational characteristics, we are able to observe differences in the nature of cooperatives, cartels, trade associations, joint ventures, and research consortia. They vary in the complexity of the coordination modes they use across time and national borders, and they will certainly evolve across time depending upon the specific cultural and historical circumstances. Future work needs to concentrate on the patterns of structural evolution, a topic beyond the scope of this paper. Our dimensions of complexity, differentiation, and the particularism of organizational partners provide an attractive way of describing this evolution, even if they leave unanswered a number of questions.

Another undeveloped idea is the role of third parties such as universities, governments, trade associations, and banks in handling the coordination. In countries like Japan, the central government assumes the bulk of the coordinating function, whereas the United States government plays a more passive role, unless the network provides military equipment. U.S. universities, on the other hand, are useful facilitators, providing opportunities to negotiate between jealous competitors. Obviously, some of these coordination roles are more complex, but they provide ways of reducing inevitable conflict. There is a need for much more research on this topic as well.

ENDNOTES

1. In Chapter 1, trade associations are perceived as a distinct form of coordination, separate from networks. We classify trade associations as a kind of network because their members are organizations rather than individuals and they are contributing resources to accomplish common objectives which would be difficult to achieve on their own. In this sense, they are no different from the distributing organizations created by cooperatives to sell their products or cartels that allocate production quotas. In each instance organizations (or farms) are acting in concert through some common association or organization.
2. The typology contained in this paper is consistent with our central arguments about the importance of structural complexity in the network and the difficulties it creates for the performance of the network (see Alter and Hage, 1993: Chapter 7).
3. Ideally, we would prefer to standardize the language so that joint ventures are only contractual relationships between firms and linkages would be used when there is no contractual relationship. In fact, a close reading of the literature indicates that this is implicit in much of the discussion. For alliances, the same logic would apply except that in some alliances only the core of the alliance would have formal contracts.
4. The direction of evolution relative to the number of partners is more difficult to discern. Essentially, those within industrial groupings such as cartels are being replaced with global alliances of one kind or another and therefore have fewer members, while the joint ventures across market niches or industrial sectors are growing in numbers.
5. Although several of these citations represent studies of coordination modes internal to the organization, they apply to interorganizational relationships as well. In the future, the idea of normative appeals, taken from Etzioni's typology of compliance structures, will become more and more critical.
6. This makes the classification of interorganizational networks on the basis of their coordination mode somewhat difficult.
7. This is an application of the idea of the need for greater integration given higher structural differentiation of Lawrence and Lorsch (1967) and applied to the interorganizational network level of analysis. It also demonstrates that the latter level is a logical and further step in the evolution of organizational forms caused by the growth in knowledge, although their work has not been interpreted in this way.

BIBLIOGRAPHY

Aldrich, Howard. 1979. *Organizations and Environments.* Englewood Cliffs, N.J.: Prentice Hall.

Aldrich, Howard and S. Mueller. 1982. "The Evolution of Organizational Forms: Technology, Coordination and Control." *Research in Organizational Behavior.* 4: 33–87.

Aldrich, Howard and Toshihiro Sasaki. 1995, forthcoming. "R and D Consortia in the United States and Japan." *Research Policy.*

Alter, Catherine. 1990. "An Exploratory Study of Conflict and Coordination in Interorganizational Service Delivery Systems." *Academy of Management Journal.* 3.3: 478–501.

Alter, Catherine, W. Deutelbaum, T. E. Dodd, J. Else, and S. Raheim. 1992. "Integrating Three Strategies of Family Empowerment: Family, Community, and Economic Development." Annual meetings, Council on Social Work Education, March, Kansas City, Missouri.

Alter, Catherine and Jerald Hage. 1993. *Organizations Working Together: Coordination in Interorganizational Networks.* Beverly Hills: Sage.

Astley, W. Graham and Charles J. Fombrun. 1983. "Collective Strategy: Social Ecology of Organizational Environments." *Academy of Management Review.* 8: 576–87.

Browning, Larry, Janice Beyer, and Judy Shetler. 1995. "Building Cooperation in a Competitive Industry: SEMATECH and the Semiconductor Industry." *Academy of Management Journal.* 38, 1: 113–51.

Chandler, Alfred D. 1962. *Strategy and Structure: Chapters in the History of Industrial Enterprise.* Cambridge: MIT Press.

____ 1977. *The Visible Hand: The Managerial Revolution in American Business.* Cambridge: MIT Press.

DuBois, Martin. 1995. "Swissair to Buy 49.5 Percent of Sabena Ailing Airline." *Wall Street Journal.* May 5: A, 9:1.

Etzioni, Amitai. 1975. *A Comparactive Analysis of Complex Organizations.* New York: Free Press.

Gerlach, Michael. 1992. *Allicance Capitalism: The Social Organization of Japanese Business.* Berkeley: University of California Press.

Gibson, Richard. 1995. "McDonald's, U.S. Franchise Ventures on the Rise." *Wall Street Journal.* June 26: B 2, 3.

Gomes-Casseres, Benjamin. 1994. "Group vs. Group: How Alliance Networks Compete." *Harvard Business Review.* 92 (July–August): 62–66, et seq.

Gouldner, Alvin W. 1959. "Organizational Analysis." In Robert K. Merton, ed. *Sociology Today.* New York: Basic Books. Pp. 400–28.

Grandori, Anna and Giuseppe Soda. 1995. "Inter-firm Networks: Antecedents, Mechanisms and Forms." *Organizational Studies.* 16,2: 183–214.

Hage, Jerald. 1974. *Communication and Organizational Control: Cybernetics in Health and Welfare Settings.* New York: Wiley-Interscience.

Hage, Jerald and Charles Powers. 1992. *Post-industrial Lives.* Newbury Park, CA: Sage.

Hage, Jerald and Zhongren Jing. 1995. "Adaptive Costs: Another Issue in Institutional Economics." Revision of a paper presented at the annual meetings of the Society for the Advancement of Economics, March, New York.

Hage, Jerald and Yishu Yang. 1995. "Tacit Knowledge, Trust and Innovation." Annual meetings of the Society for the Advancement of Economics, April, Washington, D.C.

Häkansson, Häkan. 1990. "Technological collaboration in industrial networks." *European Management Journal.* 8(3): 371–79.

Häkansson, Häkan and Jan Johanson. 1988. "Formal and Informal Cooperation Strategies in International Industrial Networks." In F. Contractor and P.

Lorange, eds. *Cooperative Strategies in International Business.* Lexington, Mass.: Lexington Books. Pp. 369–79.

Henderson, Angelo. 1995. "GM Plans to Build Forklift Truck Engines for Toyota." *Wall Street Journal.* May 25: B 9, 5.

Hergert, M. and D. Morris. 1988. "Trends in International Collaborative Agreements." In F. Contractor and P. Lorange, eds. *Cooperative Strategies in International Business* Lexington, Mass.: Lexington Books. Pp. 99–109.

Hilts, P. J. 1989. "U.S. Consortium Is Formed to Commercialize Superconductors." *Washinton Post.* May 24: A, 1.

Hladik, K. 1988. "R&D and International Joint Ventures." In F. Contractor and P. Lorange, eds. *Cooperative Strategies in International Business.* Lexington, Mass.: Lexington Books. Pp. 187–204.

Houghton, J. R. 1989. "The Age of Hierarchy is Over." *The New York Times.* September 24, 3.

Hollingsworth, J. Rogers. 1991. "The Logic of Coordinating American Manufacturing Sectors." In J. L. Campbell, J. R. Hollingsworth, and L. N. Lindberg, eds. *The Governance of the American Economy.* New York: Cambridge University Press. Pp. 35–74.

Hollingsworth, J. Rogers and Ellen Jane Hollingsworth. 1987. *Controversy about American Hospitals: Funding, Ownership, and Performance.* Washington, D.C.: American Enterprise Institute.

Jarillo, J. C. 1993. *Strategic Networks: Creating the Borderless Organization.* Oxford: Butterworth-Heineman.

Johanson, Jan, and Lars-Gunnar Mattson. 1987. "Interorganizational Relations in Industrial Systems: A Network Approach Compared with the Transaction Cost Approach." *Working Paper Series (#7),* Department of Business Administration, University of Uppsala, Sweden.

Kaluzny, Arnold D., Joseph P. Morrissey, and Martha M. McKinney. 1990. "Emerging Organizational Networks: The Case of Community Clinical Oncology Programs." In S. S. Mick and Associates, eds. *Innovations in Health Care Delivery: Insights for Organization Theory.* San Francisco: Jossey-Bass Publishers, 1990. Pp. 86–115.

Kantner, Rosabeth M. 1989. "Becoming PALS: Pooling, Allying and Linking Across Companies." *Academy of Management Executives,* 3 (August): 183–193.

Kantner, Rosabeth M. 1994. "Collaborative Advantage: Successful Partnerships Manage the Relationship, Not Just the Deal." *Harvard Business Review.* 92 (July-August): 96–108.

Killing, J.P. 1988. "Understanding Alliances: The Role of Task and Organizational Complexity." In F. Contractor and P. Lorange, eds. *Cooperative Strategies in International Business.* Lexington, Mass.: Lexington Books. Pp. 55–67.

Kraar, L. 1989. "Your Rivals Can Be Your Allies." *Fortune.* March 27: 66–76.

Laage-Hellman, J. 1989. *Technological Development in Industrial Networks.* Published doctoral dissertation. Uppsala: University of Uppsala.

Lawrence, Paul and Jay Lorsch. 1967. *Organization and Environment: Managing Differentiation and Integration.* Cambridge: Harvard Graduate School of Business Administration.

Lazeron, Mark. 1988. "Small Firm Growth." *American Sociological Review.* 53 (June): 330–42.

LePoint April 14, 1994.

Moxon, R., T. Roehl, and J. F. Truitt. 1988. "International Cooperative Ventures in the Commercial Aircraft Industry: Gains, Sure, But What's My Share." In F. Contractor and P. Lorange, eds. *Cooperative Strategies in International Business.* Lexington, Mass.: Lexington Books. Pp. 255–78.

Nielsen, R. 1988. "Cooperative Strategy." *Strategic Management Journal.* 9: 475–92.

North, Douglas C. 1990. *Institution, Institutional Change, and Economic Performance.* New York: Cambridge University Press.

Pfeffer, Jeffrey and Gerald Salancik. 1974. *The External Control of Organizations.* New York: Harper & Row.

Piore, Michael J. and Charles F. Sabel. 1986. *The Second Industrial Divide: Possibilities for Prosperity.* New York: Basic Books.

Pollack, A. 1992. "Technology without Borders Raises Big Questions for U.S." *The New York Times.* January 1: A, 1 et seq.

Powell, Woodward W. 1990. "Neither Market nor Hierarchy: Network Forms of Organizations." In L. L. Cummings and B. Staw, eds. *Research in Organizational Behavior.* Greenwich, Conn.: JAI Press. Pp. 295–336.

Powell, Woodward W. and P. Brantley. 1992. "Competitive Cooperation in Biotechnology: Learning through Networks." In N. Nohria and R. Eccles, eds. *Networks and Organizations.* Cambridge: Harvard Business School Press.

Putnam, Robert D. 1993. *Making Democracy Work: Civil Traditions in Modern Italy.* Princeton, NJ: Princeton University Press.

Richards, E. 1989. "U.S.-Japanese Venture Develops New Supercomputer." *Washington Post.* April 10: A 16, 1.

Rigdon, Joan and Thomas King. 1995. "Dream Works: Silicon Graphics Team on Studio." *Wall Street Journal,* June 1: B 1, 3.

Roemer, Paul. 1985. "Increasing Returns and Long-Run Growth." *Journal of Political Economy.* 94 (October): 1002–37.

Sako, M. 1994. "Neither Markets nor Hierarchies: A Comparative Study of the Printed Circuit Board Industry in Britain and Japan." In J. R. Hollingsworth, P. C. Schmitter, and W. Streeck, eds. *Comparing Capitalist Economies: Variations in the Governance of Sectors.* Oxford: Oxford University Press.

Schneiberg, Marc and J. Rogers Hollingsworth. 1990. "Can Transaction Costs Economics Explain Trade Associations?" In Massahiko Aoki, Bo Gustafsson, and Oliver E. Williamson, eds. *The Firm as a Nexus of Treaties.* Newberry Park, Cal.: Sage Publications. Pp. 320–346.

Suleiman, Ezra. 1978. *Elites in Society: The Politics of Survival.* Princeton: Princeton University Press.

Sydow, Jorg and Arnold Windeler. 1995. "Organizing Inter-Firm Networks – A Structurationist Perspective on Management Practices." Academy of Management Meetings. August. Vancouver, British Columbia, Canada.

Wall Street Journal, January 23, 1995 A, 3: 4.

Wall Street Journal, February 14, 1995 A, 4: 6.

Wall Street Journal, April 6, 1995 A, 4: 2.

Wall Street Journal, April 13, 1995 B, 8: 5.

Wall Street Journal, April 14a, 1995 A, 5: 4.

Wall Street Journal, April 14b, 1995 B, 3: 5.

Wall Street Journal, April 14c, 1995 B, 6: 3.

Wall Street Journal, April 20, 1995 B, 3: 5.

Wall Street Journal, May 19, 1995 B, 8: 6.

Wall Street Journal, June 8, 1995 B, 6: 4.

Wall Street Journal, June 16, 1995, B, 3: 4.

Wall Street Journal, June 26, 1995 "Business Round-up." B, 4: 4.

Wall Street Journal, June 28a, 1995 B, 1: 1.

Wall Street Journal, June 28b, 1995 "Business Round-up." B, 4.

Wall Street Journal, June 30, 1995 A, 6: 3.

Wikström, Solveig and Richard Normann. 1994. *Knowledge and Value.* London: Routledge.

Williamson, Oliver E. 1975. *Markets and Hierarchies – Analysis and Antitrust Implications: A Study in the Economics of Internal Organization.* New York: The Free Press.

    1985. *The Economic Institutions of Capitalism: Firms, Markets, Relational Contracting.* New York: The Free Press.

Wolferen, Karel van. 1990. *The Enigma of Japanese Power.* New York: Vintage Books.

Womack, J., D. Jones, and D. Roos. 1990. *The Machine That Changed the World.* New York: Rawson Associates.

Work, C. 1988. "Business without Borders." *U.S. News & World Report.* June 20: 48 et seq.

Zuckerman, Howard and Arnold Kaluzny. 1990. "Strategic Alliances in Health Care: The Challenges of Cooperation." *Frontiers of Health Services Management,* 7, 3: 3–35.

4

ASSOCIATIONAL GOVERNANCE IN A GLOBALIZING ERA: WEATHERING THE STORM

William D. Coleman

The growth of international competition and trade in the postwar period, at first blush, would not appear to provide a context especially favorable for the assumption of governance roles in the economy by interest associations. In many capitalist states, neoliberal ideologies that favor the globalization of economic relations have gained significant influence within the *classe politique.* These ideologies celebrate the virtues of markets as the preeminent governing mechanisms, laud their efficiency, and postulate their capacity to increase the general good of all. Championed as extraordinary, "natural" allocative instruments, markets, it is suggested, must be left free to weave their magic. Consistent with this neoliberal ideology are policies that promote markets at the expense of other governing structures and that seek to dismantle alternative governance arrangements when they exist. The ideologically committed dismiss all attempts by the state to approach economic policy in an anticipatory fashion. The idea of state intervention is attacked as protectionist, inefficient, and self-serving for backward private interests.

Research supported by Social Sciences and Humanities Research Council of Canada, Research Grants 410-88-0629 and 410-92-0260. An earlier draft of this chapter was published in French in *Études internationales,* Vol. XXIV, No. 3 (1993): 631–51. I would like to thank Henry J. Jacek and participants at the second and third conferences of the Comparative Economic Governance Group for their comments on an earlier draft of this paper.

Interest associations might not be expected to fare well as governance mechanisms in this neoliberal world. At the sectoral level, neoliberals perceive them to be the servants of corrupt special interests that refuse to face the bracing world of international competition. At the macro level, they are branded disdainfully as "corporatist," a term that hints at market interference and at collusion among the state, big capital, and big labor. The reactive approach to policy favored by neoliberal governments has little room for associations. Willis and Grant's (1987) concept of the "company state" underlines these implications. Governments have dismantled sector branches or sponsorship divisions in industry ministries in order to place more emphasis on direct relationships with the "real" economic actors, individual entrepreneurs. Associations are dismissed as hide-bound purveyors of the lowest common denominator sectoral view.

Despite these pressures, many associations have survived as governance mechanisms in the present wave of globalization and neoliberal hostility. In this chapter, several factors are noted that help to explain this survival. First, the neoliberal perspective on economic and social policy has yet to displace many of the ongoing routines of the policy process. The policy process remains ongoing, technical in orientation, and complex. Policy development and implementation require negotiation between state agencies and societal actors and often some sharing of responsibilities and of expertise. As long as these characteristics of the policy process remain, so too will opportunities exist for associations as governance mechanisms.

Second, the commitment to neoliberal ideology varies significantly among the capitalist powers (Cox, 1987: 285ff). Outside the Anglo-American states, governments have more of a tendency to adopt a consensus-based adjustment process and thus try to balance the virtues of markets against some of their vices: the concentration of wealth and power, the inability to take account of "externalities" – environmental destruction, unsafe workplaces, depressed living conditions – and the tendency to foster collusion and monopolies. In short, markets are not seen always to work best when left alone. State intervention is not necessarily forsworn. And, when pursued, its logic often dictates close reciprocal relationships between state agencies and various intermediaries representing firms and workers in a sector, what Cox (1987: 286) calls a "state capitalist" approach.

Finally, a commitment to neoliberal ideology at the macro plane may or may not have a determining impact on policy making at the sectoral plane. In the adversarial Anglo-American polities in particular, the lack of a state tradition (Dyson, 1980), the tendency to diffuse power to autonomous bureaucratic agencies, and the fragmentation and low integration of business associational systems (Coleman and Grant, 1988; Coleman, 1990) all create conditions that allow for considerable variation in approaches to policy and in state and associational structures at the sectoral plane. Individual sectoral bureaucracies, as a result of historical conditions, can concentrate considerable expertise and develop significant autonomy of action in their own right. Associations long versed in the sharing of state authority can adapt creatively and find new governing niches. In the process, they may encourage the organizational development of companion intermediary associations and, with the state, may embark on an anticipatory path to policy making.

This chapter examines the governance roles of interest associations in four steps. First, the concept of associational governance is analyzed conceptually by reflecting briefly on the likely effects of economic globalization on the organizational development of associations. Second, the chapter assesses the impact of internationalization on associational governance at the national level. It suggests that different approaches to policy and historical legacies must be taken into account. The third section builds on this suggestion by looking at two scenarios: sectors in decline and sectors at a maturation stage. Finally, the paper reviews the prospects for associational governance at a supranational level. It argues that, at present, such developments remain highly unlikely, but that supranational governing arrangements among states may lead to an increase in the governing powers of national level interest associations.

INTERNATIONALIZATION AND ORGANIZATIONAL DEVELOPMENT

Interest associations assume governance roles as intermediary organizations, a status that distinguishes associative action from other governing mechanisms. The comparative economic governance project has defined governance broadly to include the totality of institutional arrangements that coordinate and regulate transactions inside and across the boundaries of economic sectors. Associations act as governance mechanisms by defining and procuring public goods through organizing and enforcing cooperative behavior among their members, by engaging in collective contracts with other associations, and by securing delegations of state authority to be used to the advantage of their members (Hollingsworth, Schmitter, and Streeck, 1994). To assume such a governance role, associations must reach a certain level of organizational development (Coleman and Grant, 1984; Schmitter and Streeck, 1981). A developed association is one first that is capable of ordering and coordinating the complex range of information and activity that it is asked to assume by its members and by other organizations, particularly the state (Coleman, 1988). Second, such an association is autonomous from its members and the state. It takes on a life of its own and is able to rise above the short-term, particularistic interests of its members.

The emergence of these organizational characteristics for an intermediary like an association depends on relations with its membership and with key actors in its environment. Schmitter and Streeck (1981, 1985) have suggested two organizing concepts for studying these relationships. First, they emphasize the importance of how an association defines its domain of potential members. This definition constrains the size of the association, the pattern of industrial organization and geographical location characteristic of its members, and its degree of sectoral specialization. In short, the domain sets in motion a logic of organization, the "logic of membership." Second, they take note of the environment within which an association acts on behalf of these members. Always complex, this environment is populated by various actors, of which the most important normally is the state. The characteristics of the state, including its own organizational capacity and its specific needs and objectives, have a further impact on the organizational characteristics of an interest association, an impact assimilated by Schmitter and Streeck under the concept of the "logic of influence."

As intermediary organizations, associations must accommodate the often competing demands of these two logics. Certainly, their assumption of governance roles in a sector is based on a set of conditions involving the balance between the logics of membership and influence and on the impact of this balance on internal structures for goal definition and implementation (Schmitter and Streeck, 1981; Streeck, 1989). What is evident nonetheless is that associations take on governance roles in the context of a broader institutional environment that favors dense social organization around market allocations. Any assessment, therefore, of the fate of associations as governance instruments in the present era requires a consideration of the impact of increased global competition and its supporting neoliberal ideologies on such patterns of social organization. Changes here, in turn, may affect the ability of associations to order and coordinate complex information and to maintain autonomy.

More international competition may alter the *logic of membership* in ways unfavorable to organizational development in the following ways. For example, it may encourage the rationalization of production within the nation-state leading to increased concentration of ownership and centralization of production. Consequently, the number of firms eligible for membership in a national association may diminish, the geographical distribution of production sites may change, and the very definition of the sector may broaden or narrow. Such revisions in the membership will have an impact on *the internal organization of an association* and on *relations with other associations.* Members may see less need for collective action. Or mergers may follow, new information may need to be studied and learned, and internal procedures and structures may be redefined. These kinds of changes will also affect an association's resources including its funds, the quality of its staff, and its ability to draw on the expertise of its members. To the extent that these kinds of changes hamper the ability of an association to define collective interests, to coordinate with other associations, or to retain resources, associational governance becomes less likely.

As we will indicate later in the chapter, large scale, mass production national sectors faced with serious decline in the wake of internationalization are most likely to possess associations with declining levels of organizational development. By contrast, some evidence suggests that diversified quality mass production or flexible specialization sectors that stabilize or even expand growth in the globalization process are more likely to be able to maintain and even advance developed associations.

Globalized economic competition may have an impact on the *logic of influence* in ways that might also retard organizational development. The liberalization of trade relations and financial markets has reduced the use of tariffs, quantitative barriers to trade, and controls on foreign exchange and interest rates. Policy makers find themselves with fewer policy instruments available for promoting or defending any given sector. Accordingly, individual states may be faced with very difficult questions about how to react to the rapid decline of a poorly competitive sector when the traditional remedy of higher tariffs is no longer available. But it is in the definition and management of these kinds of distributive or regulatory instruments that state actors have often sought to involve interest associations. In other sectors, increased global competition may foster the emergence of supranational "regimes" for managing the rules of the game. Not only must national governments adopt new strategies for negotiating in these fora, but also associations must assimilate a new *definition of what the state entails.* The complexity of this new state environment, in particular the diffusion of authority, may render more difficult the delegation of state authority that is often central to associational governance.

A revitalized commitment to neoliberal principles by state actors has often accompanied the internationalization of production relations and may bring attacks on associational governance. Such a commitment entails giving primacy to markets among governance mechanisms. Neoliberals have advocated less political intervention into markets and have attacked other governance structures, whether associations, informal collusive practices, or excessive state regulation that restrain the "freedom" of markets. These attacks extend, in many instances, to trade unions which are viewed as nefarious obstructions to the free development of labor markets. In short, the ideological changes among some national ruling classes that have accompanied globalized competition will affect the perceived legitimacy of associational governance. The general political environment may become considerably less hospitable to close working relationships between the state and associations and to cooperative behavior within associations.

Generally speaking, the processes involved in the internationalization of economic activity do not appear to favor associational governance. They promise to destabilize memberships, possibly to the point that the association may be forced into mergers or even defined out of existence. They favor developments in the policy process that may undermine cooperative behavior between the state and collective interests. As cooperation decreases, associations will lose their access to some information, may cut back on their own policy research, and thus may become less autonomous from members. Without this policy expertise and autonomy, they become less able to exercise a governance role.

Not all the evidence supports this thinking about the relationship between globalization and associational governance. The empirical studies in the comparative economic governance project and other research in comparative public policy suggest that a secular decline in associational governance does not emerge as clearly as might be expected. Two factors appear to counter the trend. First, despite the efforts of neoliberals, the ongoing, technical, and complex character of public policy has remained, and this character demands close working relationships between the state and affected interests. The maintenance of organizationally developed interest associations remains in the interests of many state officials. Second, the compelling logic of internationalization does not affect all social systems of production in the same way. Internationalization tends to favor stripping bare the institutional environment around markets in large-scale and small-scale mass production systems. In contrast, some evidence suggests that it promotes a redefinition and retention of associational governance in flexible specialization and diversified quality mass production manufacturing sectors, as well as in agriculture. Here associations appear to be capable of drawing on their own organizational resources to participate in the reshaping of their environments. Once in position to play a governance role, associations often "stick" and find new ways to maintain their governing status. The importance of these two factors is illustrated in the following two sections of the chapter.

INTERNATIONALIZATION AND NATIONAL ASSOCIATIONAL GOVERNANCE

POLICY APPROACH: THE IMPORTANCE OF STATE STRUCTURE

In searching for the beginnings of an identification of the factors that assist associations to resist the pressures against associational governance posed by internationalization, we suggest looking at two: state structures and the historical development of reliance on associational governance. "State structures" is an encompassing term that refers to the arrangements governing relations between executive and legislature, the role of the constitution, corresponding administrative practices and goals, and what Hall (1989: 383) has termed the "structure of political discourse." This structure includes "shared conceptions about the nature of the society and the economy, various ideas about the appropriate role of government, a number of common political ideas, and collective memories of past political experiences." When compared to the operation of the policy process at the sectoral level, these state structures would appear to be relatively fixed. In speaking about a development model of national policy networks, Lehmbruch (1990) writes that such broad state structures tend to be set in the context of major crises and then proceed to constrain national politics for a considerable period of time. Such an interpretation is quite consistent with Dyson's (1980) work on state traditions and his attempt to define a set of ideal typical polities.

A given complex of state structures will have a *variable* relationship with policy making at a sectoral level. As Maurice Wright (1988: 594) has noted:

> What actually happens within the policy process within a particular industrial sector may not only be different from what happens in other industrial sectors (and other countries), but the behavior of policy makers may also appear inconsistent with conventional explanations of, for example, the "role of the state," the bureaucracy, representative associations, and financial institutions.

Hence national state structures and the policy process in a particular sector may appear to have little in common. We should recognize that some state structures may even be particularly favorable to widespread experimentation with policy processes and instruments at the sectoral level. In other contexts, national state structures will have a direct impact on the organization of policy networks at the sectoral level. In particular, instances where the very fate of the sector is at stake are particularly likely to bring out nationally characteristic responses.

Obviously in a chapter of this length and scope, we cannot expect to trace out in detail differences in state structures and their individual impact on sectoral policy making. Rather we propose to use a summary variable, policy approach, a variable that draws an implicit contrast between two broad constellations of state structures. *Policy approach* refers to the method that a government uses to solve problems faced by a sector. Although a number of typologies exist for characterizing variations in approach, we retain for the purposes of this discussion only one of these, the distinction between *anticipatory* and *reactive* approaches. This distinction was first advanced by Richardson, Gustafsson, and Jordan (1982) and has been elaborated in subsequent work by Dyson (1982), Hayward (1982), Shepherd and Duchêne (1983), Duchêne (1987), and Atkinson and Coleman (1989a).

An anticipatory approach to problem solving emphasizes the importance of acquiring information and knowledge in order to provide a foundation for activist, innovative government (Dyson, 1982: 17). It presumes the presence of highly capable state agencies and a set of political ideas that treat skeptically neoliberal admonitions against state intervention. Anticipatory policy making gives precedence to medium- and long-term objectives; it sacrifices short-term economic growth for longer term economic stability; and it may involve significant intrusion into the affairs of private firms. "The working assumption is that for many purposes market signals will not be in accord with overriding national goals, especially the preservation and nurturing of what are considered strategically important industries" (Atkinson and Coleman, 1989a: 24). The investment decisions of individual firms are not assumed to be completely private; indeed their public character, the way in which they affect the lives of workers and other capitalists, makes them matters for public discussion.

Anticipatory policy making thus has a broad range (it will look at a whole sector rather than one firm) and a pronounced depth (it takes into account the detailed characteristics of firms in a sector). Finally, anticipatory policy normally involves the integrated application of a series of policy instruments. "Strong efforts are made to achieve a measure of complementarity, with special attention being paid to backward and forward linkages among industrial sectors" (Atkinson and Coleman, 1989a: 25).

An anticipatory approach to policy making will often require associational governance to be successful. The degree of coordination of diverse policy instruments, the level of information on the strengths and weaknesses of firms, and the need for cooperation between state actors and industry – all these factors create conditions that favor associational development. It is true that the state can act on its own and impose a policy on a sector, but these circumstances are actually quite rare in market economies. They are used only as a last resort in order to encourage participants in the policy process to make negotiation work (Dyson, 1982), at very early stages in a sector's development when no association has yet formed (Atkinson and Coleman, 1989a: Chapter 5), or in special policy areas such as monetary policy where the state wishes to limit state–society contacts (Coleman, 1991; Woolley, 1984). Normally, if an anticipatory approach is favored, state officials must set up a "negotiated order" (Whiteley, 1987) or pursue what Richard Samuels (1987) calls "the politics of reciprocal consent" between state and civil society.

Anticipatory policy will rest then on the presence of strong, highly organized interest associations capable both of developing a longer term view of the sector's development and of convincing members to abide by that view. The relationship between the state and industry in this policy environment is ongoing, intense, and highly technical in approach. Without a developed associational system, it becomes very difficult to sustain anticipatory policy making.

A reactive approach to policy making operates according to a different set of assumptions; it "rests on a neoliberal view of the importance of the state–society distinction and of the impartial role of government as a referee" (Dyson, 1982: 17). Such assumptions dictate first that governments have limited and short-term objectives when it comes to sectoral development. Structural adjustment should be left in the hands of market forces; the state only intervenes to correct short-term failures of the market mechanism. Strong government here does not necessarily mean an extensive and highly capable state bureaucracy. Reactive policy does not involve intrusion into the affairs of individual firms; rather it gives primacy to "environmental" intervention – the development of an appropriate climate for investment through the tax system, industrial relations law, and monetary policy. Reactive policy does not appear planned and coordinated like anticipatory policy; it gives the appearance of a series of ad hoc measures applied to firms and sectors as the need arises. In fact, the market is expected to take the lead role.

By implication, reactive policy making is much less likely to require associational governance in its implementation. Indeed under most, but not all, conditions, associations play an ancillary role in the delivery of reactive policy. The major exception involves situations where regulatory policy instruments are used in a reactive manner. A group may seek to exercise authority over economic activity in a sector on behalf of its members, a move largely unopposed by other potential interests (Hayes, 1978). In these circumstances, a state agency may be persuaded to delegate some of its regulatory authority to the association. In exchange, the agency experiences less conflict and delay in the administrative process, possibly lowers its costs, and receives added political support in disputes with its political masters (Chubb, 1983: 32). Such an outcome is characterized as self-regulation in the public policy literature (Hayes, 1978; Peters, 1977), with common examples being advertising (Boddewyn, 1985), accounting (Willmott, 1985), the dairy industry (Traxler and Unger, 1994), and securities (Coleman, 1989, 1994; Moran, 1989, 1990).

If state capacity is not high, such circumstances favor what many call agency capture; in order to accomplish its programmatic and political objectives, the agency incorporates the association representing the cost bearers into the policy process and gives it some responsibilities for the implementation of the regulation. Prominent examples of this phenomenon are found in the regulation of pharmaceutical pricing (Sargent, 1985) and of safety and quality in food processing (de Vroom, 1987).

Internationalization promises to destabilize these reactive forms of associational governance. The "privileges" of associational monopolies tend to be challenged from within the nation-state and from without. As a consequence, state supervision tends to increase as the securities (Cerny, 1989; Coleman, 1994, 1996; Moran, 1991) and the dairy sectors (Traxler and Unger, 1994) indicate. In some scenarios, associational governance crumbles completely as the California dairy sector (Young, 1990) illustrates.

Nonetheless, an anticipatory approach to policy making or a particular constellation of reactive policy and regulatory instruments are not sufficient conditions for the emergence of associational governance. Associational governance will also hinge very much on the level of associational development reached prior to any crisis precipitated by the internationalization of economic relations. High levels of associational development are found in agriculture and in industrial sectors whose characteristics resemble diversified quality production or flexible specialization. The focus on quality rather than price as the measure of competition in these sectors tends to require close cooperation with the state and dense social networks of organizational arrangements including associations. When these sectors are faced with increased international competition, one should not underestimate the capacity of associations to transform themselves and to adapt to new conditions. The following two sections analyze these factors under two different economic scenarios: management of decline and the transition from expansion to maturity.

MANAGEMENT OF DECLINE

Perhaps the most difficult political problem that emerges in the wake of increased international competition involves what to do when a sector can no longer compete in world markets. Two ideal typical responses might be distinguished. In the first, the state in cooperation with the sector develops a medium- to long-term plan directed either at rationalizing production to favor the firms most likely to be competitive or at abandoning the sector. Such options require an anticipatory approach to policy utilizing redistributive policy instruments. In the second response, business, possibly in conjunction with labor, pressures the state to subsidize and protect existing firms, while they seek to adapt individually to the new competitive conditions. The state responds with the required assistance when it has the resources and when it feels the pressure the most intensely. In this scenario, the state reacts rather than anticipates, and utilizes distributive [what Stråth (1994) calls the "slice of pie" approach] rather than redistributive policy instruments. If the first anticipatory-redistributive approach is followed, we would expect associations to assume some sort of governing role. By contrast, a reactive-distributive response is unlikely to require a governing role for associations.

The empirical evidence suggests that only some state structures appear open to anticipatory policy and that associations will not emerge to play a governance role in support of an anticipatory-redistributive strategy if they had not already become involved directly in the management and development of the sector at a previous stable and mature stage of the industry. Historical sediment matters. An industrial order that rests on highly concentrated, vertically integrated firms engaged in mass production seems least likely to have encouraged the requisite associative actions. Examples from the U.S. steel industry (O'Brien, 1994), the U.S. machine tool industry (Herrigel, 1994), and the German shipbuilding industry (Stråth, 1994) illustrate this point. There are exceptions to this general trend: Swedish shipbuilding and British consumer electronics. The first indicates the importance of broader political institutions where neocorporatist thinking is applied to a crisis; the second illustrates how the state's predisposition for anticipatory policy making might encourage associational governance.

In the postwar period, interest associations in the U.S. steel industry such as the American Iron and Steel Institute played a classic advocacy role. Political relationships between the industry and its environment were highly adversarial; firms and associations sought to deflect government pressures to increase capacity and fought bitterly against labor unions representing steelworkers. When competition from Europe, Japan, and Korea began to threaten the U.S. industry in the 1960s and 1970s, the steel sector found itself lacking both the experience of association self-government and the will to coordinate and plan the sector's future with state agencies. Reactive policy based on subsidies and trade restraints was the result, with associations continuing to play their lobbyist role. The "industry adjusted through a slow, painful and costly process of lagging competitiveness, falling sales, staggering losses, and company failures. Given the American system of industrial governance, no other method of adjustment may have been feasible" (O'Brien, 1994: 58).

Associations played even less of a role in the U.S. machine tools sector. Herrigel (1994) traces the development of this industry over the present century demonstrating that firms became progressively specialized while concentrating móre and more on manufacturing standardized machine tools in long production runs. Hence they adopted a mass production or Fordist strategy. In the postwar period, small and medium-sized firms were absorbed by larger firms, and these large integrated firms themselves took on most of the responsibility for governing the sector. Issues related to production strategies, training of workers, and product innovation became the internal concerns of the individual companies dominating the sector.

Such a logic of membership provided barren ground for the organizational development of interest associations; associations representing the sector were not central to its governance in the postwar period. Consequently, when new forms of international market competition based on technological innovation emerged in the 1980s, the sector had neither the experience with associative action to aid in retraining workers and studying changes in process technology, nor the cultivated expertise in the state agencies responsible for the sector. In the absence of such other institutional supports, it was up to the firms themselves to manage adjustment. But as Herrigel suggests, even with knowledge of the most advanced techniques, the U.S. firms were unable to adapt the technology for commercial use in response to foreign competition.

The West German shipbuilding industry provides a final example of a concentrated, vertically integrated sector adjusting to decline without significant previous experience with collective action. In a fashion analogous to the U.S. machine tools sector, the German shipbuilding industry had become dominated by a limited number of large, vertically integrated firms. These firms all belonged to a trade association, the Federation of German Shipbuilders, that had played no significant role in sectoral governance prior to 1975 (Stråth, 1994: 76). When markets collapsed in 1975, the association was mobilized to join a "strange coalition" with the trade union IG Metall and with Länder governments in an effort to pressure the federal government to maintain subsidy levels.

In the early stages of this partnership, IG Metall proposed a plan for adjustment involving redistributive policies in an anticipatory framework: It suggested that the shipyards most likely to succeed in international competition should be named and that capacity reduction be reserved for those that were the least competitive. This proposal gave rise to intense internal opposition within IG Metall. In addition, even though it was philosophically acceptable to the shipbuilders association, practically it was not possible to proceed. The association simply had not developed over time any capacity to govern its members' behavior in a way consistent with the realization of such a plan. Not surprisingly, the strange coalition did not become a private interest government overseeing a planned approach to adjustment. Instead, it ended up working in pressure pluralist policy networks demanding continued subsidies allocated on a nondiscriminatory basis to all yards (distributive policy).

In contrast, the Swedish shipbuilding sector shows that associations may play a governing role even in a Fordist sector. What was crucial here was a macropolitical environment that legitimized corporatism, and particularly a strong role for trade unions. The Swedish association of shipbuilders had always faced a logic of membership that obstructed organizational development. Individual firms identified with particular localities and local cultures rather than with each other. Consequently, the association never became a strong voice for the industry. But, similar to the German example, the association was mobilized to join a tripartite council formed to deal with the crisis in the sector that developed in the 1970s. The coalition began moving toward an anticipatory-redistributive approach to the problem with the closure of the Eriksberg yard in the mid-1970s. In 1977–78, the remaining shipyards were nationalized, effectively paring the policy network to include the state and labor only.

A number of different approaches to the decline of the sector were tried over the next six years. Ultimately the trade union and the state agreed on a plan to shut down the remaining yards, with Saab and Volvo contracting to take over the facilities and to retool them for the manufacture of automobiles. Stråth emphasizes the crucial role of the trade union in these negotiations with the state; in broader neocorporatist fora, the union had long accepted the need for an active labor market policy that sought to move workers from less competitive, poorly productive sectors to others that were more competitive with high productivity. Its philosophy complemented the state's own anticipatory and redistributive approach to decline.

The British consumer electronics sector illustrates how an activist state can draw an association into a governance role, even in a mass production sector faced with decline. In contrast to the U.S. steel, U.S. machine tools, and German shipbuilding industries, the industry had not proceeded to a high level of industrial concentration. In the late 1960s, over a dozen firms of medium size were producing televisions in Britain. Such an industry structure was more favorable to collective action than one dominated by only a few, vertically integrated firms. The approach of state actors also encouraged organizational development. At the time, the British policy style emphasized negotiation and consultation with associations, and different government departments were seen as "sponsors" of particular sectors (Grant, 1987b; Jordan and Richardson, 1982; Richardson and Jordan, 1979). Not surprisingly, then, when international competition, particularly from Japan, began to hurt British firms in the early 1970s, it was the industry trade association, BREMA, that assumed the lead role in negotiations with a Japanese association that produced bilateral voluntary restraint agreements (Cawson, 1994: 227).

The next significant step in the adjustment process was initiated by the Labor government of the mid-1970s as part of a broader attempt to develop an anticipatory approach to industrial policy. With the creation of a Sectoral Working Party (SWP) for consumer electronics, the policy network expanded to include stronger representation of the state and trade unions. By 1979, the parties to this policy network had produced a longer term plan consistent with the anticipatory-redistributive model. It proposed the rationalization of production units, increased incorporation of Japanese technology, more use of cost-saving innovations, and improvements in the quality and supply of UK-manufactured components. The plan collapsed when the newly elected Thatcher government rejected anticipatory approaches to industrial policy. Such a collapse illustrates the vulnerability of associational governance to political attack when it occurs in a mass production sector without a long tradition of private interest government.

FROM EXPANSION TO MATURITY

Internationalization gives rise to a second set of changes that also bring into focus the question of associational governance. A sector takes advantage of the liberalization of trade regimes following World War II and of the economic boom occasioned by reconstruction to expand rapidly, not only in the domestic economy but also in international markets. But as reconstruction ends and American market domination in many sectors is challenged by European and Japanese competition, international expansion slows. Competition intensifies and a mature sector is faced with a period of adjusting to this changed environment.

Although the evidence remains insufficient for drawing any firm generalizations, these changes do not appear to favor governance roles for national sectoral associations. If the maturing process comes to involve the transfer of some decision-making responsibility from the nation-state to a supranational level of government, national associations may lose governance powers if they have them. If no supranational regime develops, associational governance *de novo* is also not particularly favored; evidence suggests that it obtains only when there is a long tradition of associational activity in the sector. Since such a tradition is more likely in sectors with diversified quality mass production or flexible specialization patterns, or in agriculture, it is in these sectors, in particular, that we find associational governance persisting in the 1990s.

The following three examples illustrate the importance of the historical maturation of associational governance. The necessary organizational development of associations takes place over time and in circumstances much more nationally self-contained than are available in the present era of international competition. The instability brought to domestic sectors in the 1970s and 1980s discourages the development of new associations with governing capacities. Governance thus arises in sectors where this capacity had already been established in past phases of the industry cycle. These examples also illustrate the importance of national state structures. A particular set of norms, norms that valued objectivity and *Sachlichkeit* in Germany (Dyson, 1982) and negotiated reciprocal consent in Japan (Samuels, 1987), were crucial in providing a fertile national environment for collective action, even in the face of globalization.

Herrigel notes that the German state and the association representing machine tools had cooperated early on in the development of the sector. The state supported vocational training offered through the *Handwerk* chambers and financed the establishment of research institutes and technical universities. The association became active in coordinating research among the various institutions and in advising on emerging needs in vocational training. It thus shared in the governance of the industry with the state and these quasipublic institutions. This role was maintained in the expansionary periods of the 1920s and from 1950 until 1970.

When the latter boom ended, the German industry found itself faced with increased competition from Japan and with a need to make significant changes in its philosophy of product design. In contrast to the U.S. industry which, as we have noted, followed a standardized mass production approach, the German industry evolved into a pattern of diversified quality mass production (Herrigel, 1994; Streeck, 1991). The long-standing corporatist network of trade unions, business associations, public law chambers, research institutes, and the state refocused its attention on computerized technology and the problems of microelectronic applications to machine tools. Successful adaptation has followed in the changed, less expansionary era of the 1980s.

In the Japanese printed circuit board sector, the Japanese Printed Circuit Association emerged in 1962, early in the industry's development (Sako, 1994). By 1976, it had developed a monopoly on representation and was recognized by the Ministry of International Trade and Industry as the legal representative of the sector. As the sector matured in the late 1970s and early 1980s, the Japanese government, in consultation with the sector, developed a series of programs for the modernization and rationalization of firms. These changes allowed the sector to shift toward diversified quality mass production from standardized, high volume mass production. Responsibility for administering these programs was delegated to the JPCA, and the association was given the power to impose binding decisions on its members. In this instance again, associational governance emerged in circumstances where associational governance was historically established and the state was following an anticipatory approach to policy making.

Finally, the agriculture sector in many countries illustrates this phenomenon well. Both general farm organizations and more specialized commodity associations have often been part of corporatist policy networks in many OECD countries. As the era of expanding agricultural production and rapid modernization began to end in the late 1970s and early 1980s, governments were forced to reconsider the objectives of agricultural policy and to look at new ways to implement these policies. Research on Canada and Australia indicates that these crises have been met partially by a redefinition and a strengthening of the role of associations in corporatist networks (Coleman and Skogstad, 1995; Skogstad, 1990). In France, the system evolved from a broad macrocorporatism based on collaboration between general farm organizations and the state to one of more specialized sectoral corporatism involving commodity-based associations and the state (Cleary, 1989; Culpepper, 1993). Particularly important has been the expansion of formally representative *offices interprofessionnels* as places for concertation (Culpepper, 1993: 309; Pivot, 1985).

INTERNATIONAL AND SUPRANATIONAL ASSOCIATIONAL GOVERNANCE

If the impact of internationalization is likely to diminish the likelihood of associational governance at the national level, the question still remains whether this diminution might be compensated for by the emergence of associational governance at supranational levels. To investigate this question further, we concentrate our analysis in this section on two related sectors, the buying and selling of securities and banking. Activity in these sectors has moved rapidly onto an international plane over the past quarter century to an extent matched by few other sectors. A qualitative change has taken place in the amount and kinds of international activities carried out by investors, borrowers, and financial institutions in much of the capitalist world (Economic Council of Canada, 1990; Pecchioli, 1983).

Both banking and securities are sectors where significant self-regulation and bipartite policy coordination with national authorities have occurred in the past. When contemporary governance arrangements in these sectors are examined closely, there are as yet only embryonic examples of associational governance at a supranational level. What changes have occurred tend to be overshadowed by the strengthening of the governance roles of associations at the national level. Continued associational governance is not explained by anticipatory state action. Rather, coping with an internationalized sector has created a need for highly complex public policy. Managing such a policy corpus forces the state to draw heavily on the sector's own expertise and information base.

Beginning in the late 1960s, pure self-regulatory organizations began to emerge at the international level in the securities sector. Common examples are the Association of International Bond Dealers (AIBD) (later the International Securities Markets Association), the International Primary Markets Association, and the International Swap Dealers Association. These organizations tended to operate as examples of pure self-regulation; no state authorities provided either direct or indirect delegations of authority. As international business in these sectors grew and had more and more impact on national markets, national state authorities began to seek to supervise the activities of relevant firms. The AIBD illustrates this process well. In exchange for avoiding direct state regulation, the association sought and gained recognition as an "international stock exchange" based in London (Coleman, 1994). Consequently, the AIBD remained the regulatory body for international bond trading, but agreed to submit its rules and procedures for approval by British regulatory authorities. International associational governance emerged, but under national supervision!

Such limited governance has been complemented by an increase in the activity of other associations at the international level. The Fédération Internationale des Bourses de Valeurs has emerged as an important body for the exchange of information by national stock exchanges. A similar role is fulfilled by the International Council of Securities Dealers and Self-Regulatory Organizations which represents nonstock exchange self-regulatory bodies such as the National Association of Securities Dealers in the United States and The Securities and Futures Authority in Britain. At the European Union (EU) level, the Federation of Stock Exchanges of the European Union

(EU) has awakened from its previous moribund state to play an advisory role in the liberalization of Community capital markets. All of these bodies serve to monitor the progress toward policy coordination being made by the International Organization of Securities Commissions (IOSCO), a supranational organization composed of national securities supervisors.

Yet from the point of view of the governance of the securities sectors, these developments are less significant than the kinds of changes that have taken place at the national level (Coleman, 1994, 1996; Moran, 1990, 1991). The past decade has seen a significant strengthening of national agencies responsible for supervising securities markets, a redefinition and formalization of the roles of self-regulatory associative organizations, and an expansion and refurbishment of their capacities. National authorities have increased bilateral policy coordination, with the Securities and Exchange Commission of the United States being particularly active in signing information-sharing agreements with companion organizations in other states.

The continuing importance of a strong national state presence in the securities sector is reflected in the evolution of German representation to IOSCO. As the latter organization has become a forum for more policy coordination among nation-states, Germany faced the prospect of being left out. With its particular approach to universal banking, Germany did not have a national securities supervisor like the SEC eligible to join IOSCO. The securities business was supervised either by the banking regulator (Bundesaufsichtsamt für das Kreditwesen) or by Länder agencies with no power to act internationally. As a compromise, an interest association representing German stock exchanges, the Arbeitsgemeinschaft der deutschen Wertpapierbörsen, was accepted as a German representative. Yet all parties were uncomfortable with an arrangement that had an interest association acting as a national representative in a forum composed of government agencies. Late in 1990, it was agreed that the federal Finance Ministry would seek IOSCO membership and the ADW would become an associate member. Finally, in 1994, the federal government created a national securities regulator with the responsibility to act in international bodies. This example illustrates well how international organizations and national state agencies can increase in importance together; there is no necessary inverse relationship.

Developments in the banking sector are even more instructive than securities because already the outlines of an international regime have taken shape (Porter, 1993). The Group of 10 (G10) central bank governors had begun meeting on a monthly basis at the Bank for International Settlements in Basle (a kind of central bank for central banks) beginning in 1969. In 1974, they set up a working subcommittee on banking regulation. Known informally as the Cooke Committee in the 1970s and 1980s, the Committee on Banking Regulations and Supervisory Practices has promoted increased harmonization of banking supervision practices at the national level and more sharing of information among banking supervisors.

Increases in interest rate risk, country risk, and exchange rate risk in the early 1980s raised the question of whether the capital maintained by banks as a hedge to that risk was adequate and whether different national definitions of this capital were forcing the international banking system to a lowest common denominator definition. Following an Anglo-American compromise proposal in 1987, the Cooke Committee released a consultative paper with proposals for a new definition of capital standards (BIS, 1987). The paper proposed a two-tier system for capital composed of core capital and supplementary capital. Components of capital were to be weighted by their degree of risk, particularly credit risk. The paper then served as a beginning point for discussion and consultation within each member country. In July 1988, the central bank governors finally accepted a proposal that defined new minimum capital adequacy requirements for banks operating internationally (Kapstein, 1989). "Capital adequacy" refers basically to the ratio between a bank's total assets and its equity capital plus its disclosed reserves. This agreement set out the new definition of capital, with some discretion left to national authorities, and members agreed to abide by the new standards by 1992.

Several aspects of this international agreement are instructive for assessing the evolution of associational governance. First, to date, the movement toward this international regime has not fostered the creation of any new international association, nor has it occasioned any strengthening of the International Bankers Association. Second, the impact on national banking associations is mixed but generally in the direction of increasing their governance powers. Some national associations, particularly those in Canada and Germany, reported being frozen out of the earlier stages of the Cooke Committee's work. Interstate negotiations on the international level allowed national banking supervisors to take their distance from national associations. Yet the evolution of the supranational banking regime has also encouraged further associational governance at the national level. The attempts to define capital requirements and more importantly the design of regulations to put the agreement in place have required very close collaboration in all affected states between banking supervisors and associations. The level of technical detail and the complexity of new financial instruments are such that no agency itself has the requisite expertise to develop policy on its own. Such close collaboration is reinforced in some countries like France (Burgard, 1989: 259–60) and Germany (Ronge, 1979) by the fact that the state has delegated responsibility for managing depositor protection funds to national bankers' associations.

When the focus of analysis is limited to the more narrow arena of the European Union, again the evidence suggests a strengthening of national associations in tandem with a more prominent role for EC level associations. The development of a communitywide banking regime has moved quickly since passage of the Single European Act. The Second Banking Directive, plus accompanying directives on "own funds" and on solvability agreed to by the European Council in December 1989, ensure that an *espace financier européen,* at least in the area of banking, was to be a reality by 1993. National associations have been closely associated by respective nation-states in the negotiations leading up to these directives and in the development of national regulations to put the directives into effect.

In addition, on the EC plane, the European Banking Federation composed of the respective national associations, has become the Commission's channel of communication to Europe's banking sector. The Federation has also been an important site for bargaining among national banking sectors who recognize that their influence is multiplied significantly when they can define a common position. In these respects, the European federation has made significant progress toward assuming a governance role. Yet the Federation remains somewhat dependent on its national members. Its staff complement is barely one-fifth of any of the larger member bankers associations (France, Germany, Britain, Italy). Nor has it shown any ability to discipline its members. When negotiations have broken down, the national associations use their own impressive resources to target the Commission and the Council directly. Some national associations have even set up their own offices in Brussels. In short, on balance, any increase in influence for supranational associative action has been countermanded, if not superseded, by increased governing powers for national-level associations.

CONCLUSION

Associations continue to serve as governance mechanisms at the national level despite the pressures of internationalization. They have yet to emerge as significant governance structures on the supranational plane. Yet even the survival of associative governance in internationalizing sectors might not have seemed highly probable. Such governance is often associated in public discourse with loaded terms: corporatism, clientelism, special interests, self-regulation. Frequently, it has served as an obvious object for attack by governing politicians or those in opposition. We have suggested in this chapter several explanations for the persistence of associational governance under somewhat trying circumstances: the complexity of the policy process, the desire by some state agencies to pursue anticipatory policy over a longer term, and the resilience of associations as organizations. This latter property deserves some further consideration.

Whatever one's definition of associational governance, it will virtually always involve an interpenetration of state and society and a transfer of public functions to recognized private actors. Associations are closely consulted in the formulation of policy and are involved in its implementation. They are normally embedded in informal networks that include research institutes, training organizations, and local government agencies. In exchange, the state receives a measure of freedom to intervene in the definition of the structure of the association (Jobert, 1988) and in the organization of the sector. As such, associational governance is not only an affair of members of the association but also of the state itself. Both parties become highly familiar with one another through working groups and frequent consultation. Both parties gain easier access to informal information and are in a good position to influence decisions taken by the other that may be crucial to the governance of the sector. Consequently, as Segestrin (1985) has emphasized, associational governance becomes more than a mechanism for regulating a particular market segment. The association becomes an actor in its own right. It develops a collective identity that comes to infuse the consciousness of its members and that is recognized by state actors.

When faced with the challenge of liberalizing markets associated with internationalization, all of these elements of associational governance may come into question. The style and mechanisms of regulation of the given market segment appear restrictive. As an actor, the association takes on the image of a dinosaur – old, lumbering, and soon to be extinct. The collective identify fashioned carefully over time becomes less and less consistent with the reality of the marketplace, provoking dissension in the membership and challenges from outside the traditional domain. All of these changes will be familiar to the state because of its long-standing and close association with the group.

Why then should associational governance survive in the face of such a multidimensional challenge? It may not. A sector may shrink to the point where collective action loses its meaning. Or an association may disappear following a merger with another. That said, Segestrin (1985: 109–113) notes that an association may draw on its long-standing relationship with the state and seek to negotiate a new order. Both parties are long conditioned to discussion and are often tied together in a dense network of private and parapublic organizations. The association finds itself thus in an organizational environment that favors the pursuit of negotiations of a new, more inclusive arrangement. The continued complexity of the policy process and the presumed benefits of some market stability will often tempt state actors to agree to such negotiations. The weight of historical experience in mutual consultation and the relative familiarity of the partners with one another raise significantly the probability that these negotiations will succeed.

The considerable organizational development of the association is also an asset in this process. As an autonomous actor in its own right, it is able to pursue the redefinition of its domain or the merger with other groups that is necessary to embrace a membership more consistent with reshaped markets. Possessed of a long-standing responsibility for defining the collective identity of its members, the association will usually control educational institutes that play a central role in the training and accreditation of workers, farmers, or professionals. Courses can be redesigned, the requirements for certificates reassessed, and new instructors hired. If the manufacture of machine tools must assimilate the concept of computer-assisted design or the business of a stock broker must expand to include futures or swaps or farm management demands knowledge about environmental degradation, then the association is well placed to control this process of change. It is also in a strong position to convince the state that necessary adaptations are being made. In the process, the association will oversee the redefinition of the collective identity of its members and will build a new base of support for its own autonomy.

The reconstitution of associational governance in the face of the kinds of crises precipitated by internationalization is by no means a certainty. The process of change may take place so quickly or the decline of a sector may be so precipitous that the association cannot react in time. Yet, as this chapter has emphasized, in many instances, the change may be more gradual and the decline far from self-evident. Under these conditions, associations have proved remarkably resourceful in drawing upon their interpenetration with the state, their control over the definition of their domain, their influence over companion research and training organizations, and their responsibility for developing a collective identity. All these factors assist the association to weather the storm of market liberalization prompted by the globalization of markets.

REFERENCES

Atkinson, M. M. and W. D. Coleman. 1989a. *The State, Business and Industrial Change in Canada.* Toronto: University of Toronto Press.

    1989b. "Strong States and Weak States: Sectoral Policy Networks in Advanced Capitalist Economies." *British Journal of Political Science.* 19: 47–65.

Bank for International Settlements, Committee on Banking Regulations and Supervisory Practices. 1987. *Consultative Paper: Proposals for International Convergence of Capital Measurement and Capital Standards.* Basel: BIS.

Boddewyn, J. J. 1985. "Advertising Self-Regulation: Organization Structures in Belgium, Canada, France and the United Kingdom." In W. Streeck and P. C. Schmitter, eds. *Private Interest Government: Beyond Market and State.* London: Sage. Pp. 30–43.

Burgard, Jean-Jacques. 1989. *La banque en France.* Paris: Les Presses de la Fondation nationale des Sciences politiques & Dalloz.

Cawson, Alan. 1994. "Sectoral Governance in Consumer Electronics in Britain and France." In J. Rogers Hollingsworth, Philippe Schmitter, and Wolfgang Streeck, eds. *Governing Capitalist Economies: Performance and Control of Economic Sectors.* New York: Oxford University Press. Pp. 215–43.

Cawson, Alan, Peter Holmes, and Anne Stevens. 1987. "The Interaction between Firms and the State in France: The Telecommunications and Consumer Electronics Sectors." In Stephen Wilks and Maurice Wright, eds. *Comparative Government-Industry Relations.* Oxford: Oxford University Press. Pp. 10–34.

Cerny, P. 1989. "The 'Little Bang' in Paris: Financial Market Deregulation in a *dirigiste* System." *European Journal of Political Research.* 17: 169–92.

Chubb, John. 1983. *Interest Groups and the Bureaucracy: The Politics of Energy.* Stanford: Stanford University Press.

Cleary, M. C. 1989. *Peasants, Politicians and Producers: The Organisation of Agriculture in France since 1918.* Cambridge: Cambridge University Press.

Coleman, W. D. 1988. *Business and Politics: A Study of Collective Action.* Montreal: McGill-Queen's University Press.

1989. "Self-Regulation in the Canadian Securities Industry: A Case Study of the Investment Dealers Association of Canada." *Canadian Public Administration.* 32: 503–23.

1990. "State Traditions and Comprehensive Business Associations: A Comparative Structural Analysis." *Political Studies.* 38: 231–52.

1991. "Fencing off: Central Banks and Networks in Canada and the United States." In Bernd Marin and Renate Mayntz, eds. *Policy Networks: Empirical Evidence and Theoretical Considerations,* Band 9. Schriften des Max-Planck-Instituts für Gesellschaftsforschung Köln. Frankfurt and Boulder, Col.: Campus/Westview.

1994. "Keeping the Shotgun behind the Door: Governing the Securities Industry in Canada, the United Kingdom and the United States." In J. Rogers Hollingsworth, Philippe Schmitter, and Wolfgang Streeck, eds. *Governing Capitalist Economies: Performance and Control of Economic Sectors.* New York: Oxford University Press. Pp. 244–69.

1996. *Financial Services, Globalization, and Domestic Policy Change: A Comparison of North America and the European Union.* London: Macmillan.

Coleman, W. D. and Wyn P. Grant. 1984. "Business Associations and Public Policy: A Comparison of Organisational Development in Britain and Canada." *Journal of Public Policy.* 4: 209–35.

1988. "The Class Cohesion and Political Influence of Business: A Study of Comprehensive Associations." *European Journal of Political Research.* 16: 467–87.

Coleman, W. D. and Grace Skogstad. 1995. "Neo-Liberalism, Policy Networks, and Policy Change: Agricultural Policy Reform in Australia and Canada." *Australian Journal of Political Science.* Vol. 30: 242–63.

Cox, Robert. 1987. *Production, Power and World Order: Social Forces in the Making of History.* New York: Columbia University Press.

Culpepper, Pepper, D. 1993. "Organizational Competition and the Neo Corporatist Fallacy in French Agriculture." *West European Politics.* 16: 295–315.

de Vroom, Bert. 1987. "The Food Industry and Quality Regulation." In Wyn Grant, ed. *Business Interests, Organisational Development, and Private Interest Government: An International Comparative Study of the Food Processing Industry.* Berlin: de Gruyter. Pp. 180–207.

Duchêne, François. 1987. "Policies for a Wider World." In Duchêne and G. Shepherd, eds. *Manging Industrial Change in Western Europe.* London: Frances Pinter.

Dyson, Kenneth. 1980. *The State Tradition in Western Europe.* Oxford: Martin Robertson.

———. 1982. "West Germany: The Search for a Rationalist Consensus." In J. J. Richardson, ed. *Policy Styles in Western Europe.* London: George Allen & Unwin: Pp. 17–46.

Economic Council of Canada. 1990. *Globalization and Canada's Financial Markets: A Research Report.* Ottawa: Supply and Services Canada.

Grant, Wyn P. 1987a. "Introduction." In Wyn P. Grant, ed. *Business Interests, Organizational Development and Private Interest Government: A Study of the Food Processing Industry.* Berlin: de Gruyter. Pp. 1–17.

Grant, Wyn P. with Jane Sargent. 1987b. *Business and Politics in Britain.* London: Macmillan.

Grant, Wyn P. and William Paterson. 1994. "The Chemical Industry: A Study in Internationalization." In J. Rogers Hollingsworth, Philippe Schmitter, and Wolfgang Streeck, eds. *Governing Capitalist Economies: Performance and Control of Economic Sectors.* New York: Oxford University Press. Pp. 129–55.

Grant, Wyn P., William Paterson, and Colin Whitson. 1988. *Government and the Chemical Industry: A Comparative Study of Britain and West Germany.* Oxford: The Clarendon Press.

Hall, Peter A. 1989. "Conclusion: The Politics of Keynesian Ideas." In Peter A. Hall, ed. *The Political Power of Economic Ideas: Keynesianism Across Nations.* Princeton: Princeton University Press. Pp. 361–91.

Hayes, Michael T. 1978. "The Semi-Sovereign Pressure Groups: A Critique of Current Theory and an Alternative Typology." *Journal of Politics.* 40: 134–61.

Hayward, Jack. 1982. "Mobilising Private Interests in the Service of Public Ambitions: The Salient Element in the Dual French Policy Style?" In J. J. Richardson, ed. *Policy Styles in Western Europe.* London: George Allen & Unwin. Pp. 111–40.

Herrigel, Gary 1994. "Industry as a Form of Order: A Comparison of the Historical Development of the Machine Tool Industries in the United States and Germany." In J. Rogers Hollingsworth, Philippe Schmitter, and Wolfgang Streeck, eds. *Governing Capitalist Economies: Performance and Control of Economic Sectors.* New York: Oxford University Press. Pp. 97–128.

Hollingsworth, J. Rogers, Philippe Schmitter, and Wolfgang Streeck. 1994. "Capitalism, Sectors, Institutions and Performance." In J. Rogers Hollingsworth, Philippe Schmitter, and Wolfgang Streeck, eds. *Governing Capitalist Economies: Performance and Control of Economic Sectors.* New York: Oxford University Press. Pp. 3–16.

Jobert, Bruno. 1988. "La version française du corporatisme: définition et implications pour la modernisation de l'Etat dans une économie en crise." In Dominique Colas, ed. *L'Etat et les Corporatismes.* Paris: Les Presses Universitaires de France. Pp. 3–18.

Jordan, A. G. and J. J. Richardson. 1982. "The British Policy Style or the Logic of Negotiation?" In J. J. Richardson, ed. *Policy Styles in Western Europe.* London: George Allen & Unwin. Pp. 80–110.

Kapstein, Ethan. 1989. "Resolving the Regulator's Dilemma: International Coordination of Banking Regulations." *International Organization.* 43: 323–47.

Lehmbruch, Gerhard. 1990. "The Organization of Society, Administrative Strategies, and Policy Networks: Elements of a Developmental Theory of Interest Systems." In Roland Czada and Adrienne Windhoff-Héritier, eds. *Political Choice. Institutions, Rules, and the Limits of Rationality.* Frankfurt and Boulder, Col.: Campus/Westview Press.

Moran, Michael. 1989. "Investor Protection and the Culture of Capitalism." In Leigh Hancher and Michael Moran, eds. *Capitalism, Culture and Economic Regulation.* Oxford: Clarendon Press. Pp. 49–77.

———. 1990. "Regulating Britain, Regulating America: Corporatism and the Securities Industry." In Colin Crouch and Ronald Dore, eds. *Corporatism and Accountability: Organized Interests in British Public Life.* Oxford: Clarendon Press: Pp. 103–24.

———. 1991. *The Politics of the Financial Services Revolution: The USA, UK, and Japan.* London: Macmillan.

O'Brien, Patricia A. 1994. "Governance Systems in Steel: The American and Japanese Experience." In J. Rogers Hollingsworth, Philippe Schmitter, and Wolfgang Streeck, eds. *Governing Capitalist Economies: Performance and Control of Economic Sectors.* New York: Oxford University Press. Pp. 43–71.

Pecchioli, R. M. 1983. *The Internationalisation of Banking: The Policy Issues.* Paris: OECD.

Peters, B. Guy. 1977. "Insiders and Outsiders: The Politics of Pressure Group Influence on Bureaucracy." *Administration and Society.* 9: 191–218.

Pivot, Catherine. 1985. "Offices d'intervention et régulation contractuelle en agriculture." *Revue d'Économie financière.* 95: 66–86.

Porter, Tony. 1993. *States, Markets and Regimes in Global Finance.* Basingstoke: Macmillan.

Richardson, J. J., G. Gustafsson, and A. G. Jordan. 1982. "The Concept of Policy Style." In J. J. Richardson, ed. *Policy Styles in Western Europe.* London: George Allen & Unwin. Pp. 1–16.

Richardson, J. J. and A. G. Jordan. 1979. *Governing Under Pressure: The Policy Process in a Post-Parliamentary Democracy.* Oxford: Martin Robertson.

Ronge, Volker. 1979. *Bankpolitik im Spätkapitalismus: Politische Selbstverwaltung des Kapitels?* Frankfurt: Suhrkamp Verlag.

Sako, Mari. 1994. "Neither Markets nor Hierarchies: A Comparative Study of the Printed Circuit Board Industry in Britain and Japan." In J. Rogers Hollingsworth, Philippe Schmitter, and Wolfgang Streeck, eds. *Governing Capitalist Economies: Performance and Control of Economic Sectors.* New York: Oxford University Press. Pp. 17–42.

Samuels, Richard. 1987. *The Business of the Japanese State.* Ithaca: Cornell University Press.

Sargent, Jane. 1985. "The Politics of the Pharmaceutical Price Regulation Scheme." In W. Streeck and P. C. Schmitter, eds. *Private Interest Government: Beyond Market and State.* London: Sage. Pp. 105–28.

Schmitter, Philippe C. and Wolfgang Streeck. 1981. "The Organization of Business Interests." Discussion Paper IIM/LMP 81-13. Berlin: Wissenschaftszentrum Berlin.

———. 1985. "Community, Market, State and Associations? The Prospective Contribution of Interest Governance to Social Order." In Wolfgang Streeck and Philippe C. Schmitter, eds. *Private Interest Government.* London: Sage. Pp. 1–29.

Segestrin, Denis. 1985. *Le Phénomène Corporatiste: Essai sur l'avenir des systèmes professionnels fermés en France.* Paris: Fayard.

Shepherd, G. and F. Duchêne. 1983. "Introduction: Industrial Change and Intervention in Western Europe." In G. Shepherd, F. Duchêne, and C. Saunders, eds. *Europe's Industries.* London: Frances Pinter. Pp. 1–25.

Skogstad, Grace. 1990. "The Farm Policy Community and Public Policy in Ontario and Quebec." In W. D. Coleman and G. Skogstad, eds. *Policy Communities and Public Policy in Canada: A Structural Approach.* Toronto: Copp Clark Pitman. Pp. 59–90.

Stråth, Bo. 1994. "Modes of Governance in the Shipbuilding Sector in West Germany, Sweden and Japan." In J. Rogers Hollingsworth, Philippe Schmitter, and Wolfgang Streeck, eds. *Governing Capitalist Economies: Performance and Control of Economic Sectors.* New York: Oxford University Press. Pp. 72–96.

Streeck, Wolfgang. 1989. "The Territorial Organization of Interests and the Logics of Associative Action: The Case of Handwerk Organization in West Germany." In W. D. Coleman and H. J. Jacek, eds. *Regionalism, Business Interests, and Public Policy.* London: Sage. Pp. 59–94.

———. 1991. "On the Institutional Conditions of Diversified Quality Production." In Egon Matzner and Wolfgang Streeck, eds. *Beyond Keynesianism: The Socio-Economics of Production and Full Employment.* Aldershot, Hants: Edward Elgar. Pp. 21–61.

Traxler, Franz and Brigitte Unger. 1994. "Industry or Infrastructure? A Cross-national Comparison of Governance: Its Determinants and Economic Consequences in the Dairy Sector." In J. Rogers Hollingsworth, Philippe Schmitter, and Wolfgang Streeck, eds. *Governing Capitalist Economies: Performance and Control of Economic Sectors.* New York: Oxford University Press. Pp. 183–214.

Whiteley, Paul. 1987. *Political Control of the Macro-Economy: The Political Economy of Public Policy-Making.* London: Sage.

Willis, D. and Wyn Grant. 1987. "The United Kingdom – Still a Company State?" In M. P. van Schendelen and R. J. Jackson, eds. *The Politicisation of Business in Western Europe.* London: Croom Helm. Pp. 158–83.

Willmott, Hugh C. 1985. "Setting Accounting Standards in the UK: The Emergence of Private Accounting Bodies and Their Role in the Regulation of Public Accounting Practice." In W. Streeck and P. C. Schmitter, eds. *Private Interest Government: Beyond Market and State.* London: Sage. Pp. 44–71.

Woolley, John. 1984. *Monetary Politics: The Federal Reserve and the Politics of Monetary Policy.* Cambridge: Cambridge University Press.

Wright, Maurice. 1988. "Policy Community, Policy Network and Comparative Industrial Policies." *Political Studies.* XXXVI: 593–612.

Young, Brigitte. 1990. "Does the American Dairy Industry Fit the Meso-Corporatism Model?" *Political Studies.* XXXVIII: 72–82.

Young, Brigitte, J. Rogers Hollingsworth, and Leon Lindberg. 1989. "The Governance of the American Dairy Industry: From Regional Dominance to Regional Cleavage." In W. Coleman and H. J. Jacek, eds. *Regionalism, Business Interests, and Public Policy.* London: Sage. Pp. 127–52.

5

CONSTITUTIONAL ORDERS: TRUST BUILDING AND RESPONSE TO CHANGE

Charles F. Sabel

HIERARCHIES, MARKETS, AND CONSTITUTIONAL ORDERS

To capture what is theoretically distinctive about the commonalties of the new organizational forms in the public and private sectors, and to understand why current theories are blind to this distinctiveness, it is helpful to contrast more familiar governance structures – markets and hierarchies – with a third. I will call this type of governance structure a *constitutional order.* In introducing this category, however, I do not mean to attempt to supply the missing member of an exhaustive, three-part typology of governance structures. On the contrary, it seems in principle unlikely that the set of these structures is closed. Just as firms operate in markets defined by other firms, governance structures are at bottom strategic responses to competitive environments composed of other governance structures. Under highly restrictive assumptions it is conceivable that the mix of institutional strategies embodying the current governance structures will arrive at a stable equilibrium. But unless the context in which existing governance structures operate is frozen, so long as it is impossible to invent a new strategy that takes advantage of rigidities created by the self-reinforcing mesh of the current ones, equilibrium seems unlikely. In any case, the arguments here for a third governance structure of particular substantive moment are meant to encourage consideration of a class of trust-based coordination mechanisms that parallel the dichotomy of markets and hierarchies. In what follows, I reproduce only as much of the conventional account of this latter dichotomy as needed to create a backdrop for a discussion of an alternative category.

HIERARCHIES

Hierarchies are composed of bureaucratic units (bureaus, workshops, etc.) and a head or central office. Every bureaucratic unit is directly subordinate to one, but only one, other bureaucratic unit, or to the head office. The head office is directly or indirectly superordinate to all bureaucratic units. This form of organization is sometimes called near-decomposable to emphasize its capacity to transform intractably complex tasks into a coordinated series of manageably simple ones, each so loosely connected to the others that its operation can be perfected without disturbing theirs (Simon, 1973). Sometimes it is called a tree or semitree structure to emphasize the formal constraints on the flow of commands and the resulting counterflow of products or services (Aoki, 1984: 26–34). The head office determines the responsibilities and jurisdictions of the bureaucratic units, endows them with resources, installs supervisors accordingly, and monitors their performance (Williamson, 1991).

The hierarchy is distinct from its competitive environment in the sense that changes in that environment affect the organization only when, and in the manner that, the head office judges they will. As long as the head office regards its organizational plan as consistent with competitive conditions, shortfalls in performance result in small adjustments of jurisdiction or substitution of supervisors. Significant inconsistencies should result in major reorganizations. If headquarters had available all the information available to its subordinate agents, hierarchies could, in theory, mimic the optimizing capacities of markets, and solve coordination problems that markets often have difficulty solving to boot. But subordinates withhold information from headquarters as a way of advancing their personal interests within the hierarchy. For this reason a hierarchy functions best when the pace of change does not outrace headquarters' information gathering and processing capacities.

MARKETS

Markets, in contrast, consist only of independent agents (firms, "privatized" government agencies, persons, etc.) trading for their own account. No agent is superordinate to any other; each is entitled to engage in any kind of transaction permitted to the others. The rules governing transactions, and relatedly the formal capacities and responsibilities of the market participants, are determined collectively in the long run by the agents themselves. By a process analogous to Darwinian natural selection, efficient behaviors – those that encourage the intensification and extension of exchange – survive the test of competition and become generally recognized as binding rules. Infractions are punished by procedures established by the same process. Hayek calls the resulting corpus of rules a spontaneous or extended order (Hayek, 1973: 35–54, 1988).

In the sense that agents adapt reflexively to their environment (or, in more sophisticated variants of the argument, reshape their environment in the very act of adapting to it), they are integrated into, not distinct from, their competitive context. But there is disagreement regarding the robustness of this connection under various circumstances. Given the autonomy of market actors and their incentives to put information to an economically efficient use rather than withholding it, markets plainly respond more efficiently to limited perturbations than hierarchies – provided, of course, that hold-up problems of the kind noted earlier are inconsequential. But it is not obvious, even to advocates of market coordination, that natural selection is always superior to authoritative deliberation as a way of redrawing transaction rules. Consider, for example, the recurrent debates about whether firms are best reorganized through changes of ownership through equity markets, bank monitors whose fate is tied to their clients' through equity holdings and long-term lending relations, other firms obliged to solidary interventions through cross-holdings of stock, as in the Japanese *keiretsu,* or still other arrangements (Gilson and Kraakman, 1991). In their pure form, then, markets do best when the possible states of the world are fully known, hold-ups are irrelevant, and the problem is to adjust the allocation of resources, given preferences and budget constraints as the world shifts from one state to another.

CONSTITUTIONAL ORDERS

Constitutional orders consist of constituent units and a superintendent. The constituent units may be market agents such as independent firms or, analogously, the citizens of a democracy or the members of a trade union or other association. But they may also be entities such as divisions of corporations, branch plants, or governmental agencies that would count as bureaucratic units in a hierarchical system. The superintendent may be, for example, a court of law, the head office of a public or private hierarchy, the elected officers of an association, a bureaucratic entity, or an arbitration committee. Or the superintendent might be a body that is a composite of such entities, as, for example, a local economic development cartel formed of representatives of trade associations, unions, local banks, large and small firms, social welfare agencies, and various educational and training institutions. The superintendent of one constitutional order, moreover, can be and typically is a constituent of another, more encompassing order: A court of administrative law is bound by the rulings of a court of constitutional law; the divisional office of a highly decentralized holding company monitors the performance of certain business units, but is itself monitored by the holding company's head office. As these last examples suggest, the role of the superintendent is to determine the justification and responsibilities of the constituent units and set the rules by which they conduct transactions and resolve disputes arising under those rules insofar as the constituents cannot do so themselves. The superintendent may subordinate one constituent unit to another and any or all to itself. But limitations on its jurisdictional and rule setting authority render the superintendent's own hierarchical relation to the constituents indeterminate.

This jurisdictional and rule making authority is limited in two fundamental ways. First, the rules set for the constituent units must be consistent with the rules by which the superintendent itself is bound as constituent of a more encompassing constitutional order. Thus, the findings of the labor–management arbitration board must conform to the relevant provisions of labor law, which must be consistent with the constitutional court's interpretation of contract law; the board of director's decision to acquire a new company must be sustainable under current antitrust and securities law; a committee of transportation companies serving a single metropolitan area must devise a system of coordination consistent with the general guidelines established by the regional office of the national transportation agency which subsidizes mass transit in the region.

The second limitation is that all rules must be set in consultation with the constituents. Consultation may take the form of democratic rule making by the constituents' representatives, as in the legislature of a polity, or by the elected officers of a labor union, employers' federation, or other association. Or it might take the form of customary rights to a hearing of constituent views in various rule making fora: The widely acknowledged but only partially formalized rights of Japanese company unions (Aoki, 1988) and German enterprise councils (Streeck, 1984) to participate in the discussion of many matters affecting labor through the eventual reorganization of work are examples. The form of consultation will naturally reflect the constitutional order's history. Consultation in a constitutional order formed by a compact among previously independent constituents will tend to be manifestly democratic, because under most historical circumstances the constituents will not cede power to the monitor without the assurances that democratic procedures provide. Conversely, consultation in constitutional orders formed by the decentralization or devolution of a central authority tends to rely more on hearings, because the central authority too tries to preserve as much of its authority as is consistent with incorporation in the new constitutional order.

The superintendent's obligation to consult the constituents, by whatever means, derives from the presumption that the constituents typically know more about the general features of their situation and how to order it than the superintendent. Normally, the superintendent should reconcile, promulgate, and enforce rules proposed by the constituents and derived from their practical experience. In extraordinary circumstances – a division among the constituents, a disorienting change in the environment – the superintendent may reserve the right to impose rules by fiat (as in a private company acting under the authority of the legal majority of its board of directors), to dissolve the constitutional order (as in the case of a legislative decision to abolish a particular administrative agency or program), or, in rare cases at the highest level of politics, to demand that the constituents either formulate a definitive rule or reshape the powers of the superintendent (as in the case of a constitutional court that by its decision forces the citizenry to choose among acceptance of the decision, revision of the substantive or procedural provisions of the constitution according to the constitutional provisions for self-amendment, or extraconstitutional change – for instance, by the (re)convocation of a constituent assembly). Consultative rule making, culminating in the possibility of a constitutional crisis, makes the ranking of constituents and superintendent indeterminate.

For related reasons the connection between the constitutional order and its environment is also ambiguous. Because the superintendent must make rules in conformity with higher order entities and in consultation with its constituents, it lacks the head office's freedom to respond to shifts in the environment. Similarly, the superintendent's mediation deprives the constituents of the immediate freedom to respond to environmental changes that distinguishes market actors. Whether these constraints are burdensome or beneficial is, of course, no less controversial than the respective adaptive capacities of markets and hierarchies.

On the other hand, constitutional orders can solve coordination problems that neither markets nor hierarchies can solve. Unlike the former, they have superintendents who can align and redraw the jurisdictions of the operating units. In contrast to the latter, those superintendents can rely on alignment of interests between themselves and their constituents secured by consultation to provide them with reliable information about current conditions. Thus, as I will argue more fully, constitutional orders do best when there are coordination problems that markets in their pure form cannot solve and the pace of change – the rate at which new states of the world are being created – outpaces the adaptive capacities of hierarchies.

Constitutional orders adjust to changes in the environment according to distinctive principles. Indeed the combination of elements of horizontal coordination by market and vertical coordination by hierarchy in a single governance structure – the very combination that invites the efforts to subsume and reduce that structure to triviality – transforms the operation of both and produces an irreducibly distinct pattern of adjustment to environmental changes.

It is as if – imputing deliberation where it may have been scarce – the architects of a constitutional order sought a governance structure that adjusts to changes in its context of operations, as opposed to changes within a particular context. Put otherwise, it is as though those architects, dubious of the plasticity of markets and hierarchies, and without fixed ideas of their respective virtues and vices, sought a regime that redefines centralization and decentralization as required to move successfully from the old context to the new, without jeopardizing subsequent adjustment by the same process.

More precisely, they set out to design a structure in which "horizontal" relations can be redefined through "vertical" consultation as the context of cooperation shifts. What is "transitional" about this governance structure is its ability to facilitate transitions; the structures that do this work remain in their constitutional features invariant through the changes. What is invariant in these features is their institutionalized presumption that adjustment is risky and precarious because the consequential features of the new context are hard to identify – so hard, indeed, that only the deliberate consultation of constituents and superintendent can achieve a provisional success beyond the reach of the reflexive maximizing adjustments of either alone. What is distinctive about constitutional orders, in short, is that they do not take the success of their powers of self-adjustment for granted. Depending on the context, adjustment may require a reordering of the order itself: a redefinition not just of which unit is responsible for what (a redrawing of organograms that is consistent with a reshuffling of the hierarchy or even a new division of labor in the market), but also and more importantly a redefinition of who is entitled to be heard on which questions.

But how are these prodigies of plasticity possible in the first place? Why, if they are possible at all, do they prove so vulnerable to changes in historical circumstances? Should we care about their possibility given their vulnerability?

HOW IS TRUST POSSIBLE? TRUST, REFLEXIVITY, AND SOCIABILITY

There is no dearth of theories that warrant the expectation that trust is broadly possible, yet not inevitable in any particular exchange or situation. Some of these theories derive from intellectual traditions that always rejected the liberal postulate of the autonomous individual as antecedent to and (through the pursuit of self-interest) constitutive of all social relations. Others reject this postulate after analysis of the inconsistencies of the liberal system itself. What the theories assert in common, either as assumption or conclusion, is that trust in the sense just defined is the foundation of the very sociability that makes us human. To be a person at all, in this view, it is necessary to make oneself vulnerable to some other persons. But it does not follow from this assertion – nor do the theories I have in mind claim – that we must trust everyone all the time because we must always trust someone at any particular time. On the contrary, the theories imply, if they do not explicitly claim, that trust relations can be formed and broken. In explaining this capacity, the theories rely on the notion of a reflexive self: a self taken as a hierarchy of identities or a cacophony of voices that somehow decides which of its many possible selves the self will be. Thus these alternative theories reject as misguided and misleading the liberal question, How might trust be possible?

Yet they invite two others. First, given that some trust is unavoidable in human relations, how do we come to trust some persons, groups, or institutions rather than others? Second, what can trust be if, despite its apparently unconditional character as an uncalculating relation, it can be made and destroyed? Examination of these questions, we will see, improves our grasp of the role of the superintendent in constitutional orders and the process by which such orders are constituted in the first place.

The most encompassing of the alternative theories of trust simply assume that individuality and sociability – here, unthinking attachment to a body of collectively defined routines and precepts – are indissolubly linked. Just as artists define their styles by varying some – but only some – of the elements defining the commonly acknowledged genres, so the individual becomes an individual by applying the repertoire of socially acknowledged behaviors in a distinctive way. A condition of individuality is thus to accept as natural and (for the moment at least) unquestionable a substantial part of the complex bundle of beliefs and relations, including many meeting the definition of trust, that the others take for granted too (Bourdieu, 1977, 1990). Marxism is a special case of this general position: Work is taken to

be a collective enterprise, and it is only by relying on the collectivity in production that persons come to make things that distinguish them as individuals (Lukács, 1986).

Liberal self-criticism reaches a similar result by showing that primitive
acts of individualism (including self-definition, self-expression that is intelligible to others, and prudential behavior) tie individuals to society or to
a future self that is like society in that it is as different from one's current
self as that current self is from contemporary others. To complete my understanding of who I am, for example, I must know how others see me. But
to do that I must grasp myself from their perspective, questioning my absolute individuality in ways that make what I may share with and what I
may owe to society more and more manifest (Nagel, 1970). Or consider
conversation including (to borrow a line from Lubitsch's *To Be or Not to Be*)
the limiting case of conversation about what you think of me. Given the
ambiguities of language, I must assume that you are saying things you take
to be correct most of the time. If I tried to figure out what you were really thinking while I tried to simply understand what you were apparently
saying, I could never understand your real beliefs or your meanings.[1] Thus
even my ability to articulate a disagreement with you rests on trust – arguably as deep as that implicated in the exchange of material things – that
you are not taking advantage of my linguistic vulnerabilities. Or take, finally, the case of my prudent decision to do something that I would rather
not do now, but that I one day will be glad to have done. Surely normal individuals do such things all the time. But why should they care for the future bundle of desires they will accidentally become any more than for the
other various bundles of desires that define their contemporaries? The answer is that if individuals can see themselves only from the point of view
of their momentary bundle of interests – the unique vantage point liberalism concedes them – they would no more act prudently than trustingly.
But people can be prudent; so other perspectives are possible. Just as each
person can regard him- or herself as someone, so each is apparently able to
imagine various future selves and act (with more or less determination) in
the interest of actually creating one of these selves in preference to another (Nagel, 1970).

More generally, in fact, it is the interplay of reflexivity and sociability
that is doing the work in all the alternatives to standard liberal theory considered so far. Because individuals can self-reflexively imagine and act to
realize different strategies corresponding to different variations of themselves, they do not merely execute social routines or work practices, or
blindly pursue the passions that move them at the moment. But because
those strategies can be articulated only in reference to particular social set-

tings and presumed alliances or associations accordingly, reflexivity reconnects individuals to one another even as it momentarily relaxes the collectivity's grip. Put another way, reflexivity connects individuality to sociability by making vulnerability to others – trust – a constituent of autonomous self-hood.

How is reflexivity possible? What, precisely, is the relation between reflexivity and sociability? I do not know, and suspect I have lots of excellent company in my ignorance. There is no agreement, for example, on such basic questions as whether the reflexive self should be conceived hierarchically – the self, in Sen's language, as a "ranking of preference rankings" (Sen, 1979) – or polyarchically – the self, in Minsky's terms, as a community of "agents" or "voices" jabbering at each other until, by rules that may differ from occasion to occasion, one opinion prevails (Minsky, 1986). Still less is there a settled understanding of the reflexive self in relation to social groups. Perhaps our sociability is exhausted, as much self-critical liberalism suggests, in the realization that buried within each of us there is a human essence, defined by the capacity for reason and autonomy and conscious of its own insufficiency, from which we draw moral conclusions that frame all social development. Then the abstract recognition of our mutual vulnerability, and whatever political convictions that entails, would be all we really had in common.[2] Or perhaps, as many alternative traditions suppose, the self is so thoroughly implicated in social life that the exercise of reason and autonomy, including the ability to reason about them, is possible only with reference to (and thus limited by) the ideas and choices available in a particular society at a particular time. Then we would argue about what common obligations our history does or should oblige us to recognize, not about our duties as reasonable beings (Rorty, 1990; Rosenblum, 1987; Taylor, 1989; Walzer, 1983, 1987).[3] Considering how good we are getting at posing such questions, I (optimistically) presume that the time is nearing when we shall either begin to answer them or put them aside as unanswerable.[4]

For purposes, however, of constructing an alternative to presumptive opportunism as the motive and limit of institutional design, it is, I think, enough to know that the self is reflexively sociable. First, reflexivity makes trust broadly possible. The capacity for reflexivity, by definition, implies both the experience of trusting vulnerability in many spheres of life, and the ability to envisage and pursue different life spans, including presumably relations of trust with correspondingly different persons. Second, by further and more surprising implication, the presumption of reflexivity leads to a redefinition of what trust is that brings some of the most elusive features of the constitutional order into focus.

REFLEXIVITY AND DELIBERATE TRUST IN ACTION: FOUR EXAMPLES

Recall that in an opportunistic world, trust is an all-or-nothing – and almost always a nothing – proposition. Either a community of fate exists in which adverse individual interests can barely be articulated and if pursued, are punished by social extinction, or this community of fate does not exist, and no series of exchanges can produce more than a *modus vivendi* that simulates trust, but whose foundation of selfishness cannot bear even a suspicion of bad faith. But in a world of reflexive agents, everyone knows what it means to trust, and everyone can imagine trusting persons one does not currently trust, and ceasing to trust persons one currently does. This reflective footlooseness plainly collides with our understanding of trust as something unconditional. What gives?

The best demonstration of the explanatory grip of this view of reflexive cooperation is its ability to make sense of the institutional complexity of constitutional orders that all-or-nothing notions of trust ignore. If trust were a matter of the (accidental) alignment of beliefs and associated interests, the institutional life of a constitutional order would plausibly be limited to periodic rituals which reinforced those beliefs by making them manifest. But as the earlier definition of a constitutional order suggested, and as we shall see in more detail in a moment, trust-based governance structures have rich, consultative institutional structures whose very existence belies the assumption that the agents expect their actions automatically to be harmonized by a confluence of belief. The central effect of these institutions, moreover, is to blur the line between policing behavior and articulating consensus that all-or-nothing views draw to distinguish systems presuming opportunism from those presuming trust. They do this by allowing the parties to monitor one another's behavior while encouraging them to jointly reevaluate their situation in the light of these observations and adjust their reciprocal expectations accordingly. Constitutional orders thus constantly recreate themselves in the sense that their operation reinvokes, by redefining, the consensus on which they were founded. Four brief examples will illustrate deliberative trust in institutional action.

The first is drawn from the current redefinition of customer–supplier relations in both the industrial and service sectors in many advanced economies. Instead of presenting, say, a blueprint specifying precisely a particular part or subassembly and then awarding the contract for the job to the lowest bidder, large firm customers are increasingly negotiating the relevant performance and price specifications with their major suppliers, and allowing the latter to determine the best way first to meet and then to improve them. Typically the customer offers the supplier a long-term (often five-year) contract as a major, and sometimes sole, source for a particular class of components. This induces the supplier to dedicate resources to the project, but makes the customer vulnerable to hold-ups for reasons noted earlier. At the same time the customer obtains the contractual right to specify at least some of the technologies and process control measures that will be used in production, and to be regularly informed of changes in production costs (Helper, 1991a; Ikeda, 1987; Mendius and Wendeling-Schröder, 1991).

If you think monitoring is incompatible with trust relations, then you will take the disclosure requirements as a sign of mistrust and try to weigh – despite the incomparability of the measures – what the company gains in control through increased powers of supervision against what it loses through increased vulnerability to hold-ups. Looked at from the perspective of a regime of deliberative trust, however, the two parts of the bargain look less like the ground rules for a tug of war than two mutually reinforcing fundamentals of the same institutional structure. The monitoring reduces the possibility of duplicity, but its central function is to regularize consultation between the parties so as to minimize the cost of mistakes and maximize the possibility of introducing improvements that benefit both. In a full-fledged version of this system, the customer becomes a superintendent in the sense introduced earlier, organizing exchanges of information between itself and all the suppliers; and the latter in time expand such exchanges among themselves and with like firms supplying other large customers. Such systems are hard to build and maintain because they create possibilities for opportunism. Yet, in conformity with Ostrom's common-pool-resources result, there is evidence that they can be built (by, for example, Japanese automobile producers in the United States; see Nishiguchi, 1992), even in environments where traditions of mistrustful, arm's-length bargaining seem to exclude them.

A second example concerns the governance of geographically clustered networks principally of small and medium-sized firms or industrial districts. In the nineteenth century, districts in places such as Lyon (silks) or Solingen (cutlery) were regulated by a tariff commission composed of representatives of different groups cooperating in production: merchants or merchant-manufacturers, large subcontractors, independent out-workers or subcontractors, and the journeymen or factory hands employed by others. One purpose of such commissions was to adjust wages, working rules, and terms of payment among firms in the course of business cycles. This distributed the burdens and rewards of adjustment fairly and prevented cycles of wage and price cutting that could have led firms to abandon their strategy of innovative adaptation to shifting demand in favor of an effort – generally fatal, because helpless in the face of new, low-wage entrants – to market standard goods at rock bottom prices. But a second and equally important purpose was to articulate a collective response to major shifts in the composition of demand or the use of technology (Sabel and Zeitlin, 1985).

In modern industrial districts the work formerly done by one or two committees is now done by many, but with partially overlapping membership (Pyke et al., 1990; Pyke and Sengenberger, 1992). Vocational training, for instance, might be the province of a tripartite commission composed of representatives of the firms, labor organizations, and training institutions. Working conditions will be regulated partially by collective bargaining agreements, but also by municipal or state bodies charged with environmental control or occupational health and safety. Firms may learn of new techniques or markets by consulting with public agencies which often must insist on access to closely held information if their interventions are to be successful. Economic development understood as a coordinated response to changing conditions of competition is typically the responsibility of a consortium of all the institutions just noted under the aegis of the municipality, regional authorities, a local bank, or a committee founded by some or all of these.

Again, I do not mean to suggest that the new structures are always successful. A rapid change in the economic environment can induce formation of two rival consortia, each with a plan for reorganizing the local economy and powerful enough to block the other but not impose its own solution.[5] I argue only that the dense and constantly changing web of institutions in the modern industrial district, like its less elaborate precursors, shows how the monitoring of current activity is connected to its periodic reconstitution in a fashion consistent with the deliberately trustful principle of testing the reliability of particular arrangements while relying on them.

A third, public sector example (in some ways an extension of the second) concerns economic development as seen from the regional or state perspective. I am thinking of experiences in the United States, and particularly in the state of Pennsylvania, although similar developments are observable in many other U.S. states and in other countries.

Throughout the 1970s, the poorer American states "chased smokestacks," outbidding each other in an ultimately self-defeating effort to attract firms to their jurisdiction through promises of tax advantages and low-cost capital. As it became clear that the firms most likely to be lured by such means were also the most likely to close or go elsewhere in the next recession, the policy shifted to encouraging the development of the local economy by providing factors of production such as venture capital or skilled workers which the regional capital and labor markets for whatever reason failed to provide (Osborne, 1988). By the mid-1980s, however, policy makers started to realize that firms often needed assistance to make use of the supplemental resources even when they realized their need for them, which was just as commonly not the case. Beginning in this period, then, many states began to create programs whose purpose was to encourage firms, trade associations, trade unions, and – in a recursive second phase – the state's own agencies to constitute themselves so as to make optimal use of the available resources and identify what was still lacking (Bosworth, 1991).

The change in the state's relation to the economy was reflected in changes in the institutionalization of economic development and corresponding innovations in governance structure. So long as it was presumed that firms made efficient use of government programs, the government's task was to identify the required programs and set standards for measuring their performance. As firms' needs were by assumption narrow and relatively homogeneous, it was natural to favor programs that, centrally administered or not, could be judged by clear, centrally established and reviewable criteria: for example, placements per dollar invested in (re)training or jobs created per dollar of investment subsidy. Clearly standards of this sort and the administrative practices underlying them were irrelevant once the state defined its task as helping to create actors who could define performance standards for themselves and eventually for the state itself.

A particularly successful bootstrapping response to the new situation was the creation in Pennsylvania of the Ben Franklin Partnership (Sabel, 1992: 229–47). The core of the program is a network of regional economic development centers, each with a board of directors drawn from the local economy and a license from the state to interpret policy guidelines according to local needs. This meant in practice that the staff and board of each institute would decide by trial and error how precisely the mandate to facilitate the development of a class of new products or the introduction of a particular production technology (such as computer integrated manufacturing) could be used to set in motion the self-reinforcing reorganization of not just the firms, but local training facilities and research institutions as well. The result was that each center embodied its own development strategy in project selection criteria. The portfolios of two centers (Pittsburgh and Philadelphia) were weighted toward start-ups, while the portfolios of the other two (Lehigh and Central Pennsylvania) balanced projects with start-ups and projects with small and medium-sized firms (Strategic Investment Committee, 1991).

The next step was crucial to the creation of the new governance structure: Each center had to defend its choices before a committee composed of the directors of all centers, their superiors in the state government, and the members of the de facto, statewide advisory board.[6] A successful demonstration of the connection between the project selection criteria and a broader analysis of the needs of the local economy, together with a showing that projects of the preferred type did succeed, then led to reelaboration of the program's mandate and the performance criteria used in evaluating the operation of each center. Continuous redefinition of performance standards is being institutionalized through the creation of a two-tier system of rolling self-evaluation. The first tier is a statewide quality council composed of the four center directors plus the head of the program. It will meet every six weeks to discuss the progress of key projects and identify emergent best practices and problems. A council with an analogous composition and responsibilities will be created in each center. Thus, as in the case of the new supplier relations, monitoring is inextricably connected to the constant, collective redefintion of goals. Because this connection is recognized by all the parties, an assessment of performance that might in another context appear as an indication of mistrust can become an occasion for the acknowledgment of mutual vulnerability and rededication to a common purpose.

A fourth example concerns the governance structures of the most successful of the newly industrializing countries: South Korea, Taiwan, Malaysia, and certain regions in Mexico, Brazil, and India (Amsden, 1989; Amsden and Hikino, 1991). These countries and regions cannot directly compete in the development of radically new products and production processes against the most advanced economies. Nor can they succeed for long on the basis of low wages, because the initial success on such foundations drives domestic wages up and draws lower-wage economies into the market. To compete, therefore, these countries license "medium tech" know-how in industries such as automobiles, consumer electronics, machine tools, computers, and semiconductors. They then improve existing designs and cut production costs through the kind of collaborative manufacturing, described earlier, in which design is closely linked to the shop floor, both in-house and in outside subcontractors. The state's role – a vastly extended variant of the experiments underway in Pennsylvania – is to help encourage the formation of private sector groups able to pursue this strategy by facilitating the acquisition of technology, supplying capital on favorable terms, protecting the domestic market and subsidizing exports until products are sufficiently improved and costs sufficiently reduced to be competitive, and monitoring the groups' performance to ensure that this protection is used for the intended purpose. The headquarters of each group has in effect the same relation to each of its constituent firms, providing capital, technical assistance, and stabilizing markets: The group's steel mill sells its plate to its shipyards, which sell tankers to its petroleum company, which insures them through another group affiliate, and so on. The groups' relation to the state, the affiliated companies' to the groups, and the production units' to the affiliated companies all depend on the consultative combination of monitoring and reelaboration of common goals evoked in the preceding examples. Thus these high-growth economies can be thought of as a nested set of constitutional orders whose purpose is to link the shop floor to world markets in a way that fosters constant, incremental innovation.

Because of the way the creation and recreation of constitutional orders blur together, each of these cases could be extended in two complementary ways. First, on closer scrutiny, consultation turns out to be more diffuse and less tied to particular, formal institutions than the examples suggest. As the parties' interests grow together, predictable, although often informal, occasions for the exchange of views multiply. The formal consultative institutions may then begin to recede into the background, only to regain their centrality in times of crisis – as we shall see in a moment. Second, a closer look at the history of particular constitutional orders reveals a complex politics of collective historical memory slighted by the institutional focus of the preceding examples. Typically the eventual parties to the kinds of constitutional orders just described have a rough idea of the benefits to themselves of participation. But they also have reason to fear the vulnerability that participation supposes. Small firms may have been squeezed by large customers proposing systems of collaborative production, or they may have competed with other small firms now offering to cooperate. The state may have tried to expropriate or simply milk the private groups, or the latter may have used state protection as an alternative rather than an aid to improving competitiveness. Under these conditions each step in the construction of a constitutional order is an exercise in deliberative trust in which the testing of mutual trustworthiness simultaneously encourages a clarification of the potential benefits of cooperation and the redefinition of past conflicts from historical enmities to comprehensible, forgivable, and forgettable misunderstandings. Developed in these ways, accounts of the creation and operation of constitutional orders suggest that the diffuse, almost institutionless historical consensus so often evoked in connection with this kind of governance structure is more an outcome of its success than a precondition for its existence (Sabel, 1992: 225–9). And given Ostrom's failure to find any trenchant list of preconditions for cooperation, moreover, this is just what we should expect.

Now I want to shift focus. Instead of examining the institutional innards of constitutional orders by considering their foundations in trust relations among persons, I want to examine crucial aspects of their historical relation to their environment by considering them in analogy to constitutions proper.

CONSTITUTIONS AND CONSTITUTIONAL ORDERS: DELIBERATIVE INSTITUTIONS TO RESPOND TO CHANGE

The eighteenth-century constitutionalism that continues to shape our own was intertwined with the liberal thought of the day. Hence it is no surprise that current constitutional debates reflect antinomies familiar from the liberal analysis of trust relations, and that the resolution of these antinomies directs attention back to the possibilities of institutionalizing deliberative cooperation. Seen this way, I will argue, a constitution is just the most encompassing of all the constitutional orders of a given society: the one in which all the others are ultimately embedded and from which their legitimacy derives. But precisely because constitutions are more encompassing than constitutional orders and are limited only by the limits they set themselves, examination of both together calls attention to relations between the historical boundaries and inner workings of trust-based governance structures that escape notice when constitutional orders are treated out of context.

At one extreme in current constitutional debate is the view that the citizens of a polity are united by their pursuit of a common good, called the public interest, and by their capacity to recognize that interest once it has been articulated. What citizens taken one by one lack in this view is the capacity to distinguish their particular interests from the general one. The purpose of a constitution, therefore, is to establish a parliament or similar forum in which the clash of opinion will cause the majority to identify the public interest sought and therefore accepted unquestionably by all. This line of interpretation derives from Rousseau; but it echoes on, for example, in the work of Habermas (1975, 1978). It is a variant of the liberal position that authentic cooperation depends on a natural alignment of interests, where "natural" here refers ambiguously to an essential, rational human nature or to the "nature" of a particular historical community, both discoverable only with the help of the cognitive machinery of constitutional democracy. The difficulty with this constitutional reading, of course, is that profound differences of opinion continue in democracies even after the revelation of the majority view. Worse yet, that view often seems to result from compromises among or the agglomeration of particular interests, not their purification through debate.

The contrary position, as most clearly represented by the proponents of the law and economics movement in the United States (Posner, 1981), carries the *modus vivendi* argument to its constitutional conclusion. The central notion is that a constitution provides background conventions regulating transactions in general, therefore freeing contracting parties from the fear that their more particular agreements could be undone by confusions about the broad rules to be applied in their interpretation. Constitutions thus provide the rules of the contractual road. And just as drivers have a strong interest that there be such coordinating conventions, they are within broad limits indifferent to the content of the conventions themselves. What matters, plainly, is that everyone drives on the same side of the road, not which side that is. Because contracting parties cannot pursue their contractual interests unless the coordinating rules are in place, each has, by a similar logic, an interest in enforcing a constitution (Hardin, 1989).

The problem is that this position seems more like a *reductio ad absurdum* of the *modus vivendi* argument than its extension back to the clarification of first principles. Naturally if the parties believe that the gains from cooperation are so large that each can afford to be indifferent to the possible distributive effects of particular conventions, the setting of conventions by constitutions will be uncontested and the constitutions self-enforcing. But if the parties held similar views about more limited contractual arrangements, and it is unclear from the general argument why narrow agreements should provoke more, not less, trepidation than broad ones, then contracts, too, would be self-enforcing, and all the liberal worries concerning the fragility of cooperation in a world of opportunism would vanish – which they plainly do not.

A third school of interpretation assumes neither that there is a latent public interest that can be made manifest by democratic debate, nor that persistent differences can be regulated by a self-enforcing regime of conventions and contracts. The assumption here is that a polity is an historical entity composed of groups with enduringly different interests and ideals of public order. These groups, it is further assumed, nonetheless recognize the need to cooperate for long but indeterminate periods in pursuit of large projects with uncertain outcomes. But they realize too that such enduring and intimate cooperation both presupposes and contributes to changes in their identities without necessarily erasing their original differences, and that such changes can only occur if facilitated by institutional arrangements, particular to the historical circumstances, that encourage the parties to make themselves mutually vulnerable by limiting the dangers of vulnerability. Finally, just as the constitution anticipates the transformation of the groups in the polity, so it anticipates that those groups, once transformed, may amend the constitutional rules to conform to their new relations. The process by which identities are changed through the accommodation of different interests is called *deliberation;* the institutional arrangements that in their ensemble encourage this are called the *constitution;* the periods in which the constitutional rules are themselves the subject under deliberation are called *constitutional crises* (Ackerman, 1991; Michelman, 1988; Sunstein, 1988).[7]

These views plainly have deep affinities with the account of science as a continuous exchange among dubious orthodoxies and redoubtable heterodoxies. Like this notion of science, the idea of deliberative constitutionalism takes continuing differences of opinion as constitutive of a process of self-(re)definition, not an obstacle to it. Like the former, the latter calls attention to the difficulties of holding the world fixed enough in particular circumstances to assess which parts of it can be fruitfully questioned. Like this view of science, deliberative constitutionalism also assumes that answers regarding the questionable parts will eventually call into question the parts held fixed, but that these "crises" or "revolutions" will (usually) be manageable precisely because they are ultimately recognized as a heightened form of everyday deliberation or debate. Thus deliberative constitutionalism presumes that citizens have and can exercise in public debate the same cognitive faculties as the members of a disputatious scientific community (Michelman, 1988).

Given these assumptions, proponents of deliberative constitutionalism have historically been more concerned with building or justifying the construction of institutions to facilitate deliberation among particular social groups in particular historical circumstances than in resolving "the" problem of constitutional cooperation once and for all. In this sense they have tended to be theoretically versed puzzle solvers – practically minded intellectuals or professionals rather than theoreticians specializing in constitutional law or in political or social theory. Journalists like Walter Lippmann (1965) wanted to reconcile elites and masses. Some political leaders, such as Masaryk, wanted to reconcile different ethnic groups (Szporluk, 1981); others, such as Wigfoss, Gustav Möller, and Guizot, wanted to reconcile various social classes (Rosanvallon, 1985; Rothstein, 1986). Administrative lawyers (such as Jaffe or Landis) wanted to solve problems concerning labor–management relations or nonjudicial monitoring of private sector activities (Jaffe, 1937; Landis, 1938). In the rare cases, such as that of J. S. Mill (Thompson, 1976), where proponents of such ideas did have unabashedly theoretical ambitions, their programmatic ideas are so idiosyncratically tied to their own and public experience that even their most enthusiastic advocates feel obliged to argue that the corpus of ideas they are urging is more systematic than usually presumed. Many of the most persuasive contemporary advocates of deliberative constitutionalism, such as Ackerman, play artfully on this practical tradition. In their theoretical writ-

ings, they claim to be recovering the discourse of the practitioners themselves from misleading attempts by philosophers to assimilate those ideas to
either of the other schools of interpretation (Ackerman, 1991). Conversely,
for reasons to be discussed in a moment, efforts to extract timeless substantive conclusions or even principles of interpretation from the premises of deliberative constitutionalism skirt vacuity.[8]

Yet in emphasizing their practical bent, I do not mean to suggest that
proponents of deliberative constitutionalism have historically had no influence on the way we conceive of cooperation or that their ideas are not theoretically provocative. On the contrary, precisely because much of what they
advocate is embodied in institutions that often have exemplary character
and because, as this line of argument itself suggests, even our most general
understandings of cooperation are grounded in particular examples, their
constitutional programs often profoundly shape our reflections on problems
of coordination in unsuspected ways.

Take as an example of such complex historical influence the notion of
the relational contract – a form of contract, we saw, in which the parties anticipate that they will fail to anticipate all sources of disagreement, and provide under the contract procedures for resolving eventual disputes. Assume
for the moment that I was right earlier to dismiss the argument that such
contracts represent an intermediate or transitional form between markets
and hierarchies. The category still stands as a rough description of the class
of arrangements I have been calling constitutional orders.

The surprise is that, as established by Macneil (1978) in an essay that is
still a central (and often sole) point of reference in the debate, the concept
of the relational contract was not defined by extrapolation from typical private party contracting. It was constructed rather by analogy to developments in a border land between constitutional, administrative, and labor
law: American collective bargaining, whose doctrinal and institutional history, we will see in the penultimate section, is deeply rooted in the third
school of constitutional analysis. Just as the parties to collective bargaining
agreements formed what have been called "minirepublics" (Stone, 1981), so
the relational contract argument runs, the parties to increasingly complex
commercial transactions should establish themselves as quasipolities, endowed with the institutions necessary to maintain their relations under
changing circumstances. Thus, ironically enough, insofar as the standard
analysis simply incorporates relational contracting into its typology of organizational forms on the unspoken assumption that everything must be
consistent with the presumption of opportunism, it is relying on a category that is not.

But such "economic" analysis of governance structures, moreover, borrows from the tradition of deliberative constitutionalism while depriving that tradition of its chastening historicity. Deliberative constitutionalism, like deliberative trust, assumes that individuals and groups must, to survive, enter into agreements with others that create unanticipated states of the world, including changes so great in the parties' identities that their original measures of advantage may be inapplicable in the world thus created. We saw in the analysis of the relation between monitoring and the setting of performance criteria in the institutions of constitutional orders that entering such agreements in a range of contemporary contexts does not necessarily make one a hostage to fortune, and this is more like the first than the last word to be said on that account.

But it is one thing to say that entering such agreements is not always a leap in the dark, and quite another to suggest that there is a well-understood institutional device – the relational contract – always available to resolve whatever difficulties arise. On the contrary, deliberative constitutionalism assumes that constitutional arrangements that facilitated deliberation in one epoch may not in another, not least because of the changes in the environment caused by the very successes of deliberation. Hence the constitution itself can be viewed in this tradition as semiotic or iconoclastic: semiotic insofar as the provisions for self-amendment underscore that the current constitutional document is only the representation or sign of a larger, changing institutional plan (Ackerman, 1991); iconoclastic insofar as the same confession of incompleteness, like the blank slab jutting at the vast beyond, is meant to suggest that no document or institutional monument can represent the full range of potential forms of human association.

And what is true of constitutions is true in spades of the constitutional orders embedded in them. Think of the latter as the deliberative institutions authorized by the former, and hence limited in their adaptive capacities by the dominant interpretation of the relevant constitutional provisions. But the adaptiveness of a constitutional order may also be limited by the particular resolution, in the course of its formation, of ambiguities in those provisions regarding, for example, its jurisdiction, consultative procedures, or autonomy from review by judicial or legislative authorities. Thus a constitutional order may come to grief because it has outrun its past, encouraging forms of deliberation that press against the limits of what is constitutionally authorized, perhaps provoking a constitutional crisis. Or it may come to grief because it is mired in the past in a way that prevents it from making use of all the possibilities for deliberation that the constitution provides.

A CONSTITUTIONAL ORDER IN HISTORICAL CONTEXT: WATER DISTRICTS AS DELIBERATIVE INSTITUTIONS AND CONSTITUTIONAL FIGURES

The vicissitudes of American water districts, as institutional solutions to a classic common-pool-resource problem and as figures in American constitutional debate, cast into sharp relief the historical vulnerability of constitutional orders and constitutions.

A water district is a quasigovernmental entity whose purpose is to regulate many aspects of the provision of water and any jointly produced hydroelectric power to a particular locale. A water district is typically formed when a fixed proportion of the potential members petitions that state government to put an appropriate plan to a vote and a majority of the eligible voters approves the plan. A district can appropriate property, including water rights, under powers of eminent domain, construct water works to transport, store, and distribute water, and collect fees for its distribution. To finance its activities, a district may tax property within its jurisdiction and use the revenues to pay for projects directly and to service the debt on bonds it may sell, as a subdivision of state government, exempt from federal taxes to the general public. Some districts are authorized to assess a pump tax on groundwater withdrawn within their boundaries from underlying basins. Many districts may contract the purchase and sale of services with like entities. Districts are typically governed by a board of directors elected either by land-owning members or frequently by all citizens living within their boundaries (Sax et al., 1991: 117–20; Ostrom, 1990: 107–10). In short, the water district is an institutionalized, cooperative solution to the common-pool-resources problem and a model of a constitutional order.

For our purposes the water district is significant, because its precedential role in American constitutional debate and a comparison of its development with that of a constitutional order it helped inspire illustrate the historicity of deliberative institutions. From the 1890s until the Supreme Court reversed itself to approve the New Deal legislation of the 1930s, the right to contract, understood as the unrestricted capacity of private parties to stipulate the terms of their exchanges, was regarded as a property right. Hence the Court often regarded state efforts to restrict the terms of such agreements by, for example, regulation of wage rates or working hours as an unlawful taking of property. Similar arguments could nullify collective bargaining agreements between representatives of labor and management that limited what could be contracted by others not party to the bargain but subject to it. Similarly, trade unions could be enjoined from soliciting new members if the potential members had signed a yellow-dog contract with their employer forswearing union membership. Here the mere invitation to join the forsworn organization was treated as an inducement to breach the employment contract and hence an assault on the employers' right to contract. In this interpretation of contract law, it was all but illegal for the state to regulate the economy directly or to enable groups to regulate their own affairs under its aegis (Sunstein, 1988).

The water district was one of the important exceptions to this constitutional regime, and served as a precedent in formulating the alternative rule in the succeeding one. Through the late nineteenth century, common use of water resources was regulated by traditional institutions (the Hispanic *acequias* in New Mexico) or by more or less formal arrangements based on community consent (the Mormons in Utah) (Sax et al., 1991: 617). A decision by the California Supreme Court in 1886 threatened these solutions by favoring the rights of riparian owners over those whose holdings did not border a stream bed (Sax et al., 1991: 335). The California legislature responded by legalizing water districts in their modern form, and the legislation was upheld by the U.S. Supreme Court in 1896. The decision took for granted the capacity of a self-constituted group to coordinate the activities of its members more efficiently than could a court or legislature, and regarded concomitant restrictions on the freedom to contract of dissident members as the price of efficient results (Sax et al., 1991: 619–20, 631–34).

Water districts, together with school and road districts, and other entities endowed with the powers to tax and regulate normally reserved to the state, then became central examples in the New Deal jurists' attack on contractarian orthodoxy (Jaffe, 1937). Their core argument was that the notion of a universal, individual, and absolute right to contract was meaningless because *all* contractual orderings sanctioned by the state infringed the contractual powers of some parties. In the case of self-constituting groups such as water districts or in the collective bargaining between labor and management, the rights of dissident members or third party bystanders are restricted; where the latter's rights to contract are protected, then the rights of the potential members of districts and trade unions to order their affairs collectively are impaired.

The state, in this view, is therefore always obligated to choose substantive criteria for judging which contractual order is preferred. Evasion of this obligation through talk of the absolute right to contract only entrenches the status quo. Established rights are inconspicuous because they frequently suppress and thus render hard to define the adverse rights to which they are opposed. The assertion of incipient rights, on the contrary, requires an express attack on the settled ones. By joining this demonstration of the pervasive inevitability of the state's ordering authority to showings of the growing importance of collective self-organization as pioneered by water and related districts, the New Deal jurists extended the regulatory reach of the state while creating the possibility of self-regulation for many new constitutional orders through "law making by private groups" (Jaffe, 1937).

To this point the story can be assimilated to a larger account of the evolution of law in response to increasing social complexity that identifies a developmental pattern in the crises that deliberative constitutionalism treats as historical contingencies. The claim is that small firms and individuals were the principal actors in simple market economies, and this explains the serviceability of the regime of absolute, individual contract rights. With increasing specialization of tasks, coordination by large managerial hierarchies displaces much market coordination, and workers, farmers, or pensioners can only defend their interests in collectivities. Contracts among collectivities accordingly take precedence over the contractual rights of individuals. As contracting among groups produces growing costs not directly borne by those groups, the argument continues, fear of the incalculable consequences presses society to elaborate a third, self-reflexive stage of law: Now bargaining collectivities are induced to account for the effects of their bargains on the larger environment while negotiating them. Thus the historical crises of deliberative constitutionalism are revealed in this scheme as the unfolding of an historical teleology in which the agents' actions have more and more complex ramifications, and the agents recognize this and their accountability for it (Teubner, 1983).

Viewed by itself, the development of the water district supports the teleological account. Contiguous water districts in southern California, for instance, were linked in the late 1960s by intergovernmental networks to create complex, federated structures able to address problems beyond the reach of each. Such Joint Powers agencies manage water resources and serve as forums for the resolution of disputes arising in connection with that management (Trager, 1988). Here, surely, is a case of increasingly extensive "coordination without hierarchy" that apparently demonstrates the adaptiveness of constitutional orders embedded in the constitution.

But the briefest comparison of the fate of the water district and one of its close cousins, collective bargaining, demonstrates that this evolutionary view overstates the robustness of constitutional orders by ignoring how their adaptability depends on the historical context in which they were formed. As articulated in legislation, judicial decisions, and administrative rulings from the New Deal on, American labor law came to obstruct just the kind of trusting cooperation based on the fusion of monitoring and consultation that is central, in the present analysis, to currently successful economic organizations. The law, for example, discourages supervisors from belonging to the same unions as the employees they direct, thus creating adverse interests at the workplace and emphasizing hierarchical distinctions instead of encouraging consultative relations, as between team leader and team. While supervisors are not prohibited outright from joining unions, their support for such organizations is not protected against employer reprisals as is the activity of nonsupervisory employees; nor may they hold office, serve on bargaining committees, or otherwise direct the affairs of unions including members under their authority. Moreover, union members who take on the leadership of work teams may be regarded as supervisors and stripped of their legal immunities.[9]

American labor law, more generally, obstructs cooperation at the level of the firm by distinguishing a core of managerial prerogative regarding which collective bargaining is permitted but not mandatory. This invites firms to take the most important, strategic decisions unilaterally, rather than obligating them to agree on a strategy in compromise with their employees, as in many other labor law regimes (Stone, 1988, 1990). Some firms and unions ignore the law or put their faith in dissident precedents authorizing experiments in these areas and establish workplace teams with de facto supervisors as team leaders. Some firms negotiate strategic plans with unions even though it is not mandatory to do so. But many more firms, unwilling or unable to find union partners with whom to build such governance structures, are going it alone. As a result, the fiftieth anniversary of the New Deal legislation that created collective bargaining as a constitutional order was commemorated in articles with titles such as "Milestone or Tombstone: The Wagner Act at Fifty" (Weiler, 1986).

The failure of American collective bargaining to adjust to the new environment has, moreover, become self-reinforcing. Unable to secure their interests through collective representation, employees are appealing directly to the courts for protection against, for example, unfair dismissal under individual employment contracts. The success of these appeals creates case law precedents and then, as these are digested in public debate, legislation limiting what can be collectively bargained. From the vantage point of evolutionary or self-reflexive views of law, this is history run incomprehensibly in reverse. It returns at the limit to a regime where group bargains fill gaps left in the pattern created by individuals and the polity (Kempf and Taylor, 1991). Whether or not it will take a constitutional reform to revitalize collective bargaining in the United States is an open question; that American collective bargaining as a constitutional order has not revitalized itself is not.

SOCIAL ORDER AND CONSTITUTIONAL ORDERING

Reference to the failure of the Wagner Act and the historical vulnerability of American collective bargaining re-evokes the opening setting of this essay: the current, general skepticism about the possibilities of effective collective action that leads observers to see markets as paralyzed by the threat of hold-ups, and hierarchical responses to that threat as hamstrung by conflicts between principals and agents. Behind this skepticism and the fascination with the science of suspicion that it engenders, I believe, is a deeper worry. Even as we discover the need for greater and greater reserves of trust in the complex exchanges directing our division of labor, we are coming to fear that our disposition to cooperate is being undermined by the exchanges themselves. Sometimes that fear is expressed in the idea that the economic agents' precapitalist notions of goodwill, forbearance, and equity in trading is the precondition of modern capitalist exchanges, but the consequence of the trades is self-reinforcing, self-defeating mistrust. The dependence of the modern culture of exchange on the premodern culture of reciprocity is the "cultural contradiction" of capitalism (Bell, 1976). Sometimes an analogous worry is expressed more generally in the fear that society is somehow depleting its "social capital," understood as the stock of institutions such as the family, voluntary associations, and religious organizations which together provide the reserves of sociability necessary to renew the instruments of collective action – the state, the political parties – when those instruments neither have a grip on the problems of the day, nor can be used to refashion themselves so that they do (Coleman, 1988, 1990: 300–21). By way of conclusion, I want to illuminate the theoretical underpinnings of the notion of a constitutional order by showing how in the light of that idea these despairing concerns seem misplaced.

Worries that the capitalist economy might corrode its social foundations have, to be sure, been central themes in popular debate and social-theoretic controversy since the late nineteenth century. Durkheim (1992), for example, argued that the *homo economicus,* controlled by the desire for more wealth, was a psychologically self-destructive creature. Ceaseless striving for a goal that was unattainable because limitless was, he thought, one definition of suicidal madness. The more the agents set themselves the goals that economic theory set for them, the greater was the actual danger of catastrophic insanity and social disorder. Durkheim's hope was that each participant in the division of labor would come to recognize his or her indispensability and vulnerability to the others, and that the ambition to fulfill one's particular obligation to the collectivity would give a tolerably human shape to the individual and collective yearnings for progress. In his early years Marx, too, was preoccupied with the psychologically deformative effects of life in an economy that broke the bonds between humans, their experiences, and their works by turning everything into a salable commodity (Marx, 1970). But his chief concern, of course, was that accumulation in a regime of private property induced a use of automatic production machinery that displaced much of the workforce and condemned most of the rest to mindless machine tending. Only collective ownership of property could create the incentives for using humankind's cumulative technical prowess as a tool for the self-development of each and the enrichment of all. Views of these kinds had broad resonance in all social classes because, whatever capitalism's material benefits, it was clear that the new economy was destroying traditional communities and callings without creating the prospect of a society in which striving was more than an end in itself. Throughout much of the industrializing world in the last half of the nineteenth century, "Manchesterism" was the popular name for a form of commercial development that ultimately destroyed trade by destroying the foundations of worthy life.

The novelty of our current situation and the source of widespread skepticism of collective action in all its various degrees of refinement is that the theoretical alternatives to capitalist self-interest as the motor of progress have been swept aside by capitalism. Yet the capitalists and the theorists of capitalism have begun openly to explore the potential shortcomings of many forms of self-interest as a self-regulating motor force. The failure of American collective bargaining – a story that could be extended to include the disruption of similar "neocorporatist" arrangements in most of the industrialized world[10] – raises a fundamental doubt about the Durkheimian notion that the increasing complexity of the division of labor automatically gives rise to institutions that give meaning to individual lives while regulating the needs of the collectivity. The implosive collapse of the Soviet-type plan economies provides all the experimental proof anyone will want for generations that the productive power of the human capacity for expressive self-development cannot be unchained by collectivizing the ownership of property. Even theoretically modest, "postideological" appeals to temper capitalist appetites through the reaffirmation of religious or moral values have been tainted by the explosion of religious fundamentalism and ethnic hatred as constant reminders of the violent ambiguities of "traditional" order. Meanwhile, as the returns to collective action become more and more palpable, self-interest appears at war with itself, at least as disposed to paralyzing selfishness as to mutually beneficial cooperation.

But if the arguments regarding constitutional ordering in historical context presented here carry conviction, then however burdensome the current problems of collective action, the fear that they are in principle insoluble is an unnecessary addition to the load. The starting point of my argument is precisely the rejection of the claim that collective action problems can be solved only by the action of self-interest as depicted in modern game theory, or by a disposition to trusting cooperation understood as product of an historical accident, or as the outcome of social evolution linked to changes in the division of labor. To the contrary, my claim is that the capacity to address collective action problems is as unalterably human as human can be.

Because individuals are sociable, depending on the relations with others for self-definition, I argue we must know how to trust others if we are to know ourselves. Because we are self-reflexive, we can always imagine reordering our relations of trust. Hence, just as we identify potential gains to cooperation we can imagine what it is like to cooperate with the potential partners. We may, in the end, fail to cooperate. But it would make no more sense to explain the lack of cooperation by an incapacity to cooperate than it would be to say that being at a loss for words results from running down a tradition of speech or depleting our linguistic capital.

But, finally, because the capacity to cooperate in this view is rooted in human nature, cooperation is always historically contingent in two senses. First, whether the actors cooperate at all depends on their assessments of the particulars of the proposed arrangements. Second, whether and for how long the eventual cooperation endures is also hostage to historical circumstances, of which some may be shaped by the unintended consequences of the actors' joint efforts. If cooperation is viewed as the consequence of self-interest properly understood or the upshot of social evolution, then history "causes" cooperation only in the trivial sense of providing the medium, the permissive environment in which collective action unfolds. Even when cooperation is explained "historically" as the result of a one-time accident that created an enduring culture of trust, history as a continuous interweaving of irreducibly different strands of causality plays no part in the explanation of causality. Thus the notion of constitutional ordering in historical context affirms our inextinguishable capacity for collective action at the price of cutting all ties to spent theories whose enduring attraction was the implicit promise that those capacities would, for some at least, inevitably be realized.

Three different kinds of arguments have been combined in support of these broad claims. The first is Ostrom's finding – which might be called sociological in that it characterizes social aptitudes – that cooperation is possible just about anywhere it is advantageous. This is the stylized fact that encompasses the despairing and the complacent views of the grounds of co-operation in a way that reveals the insufficiency of both. If the disposition to cooperate were an attribute of social groups, resulting from their cultural endowments or their evolution, then plainly, it should be possible to list the social preconditions that must be fulfilled if groups are to take advantage of their potential advantages. But there is no such list. If, on the other hand, the promise of advantage were enough to induce self-interested cooperation, then cooperation should be all but inevitable whenever it is advantageous. But it is not. In the face of Ostrom's finding, I conclude that the first problem is not to explain particular cases of cooperation, but rather how human agents might be constituted so that particulars matter to their disposition to cooperate.

Second, the argument draws on philosophy and philosophical anthropology to fix a notion of personhood consistent with this record of performance. The central finding is that the distinctively human power of intelligibility – the capacity to venture an explanation of anything in the world, including one's self – depends on the same kind of tolerance for mutual vulnerability in collaboration that marks joint economic activity. In this realm understanding is always possible wherever it is advantageous, and if disagreements persist it is because the disputants disagree, not because they do not understand what it would mean to come to an understanding. Feyerabend's groups of scientists pursuing their conceptual projects in awareness of and even at the partial instigation of alternative conceptions occupy the middle ground between the dialogue of truth seekers and *mundane* economic exchanges, and illustrate how the same motifs can guide actions at every range of activity.

The third constituent of the general argument consists of the historical and doctrinal arguments concerning constitutions in general and water districts and industrial relations as constitutional orders in particular. They are invoked to show that institution builders know or sense what participants in a debate or scientific controversy know or sense: that solutions are not once and for all, and that understandings must be reinterpreted to account for changing circumstances. In providing for self-amendment, constitutions say the last official word on the possibilities of reconciling permanency and contingency. Their plausibility as amendable frameworks of action depends crucially on the citizens' convictions that they possess the sociable and self-reflexive powers to address problems of collective action that the notion of constitutional ordering attributes to them.

Beyond, perhaps, the particular arrangement of its elements, nothing in this general argument is novel. At bottom it is an effort to begin understanding the ambiguities of economic exchange from the vantage point of the analysis of efforts to negotiate ambiguities of meaning. In a sense, therefore, it represents nothing more than an application to questions in the pedestrian heartland of *do et des* social life of many figures of analysis long current in the intellectual marches, and its sources therefore are too numerous and general to count. Yet in tracing both the foundations of central constitutional orders in contemporary America and the twentieth-century exploration of ambiguity through action, I came again and again upon the work of the American pragmatist John Dewey. In the looking glass of a conclusion he appears as the demon of the essay, building its motion, unseen, from the background. Recalling the categories of his analysis and the circumstances under which it arose seems the most succinct way to underscore the motives and intent of my own argument.

Dewey began with the idea of sociable individuals. Drawing an unbreakable distinction between individuals and society was as misguided as making a "problem out of the relation of the letters of an alphabet to the alphabet. An alphabet *is* letters and 'society' is individuals in their connections with each other" (Dewey, 1927: 69). Individuals thus conceived can perceive through public debate when the cumulative effects of their separate transactions become objectively burdensome, and they can jointly regulate their affairs accordingly. The group formed in the act of identifying the problem for collective action Dewey calls the public. The agents this public appoints to execute its program of reform are the officials; together these officials constitute the state. The intended and unintended consequences of state action reshape the conditions of private transactions. This leads in time to the creation, discovery, and redress of new problems of collective action by way of dissatisfaction with current arrangements, reconstitution of the public, and reform of the state and its officials.

Dewey's view on *The Public and Its Problems* appeared in 1927, occasioned by growing public realization of the inadequacies of the institutions of American democracy in addressing the problems of the giant, bureaucratic institutions that were manifestly coming to dominate American life (Dewey, 1927). His formulation of the problem of collective self-regulation as a continuous experiment rendered possible by extending the scope of democratic deliberation formed the matrix for much New Deal experimentation. Above all, it helped inspire Senator Robert Wagner's efforts to reconstitute American institutions so that they could better reconstitute themselves (Barenberg, forthcoming).

Looking back on that period at a time when some of its most notable successes have become failures, it is comforting to think – as I have tried to do here – that whatever their ultimate issue, the institutional innovations of that day are self-conscious testimony in support of the theoretical claim that collective failure can be the springboard for debate about collective action, and that debate can, for a time, lead to collective success. Indeed, amid the current dissatisfaction with our institutions and the general skepticism about the possibilities of collective action, this is one of the few comforting thoughts we have.

ENDNOTES

1. More precisely, to understand your meanings I need to understand your beliefs – what it means for you to assert something in general and in the given case – and vice versa. Unless I assume that you think you have good reasons to say what you say, and can say what those reasons are, I can't hold the conversation steady enough to get a fix on your meanings (Davidson, 1985, 1986).
2. This position is often attributed to John Rawls (Sandel, 1982). For a contrary interpretation, see Rorty (1990).
3. Note that these authors disagree about the extent to which our current historical obligations should be interpreted in a language approximating that of Anglo-American liberalism, and further about the implications of these interpretative differences for evaluations of contemporary political and social life.
4. There are, of course, schools of thought in which sociability and reflexivity are treated as mutually exclusive, not complementary. One argument is that individuals are so thoroughly socialized or disciplined by group life that reflexivity, even in the sense of an improvised reading of the social script, is impossible (Durkheim, 1966; Foucault, 1977). A contrary view is that reflexivity is possible only on condition that rare individuals, by an almost superhuman assertion of will, break free of social convention and impose their way of being on unreflective others (Nietzsche, 1967; Sorel, 1925). Such views, however, substitute in effect "social groups" and "great persons" respectively for the individuals of liberal theory, and hence do no better than the latter at explaining the stylized facts of cooperation introduced earlier.
5. Prato, the woolens district just north of Florence, is a current case in point. During the boom of the 1980s, the local Christian Democratic bank built up its clientele by providing easy credit against minimal collateral. The Communist municipality built its following by providing services – marketing, technology transfer, and the like – to firms, not least the newest and smallest started by employees of larger units going into business for themselves. The easy credit made it easy to defer adjustment to new conditions. Once adjustment could no longer be deferred, and change came with the rapidity that creates an air of crisis, the bank and the municipality began to fight over whose clientele should bear the major burden of accommodation (Balestri, 1990).
6. Discussions with Robert W. Coy, Director, Office of Technology Development, Department of Commerce, Commonwealth of Pennsylvania, and Executive Director, Ben Franklin Partnership, 1989 to the present. Coy chairs the Strategic Investment Committee of the Department of Commerce, of which I am a member.

7. I gloss over here important differences between Ackerman, for whom there is a sharp line separating constitutional crises from normal constitutional adjudication and who associates constitutional crises with the mass rediscovery of the responsibilities of citizenship, and Sunstein and Michelman, for whom the transformative is mixed up with the everyday and for whom the responsibility of deliberation is reserved to constitutionally designated bodies such as the legislature and the constitutional court. See the criticism of Ackerman's views in Sunstein (1992) and Michelman (1988: 1522–23). Thus to advocate deliberative constitutionalism is not necessarily to advocate participatory democracy. For views that do try to associate the two, see Cohen (1989) and Brest (1988).

8. See, for example, Mashaw's (1988) criticism of Sunstein (1988).

9. My account here follows Barenberg (1993).

10. On the historical contingency of neocorporatist arrangements see Kern and Sabel (1991), Schmitter (1989), and Streeck (1990).

BIBLIOGRAPHY

Ackerman, Bruce A. 1991. *We the People, Vol. 1: Foundations.* Cambridge: Harvard University Press.

Amsden, Alice H. 1989. *Asia's Next Giant: South Korea and Late Industrialization.* New York: Oxford University Press.

Amsden, Alice H. and Takashi Hikino. 1991. *Borrowing Technology or Innovating: An Exploration of Two Paths to Industrial Development.* The New School for Social Research, working paper 31.

Aoki, Masahiko. 1984. "Innovative Adaptation Through the Quasi-Tree Structure." *Zeitschrift für Nationalökonomie. 44 (supplement): 177–98.*

1988. *Information, Incentives, and Bargaining in the Japanese Economy.* Cambridge: Cambridge University Press.

Balestri, Andrea. 1990. *Cambiamento e politiche industriali nel distretto tessile di Prato.* Milan: Franco Angeli.

Barenberg, Mark. Forthcoming. "Power, Cooperation, and Endogenous Interest-Formation in Robert Wagner's Progressivism: A Reexamination of the Political and Ideological Origins of the Wagner Act." *Harvard Law Review.*

Barenberg, Mark. 1993. "The Politial Economy of the Wagner Act: Power, Symbol, and Workplace Cooperation." *Harvard Law Review*, 106 (7): 1379-1496.

Becattini, Giacomo. 1990. "The Marshallian Industrial District as a Socio-Economic Notion." In Frank Pyke, Giacomo Becattini, and Werner Sengenberger, eds. *Industrial Districts and Inter-Firm Cooperation in Italy.* Geneva: International Institute for Labour Studies. Pp. 37–51.

Bosworth, Brian. 1991. *State Strategies for Manufacturing Modernization.* Washington, D.C.: National Governors' Association.

Bourdieu, Pierre. 1977. *Outline of a Theory of Practice.* Translated by Richard Nice. Cambridge: Cambridge University Press.

1990. "A Reply to Some Objections." In P. Bourdieu. *In Other Words: Essays towards a Reflexive Sociology.* Stanford: Stanford University Press. Pp. 106–23.

Brest, Paul. 1988. "Further beyond the Republican Revival: Toward Radical Republicanism." *Yale Law Journal*, 97 (8): 1623–1631.

Cohen, Joshua. 1989. "Deliberation and Democratic Legitimacy." In *The Good Polity: Normative Analysis of the State*, eds. Alan Hamlin and Philip Petit, pp. 17–34. Oxford: Blackwell.

Coleman, James S. 1988. "Social Capital in the Creation of Human Capital." *American Journal of Sociology.* 94 (supplement): 95–121.

Davidson, Donald. 1985. "On the Very Idea of a Conceptual Scheme." In *Post-Analytic Philosophy*, eds. John Rajchman and Cornel West, pp. 5–20. New York: Columbia University Press.

Davidson, Donald. 1986. "A Coherance Theory of Truth and Knowledge." In *Truth and Interpretation: Perspectives on the Philosophy of Donald Davidson*, ed. Ernest LePore, pp. 307–319. Oxford: Basil Blackwell.

Dewey, John. 1927. *The Public and Its Problems.* New York: H. Holt.

Durkheim, Emile. 1992. *Professional Ethics and Civic Morals,* new ed. New York: Routledge.

Foucault, Michel. 1977. *Discipline and Punish: The Birth of the Prison.* Trans. Sheridan, Alan. New York: Pantheon Books.

Gilson, Ronald J. and Reinier Kraakman. 1991. "Reinventing the Outside Director: An Agenda for Institutional Investors." *Stanford Law Review.* 43: 863–906.

Habermas, Jürgen. 1975. *Legitimation Crisis.* Translated by Thomas McCarthy. Boston: Beacon Press.

Hardin, Russell. 1989. "Why a Consititution?" In *The Federalist Papers and the New Institutionalism*, eds. Bernard Grofman and Donald Wittman. New York: Agathon Press. Pp. 100–120.

Hayek, Friedrich A. von. 1973. *Law, Legislation and Liberty: A New Statement of the Liberal Principles of Justice and Political Economy,* vol. 1. Chicago: University of Chicago Press.

1988. *The Fatal Conceit: The Errors of Socialism.* Chicago: University of Chicago Press.

Helper, Susan. 1991. "An Exit-Voice Analysis of Supplier Relations." In Richard M. Coughlin, ed. *Morality, Rationality, and Efficiency: New Perspectives on Socio-economics.* Armonk, N.Y.: Sharp. Pp. 355–72.

Ikeda, Masayoshi. 1987. "Small and Medium-sized Firms: Evolution of the Japanese Subcontracting System." *Tradescope.* 7(7): 2–6.

Jaffe, Louis. 1937. "Law Making by Private Groups." *Harvard Law Review.* 51 (2): 201–53.

Kempf, Donald G. and Roger L. Taylor. 1991. "Wrongful Discharge: Historical Evolution, Current Developments and a Proposed Legislative Solution." *San Diego Law Review.* 28 (1): 117–57.

Kern, Horst and Charles F. Sabel. 1991. "Trade Unions and Decentralized Production: A Sketch of Strategic Problems in the West German Labor Movement." *Politics & Society.* 19 (4): 373–402.

Landis, James M. 1938. *The Administrative Process.* New Haven: Yale University Press.

Lippmann, Walter. 1965. *Public Opinion.* New York: Free Press.

Lukács, Georg. 1986. *Zur Ontologie des gesellschaftlichen Seins.* Darmstadt: Luchterhand.

Macneil, Ian R. 1978. "Contracts: Adjustments of Long-term Economic Relations under Classical, Neoclassical, and Relational Contract Law." *Northwestern University Law Review.* 72 (6): 854–905.

Marx, Karl. 1970. *The German Ideology.* Ed. by C. J. Arthur. New York: International Publishers.

Mashaw, Jerry. 1988. "As if Republican Interpretation." *Yale Law Journal,* 97 (8): 1685–1701.

Mendius, Hans Gerhard and Ulrike Wendeling-Schröder, eds. 1991. *Zulieferer im Netz – Zwischen Abhängigkeit und Partnerschaft.* Neustrukturierung der Logistik am Beispiel der Automobilzulieferung. Cologne: Bund-Verlag.

Michelman, Frank. 1988. "Law's Republic." *Yale Law Journal.* 97 (8): 1493–537.

Nagel, Thomas. 1970. *The Possibility of Altruism.* Oxford: Clarendon Press.

Nishiguchi, Toshihiro. 1992. *Strategic Industrial Sourcing: The Japanese Advantage.* New York: Oxford University Press.

Nietzche, Friedrich Wilhelm. [1887] 1967. *On the Genealogy of Morals.* Trans. Kaufmann, Walter Hollingdale, R.J. New York: Vintage Books.

Osborne, David. 1988. *Laboratories of Democracy.* Boston: Harvard Business School Press.

Ostrom, Elinor. 1990. *Governing the Commons: The Evolution of Institutions for Collective Action.* New York: Cambridge University Press.

Posner, Richard A. 1981. *The Economics of Justice.* Cambridge: Harvard University Press.

Pyke, Frank, Giacomo Becattini, and Werner Sengenberger, eds. 1990. *Industrial Districts and Inter-Firm Cooperation in Italy.* Geneva: International Institute for Labour Studies.

Pyke, Frank and Werner Sengenberger, eds. 1992. *Industrial Districts and Local Economic Regeneration.* Geneva: International Institute for Labour Studies.

Rorty, Richard. 1990. "The Priority of Democracy to Philosophy." In Alan R. Malachowski, ed. *Reading Rorty: Critical Responses to Philosophy and the Mirror of Nature.* Oxford: Basil Blackwell. Pp. 279–302.

Rosanvallon, Pierre. 1985. *Le moment Guizot.* Bibliotheque des sciences humaines, Paris: Gallimard.

Rosenblum, Nancy L. 1987. *Another Liberalism: Romanticism and the Reconstruction of Liberal Thought.* Cambridge: Harvard University Press.

Rothstein, Bo. 1986. *Den social-demokratiska staten.* Avhandlingsserie 21, Lund: Arkiv.

Sabel, Charles F. 1989. "Flexible Specialization and the Re-emergence of Regional Economies." In Paul Hirst and Jonathan Zeitlin, eds. *Reversing Industrial Decline? Industrial Structure and Policy in Britain and Her Competitors.* Oxford: Berg. Pp. 17–70.

———. 1991. "Moebius-Strip Organizations and Open Labor Markets: Some Consequences of the Reintegration of Conception and Execution in a Volatile Economy." In Pierre Bourdieu and James S. Coleman, eds. *Social Theory for a Changing Society.* Boulder, Col.: Westview Press. Pp. 23–63.

———. 1992. "Studied Trust: Building New Forms of Co-operation in a Volatile Economy." In Frank Pyke and Werner Sengenberger, eds. *Industrial Districts and Local Economic Regeneration.* Geneva: International Institute for Labour Studies. Pp. 215–50.

Sabel, Charles F. and Jonathan Zeitlin. 1985. "Historical Alternatives to Mass Production." *Past and Present.* 108: 133–76.

Sandel, Michael J. 1982. *Liberalism and the Limits of Justice.* Cambridge: Cambridge University Press.

Sax, Joseph L., Robert H. Abrams, and Barton H. Thompson. 1991. *Legal Control of Water Resources,* 2nd ed. American Case Book Series, St. Paul: West Publishing Co.

Schmitter, Phillippe C. 1989. "Corporatism Is Dead! Long Live Corporatism!" *Government and Opposition,* 24 (1): 54–74.

Sen, Amartya K. 1979. "Rational Fools: A Critique of the Behavioral Foundations of Economic Theory." In Henry Harris, ed. *Scientific Models and Man.* New York: Oxford University Press. Pp. 317–44.

Simon, Herbert A. 1973. "The Organization of Complex Systems." In Howard H. Pattee, ed. *Hierarchy Theory: The Challenge of Complex Systems.* New York: George Braziller. Pp. 1–28.

Sorel, Georges. 1925. *Reflections on Violence.* Trans. T.E. Hulme. London: Allen & Unwin.

Stone, Katherine Van Wezel. 1981. "The Post-War Paradigm in American Labor Law." *Yale Law Journal.* 90 (7): 1509–80.

1988. "Labor and the Corporate Structure: Changing Conceptions and Emerging Possibilities." *University of Chicago Law Review.* 55 (1): 73–173.

1990. "Labor Relations on the Airlines: The Railway Labor Act in the Era of Deregulation." *Stanford Law Review,* 42 (6): 1485–1547.

Strategic Investment Committee, Pennsylvania Dept. of Commerce. 1991. *An Analysis of the Research and Development Component of the Ben Franklin Partnership Program.* Harrisburg, Penn.: Office of Technology Development.

Streeck, Wolfgang. 1984. *Industrial Relations in West Germany: A Case Study of the Car Industry.* New York: St. Martin's Press.

1990. *Interest Heterogeneity and Organizing Capacity: Two Class Logics of Collective Action.* Estudio/Working Paper 1990/2. Madrid: Instituto Juan de Estudios e Investigaciones.

Sunstein, Cass R. 1988. "Beyond the Republican Revival." *Yale Law Journal.* 97 (8): 1539–90.

Szporluk, Roman. 1981. *The Political Thought of Thomas G. Masaryk.* Boulder, Col.: East European Monographs.

Taylor, Charles. 1989. "Cross-Purposes: The Liberal-Communitarian Debate." In Nancy L. Rosenblum, ed. *Liberalism and the Moral Life.* Cambridge: Harvard University Press. Pp. 159–82.

Teubner, Gunther. 1983. "Substantive and Reflexive Elements in Modern Law." *Law and Society Review.* 17 (2): 239–85.

Thompson, Dennis F. 1976. *John Stuart Mill and Representative Government.* Princeton: Princeton University Press.

Trager, Susan M. 1988. "Emerging Forums for Groundwater Dispute Resolution in California: A Glimpse at the Second Generation of Groundwater Issues and How Agencies Work Towards Problem Resolution." *Pacific Law Journal,* 20 (1): 31–74.

Walzer, Michael. 1983. *Spheres of Justice: A Defense of Pluralism and Equality.* New York: Basic Books.

1987. *Interpretation and Social Criticism.* Cambridge: Harvard University Press.

Weiler, Paul C. 1986. "Milestone or Tombstone: The Wagner Act at Fifty." *Harvard Journal on Legislation.* 23 (1): 1–31.

Williamson, Oliver E. 1991. "Comparative Economic Organization: The Analysis of Discrete Structural Alternatives." *Administrative Science Quarterly.* 36 (2): 269–96.

PART II

HOW AND WHY DO SOCIAL SYSTEMS OF PRODUCTION CHANGE?

Robert Boyer and J. Rogers Hollingsworth

In this section, the focus shifts from a tentative theorizing about institutional arrangements for coordinating economic activity to an analysis of the contemporary transformations in social systems of production. In the previous chapters, we have touched on the following issues. Boyer has argued that societies with more market oriented firms have not enhanced their structural competitiveness (i.e., the ability to innovate and obtain market shares), contrary to the expectations of the early 1980s (Chapter 2). Similarly, networking, joint ventures, and alliances have increased to unprecedented levels, and this is not unrelated to the complexity and uncertainty associated with innovation and restructuring of production methods (Chapter 3). Furthermore, states as well as business associations may deploy contrasted strategies when facing the internationalization of economic activity: One of the most promising avenues is no longer to rely on the demand-type strategies reflected in Keynesian economics but to anticipate the

challenge for national competitiveness and to develop policies on the production side of the economy (Chapter 4).

Obviously, how production is organized is an important issue for social
scientists to address. Is not the long-run performance of capitalist
economies largely shaped by their varying abilities to use, direct, or foster
organizational and technical change? Did not Soviet-type economies collapse in large part due to their inability to raise standards of living and to
promote a minimum democratic order? Since most observers probably respond positively to all these questions, the challenge is to make some
progress in comprehending at a theoretical level the sources of success in
production and innovativeness.

At a microeconomic level, the organization of production is composed
of a set of techniques and a spectrum of products with varied quality grades.
This is complemented by other aspects of the production system: a particular structure in the division of labor, a style in informational exchanges and
hierarchical controls, a pay system, and a management style. *A priori,* many
ways of organizing production may exist or have existed, but for theoretical
purposes, it is important to focus on ideal types, against which existing diversity can be gauged. The core hypothesis of the subsequent chapters is
twofold:

- On the one hand, there exists at the level of the firm a limited number
  of production systems, since they have to make compatible a series of
  features which cannot be independent one with another: The product
  must fit with the technology, the techniques with the division of labor,
  jobs with the pay system, the information flow with the design of incentives, and the market niche with productive constraints. Historical
  investigations have proposed a series of production configurations, and
  some ideal types can be abstracted from these findings.
- On the other hand, production systems cannot operate in isolation from
  the rest of the society. Technological innovation originates from learning by doing within the firm, but the deepening of the division of labor
  means that innovations result more and more from the activity of crafts-
  men, technicians, engineers, and scientists within firms as well as from
  their relations with research centers and universities. Moreover, the
  skills of workers have to be acquired either within schools and training
  institutes or on the job within the firm. The pay system and the nature
  of the hierarchy within the firm are influenced by the style in industrial relations and the stratification of competences at a societywide level.
  Conceptions about fairness necessarily interfere with the internal man-

agement style and influence income differentials across skill levels, firms, or regions. Even the organization of capital markets must be considered. Some mass production industries require such a vast amount of capital that the very characteristics of financial intermediation play an important role in the viability of any production system. Finally the state delivers – or does not – some general preconditions for productive efficiency to prosper: clear rules of the game concerning property rights, but also labor laws, international trade, access to knowledge, etc.

The notion of a social system of production (SSP) captures this complementarity between private management tools and their embeddedness into more general, societywide relationships. An SSP is a configuration of complex institutions which include the internal structure of the firm along with the society's industrial relations, the training system, the relationships with competing firms, their suppliers and distributors, the structure of capital markets, the nature of state interventions, and finally the conceptions of social justice. Given these complementarities at each period and for a given society, there exist a limited number of such social systems of production, since a coalescence of various institutional arrangements is not a trivial thing and assumes a mutual adjustment among a number of different costly institutions. And even if a society may have more than one social system of production, one generally imposes its flavor, constraints, and opportunities on other production systems. One may label such an SSP, *the dominant social system of production:* This is the one that is tuned to the core national institutions concerning labor, finance, and state interventions, and is more involved with an international regime. And while there is considerable variability in the way production is organized within a particular society, that variability generally exists within the broad parameters of a single social system of production.

The concept of social systems of production (SSP) is closely correlated with parallel efforts to theorize about alternative ways of organizing production. For example, technical change is more and more analyzed within the institutions that shape the innovativeness process, the nature of the linkages between firms and universities, basic science and applied research, the role of associations or public agencies in internalizing the spillover effects of innovation, the nature and duration of patents, etc. Richard Nelson (1993) in writing about national systems of innovation (NSI) uses an approach analogous to the one used here, studying the relationship of social systems of production to production organization (also see Lundvall, 1992). Starting from issues in labor markets, macroeconomic modeling, and the impact of macroeconomic policies, David Soskice has emphasized the major role of "productive organization" in comprehending contrasted economic performances (Soskice, 1990). Similarly, the "régulation" school in France has investigated why variations in institutional forms matter for growth, economic stability, and competitiveness (Boyer, 1987). The régulation school has demonstrated that a viable economic regime derives from the compatibility of five major institutional forms: a wage-labor nexus, a configuration for competition, a monetary (and credit) regime, a set of state interventions, and finally an international regime. It is obvious that this complements many of the components of a social system of production. Finally, Piore and Sabel (1984) elaborated a flexible specialization approach, which placed emphasis on the variety of production systems. Their emergence and stability are dependent on their compatibility with societywide social relations, such as industrial relations and skills formation, along with some forms of state interventions.

Thus, one of the interests of this part of the book is to provide several analyses that explore one or another of these theoretical frameworks. In spite of their diversity, Chapters 6 through 9 converge toward a common set of conclusions.

- For many industrialized countries, the social system of production after World War II was framed by the mass production of relatively standardized goods and had a distinctive configuration involving industrial relations, pay systems, on the job training, and the management style of firms (see Chapters 6, 7, 8, 9).
- In retrospect, it is obvious that there was variability in the extent to which OECD countries implemented such a social system. In Germany, for example, a highly institutionalized apprenticeship system and a cooperative type of industrial relations system led to a rather different SSP, one based upon diversification and quality much more than on standardization and price reduction (Chapter 9).
- These chapters engage in a fundamental confrontation with those neoclassical economists who have argued that an economy improves in its performance as the social constraints are removed on the ability of individuals to pursue their self-interest. Indeed, these chapters argue that societies perform best when economies are embedded in well-integrated societies, capable of imposing normative constraints or social obligations on individuals pursuing their self-interests (see especially Chapter 6 by Streeck).
- Each author proposes a different label for a social system of production that emphasizes diversification and quality, but the basic features are quite similar: a variant of flexible specialization (Chapter 7) or diversified quality production (Chapter 9).

- During the last two decades, alterations in forms of competition, in consumers' requirements, in uncertainty about macroeconomic outcomes, and in new technological opportunities and skills have made the limitations of a social system of mass standardized production very evident (Chapters 6, 7, 8, 9).
- The future direction of social systems of production in advanced industrial societies is not clear, since the possibility of alternative social systems of production is a complex process which usually requires several decades to develop. For a new social system of production to occur, there must be a new configuration of institutions concerning industrial relations, training systems, state interventions, and financial intermediation, as well as a complementary international regime. This is a significant departure from the conventional neoclassical analysis of production, which contemplates a smooth and quasiautomatic process of innovations that are technologically determined and not very much influenced by the structure of organizations.

Nevertheless, the authors in Chapters 6 through 9 express differing views about the future prospects of specific kinds of social systems of production.

- For Paul Hirst and Jonathan Zeitlin, mass production will progressively decay, whereas for Benjamin Coriat, a significant portion of the production of components will remain mass produced. Thus, all social systems of production appear to be becoming more flexible, but what is problematic is how a total social system of production is related to the production of goods and services. Are economies of scope and customization sufficient to generate a virtuous circle of productivity growth, or will they be combined with scale economies in order to launch a new era of flexible mass production?
- In markets with overcapacities, quality has become a key factor for competitiveness, and this feature is recognized by all the following authors. Nevertheless, the future of social systems of production can be conceived according to two different scenarios: They can be geared toward either short-run optimization of static oligopolistic rents or the search for dynamic efficiency by means of an adequate mix of innovation, production, and marketing (Chapter 6).

Thus, from a theoretical point of view, it is important to make a clear distinction among various alternatives to a social system of mass standardized production.

- Customized production assumes a reduction in the volume of production (Chapter 8).
- Diversified quality mass production combines the benefits derived from product differentiation with significant quantities of production (Chapters 6 and 9).
- Adaptive or reactive production builds upon a constant redefinition of market niches and the fastest possible use of new technologies in order to preserve market shares and/or productivity increases (Chapter 8).

Each type of social system of production has advantages and weaknesses and calls for specific types of organizations and institutional arrangements. This leads to another set of differences among the following authors.

Will future social systems of production converge toward a single best model, or will they lastingly exhibit significant differences? Paul Hirst and Jonathan Zeitlin appear quite confident that flexible specialization will become the dominant social system of production. Benjamin Coriat points out that at the level of principles, variety and fast reactions define a clear and general alternative to Fordism for particular sectors. Robert Boyer argues that the new principles are potentially quite general and can be implemented in many economies, but nevertheless the institutional inertia linked to obsolete social systems of production might prevent a quick and easy implementation of these superior principles. J. Rogers Hollingsworth argues against the convergence of social systems of production, since the embeddedness of industrial relations, training, financial systems, and state interventions is placing severe constraints upon the adoption of new principles.

An elegant solution to this dilemma would be to recognize that each of the features concerning quality, differentiation, reactivity, customization, and volume of production will be combined in different proportions given the nature of sectors, and the legacy of national or regional institutional forms. This part of the book does not provide a definitive answer to all of these problems, but the chapters provide stimulating analyses and hypotheses to be investigated by future research.

REFERENCES

Boyer, Robert. 1987. "Régulation." In John Eatwell, Murray Milgate, and Peter Newman, eds. *The New Palgrave. A Dictionary of Economics,* 4 vols. London: Macmillan Press. Pp. 126–28.
Lundvall, Bengt-Ake. 1992. *National Systems of Innovation.* London: Pinter Publishers.

Nelson, Richard. 1993. *National Innovation Systems.* Oxford: Oxford University Press.

Piore, Michael and Charles Sabel. 1984. *The Second Industrial Divide: Possibilities for Prosperity.* New York: Basic Books.

Soskice, David. 1990. "Reinterpreting Corporatism and Explaining Unemployment: Co-ordinated and Non Co-ordinated Market Economies." In Renato Brunetta and Carlo Dell'Aringa, eds. *Labour Relations and Economic Performance.* London: The Macmillan Press Ltd. Pp. 170–214.

6

BENEFICIAL CONSTRAINTS: ON THE ECONOMIC LIMITS OF RATIONAL VOLUNTARISM

Wolfgang Streeck

Economists have succeeded in persuading most people that the performance of an economy improves as social constraints on self-interested rational action are removed. In this essay I wish to argue that, to the contrary, socially institutionalized constraints on the rational voluntarism of interest-maximizing behavior may be economically beneficial, and that systematic recognition of this must have far-reaching implications for both economic theory and the conduct of economic policy.

Note that I am referring not to social but to economic benefits of social constraints, and to constraint rather than choice. In other words, I am not discussing whether or not societies may or should impose constraints on economic behavior *for moral reasons;* even most economists agree that people should not be allowed to sell and buy babies, regardless of whether this was the free will and perceived rational interest of all parties involved.[1] And I am arguing for the economic benevolence not of individual freedom, but of *limitations on individual volition and the pursuit of self-interest.* To support high economic performance, I am claiming, a society requires a capacity to prevent advantage-maximizing rational individuals from doing things that they would prefer to do, or to force them to do things that they would prefer not to do.

Contribution to the Fifth Annual International Conference, *The Society for the Advancement of Socio-Economics,* March 26–28, 1993, New York, NY.

The suggestion that *social institutions* constraining the rational voluntarist pursuit of economic advantage, and thereby interfering with the spread and operation of *markets,* may be economically beneficial directly contests the leading premises of mainstream economics with its *laissez-faire* conceptual heritage, and strikes right into the heart of darkness of liberal individualism. For standard economics, rules and institutions are legitimate in principle only if they are confined, like contract or competition law, to ensuring the continued viability of rational voluntarism. By comparison, the notion of beneficial constraint implies that the performance of an economy may be improved by the surrounding society retaining and exercising a right for itself to interfere with the choice and pursuit of individual preferences, i.e., to *govern* "its" economy. Note that this goes further than three other qualifications of rational voluntarism that are more easily acceptable within the economic paradigm:

1. That good economic policy cannot consist *exclusively* in the removal of constraints on rational actors, and that it in addition must include subsidies and services from public institutions ("industrial policy"). While supportive governmental intervention of this kind may indeed be meritorious, such policies typically no more than cater to the existing preferences of market actors, for example by offering them an attractive infrastructure or other "incentives" in exchange for (still "voluntary") investment. I maintain, by contrast, that sometimes economic performance may be improved not by servicing, but by constraining actors' preferences, employing governance to bar them from doing what they would want to do, and making them do what they would not want to do on their own.

2. That societies may have the right to intervene authoritatively in markets and correct their outcomes in pursuit of objectives other than economic efficiency, like equity, at the expense of efficiency. While there may or may not be trade-offs of this kind, I argue that efficiency is to an important extent conditional on the effective enforcement of social constraints, and that rational voluntarism *alone* generates fewer resources than might otherwise be available for political intervention to reallocate to the pursuit of social values or collective political preferences. In other words, the notion of beneficial constraint implies that there is no such thing as a self-sufficiently "rational," efficient economy apart from and outside society, into which the later may or may not decide to intervene; and that how "rational" an economy is depends on the social institutions within which it is enclosed.

3. That constraint may be required and legitimate for the correction of "market failure," to enable rational individuals to contribute to collective goods which they in principle want but are unable to generate, caught as they are in prisoners' dilemmas and similar rationality traps. While this is an important and underestimated productive function of constraints on rational voluntarism, social constraint may also contribute to performance by *transforming* the preferences of actors – i.e., instead of enabling them to act on their *given* preferences, teaching them that what they *really* want is something else. More generally, the idea of productive constraint is premised on the principle that rational choice alone is less than fully instructive for the selection of preferences and courses of action, including economic action; that choices between preferences, as Hirschman (1992) has shown, are choices between alternative social identities; and that by socializing their members through constraint, societies implicitly select between alternative models and standards of economic performance which may be more less sustainable in competition with others.

Summing up so far, I am proposing to apply a *Durkheimian perspective* to economic action.[2] Specifically, the point I am setting out to make is that a society, when it leaves market-rational economic actors the freedom to act as they see fit, fails to utilize optimally its productive potential, and ends up performing less well economically than it might. The general principles this invokes are that an economy can perform well only to the extent that it is embedded in a well-integrated society, and that a society exists only to the extent that it is capable of imposing normative constraints, or social obligations, on the pursuit of individual interest.[3] Without such constraints, social order gives way to anomy, ultimately depriving self-interested rational actors of essential conditions for the pursuit of self-interest, in part by allowing them to consume those conditions through their own activities.

An argument like this sits uncomfortably not only with liberal *laissez-faire,* but also with left libertarianism. This is because of its emphasis on the limits of individual rationality, including self-interested, voluntary long-term "prudence," and the need derived from this for governance of social and economic behavior by social – i.e., not themselves rationally or contractually constituted – institutions that limit options, foreclose choice, and override actors' "free will" against their resistance.[4] While I am not saying that *all* social constraints on economic rationality and rational voluntarism are economically beneficial, I do claim that some are, and in a fundamentally important way. It is at this point that I expect other critics of the neoclassical worldview to part company with me. But since I believe that the single most important issue in political economy is indeed the extent to which theory and policy must allow for *rational voluntarism being beneficially corrected by social constraint,* this is very welcome.[5]

BENEFICIAL CONSTRAINTS: SELECTED EXAMPLES

Economically beneficial constraints are of many kinds, and I do not pretend to have a conceptual schema to cover them all. For the time being, I can do no more than offer a number of *examples* – most of which I have come upon in my own research on industrial relations and industrial change in a number of Western countries[6] – as a point of departure for an exploration of some of the theoretical and practical implications of my general point: that social constraints on rational economic action may be economically beneficial.

ECONOMIC PRESSURES AND THE COUNTERPRODUCTIVE TEMPTATIONS OF SHORT-TERMISM

Employers, if given a choice and everything else being equal, usually prefer low over high wages; want to have easy access to external labor markets for hiring and firing workers, rather than being constrained by rules of employment protection; and wish to make decisions unilaterally, without having to inform their workers or to consult and share decision-making powers with them. At the same time, employers often realize that paying workers above the "going rate," keeping them in long-term employment, and giving them opportunities for participation may improve workers' performance and that of the firm as a whole. However, the voluntary supply by employers of "efficiency wages," employment security, and workforce participation is limited by opposing pressures on managements for cost cutting, "flexibility," and insistence on "managerial prerogative" allowing rapid response to fast-changing business conditions. In particular, short-term economic contingencies typically create temptations for employers to defect from long-term beneficial arrangements, if only temporarily until a present crisis has been resolved.

Employer defections, however temporary, toward what might be called the market and hierarchy minimum of the employment relationship (Streeck, 1992: 1 ff) may be highly counterproductive. Wage cutting can have devastating consequences for worker morale precisely in firms that have previously availed themselves of worker "involvement" through generous wage regimes. Firing workers who had informally been promised secure employment is likely to limit severely the beneficial results of the same promise being held out to the remaining workforce. And a participation regime that has once been circumvented by an employer in an emergency may never regain its credibility, making workers permanently hold back on participation effort. A single instance of defection may thus annihilate all of an employer's previous investment in the "X-efficiency" (Leibenstein, 1987) derived from high wages, secure employment, and worker participation. In fact, the mere *possibility* of defection, as is by definition inherent in *any* voluntary arrangement, is likely to reduce the behavioral effects on workers of even the best designed X-efficiency-oriented labor regime.

Vice versa, employers that do not have the freedom unilaterally to opt out of high wages, long-term employment, and participation may enjoy the benefits these produce more predictably and indeed in greater supply. Workers who can be certain that their participation rights will continue to exist when the returns on sacrifices they are asked to make will be available for distribution, or conversely when losses have to be allocated in harder times, are likely to be more willing to adopt a long-term perspective and extend "credit" to their employers, than workers who cannot be sure how long participation will last. Similarly, workers whose employment security is not just dependent on their employers' good will – that is, is based on employment protection rules or, as in Japan, on a common culture strong and instructive enough to act as a break on managerial unilateralism – are likely to identify more closely with the firm as a community of fate and find it in their interest to contribute to its prosperity. And workers whose wages are not determined by narrow metering of actual performance will feel less pressed to assume a narrow, calculative attitude towards their work. Employers, that is, that are *constrained* to adopt a productivity-enhancing labor policy – that are forced to operate on a *high general wage floor* under a binding wage agreement negotiated for an entire economy or industry; under strict *rules of employment protection;* and under constitutional or quasiconstitutional status rights for workers to *industrial democracy and codetermination* – may in fact find it *in their economic interest* to be so constrained, as this protects them from temptations to seek temporary relief through long-term costly defections, which increases their labor policy's credibility, which in turn improves its effectiveness.

THE ECONOMIC LIMITS OF SELF-INTERESTED PRUDENCE AND VOLUNTARY BENEVOLENCE

While trust can vastly improve the performance of both markets and hierarchies, it cannot be requested and extended *solely* because of its beneficial economic consequences. Trust is the belief that another party will continue to adhere to rules of reciprocity or "fairness" even in circumstances in which it might be advantageous to defect. Such belief will be weak at best where another's not breaking one's trust is perceived as being based only on self-interest. In fact, "You can trust me because it is in my best interest to be fair with you," will very likely be understood as simply announcing that, should the party's trustworthy behavior cease to be profitable, it will cease to be forthcoming. The resulting *lack of trust* is mitigated, but by no means over-come, if the party in question has made itself known as a *prudent trader* in-terested in long-term relations and capable of taking into account the value of other traders' "goodwill"; the possibility of a change in its payoff matrix causing it to break the trust remains in principle unabated.

Social constraints on rational behavior can reinforce trust, and thus fa-cilitate the rational pursuit of economic objectives, by reassuring potential-ly suspicious parties of continued adherence to reciprocity regardless of changes in circumstances. Credible information that the other side has noneconomic *in addition to* economic reasons not to defect accelerates and consolidates the growth of trustful relations. Such reasons may consist of culturally supported moral commitments that preclude or inhibit oppor-tunistic behavior. Or they may consist of impersonal rules, especially formal law, that provide for sufficiently strong sanctions to make opportunistic withdrawal from reciprocal obligations highly unlikely or factually impos-sible. Both cultural values, enshrined in traditions and enforced through in-formal group relations, and formal laws promulgated and enforced by the public power, are social constraints in Durkheim's sense that, by containing self-interested rational action within socially determined limits, make it more effective.

In modern Western societies – where one believes in another's good-will only at one's own risk, where social disapproval for a "sucker's" lack of sophistication tends to be almost as strong as for the betrayer's oppor-tunism, and where "healthy skepticism" regarding the behavioral signifi-cance of another's professed moral orientations is almost in itself a social norm – formally institutionalized constraints may have become the most important defense against erosion of trust. This seems to hold in particular where trust is to emerge in relations between actors of unequal power, such as between employers and workers. Typically, employers invoking their own normative commitments as a reason why workers should trust them are suspected of paternalism, while workers who refuse to be suspicious are suspect of being less than wise. To the extent that Western businesses can-not therefore be normatively integrated enterprise communities on the Japanese model, pluralist industrial relations with secure rights for workers to collective bargaining and, even better, codetermination – that is, with strongly institutionalized constraints on employer unilateralism[7] – may be the most suitable mechanism for generating economically beneficial trust.

THE SUBOPTIMALITY OF EXCESSIVE CHOICE AND THE PRODUCTIVITY OF CONSTRAINING OBLIGATIONS

Political conversion of productivity-enhancing labor practices from managerial techniques into rights for workers, and thus into constraints on management, may force managements to invent other techniques enabling firms to continue to operate successfully under changed external conditions. By foreclosing certain strategic options for employers, imposition on the economy of a safely institutionalized floor of obligatory social standards may start a process of *learning* among managements that may lead to successful restructuring, amounting to nothing less than a *redefintion of firms' identities.* Employers who find themselves permanently prevented by rigid high labor standards from being competitive low-wage mass producers may discover that what they *really* want to be is producers of quality-competitive, customized products, oriented towards markets in which the expensive social system of production that they have to live with may not just be competitive, but may in fact be a source of competitive advantage.

Constraints, in other words, can open up as yet unknown *opportunities* by making learning unavoidable. Firms that are barred from responding to competitive pressures by paying lower wages, employing more unskilled workers, cutting training programs, and terminating participation schemes may come to realize that, for example, higher investment in research and development may enable them to move on to competitive arenas where worker involvement and skills are an asset instead of a liability, and where what they are socially mandated to do and to be may provide the basis for a successful economic strategy. Comparison of industrial restructuring in countries like Germany, the United States, and Britain has assembled ample evidence that a high mandatory wage level and strong employment protection may create incentives for firms to train and retrain workers; that a training regime that results in "excess skills" may lead to changes in work organization towards broader job definitions and decentralized competence; that such changes can be solidified by union-imposed obligations for employers to "humanize" working conditions, changing the way in which new technology is deployed on the shop floor; that legally enshrined codetermination rights of workers may force managements to seek out strategies of adjustment that are capable of mobilizing worker consent – and that together a set of constraints of this kind may virtuously move the production profile of a company, industry, or economy towards more demanding markets that can sustain both high wages and high profits (Streeck, 1992: Chapter 6).

If improved economic performance requires a restructuring of identity, it will not normally be sought for economic reasons and voluntarily. This is because rational choice cannot in principle adjudicate between alternative identities, but makes sense only under established second-order preferences (Hirschman, 1992). Changes in the latter, in the kind of actor one wants to be, are accomplished through socialization and resocialization, i.e., through collective normative pressure rather than individual interest maximization. While actors can be expected to know and choose what is good for them in their present identity, they cannot be expected to know or to investigate what would be good for them if they were someone else, or whether it would be in their interest to become someone else.[8] To stimulate strategic creativity beyond present interests and structures, having fewer options and less choice may be better for rational actors than having more, if foreclosed options are short-term remedies under unreformed second-order preferences.[9] Constraining, choice-limiting social obligations, like a high floor of general labor standards, may be economically beneficial because they may protect rational actors from spending time and resources on exploring suboptimal options, and force them to concentrate their efforts on making successful use of potentially more productive alternatives.

Without social constraints, rather than embarking on an uncertain search for new structures and strategies, actors are likely to look for ways of defending present ones. Social constraints that foreclose this are typically not welcomed, even though they may eventually open up new and more profitable economic opportunities. German codetermination, for example, whose economically beneficial influence on management has come to be widely acknowledged, had to be introduced and expanded against employer resistance, confirming that authoritative intervention may be required even where its outcome might conceivably have been voluntarily adopted by rational economic actors in their own interest. The same holds for an institution like the German training regime, where self-defeating temptations on the part of employers to limit their efforts to the creation of narrow, firm-specific skills are kept in check by a host of regulations and enforcement agencies, making employers act as they conceivably might themselves want to act in pursuit of competitive advantage.

THE LIMITS OF RATIONAL ACCOUNTING AND THE COSTS OF EXCESSIVE RATIONALITY

Economic performance may require that producers not be excessively calculative, "economistic," or "hyperrational" – i.e., that their behavior not be exclusively motivated by rational-economic objectives.[10] Economic actors that are too singlemindedly concerned with "making money" may find themselves making less money than less economically rational competitors; "greed," it is often observed, "is not enough." The reason appears to be that markets often value aspects of products and services whose provision is not easily motivated by economically rational considerations, i.e., that require production inputs that rational cost accounting would be inclined to regard as excessive or "fuzzy." Such inputs are therefore more likely to be provided if their provision is socially or culturally mandated.[11]

Nonrational, norm-bound behavior seems to be particularly beneficial economically when it comes to *investment decisions.* Individuals who invest in knowledge in order to increase their earnings capacity in the labor market, rationally limiting their efforts to learning what they will "need," tend to learn less, and often subsequently to earn less, than individuals who learn for other than economic reasons – because they identify with their teachers or because they have been socialized into a culture of learning. Similarly, firms that have a choice to train or not to train workers, and to train only insofar as this "makes sense" to them economically, tend to train less than they should in their own rational interest, due to the difficulties of calculating with any degree of certainty the costs and benefits especially of training at the workplace and in the work process (Streeck, 1992, Chapter 1). Note that workplace training, while undoubtedly economically beneficial, flourishes only where its provision is largely removed from rational-economic calculation by a socially or legally obligatory training regime.

More generally, where accountants, as organizational representatives of economic rationality, are allowed to enforce rational return-on-investment calculations on investment decisions, ranging from worker training to the acquisition of new technology, investment will often fall short of the economically optimal. This holds in particular where high economic performance requires *redundant capacities,* i.e., excess production resources that are kept in reserve for coping with as yet unknown future contingencies. An example is a broadly based vocational training regime, like the German one, that generates skills, including the skill to acquire more skills, far in excess of present needs. Excess skills make possible an organization of work capable of flexibly restructuring itself in response to fast-changing, highly uncertain environmental conditions. Such capacity, which tends to be costly to build and whose pro-

ductive contribution is difficult to measure directly at any given point in time
– because it contributes only indirectly to production and remains unused
most of the time – is always in danger of being rationalized away under pressures for detailed cost accounting, even though such rationalization may deprive the organization of crucial capacities for flexible adjustment.

While the costs and returns of redundant capacities are particularly hard
to assess, the principle would appear to hold also for less intangible and less
"useless" production factors. Given the requirements of rational calculation,
productive investment determined exclusively by its foreseeable return is
likely to be underinvestment. That investment decisions may in this sense
be excessively rational, and therefore suboptimal, is consistent with the insight that rational principles alone are not sufficient to instruct organizational behavior or, for that matter, social behavior in general. As the neoin-
stitutionalist school of organization theory has pointed out (Powell and
DiMaggio, 1991), organizations depend on imitation, social norms, or legal
requirements to "close" their structures – i.e., on socialization in a culture.
Relying on rational accounting for guidance of investment decisions is just
one possible cultural-institutional solution, with the more important drawback that a culture of rational accounting, as prevails in British firms, may
be less economically successful and internationally competitive than, for example, a culture of technological perfectionism, like in Germany (Lawrence,
1980) or Japan, where certain investments are socially or legally obligatory
and in this way protected from economism and excessive rationality.

ECONOMY AND SOCIETY

In emphasizing the limitations of rational voluntarism as a basis for economic performance, the concept of beneficial constraint posits the indispensability for an economy of a well-integrated surrounding society – i.e.,
one that has the power to make economic liberties conditional on compliance with social obligations – and to a need for the noneconomic to control
the economic, *for the sake not only of the former, but also of the latter.* It thus leads
to a view of the "embeddedness" of economy in society that differs profoundly from current sociological models (e.g., Granovetter, 1985), in that
social structure is conceived as much more than a mere lubricant for the efficient conduct of economic transactions, enabling individuals to do better
and faster whatever they may rationally wish to do in pursuit of self-defined
interests. While there is no reason to deny that embeddedness may serve
this function, the more fundamental contribution of social structure to economic action is that it *imposes limits on it.*

A perspective like this refers back to Durkheim [1984 (1893)] whose image of economy-in-society is informed by his basic sociological principle that a good society is one that is capable of disciplining its members' pursuit of egoistic advantage. An economy, then, being dependent on social cohesion, can be a good economy only to the extent that it is embedded in a good society, and may decline in performance if the surrounding society allows its rational actors to become excessively rational – for example, defect for short-term advantage from long-term relations of reciprocity, make trusting behavior conditional on its economic payoff, or avoid uncertainty by requiring exact calculations of return on investment instead of submitting to cultural expectations. The uncomfortable implication of this, which is indeed inseparable from the notion of beneficial constraint, is that rational actors may not always be the best judges of what is in their rational interest, that they may need to be governed for protection from themselves, and that they may have to be constrained to do what is good for them.

Beneficial constraint, that is to say, is a *dialectical concept,* suggesting a relationship of *both mutually subversive and mutually supportive conflict* between the economic and the social, ruling out any lasting harmony between the two, and harboring a permanent possibility of pathological decay in both. Social structures that are streamlined to support rational-voluntaristic economic action are likely to be less supportive of it than social structures that defend their distinctive, nonvoluntaristic logic by subjecting economic action to collective social obligations. Nevertheless, economic action in pursuit of self-interest will always work to undermine social cohesion, and, to the extent it is successful in liberating itself from social constraints, will in turn undermine its own success. Just as on Durkheim, the notion of beneficial constraint draws on Polanyi's [1957 (1944)] central proposition that a self-regulating free market that makes the rational pursuit of economic gain the only maxim of social action, will ultimately destroy its own human, social, and natural conditions. In both theories, rational individualism is described, not just as socially destructive, but as inherently self-destructive and *unable to attain even narrow economic objectives unless properly harnessed by noneconomic social arrangements.*

Rather than a network of loose ties that benevolently facilitates economic exchange,[12] this suggests a more complex image of the embeddedness of the economic in the social. In the metaphor that I prefer the economy is socially embedded, *in the sense of contained and constrained,* like a hot plasma in a fusion reactor – where it is made *productive* by being *pressed together* and *kept in place* by strong *opposing forces.* If these recede, i.e., if the containment becomes too weak, the plasma disintegrates and ceases to produce energy. In fact, I would like to be able to say that if the constraining pressure loses strength, the whole machine, economy, *and* society, is blown apart. I understand, however, that the metaphor cannot model what one might call the "Polanyi effect" since, unfortunately, fission reactors refuse to explode.

As an aside, taking seriously the idea of the *primacy of the society over its economy* may lead one to think anew about the reasons for the collapse of Communism. Received wisdom has it that Communism fell apart because it prevented people from rationally pursuing their individual economic advantage, in the name of social objectives like low income differentiation and high social security. But while it is true that the Communist model of society had no markets, *it is equally true that it had no citizenship.* In Western societies, as Marshall (1964) and others have pointed out, citizenship "distorts" markets in favor of political participation and material equality, containing the domain and the outcomes of self-interested rational economic action within borders defined by social values. As a system of politically generated status rights and obligations that precede and are excluded from voluntary market exchanges, citizenship imposes social conditions on rational-economic action that legitimate it socially.[13] By giving rise to an interventionist politics, it also enables societies to protect themselves from at least some of the dislocations wrought on them by self-regulating markets, just as it safeguards them against economistic temptations to streamline their structures and succumb to a rationalist monoculture undervaluing the nonrational conditions of social and economic action. Allowing for the expression of a *political logic of social integration* balancing and, if necessary, overriding the competing logic of economic efficiency, citizenship not only protects the cohesion of society, but also and at the same time supports the operation of its economy.

In the West, in other words, pluralism between institutional spheres, as enshrined in citizenship, sustains the economy by encasing it in an institutional framework that prevents it from eating into and dominating its surrounding society. No such possibility for *reconstructive opposition* of social norms to economic rationality existed in Communist societies. While Communism had no markets, it had in common with unreconstructed capitalism that it subordinated the social order entirely to rational-economic objectives – if not determined by a blind aggregate of individually rational traders, then by an equally blind central planning bureaucracy. In particular, citizenship was suspended to enable the provision of social integration, not in opposition to rational-economic action, but as its planned result. Deprived of an institutional base for independent political representation, Communism's social values became, in the everyday practice of "really existing" Communism, absorbed into a monolithically rationalized order that, unchallenged by independently articulated conditions and limitations on its operation, was doomed to become both irrational and socially destructive.

Like Polanyi's "self-regulating market," the all-powerful Leninist economy-*cum*-state was unconstrained by social institutions capable of representing a logic other than that of economic accumulation. See, for example, the ease with which Communist bureaucracies were able to override environmental concerns or health and safety regulations at the workplace in the name of increased production. It is true that Communist accumulation was driven by *bureaucratic rationality* whereas capitalist accumulation is governed by *market rationality.* But the really important difference, and the reason for the ultimate superiority of capitalism, may not have been the absence of market incentives in Communist *economies,* but the fact that Communist *society* was too monistically rationally organized to be able to produce economically beneficial constraints on the economy and thereby protect and replenish the social supply of confidence, good faith, trust, long-term obligations, "work ethic," and legitimate authority required for economic performance. As Bendix has shown in his analysis of industrial management in East Germany after 1949 (Bendix, 1956), not only markets, but also bureaucracies require citizenship to prevent pathological overextension of instrumental rationality into core social relationships – that is, as a condition for their own efficient operation. Communism may have had a bad economy, not primarily because it had no market, but because, having sacrificed citizenship to instrumental rationality, it found itself saddled with *a bad society incapable of sustaining a good economy.*

Capitalism, by comparison, having been unable so far – to be sure, not for lack of trying – to dispose of citizenship and the economically unruly social values it articulates, would have prospered, not because it gives free reign to rational individualism, but because, *and only to the extent that,* it has historically developed or retained an ability to contain such individualism within a politically reconstructed or culturally inherited social community. From this it would follow that restoring economic performance to post-Communist societies would require more than the mere removal of institutional constraints on advantage-seeking individuals and the creation of an institutionally unobstructed, "free" market. Instead, the construction of social constraints on rational economic behavior, in particular the introduction of citizenship as a constraining context for the "free operation of market forces," would seem to be as important for the economic performance of post-Communist countries as market making, and may become ever more so as time passes.

In the rest of this paper, I will touch on some rather puzzling implications of the notion of beneficial constraint, as developed in this essay. If to perform well an economy requires social constraints on the exercise of eco-

nomic rationality, the social institutions it needs for this cannot primarily
be created or sustained for economic purposes in pursuit of a logic of economic efficiency, but must legitimate themselves as elements of a good society. (Put otherwise, it would appear that they can be economically functional only to the extent that their primary functions are *not* economic or
that their economic functions are unintended.) Moreover, to complicate
matters further, obviously not all social constraints on rational-economic action are equally economically beneficial, and some may in fact be the opposite. However, since beneficial constraints are not, and cannot be, designed
for economic purposes, both theory and policy face the fundamental problem of how to distinguish benevolent from malevolent constraints, and how
the uncertainties of that distinction might be dealt with.

THE FUNCTIONALITY OF THE NONFUNCTIONAL

While an economy can perform well only within an integrated social order,
a social order cannot be integrated for the purpose of good economic performance. This is just another way of saying, with Weber (1978: 31, 213,
passim), that there can be no purely instrumentally rational (*zweckrational*)
legitimacy. A social order that is not based on principles that are sufficiently different from, and even opposed to, those governing its economy will be
unable to contain and thereby sustain that economy; instead, it will gradually be decomposed by it. Economic rationality, in turn, that is allowed to
decompose the society in which it is embedded, undercuts itself.

Social institutions that are to support rational economic action by governing it must have other *raisons d'etre* than economic efficiency alone. Social
constraints on economic action that are justified on the ground that they help
individuals maximize their perceived advantage are impossible to defend
against individuals refusing to perceive their advantages as advantageous. For
example, if individuals prefer short-term over long-term gratifications, constraints that force them to forego the former and seek the latter cannot be
"sold" to them as increasing economic performance: Unless and until their
preferences have been resocialized in response to the constraints, they can always rightly insist that *for them,* at least, performance is clearly not improved.
While constraints might be legitimated by distributional or general welfare
objectives, these are social and political in character, even though as a side-
effect their pursuit may result in higher economic output overall or over
time. In this case as in others, the contribution of social institutions to economic performance is not intended and manifest, but unintended and latent.

In fact, and certainly in most of our examples, social constraints on economic rationality, beneficial or not, are typically created for noneconomic, i.e., political or moral, reasons. While removal of constraints for economic purposes – "deregulation" – is possible although, if excessive, self-defeating, imposition of constraints cannot in principle be motivated economically even though it may have economically beneficial effects; if it was so motivated, trying to be *directly instead of dialectically supportive* of economic performance, this might make it less supportive than it could be. The uncomfortable implications of this include not only that the beneficial economic functions of social institutions cannot easily be directly targeted as institutions are built, but also that whether or not a social institution will be economically productive is hard to know beforehand. This holds in at least three ways:

1. As has been said, important economic benefits often accrue as *nonintended consequences* of institutional arrangements created for noneconomic reasons. An example is the legal protection of artisanal firms in Germany in the late nineteenth century, which helped preserve the apprenticeship system and enabled it to develop in a way that later, especially after World War II, contributed greatly to German economic performance and competitiveness. At the time, the legal constraints on *Gewerbefreiheit* (freedom of enterprise and trade) that saved the artisanal economy were attacked by liberals and economists as an economically wasteful political distortion of markets and free competition, and as sacrificing the modernization of the German economy to the political purpose of creating a reliable base of support for conservative parties.

2. Social arrangements that may be economically irrelevant or counterproductive under given conditions *may unexpectedly turn out to be beneficial as conditions change.* In the 1960s the predominance of small artisanal family firms in Northern Italy was widely deplored as a sign of economic backwardness. When the technological and market environment changed in the 1970s and 1980s, favoring flexible producers of semi-customized high quality products, the embeddedness of the economy of the Third Italy in dense family ties and local networks of parties, unions, and employers' associations came to be regarded as a principal source of the region's suddenly impressive competitive performance in national and international markets. Hardly any of the social structures that were now found to be economically beneficial had originally been devised for economic purposes; the solidarity between Communist party members in the various interconnected spheres of Bologna's civil society was not based on a shared desire to get rich. Prosperity ensued

as a *secondary effect* of a social system that happened to find itself well-aligned with a specific period's economic opportunities and requirements. There is no guarantee, however, that this will always be so; as conditions continue to change, the favorable conjuncture for the social structure of *Terza Italia* may well disappear, and continuing prosperity may depend on discovery of a different noneconomic rationale for a social compact that also happens to support economic performance.

3. When first imposed, social constraints on economic action may seem nothing but economically stifling, and it may *take time* for rational actors to discover the economic opportunities they entail. Turning institutional constraints into opportunities may in fact be one of the most important functions of Schumpeterian entrepreneurialism. Generally, advantage-seeking individuals may be credited with an *unpredictable, creative capacity,* both to work around social constraints by circumventing or breaking insufficiently enforced rules, as well as to detect unforeseen possibilities of using them productively. A high minimum wage may at first detract from a firm's or economy's competitive performance; but as time passes it may also make employers realize that high wages can lead to high profits if products and processes are redesigned for high product quality and diversity.

One of the most disturbing conclusions this suggests is that, even in economic life, it is often the nonfunctional that is the most functional, and indeed that where everything is functional, functions may be less than optimally performed. Protecting the nonfunctional from rationalist pressures for functionalist streamlining, even though its benefits can, at best, only be guessed, may well be the most difficult challenge today for societies and decision makers, economic and noneconomic, private and public. That challenge is difficult because protecting a society's "requisite variety" is ultimately impossible under a functionalist rationale, even an enlightened, long-term prudent one, given that some of the most important social contributions to economic performance can be ascertained only ex post.[14] Preservation of economically beneficial preeconomic resistance to the dictates of the economic requires preeconomic and prerational tolerance of social objectives that, *to the best of the available knowledge,* may have negative or uncertain or no economic consequences at all. Such tolerance, where it is not prescribed by religious respect of the "sacred," must be politically constitutionalized, that is, secured by independent forces, such as a politics or culture, that refuse to be enlisted for the pursuit of economic rationality. Just as individuals need protection from hyperrationality, so do modern societies, the former through social constraints and the latter through constitutionally guaranteed pluralism.

POLICY AND POLITICS

A well-integrated social order capable of sustaining a well-performing economy may be inherited from tradition, or constructed through politics, or both. Traditional and politically constructed institutions seem in principle equally capable of imposing beneficial constraints on economic behavior. At the same time, the fact that some social constraints may be economically beneficial does not rule out that others may be economically counterproductive. What seems worse, since the economic functions of social institutions are often latent and unintended, or cannot be directly intended at all, and in fact are frequently contradictory and "dialectical," telling productive from counterproductive constraints in advance may more often than not be difficult or impossible.

The consequences of this for policy, and for theory that tries to inform policy, appear at first more unsettling than reassuring. In the abstract, it may be interesting to know that good economic performance is often an unintended consequence of a social order supported for noneconomic or, if the word exists, countereconomic reasons, and that excessive economic streamlining of social arrangements may undermine performance. But since it is no less the case that *not all* constraining social institutions are economically beneficial, this seems to offer little guidance for practical action, especially compared to the sense of accuracy and certainty conveyed by technical economics. While I agree with this in part, I wish to argue in the remainder of this paper that insight in the economic benevolence of some social constraints on economic action, and in our limited ability to predict the latent economic functions of social institutions, is of potentially great practical value, and that the impressive certainties of functionalist economism are deceptive and may be dangerously misleading.

To begin with, that some social institutions improve economic performance by refusing to be economically rational is simply true, and knowing the truth is better than not knowing it. Recognition of the economic benefits of *some* social constraints immunizes against the received wisdom that *all* constraints are counterproductive by definition, which implies that a good economic policy is always one that replaces institutional constraints with free markets. There is no doubt that accepting the possible benevolence of social constraints makes theory less elegant and practice more complicated. But it also makes theory more truthful and practice potentially more successful. Instead of simply destroying social cohesion to eliminate restraints on trade, "collusion," "price fixing," "monopoly," "market distortion," etc., a more enlightened economic policy knows that it may face a double task: to preserve or create social order through institutional constraints, and then put such order to good economic use by preventing constraints from becoming economically counterproductive. An example would be the imposition of codetermination by legal constraint on German firms, contributing importantly to cooperation between management and labor, and its association with a liberal trade and tough competition policy exposing labor–management coalitions to relentless efficiency pressures and preventing them from using their cooperation for joint rent-seeking (Streeck, 1992, Chapter 6).

Similarly, knowing that good economic performance may hinge on latent or unintended functions of constraining social institutions, and realizing that such functions may be difficult to plan or even to ascertain, may as such improve policy. Uncertainty over the economic consequences of social institutions is not necessarily due to bad theory, but is an essential and inevitable element of economic life. Rather than trying to eliminate it with the help of theories that pretend to be what no theory can be – a manual for economically correct institutional engineering, or deengineering – uncertainty must be incorporated in political-economic practice as one of its defining conditions. This will restore to its rightful place the shrewd, experienced, common sense judgment of the practitioner, as distinguished from the deductively-based knowledge of the expert, emphasizing the importance of political skills such as empathy, tolerance of compromise and ambiguity, capacity to bargain, sense of legitimacy and power, and intuitive appreciation of intangible assets like goodwill and consensus. Most importantly, understanding the essential but uncertain economic contribution of constraining social institutions will foster a sense for the preciousness of social order and cohesion in a rapidly modernizing world, inhibiting easy recourse to deregulation and marketization, and supporting a general presumption for conservation of social cohesion where it still exists, and for restorative institutional gardening instead of rationalist-constructivist institutional engineering.

Perhaps most importantly, insight in the complex institutional conditions of economic performance reminds one that economic policy, as conventionally defined, covers only very few of a wide range of conditions responsible for an economy's performance and competitiveness, and very likely not even the most important ones. While far from offering a magic solution, the notion of beneficial constraint implies that restoring performance to an economy through economic policy as we know it is likely to work only in the simplest of cases. Just like an enterprise, an economy is not a machine, and governance, just like management, is not an applied science consisting of pressing the right buttons. At the minimum, good economic policy must be embedded in family policy, social policy, and educational policy, all having to do as much with the socialization as with the satisfaction of preferences, in the same way as the economy is embedded in the society. Rather than merely offering incentives for desirable rational individual behavior, good economic policy must be involved in the creation of social obligations as well as individual opportunities, and in institution building as well as market making. To the extent that economic policy needs to strengthen the social fabric as a condition of strengthening economic performance, there is no simple technique it can apply, and there cannot be one. However, that the problem is messy and not well understood, and indeed may appear so daunting that one would like it to go away, does not make it go away.

Finally, it is only after the existence of economically beneficial social constraints has been recognized that systematic efforts can be made to understand their nature, and to assign them a place on the economic and sociological research agenda that corresponds to their importance. While distinguishing between benevolent and malevolent constraints will for intrinsic reasons always be difficult, this does not mean that more focused empirical research could not uncover important differences and similarities, or generate useful analytical concepts, typologies, and even theories. Similarly, there is no reason in principle why economic theory should not for once try to escape from the prison of laissez-faire voluntarism, give up parsimony for realism, and include the economic effects of benevolent noneconomic constraints in formal models – instead of treating constraints as exogenous or as theoretically irrelevant anomalies.[15]

Short of a theory, two general conclusions stand out concerning the relationship between the political and the economic, both allowing for and indeed demanding a measure of autonomy of the former from the functionalist dictates of the latter. First, since economic rationality is inherently incapable of instructing the design of a viable social order, since furthermore the economic consequences of social institutions are often unpredictable, and since above all some of the most economically functional institutions – like the Asian family – are sustained by principles of social organization that are decidedly noneconomic, or even antieconomic, policy and politics may just as well not even try to become "economically rational," and indeed may have to refuse to do so precisely in order to produce good economic results. Economic rationality alone cannot define social institutions; to the contrary it needs itself to be defined by them. A society that fails to provide such definition will suffer from low economic performance. While the same applies to a society whose social institutions suffocate its economy, it is also true that the kind of social embedding good economic performance requires can be built only for reasons other than good economic performance, enabling it to support rational-economic action by containing it. While letting politics operate on its own terms may sometimes go wrong economically, making politics subservient to economics always will.

A good society can only be constructed for its own sake; economic benefits may or may not ensue, but they cannot be the purpose. Political governance must above all provide for the construction and reconstruction of a legitimate social order, protecting social commitments from erosion by excessive rationality ("greed") and safeguarding a space in which people can be expected to treat each other and their community as ends and not as means. Such politics will often also, unintendedly, be good economic policy. For example, the pursuit of social justice *as an end in itself* may be supportive of economic action to the extent that it safely establishes the limits within which it may take place. And by foreclosing certain strategies of rational interest maximization, norms of social justice may stimulate a creative search for alternative, possibly more economically productive strategies. Where, however, justice is pursued only insofar as it fits "economic needs," it will very likely fail to generate the legitimacy and trust an advanced economy requires to perform well. The space for political choice and for autonomy of politics from the economy, this suggests, may easily be underestimated.

Second, if social institutions may generate beneficial economic consequences by constraining rational economic action, economic policies that aim at improving economic performance are not in principle required to accommodate the expressed preferences and perceived interests of "the marketplace." The notion of beneficial constraint points to an inherent need of economies to be *governed,* as opposed to just *supported,* by public policy, recalling the essential sociopolitical constructedness of markets emphasized in Polanyi's [1957 (1944)] work. This need is clearly *not* satisfied by negative policies of liberating "market forces," or not by them alone. Nor can it be filled by simple subsidization of market participants helping them attain their self-determined objectives, for example through the provision of infrastructure or through public research and development projects. Governance implies that society, through culture, politics, and policy, must retain the power to review the self-chosen objectives of rational economic actors *under other than rational economic criteria.* Government, that is, must be more than, however technocratically intelligent, service provision. Turning the interventionist state into an "entrepreneurial state," and thereby depriving it of its distinctive status as wielder of public authority, falls significantly short of what may be required for good economic performance.[16]

Imposing and enforcing constraints requires power, and there is no guarantee that such power can always be mobilized. Where, as in today's global financial markets, mobile economic agents can credibly threaten to exit to more accommodating political jurisdictions, taking vital productive resources with them, they stand a good chance of protecting their current preferences, even if economically suboptimal, from public intervention, and may ultimately succeed in forcing the political to become subservient to the economic. Insight in the economic benefits of social constraints may not as such be able to prevent this; at the minimum, however, it can warn us against celebrating it as progress towards a more "responsive" economic policy or a less "bureaucratic" state. The fact that a decline of the public power may lead to an institutional politics and economic policy with economically suboptimal results does not mean that it cannot happen; but it is also true that the fact that it may already be happening does not mean that its results cannot be suboptimal.

ENDNOTES

1. However, there are economists who would like to see the Chicago Mercantile Exchange quote baby futures alongside soybean futures, in order to provide adequate information for production to match demand.
2. I am referring here to the Durkheim of *The Division of Labor in Society* [1984 (1893)] and *The Rules of the Sociological Method* [1964 (1895)].
3. Such constraints may be based in formal law or in a common culture; what is important is that, where they exist, individuals who are subject to them, especially if they are inclined towards rational cost-benefit calculation, may typically experience a *conflict* between what they would be doing if they were allowed to maximize their utility, and what they are expected to do by "society" or by the ethical code with which they identify.
4. That is, institutions that wield *power,* and indeed *authority,* in a Weberian sense.
5. I am aware that the position I am presenting here can easily be denounced as socialist, paternalistic, authoritarian, etatistic, bureaucratic interventionist, or something similarly old-fashioned. I also understand that many, while not wanting to sit with the economists, may not want to be seen as any of the above either. The unpleasant truth, however, is that one cannot have it both ways, and that even a mixed economy cannot be founded on muddled concepts. Ultimately, one can have either a contractual or an institutional theory of social order, not both at the same time. Softening up institutionalism by recasting institutions as contractual, or hiding the ugly face of the voluntarist state of nature behind cosmetic assumptions on the innate farsightedness or benevolence of human beings, or on the civilizing potential of business school courses in "management ethics," may make one feel better, but only at the cost of confusing the issue.
6. Some are reported in Streeck (1992), especially in Chapters 1, 5, and 6.
7. As anchored, in Germany, in a law that, not by chance, is called the Works Constitution Act (*Betriebsverfassungsgesetz*). Compare this to the American unilateral practice of "unionism without unions" (Garbarino, 1984) and its comparatively low capacity to generate trust between employers and employees.
8. More precisely, whether redefinition of their identity would serve a yet to be discovered *extended interest* that would make it rational for them to have *different interests* from those they have now.

9. Put otherwise, actors may be worse off for having more options. For a similar argument, see Herrnstein and Prelec (1991).

10. It is interesting to note, incidentally, that this principle is widely recognized with respect to workers, but much less with respect to managements, investors of capital, or business organizations.

11. In his comparative ethnographic study of British and German management, Lawrence notes that, "perhaps paradoxically, German ideas of *Technik* have conditioned the approach to profits, *this approach being both less overt and more successful*. German companies show an implicit grasp of the fact *that profits are not to be pursued directly*. ... Companies do not make money, only the mint does that; they make goods and services and if people want to buy them, *profits ensue*. In the author's experience there is far less obsession with the various indices of performance and profitability in German companies. ... The German corporate obsession is products. Their design, construction and quality ..." (1980: 187; italics mine, WS).

12. And that can conveniently be presented, explicitly or implicitly, as owing its origin to the desire of prudent economic actors to reduce their "transaction costs" (Williamson and Ouchi, 1981).

13. See, for example, Marshall's famous description of citizenship as "a single uniform status" providing "the foundation of equality on which the structure of inequality could be built" (1964: 87).

14. As Eva Pichler has pointed out to me, this amounts to a Hayekian rationale for protecting collective nonmarket institutions from being dissolved into markets.

15. For an interesting attempt to model the effects of works councils on economic performance, and especially to demonstrate that legally mandated councils are economically preferable to voluntary ones, see Freeman and Lazear (1985).

16. For example, if vocational training policy in the United States were to serve the presently perceived skill needs of American employers, it would limit itself to reproducing a skill structure that is internationally not competitive. An effective training policy would therefore have to be linked with a technology transfer and work reorganization policy aimed at reshaping the demand side of the skill equation, politically creating a "market" for the kind of skills that are needed to raise economic performance to a socially desirable level. This, in turn, may require imposition of institutional rigidities on work organization, and limitations on managerial prerogative, through "culture" or, more likely, trade unions, to rule out resort to a traditional "Taylorist" organization of work.

BIBLIOGRAPHY

Bendix, R. 1956. *Work and Authority in Industry: Ideologies of Management in the Course of Industrialization.* Berkeley: University of California Press.

Durkheim, Emile. 1964 (1895). *The Rules of Sociological Method.* Translated by Sarah A. Solovay and John H. Mueller. New York: Macmillan.

   1984 (1893). *The Division of Labor in Society.* Translated by W. D. Halls. New York: The Free Press.

Freeman, R. and E.P. Lazear. Forthcoming. "An Economic Analysis of Works Councils." In: J. Rogers and W. Streeck, eds. *Works Councils: Consultation, Representation, and Cooperation in Industrial Relations.* Chicago: University of Chicago Press. Pp. 27–50.

Garbarino, J. W. 1984. "Unionism Without Unions: The New Industrial Relations." *Industrial Relations.* 23: 40–51.

Granovetter, M. 1985. "Economic Action and Social Structure: The Problem of Embeddedness." *American Journal of Sociology.* 91: 481–510.

Herrnstein, R. J. and D. Prelec. 1991. "Melioration: A Theory of Distributed Choice." *Journal of Economic Perspectives.* 5: 3, 137–56.

Hirschman, A. O. 1992. "Against Parsimony: Three Easy Ways of Complicating Some Categories of Economic Discourse." In A. O. Hirschman. *Rival Views of Market Society and Other Recent Essays.* Cambridge: Harvard University Press. Pp. 142–60.

Lawrence, P. A. 1980. *Managers and Management in West Germany.* New York: St. Martin's Press.

Leibenstein, H. 1987. *Inside the Firm.* Cambridge: Harvard University Press.

Marshall, Th. H. 1964. *Class, Citizenship and Social Development.* Garden City, N.Y.: Doubleday & Company.

Polanyi, K. 1957 (1944). *The Great Transformation: The Political and Economic Origins of Our Time.* Boston: Beacon Press.

Powell, W. W. and P. J. DiMaggio. 1991. *The New Institutionalism in Organizational Analysis.* Chicago: University of Chicago Press.

Streeck, W. 1992. *Social Institutions and Economic Performance: Studies of Industrial Relations in Advanced Capitalist Economies.* London: Sage.

Weber, Max. 1978. *Economy and Society,* 2 vols. Ed. by Guenther Roth and Claus Wittich. Berkeley: University of California Press.

Williamson, O. E. and W. G. Ouchi. 1981. "The Markets and Hierarchies and Visible Hand Perspectives." In A. H. van de Ven and W. F. Joyce. *Perspectives on Organization Design and Behavior.* New York: Wiley. Pp. 347–70.

7

FLEXIBLE SPECIALIZATION: THEORY AND EVIDENCE IN THE ANALYSIS OF INDUSTRIAL CHANGE

Paul Hirst and Jonathan Zeitlin

There is widespread agreement that something dramatic has been happening to the international economy over the past two decades: rapid and radical changes in production technology and industrial organization, a major restructuring of work markets, and consequent large scale changes in the policies of economic management at the international, national, and regional levels. At the same time there is a great deal of confusion about how to characterize these changes, the mechanisms at work, and the policy implications for different groups of economic and political actors. One way of accomplishing these tasks is to postulate a change of basic manufacturing organization from a "Fordist" pattern that prevailed in the years of the long post-1945 boom to a "post-Fordist" successor in the later 1970s and 1980s. Many people habitually conflate a variety of approaches to industrial change under this heading, such as flexible specialization, regulation theory, disorganized capitalism, or diversified quality production. The resulting problem is that significant differences of approach are concealed by a superficial similarity between the proponents of flexible specialization and a set of apparently similar but underlyingly divergent ideas. The purpose of this paper is thus to set out the distinctive properties of flexible specialization as a theoretical approach to the analysis of industrial change and examine its relationship to problems of empirical evidence.[1]

FLEXIBLE SPECIALIZATION: TECHNOLOGICAL PARADIGMS AND POSSIBLE WORLDS

Despite their apparent similarities, flexible specialization and post-Fordism represent sharply different theoretical approaches to the analysis of industrial change. Where post-Fordism sees productive systems as integrated and coherent totalities, flexible specialization identifies complex and variable connections among technology, institutions, and politics; where post-Fordism sees industrial change as a mechanical outcome of impersonal processes, flexible specialization emphasizes contingency and the scope for strategic choice. The distinctiveness of flexible specialization as a style of analysis can best be appreciated by examining the way in which its theoretical architecture builds upwards from simple ideal types to a complex and multileveled system of concepts applicable to a diverse range of empirical cases.[2]

The central building block of this approach is its distinction between mass production and craft production or flexible specialization as technological paradigms, ideal-typical models or visions of industrial efficiency. *Mass production* for these purposes can be defined as the manufacture of standardized products in high volumes using special-purpose machinery and predominately unskilled labor. *Craft production* or *flexible specialization,* conversely, can be defined as the manufacture of a wide and changing array of customized products using flexible, general-purpose machinery and skilled, adaptable workers.[3]

Neither mass production nor flexible specialization on this view is inherently superior to the other. Each model is theoretically capable of generating a virtuous circle of productivity improvement and economic growth. Under mass production, subdivided labor and dedicated equipment can reduce unit costs through economies of scale, extending the market for standardized goods, and facilitating new investments in special-purpose technologies, which further reduce costs, extend the market and so on. Under flexible specialization, conversely, versatile labor and universal equipment can reduce the cost of customization through economies of scope, extending the market for differentiated goods, and facilitating new investments in flexible technologies, which narrow the price premium for customized products, extend the market, and so on. But the practical realization of either possibility depends on a contingent and variable framework of institutional regulation at the microlevel of the firm or region and the macrolevel of the national and international economy. Hence the technological dynamism of each model and its potential for sustained development cannot be evaluated outside of definite institutional and environmental contexts. Thus just as there may be technologically innovative forms of both mass and craft production, so too are there stagnant variants of each model in which firms compete through squeezing wages, working conditions, and product quality, practices as common in large, declining enterprises as in small sweatshops.

The structural properties of each technological paradigm define a set of micro- and macroregulatory problems whose resolution is crucial for their long-term economic success.[4] In each case, however, similar problems may be solved in different ways, and a plurality of institutional frameworks can therefore be observed within both mass production and flexible specialization alike. For mass production, the crucial microregulatory problem is that of balancing supply with demand in individual markets: coordinating the flow of specialized inputs through the interdependent phases of production and distribution, and matching the output of productive resources that cannot easily be turned to other uses with the normal level of demand for each good. But as Piore and Sabel argue in *The Second Industrial Divide* (1984), these common goals may be pursued through a range of individual strategies, such as market segmentation, inventory variation, and superficial product differentiation, while the institutional framework provided by the large, hierarchical corporation likewise varies considerably both within and across national economies. Thus the organization of mass production firms in the United States, West Germany, and Japan, to choose some notable examples, differs significantly along key dimensions such as levels of administrative centralization and vertical integration, relationships with financial institutions, and systems of shop floor control.

For flexible specialization, by contrast, the crucial microregulatory problem is that of sustaining the innovative recombination of resources by balancing cooperation and competition among productive units. Two major types of institutional framework may be identified for the performance of these functions: "industrial districts" of small and medium-sized firms, and large, decentralized companies or groups. In the industrial districts, geographically localized networks of firms subcontract to one another and share a range of common services that are beyond the capacity of individual enterprises to provide for themselves, such as training, research, market forecasting, credit, and quality control. Successful districts are also typically characterized by collective systems of conflict resolution that encourage firms to compete through innovation in products and processes rather than through sweated wages and conditions. Within any particular district, however, there may be substantial differences in the roles played by specific institutions, from trade or employers' associations and cooperative banks or credit unions to trade unions, churches, and local government; and the political complexion may also vary sharply from "red" regions such as Tuscany or Emilia to "white" ones such as the Veneto or Baden-Württemberg.

In large, decentralized companies, on the other hand, the relatively autonomous productive units often resemble small, specialized firms or craft workshops, while obtaining services such as research, marketing, and finance from other divisions of the parent enterprise. As in the case of mass production corporations, however, large, flexible firms may also differ significantly from one another – for example, in their relationship to banks or trade unions – depending on their individual histories and the national institutional context. There are signs, too, that the extended period of volatility in international markets since the mid-1970s is giving rise to what Sabel calls a "double convergence" of large and small firm structures, as small firms in the industrial districts build wider forms of common services often inspired by large firm models, while the large firms themselves increasingly seek to recreate among their subsidiaries and subcontractors the collaborative relationships characteristic of the industrial districts.[5]

As the Great Depression of the 1930s demonstrated, the market stabilization strategies of large corporations by themselves could not solve the central regulatory problem of mass production: how to ensure a continuing balance between consumption and production across the national economy in order to amortize lumpy investments in product-specific equipment. While the Keynesian welfare state emerged as the dominant form of macroregulation during the postwar period, here too the differences among national economies remained striking: differences, for example, in the methods of managing budgetary aggregates, in the commitment to countercyclical deficit finance and public welfare provision, and in the role of collective bargaining agreements and other "private" means for relating purchasing power to productivity growth. Like mass production itself, Keynesian macroregulation was as much a project as an accomplished fact, and nowhere was this more true than at the international level. Despite Keynes's own postwar proposals, no effective institutional mechanisms were created to ensure a steady expansion of global demand in line with productive capacity or recycle purchasing power from surplus to debtor countries in the world economy.

If the macroregulatory requirements of mass production are relatively well-defined, those of flexible specialization remain the least developed aspect of the model. Thus Piore and Sabel argued that the superior capacity of flexibly specialized firms to accommodate changes in the level and composition of demand makes macroregulation less vital than in mass production, giving the price mechanism a greater role in equilibrating supply and demand than in the nineteenth-century competitive economy. But Piore and Sabel also emphasized the microregulatory need for such an economy to take wages out of competition and maintain welfare services in order to avoid debilitating breakdowns of solidarity among economic actors, distinguishing possible low- and high-consumption variants of a flexible specialization regime through the contrasting images of Bourbon Naples and a Proudhonian artisan republic.

More recently, Sabel has developed these ideas by treating macroeconomic regulation as a problem of reinsurance. Whereas for mass production, the key problem is that of reinsuring firms against unpredictable fluctuations in the level of demand through macroeconomic management, the problem for flexible specialization is that of reinsuring regional economies against large-scale shifts in its composition by establishing interregional mechanisms to facilitate structural adjustment. On this basis, in turn, he distinguishes two possible futures for the welfare state under a regime of flexible specialization:

- An exclusive or dualist variant in which regional economies increasingly opt out of the national welfare state while remaining vulnerable to unpredictable external shocks as well as to disruption from those left outside the system.
- An inclusive variant which would integrate firms and industrial districts into national systems of training and reinsurance, extend flexible specialization to less successful regions and social groups, and build on existing trends towards the decentralization of the welfare state itself.[6]

A final macroregulatory issue concerns the implications of flexible specialization for the international division of labor. In *The Second Industrial Divide,* Piore and Sabel suggested that one possible scenario might be the emergence of new forms of interdependence in the world economy, as mass production migrated to underdeveloped countries, while advanced economies increasingly shifted over to flexible specialization. Under these conditions, the First and Third Worlds might also come to share a common interest in a new institutional framework of multinational Keynesianism to regulate world demand and ensure macroeconomic stability (Piore and Sabel, 1984: 279–80). But flexible specialization might also be conceived as an alternative development strategy for parts of the Third World itself. Such a strategy might build on existing forms of small-scale enterprise concentrated in the substantial "informal" sectors of many developing economies, and it might also build on the unavoidable flexibility of preexisting forms of mass production imposed by the constraints of narrow markets and shortages of appropriate skills and materials. Either way, flexible specialization might offer an attractive route to economic development for such countries in which "appropriate technologies" were not necessarily inferior and modern forms of industrial organization could more easily be adapted to local conditions.[7] Like any development strategy for the Third World, flexible specialization would clearly be advanced by the creation of effective mechanisms of international macroeconomic coordination, but unlike mass production it could also be successfully pursued under the more likely conditions of continued volatility in the world economy. Which of these possible worlds may in fact be realized, and to what extent, like the institutional frameworks or micro- and macroregulation, cannot be derived from flexible specialization as an abstract model, but depends instead on the outcome of strategic choices and political struggles.

From this account it should be clear that flexible specialization is at once a general theoretical approach to the analysis of industrial change, and a specific model of productive organization whose micro- and macroregulatory requirements may be satisfied through a variety of institutional forms. But in no sense can this general approach be understood as an evolutionary teleology in which the triumph of flexible specialization as a specific model is a necessary consequence of some immanent logic of economic or technological development. Much of the debate over flexible specialization has in fact missed the mark by construing the latter as a similar type of theory to post-Fordism in its many variants.

Contrary to what many critics have supposed, for example, mass production and flexible specialization are ideal-typical models rather than empirical generalizations or descriptive hypotheses about individual firms, sectors, or national economies.[8] As the original formulations made clear, neither model could ever be wholly predominant in time or space. Thus mass production requires a continuing role for skilled workers and craft production both inside and outside the large firm, to design, set up, and maintain special-purpose machinery on the one hand and to manufacture goods for which demand is too small or unstable to justify investments in dedicated equipment on the other. Conversely, some standardization of intermediate goods and components is a necessary condition for the flexible manufacture of diversified final products.[9] Hence the persistence of firms, sectors, and even whole national economies organized on alternative principles does not in itself undercut the notion of a dominant technological paradigm in any given period.

At a deeper level, moreover, the analytical distinction between mass production and flexible specialization is also compatible with the empirical finding that hybrid forms of productive organization are the rule rather than the exception. As historical research conducted within this framework shows, firms in most countries and periods deliberately mix elements of mass production and craft or flexible production because they are acutely aware of the dangers involved in choosing an unalloyed form of either model. Thus economic actors' understanding of the pure models paradoxically leads them to hedge against risks in ways that blur the lines between them. The resulting interpenetration of elements of flexible and mass production also means that firms often find it easier to shift strategies from one pole to another than an abstract consideration of the two models might lead one to expect.[10]

Contrary to another widespread misconception, therefore, flexible specialization is neither a technological nor a market determinism.[11] Just as trajectories of technological development in this approach are shaped by competing visions of production, so too are patterns of demand shaped by competing visions of consumption. Thus, for example, the realization of either virtuous circle between investment, productivity, and the extension of the market depends not only on the creation of an appropriate institutional framework but also on the relative success of flexible and mass producers in persuading consumers to accept or reject a price premium for differentiated goods over their standardized counterparts. This dynamic interaction between production and consumption means that the flexible specialization approach regards market structures not as fixed parameters that impose a uniquely appropriate form of conduct on economic actors, but rather as contingent historical constructs that reflect the competitive strategies of the actors themselves. Hence, for example, current trends towards the diffusion of flexible specialization as a productive strategy result not only from the pervasive volatility of demand but also from the conscious efforts of firms organized along these lines – most notably in Japan – to fragment the mass market still further through the constant introduction of new specialty products.[12]

While flexible specialization strategies may be pursued within a plurality of productive and institutional forms, the range of variation is neither infinite nor arbitrary. Thus, for example, the regulatory requirements of flexible specialization are incompatible with a neoliberal regime of unregulated markets and cut-throat competition. In each of its institutional forms, flexible specialization depends for its long-term success on an irreducible minimum of trust and cooperation among economic actors, both between managers and workers within the firm and between firms and their external subcontractors. And as we have already noted, such cooperation depends in turn on the establishment of rules limiting certain forms of competition such as sweated wages and conditions, as well as on collective institutions for the supply of nonmarket inputs such as technological information or trained labor. Hence flexible specialization should not be conflated with opposed conceptions of "flexibility" as labor market deregulation that have become common currency not only among businesspeople, policy makers, and trade unionists, but also among post-Fordists and their critics.[13]

If flexible specialization depends on trust and cooperation, finally, this does not imply the absence of any conflict. On the contrary, flexible specialization, like any system of production, is prone to potentially debilitating conflicts among economic actors, not only between employers and workers, but also between firms and their subcontractors or subsidiaries. The reproduction of social consensus within these systems, though it may build on formative experiences in the past, can only be sustained in the longer term through the creation of institutional mechanisms for the resolution of disputes whose operation is broadly satisfactory to all the parties concerned. While the maintenance of consensus is always provisional and contingent, so too is the crystallization of particular conflicts into durable antagonisms between social groups: Neither outcome is predetermined by flexible specialization as a technological paradigm without reference to a definite social and institutional context. For flexible specialization, unlike post-Fordism and its Marxist antecedents, social and political identities cannot be derived from the structure of production through the ascription of objective interests to abstract categories or classes of actor; therein lies another fundamental difference between these two contrasting approaches.

FROM THEORY TO EVIDENCE

The flexible specialization approach takes its start from a criticism of social theories that assume that society is a "totality," a set of relationships governed by a single general principle and consistent in their character with such a principle. It also entails the criticism that such theories frequently presume a process of necessary social development or evolution based on certain fundamental "tendencies" operative in such a totality.[14] These criticisms apply to both Marxist and non-Marxist general sociological theories alike. Flexible specialization emphasizes the contingency and complexity of the connections between social relations, it insists on the distinctiveness of the national and regional routes to the establishment of such connections between social relations, it recognizes the crucial role of strategy and bodies of ideas in constructing such routes, and it is aware that things could have been otherwise. It is therefore alert to the specific conditions producing certain outcomes and to the possible coexistence of several distinct sorts of outcomes. The variety of possible outcomes that can be constructed from the basic ideal-typical concepts of flexible specialization is therefore considerable and each establishes a different relation between concepts, constructed social objects, and type of evidence that will demonstrate whether or not the social outcomes connected to such objects are operable.

To illustrate this complexity we shall outline three kinds of relation between theory and evidence in flexible specialization.

First, flexible specialization can be used in a mode we call the normative-empirical. Flexible specialization emphasizes that each social "world" contains a number of possibilities. A prevalent technological paradigm and the typical modes of social organization connected to it arises for a complex variety of factors, and has predominance over other possible outcomes for reasons that fall far short of social-structural or historical logics or necessities. This means that we must be alert to competing strategies and assess outcomes in terms that do not predetermine which of them will prevail. Hence the attention given to historical alternatives to mass production and the search for other reasons for the saliency of mass production strategies than an assumption of their inherent efficiency due to economies of scale.[15] Part of the role of evidence here consists in showing that other alternatives were possible, that they coexisted with the dominant paradigm, and that they offer distinct routes to innovation and change should the specific complex of conditions favoring the dominant paradigm cease to apply.

Thus flexible specialization is concerned to rewrite history in order to show that the complexity of the past helps us to recognize that there are a variety of options in the present. The relation of theory and evidence in such historical work is complex. In particular such claims cannot be refuted by pointing to the importance of mass production; rather they depend crucially on the conditions under which it came to prevail and national and regional variations in the forms of mass production strategies themselves. The same complexity of evidence about the coexistence and possibility of a number of worlds relates to present debates as well. Part of the role of theory is to identify certain instances or cases of progressive flexible specialization strategies, to show that such things are socially possible, and to investigate whether they can be generalized given appropriate policy commitments and satisfactory conditions. If flexible specialization strategies are possible, if their conditions are not too difficult to satisfy, and if certain of their policy consequences and social outcomes are attractive from a certain normative standpoint, then the role of evidence here is to serve as a support for advocacy and a means of generalizing the process of learning from certain national, regional, or enterprise experiences.[16] Simply showing that flexible specialization strategies have not been generalized, that they exist only in certain cases, and that they do not exist in a pure ideal-typical but in a hybrid form thus does not constitute a refutation of flexible specialization as advocacy. All the advocate of flexible specialization as a normative approach has to do is to show that such strategies are possible and that they can be expanded beyond given cases, even if in a hybrid form. Thus much of the "empirical" criticism of flexible specialization analysis is beside the point, since the use of such concepts is not confined to the hypothesis that flexible specialization is the prevailing or generalized mode of manufacturing organization.

Second, flexible specialization serves as a positive heuristic. Thus flexible specialization theory includes a battery of concepts drawing attention to a number of distinct ideal-types of production systems, progressive and stagnant variants of the same, possible forms of hybridization, and also ways in which these various forms can be combined in large and small companies, as well as in national and regional economies. The result is a very large range of possible situations and complex cases, a wide variety of types of hypotheses. Thus it will not do to select one of these types of hypotheses and seek to "refute" it without reference to the others. This is a common failing of the critical literature, which tends to operate as if flexible specialization were a theory that gives necessary prominence to small firms over large ones, or that supposes that the industrial district based on small firms is the sole or major form of flexible production. The ideal-type is not to be taken as an empirical generalization, and therefore it should not be treated as if it consisted in a proposition that the majority of firms in a given national economy would conform to its features. Moreover, the simple ideal-type is just a part in a more complex and multilayered process of theorization. This process emphasizes the importance of social context, the complexity of coexisting strategies and structures of manufacturing, the contingent nature of their conditions of existence, and the variety of possible outcomes. Flexible specialization cannot be reduced to a few simple hypotheses. At the same time, this theoretical complexity is not the result of ad hoc argumentation and incoherence.

Third, flexible specialization serves as a negative heuristic. Flexible specialization is a theory about the nature of manufacturing as a form of social organization. Even if flexible specialization were not widespread, the concept would still be valuable. For the analysis of mass production and its conditions of existence could not remain the same, and the specific social routes to its generalization as a paradigm and the variant forms of its institutionalization would gain in saliency as against traditional claims that mass production prevailed because of technological necessities and economies of scale. Flexible specialization is thus not merely an hypothesis about one type of production but is part of a much wider theory about production systems in general and their sociopolitical conditions of existence.

Given this complex and multiple relationship between theory and evidence, the central problem for flexible specialization is not to demonstrate the truth or falsity of its basic concepts, since these are explicitly conceived as ideal-types instead of real forces operating behind the observable phenomena themselves. The appropriate criterion for the assessment of such ideal-types is not their truth value but rather their heuristic productivity: How far does the conceptual framework of flexible specialization illuminate observable processes of industrial change? As we have seen in previous sections, flexible specialization as a general theoretical approach is compatible with a broad spectrum of possible forms of productive organization – including the continued predominance of mass production. But a hypothesis whose validity does depend on empirical evidence is whether – as much of the literature argues – current manufacturing practice is moving in the direction of flexible specialization as a specific model of productive organization, taking account both of the plurality of institutional forms within which it may be pursued and of the possibilities of hybridization.

What sort of evidence might permit us to test this hypothesis? Both macro- and microlevels of analysis are in principle relevant. At the macrolevel, one would ideally like to establish statistical indicators of cross-sectional variations and changes over time in the distribution of different forms of production across industrial sectors, national economies, and the international economy as a whole. Thus one would need large-scale data about such issues as:

- Product diversification (number of distinct products manufactured, rate of introduction of new models, average batch size).
- Productive flexibility (costs of product changeover, nature of equipment used, minimum efficient scale of operation).
- Workforce versatility (skill composition, job content, training).
- Interfirm relationships (extent and nature of subcontracting, reliance on collective services).
- Geographical agglomeration of economic activity.

But there are good reasons, both practical and theoretical, why reliable macro data of this type are likely to be difficult if not impossible to obtain. The first arises from the nature of the available industrial statistics. Like all official statistics, the classification systems used by industrial censuses in different countries reflect particular sets of theoretical assumptions and administrative practices. Thus as Storper and Harrison rightly point out, national statistical accounts cannot be used to analyze the operation of real input-output systems or industrial sectors "since they tend to classify whole firms or establishments according to their 'principal' activities" (Storper and Harrison, 1991). And even within these limitations, as Luria has shown, there are fundamental difficulties in measuring intertemporal variations in product diversity because of widespread inconsistency in classification, frequent code changes, and suppression of data to protect proprietary information (Luria, 1990). The more rapid the rate of product diversification, moreover, the more serious these difficulties become, since earlier classifications become obsolete more quickly and incommensurability of data from different periods increases.

For many of the other empirical questions thrown up by the flexible specialization hypothesis such as product batch sizes, workforce versatility, or patterns of subcontracting, little large-scale data is available because official statistics have not been compiled with these issues in mind.[17] But even were industrial census classifications rewritten with an eye to flexible specialization, significant conceptual problems would still remain in the interpretation of such evidence. The key issue is the context and strategy dependence of each element of a productive system within the flexible specialization approach. Each industrial branch or sector, for example, has its own specific market and technological characteristics against which any particular indicator must be assessed. Thus a given product batch size will have a different significance in, say, clothing, steel, or automobiles, and there is no obvious way to aggregate such data across the economy as a whole. At a deeper level, moreover, the same component or practice may have a different significance depending on its place in the broader strategy of the individual firm: Thus as a substantial body of research has demonstrated the same equipment, such as numerically controlled machine tools or flexible manufacturing systems, can be used in contrasting ways in different national and industrial settings.[18] Similarly, even the most determined mass producer may be obliged to manufacture some specialty lines in small batches, while the best-selling lines of a successful flexible specialist may likewise be turned out in significant volumes.

For all these reasons, such macrolevel indicators can only provide a suggestive guide to broad trends in industrial reorganization rather than a definitive test of the flexible specialization hypothesis. The preferred form of evidentialization for flexible specialization is instead the analytical case study conducted at the microlevel of particular firms, regional economies, or industrial sectors. Only detailed case studies permit the close attention to context and strategy that is the hallmark of a flexible specialization approach; and only this method makes possible the comparative analysis of relationships between forms of production and institutional frameworks that is central to its theoretical architecture.[19]

Two major problems arise from this strategy of evidentialization through case studies: interpretation and representativeness. As we have already noted, most firms or regional economies characteristically combine elements from both flexible and mass production rather than embodying pure examples of either model. How then can one assess the precise balance between the two models in any given case from the standpoint of the flexible specialization hypothesis? In principle, the solution might appear to lie in a search for objective indicators of flexible specialization such as those discussed at the macrolevel which could more successfully be applied to less heterogeneous micro data. Considerable mileage can undoubtedly be obtained through this route in documenting the spread of flexible specialization, as a number of suggestive studies have indicated.[20] In practice, however, the conceptual problems raised by such indicators remain the same: Their precise meaning in any case cannot be determined without reference to the strategies of the actors concerned. Hence the case study method necessarily entails an ineradicable element of subjective interpretation, in which there is considerable scope for legitimate disagreement among different observers. But if there is an unavoidable degree of indeterminacy about the interpretation of case study evidence, this does not mean that there is no valid basis for discriminating among competing views, contrary to what current fashions in literary theory might appear to suggest.[21] Competing interpretations, like competing theories more generally, can properly be ranked in terms of their plausibility in accounting for agreed features of a common body of evidence according to internally consistent criteria.

These considerations can be illustrated more fully through a brief examination of current debates about the nature of Japanese manufacturing practices. How far can the success of Japanese firms be properly interpreted as evidence of the diffusion of flexible specialization, and how far instead as evidence of the development of increased flexibility within mass production itself? At one level, as Sayer points out, this question may be considered largely semantic, since there is considerable agreement among apparently conflicting interpretations about key features of the Japanese system: the rapid pace of model renewal and new product development; the productive flexibility obtained through organizational innovations such as just-in-time component supply, quick die changes, or mixed model assembly lines; the prevalence of job rotation, teamworking, and other forms of functional flexibility among large sections of the labor force; and the importance of "relational subcontracting" between large and small firms.[22] At another level, however, this question is crucially important, given the centrality of Japanese manufacturing to the characterization of current trends in competitive strategy and productive organization in the international economy.

Some differences between the two interpretations are based on a misspecification of the opposed view: Thus it is no objection to the flexible specialization hypothesis properly understood to emphasize the continued role of large firms in Japan, nor the high overall volume of different products manufactured within the same firm or plant. Others arise from the results of new empirical research, such as David Friedman's (1988) demonstration of the limited role of MITI and the importance of small firm industrial districts in the development of key Japanese export industries such as machine tools. But many differences of interpretation arise from ambiguities in Japanese industry itself. There can be little doubt that most Japanese innovations in sectors such as automobiles or consumer electronics originated in domestic firms' adaptation of mass production methods to local conditions during their postwar drive to catch up with the West.[23] And important features of more recent Japanese practice can still be legitimately interpreted in this light, from the limited range of variation on certain models and the long production runs of key components through the continued importance of hard automation and the relatively narrow skills required for many jobs to the dominance of large firms over their subcontractors. But there are also signs that many Japanese manufacturers are pushing these innovations in a more radical dimension in order to trade on their competitive advantage in catering for fragmented markets and volatile demand. Thus leading firms in these sectors appear to be dramatically increasing the pace of product innovation, expanding the range of distinct models that can be manufactured with a given combination of workers and machinery, and devolving responsibility not only for component supply but also for final assembly and product development to suppliers whom they often encourage to work for other manufacturers as well. Such strategies may not lead Japanese manufacturers to converge on a pure model of flexible specialization, but, like many Western experiments at industrial reorganization, they have already progressed too far to fit comfortably into an alternative conception of neo-Fordism or flexible mass production.[24]

But even if it were agreed that particular cases could legitimately be interpreted as examples of flexible specialization, a significant problem of representativeness would still remain. As Sabel himself remarks, "for example is not a proof" (Sabel, 1989a: 23), and no quantity of case studies, however convincing, could demonstrate the validity of the broader flexible specialization hypothesis. In the absence of a comprehensive macrolevel map of the relative importance of competing models of productive organization, this difficulty may appear insuperable. But the Japanese case just discussed suggests an alternative strategy — common to most approaches to the analysis of industrial change — of focusing on those national economies, regions, and firms that have proved most successful in the current phase of international competition. Beyond Japan itself, for example, flexible specialization analyses have concentrated on regions such as Emilia-Romagna and Baden-Württemberg whose technological dynamism, export, competitiveness, and importance to the national economy are relatively well documented.[25] Other analyses, conversely, have concentrated on countries such as Britain in which flexible specialization has been weakly developed, highlighting its role in explaining their poor performance in manufacturing competition during the 1980s.[26] In either case, finally, the claim is not that international competition imposes a single form of productive organization on economic actors, given the plurality of institutional frameworks and the possibilities of hybridization, but rather that tendencies can be observed towards the displacement of mass production by flexible specialization as the dominant technological paradigm of the late twentieth century.

ENDNOTES

1. In a longer version of this paper, we contrast systematically the theoretical architecture, strategies of evidentialization, and policy implications of flexible specialization with those of regulation theory and other post-Fordist analyses (see Hirst and Zeitlin, 1991).

2. This exposition is based primarily on Piore and Sabel (1984), Sabel and Zeitlin (1985), Sabel (1989a), and Sabel (1990).

3. It will be evident that this definition of flexible specialization as a form of craft production entails a revaluation of the conventional stereotype of the latter as the manufacture of luxury goods in tiny volumes using hand tools and obsolete methods. The historical basis for a more positive interpretation of the technological dynamism of craft production is presented in Sabel and Zeitlin (1985). For a related approach that seeks to distinguish between craft production and "diversified quality production" on the basis of the volumes involved, see Streeck (1987, 1991) and Sorge and Streeck (1988).

4. As Piore and Sabel acknowledge (1984: 4–5), their notion of regulatory requirements of the technological paradigm is borrowed from the French regulation school, but used in very different ways.

5. For fuller discussions of the reorganization of large corporations and the process of "double convergence," see Sabel (1989a), Sabel et al. (1989), and Sabel (1991). This process implies, as Sabel (1989b) observes, not only that corporate operating units are coming to resemble the constituent elements of the industrial districts, but also that there are increasing numbers of exchanges and alliances between large-firm subsidiaries and their small-firm counterparts in the districts themselves.

6. For an extended account of these ideas, see Sabel (1989a: 53–9) and Sabel (1989b); and for the potential role of a reorganized labor movement in the transformation of the welfare state, see Kern and Sabel (1991).

7. For a fuller account of flexible specialization as a development strategy, see Sabel (1986); and for a thoughtful critical discussion, see Schmitz (1989). For an extended attempt to apply this approach to the problems of a small semi-developed economy on the European periphery, see Murray (1987).

8. Cf. Williams et al. (1987), Pollert (1988), Wood (1989). For an insightful discussion of the critical debates surrounding flexible specialization, see Badham and Mathews (1989).

9. Piore and Sabel (1984: 26–28, 219, 279–80), Sabel and Zeitlin (1985: 137–38), and Sabel (1989: 40).

10. These arguments draw on the work of the international working group on Historical Alternatives to Mass Production, sponsored by the Maison des Sciences de l'Homme in Paris. See Sabel and Zeitlin (1997); and for a discussion of contemporary problems of technological hybridization, see Sabel (1991).

11. Cf., for example, Elam (1990). Thus flexible specialization is not, among other things, an optimistic general theory of the labor process: cf. Thompson (1989: 218–29) and Wood (1989).

12. Piore and Sabel (1984: 261–63), Sabel (1989a: 37–40), Sabel et al. (1990), and Sabel (1991).

13. Cf. especially Pollert (1988).

14. See, for example, the theoretical arguments in Sabel (1982).

15. See Sabel and Zeitlin (1985, 1997).

16. Good examples of such normative-empirical advocacy using flexible specialization concepts are found in Mathews (1989a, 1989b).

17. For an ingenious but ultimately unsatisfying attempt to use existing data to test the flexible specialization hypothesis for the U.S. manufacturing industry, see Luria (1990). Thus, for example, Luria uses share of value added in manufacturing output (VA/M) as an indicator of product batch sizes, on the assumption that VA/M rises proportionately as batch sizes fall, and explores its relationship with labor productivity (value added per employee) for SIC industries over the past two decades. But there may be many reasons for an industry to be characterized by a high VA/M ratio besides small batch production, while the use of this indicator also depends on the absence of any significant shift in the relative productivity of small and large batch production, the very question to be examined.

18. See, inter alia, Sorge et al. (1983), Jones (1982, 1989), Maurice et al. (1986), and Adler (1989).

19. For a selection of case studies written from a flexible specialization perspective, see Best (1989), Brusco and Sabel (1981), Friedman (1988), Herrigel (1989), Hirst and Zeitlin (1989b), Katz and Sabel (1985), Lorenz (1989), Lyberaki (1988), Michelsons (1987, 1989), Piore and Sabel (1983), Regini and Sabel (1989), Sabel (1986, 1989a), Sabel and Zeitlin (1997), Sabel et al. (1989), Storper (1989), Tolliday and Zeitlin (1986), and Zeitlin and Totterdill (1989). The major statements of the flexible specialization approach, such as Piore and Sabel (1984), Sabel and Zeitlin (1985), and Sabel (1989), are all built up from a comparative analysis of such case studies.

20. See Michelsons (1987), Storper and Christopherson (1987), Christopherson and Storper (1989), Storper and Salais (1992).

21. For a discussion of current debates about the interpretation of texts in the history of political ideas, see Tully (1988).

22. Compare, for example, Piore and Sabel (1984), Tolliday and Zeitlin (1986), Friedman (1988), and Sabel (1989) with Williams et al. (1987), Wood (1988), Sayer (1986, 1989), and Kenney and Florida (1988, 1989).

23. For a major case study, see Cusumano (1985).

24. See Tolliday and Zeitlin (1986), Sabel (1989, 37–39), Regini and Sabel (1989: 33–44), Sabel et al. (1989b), and Sabel (1991). But cf. also Sayer (1989: 685–89), and Kenney and Florida (1988, 1989).

25. On Emilia-Romagna and the "Third Italy" more broadly, see, in English, Brusco (1982), Sabel (1982: 220–26), Piore and Sabel (1983), Zeitlin (1989b), Goodman et al. (1989), Pyke et al. (1990). Contrasting interpretations can be found in Murray (1987) and Amin (1989). On Baden-Württemberg, see Sabel et al. (1989) and Herrigel (1989). For a more general debate on the interpretation of regional case studies in relation to the flexible specialization hypothesis, see Amin and Robins (1990) and the responses by Michael Piore, Charles Sabel, and Michael Storper in Pyke et al. (1990: 220–37).

26. See Hirst and Zeitlin (1989a and b) and Lane (1988). Attempts to use predominately British evidence to criticize the flexible specialization hypothesis therefore badly miss the mark: see, for example, Pollert (1988).

BIBLIOGRAPHY

Adler, Paul and Brian Borys. 1989. "Automation and Skill: Three Generations of Research on the NC Case." *Politics and Society.* 17 (3): 353–76.

Amin, Ash. 1989. "Flexible Specialisation and Small Firms in Italy: Myths and Realities." *Antipode.* 21 (1): 13–34.

Amin, Ash and Kevin Robins. 1990. "Industrial Districts and Regional Development: Limits and Possibilities." In Pyke et al. 1990. Pp. 185–219.

Badham, Richard and John Mathews. 1989. "The New Production Systems Debate." *Labour & Industry.* (2) 2: 194–246.

Bagnasco, Arnaldo. 1988. *La costruzione sociale del mercato.* Bologna: Il Mulino.

Best, M. 1989. "Sector Strategies and Industrial Policy: The Furniture Industry and the Greater London Enterprise Board." In Paul Hirst and Jonathan Zeitlin, eds. *Reversing Industrial Decline? Industrial Structure and Policies in Britain and her Competitors.* Oxford: Berg/NewYork: St. Martins. Pp. 191–222.

Brusco, Sebastiano. 1982. "The Emilian Model: Productive Decentralization and Social Integration." *Cambridge Journal of Economics.* 6: 2, 167–84.

Christopherson, Susan and Michael Storper. 1989. "The Effects of Flexible Specialization on Industrial Politics and the Labor Market: The Motion Picture Industry." *Industrial and Labor Relations Review.* 42 (3): 331–47.

Cusumano, Michael. 1985. *The Japanese Automobile Industry.* Cambridge: Harvard University Press.

Elam, Mark. 1990. "Puzzling out the Post-Fordist Debate: Technology, Markets and Institutions." *Economic and Industrial Democracy.* 11 (1): 9–37.

Friedman, David. 1988. *The Misunderstood Miracle: Industrial Development and Political Change in Japan.* Ithaca: Cornell University Press.

Goodman, Edward and Julia Bamford with Peter Saynor, eds. 1989. *Small Firms and Industrial Districts in Italy.* London: Routledge.

Herrigel, Gary. 1989. "Industrial Order and the Politics of Industrial Change: Mechanical Engineering." In Peter Katzenstein, ed. *Industry and Political Change in West Germany: Towards the Third Republic.* Ithaca: Cornell University Press. Pp. 185–220.

Hirst, Paul and Jonathan Zeitlin, eds. 1989a. *Reversing Industrial Decline? Industrial Structure and Policies in Britain and her Competitors.* Oxford: Berg/New York: St. Martins

Hirst, Paul and Jonathan Zeitlin. 1989b. "Flexible Specialization and the Competitive Failure of UK Manufacturing." *Political Quarterly.* 60 (3): 164–78.

1991. "Flexible Specialization Versus Post-Fordism: Theory, Evidence and Political Implications." *Economy and Society.* 20 (1): 1–55.

Hyman, Richard and Wolfgang Streeck, eds. 1988. *New Technology and Industrial Relations.* Oxford: Basil Blackwell.

Jones, Bryn. 1982. "Destruction or Redistribution of Engineering Skills? The Case of Numerical Control." In Stephen Wood, ed. *The Degradation of Work?* London: Hutchinson. Pp. 179–200.

1989. "Flexible Automation and Factory Politics: Britain in Comparative Perspective." In Hirst and Zeitlin 1989a. Pp. 95–121.

Katz, Harry and Charles Sabel. 1985. "Industrial Relations and Industrial Adjustment in the Car Industry." *Industrial Relations.* 24 (3): 295–315.

Kenney, Martin and Richard Florida. 1988. "Beyond Mass Production: Production and the Labor Process in Japan." *Politics and Society.* 16 (1): 121–58.

1989. "Japan's Role in a Post-Fordist Age." *Futures.* 21 (2): 136–51.

Kern, Horst and Charles Sabel. 1991. "Trade Unions and Decentralized Production: A Sketch of Strategic Problems in the West German Labor Movement." *Politics and Society.* 19 (4): 373–402.

Lane, Chrystel. 1988. "Industrial Change in Europe: The Pursuit of Flexible Specialisation in Britain and West Germany." *Work, Employment and Society.* 2 (2): 141–68.

Lorenz, Edward. 1989. "The Search for Flexibility: Subcontracting Networks in French and British Engineering." In Hirst and Zeitlin 1989a. Pp. 122–32.

Luria, Dan. 1990. "Automation, Markets and Scale: Can 'Flexible Niching' Modernize American Manufacturing?" *International Review of Applied Economics.* 4: 127–65.

Lyberaki, Antigone. 1988. "Small Firms and Flexible Specialisation in Greek Industry." Ph.D. thesis, University of Sussex.

Mathews, John. 1989a. *Tools of Change: New Technology and the Democratization of Work.* Sydney: Pluto Press.

1989b. *Age of Democracy: The Politics of Post-Fordism.* Melbourne: Oxford University Press Australia.

Maurice, Marc, François Eyraud, Alain d'Iribarne, and Frédérique Rychener. 1986. *Des enterprises en mutation dans la crise: Apprentissage de technologies flexibles et emergence de nouveaux acteurs.* Aix-en-Provence: Laboratoire d'Économie et de Sociologie du Travail.

Michelsons, Angelo. 1987. "Turin Between Fordism and Flexible Specialization: Industrial Structure and Social Change, 1970–85." Ph.D. thesis, University of Cambridge.

1989. "Local Strategies of Industrial Restructuring and the Changing Relations between Large and Small Firms in Contemporary Italy: The Case of Fiat Auto and Olivetti." In Zeitlin 1989a. Pp. 425–47.

Murray, Feargus. 1987. "Flexible Specialisation in the 'Third Italy.'" *Capital and Class.* 33: 84–95.

Murray, Robin, ed. 1987. *The Cyprus Industrial Strategy: Report of the UNDP/UNIDO Mission,* 8 vols. Institute of Development Studies, University of Sussex.

Piore, Michael and Charles Sabel. 1983. "Italian Small Business Development: Lessons for U.S. Industrial Policy." In John Zysman and Laura Tyson, eds. *American Industry in International Competition.* Ithaca: Cornell University Press. Pp. 391–421.

1984. *The Second Industrial Divide: Possibilities for Prosperity.* New York: Basic Books.

Pollert, Anna. 1988. "Dismantling Flexibility." *Capital and Class.* 34: 42–75.

Pyke, Frank, Giacomo Becattini, and Werner Sengenberger, eds. 1990. *Industrial Districts and Inter-firm Co-operation in Italy.* Geneva: International Institute for Labour Studies.

Regini, Marino and Charles Sabel. 1989. *Strategie di riaggustimento industriale.* Bologna: Il Mulino.

Sabel, Charles. 1982. *Work and Politics: The Division of Labour in Industry.* Cambridge: Cambridge University Press.

1986. "Changing Models of Economic Efficiency and their Implication for Industrialization in the Third World." In Alejandro Foxley, Michael McPherson, and Guillermo O'Donnell, eds. *Development, Democracy and the Art of Trespassing: Essays in Honor of Albert O. Hirschman.* Notre Dame: Notre Dame University Press. Pp. 27–55.

1989a. "Flexible Specialisation and the Re-emergence of Regional Economies." In Hirst and Zeitlin 1989a. Pp. 17–70.

1989b. "Equity and Efficiency in the Federal Welfare State." Unpublished paper presented to the Nordic Working Group on the New Welfare State, Copenhagen, August 8.

1990. "Studied Trust: Building New Forms of Cooperation in a Volatile Economy." Paper presented to the conference on Industrial Districts and Local Industrial Regeneration. International Institute for Labour Studies, Geneva, October 19–20.

1991. "Moebius-Strip Organizations and Open Labor Markets: Some Consequences of the Reintegration of Conception and Execution in a Volatile Economy." In James Coleman and Pierre Bourdieu, eds. *Social Theory for a Changing Society.* Boulder: Westview Press. Pp. 23–63.

Sabel, Charles and Jonathan Zeitlin. 1985. "Historical Alternatives to Mass Production: Politics, Markets and Technology in Nineteenth-Century Industrialization." *Past and Present.* 108: 133–76.

Sabel, Charles and Jonathan Zeitlin, eds. 1997. *Worlds of Possibility: Flexibility and Mass Production in Western Industrialization.* Cambridge: Cambridge University Press/Editions de la Maison des Sciences de l'Homme.

Sabel, Charles, Gary Herrigel, Richard Deeg, and Richard Kazis. 1989. "Regional Prosperities Compared: Massachusetts and Baden-Württemberg in the 1980s." In Zeitlin, 1989a. Pp. 374–404.

Sabel, Charles, Horst Kern, and Gary Herrigel. 1990. "Collaborative Manufacturing: New Supplier Relations in the Automobile Industry and the Redefinition of the Industrial Corporation." In H. G. Mendius and U. Wendling-Schroeder, eds. *Zulieferer im Netz: Zwischen Abhängigkeit und Partnerschaft.* Cologne: Bund Verlag. Pp. 203–27.

Sayer, Andrew. 1986. "New Developments in Manufacturing: The Just-in-Time System." *Capital and Class.* 30: 43–72.

1989. "Post-Fordism in Question." *International Journal of Urban and Regional Research.* 13 (4): 666–93.

Schmitz, Hubert. 1989. "Flexible Specialisation – A New Paradigm of Small-Scale Industrialisation?" *Institute of Development Studies Discussion Paper.* No. 261, University of Sussex.

Sorge, Arndt, G. Hartmann, Malcolm Warner, and Ian Nicholas. 1983. *Microelectronics and Manpower in Manufacturing.* Aldershot: Gower.

Sorge, Arndt and Wolfgang Streeck. 1988. "Industrial Relations and Technical Change: The Case for an Extended Perspective." In Hyman and Streeck, 1988. Pp. 19–47.

Storper, Michael. 1989. "The Transition to Flexible Specialization in the US Film Industry: The Division of Labour, External Economies and the Crossing of Industrial Divides." *Cambridge Journal of Economics.* 13 (2): 273–305.

Storper, Michael and Susan Christopherson. 1987. "Flexible Specialization and Regional Industrial Agglomerations: The Case of the US Motion Picture Industry." *Annals of the Association of American Geographers.* 77 (1): 104–17.

Storper, Michael and Bennett Harrison. 1991. "Flexibility, Hierarchy and Regional Development: The Changing Structure of Industrial Production Systems and their Forms of Governance in the 1990s." *Research Policy.* 20: 407–22.

Storper, Michael and Robert Salais. 1992. "The Division of Labour and Industrial Diversity: Flexibility and Mass Production in the French Automobile Industry." *International Review of Applied Economics.* 6 (1): 1–37.

Streeck, Wolfgang. 1987. "Industrial Change and Industrial Relations in the Motor Industry: An International View." *Economic and Industrial Democracy.* 8 (4): 437–62.

1991. "The Social Conditions of Diversified Quality Production." In Egon Matzner and Wolfgang Streeck, eds. *Beyond Keynesianism: The Socio-Economics of Production and Full Employment.* Aldershot: Gower. Pp. 21–61.

Thompson, Paul, Jr. 1989. *The Nature of Work: An Introduction to Debates on the Labour Process,* 2nd ed. London: Macmillan.

Tolliday, Steven and Jonathan Zeitlin, eds. 1986. *The Automobile Industry and Its Workers: Between Fordism and Flexibility.* Cambridge: Polity Press/New York: St. Martins.

Trigilia, Carlo. 1986. *Grandi partiti e piccole imprese.* Bologna: Il Mulino.

Tully, James, ed. 1988. *Meaning and Context: Quentin Skinner and his Critics.* Cambridge: Polity.

Williams, Karel, Tony Cutler, John Williams, and Colin Haslam. 1987. "The End of Mass Production?" *Economy and Society.* 16 (3): 404–38.

Wood, Stephen. 1988. "Between Fordism and Flexibility?: The Case of the US Car Industry." In Hyman and Streeck, 1988. Pp. 101–27.

Wood, Stephen, ed. 1989. *The Transformation of Work.* London: Unwin Hyman.

Zeitlin, Jonathan, ed. 1989a. "Local Industrial Strategies." Special issue of *Economy and Society.* 18 (4).

Zeitlin, Jonathan. 1989b. "Italy's Success Story: Small Firms with Big-Firm Capability." *QED: Quarterly Enterprise Digest.* October: 5–9.

1992. "Industrial Districts and Local Economic Regeneration: Comments and Overview." In Frank Pyke and Werner Sengenberger, eds. *Industrial Districts and Local Industrial Regeneration.* Geneva: International Institute for Labour Studies. Pp. 279–94.

and Peter Totterdill. 1989. "Markets Technology and Local Intervention: The Care of Clothing." In Paul Hirst and Jonathan Zeitlin, eds. *Reversing Industrial Decline: Industrial Structure and Policies in Britain and her Competitors.* Oxford: Berg/New York: St. Martins. Pp. 155–190.

8

GLOBALIZATION, VARIETY, AND MASS PRODUCTION: THE METAMORPHOSIS OF MASS PRODUCTION IN THE NEW COMPETITIVE AGE

Benjamin Coriat

INTRODUCTION

In the last fifteen years, there have been many theoretical efforts to explain the breaking down of the old Fordist model of accumulation. Thus, it is not our intent to review the many causes which explain the erosion of this model.[1] In this paper, we choose to focus on new social institutions that are emerging from the breakdown of the Fordist model, and to focus on the "transition" towards new institutional configurations of "post-Fordism." We are concerned with new patterns and industrial routines at the level of both intra- and interfirm relationships. By doing this, we hope to contribute to the understanding of the embeddedness of institutions in modern capitalism.

In our judgment, there are two determinants of crucial importance to understand the transitory period in which we are living. These two determinants, largely interdependent and interrelated, are, on the one hand, the process of "globalization" and, on the other, an ongoing technological and organizational revolution. These two determinants are crucial, for they contribute to eroding and destroying the classical forms of production and principles of efficiency of the old Fordist model, and as they push societies toward

240

the adaptation of new institutional configurations. In this sense, these two determinants contribute to the new "post-Fordist" regime(s) of accumulation.

To explore these aspects of the transitory regime towards post-Fordism, we concentrate on several interrelated issues. Considering the process of the internationalization of capital in the long run and the technological and organizational revolution, the first question addressed by this paper is how and for what reason does it matter whether we have a precise definition of globalization, and a correct evaluation of its meaning for production issues? In other words, what do globalization and the revolution in production management mean for firms and industries in terms of new requirements and opportunities for competitiveness? The first section of the chapter is dedicated to these issues.[2]

Having provided some evidence on the direction driven by the process of adaptation to the new constraints, we then turn to a more abstract level. The question then is how to define and characterize the new regime of production emerging from the adaptation to globalization. Based on data and finds from ongoing research on the restructuring of the auto industry and presented as a typical sector for mass production techniques, the central hypothesis put forward by this paper is that a new regime of production is emerging in advanced capitalist societies. In contrast to the previous regime, the characteristics of the emerging regime are based on a set of new institutional routines and protocols specifically designed to face the constraints of variety. Thus, variety is posed as the main challenge driving the metamorphosis of mass production arrangements. The second section focuses on this as a general characterization of this new regime of production.

The paper then explores and analyzes several dimensions of the basic constitution of the new regime. The third section presents some of the new trends in the relations between suppliers and subcontractors, and analyzes the content of the contractual relationships between firms operating inside the same industry. The fourth section focuses on some of the most innovative protocols in the field of production management, recently implemented inside the auto industry to face the just-in-time requirements driven by the regime of variety. Finally, there is a short conclusion.

"GLOBALIZATION" AND ITS MEANING FOR PRODUCTION ISSUES: IDENTIFYING THE NEW CHALLENGES

If there is a strong agreement within the scientific community that "globalization" as an idea is something important to both firms and industries, one must nevertheless admit that the meaning of the word "globalization" remains elusive, and that it has not received a full and accepted definition. So despite the thousands of articles about globalization within the last several years, it is nevertheless useful for our discussion to put forward our own definition – a definition designed to include both production and industry issues. The idea of globalization should first be defined by distinguishing it from the code word of an earlier era, internationalization.

GLOBALIZATION "VERSUS" INTERNATIONALIZATION: TOWARD A USEFUL DEFINITION

In practice, internationalization has historically had two components. The first was the spread across national borders of a single dominant style of production – mass production. Essentially, this style consisted of American Fordist methods with more or less marginal adaptations to local conditions, typically under the sway of American-based multinationals. Second, internationalization contained mirror-like responses to this kind of production process by foreign-based competitors. The diffusion was slow, but, since it was mainly confined to Europe, a good deal of the lag in response time can be legitimately attributed to a range of factors. These include disruptions of war, chaos, and depression, as well as a generally slower rate of diffusion of organization, product, and technology innovation. Globalization, by contrast, can be characterized by the existence of a multiplicity of innovative methods that originate in a variety of places in the world. Both directly impact on national producers.

Continuing with stylized facts, internationalization could be characterized by the typical configuration of one basic innovator and a set of followers, thus fitting traditional diffusion models rather well. While internationalization generated intense competitive pressures for national producers, it generated major dislocations and reorganizations for governments. However, it did not generate much in the way of uncertainty. For many countries (including the main countries of Europe and Japan) in the postwar period, the task was to catch up with the future, not invent it. By contrast, globalization today is characterized by heightened uncertainty as well as intense new competitive pressures, which come from rival innovators located in all parts of the world. Competition has become multidimensional, with emphasis on price, quality, speed of production, and product differentiation. In the organization of production, heightened economies of scale, scope, and propinquity appear to be one side of the coin. On the other side, we find clear indications of the competitive power of worldwide sourcing, diseconomies of organization scale, and the rise of many new productive arrangements trying to take advantage of economies of scope, and different combinations of flexible organization. The uncertainty inherent in the process of globalization is not just confined to firms in a few particular sectors, but extends across a broad swatch of sectors. It extends most to the very heart of national economic policy: What should a nation do (and not do) to improve its wealth of power, with national responses varying as much as firm responses?

One can observe that the link among these competing visions of globalization is rooted in a common observation: the end of mass production – Fordist production – as the ascendant and dominant mode of production organization. The definition of globalization that emerges from these considerations must give consideration to rival innovators operating in multiple dimensions from at least several national bases in a more open world market – the result of which heightens competition and, critically, uncertainty.

GLOBALIZATION AND THE ENVIRONMENT OF THE FIRMS: THE NEW COMPETITIVE CHALLENGES

As firms have struggled to adapt, they have focused on a variety of key operational elements. Each element is an adventure in its own right, and an experiment with new forms of corporate strategy and organization. Start with any particular element, and you will find yourself in the broader story. For example, product variety and business speed have become critical. Today, competitive position increasingly rests on a firm's ability to differentiate and adapt its products, to do so rapidly in response to demand changes, and to anticipate such changes so as to identify and occupy lucrative market niches. To accomplish this, automobile firms (under the pressure of the Japanese) have sought to shorten their product cycles drastically. In the auto industry, for example, product life cycles have dropped from ten to four years. The need for flexibility and speed has compelled firms to modernize and substantially revitalize their commercial operations and marketing methods. Firms now find that it has become necessary to have much closer proximity to the market, to clients' needs and demands. This kind of marketing need has affected production in unexpected ways. Except for a few specific market segments where mass production of undifferentiated products remains viable, in most cases firms must be able to address constantly changing demands for shorter series of products.

The choices are certainly technological, but, as we will see, they are much more organizational ones. Thus, telecommunication networks enter the very heart of the production process as they transmit, often in real time, the information needed to program equipment and match actual production to the orders received.[3] Firms certainly can draw upon a variety of new technological tools, from NC machine tools to very sophisticated CAD/CAM systems. But what do they do with them and how do they use them? In previous works, I have heavily argued that the ongoing organizational revolution is much more important than any other consideration (Coriat, 1990, 1991a, 1992).

The range of new manufacturing arrangements (beginning with the various implementation of just-in-time methods), new logistics know-how (e.g., autonomous production islands linked through new parts circulation schemes), group technology, and stock management methods collectively provide firms with a substantially rejuvenated and enriched reservoir of methods to organize work and production.[4] The relationships between headquarters and subsidiaries, and those with partners and subcontractors have similarly been reorganized. In short, the basic principle behind the new forms of interaction is to retain the economic advantages of integration, while decentralizing activities, in order to lower fixed costs and better share the cost of innovation as a means of facing variety and uncertainty. Thus, the combination of internal organizational innovations with new kinds of external links has led firms towards new and varied social "network" forms,[5] which are integral parts of their competitive drive and their adaptation to the environmental changes just described.

These constraints boil down to one essential challenge: Can firms create relative advantages and establish long-term competitiveness by developing the capacity to combine economies of scale and economies of scope, mass production, and differentiated products in new organizations? For our purposes, what matters is that all of these things call for a new art of manufacturing and production.

The sections that follow are devoted to the series of questions that we have just posed. By using the results of ongoing research on the recent restructuring that has affected the relationships among agents in the automobile industry,[6] the analysis demonstrates how a new production regime is emerging as rising new constraints confront firms. This new regime, as it gets stronger, is increasingly substituting itself for the previous Fordist regime, which was long organized along the principles of mass production.

VARIETY AND MASS PRODUCTION: CHARACTERIZING THE NEW EMERGING REGIME

THE ORDER OF VARIETY

Many changes in the firm's environment can be linked to the emergence of a general constraint of variety, which is the central determinant of the industrial reorganization concerning both "internal" methods of production management and the relationships that exist among firms in an industry. In this paper, the automobile industry is the sector of reference, and is discussed as the archetype of the sectors of mass production.

The present moment represents the passing of a regime of production centered and organized around the principles of specialization to a new one whose organizing logic is dictated by the constraints of variety. Confronted with supplier markets in which the capacity to move about in a universe organized around multiplicity has become both a condition of survival and a source of multiple advantages, automobile makers have progressively dealt with variety no longer as a simple "constraint" of the demand, but as the central axis of their production and supply strategies. The entire productive order has swung toward new forces and bases that have come into their own with the movement toward variety.

Approaches to Variety

From a strictly empirical viewpoint, the emergence of a regime of variety can be demonstrated with a few simple figures. The combined results of the multiplication of products that customers demand are more and more widely diversified and specified, as seen by the fact that the number of final specifications has increased from 322 in 1966 to more than 100,000 in 1978 (see Table 8-1).

Nowadays, it has become commonplace for a major automobile maker to be able to produce a hundred thousand or so variants for each basic model offered (e.g., the Peugeot 205 or the Toyota Corolla). For Peugeot, the result of this is that a particular model may have only a handful of the same variants in a given year (Coriat, 1993a). Of course, it is a relatively limited number of variants that ensure sales. However, auto firms today are benefiting enormously from the effects of mass production and repetition. Clearly, this production regime is different from the previous one in which "customers could choose the color of the car they wanted so long as it was black" – to recoin the well-known words of Henry Ford. From a conceptual point of view, the production regime that is required by this general change in the market and the behavior of suppliers is that of variety, and must be differentiated from the previous regime of specialization. Even though the demand for every variant is unequal, the productive structure is designed to satisfy each potential demand as much as possible. In order to produce such variety, the entire automobile industry has had to undergo a series of major transformations.

Features of the Regime of Variety

If variety is accepted as an ordinary regime, it strongly contradicts several principles of a "specialization economy" that preceded its existence, that

Table 8-1. Number of Toyota Crown Types Produced in 1966 and 1978: An Example of the Trend Toward Variety

Name of Item	The number of different kinds available as of April 1966	The number of different kinds available as of April 1978
Body type	2	4
Engine	2	4
Carburetor	2	2
Fuel to use	2	3
Transmission	3	7
Grade of luxury	4	8
Seat shape	2	5
Option	1	20
Color	14	13
Final specification of the vehicle	322	101,088

Note: The number of orderable different final specifications of the vehicle is not equal to the number of all possible combinations of selectable items calculated by simple multiplication. This is because some combinations are not offered by the company.

Source: Jidosha Kogaku Zensho Henshu Iinkai (1980), as cited in ASANUMA (1989), p. 186.

brought about its dissolution, and that led to a new regime with new principles. They can be identified as follows:

1. *Variety is a regime of "virtual" production, based on the property of reactivity.* First, it is clear that variety demands not only flexibility and adaptability of a production structure, but also a rapid response to a large range of demands. Market time-span is not production time-span. Flexibility is useless unless its effective time-span lets it satisfy variety and its own order. Thus, in order to obtain variety, market time-span and production time-span must be brought closer together.

   In practice, the growth of variety and its corollary, reactivity, both induce production rationalization. Two important new lines of rationalization are opened up by the new economy of time that comes from variety. The first concerns stock and work in process economy. The second concerns quality.

2. *Variety is a regime of zero inventory and just-in-time production.* The passing over to a permanent regime of variety can be done only at the ex-

pense of reducing work in process and every type of stock. It is out of
the question to stock the supplies necessary for the manufacturing of
hundreds of thousands of variants that consist only of pure virtual demands. Variants get their true existence, and are only an object for a
manufacturer, when the customer demands a particular product. In
this sense, the regime of variety can only be that of a just-in-time production system. To exist in variety means to react only in a very short
time period. To exist in variety is not only to exist without stock, but
also to be able to produce the item demanded just-in-time. Thus, as
we shall see, this property of variety creates an upheaval in the relationships among the car makers/contractors and their suppliers and
subcontractors.

3. *Variety means a regime of original and better quality.* In its turn, production
   "without stock" means a leap forward in the quality of the finished
   product as an intermediary asset. Even though market time schedules
   have to be respected without stock, the manufactured products must
   still be faultless. Even though the security net of stock has disappeared,
   production must nevertheless leap forward with respect to quality.
   Thus, a regime of variety necessarily means a regime of better quality,
   and this characteristic becomes a central element in defining the relationship between contractors and subcontractors. In practice, the emergence of a regime of variety is part and function of the assembler's decision to set up drastic procedures of selection for subcontractors,
   especially when quality criteria are decisive. These procedures are carried out by following finely and precisely codified protocols that are reflected in the concept of "supplier quality assurance."

Variety as a Permanent Regime Is a Regime of Supply

We have previously focused on considerations of demand in an effort to
understand variety. But as we study the regime of variety as a new permanent regime, we must also analyze it as a regime of supply. Even if the consumer appears to be king, with the possibility of choosing among hundreds
of thousands of variants of one particular model, we must not forget that the
firm chooses to offer this possibility. It is the firm that chooses to put itself
into a situation of virtual variety that gives existence to the regime itself.
Even though such a choice was made by firms, paradoxically, the transition
to a regime of virtual supply becomes a means of limiting the commercial
and financial risks that accompany every act of production. In a situation of
quasipermanent innovation, of unpredictability of product life, and of shorter product life cycles, firms encounter certain advantages as they make the
transition to a regime of supply.

Entering into the regime of variety means entering into a series of new constraints that are linked to the general remolding of production routines. Production without stock and the tightening of the regime of quality means the transformation to forms of internal organization and to modes of inter-firm coordination that were quite unknown hitherto. Virtual variety means a policy of design that can both shorten a product's life cycle and can develop the product in order to meet the potential demands for hundreds of thousands of virtual variants.

Many observers characterize this new production system as a transition stage, whereby a regime of variety is well on its way, but where the actors try, whenever possible, to continue to use the routines of the previous specialized production economy. The outcome is a subtle game of balance of power by which different actors try to protect their traditional routines. In this game, it is obvious that assembler contractors have more weight, and can impose rules that are more favorable to themselves than their partners, component makers, or their agents.

PLACE AND ROLE: THREE KEY CHANGES BROUGHT ABOUT BY THE TRANSITION TO VARIETY

The Place of the Market and the New Role of Distributors and Agents

The first change is the one that concerns the place of the marketplace in the global production cycle of the industry. In a specialized economy, the market constituted the departure point for sparking off the whole of the manufacturing cycle. It is indeed from customer orders (notably those that come from the dealers) that the core of the production cycle is put into motion. Information finds its way to the manufacturer, and the firm then starts the manufacturing process. From that point, production and delivery orders go to subcontractors and suppliers. The exchange of information between the dealers – who have a direct relationship with the market – and the car manufacturer thus plays a decisive role in parenting and planning the exchange of products at the core of the industry. The quality of the exchange of information between agents – often backed up by information networks – plays a decisive role in influencing the general efficiency of the system.

In practice, each industrial actor tries not to be subjected to the direct and permanent dictatorship of the market and its risks. Thus the dealer is not reduced to the simple role of order processor. Obliged by the manufacturer to buy a certain quantity of each of its models, the dealer will try to influence the customer's choice in order to sell them. As a result, agents find themselves in a situation where they have to absorb part of the risk in order to give the car manufacturer's production cycle a minimum of regularity and predictability.

Subcontractors and suppliers are subject to highly variable delivery schedules – from one to two hours to several days – depending on the type of part and component they produce. Thus, subcontractors try to defend themselves against the excesses of unpredictability by using different techniques. One consists of having strategic stocks and reserves to ensure the continuity of supplies over and above the unknown factors of orders that are sent to them by their contractors.

The Place of the Final Assembly Plant

The second change is that the final assembly plant no longer resembles the Fordist picture of a "long river with its converging tributaries." As the point of final assembly has a direct relationship to the market, it has become a "nerve center" of production operations. From now on, the point of final assembly receives and distributes essential information. It becomes a sort of "revolving point," as much for information flows as for merchandise flows. Receiving and redirecting orders to the point of final assembly, telecommunication networks play an essential part in ensuring the workings of the regime of variety.

The New Role of Subcontracting

The subcontractor is visibly and profoundly affected by the transition to variety in three different ways. At the most visible level, the subcontractor is put into a situation where it is necessary to operate completely "reactively" with respect to the demands of the order giver, and deliver "just-in-time" the components that have been requested. Even if the "time" considered is a variable (hour, day, week) and even if the stocks held in reserve can help in certain cases against the excesses of variety, a new order nevertheless demands a refocusing of routines.

A second consequence involves the quality of supplies. If the car maker produces without stocks held in inventory, all supplies from the subcontractor must be usable in the finished product and delivered in the just-in-time mode. Under these conditions, the subcontractor is subjected to the pressure of producing high quality products in a very short period of time. Thus, the regime has complex and harsh protocols about quality, which affect the relationships between contractors and subcontractors.

The third consequence of variety is a gradual but steady transformation by subcontractors passing from the status of ordinary suppliers who simply manufacture components to that of designers of component makers.

VARIETY, DIVISION OF LABOR INSIDE THE INDUSTRY, AND NETWORKING: THE BUILDING OF NEW ROUTINES

Having exposed the wider characteristics of the change to variety, the analysis now explores the ways in which protocol and production routines have been modified.

Under the joint impulse of variety and globalization, automobile groups as early as the 1980s took new directions concerning production strategies. At least three of these directions were essential, for they introduced a series of crucial changes in the relationships among suppliers who were at the origins of new routines. This meant that the manufacturers frequently sought to reduce the number of suppliers, by forcing them to merge with one another. The pursuit of high volume output and its consequences on the economy of scale, costs, and delivery prices were basic motivating factors in generating the pressures for the merger of suppliers and subcontractors. As the number of subcontractors declines, an extremely rigorous process of quality upgrading is established, but the burden of generating higher volume tends to fall on the subcontractor. Moreover, the subcontractor becomes more involved in the overall design of all the subunits of the automobile, thus acquiring a technical capacity on R&D issues.

REDUCTION IN THE NUMBER OF SUPPLIERS AND TENDENCIES TOWARD CONCENTRATION AND MULTINATIONALIZATION

This process came to its climax at the end of the 1980s, though it presently continues. In 1980, Peugeot had approximately 2,000 direct suppliers for mass produced parts. In 1988, this figure was halved, and in recent years the process has even increased. In July 1990, there were no more than 770 official suppliers (a fall of 21.8 percent in two years). And the aim was to reach a figure of about 650 suppliers by the end of 1994. For the other automobile manufacturers operating in France (Renault and Ford), the tendency was essentially the same.

The most remarkable aspect of this movement was the decisive part played by the manufacturers. Even if the most important component makers followed their own strategies, manufacturers were particularly active in accelerating the process of merger. First, the weight of their intervention was most visible in a series of assessment procedures called "Quality Assurance," which allowed them to give (or to take back) the approval that led to the production of component parts in the first place. By this means, and sometimes by more direct financial intervention, they favored regrouping on criteria that were specific to them and that were aimed at several objectives. Two of these were to keep at least two suppliers by product type to maintain the principle of competition among suppliers, and not to risk being subjected to the effects of abusive monopolization. In practice, most subcontractor mergers meant that manufacturers increased their profits by imposing lower prices on subcontractors.

Meanwhile, this process was designed to ensure that suppliers took on an international dimension as production became more global. Thus, regrouped suppliers had to aspire at least to a European dimension and not be simply local firms. Indeed, the expectation has been that suppliers would become European leaders in their respective areas of competence. Thus, they must not only be established on a national and an international basis, but also near the manufacturers' assembly plants. This condition is linked to the new "synchronous" production techniques of just-in-time delivery. The suppliers who survived the selection process have tended to have at least 25 percent of their productive sites situated abroad near the manufacturers' foreign sites. In the process of becoming more concentrated, French manufacturers have tended to favor French or at least European concentrations, in order not to be dependent on non-European groups. This criterion is linked to the idea that information should not leak to networks over which the manufacturer has no control.

QUALITY SELECTION

A second direction in manufacturer–supplier relationships was connected with a general redevelopment in quality criteria. In 1987, various French groups set up a common reference system of Supplier Quality Assurance, which elaborated a five-stage protocol.

- The first stage consisted of a procedure for determining the attitude of the supplier toward quality, after a minute inspection of the subcontractors' production units.
- The second stage centered around suppliers' improvement of the handling of the production process. Help was eventually offered by the manufacturer through various types of know-how transfers.
- In the third stage, suppliers' first samples were accepted by the manufacturer.
- The fourth stage was a decisive one, and permitted the supplier to enter into the Product Quality Assurance (QPA) circle. A supplier who

reached this stage retained entire responsibility for the quality of the products. Thus, following the "quality charter" that governs relationships among firms in the automobile industry, "the QPA marked the beginning of an approach toward a permanent improvement of quality."
  • The fifth stage represented a continual assessment of the quality performance of the supplied products, whereby demerits were received if delivery did not conform to the QPA contract.

Firms were assessed right from the first stage, and they were given grades (from A to D). In practice, only those suppliers were retained who had grades of A. Adaptation time-spans were set up to allow suppliers receiving grades of B to become A graded firms. In practice, B firms had two years to meet A standards. This rigorous process of selection rapidly established severe selection effects.

Quality is appreciated in its wider sense, as it includes criteria of time-span and reactivity. These are understood to represent a rapid response capacity to unforeseeable demand from contractors.

An essential criteria for an A grade is to be capable of product development and to develop the QPA approach when acting alone. Essential criteria for suppliers to be selected were not only to meet high quality standards, but also to have high organizational and technical capacity in matters of design.

REACTIVITY AND TECHNICAL CAPACITY IN PRODUCT DEVELOPMENT

Once assembly line plants select a supplier on the basis of quality auditing, they become very loyal to the supplier. The outcome is a series of requirements and complementary constraints that the supplier must possess. In practice this assumes that the supplier has the organizational capacity to provide the "rapid change of tools" that is required by tight flow production techniques.

Parallel to organizational capacity is the technical capacity to participate in the design of products. The objective here is to make certain that any delay in the design of certain elements of subunits does not interfere with the launching of new products. This method has required the establishment of a permanent innovation group made up of manufacturers and suppliers that functions as an innovation bank. In this way, management is able to follow projects from the onset of the design through the launching of production.

PRODUCING VARIETY IN "REAL TIME": THE NEW PROTOCOLS FOR MASS PRODUCTION

The growth of the regime of variety brings about an increase in diverse forms of production because of the acceptance of the idea that customer demand is primordial. They are carried out by a series of protocols and routines that have reshaped the entire relationships among the various actors at the core of the automobile industry. The following are the main principles of these new protocols.

A FIRST PRESENTATION OF THE NEW TECHNIQUES OF JUST-IN-TIME PROGRAMMING

Once the idea of manufacturing and delivering some 100,000 variants per model has been accepted, a revolution in the principles of manufacturing is underway. As far as possible, only variants that have actually been ordered and sold beforehand should be made, and the manufacturing process should be organized on this basis. The universe of just-in-time production, under the authority of the manufacturer and final assembler, necessarily becomes the reference universe for the agents of the industry.

In practice, "tight production flows" function under tensions that require the establishment of specific procedures. Procedures on the information exchange systems differ from those involving the preparation and launching of manufacturing and delivery techniques. Note that in certain cases temporal constraints can become special ones: The tighter the flow of products, the shorter the distance between actors. The result is that certain just-in-time procedures imply paradoxically a multiplication of stocking points and new sites. The result is new "mobile" logistics, built in a proximity compatible with the constraints involving supplier time.

The essential change brought about by just-in-time production is a new pacing of programming. From the information that comes from the manufacturers and that is destined for the subcontractors, everything is built on the principle of three series of temporality corresponding to shorter and shorter time spans. Each series of information and delivery instructions is more and more precise. In principle, the last instructions can consist of delivery orders consistent with strict just-in-time principles – with a time limit occasionally of less than one hour separating the delivery order from the actual delivery. But, in fact, everything happens in three phases.

- *Phase 1:* The contractor, on the basis of an analysis of customer orders, communicates monthly load plans to subcontractors. At this stage these load plans are still highly provisional, but they allow subcontractors to organize their own provisional plans of how to use workers and machines.
- *Phase 2:* Clearly defined programs are sent out on a weekly basis, corresponding to definite production orders. The subcontractors then commit themselves to production.
- *Phase 3:* Finally come demands for daily deliveries, following a schedule that varies from a delivery order of one day for the next product to only a few hours. On the basis of such a general principle, several just-in-time protocols are applied that correspond to a more or less strong subcontractor integration into the rhythms of the manufacturers' programming and production. This concerns the looped or synchronous production methods, the essential principles of which we now lay out.

SYNCHRONOUS PRODUCTION

This is the most demanding and rigorous method for the subcontractor and the one that, corresponding to strict just-in-time principles, fulfills the highest possible level of virtual integration of the subcontractor with the manufacturer. At this point, the protocols of information exchange and effective delivery are highly formalized and codified. Nothing is left to improvisation. It is also the technique in which telecommunication networks are the most systematically developed. Messages must be particularly speedy and reliable, and the information contained in them must be perfectly readable. The conditions for the application of this method are also very strict. Only large-volume parts are concerned (seats, exhaust pipes, tanks) or parts of great diversity (several dozen references for the same part). The risk factor of variety is thus carried by the supplier whose final and daily load plan is highly uncertain, both for quality and, sometimes, quantity.

In all strict just-in-time configurations, the subcontractor has to deliver the different parts in the exact order in which they will be assembled and deliver them to the assembly line at the exact moment when parts are needed. Because of this, geographical proximity is a prerequisite, for the manufacturer has no stocks of supplies. The parts are delivered directly to the assembly line. For this reason, this method of production is also called "looped," since the subcontractor is perfectly integrated into the manufacturer's production cycle. This type of looped production at Peugeot presently makes up about 15 to 20 percent of the total volume of subcontracted supplies, which is a remarkably high percentage considering the very demanding nature of these techniques.

As soon as the automobile is in a phase of its production when the next required part can be forecast, a requisition order is sent to the appropriate supplier who can then begin its production. The supplier firm then knows exactly when it will intervene and the order in which it can introduce the variety of its subassembly parts into the more global assembly of the manufacturing process. In practice, and in a very short interval, two distinct messages are sent to the supplier. The first is sparked by a camera that is linked to an electronic system of information transmission. As soon as a given section in the manufacture of the automobile is picked up by the camera, a message to go into production is automatically sent to the supplier. The second message, which deals with the effective delivery order, is sent out moments after, once the theoretical cycle has been checked. If any unknown factors have occurred, the message then integrates them.

In such a regime of synchronous flow production, the supplier must start up and function according to a definite delivery plan. The supplier's plan must include the means to anticipate and absorb the solution to all types of unknown factors that could arise, since final assembly cannot be subjected to some form of disfunctioning. Should this occur, the suppliers are attributed demerit points according to QPA conventions.

THE SPARTE METHOD

The SPARTE method, or "system of rationalized supply," is a very strict variant of just-in-time principles, and is based on a principle of coordinated, quick-selling automobile production. Citroen has used this method for a number of years, particularly at Rennes.

The principle applied is that of "consumer anticipation." In practice, everything functions in the following way: Definite manufacturing orders for six days are sent to suppliers on a daily basis on teleinformation networks. These orders are brought up to date and clarified every day, and are then transformed into delivery orders which must be carried out at least on a daily basis and in the majority of cases several times per day.

The advantage of this method is that it allows the final assembler to function in "near synchrony" with suppliers, but it also allows the supplier firm the time for its production programming. The proximity of the supplier in this particular case is not an absolute prerequisite. This method, which offers almost the same advantages as synchrony, but is less restricting, is being used more and more. The SPARTE and Synchronous methods at the Citroen Rennes site make up some 45 percent of the plant's supplies.

RECOR OR KANBAN *DELIVERY*

The Recor method is a classic application of the initial Japanese *kanban* method and is now very well known. With this method, the suppliers work with reduced stock, and production start-up replenishes these stocks as they become the object of delivery to the automobile makers. The procedure follows the classic method of using tags and *kanban* boxes. When an empty box arrives, this is an order to set up production to replenish the stock that has just been delivered.

This method is suitable for the production of certain types of parts (e.g., door panels and certain mass produced small parts), but it is also seldom used. It has proved to be too restricting, allowing only limited economic profit. In the case of high variety in the products, the stocked quantities are a heavy burden on cost if the firm wants to have all the variant parts available.

SUMMING UP: VIRTUAL INTEGRATION AND ITS MODES OF COORDINATION

In conclusion, the discussion concentrates on several aspects of the regime of variety and focuses on the characteristics that set it apart from other forms of production that emerged following the Fordist system of production.

THE REGIME OF VARIETY AS A NEW PRODUCTION REGIME

The regime of varied mass production is a variant of post-Fordian production regimes. From the Fordist regime, it maintains the principle of high volume, but it emphasizes variety, a process that was previously unheard of.

Virtual Integration

First of all, these changes affect the entire industry. They are not intelligible if they are considered at the level of the individual firm. Variety and the virtual regime that it implies assume a new division of tasks and functions at the core of the entire industry. These processes take on several new characteristics.

- The tasks of interface and market approach are passed over to the agents, with the pacing coming from the orders they collect and then pass on to the car manufacturer. This is the key to the swing from the "pushed flow" Fordian principle of production organization toward a "pulled flow" principle of production. It is the agent's orders that transform virtuality into reality.

- The part that the final assembly plants play is modified and gains in importance. They are more than terminal "pouring out" points. Rather, they take on fine-tuning tasks of subcontractor management and of production flow management at the core of the industry.
- Finally, the subcontractors take on the task of the design of entire subunits.

Thus, the industry as a whole is built around the principle of a virtual network that requires separate firms to be much more intricately involved with each other than they could have been during the preceding production regime. Thus, the new regime has brought about a greater integration of relationships among firms, since the tasks and functions that were previously addressed inside a single firm are now thinned out and decentralized to other firms. We call this process "virtual integration."

Hierarchical Networks

These networks are built on the basis of hierarchical principles under the influence of the car manufacturer. This process pervades all the essential practices of the new regime. On the one hand, dealers are subjected to quota and price negotiation processes that leave them with little initiative and with small profit margins in the sale of new models. Nevertheless, they do gain more help and assistance from the car manufacturer. On the other hand, the suppliers are subjected to a very harsh process of selection that:

- Uses drastic criteria such as quality, reactivity, and design.
- Operates through an industrial restructuring process and strives towards a concentration and regrouping of the component makers.
- Moves the firms towards multinationalization.

This results from the fact that suppliers are selected on the basis of several criteria: economy of scale and price competition, the transferring of activity and a diminution of stock, delivery time schedules, and quality and economy of variety on the products manufactured.

Embodying Cooperation and Long-Term Contractual Relationships

The establishment of the protocols that establish a network of actors within the industry has its counterpart in tacit contracts for long-term orders. Thus, the result of the setting up of these new firms is a special partnership that operates by externalizing its functions while multiplying the bonds of dependency. In order to understand the relationships among the various actors, however, one must turn to the social relationships among firms that are essential for the building of a regime of variety.

VARIETY AND ITS SOCIAL FORMS OF PRODUCTION ORGANIZATION: "PARTNERSHIP" AND THE BUILDING OF "RELATIONAL RENTS" THROUGH NEW ROUTINES

In practice, two series of new routines are established with the breakthrough and strengthening of the regime of variety.

New Interfirm Routines

These routines concern interfirm relationships involving car manufacturers, their subcontractors, and component makers. The core of the network is established from certification procedures which were established by codifications that were part of AWF procedures. What is remarkable about these procedures is that at all stages there is the presence of a highly visible hand that substitutes itself for the market. This can be verified at the interfirm network formation stage, the stage of subcontractor selection, and during the functioning of the ordinary regime once the network has been established.

1. *Selection: administrative practice versus auction mechanisms.* The procedures used to establish the network do not follow the commercial procedures of "auctioning" the products to be made. The supplier network is based on the procedures of inspection, assessment, and certification. Practices of a cooperative nature permit those who do not initially satisfy the required certification criteria to improve their performance and to be admitted eventually into the network. Once a stable functioning regime has been established, demerits are directed against the subcontractor if flaws are found in the criteria of quality, reactivity, or scheduling. This overall process, of course, is quite distinct from traditional practices of market coordination.

2. *Cooperation.* Once subcontractors have been selected, they benefit from a relative guarantee of continuity concerning the orders that are sent to them. The explanation is that the establishment of just-in-time production modes corresponds to the establishment of minute, complex routines, and investment in the training of new subcontractors is heavy and costly. Thus, as far as possible, due weight must be given to the learning "apprenticeship effects" that result from the repetition of co-

operation between subcontractors and manufacturing firms. Of course, market procedures based on auction mechanisms are not completely eliminated, as car manufacturers attempt to maintain some competition among suppliers. Nevertheless, both in the selection procedure and in the functioning modes of a stable regime network, the coordination of firms both at the signing of contracts and at the implementation level is not that of the market.

In fact, "the partnership" is unusual in that it is made up of a very special mix of selection and cooperation. From a theoretical point of view this is governance by an administrative procedure and not by an auction procedure, even if, at the core of the network a principle of competition is maintained between the suppliers.

The substitution of administrative selection and cooperation principles for commercial forms of governance according to "auction logic" is neither accidental nor contingent. Indeed, if the regime of variety is a just-in-time and quality regime, a unity of codification and minute routine is a required substitute for auction procedures.

Intrafirm: Sequential versus "Dialogue" Model

If one examines intrafirm relationships, remarks of a similar nature can be made. The new routines consist of new modes of distribution of, access to, and sharing of information. This is an area defined by Arrow (1976) as nanoeconomics, and is characteristic of the new institutional microeconomy. The establishment of these new routines involving information management happened at the same time there was a change in organizational forms. Meantime, the traditional Fordist firm faded away to allow less hierarchical forms to emerge. Thus, the final assembly plant manages the subcontractor network in just-in-time production processes. In the Fordist division of work mode, this activity was under the exclusive monopoly of the group's purchasing department. Thus, the firm has swung from a sequential model to what Clark and Fujimoto (1989) have labeled a "dialogue" model.

Partnership and the Building and Sharing of a Relational Rent

This new partnership is a social procedure of building and sharing in long-term relationships. This is a regime of variety, and the constraints that go with it are too serious to be left in the hands of market arbitration. The establishment of routines and multiple procedures have bonded agents together with forms of coordination and arbitration that are essentially non-commerical. And these forms of coordination can be developed only through the building of complex social networks.

THE REGIME OF VARIETY VERSUS OTHER POST-FORDISTS SOCIAL FORMS OF PRODUCTION

Of course, varied mass production was not the only social form of production that emerged following the breakdown of traditional Fordism. There were forms of flexible specialization (Piore and Sabel, 1994) and the contrasting forms that Boyer and Coriat (1986) described as flexible mass production. In previous publications, I have tried to demonstrate that forms of "flexible specialization" center on economies of scope, while forms of industrial organization that emerge from flexible mass production attempt to gain economies of scale while pursuing some of the benefits provided by economies of scope (Coriat, 1991, 1992). Moreover, Streeck (1991), referring notably to the German example, focused on a regime that he described as diversified quality production, one that has much in common with flexible mass production.

Thus, where do we fit the regime of variety that we have just described? Two sets of propositions provide a model that reveals similarities to and differences from other forms of production.

Common Ground

On the one hand, the regime of variety, like all the other regimes previously described, is organized in such a way that it can confront both the flexibility of demand and strategies of differentiated supply. It also has the distinctive feature of being concerned with inter- as much as intrafirm relationships. Indeed, all the post-Fordist models involve different networks of actors implicated in the global cycle of product design and manufacturing.

What Is Different about the Regime of Variety?

First, this regime consists of a systematic pursuit of scale effects of mass production while taking on an exceptionally high level of product differentiation (the more than 100,000 variants discussed). Such a strategy involves not only the car makers but also the subcontractors and assemblers who are pressured into becoming bigger, more concentrated, and more multinational. The requirement for standardized elementary parts has demanded greater cooperation among firms as they jointly design and produce certain parts (carburetors, gear boxes, engines). In the case of Peugeot, the reference in this chapter, the two divisions of the group, Peugeot and Citroen, both in search of economies of scale, systematically "put their heads together" where parts supply was concerned. Thus, not only has the oligopolistic structure of the market remained tight but it has become even tighter because of the reinforced mutual cooperation between divisions within groups and because of the greater concentration of subcontractors and fitters.

A "variety regime" is a distinct application of the principle of dynamic flexibility in combining economies of scale and differentiation. In this respect, a variety regime clearly belongs to the family of flexible mass production models. From our point of view, however, it is a "specific variant" of these forms, as it pushes the concept variety to levels of analysis that were still beyond reach when the first hypotheses on flexible mass production were formulated.

The second particularity of this regime is the central part that "just-in-time" procedures and protocols play. As we have demonstrated, these procedures and protocols are part and parcel of variety, since it derives its force and coherence from just-in-time implementation. Enhanced performance is observed on all fronts: in part and model design time, thanks to simultaneous engineering methods, economy of means and stock, and economy of human capacity. And this is how Japanese production methods have made headway, going deeply into the heart of industry, changing its shape and protocols and eventually the general economy. Apart from national or sectorial differences in the ways and conditions in which these methods are established, various Japanese production methods bear a new general principle of production organization that will progressively be the successor to Taylorian and Fordian methods (Coriat, 1991a, 1992). Just-in-time methods have become a lever and a form of rationalization in production as powerful as was the principle of Taylor's "one best way" in its time.

Even if there is no doubt that the variety social system of production has enhanced profits and higher productivity, one should note that this kind of microeconomic progress is not parallel with equivalent progress at the macroeconomic level. It should not be forgotten that Fordism, while increasing profits from greater levels of productivity, had provided new ways of sharing profits in a social formula. Some of this was revealed in the Fordists regime of accumulation through forms of collective and connective bargaining (Coriat, 1990).

The present production revolution has nothing resembling this. If new strategies are not found that permit the sharing and spreading of gains in productivity throughout the economy, the new regime of variety runs the risk of being a regime of growth without employment or with decreasing employment. In other words, additional contractual agreements must develop alongside the regime of variety as a new regime of high productivity. Only if this condition is met can the production management of variety maintain its vitality and stability at a macroeconomic level. Unfortunately, we are still far from achieving such a goal. Thus, the prospects for long-term macroeconomic vitality and stability are not very good.

ENDNOTES

1. On this point, see Coriat (1990, 1992).
2. This section of the paper relies heavily on a paper that I wrote jointly with J. Zysman, S. Cohen, and other BRIE researchers (BRIE, 1989).
3. See Bar, Borrus, and Coriat (1989). On the same issue see Arrow (1976).
4. In Coriat (1990), I define three successive but interrelated "schools" in production organization (the first being the American school – based on the principles of Scientific Management – the second the (Swedish) "Socio-Technical" one, and the third being the Japanese). For the specific contributions of Taiichi Ohno and of the Japanese School, see Coriat (1991a), which is entirely dedicated to a comparison between the American and the Japanese schools of production management.
5. Elaborations on this theme of the network firm can be found in Thorelli (1986) and Antonelli (1988).
6. The main results of a comparative study between the French car maker Peugeot and General Motors are published in Coriat (1993a). In the following discussion, I shall draw heavily on these results. Gorgeu and Mathieu (1990, 1991) are very useful for empirical findings on recent mutations in the French auto industry.

REFERENCES

Aoki, M. 1988. *Informatin, Incentives, and Bargaining Structure in the Japanese Economy.* Cambridge: Cambridge University Press.
    1990. "Towards an Economic Theory of the Japanese Firm." *Journal of Economic Literature.* (March) XXVI.
Antonelli, C. 1988. *New Information Technology and Industrial Change: the Italian Case.* Dordrecht: Kluwer Academic Publishers.
Arrow, K. J. 1976. "Vertical Integration and Communication." *Bell Journal of Economics.* (Spring): 173–83.
Asanuma, B. 1988. "Transactional Structure of Parts Supply in the Japanese Automobile and Electric Machinery Industries: A Comparative Analysis." Working paper. Faculty of Economics, Kyoto University.
    1989. "Manufacturer–Supplier Relationships in Japan and the Concept of Relation Specific Skill." *Journal of the Japanese and International Economies.* (March) 3: 1–30.
Bailey, E. and A. Friedlander. 1982. "Market Structure and Multi-Product Industry." *Journal of Economic Literature.* September.
Bar, F., M. Borrus, and B. Coriat. 1989. "Information Networks and Competitive Advantage. Issues for Government Policies." OECD/BRIE Telecom Users. International Synthesis, final report. Published by the Commission of the European Community, Brussels.
Baumol, W., R. Panzar, and J. Willig. 1982. *Contestable Markets and the Theory of Industry Structure.* New York: Harcourt Brace Jovanovich.
Bounine, J. and S. Kiyoshi. 1986. *Produire juste à temps.* Paris: Masson.

Boyer, R. and B. Coriat. 1986. "Technical Flexibility and Macro-Stabilization." *Ricerche Economiche.* 4.

BRIE. 1989. "Globalization and Production." Working Paper, Berkeley Round-table on the International Economy, UCB.

Clark, K. G. and T. Fujimoto. 1989. "Product Development and Competitiveness." Paper Presented to the International Seminar on Science, Technology and Growth. OECD, April.

Cohen, S. and J. Zysman. 1987. *Manufacturing Matters.* New York: Basic Books.

Commissariat General du Plan. 1992. "L'Automobile, les défis et les hommes." Rapport du GSI "Automobile." La Documentation Française.

Coriat, B. 1990. *L'Atelier et le Robot − Essai sur le Fordisme et la production de masse à l'age de l'Electronique.* Paris: Christian Bourgeois Editeur.

1991a. *Penser à l'Envers − Travail et Organisation dans l'Entreprise japonaise.* Paris: Christian Bourgeois Editeur.

1991b. "Technical Flexibility and Mass Production: Flexible Specialisation versus Dynamic Flexibility." In G. Benko and M. Dumford, eds. *Industrial Change and Regional Development: The Transformation of the New Industrial Spaces.* London: Belhaven, Pinter Press Publishers. Pp. 134–158.

1992. "The Revitalization of Mass Production in the Computer Age." In M. Storper and A. Scott, eds. *Pathways to Industrialization and Regional Development.* London: Routledge.

1993a. "Variété, Informations et Réseaux dans la Production de Masse − Le cas de l'Industrie Automobile." Rapport Final de recherche AMES/MRT.

Coriat, B. and P. Petit. 1991. "De-industrialisation and Tertiarisation, Towards a New Growth Regime." In D. Amin and M. Dietrich, eds. *Towards a New Europe, Evolutionary Economic Association.* London: Edward Elgar Publisher. Pp. 18–45.

Dosi, G., C. Freeman, R. Nelson, G. Silverberg, and L. Soete. 1988. *Technical Change and Economic Theory.* London: Pinter Publishers.

Gorgeu, A. and R. Mathieu. 1990. "Partenaire ou sous-traitant?" Dossier de recherche no. 31, Paris: Centre d'Etudes de l'Emploi.

1991. "Les pratiques de livraison en juste a temps en France entre fournisseurs et constructeurs automobiles." Dossier. Paris: Centre d'Etudes de l'Emploi.

Klein, B. 1986. "Dynamic Competition and Productivity Advances." In Ralph Landau and N. Rosenberg, eds. *The Positive Sum Strategy: Harnessing Technology for Economic Growth.* Washington: National Academy Press. Pp. 77–88.

Menard, C. 1990. *L'Economie des organisations.* Paris: La Découverte.

Midler, C. 1991. "L'Apprentissage de la gestion par projet dans l'industrie automobile." *Réalités industrielles, Revue des Annales des Mines.* Octobre.

Nelson, R. and S. Winter, eds. 1982. *An Evolutionary Theory of Economic Change.* Cambridge: Harvard University Press.

Ohno, T. ed. 1989. *L'esprit Toyota.* Paris: Masson.

Piore, M., and C. Sabel. 1984. *The Second Industrial Divide.* New York: Basic Books.

Streeck, Wolfgang. 1991. "On the Institutional Conditions of Diversified Quality Productione." In Egon Matzner, Wolfgang Streeck, eds. *Beyond Keynesianism: The Socioeconomics of Production and Full-Employment.* Aldershot, Hants, England: Edward Elgar. Pp. 21–61.

Taddei, D. and B. Coriat, eds. 1993. *Made in France: L'Industrie française dans la compétition mondiale.* Paris: Livre de Poche, Hachette.

Thorelli. 1986. "Networks: Between Markets and Hierarchies." *Strategic Management Journal.* 7: 37–51.

Volle, M. and D. Henriet. 1987. "Services de télécommunication: intégration technique et différenciation économique." In *La Revue Economique: L'économie des télécommunications.* Mars.

Williamson, O. E. 1975. *Markets and Hierarchies.* New York: Free Press.

Womack, P. et al. 1990. *The Machine That Changed the World.* New York: MacMillan.

9

CONTINUITIES AND CHANGES IN SOCIAL SYSTEMS OF PRODUCTION: THE CASES OF JAPAN, GERMANY, AND THE UNITED STATES

J. Rogers Hollingsworth

In twentieth-century capitalism, there have been several changes in perceptions about the relative effectiveness of specific management styles and work organizations (Boyer, 1991; Chandler, 1962, 1977, 1990; Piore and Sabel, 1984; Sabel, 1982). Changes in technology, relative prices, and consumer preferences have been instrumental in altering the perception as to why one form of management style and work practice is superior and should supplant existing forms (North, 1990). Economic actors not only defend specific forms of management and work practices as means of achieving particular economic outcomes and performances (Marglin, 1991), but they also attempt to borrow from other societies what they consider to be "best practices."

This paper argues that forms of economic coordination and governance *cannot* easily be transferred from one society to another, for they are embedded in social systems of production distinctive to their particular society. Societies borrow selected principles of foreign management styles and work practices, but their effectiveness is generally limited. Economic performance is shaped by the entire social system of production in which firms are embedded and not simply by specific principles of particular management styles and work practices. Moreover, a society's social system of production tends to limit the kind of goods it can produce and with which it can compete successfully in international markets.

The chapter suggests, with empirical references to the Japanese, German, and American economies, that a society's social system of production is very path dependent and system specific. Because a society's modes of economic governance and coordination develop according to a particular logic and are system specific, the overall theme of the chapter is that there are serious limitations in the extent to which a society may mimic the forms of economic governance and performance of other societies. The focus of the chapter throughout is exclusively on manufacturing sectors.

SOCIAL SYSTEMS OF PRODUCTION: FURTHER CLARIFICATION AND TWO EXAMPLES

In recent years, some scholars (Florida and Kenney, 1991; Kenney and Florida, 1988, 1993; Oliver and Wilkinson, 1988) have assumed that the diffusion of particular forms of management styles and work practices across societies would lead to convergence in performance. However, the argument of this paper is that, even though British, French, and American firms may adopt certain aspects of Japanese management styles – e.g., just-in-time production complexes, self-managing teams, quality circles, the use of "statistical process controls" etc. – or some variant of the German vocational system, one should not conclude that their economies will be transformed. A nation's financial markets, educational system, industrial relations system, and other sociopolitical factors influence sectoral and national economic performance. In order to understand how and why a society's economy performs, it is necessary to understand its entire social system of production. If a society is to improve substantially the performance of its economy, it must do more than adopt some of the management and work practices of its foreign competitors. It must alter its entire social system of production.

In the history of modern capitalism, there is a logic by which institutions coalesce into a social system of production (Hollingsworth, 1991a, 1991b). This occurs – in part – because institutions are embedded in a culture in which their logic is symbolically grounded, organizationally structured, technically and materially constrained, politically defended, and historically shaped by specific rules and norms. Though institutions are constantly changing, there are sharp limits to the type and direction of change that any particular institution can undergo because of its linkages with other institutions. Thus, a society's business firms, educational system, capital markets, industrial relations system, etc. can engage in serious restructuring only if the norms and rules, as well as most of the other institutions with which they are linked, also change.[1]

In any social system, there are pressures to have consistency in the rules and norms across institutional sectors, though in any complex society, social systems are obviously imperfectly integrated. Indeed, the degree to which the institutional norms and rules making up a social system of production are loosely or tightly coupled is a variable of considerable importance. In general, however, the institutions making up a social system of production are interdependent, and changes in one institution generally result in changes in other institutions. Each institutional sphere is dependent on the others for various types of resources, so there is interdependence among the differing institutional spheres. Moreover, each society has its norms, moral principles, rules and laws, recipes for action, as well as its own idiosyncratic customs, traditions, and principles of justice (Burns and Flam, 1987).

There are inherent obstacles to convergence among social systems of production of different societies, for where a system is at any one point in time is influenced by its initial state. Systems having quite different initial states are unlikely to converge with one another's institutional practices. Existing institutional arrangements block certain institutional innovations and facilitate others (Roland, 1990). Thus, the institutions making up a social system of production provide continuity, though institutional arrangements are always changing, but with a logic that is system specific. While Williamson (1975, 1985) suggests that actors tend to choose the institutions that are most efficient, North (1990) is much closer to the mark in his argument that most social institutions exist as a result of custom and habit and are therefore inefficient. At any moment in time, the world tends to appear to its actors as very complex and uncertain. For this reason, actors often engage in contradictory forms of behavior – pursuing different strategies as hedges against what is viewed as a very uncertain world. And their hedging and contradictory forms of behavior may lead to somewhat different societal directions, but ones constrained by the institutional fabric within which the actors are embedded.

Despite the emphasis on the logic of institutional continuity, this is not an argument that systems change along some predetermined path. There are critical turning points in the history of highly industrialized societies, but the choices are limited by the existing institutional terrain. Being path dependent, a social system of production continues along a particular logic until or unless a fundamental societal crisis intervenes (David, 1988; Durlauf, 1991; Hollingsworth, 1991a, 1991b; Krugman, 1991; Milgrom, Qian, and Roberts, 1991; Pred, 1966).

In the presentation that follows, the focus is on two social systems of production: the social system of mass standardized production and variants of a social system of flexible production. A major argument of the discussion is that at the core of each social system of production is a set of social institutions that are system specific and that are unlikely to diffuse to other societies. On the other hand, within a country's social system of production, there may be narrow dimensions of its management style, work organization, and policies and practices that are more mobile than others. Depending on the social system of production of a host society, these may be adopted from another system (for examples, see Ackroyd et al., 1988; Boyer, 1991; Cool and Leng-nick-Hall, 1985; Freeman, 1982; Fucini and Fucini, 1990; Gordon, 1988; Graham 1988; Kujawa, 1980; Levine and Ohtsu, 1991; Oliver and Wilkinson, 1988; Shibagaki, Trevor, and Abo, 1989; Trevor, 1987, 1991; Turnball, 1988). But even though some dimensions of a society's social system of production are more susceptible of diffusing across societies than are other dimensions, all the component parts of a social system of production are socially constituted, contextually defined, and shaped by historical circumstances.

At this point, it is important to reemphasize a point made earlier in this volume. Some advanced industrial societies have more than one social system of production. But where this occurs, one tends to be dominant, and it usually imposes its flavor, constraints, and opportunities on other systems. In other words, the dominant system dictates the labor practices, finances, and the way that the state intervenes elsewhere in the society. Thus, over time, there tends to be some integration and/or diffusion of social systems of production within the same nation-state (Herrigel, 1995).

MASS STANDARDIZED SOCIAL SYSTEMS OF PRODUCTION

Until the 1960s, the model of mass production was widely held by American scholars to be the undisputed means of enhancing industrial efficiency. For at least three quarters of a century, most American industrial economists assumed that the most efficient means of reducing costs was by employing economies of scale and a standardized system of production. Mass production became the strategy for expanding a firm's market, and expanding markets became the means of minimizing costs. Many observers assumed that this was the direction in which industrial sectors were converging both within and across countries (Kerr et al., 1960).

Firms that successfully employed a mass production strategy had to engage in a particular form of industrial relations, use specific types of machinery, and relate in particular ways to other firms in the manufacturing process. Increasingly, mass producers took seriously Adam Smith's prescription that the most efficient way of organizing a factory was to routinize and differentiate workers' tasks down to the smallest detail. One way to break down manufacturing into ever more detailed operations was to employ specific purpose machinery which would focus on each manufacturing task along an assembly line. In much neoliberal thinking about mass production, employment was viewed as an impersonal economic exchange relationship, and machines, when it was profitable to do so, could easily be substituted for workers. Whatever labor was needed to work on assembly lines could be hired or dismissed on short notice. As machinery became more and more specialized, the skill and autonomy of individual workers often declined – although there was variation in the "deskilling" process from industry to industry and country to country.

Widespread adoption of mass production had major implications for the relationship between manufacturing firms and their suppliers. Because specific purpose machines operated in relatively stable markets, firms either engaged in backward integration or were in a strategic position to force their suppliers to invest in complementary supplies and equipment. Once firms announced their need for specific types of parts, suppliers had to produce at very low costs or lose their business. Over time, those firms that excelled in mass production tended to develop a hierarchical system of management, to adopt strategies of deskilling their employees, to install single-purpose, highly specialized machinery, and to engage in arm's-length dealings with suppliers and distributors based primarily on price. In the long run, the more a firm produced some standardized output, the more rigid the production process became – e.g., the more difficult it was for the firm to produce anything that deviated from the programmed capacity of its special purpose machines. On the other hand, such firms were extraordinarily flexible in dealing with the external labor market. As employees in firms engaged in standardized production had relatively low levels of skill, one worker could easily be exchanged for another. Management had little incentive to engage in long-term contracts with their workers or to invest in the skills of their employees.

This form of production was dependent on large, stable, and relatively well-defined markets for products that were essentially slow in their technological complexity and relatively low in their rate of technological change. Using transaction cost economics, some have argued that hierarchical structures were particularly well suited for mass production and distribution. When the transaction costs of working with external suppliers and distributors became too high, firms frequently resorted to a vertically integrated structure and assumed diverse functions in house (Chandler, 1962, 1977; Teece, 1988; Williamson, 1975, 1985).

Even in a country in which standardized mass production was the dominant technological paradigm, there were always industries that were organized differently (Sabel, 1988, 1991, 1992; Sabel and Zeitlin, 1985). Because heterogeneous markets existed for many products, many firms often competed with mass producers, sometimes by upgrading traditional skills and by producing carefully differentiated, high quality products. There is considerable historical literature replete with examples of mass and flexible producers existing in the same society (Friedman, 1988; Herrigel, 1989, 1993, 1995), although many observers viewed those who refused to engage in mass production to be "premodern" centers of production (Lamoreaux, 1985; Sabel and Zeitlin, 1985).

Not just any country could have a mass standardized production system as its dominant form of production. For such a social system to be dominant, firms had to be embedded in a particular environment, one with a particular type of industrial relations system, educational system, and financial markets, one in which the market mentality was very pervasive and civil society was weakly developed. Because firms engaged in mass standardized production required large and stable markets, they tended historically to succeed best in large societies. But the larger the spatial area in which this form of production was embedded, the greater the heterogeneity of interests of both labor and capital and thus the greater the difficulty of labor and management to organize effective associations..

Many historians have demonstrated how American schools historically were integrated into a social system of mass standardized production and how the education system was vocationalized (Hogan, 1982; Kantor and Tyack, 1982; Katz, 1971; Tyack, 1974). In such a system, schools for most of the labor force tended to emphasize the qualities and personality traits essential for performing semiskilled tasks: punctuality, obedience, regular and orderly work habits. Because labor markets in such a system were segmented, however, educational systems also tended to be segmented, but intricately linked with one another. Thus, such a system also had some schools for well-to-do children that emphasized student participation and less direct supervision by teachers and administrators (Bowles and Gintis, 1976). Hogan (1982: 163) argues that schools in a social system of mass production provide skills that are less technical than social and are less concerned with developing cognitive skills and judgments than attitudes and behavior appropriate to organizations and their labor process. Obviously, such an educational system is very useful for a social system of production that does not require a labor force with high technical skills or a high degree of work autonomy.

The historical development of capital markets, as part of an institutionalized social system of mass production, is very complex and will not be elaborated here. However, where social systems of mass standardized production have been highly institutionalized, the financial markets have also been highly developed. Large firms in such systems – in comparison with those in other societies – have tended to expand from retained earnings or to raise capital from the bond or equity markets, but less frequently from bank loans.

Once financial markets become highly institutionalized, securities become increasingly liquid. And the owners of such securities tend to sell their assets when they believe their investments are not properly managed. Since management embedded in such a system tends to be evaluated very much by the current price and earnings of the stocks and bonds of their companies, it has a high incentive to maximize short-term considerations at the expense of long-term strategy (Cox, 1986a, 1986b; Kotz, 1978; Navin and Sears, 1955; Zysman, 1983). This kind of emphasis on a short-term horizon limits the development of long-term stable relations between employers and employees – a prerequisite for a highly skilled and broadly trained workforce. Instead, the short-term maximization of profits means that firms in a social system of mass standardized production tend to be quick to lay off workers during an economic downturn, thus being heavily dependent on a lowly and narrowly skilled workforce.

A social system of mass standardized production is most likely to be dominant in a society in which the economy is weakly subordinated to religion, politics, and/or other social arrangements. Where the noneconomic aspects of society are weakly developed – e.g., a weak civil society – a market mentality tends to become pervasive. And the dominant institutional arrangements for coordinating a society's economy tend to be markets, corporate hierarchies, and a weakly structured regulatory state (Polanyi, 1957).

SOCIAL SYSTEMS OF FLEXIBLE PRODUCTION

For purposes of this discussion, flexible production is simply the inverse of mass production. It is the production of goods by means of general purpose resources rather than vice versa, a system of production which can flexibly adapt to different market demands. In systems in which flexible production is dominant, there is an ever-changing range of goods with customized designs to appeal to specialized tastes (Friedman, 1988; Herrigel, 1995; Kristensen, 1986; Sabel, 1987, 1991, 1992; Sabel and Zeitlin, 1985; Piore and Sabel, 1984; Streeck, 1987a, 1987b).

In the contemporary world, markets for many products are changing with great speed, and in those sectors where this is the case, it is less appropriate for firms to invest in product-specific machines and workers who are capable of doing only one thing. Production systems are closely linked to and influenced by available technology, and in numerous industries the emergence of microelectronic circuitry has done much to revolutionize systems of production, giving rise to what are widely called "economies of scope." The flexibility of microelectronic circuitry now permits large and small firms to introduce both quality and variety, in both small and large batches of production (Sorge and Streeck, 1988; Sorge et al., 1983; Streeck, 1987a). Because employees and general purpose machines in a flexible production system can be used for many different purposes, the flexibility of manufacturing systems is increasingly being defined by the extent to which its various parts can be combined and recombined and by the ease with which machinery and workers can be assigned to different tasks and products (Kristensen, 1986; Sabel, 1991, 1992). In contrast to mass standardized producers, flexible production requires workers who have high levels of skills and who can make changes on their own. This means that there is much less work supervision than in firms engaged in mass production. Because of the need to shift production strategies quickly, management in firms engaged in flexible production must be able to depend on employees to assume initiative, to integrate conception of tasks with execution, and to make specific deductions from general directives. Moreover, firms engaged in flexible production methods tend to become somewhat more specialized and less vertically integrated than firms engaged in mass production. As a result, such firms must be in close technical contact with other firms. In short, flexible producers require a highly skilled work force operating with minimal supervision, general-purpose machinery, and intense coordination-even frequent collaboration with other producers (Friedman, 1988; Hollingsworth and Streeck, 1993; Pyke, Becattini, and Sengenberger, 1991; Pyke and Sengenberger, 1992; for somewhat different, but very stimulating perspectives, see Pollart, 1991).

A key indicator to the development of a social system of flexible production in a society is its industrial relations system. Highly institutionalized social systems of flexible production require workers with broad levels of skills and some form of assurance that they will not be dismissed from their jobs. Indeed, job security tends to be necessary for employers to have sufficient incentives to make long-term investments in developing the skills of their workers.

To be most effective in employing technologies of flexible production, management must have a willingness to cooperate and have trusting relationships with their competitors, suppliers, customers, and workers (Sabel, 1990). But the degree to which these trust relationships can exist depends on the institutional environment in which firms are embedded (see Table 9-1 for characteristics of social systems of flexible production).

Social systems of mass standardized production tend to have firms embedded in environments that are impoverished in terms of collective forms of governance – e.g., trade unions, trade associations, employers' associations, etc. – and in societies in which the market mentality is pervasive.[2] But firms in social systems of flexible production are embedded in environments with highly developed institutional forms of a collective nature which promote long-term cooperation between labor and capital as well as between firms and suppliers. And the market mentality of the society is less pervasive. The collective nature of the environment also facilitates cooperation among competitors. The economic importance of institutional arrangements for rich and long-term relationships between labor and capital and among suppliers, customers, competitors, governments, universities, and/or banks is that such arrangements link together economic actors having relatively high levels of trust with each other, and having different knowledge bases – a form of coordination that is increasingly important as technology and knowledge become very complex and change very rapidly (Hollingsworth, 1991b; Hollingsworth and Streeck, 1993).

These comments may suggest that a social system of flexible production can exist on a voluntaristic, contractual basis – that is, economic actors simply have to structure their industrial relations system and their relations with their suppliers and customers in a prescribed way and a social system of flexible production will follow. However, the processes are far more complex. For a social system of flexible production to thrive, firms must be embedded in a *community, region,* or *country* in which many other firms share the same and/or complementary forms of production (Amin and Roberts, 1990). Firms that adhere to the principles of a social system of production over long periods of time tend to do so either because of communitarian obligations or because of some form of external coercion.

Moreover, for a social system of flexible production to sustain itself, firms must invest in a variety of redundant capacities. Such redundancies are likely to result only if firms are embedded in an environment in which associative organizations and/or the state require such investments. Firms act-

Table 9-1. A Typology of Social Systems of Production

Variables	Mass standardized production	Flexible production
Size and nature of the market	Large homogeneous markets, with competition based very much on price	Smaller markets; more heterogeneous tastes with competition based very much on quality
Technology of the product	Stable and slow to change; not highly complex. Products produced in large volume	Rapidly changing and highly complex; products produced in small batches
Organizational characteristics of firms		
Chain of production	Tendency for production to be vertically integrated	Vertical disintegration, with various types of obligational networks linking various actors together; subcontracting, cooperative contracting among small firms, joint ventures, and strategic alliances common
Work skills	Narrowly defined and very specific in nature	Well-trained, highly flexible, and broadly skilled workforce
Labor–management relations	Low trust between labor and management; poor communication but hierarchical in nature	Relatively high degree of trust
Internal labor market	Rigid	Flexible
Centralization	Very hierarchical and semiauthoritarian	Decentralized, consensual, and participatory type organization
Production equipment	Product-specific machines	General purpose machines
Work security	Relatively poor security except due to considerable class conflict	Long-term employment, relatively high job security
Investment in work skills by firm	Low	High
Conception of property rights	High degree of consciousness of property rights	Lower level of consciousness of property rights

Table 9-1 *(cont.)*

Variables	Mass standardized production	Flexible production
Environmental Structures		
Relationship with other firms	Highly conflictual, rather impoverished institutional environment	Highly cooperative relationships with suppliers, customers, and competitors in a very rich institutional environment
Collective action	Trade associations poorly developed and where existent are lacking in power to discipline members	Trade associations highly developed with capacity to govern industry and to discipline members
Modes of capital formation	Capital markets well developed; equities are highly liquid, frequently	Capital markets are less well developed, strong bank–firm links, extensive cross-firm ownership, long-term ownership of equities
Antitrust legislation	Designed to weaken cartels and various forms of collective action	More tolerance of various forms of collective action
Institutional training facilities	Public education emphasizing low levels of skills	Greater likelihood of strong apprenticeship programs linking vocational training and firms
Performance measures which get high priority in sectors	Wage inequality, lower quality products, innovativeness in new industries, conflictual labor–management relations	High wage equality, high quality products, innovativeness in product improvement, high social peace between labor and management
Type of civil society in which firms are embedded	Weakly developed	Highly developed
Degree of pervasiveness of market mentality of society	High	Low

ing voluntarily and primarily from a sense of a highly rational calculation of their investment needs are unlikely to develop such redundant capacities over the longer run. Manufacturing firms engaged in flexible forms of production require a workforce that is broadly and highly skilled, and capable of shifting from one task to another and of constantly learning new skills. But firms that are excessively rational in assessing their needs for skills are likely to proceed very cautiously in their skill investments; in such firms, accountants and cost benefit analysts are likely to insist that only those investments be made that will yield predictable rates of return. In a world of rapidly changing technologies and product markets, firms that invest *only* in those skills for which there is a demonstrated need are likely over time to have a less skilled workforce than they need. Moreover, firms that invest only in those skills that management is convinced they need, over time, run the risk of not being able to utilize the skills in which they have invested. With knowledge and technology becoming more complex and changing very rapidly, excessive rational economic thinking along the principles inherent in a social system of mass production may well result in poor economic performance. Thus, firms engaged in flexible production require excess or redundant investments in work skills, and can sustain this over time only if they are embedded in a social system of flexible production – which by definition has highly developed collective forms of behavior with the capacity to impose communitarian obligations among actors (for an excellent development of this argument for the German case, see Streeck, 1991b; also see Hollingsworth and Streeck, 1993).

Another redundant investment – one that is somewhat complementary – involves efforts to generate social peace. High quality and flexible production can persist only if there is social peace between labor and management. The maintenance of peace is costly, and it is impossible for cost analysts to demonstrate how much investment is needed in order to maintain a high level of social peace. Thus, just as highly rational managers are tempted to invest less in skills than will be needed over the longer term, so also they tend to underinvest in those things which lead to social peace. But for a firm to have a sufficient supply of social peace when needed, it must be willing to incur high investments in social peace when it does not appear to need it. In this sense, investment in and cultivation of social peace create a redundant resource which is exposed to the typical hazards of excessive rationality and short-term opportunism. Social peace as a redundant resource is more likely to be created as matter of legal or social obligation than as a rationally calculated economic interest (Hollingsworth and Streeck, 1993; Sorge and Streeck, 1988; Streeck, 1991b).

Investment in the redundant capacities of general skills and social peace tend to require long-term employment relationships. And while firms may occasionally develop such capacities based on *voluntarily* imposed decisions, such decisions tend to be less stable and less effective for the development of broad and high level skills and social peace than socially imposed or legally compulsory arrangements which originate from institutionalized obligations. Social systems of mass standardized production represent a social order based on contractual exchanges between utility-maximizing individuals (Williamson 1975, 1985), and most firms in such systems underinvest in the skills of their workers and in social peace. Social systems of flexible production require cooperative relations and communitarian obligations among firms, as well as collective inputs that firms would not experience based purely on a rational calculation of a firm's short-term economic interests (Hollingsworth, 1991a, 1991b; Streeck, 1991b).

In sum, societies with social systems of flexible production tend to have most – if not all – of the following characteristics:

- An industrial relations system that promotes continuous learning, broad skills, workforce participation in production decision making, and is perceived by employees to be fair and just.
- Less hierarchical and less compartmentalized arrangements within firms, thus enhancing communication and flexibility.
- A rigorous education and training system for labor and management, both within and outside of firms.
- Well-developed institutional arrangements which facilitate cooperation among competitors.
- Long-term stable relationships with high levels of communication and trust among suppliers and customers.
- A system of financing that permits firms to engage in long-term strategic planning.

All of these practices are mutually reinforcing. Because the institutional arrangements of each social system of flexible production are system-specific, they are not easily transferable from one society to another.

THE PATH DEPENDENCY OF SOCIAL SYSTEMS OF PRODUCTION

One gains some insight to the path dependency and distinctiveness of social systems of production by focusing on one historical process important in shaping a society's social system of production: the timing of its industrialization (Cole, 1978; Dore, 1987; Gerschenkron, 1962). Slow developers such as Britain and the United States had a long period of capital accumulation with numerous firms drawing workers from highly competitive labor markets. From such a tradition emerged the practices in the twentieth century of considerable job mobility from firm to firm, few constraints on the ability of employers to dismiss their workers, a tendency for employers to pay employees substantially different rates for different job tasks, and a practice of workers having narrow job assignments so that workers were easily substitutable. Relative to their size, these early developers had complex economies – e.g., many industries – coordinated by markets and corporate hierarchies. Their industries were *not* well embedded in an environment with such collective institutional arrangements as highly developed business associations, trade unions, or apprenticeship systems. In such an environment, there evolved over a long period of time a capitalist class with a high degree of consciousness about property rights; a workforce with a low degree of job security; a low degree of cooperative relations among competitors; a high degree of distrust and instability between firms and their suppliers; a high degree of distrust between labor and capital; and a political culture that emphasized a high degree of individualism. In such highly individualistic societies, the state was primarily regulatory in its function. Thus, there developed a social system of production with a low degree of communitarian obligations on the part of both capital and labor; an industrial relations system with low worker participation in managerial decisions, narrow job skills, and low levels of social peace; and a managerial style of decision making with a high degree of hyperrationality with heavy emphasis on short-term consequences (Elbaum and Lazonick, 1986; Hounshell, 1984; Whitely, 1991). Most of these characteristics are associated with a social system of mass standardized production and have persisted to the present day. Late developers – such as Sweden, Germany, and Japan – are toward the opposite end of the continuum on most of these characteristics, although these three countries vary in terms of their historical development and their social systems of production (for a discussion of regional variation within Germany, see Herrigel, 1995).

The way local, regional, and national economies are coordinated is the result of complex configurations of forces that seem to be deeply rooted in the histories of societies (Hollingsworth, 1991a, 1991b). Because the social processes which have resulted in social systems of flexible production are quite historically specific, the institutional arrangements that give support to such systems are not easily transferable from one country to another. As a result, it is unlikely that there will be rapid convergence in the way manufacturing sectors are coordinated across countries.

Thus far, the discussion has focused on why social systems of flexible production are more institutionalized in some societies than in others, without giving much consideration to the considerable variation that exists from country to country in such a social system. The discussion now focuses on two countries – Japan and Germany – the institutional configuration of which represents two contrasting examples of social systems of flexible production. The Japanese case is an example of a social system that emphasizes diversified quality *mass* production, while the German system emphasizes diversified quality production. Of course, there are other forms of social systems of flexible production in which the emphasis is less on large- and more on small-scale productions. Examples are the social systems of flexible production in parts of Northern Italy or Western Denmark, but for lack of space they are not discussed here. But it is in Germany and Japan that there are social systems of production that have been conducive to high and continued investment in human resources in large firms (Coriat, 1990).

The following discussion also includes the institutional configuration of the United States' social system of production as an example of a powerful economy that has historically been embedded in a social system of mass standardized production, and largely for that reason its economic actors find it very difficult to mimic the more effective practices and performance of their Japanese and German competitors. The analysis demonstrates with these three cases how a society's social system of production limits its capacity to compete in certain industrial sectors, but enhances its competitiveness in others.

LONG-TERM AND CONTINUOUS LEARNING: JAPANESE DIVERSIFIED QUALITY MASS PRODUCTION

In explaining the governance of Japanese manufacturing firms, one of the most important features, from which many others have been derived, is the distinctiveness of the Japanese capital markets. In both Japan and Germany, where industrialization occurred later and where mass markets have historically been much smaller than in the United Sates, firms have long been more dependent on outside financiers for capital – the large banks in Germany and the major financial groups (e.g., *zaibatsu, keiretsu*) in Japan (Aoki, 1988, 1990; Cox, 1986; Chandler, 1977: 499; Chandler and Daems, 1980: 6; Gerlach, 1989; Kocka, 1980). Historically, with the equity and bond markets poorly developed, it was quite common for Japanese firms – especially large firms – to rely on one lead bank for capital. Not only has that bank monitored the firm's operations very carefully, but it often has held equity in the firm, making the bank–firm relationship quite tight. In addition, there are large groups of business firms (e.g., Mitsubishi, Mitsui, Sumitomo), each having a major bank as its main lender. Not only is each group heavily dependent on a single bank, but within each group there is extensive interlocking stockholding, creating strong ties among firms within the group (Ballon and Tomita, 1988; Gerlach, 1989; Lincoln, 1980; Okimoto et al., 1984: 207–13).

In addition to the bank-centered groups of the *keiretsu,* there is a second form of industrial grouping, deriving from the subcontracting relationships between large firms and their suppliers. Like the *keiretsu* or bank-centered groups, these relationships are strengthened by mutual stockholding and interlocking directorships. In both types of institutional arrangements, this kind of mutual stockholding diversifies risk and buffers firms from the uncertainties of labor and product markets.

The role of these groups in channeling capital to firms has tended to lower the cost of capital relative to that in most western countries. The extensive cross-company pattern of stock ownership in Japan is an important reason why Japanese firms can forsake short-term profit maximization in favor of a strategy of long-term goals – a process very much in contrast with the pressures on American managers to maximize short-term gains. Moreover, the pattern of intercorporate stockholding encourages many long-term business relationships in Japan, which in turn reinforces ties of interdependence, exchange relations, and reciprocal trust among firms. These kinds of relationships have also led to low transaction costs among firms, high reliability of goods supplied from one firm to another, close coordination of delivery schedules, and meticulous attention to servicing (Abegglen and Stalk, 1985; Aoki, 1987, 1988, 1992; Dore, 1987; Lincoln and McBride, 1987; Okimoto and Rohlen, 1988: 266; Wallich and Wallich, 1976).

Having the option to develop long-term strategies, large Japanese firms have had the ability to develop the kind of long-term relations with their employees, on which investment in worker training and flexible specialization are built (Shirai, 1983). And because of their intercorporate ties, many large firms – particularly in steel, shipbuilding, and other heavy industries – have often shifted employees to other companies within their industrial group during economic downturns rather than dismissing their workers. Firms with long-term job security have the capacity to implement a seniority-based wage and promotion system, company welfare capitalism, consensus decision making, employee loyalty, job rotation and flexible labor assignments, and intensive in-firm instruction and on-the-job training (Aoki, 1988; Koike, 1983; O'Brien, 1993; Shigeyoshi, 1984; Stråth, 1993).

Across countries, there are also interesting linkages between labor markets and the system of training for management and labor. Whitley (1991) points out that where unitary educational systems exist – as in Japan and France – academic performance is the key to economic success (also see Hage, Garnier, and Fuller, 1988). Thus, schools provide a set of filters to select the most academically talented who are then guaranteed elite positions in industry and state. Such school systems have a poorly developed system for providing practical or vocational training. Thus, in Japan, business firms provide this type of training, and because of the existence of long-term job security, the training is high in firm-specific terms and not very generalizable to other organizations. This, of course, increases inflexibility in the external labor market.

When workers acquire most of their training, pursue their careers, and receive most of their benefits from a single firm, company unions rather than industrial unionism become quite common (Lincoln and Kalleberg, 1990; Lincoln and McBride, 1987; Shirai, 1983). Moreover, because large Japanese firms provide long-term job security, they do not classify jobs and occupations with the precision which the Americans do, thus adding greater flexibility to Japanese internal labor markets (Cole, 1979; Koike, 1988). Where employees have long-term job security, firms invest extraordinary resources in developing a distinctive firm culture and a set of practices designed to generate loyalty to and pride in the firm (Cole, 1992; Dore, 1973, 1987; Shimada, 1992; Whitley, 1992).

Japanese firms not only provide broad and high levels of skills within firms, but they emphasize job rotation in work teams. This results not only in considerable skill enhancement but also in teamwork and flexibility. Moreover, workers in teams operate as quality control over each other. And workers become accustomed to participating in solving problems, also in small groups. Rohlen (1992), Cole (1992), and Koike (1987) emphasize that this works successfully, for the Japanese have been socialized since grade school to pursue their own self-interests within small group processes. Another way of understanding the Japanese work process is to keep in mind the idea that the Japanese have long been socialized to integrate the obligations to the social group with one's own self-interest. In Japan, one learns to do this almost intuitively.

This form of industrial relations does not exist throughout Japan, as there are dualistic elements in the Japanese economy (Hashimoto and

Raisian, 1985; Levine and Ohtsu, 1991). Many Japanese employees – particularly women (Lebra, 1992) – are subject to layoffs, and wage levels in small firms are substantially less than in larger firms (Levine and Ohtsu, 1991). As the Japanese have had impressive rates of economic growth, however, even smaller firms have not laid off workers on the same scale as a number of western countries (Koike, 1983, 1988). Also, there is considerable evidence that small, fast-growing firms in high-tech sectors pay relatively high wages and provide long-term opportunities to their employees. Because of the existence of a business culture which emphasizes the appropriateness of long-term employment and a paternalistic attitude toward employees, the kind of dualism that is quite prevalent in the United States and other western economies is much less common in Japan, even in smaller firms that are not very profitable (Friedman, 1988; Kumon and Rosovsky, 1992; Lincoln and Kalleberg, 1990; Lincoln and McBride, 1987).

For some scholars, the distinctive features of the Japanese work organization – lifetime employment, seniority-based wage and promotion systems (e.g., *nenko*), welfarism, employee loyalty, consensus decision making, and participatory work structures – are part of a long tradition of corporate familism derived from Japanese feudalism. However, most present day scholars writing about the Japanese economy blend this cultural explanation with rationalist explanations (Cole, 1979; Dore, 1973, 1987; Lincoln and Kalleberg, 1990; Lincoln and McBride, 1987).

Each year, the profits of the firm are distributed to workers under a variable wage system, with a much smaller gap between the top executives and lowest starting wages than in the United States. Human resources are considered the most valuable asset of the firm, and decisions are diffused, consensual, and participatory. The compensation system is designed to maintain high overall morale of the workforce through a system of merit and seniority pay and bonuses based on the profits of the firm. In highly profitable years, a bonus can be as much as four or five months of regular salary (Ozaki, 1991: especially 23, 187).

This discussion of the Japanese institutional configuration would be incomplete without some mention of the Japanese state. Unlike the American case where the state is highly regulatory in nature (Campbell, Hollingsworth, and Lindberg, 1991; Hollingsworth and Lindberg, 1985), the Japanese state has been more involved in industrial development – though its role is less important today than in the 1950s. The Japanese state has developed many forms of protection to keep out foreign competition, it has fostered an environment for cooperation among fierce competitors, and it has channeled subsidies into targeted areas of research and development.

For many years, it adopted a set of macroeconomic policies designed to fuel economic growth with an undervalued yen vis-à-vis the dollar (Friedman, 1988; Johnson, 1982; Pempel, 1982; Samuels, 1987). However, some authors tend to overemphasize the role of the state in the Japanese economy (Anchordoguy, 1989; Brock, 1989). While the state does play an important role in helping firms to mobilize internal research resources, most Japanese research and development takes place within firms, and according to Kenney and Florida (1993: 58) "the Japanese state funds far less R & D than any other major capitalist economy, as measured on either a per capita or per unit of output basis." And the Japanese state has been quite unsuccessful in encouraging firms to mobilize internal resources when they have chosen not to do so.

Japan, like all other countries, does not have firms that compete and perform well in all industrial sectors. Indeed, Japan, like all other countries, has firms that succeed in some sectors, but not very well in others. By focusing attention on Japan, Germany, and the United States, it becomes quite obvious that why countries succeed in certain sectors depends less on such classic factor endowments as climate, natural resources, and land than on their national traditions, values, institutional arrangements, quality of labor and management, and the nature of capital markets.

In most societies, country specific traits are important in influencing which industry the nation's firms will be highly competitive in at a global level. Because of crowded living conditions and tight space constraints throughout the country, the Japanese have long concentrated on producing compact, portable, quiet, and multifunctional products. They have excelled in producing compact cars and trucks, small consumer electronic equipment (TV sets, copiers, radios, and video sets), motorcycles, machine tools, watches and clocks, and a number of business related products such as small computers, fans, pumps, and tools. Clustering of firms has benefitted from the long-term stable relationships that have existed between producers and suppliers and the *keiretsu* type institutional arrangement that has facilitated cooperation among complementary firms. As Porter observes, "With firms and their suppliers typically located close to each other, information flows freely, service is superb, and change is rapid. Larger firms sometimes have equity stakes in their suppliers, opening information further" (1990: 407). Because Japanese trade associations are highly developed and span a variety of suppliers, buyers, and related industries, they too have played an important role in developing cooperation among competing and complementary firms, as well as in facilitating the clustering of industries (Friedman, 1988; Levine, 1984; Miyamoto, 1988; Schneiberg and Hollingsworth, 1990).

The Japanese disadvantage in various national resources has ironically resulted in the development of several highly competitive industrial sectors. For example, the determination to overcome national disadvantages helped give rise to the Japanese steel and shipbuilding industries. In the case of steel, Japanese lack of raw materials and heavy dependence on foreign energy led to such intense innovation in acquisition of supplies and in development of highly efficient production processes that the Japanese emerged as one of the world's most competitive steel producers. Similarly, given Japan's remote location and its strong shipping needs both for exports and for the importation of oil and other raw materials, Japan developed one of the world's leading shipbuilding industries (O'Brien, 1993; Stråth, 1993).

Even though the Japanese have been enormously successful in improving upon existing products, they have been less successful in developing new products – primarily because of their particular institutional configuration. Their educational system emphasizes rote learning rather than creative synthesis or critical analysis. Their universities are structured to facilitate consensus decision making and group conformity. Moreover, the allocation of research funds within universities is poorly distributed on meritocratic criteria. The overall weakness of Japanese universities as research institutions is an important reason why the Japanese have lagged behind in industries involving chemistry, biotechnology, and other fields heavily dependent on basic science, and why the Japanese have won substantially fewer international prizes in the basic sciences than several much smaller European countries. Moreover, the poorly developed Japanese venture capital market has meant that there is little capital to assist entrepreneurs in bringing creative ideas to the marketplace. Among five advanced industrial societies, the number of new products developed by small firms was lowest in Japan. The way Japanese banks are tied into large groups also discourages investment in small start-up companies. And the fact that the most successful students in Japanese universities tend to enter large firms means that it is difficult for start-up firms to attract outstanding young talent. Most Japanese prefer long-term job security to the possibility of a personal fortune (Okimoto, 1986).

SOPHISTICATED INDUSTRIAL RELATIONS AND TRAINING: GERMAN DIVERSIFIED QUALITY SYSTEM OF PRODUCTION

Like Japan, German firms are not embedded in a strong neoliberal institutional environment. These two cases provide excellent evidence that societies are not converging along a common path of neoliberal modernization that was strongly predicted by American social science during the 1960s and 1970s. Rather, the two cases are strong testimony to the argument that firms in advanced capitalist societies are embedded in distinctive social systems of production which have emerged from different institutional trajectories. Nevertheless, a few scholars, focusing primarily on the West German society that emerged after World War II, have erroneously concluded that Germany has been "Americanized" (Berghahn, 1985). True, following World War II, stable parliamentary institutions were established, but most of the existing institutional arrangements in the German social system of production developed along a path of development that was established before World War I (Herrigel, 1995; Jaeger, 1988; Nocken, 1978; Winkler, 1974). A number of recent political economists argue that the German histories of banking, education, and corporatism are key parts of this path of development, resulting in what Katzenstein (1987) labels as a decentralized state in a highly centralized civil society.

In contrast to the Anglo-American economies, the German securities industries, as in Japan, have historically been less well developed, with the result that banks have long been much more important in supplying capital to firms than the equities and bond markets. Moreover, banks have also been important in exercising the stock voting rights of a substantial proportion of outstanding shares of the country's largest firms. Because banks have been so important in these two roles, bank officers have long served on the supervisory boards of hundreds of large companies and have even served as board chairmen of numerous firms. This type of long-term relationship between firms and banks has encouraged firms to be much more immune to the short-run fluctuations of the price of equities than their competitors in the United States and to take a long-term perspective concerning their industry needs (Cox, 1986a, 1986b; Deeg, 1992; Dyson, 1984; Esser, 1990; Kocka, 1980; Neuberger and Stokes, 1974; Tilly, 1976, 1982, 1986; Vittas, 1978; Zysman, 1983: 251–65). This capacity on the part of management has meant that German firms have had more incentive to engage in the long term development of products and have been less likely to lay off workers during a modest economic downturn, as has so often been the case with their American competitors who have been more constrained by short-run fluctuations in the financial markets.

Capitalist economies are very dynamic, and, as the relationships among German banks and business firms continue to evolve, some recent scholars (Deeg, 1992) argue that the historic importance of banks in coordinating the German economy is declining. This argument is based on the facts that (1) due to their retained earnings, many large German firms have been able to increase their independence from large banks (Welzk, 1986), and (2) savings banks and large regional banks (*Landesbanken*) have captured an increasing portion of the market of industrial lending which previously was dominated to a greater extent by three "big banks." While these trends have occurred, holdings by very large banks of shares in major firms and the cross-shareholdings among major firms still contribute to stability in the management of German firms and to the deterrence of hostile takeovers in contrast to the market and volatile pattern of ownership of large American firms (Vitols, 1995a, 1995b, 1995c, 1995d).

Another set of institutional arrangements which contribute to long-term strategic thinking within German firms is the country's industrial relations system. And the key to the German industrial relations system – and in my judgment much of the recent success of the German economy – is shaped by the highly developed centralized employer and business associations as well as trade unions. Peak association bargaining, mediated by the state, not only has played an important role in shaping distributional issues but also has played a role of great importance in influencing the quality and international competitiveness of German products. Employer associations and trade unions in Germany have had relatively encompassing and centralized organizational structures. The German Trade Union Federation (DGB Deutscher Gewerkschaftsbund) consists of 17 industrial unions which organize both blue and white collar workers. In 1987, approximately 39 percent of the employed workforce belonged to unions, though the proportion of manufacturing workers who were unionized was substantially higher. At the national level, employers are organized in the Federal Associations (BDA, the Bundesvereinigung Deutscher Arbeitgeberuerbände), a federation of 47 sectorial employer associations representing between 80 and 90 percent of private employers (Bunn, 1984; Markovits and Allen, 1984; Streeck, 1984b, 1991a).

Unions are responsible for collective bargaining and participation – through policies of codetermination – in corporate boardrooms, while elected work councils participate in organizing working conditions inside firms and ensuring that employment protection laws are obeyed by management. In the mid-1980s, among 480 of West Germany's largest companies – amounting to approximately half of the national output – workers and their representatives held approximately one half of the seats on the supervisory boards of firms. Collectively, these arrangements have been instrumental in reducing conflict between labor and management and in enhancing flexible production inside firms. The job security enjoyed by labor, under codetermination policies, has encouraged firms to invest in the long-term training of their labor force. When management has realized that it cannot easily dismiss workers in the event of economic adversity, it has had an incentive to engage in the investment of employees with skills high and broad enough to adjust to complex and rapidly changing technologies and unstable markets. And in Germany, the rigidity imposed by strongly organized industrial unionism and works councils has encouraged firms to invest in more skills and social peace than management would otherwise have invested under flexible external market conditions, a process which has directly contributed to a diversified quality, flexible social system of production – the key to Germany's high level of competitiveness in the world economy.

Managers of many German firms found the system quite distasteful. They would like to have followed the practices of their American colleagues in the face of stiff international competitiveness by cutting wages and reducing the size of the workforce. Yet, because they were constrained by the system of codetermination (regulated at the plant level by the Works Constitution Act of 1972 and at the enterprise level by the Works Constitution Act of 1952, superseded in 1976) which resulted in a high wage system, German firms were forced – with little choice – to become engineering and high skill intensive, with diversified and high quality producers. With the rigidities that firms faced in dealing with job protection and high wages for their workers, it was highly rational for management to invest more in the training of their workforce than they would have been inclined to do were they simply following market signals. Almost unintentionally, German firms were pushed to develop one of the world's most skilled labor forces (Hollingsworth and Streeck, 1993; Streeck, 1984b, 1987b, 1991b).

However, the structure of the system has also led to a highly skilled labor force and high quality products in another way. The peak associations of employers and labor have resulted in an enterprise-based vocational training or apprenticeship program whereby young workers learn the theory behind their trade, the theoretical principles of related trades, as well as rich practical training for particular tasks. In the mid-1980s, approximately 60 percent of West German teenagers were engaged in such vocational training, which now tends to last approximately three and a half years. Employers' associations and unions have jointly developed different training programs directed to young people who, upon the completion of their training, go into more than 400 different occupations.

Since 1984, the number of training programs has been reduced to eighteen in order to provide a broader-based and less specialized curriculum, while at the same time the level of training has been substantially upgraded. Significantly, those who have gone through this form of apprenticeship training program have had lower rates of unemployment than young people in other countries with less developed training systems. Because of the rich theoretical training that is integrated into their apprenticeship, German workers have a high capacity to continue advancing their training (Hamilton, 1987; Streeck, 1991b; Streeck et al., 1987).

With a high level of worker training, German firms are less hierarchical than American firms – with workers more involved in both conceptualizing and executing projects. This, of course, has led to a strong emphasis on product quality, which in turn has increased opportunities for long-term close cooperation between assemblers and suppliers in controlling quality and in product research and development.

Streeck (1984a) and others (Shigeyoshi, 1984) have suggested that there is some similarity in the social systems of flexible production of West Germany and Japan, including a high degree of social peace, a workforce that is highly and broadly trained, a flexible labor market within firms, a relatively high level of worker autonomy, a financial system with close ties between large firms and banks, a high degree of stable and long-term relationships between assemblers and their suppliers: overall, a social system of production which results in very high quality products. Despite similarity in these characteristics, there are, of course, major differences in the social systems of production in the two countries. To mention but a few, the routes by which their systems evolved were very different. In Germany industrial unions have been highly developed, whereas in Japan the emphasis has been more on company unions. In Germany, both labor and business are politically well-entrenched in most levels of politics, whereas this is not at all the case with labor in Japan (Pempel and Tsunekawa, 1979). And in Germany, there is nothing resembling the *keiretsu* structure which is so prevalent among large Japanese firms. Moreover, the Germans tend to focus on the upscale, high-cost segments of many markets, whereas the Japanese – with their emphasis on large market share of various products – tend to be more concerned with low-priced, but high quality products. In Germany, the institutional arrangements underlying the rich development of skills have some continuity with corporate associations, which historically have strongly supported and sponsored vocational training. Vocational education has long been important as a precondition for access to certain sectors of the labor market in Germany, whereas historically Japan has had a much more limited public vocational training program.

In Germany, labor and employers' associations emerged to coordinate the class interests of the two sets of actors, and their strategies originally tended to focus very much on the demand rather than the supply side of the economy. And as they negotiated along class lines, the emphasis tended to concentrate more on distributional rather than on production issues. However, macro considerations rest on microlevel performance criteria. Paradoxically, the class mobilization of labor facilitated the codetermination policies in Germany, but over the long term, as German workers have more secure tenure at the firm level, they tend to become more attached and loyal to particular firms. Moreover, their participation on supervisory boards has led to labor's becoming more involved in production, supply side, and microlevel decisions. In the words of Streeck (1992: 100), the concerns of the workers are "shifting from distribution to production, from demand to supply management, and from macro- to the microlevel." In this sense, German industrial relations shifted during the 1980s from traditional issues of reconciling conflicting class interests of labor and capital to issues of integrating labor to the production strategies at the firm level. As the interests of labor shifted from the pursuit of class interests to the enhancement of the well-being of individual companies, there was increasing convergence in the interests of labor and management of individual firms. But as this happened, class solidarity weakened, the center of gravity of German politics shifted from the left toward the center, and the weakening of the welfare state became a distinct possibility. And while there was no likelihood that the German workers and managers would develop the same level of cooperation as existed between workers and managers in many large Japanese firms, there was less divergence in the industrial relations of the two systems as the concerns of German workers shifted to production, supply, and microlevel considerations from a primary emphasis on distributional concerns (for further elaboration, see Streeck, 1992).

The structure of the German political economy has influenced the industrial sectors in which the economy performs well. And like all other countries, Germany has excelled in competing in only particular industrial sectors – not all across the board: the production of machine tools, automobiles, and chemical products, as well as many traditional nineteenth-century industrial products. They have been especially successful in applying the latest microelectronic technology to the production of traditional products and to new production processes. On the other hand, the Germans have been less competitive in many newer industries, e.g., computers, semiconductors, and consumer electronics. In other words, the Germans have placed less emphasis on developing entirely new technologies and industries than in applying the latest technologies to the production of more traditional products. And it is the specific type of German industrial relations system (high job security, the high levels of qualification, and continuous training of German workers) which is conducive to the rapid diffusion of the latest technology to the production of more traditional but high quality products (Junne, 1989). In addition the strong engineering and technical background of senior management, the high levels of skill of the workforce, and a strong consumer demand for high-precision manufacturing processes have contributed to the development of various manufacturing sectors with very high quality products. These characteristics influence the particular product markets and niches in which the Germans are highly competitive.

At the global level many German manufacturing industries have competed extremely well on the basis of high performance product segments rather than costs. Despite Germany's relatively small population, during the 1980s, it was the world's largest exporter of manufactured goods – substantially ahead of both Japan and the United States. Approximately one half of the country's manufactured products were exported, while with automobiles, machine tools, and chemicals, it was in excess of 60 percent (Streeck, 1991a).

The German chemical industry is an excellent example of a sector whose success is based on the technical competence of its workforce. Moreover, this sector demonstrates that when an industry is highly successful in a country and is closely linked to complementary sectors in the same country, it tends to be involved in making up a cluster of industries. Thus, the Germans have a history of being strong in such complementary industries as synthetic fabrics, dyes, and plastics, as well as such related industries as the production of pumps, measuring instruments, plastics processing machinery, and even the construction of chemical plants.

In addition to chemically related sectors, the number of clusters in which German industries are highly competitive at a global level is considerable. Some of the most impressive are in steel (around Dortmund, Essen, and Dusseldorf), automotive industries (around Stuttgart, Munich, Ingolstadt, Neckarsulm, and Regensburg), machine tools (around Stuttgart), printing presses and printed materials (around Offenbach, Heidelberg, and Wurzburg), medical instruments (Tuttlingen), cutlery (Solingen), and machinery of many types. Significantly, German firms have been less successful in global competition in sectors involving consumer goods and services – in other words, in industries in which mass advertising and rapid development of new products are important (Chandler, 1990; Porter, 1990). As this discussion suggests, the key to the success of German industrial sectors results from the social configuration of a host of institutional arrangements, all complementing one another: the financial markets, the business associational and trade union structure, the system of training for labor and management, the industrial relations system, the structure of firms and their relationships with their suppliers and customers, and the role of the state in the German economy. All of these institutional arrangements are intertwined and are the outcomes of a unique path of development.

Germany's social system of production performed extraordinarily well during the 1970s and 1980s. However, it is facing a number of serious problems which are likely to influence its performance during the next decade. Because of space limitations, only two will be mentioned here.

First, as a result of the increasing intensity of international competitiveness and the overcapacity of industrial sectors, some sectors of the German economy will undoubtedly be faced with declining profits. This is already the case in the shipbuilding industry, certain segments in the steel industry, and more recently in the automobile industry. German labor costs have long been very high, but this was in large part offset by high skills and high productivity levels. But the high deutschmark vis-à-vis the dollar, combined with high production costs and the threats of reduced trade, have encouraged German firms in a number of industries to invest more of their production abroad (Mueller and Loveridge, 1995). The very high costs of German production – a consequence of the German social system of production – will over time place constraints on Germany's growth rates. There are a number of recent studies that demonstrate that for some years German foreign investment has contributed – on average – to an increase of at least 100,000 unemployed people annually (see articles in *German Brief* during the past three years).

Second, many German firms have performed extremely well in recent years because of their capacity to shift the latest technologies to traditional products and processes (see the discussions in Ergas, 1986; Junne, 1989; and Sabel et al., 1989). However, the speed with which technological innovation is occurring is increasing, and it is questionable – in the mind of this observer – whether the Germans can match the Japanese both in the quality of many products and in the speed with which the Japanese will be able to bring new products to international markets.

The social system of production within which firms are embedded is important in shaping the response of firms to the transformation that is occurring. But because of the *keiretsu* type system which is so prevalent in Japan, their firms in more traditional industries are closely linked with firms that are shaping the high technology, information intensive industries, which are defining the character of the emerging twenty-first century. Japanese firms – whether in traditional industries or in high-tech ones – are closely linked with state-of-the-art basic research and the industrial infrastructure which is rapidly shaping the new industrial revolution. The speed with which new and traditional industries can integrate the latest technology provides the Japanese the ability to pull away from their major competitors – Germany and the United States. Moreover, Japanese firms in the aggregate are spending a higher percentage of their resources on research and development than any other country.

But in Germany as in most other western countries, firms are not as effectively linked to others in so many different industries. And while Germany excels – by international standards – in the way that its firms are linked to its suppliers and distributors, its social system of production on this dimension is less effective than that of the Japanese, and, for this reason, the Japanese are likely to increase their share of international markets vis-à-vis many German firms.

SHORT-TERMISM AND INSTITUTIONAL INERTIA: THE DIFFICULT AMERICAN TRANSITION

The ability of the United States to move rapidly toward a social system of flexible production is very much limited by its prevailing practices of industrial relations, its education system, and its financial markets – in short, the constraints of its past social system of production. The type of industrial relations that facilitate diversified and high quality production strategies are those in which workers have broad levels of skills and some form of assurance that they will not be dismissed from their jobs. Indeed, job security or other arrangements which provide long-term employment tend to be necessary for employers to have incentives to make long-term investments in the skills of their workers. And while these types of incentive and skill systems have become quite widespread in the core of the Japanese and German economies, in the United States manufacturing employment has tended to be much more job-specific, workers have been less broadly trained, internal labor markets have been more rigid, and employers have had much less incentive to invest in their workers' skill development. Because the United States has had one of the world's most flexible external job markets, it has been much easier for American workers to leave jobs for other firms than is the case in countries where workers have long-term job security. This has also provided disincentives for American employers to invest in worker training.

The American industrial relations system is shaped in large part by the weakly developed business associations and trade unions. The large size and complexity of the American economy, combined with the racial, ethnic, and religious diversity of the working class have created substantial heterogeneity of interests among both labor and capital, making it difficult for each to engage in collective action. And the weak capacity of both capital and labor to organize collectively has placed severe limits on the ability of the United States to move more rapidly in developing a social system of flexible production.

Countries with firms tightly integrated into highly institutionalized systems of business associations (e.g., Japan and Germany) have rather rigid ex-

On the other hand, the American system of education is highly stratified, and *highly educated Americans* are socialized by their educational background to be creative as individuals, a trait that frequently gets translated into the development of new products. In contrast, the Japanese are socialized to be highly attentive to detail, to improve upon existing products, and to work effectively as part of a group. Whereas the Americans excel as individuals in communicating across different organizations, the Japanese excel in establishing horizontal feedback types of communication "from marketing to production and production to redesign," all within the same firm (Aoki, 1988: 247). In other words, the Japanese emphasis is clearly on group activity and the production phases of the industrial process, whereas the Americans have tended to be less creative in this area. This difference in where and how economic actors focus their energies in the two countries does much to explain why the Japanese have over the long run been so successful in commercially producing and marketing products that the Americans first developed.

Markets and hierarchies work well when firms are embedded in an institutional environment impoverished with collective forms of economic coordination. But the Japanese and German cases demonstrate that diversified quality forms of production work best when they are embedded in an environment with institutional arrangements which promote cooperation between producers and suppliers, and among competitors, especially an environment which facilitates the exchange of information among competitors. It requires firms to engage in collective behavior far in excess to what is needed for markets and hierarchies to function effectively and in excess of what single firms are likely to develop for themselves. Flexible and diversified quality production systems function best when they are embedded in an institutional environment with rich multilateral or collective dimensions: cooperative action on the part of competitors, rich training centers for workers and managers, and financial institutions willing to provide capital on a long-term basis.

Of course, a number of American industries have long been embedded in a dense collective environment, and it is these industries that perform extremely well globally. For example, American agriculture owes much of its twentieth century success to the way that agricultural producers have been embedded in a rich institutional environment that has provided cooperative activity among producers, the dissemination by the state of university-based knowledge to agricultural scientists, and financial assistance from a number of public and quasipublic institutions. Another sector with a long history of being embedded in a rich institutional environment is the American chemical industry. Since the turn of the century, chemical firms have been extensively involved in cooperative networks that have consisted of university-based scientists and from time to time, the federal government.

Like the Japanese and German cases, the successes and failures of most American manufacturing sectors at the global level also reflect certain national characteristics and historical traditions. Because of the low levels of skill of American labor in most manufacturing sectors and because American management has tended to be recruited from marketing, financial, and legal rather than engineering and production backgrounds, American manufacturing firms have been less successful in improving upon products once developed than their Japanese and German competitors. And because American consumers are less demanding of product quality than the Japanese and Germans, American firms – particularly in the consumer goods industries – have been more competitive in the production of low-cost standardized products which can be mass marketed and easily discarded. Also, in contrast to the German and Japanese, the Americans – particularly in many manufacturing industries – have been more willing to compromise on design, quality, and service and to compete in terms of price.

Relationships among producers and suppliers in the United States have been more opportunistic and based more on hard-nosed bargaining over prices than in Japan and Germany. This kind of intense bargaining over price has also had an adverse effect on the Americans' ability to sustain product quality and to achieve a high level of competitiveness in global markets. There are industries in which the technology is not very complex and does not change, and, given the large size of the American market, mass standardized production is still effective in such industrial sectors. For example, paper products, breakfast cereals, soft drinks, bug sprays, floor wax, deodorants, soaps, shaving cream, and hundreds of other products remain symbolic of the familiar hierarchical form of corporate America. However, even these industries are slowly shifting to other countries where the labor costs are much lower. On the other hand, some American sectors that are spin-offs from mass marketing strategies are relatively successful at the global level. For example, some of the world's most successful firms in the advertising, entertainment, and leisure industries are American. Finally, because of the heavy emphasis American managers place on the performance of their firms' prices on stock exchanges, there is heavy emphasis on the rate of return on investment as the key performance indicator. Thus, American firms, more than those in any other country, resort to acquisitions and mergers in order to influence quarterly and annual reports, but tend to underinvest in new plants, products, and skills, none of which improves the long-term competitive advantage of American firms at the global level.

PATH DEPENDENCY VERSUS CONVERGENCE OF SOCIAL SYSTEMS OF PRODUCTION

Whether or not a social system of production can sustain its particular performance standards depends not only on its intrinsic economic "rationality," but also on where it fits into a larger system. If a particular social system of production is immune from the competition of an alternative system, survival can be long-lasting. But if different social systems of production – with diverging criteria of good economic performance – meet in the world arena, the arbitrariness of nationally imposed constructed performance standards may be superseded by alternative performance criteria as a result of international competitiveness.

As Wallerstein (1980) and others (Chase-Dunn, 1989; Chirot and Hall, 1982) have demonstrated, the world economy is also socially constructed, just as are national economies. Even if different social systems of production are competing in the international arena, it is not always possible to determine which is more competitively effective at any moment in time. Hegemonic nation-states can shape, *within the short run,* the rules of trade that favor their industrial sectors and firms. But the history of hegemonic powers suggests that in the longer run, social systems of production, sustained largely by military and political power, eventually give way to more dynamic and competitive social systems of production (Gilpin, 1987; Kennedy, 1987; Keohane, 1984; Krasner, 1983; Lake, 1984). In our own day, as nation-states are increasingly integrated into a world economy, economic competition is likely to turn into competition over social systems of production. As a country's social system of production loses its international competitive advantage, its share of world output decreases – even if it is a hegemonic power. Such a country will slowly experience deindustrialization and/or will attempt to restructure its institutional arrangements and to readjust its performance preferences. But such a restructuring generally calls for a major redistribution of power within a society. Largely for this reason, societies have historically had limited capacity to construct a social system of production in the image of their major competitors.

But firms in lagging economies do attempt to mimic some of the management styles and work practices of their more successful competitors. We observe this in both the United Kingdom and the United States, where there has emerged the concept of "the Internationalization of Japanese Business" (Trevor, 1987). However, this phenomenon has been grossly exaggerated. Many who contend that there is an emerging Japanization of the world economy have not confronted the problem of what is distinctively Japanese. True, some Japanese practices are exported elsewhere. But much of our scholarship on Japanese firms in foreign settings demonstrates that they pragmatically adapt to foreign conditions rather than duplicate Japanese practices. As Levine and Ohtsu (1991) observe, Japanese companies in foreign settings generally find that they must contend with the foreign culture as well as the laws and rules of alien governments, foreign unions, and employers – all of which are at great variance with Japanese institutions. Of course, one may point to the joint venture between Toyota and General Motors in Fremont, California, as well as the cases of Honda and Nissan in the United States, as examples in which a number of Japanese management practices appear to have diffused to the American setting. But close examination of even these more extreme cases demonstrates a hybridization of Japanese and American practices. Nevertheless, this kind of hybridization has resulted in much more flexible patterns of production than were previously observed in the American automobile industry.

This, of course, raises the larger issue of joint ventures and strategic alliances taking place in advanced capitalist societies. In an era when the rate of technological change was relatively low, production processes in an industry were relatively standardized, and production runs were quite long, vertical integration was an appropriate strategy for firms that faced high uncertainties and small numbers in their interdependent relationships with other firms. However, when technology changes very rapidly and the costs of technology are very expensive, firms are less inclined to engage in vertical integration, and joint ventures and strategic alliances become more frequent – particularly among firms in different societies. Of course, the motives for this form of coordination are varied: the search for economies of scale, the need for market access, the sharing of risks, the need to have access to technology, and the need to pool know-how if no one firm has the capability to achieve its goals. Such projects have occurred in a variety of sectors, but especially in the pharmaceutical, computer, aerospace, nuclear energy, electronics, and automobile industries. Is the increasing frequency of this form of coordination leading to the convergence of national economies?

Undoubtedly, the increased frequency of joint ventures and strategic alliances does lead to some convergence in certain management styles and work practices among cooperating partners. However, the diffusion of these practices does not bring about convergence in social systems of production. Before World War II, foreign firms attempted to borrow certain principles of scientific management that had become widespread in the United States, but in general the American practices were greatly modified when implemented. Moreover, in making these modifications, foreign actors did so within the developmental trajectory of their own social systems of production. Similarly in our own day, selected principles of Japanese management styles and work practices diffuse to other countries, but they are selectively integrated into local institutional arrangements.

Each country's social system of production is a configuration of a host of institutional arrangements. Each system is constantly changing and is open to influence from other systems. And indeed many technologies and practices diffuse from one society to another, but the direction of change is constrained by the existing social system of production. Thus, the same technology may exist in numerous countries, but how it is employed varies from one institutional configuration to another.

One recent comparative study (Hollingsworth, Schmitter, and Streeck, 1993) has demonstrated that, across countries, clusters of industries develop along particular trajectories, each having its distinct microeconomic dynamics within which markets, corporate hierarchies, networks, associations, and governments operate. Because skills, management techniques, and modes of governance are embedded in distinctive social systems of production, they do not easily diffuse from one nation to another. As a result, variation across countries in social systems of production remains substantial, even if there is convergence at the global level in how selected industries (e.g., chemical, oil, large scale aircraft, etc.) are coordinated.

This variation remains substantial for there have been great differences in the path dependencies of countries. For more than a century, the German economy has explored a diversified quality social system of production (Herrigel, 1995), whereas since the 1950s, the Japanese have hybridized mass production along with diversified quality production. In both countries, specific institutional arrangements have allowed for the cohesiveness of their distinctive social systems of production. In contrast, the United States has been very much constrained by its earlier Fordist mass production system and its "short-termism" under the influence of its distinctive financial markets, weak unions and business associations, norms, rules, and recipes for action.

Under what circumstances may such distinctive trajectories be reversed? Because the contemporary tools of social science do not provide a clear answer, this is an important agenda for future research.

ENDNOTES

1. With this line of argument, we should reread Parsons and Smelser (1965), Smelser (1959), and Eisenstadt (1964, 1965, 1977). Indeed, this line of argument is also consistent with a more recent complex body of social theory. For example, DiMaggio and Powell (1983) argue that organizations are "isomorphic" vis-à-vis their environment and that they gradually assume the characteristics of the environment and organizations with which they interact. Similarly, many of

the "new institutionalists" in the discipline of sociology (Meyer and Scott, 1983; Granovetter, 1985; Zucker, 1987, 1988) contend that organizations conform to the prevailing social and cultural conditions of their environment and therefore have limited capacity to diffuse to other societies. However, the new institutionalists also argue that organizations can modify their environment (Pfeffer and Salancik, 1978; Young, 1988).

2. Historically, there were always examples of flexible production in societies where a social system of mass standardized production was dominant, and examples of standardized production occurred in societies in which flexible production was most common (Friedman, 1988; Herrigel, 1990; Sabel and Zeitlin, 1985).

BIBLIOGRAPHY

Abegglen, James C. and George Stalk, Jr. 1985. *Kaisha: The Japanese Corporation.* New York: Basic.

Ackroyd, S., G. Burell, M. Hughes, and A. Whitaker. 1988. "The Japanization of British Industry?" *Industrial Relations Journal.* 19: 11–23.

Amin, Ash and Kevin Roberts. 1990. "The Re-Emergence of Regional Economies? The Mythical Geography of Flexible Accumulation." *Society and Space.* 8 (March): 7–34.

Anchordoguy, Marie. 1989. *Computers, Inc.: Japan's Challenge to IBM.* Cambridge: Harvard East Asian Monograph.

Aoki, Masahiko. 1987. "The Japanese Firm in Transition." In Kozo Yamamura and Yasukichi Yasuba, eds. *The Political Economy of Japan,* vol. 1. Stanford: Stanford University Press. Pp. 263–88.

1988. *Information, Incentives and Bargaining in the Japanese Economy.* Cambridge: Cambridge University Press.

1990. "Toward an Economic Model of the Japanese Firm." *Journal of Economic Literature.* 28: 1–27.

1992. "Decentralization-Centralization in Japanese Organization: a Duality Principle." In Shumpei Kumon and Henry Rosovsky, eds. *The Political Economy of Japan: Cultural and Social Dynamics,* III. Stanford: Stanford University Press. Pp. 142–69.

Ballon, Robert and Iwao Tomita. 1988. *The Financial Behavior of Japanese Corporations.* Tokyo: Kodansha International.

Berghahn, Volker. 1985. *Unternehmer und Politik in der Bundesrepublik.* Frankfurt: Suhrkamp.

Bowles, Samuel and Herbert Gintis. 1976. *Schooling in Capitalist America.* New York: Basic Books.

Boyer, Robert. 1991. "New Directions in Management Practices and Work Organization: General Principles and National Trajectories." Revised draft of paper presented at the OECD Conference on Technological Change as a Social Process, Helsinki, December 11–13, 1989.

Brock, Malcolm. 1989. *Biotechnology in Japan.* London: Routledge.

Bunn, R. F. 1984. "Employers Associations in the Federal Republic of Germany." In J. P. Windmuller and A. Gladstone, eds. *Employers Associations and Industrial Relations.* Oxford: Clarendon Press. Pp. 169–201.

Burns, Tom R. and Helena Flam. 1987. *The Shaping of Social Organization.* London and Beverly Hills: Sage Publications.

Campbell, John, J. Rogers Hollingsworth, and Leon Lindberg, eds. 1991. *The Governance of the American Economy.* Cambridge and New York: Cambridge University Press.

Carosso, Vincent P. 1970. *Investment Banking in America: A History.* Cambridge: Harvard University Press.

Chandler, Alfred D. 1962. *Strategy and Structure.* Cambridge: MIT Press.

——— 1977. *The Visible Hand: The Managerial Revolution in American Business.* Cambridge: Harvard University Press.

——— 1990. *Scale and Scope: The Dynamics of Industrial Capitalism.* Cambridge: Harvard University Press.

Chandler, Alfred D. and Herman Daems. 1980. *Managerial Hierarchies: Comparative Perspectives on the Rise of the Modern Industrial Enterprise.* Cambridge: Harvard University Press.

Chase-Dunn, Christopher. 1989. *Global Formation: Structures of the World Economy.* Cambridge: Basil Blackwell.

Chirot, Daniel and Thomas D. Hall. 1982. "World-System Theory." *Annual Review of Sociology.* 8: 81–106.

Cole, Robert E. 1978. "The Late-Developer Hypothesis: An Evaluation of Its Relevance for Japanese Employment Practices." *The Journal of Japanese Studies.* 4: 247–65.

——— 1979. *Work, Mobility, and Participation.* Berkeley: University of California Press.

——— 1991. "Some Cultural and Social Bases of Japanese Innovation: Small-Group Activities in Comparative Perspective." In Shumpei Kumon and Henry Rosovsky, eds. *The Political Economy of Japan: Cultural and Social Dynamics,* III. Stanford: Stanford University Press.

Cool, Karol and Cynthia A. Lengnick-Hall. 1985. "Second Thoughts on the Transferability of the Japanese Management Style." *Organization Studies.* 6: 1–22.

Coriat, Benjamin. 1990. "The Revitalization of Mass Production in the Computer Age." Unpublished paper presented at Conference on Pathways to Industrialization and Regional Development in the 1990s, Lake Arrow Head Conference Center, March 14–18, 1990.

Cox, Andrew. 1986a. "State, Finance and Industry in Comparative Perspective." In Andrew Cox, ed. *The State, Finance, and Industry.* New York: St. Martin's.

——— 1986b. *The State, Finance, and Industry.* New York: St. Martin's.

David, Paul A. 1988. "Path-Dependence: Putting the Past in the Future of Economics." *IMSSS Technical Report.* No. 533 Stanford University.

Deeg, Richard E. 1992. "Banks and the State in Germany: The Critical Role of Subnational Institutions in Economic Governance." Ph.D. dissertation, MIT.

DiMaggio, Paul and Walter W. Powell. 1983. "The Iron Cage Revisited: Institutional Isomorphism and Collective Rationality in Organizational Fields." *American Sociological Review.* 48: 147–60.

Dore, Ronald. 1973. *British Factory, Japanese Factory: The Origins of Diversity in Industrial Relations.* Berkeley: University of California Press.

1987. *Taking Japan Seriously.* Stanford: Stanford University Press.

Durlauf, Steven N. 1991. "Path Dependence in Economics: The Invisible Hand in the Grip on the Past." *American Economics Association Papers and Proceedings.* 81: 70–74.

Dyson, Kenneth. 1984. "The State, Banks, and Industry. The West German Case." In Andrew Cox, ed. *State, Finance and Industry.* Brighton: Wheatsheaf.

Eisenstadt, Shmuel N. 1964. "Institutionalization and Change." *American Sociological Review.* 29 (April): 235–47.

1965. *Essay on Comparative Institutions.* New York: Wiley.

1977. "Convergence and Divergence of Modern and Modernizing Societies: Indications from the Analysis of Structuring Social Hierarchies in Middle Eastern Societies." *International Journal of Middle East Studies.* 8: 1–27.

Elbaum, Bernard and William Lazonick, eds. 1986. *The Decline of the British Economy.* Oxford: Clarendon Press.

Ergas, Henry. 1986. "Does Technology Policy Matter?" *CEPS Papers* No. 29. Brussels: Centre for European Policy Studies.

Esser, Josef. 1990. "Bank Power in West Germany Revisited." *West European Politics* 13: 17–32.

Esser, Josef and Wolfgang Fach. 1989. "Crisis Management 'Made in Germany': The Steel Industry." In Peter J. Katzenstein, ed. *Industry and Politics in West Germany.* Ithaca: Cornell University Press. Pp. 221–48.

Florida, Richard and Martin Kenney. 1991. "Transplanted Organizations: The Transfer of Japanese Industrial Organization to the U.S." *American Sociological Review.* 56: 381–98.

Freeman, Audrey. 1982. *Japanese Management of U.S. Work Forces.* New York: The Conference Board.

Friedman, David. 1988. *The Misunderstood Miracle: Industrial Development and Political Change in Japan.* Ithaca: Cornell University Press.

Fucini, Joseph J. and Suzy Fucini. 1990. *Working for the Japanese: Inside Mazda's American Auto Plant.* New York: Free Press.

Gerlach, Michael L. 1989. *Alliance and Social Organization of Japanese Business.* Berkeley: University of California Press.

Gerschenkron, Alexander. 1962. *Economic Backwardness in Historical Perspective.* Cambridge: Harvard University Press.

Gilpin, Robert. 1987. *The Political Economy of International Relations.* Princeton: Princeton University Press.

Gordon, Andrew. 1985. *The Evolution of Labor Relations in Japan: Heavy Industry, 1853–1955.* Cambridge: Harvard University Press.

Gordon, Donald Duncan. 1988. *Japanese Management in America and Britain.* Aldershot, U.K.: Avebury.

Graham, Gordon. 1988. "Japanization as Mythology." *Industrial Relations Journal.* 29: 69–75.

Granovetter, Mark. 1985. "Economic Action and Social Structure: The Problem of Embeddedness." *American Journal of Sociology.* 91: 481–510.

Hage, Jerald, Maurice Garnier, and Bruce Fuller. 1988. "The Active State, Investment in Human Capital, and Economic Growth: France 1825–1975." *American Sociological Review* 53: 824–37.

Hamilton, Stephen. 1987. "Apprenticeship as a Transition to Adulthood in West Germany." *American Journal of Education.* 95 (February): 314–45.

Hashimoto, M. and Raisian J. 1985. "Employment Tenure and Earnings Profiles in Japan and the United States." *American Economic Review.* 75: 721–35.

Herrigel, Gary. 1989. "Industrial Order and the Politics of Industrial Change: Mechanical Engineering." In Peter J. Katzenstein, ed. *Industry and Politics in West Germany: Toward the Third Republic.* Ithaca: Cornell University Press. Pp. 185–220.

———. 1993. "Industrial Order in the Machine Tool Industry: A Comparison of the United States and Germany." In J. Rogers Hollingsworth, Philippe Schmitter, and Wolfgang Streeck, eds. *Governing Capitalist Economies: Performance and Control of Economic Sectors.* New York: Oxford University Press. Pp. 97–128.

———. 1995. *Industrial Constructions: The Sources of German Industrial Power.* New York: Cambridge University Press.

Hogan, David. 1982. "Making It in America: Work, Education, and Social Structure." In Harvey Kantor and David B. Tyack, eds. *Work, Youth, and Schooling.* Stanford: Stanford University Press. Pp. 142–79.

Hollingsworth, J. Rogers 1991a. "Die Logik der Koordination des verabeitenden Gewerbes in Amerika." *Kolner Zeitschrift fur Soziologie und Sozial Psychologie.* 43 (March): 18–43.

———. 1991b. "The Logic of Coordinating American Manufacturing Sectors." In John Campbell, J. Rogers Hollingsworth, and Leon Lindberg, eds. *The Governance of the American Economy.* Cambridge and New York: Cambridge University Press. Pp. 35–73.

Hollingsworth, J. Rogers and Leon Lindberg. 1985. "The Role of Markets, Clans, Hierarchies, and Associative Behavior. In Philippe Schmitter and Wolfgang Streeck, eds. *Private Interest Government: Beyond Market and State.* London and Beverly Hills: Sage Publications. Pp. 221–54.

Hollingsworth, J. Rogers and Wolfgang Streeck. 1993. "Performance and Control of Economic Sectors." In J. Rogers Hollingsworth, Philippe Schmitter, and Wolfgang Streeck, eds. *Governing Capitalist Economies: Performance and Control of Economic Sectors.* New York: Oxford University Press. Chapter 11.

Hollingsworth, J. Rogers, Philippe Schmitter, and Wolfgang Streeck, eds. 1993. *Governing Capitalist Economies: Performance and Control of Economic Sectors.* New York: Oxford University Press.

Horn, N. and Jürgen Kocka, eds. *Recht and Entwicklung der Grossunternehmen im 19 Jahrhundert und fruehen 20 Jahrhundert.* Goettingen: Vanderhoek and Ruprecht.

Hounshell, David A. 1984. *From the American System to Mass Production, 1800–1932.* Baltimore: Johns Hopkins University Press.

Jaeger, Hans. 1988. *Geschichte der Wirtschaftsordnung in Deutschland.* Frankfurt: Suhrkamp.

Johnson, Chalmers. 1982. *MITI and the Japanese Miracle.* Stanford: Stanford University Press.

Junne, Gerd. 1989. "Competitiveness and the Impact of Change: Applications of 'High Technologies.'" In Peter J. Katzenstein, ed. *Industry and Politics in West Germany.* Ithaca: Cornell University Press. Pp. 249–74.

Kantor, Harvey and David B. Tyack, eds. 1982. *Work, Youth, and Schooling: Historical Perspectives on Vocationalism in American Education.* Stanford: Stanford University Press.

Katz, Michael. 1971. *Class, Bureaucracy and Schools.* New York: Praeger Publishers.

Katzenstein, Peter J. 1987. *Policy and Politics in West Germany: The Growth of a Semi-Sovereign State.* Philadelphia: Temple University Press.

Katzenstein, Peter J., ed. 1989. *Indusry and Politics in West Germany: Toward the Third Republic.* Ithaca: Cornell University Press.

Kennedy, Paul. 1987. "The Relative Decline of America." *The Atlantic.* 260: 29–38.

Kenney, Martin and Richard Florida. 1988. "Beyond Mass Production and the Labor Process in Japan." *Politics and Society.* 16: 121–58.

———. 1993. *Beyond Mass Production: The Japanese System and Its Transfer to the U.S.* New York: Oxford University Press.

Keohane, Robert. 1984. *After Hegemony: Cooperation and Discord in the World Political Economy.* Princeton: Princeton University Press.

Kern, Horst and Michael Schumann. 1987. "Limits of the Division of Labour: New Production and Employment Concepts in West German Industry." *Economic and Industrial Democracy.* 8: 152–70.

———. 1989. "New Concepts of Production in West German Plants." In Peter Katzenstein, ed. *Industry and Politics in West Germany.* Ithaca: Cornell University Press. Pp. 87–109.

Kerr, C., J. T. Dunlop, F. H. Harbison, and C. A. Myers. 1960. *Industrialism and Industrial Man: The Problems of Labor and Management in Economic Growth.* Cambridge: Harvard University Press.

Kocka, Jürgen. 1980. "The Rise of the Modern Industrial Enterprise in Germany." In Alfred Chandler and Herman Daems, eds. *Managing Hierarchies: Comparative Perspectives on the Rise of the Modern Industrial Enterprise.* Cambridge: Harvard University Press. Pp. 77–116.

Koike, Kazuo. 1983. "Internal Labor Markets: Workers in Large Firms." In Taishiro Shirai, ed. *Contemporary Industrial Relations in Japan.* Madison: University of Wisconsin Press. P. 29–62.

———. 1987. "Human Resource Management and Labor-Management Relations." In Kozo Yamamura and Yasukichi Yasuba, eds. *The Political Economy of Japan.* Stanford: Stanford University Press. Vol. 1: Pp. 289–330.

———. 1988. *Understanding Industrial Relations in Modern Japan.* London: Macmillan.

Kotz, David M. 1978. *Bank Control of Large Corporations in the United States.* Berkeley: University of California Press.

Krasner, Stephen D. 1983. *International Regimes.* Ithaca: Cornell University Press.

Kristensen, Peer Hull. 1986. *Industrial Models in the Melting Pot of History and Technological Projects and Organizational Changes.* Roskilde, Denmark: Institut for Samfun Dsokonomi.

Krugman, Paul. 1991. "History and Industry Location: The Case of the Manufacturing Belt." *American Economic Association Papers and Proceedings.* 81: 80–83.

Kujawa, Duane. 1980. *The Labor Relations of United States Multinationals Abroad: Comparative and Prospective Views.* Geneva: International Institute for Labor Studies, Research Series, No. 60.

Kumon, Shumpei and Henry Rosovsky, eds. 1992. *The Political Economy of Japan: Cultural and Social Dynamics,* III. Stanford: Stanford University Press.

Lake, David. 1984. "Beneath the Commerce of Nations: A Theory of International Economic Structures." *International Studies Quarterly.* 28: 143–70.

Lamoreaux, Naomi R. 1985. *The Great Merger Movement in American Business, 1895–1904.* Cambridge: Cambridge University Press.

Landau, Ralph and George N. Hatsopoulos. 1986. "Capital Formation in the United States and Japan." In Ralph Landau and Nathan Rosenberg, eds. *The Positive Sum Strategy.* Washington: National Academy Press. Pp. 583–606.

Lebra, Takie Sugiyama. 1992. "Gender and Culture in the Japanese Political Economy: Self-Portrayals of Prominent Businesswoman." In Shumpei Kumon and Henry Rosovsky, eds. *The Political Economy of Japan: Cultural and Social Dynamics,* III. Stanford: Stanford University Press. Pp. 364–419.

Levine, Solomon B. 1984. "Employers Associations in Japan." In John P. Windmuller and Alan Gladstone, eds. *Employers Associations and Industrial Relations: A Comparative Study.* Oxford: Oxford University Press. Pp. 318–56.

Levine, Solomon B. and Makoto Ohtsu. 1991. "Transplanting Japanese Labor Relations." *The Annals of the American Academy of Political and Social Science.* 513 (January): 102–16.

Lincoln, Edward J. 1980. "Financial Markets in Japan." *United States-Japan Trade Council Report,* No. 47. December 19.

Lincoln, James R. and Arne L. Kalleberg. 1990. *Culture, Control, and Commitment: A Study of Work Organization and Work Attitudes in the U.S. and Japan.* Cambridge: Cambridge University Press.

Lincoln, James R. and Kerry McBride. 1987. "Japanese Industrial Organization in Comparative Perspective." *Annual Review of Sociology.* 13: 289–312.

Marglin, Stephen A. 1991. "Understanding Capitalism: Control Versus Efficiency." In Bo Gustafsson, ed. *Power and Economic Institutions.* Aldershot, Hants, England: Edward Elgar. Pp. 225–52.

Markovits, A. S. and C. S. Allen. 1984. "Trade Unions and the Economic Crisis: The West German Case." In Peter Gourevitch et al. eds. *Unions and the Economic Crisis: Great Britain, West Germany, and Sweden.* London: George Allen and Unwin. Pp. 89–188.

Meyer, John W. and W. R. Scott. 1983. *Organizational Environments: Ritual and Rationality.* Beverly Hills: Sage Publications.

Milgrom, Paul, Yingyi Qian, and John Roberts. 1991. "Complementarities, Momentum, and the Evolution of Modern Manufacturing." *American Economic Association Papers and Proceedings.* 81: 84.

Miyamoto, Matao. 1988. "The Development of Business Associations in Pre-war Japan." In Hiroaki Yamazaki and Matao Miyamoto, eds. *Trade Associations in Business History.* Tokyo: Tokyo University Press. Pp. 1–45.

Mueller, Frank and Ray Loveridge. 1995. "The 'Second Industrial Divide'? The Role of the Large Firm in the Baden-Württemberg Model." *Industrial and Corporate Change.* 4(3): 555–82.

Navin, Thomas R. and Marian V. Sears. 1955. "The Rise of a Market for Industrial Securities, 1887–1902." *Business History Review.* 39: 105–38.

Neuberger, Hugh and Houston Stokes. 1974. "German Banks and German Growth, 1883–1913; An Empirical View." *Journal of Economic History*. 34: 710–31.

Nocken, Ulrich. 1978. "Corporatism and Pluralism in German History." In Dirk Stegmann et al., eds. *Industrielle Gesellschaft und Politisches System*. Bonn: Verlag Neu Gesellschaft.

North, Douglass C. 1990. *Institutions, Institutional Change and Economic Performance*. Cambridge and New York: Cambridge University Press.

Oberbeck, Herbert and Martin Baethge. 1989. "Computer and Pinstripes: Financial Institutions." In Peter J. Katzenstein, ed. *Industry and Politics in West Germany*. Ithaca: Cornell University Press. Pp. 275–303.

O'Brien, Patricia. 1993. "The Steel Industry of Japan and the United States." In J. Rogers Hollingsworth, Philippe Schmitter, and Wolfgang Streeck, eds. *Governing Capitalist Economies: Performance and Control of Economic Sectors*. New York: Oxford University Press. Pp. 43–71.

OECD. 1986. *Germany: OECD Economic Survey, 1985–1986*. Paris: OECD.

Okimoto, Daniel I. 1986. "The Japanese Challenge in High Technology." In Ralph Landau and Nathan Rosenberg, eds. *The Positive Sum Strategy*. Washington, D.C.: National Academy Press. Pp. 541–67.

Okimoto, Daniel I. and Thomas P. Rohlen, eds. 1988. *Inside the Japanese System*. Stanford: Stanford University Press.

Okimoto, Daniel I. et al. 1984. *Competitive Edge: The Semiconductor Industry in the U.S. and Japan*. Stanford: Stanford University Press.

Oliver, Nick and Barry Wilkinson. 1988. *The Japanization of British Industry*. Oxford: Basil Blackwell.

Ozaki, Robert. 1991. *Human Capitalism: The Japanese Enterprise System as World Model*. New York: Penguin.

Parsons, Talcott and Neil J. Smelser. 1965. *Economy and Society*. New York: Free Press.

Pempel, T. J. 1982. *Policy and Politics in Japan: Creative Conservatism*. Philadelphia: Temple University Press.

Pempel, T. J. and K. Tsunekawa. 1979. "Corporatism without Labor? The Japanese Anomaly." In Philippe C. Schmitter and Gerhard Lehmbruch, eds. *Trends Toward Corporatist Intermediation*. Beverly Hills: Sage. Pp. 231–270.

Pfeffer, Jeffrey and Gerald Salancik. 1978. *The External Control of Organizations: A Resource Dependence Perspective*. New York: Harper & Row.

Piore, Michael J. and Charles F. Sabel. 1984. *The Second Industrial Divide: Possibilities for Prosperity*. New York: Basic Books.

Porter, Michael. 1990. *The Competitive Advantage of Nations*. New York: Free Press.

Pred, Allan. 1966. *The Spatial Dynamics of U.S. Urban-Industrial Growth, 1800–1914*. Cambridge: MIT Press.

Pyke, F. and W. Sengenberger, eds. 1992. *Industrial Districts and Local Regeneration*. Geneva: International Institute for Labour Studies.

Pyke, F., G. Becattini, and W. Sengenberger. 1991. *Industrial Districts and Interfirm Co-operation in Italy*. Geneva: International Institute for Labour Studies.

Polanyi, Karl. 1957. *The Great Transformation: The Political and Economic Origins of Our Time*. Boston: Beacon Press (originally published in 1944).

Pollert, Amna, ed. 1991. *Farewell to Flexibility?* Oxford: Blackwell.

Reed, John S. and Glen R. Moreno. 1986. "The Role of Large Banks in Financing Innovation." In Ralph Landau and Nathan Rosenberg, eds. *The Positive Sum Strategy.* Washington: National Academy Press. Pp. 453–66.

Rohlen, Thomas P. 1992. "Learning: The Mobilization of Knowledge in the Japanese Political Economy." In Shumpei Kumon and Henry Rosovsky, eds. *The Political Economy of Japan: Cultural and Social Dynamics,* III. Stanford: Stanford University Press. Pp. 321–63.

Roland, Gérard. 1990. "Gorbachev and the Common European Home: The Convergence Debate Revisited." *Kyklos.* 43: 385–409.

Sabel, Charles F. 1982. *Work and Politics.* Cambridge: Cambridge University Press.

——— 1987. "Changing Models of Economic Efficiency and Their Implications for Industrialization in the Third World." In Alejandro Foxley et al., eds. *Development, Democracy, and the Art of Trespassing.* Notre Dame: University of Notre Dame Press. Pp. 27–55.

——— 1988. "The Re-emergence of Regional Economies." In Paul Hirst and Jonathan Zeitlin, eds. *Reversing Industrial Decline.* Oxford: Berg. Pp. 17–70.

——— 1990. "Shades of Trust: The Construction and Destruction of Regional Economies." Paper presented before Technology and Competitiveness Conference, sponsored by the French Ministry for Research and Technology and OECD.

——— 1991. "Moebius-Strip Organizations and Open Labor Markets: Some Consequences of the Reintegration of Conception and Execution in a Volatile Economy." In Pierre Bourdieu and James S. Coleman, eds. *Social Theory for a Changing Society.* Boulder: Westview Press. Pp. 23–63.

——— 1992. "Studied Trust: Building New Forms of Co-operation in a Volatile Economy." In Frank Pyke and Werner Sengenberger, eds. *Industrial Districts and Local Economic Regeneration.* Geneva: International Institute for Labor Studies. Pp. 215–50.

Sabel, Charles F. and Jonathan Zeitlin. 1985. "Historical Alternatives to Mass Production: Politics, Markets, and Technology in Nineteenth Century Industrialization." *Past and Present.* 108 (August): 133–76.

Sabel, Charles F., Gary B. Herrigel, Richard Deeg, and Richard Kazis. 1989. "Regional Prosperities Compared: Massachusetts and Baden-Wurtemberg in the 1980s." *Economy and Society.* 18 (November): 374–404.

Samuels, Richard J. 1987. *The Business of the Japanese State.* Ithaca: Cornell University Press.

Schneiberg, Marc and J. Rogers Hollingsworth. 1990. "Can Transaction Cost Economics Explain Trade Associations?" In Masahiko Aoki, Bo Gustafsson, and Oliver E. Williamson, eds. *The Firm as a Nexus of Treaties.* London: Sage Publications. Pp. 320–46.

Shibagaki, Kazuo, Malcolm Trevor, and Tetsuo Abo, eds. 1989. *Japanese and European Management: Their International Adaptability.* Tokyo: University of Tokyo Press.

Shigeyoshi, Tokunaga, ed. 1984. *Industrial Relations in Transition: The Cases of Japan and the Federal Republic of Germany.* Tokyo: The University of Tokyo Press.

Shimada, Haruo. 1992. "Japan's Industrial Culture and Labor-Management Relations." In Shumpei Kumon and Henry Rosovsky, eds. *The Political Econo-*

my of Japan: Cultural and Social Dynamics, III. Stanford: Stanford University Press. Pp. 267–91.

Shirai, Tashiro, ed. 1983. *Contemporary Industrial Relations in Japan.* Madison: University of Wisconsin Press.

Smelser, Neil J. 1959. *Social Change in the Industrial Revolution.* London: Routledge and Kegan Paul.

Sorge, Arndt, G. Hartman, M. Warner, and I. Nicholas. 1983. *Microelectronics and Manpower in Manufacturing.* Aldershot, U.K.: Gower.

Sorge, Arndt and Wolfgang Streeck. 1988. "Industrial Relations and Technical Change: The Case for an Extended Perspective." In Richard Hyman and Wolfgang Streeck, eds. *New Technology and Industrial Relations.* New York and Oxford: Basil Blackwell. Pp. 19–47.

Sorge, Arndt and Malcolm Warner. 1986. *Comparative Factory Organization: An Anglo-German Comparison of Manufacturing, Management and Manpower.* Aldershot, U.K.: Gower.

Stråth, Bo. 1993. "The Shipbuilding Industries of Germany, Japan, and Sweden." In J. Rogers Hollingsworth, Philippe Schmitter, and Wolfgang Streeck, eds. *Governing Capitalist Economies: Performance and Control of Economic Sectors.* New York: Oxford University Press. Pp. 72–96.

Streeck, Wolfgang. 1984a. "Guaranteed Employment, Flexible Manpower Use, and Cooperative Manpower Management: A Trend Towards Convergence." In Tokunaga Shigeyoshi, ed. *Industrial Relations in Transition: The Cases of Japan and the Federal Republic of Germany.* Tokyo: The University of Tokyo Press. Pp. 81–116.

1984b. *Industrial Relations in West Germany. A Case Study of the Car Industry.* London: Heinemann.

1987a. "Industrial Relations and Industrial Change in the Motor Industry: An International View." *Economic and Industrial Democracy.* 8: 437–62.

1987b. "The Uncertainties of Management in the Management of Uncertainty: Employers, Labor Relations and Industrial Adjustment in the 1980s." *Work, Employment and Society.* 1: 281–308.

1989. "Successful Adjustment to Turbulent Markets: The Automobile Industry." In Peter J. Katzenstein, ed. *Industry and Politics in West Germany: Toward the Third Republic.* Ithaca: Cornell University Press. Pp. 113–84.

1991a. "The Federal Republic of Germany." In John Niland and Oliver Clarke, eds. *Agenda for Change: An International Analysis of Industrial Relations in Transition.* Sydney: Allen and Unwin. Pp. 53–89.

1991b. "On the Institutional Conditions of Diversified Quality Production." In Egon Matzner and Wolfgang Streeck, eds. *Beyond Keynesianism: The Socio-Economics of Production and Full Employment.* Aldershot, Hants, England: Edward Elgar. Pp. 21–61.

1992. *Social Institutions and Economic Performance: Studies of Industrial Relations in Advanced Capitalist Economies.* London and Newberry Park: Sage Productions.

Streeck, Wolfgang, et al. 1987 *The Role of Social Partners in Vocational Training and Further Training in the Federal Republic of Germany.* Berlin: European Centre for the Development of Vocational Training.

PART III

LEVELS OF SPATIAL COORDINATION AND THE EMBEDDEDNESS OF INSTITUTIONS

Philippe C. Schmitter

"Capitalism is a moving target" could well be the *leitmotif* for this entire volume. In Part I, not only did every essay stress the variety of capitalist institutions and the importance of explicit arrangements for coordinating exchanges and governing behavior, but they were all sensitive to changes in the mix of markets, hierarchies, associations, networks, state agencies, and corporatist arrangements over time. In Part II, an effort was made to aggregate these mixes into distinctive "social systems of production" and to specify the conditions for their emergence and subsequent evolution – again, with the objective of explaining persistent diversity across units and periods, not their imminent convergence.

Part III explores the significance of yet another potential source of variation within capitalism: space. In Parts I and II, as well as in *Governing Capitalist Economies,* the dominant technique of analysis involved comparisons according to *function* (or, more specifically, *sectors* of production and distribution) and *time* (or, more specifically, *historical periods* during which some relative equilibrium in the mix of governance mechanisms has set in).

The authors, implicitly or explicitly, limited their attention almost exclusively to the national level of spatial aggregation.[1] Following a well-worn tradition in the social sciences, they seem to have assumed either that each *nation* tended to develop a culturally distinctive "style of capitalism" based on its peculiar human and material endowment, as well as historical experience, or that each *state* embodied a unique configuration of power and authority that was reflected in the creation and operation of its intermediary institutions.[2] Given the plausibility of both assumptions, it should come as no surprise that the most common adjective placed as a qualifier in front of the noun, capitalism, has usually been a national or ethnic one: e.g., *American* capitalism, *German* capitalism, *Bolivian* or *Botswanian* capitalism, even *Jewish, Gujerati* or *Syrio-Lebanese* capitalism, and, much more recently, *Russian, Ukrainian,* or *Mongolian* capitalism. Each presumably possesses (or, will eventually possess) its own configuration of market, state, and "other" institutions for economic coordination and the governance of sectors. Where there existed no recognized national culture and/or sovereign state for a given territory, the analyst was likely to presume that its institutional mix was determined by the larger cultural or political unit of which it was a subordinate element and, hence, not worthy of attention.

This *de facto* – one is tempted to say, instinctive – monopoly of the nation/state in the choice of units of analysis has been broken. Currently, it is being challenged *from below and from above.* Scholars in several disciplines have become increasingly aware that innovative and significant "experiments with scale" were being conducted with systems of identity, production, and governance, both at the subnational and supranational levels of aggregation.[3] The territorial dimension, long regarded as a constant in Europe – supposedly frozen into place by the extraordinary resilience of the nation-state and its system of interstate conflict and cooperation – was thawing, assuming new configurations, and beginning to demand treatment as a variable.

Among the first to break the ice were those who began taking a fresh look at "industrial districts," "neolocalism," and "regional economies." They encouraged both scholars and practitioners to pay much more attention to the locationally specific conditions that permitted certain subnational units to produce very distinctive configurations of institutions, to develop such different modes of production as "flexible specialization" and "diversified quality production," and, consequently, to compete quite successfully in world markets against much larger national units possessing evident advantages of scale and scope. Although it is still relatively rare to see mention of *Emilia-Romagnola, Baden-Würtemburgische,* or *Juttlandish* capitalism, these and other regions characterized by differing mixes of small and medium-size enterprises, business associations, chambers of commerce, interfirm arrangements, research and training institutes, local and regional governments, and clan-like relations of interpersonal exchange and trust have served as the basis for creating alternative models of the likely (and desirable) course of contemporary capitalist development. Authors seem to agree that the conditions for the creation of such territorially concentrated systems are complex and demanding – and, often, culturally peculiar – yet, there is a booming industry of consultants prepared to advise less-favored regions on how they too can acquire the advanced production technology, the social networks, and the local governance mechanisms that will enable them to create other "mini-miracles" of growth, employment, innovation and competitiveness. Because this literature is so well known and its institutional implications relatively well-explored – indeed, by several of the contributors to this volume! – we have not included a review of its findings in Part III.[4]

It has taken a while for the impact of the second ice-breaker to be fully registered – if only because it was of such a magnitude and provoked such an extensive discussion that its implications for the viability of existing national governance mechanisms tended to be overlooked, at least initially. I am referring, of course, to the immense literature on globalization. This has become everyone's preferred *deus ex machina.* No chapter in this volume has failed to mention the concept or one of its synonyms. It is enough to wave even its specter, and almost any change in the performance and structure of the contemporary "world" economy can (allegedly) be explained. Defining what "it" is can be a complex and controversial matter, but no one doubts that changes occurring in recent decades in the most comprehensive system of exchanges of goods, services, capital, and labor have been so substantial and so pervasive that even the most isolated national or local economy must be feeling its effects.

Admittedly, the statistics on international imports and exports, investments, profit remittances, debts, patents, licenses, royalties, tourists, mail flows, television audiences, migrants, and refugees are impressive. They have increased almost monotonically and at rates generally exceeding those of comparable flows within national boundaries. However, as Karl Polanyi has shown, this is not the first time that such interdependencies have gone up so remarkably and yet left relatively intact the institutions and capacities of existing nation-states. Indeed, the booming world (or, better, Euro-centric) economy of the late 1900s was subsequently destroyed when its in-terdependent, but still sovereign, national rivals went to war with each other in 1914![5]

Why, with this sobering precedent staring them in the face, are con-temporary "globalists" so much more confident about the pervasive and transformative impact of international interdependence? Part of the answer may lie in its "complexity," i.e., in the fact that today these flows are more varied in their sources and motivations, are closely linked to the generation and assimilation of technological innovation, and tend to affect a much greater proportion of their respective mass publics than in the past. But most of their optimism seems to stem from a different assumption, namely, that the current trend towards globalization is irrevocably coupled with *deregula-tion*. Unlike the previous period when it was only accompanied (and partly propelled) by the *liberalization* of tariffs, exchange rates, and investment flows, now the process is going much further and compelling its most active participants to dismantle whole parts of their respective national apparatus-es for the governance of specific issue arenas, sectors, professions, localities, etc. These pressures from rising international competitiveness have also been supplemented by a significant paradigm shift in *economic ideology* that has challenged the legitimacy (and questioned the efficacy) of collective inter-vention and regulation at the national, regional, or global levels. At best, it justifies the replacement of these relatively strong governance mechanisms with weak *"international regimes"* that codify minimal rules of contract and ex-change and are based on convergent actor expectations, rather than the mon-itoring and enforcement power of a supra- or transnational state.[6]

The underlying, long-term, implication of this twin transformation in structure and ideology is clear: If one sets aside those few countries where for perverse and irrational – i.e., "political" – reasons the Sirenes are either not heard or successfully resisted, *the national economies of an increasingly glob-alized system should converge toward a similar (if not singular) set of governance mechanisms*. Their scale and scope will have shifted upward as far as they can go, eliminating national and local intermediaries. Their content and prac-tices will be freed from parochial loyalties and embedded in a new, more cosmopolitan society. According to this scenario, liberalized markets (read, the global marketplace) and deregulated hierarchies (read, large transna-tional enterprises) would "govern" the global economy – with just a little bit of help from international regimes and a great deal of benefit in terms of enhanced productivity and efficiency.

The opportunity-cum-threat of globalization is discussed in all four chapters of Part III, but evaluated in quite different ways.

Wyn Grant comes closest to envisaging a globalized outcome. Using the example of New Zealand to drive home his message, he shows how even a small and remote country with a history of very distinctive, even pioneering, institutions of governance has not been able to escape its consequences. After an initial attempt to exploit precisely these peculiarities for greater comparative advantage had failed, the newly elected government had no alternative but to embrace globalization through the liberalization and deregulation of its domestic economy – with, Grant notes, only modest success. The implicit message in his chapter seems to be that there is no way to avoid having to adapt to the trend, although those units that are larger and occupy a more central position can expect to have some influence in setting the new "global regulatory agenda" and some success in participating in its emerging cartels, joint ventures, and international regimes.

Paul Hirst and Grahame Thompson argue that the international economy is governed through the limited cooperation of major trade blocs and nation-states. And unlike many analysts, they argue that nation-states still have the potential for limiting the influence of financial markets. Some states (e.g., Japan and Germany), because of specific distributional contexts and sources of social solidarity, have more capacity than the United States and the United Kingdom to meet and to mediate international competitive pressures through national policy.

Lorraine Eden and Fen Osler Hampson are quite explicit in making a functionalist argument that a series of "politicomarket failures" in response to the inexorable rise in global interdependence will cause actors to rely increasingly on international regimes of various types. Their main difference with Grant, however, is that they envisage the likelihood that these efforts at economic governance will be less than global in scale and tend to cluster in "clubs of the like-minded." Various free trade blocs in Europe, North America, and Asia are cited as proof of this tendency.

Philippe Schmitter takes a similar position when he attempts to answer the question whether, in the aftermath of the Single European Act and the Maastricht Accord, the European Community is likely to be successful in defending the many (and varied) governance mechanisms so deeply embedded in that region's national capitalisms. However, he differs from the Eden-Hampson approach by stressing that EC members are anything but like-minded on most of these issues, and that the outcome hinges precisely on its institutions' acquiring a much greater capacity for governing the behavior of its members than would be the case in any international regime.

Readers should find a rich and diverse menu in this part of the book. The basic ingredients are similar; even the *cuisines* do not differ that much.

The final dishes, however, are quite distinctive – especially in their after-tastes and perhaps in their digestive properties. All that remains is for me to wish *bon appetit!*

ENDNOTES

1. The *locus classicus* for a "national" approach to the study of capitalisms is Shonfield (1965). Campbell, Hollingsworth, and Lindberg (1991) is an excellent example of the genre that carries the analysis over a longer time span within a single country. Lange et al. (1982), Gourevitch et al. (1984), Katzenstein (1984), Hall (1986), Scharpf (1987), and Wilks and Wright (1987) are all recent comparative studies that presume nationally distinctive capitalist institutions and doctrines.
2. "Transaction cost analysts," such as Williamson (1975, 1985) explicitly reject both normative-cultural and power-political explanations for the arrangements they study. Yet they settle exclusively on the national level of aggregation for their examples of intermediary forms of coordination. Presumably, they do so out of sheer habit since there does not seem to be any compelling theoretical reason why economizing on transaction costs must follow national boundaries – unless, of course, one takes explicitly into account prevailing discontinuities in national languages, identities, legal systems, and state sovereignties.
3. This is the central theme of a project pursued by an interdisciplinary group of the Social Science Research Council's Committee on Western Europe to appear in Schmitter (forthcoming).
4. The literature on regional economies and industrial districts is enormous and quite varied. Bagnasco (1977, 1988), Piore and Sabel (1984), Trigilia (1986), and Becattini (1987) have all made important contributions to our understanding of "flexible specialization." On "diversified quality production," see Sorge and Streeck (1988) and especially Streeck (1991).
   For treatments of the political role of subnational regions and their impact upon interest representation and sectoral governance, see Coleman and Jacek (1989) and Anderson (1992).
5. Polanyi (1944).
6. The *locus classicus* of this approach are the two 1983 articles by Krasner. For a review of this literature, see Haggard and Simmons (1987).

REFERENCES

Anderson, Jeffrey J. 1992. *The Territorial Imperative. Pluralism, Corporatism and Economic Crisis.* Cambridge: Cambridge University Press.
Bagnasco, Arnaldo. 1988. *La Costruzione sociale del mercato.* Bologna: Il Mulino.
    1977. *Tre Italie. La problematica territoriale dello sviluppo italiano.* Bologna: Il Mulino.
Becattini, Giacomo, ed. 1987. *Mercato e forze locali. Il distretto industriale.* Bologna: Il Mulino.

Campbell, John, J. Rogers Hollingsworth, and Leon Lindberg, eds. 1991. *Governance of the American Economy*. New York: Cambridge University Press.

Coleman, William D. and Henry J. Jacek, eds. 1989. *Regionalism, Business Interests and Public Policy*. London: Sage.

Gourevitch, Peter et al., eds. 1984. *Unions and the Economic Crisis: Britain, West Germany and Sweden*. London: George Allen and Unwin.

Haggard, Stephan and Beth A. Simmons. 1987. "Theories of International Regimes." *International Organization*. 41: 493–95.

Hall, Peter. 1986. *Governing the Economy. The Politics of State Intervention in Britain and France*. Cambridge: Polity Press.

Katzenstein, Peter. 1984. *Corporatism and Change: Austria, Switzerland and the Politics of Industry*. Ithaca: Cornell University Press.

Krasner, Stephen. 1983. "Regimes and the Limits of Realism: Regimes as Autonomous Variables." In S. Krasner, ed. *International Regimes*. Ithaca: Cornell University Press. Pp. 355–68.

——— 1983. "Structural Causes and Regime Consequences: Regimes as Intervening Variables." In S. Krasner, ed. *International Regimes*. Ithaca: Cornell University Press. Pp. 1–22.

Lange, Peter et al., eds. 1982. *Unions, Change, and Crisis: French and Italian Union Strategy and the Political Economy, 1945–80*. London: George Allen and Unwin.

Piore, Michael and Charles Sabel. 1948. *The Second Industrial Divide*. New York: Basic Books.

Polanyi, Karl. 1944. *The Great Transformation*. Boston: Beacon Press.

Scharpf, Fritz. 1987. *Crisis and Choice in European Social Democracy*. Ithaca: Cornell University Press.

Schmitter, Philippe E. Forthcoming. *Experimenting with Scale in Western Europe*. New York: Cambridge University Press.

Shonfield, Andrew. 1965. *Modern Capitalism*. Oxford: Oxford University Press.

Sorge, Arndt and Wolfgang Streeck. 1988. "Industrial Relations and Technical Change: The Case for an Extended Perspective." In R. Hyman and W. Streeck, eds. *New Technology and Industrial Relations*. London: Basil Blackwell. Pp. 19–47.

Streeck, Wolfgang. 1991. "On the Institutional Conditions of Diversified Quality Production." In E. Matzner and W. Streeck, eds. *Beyond Keynesianism*. Aldershot, U.K.: Edward Elgar. Pp. 21–61.

Trigilia, Carlo. 1986. *Grande partiti e piccole imprese*. Bologna: Il Mulino.

Wilks S. and M. Wright, eds. 1987. *Comparative Government-Industry Relations: Western Europe, the United States and Japan*. Oxford: Clarendon Press.

Williamson, Oliver. 1975. *Markets and Hierarchies*. New York: Free Press. 1985. *Economic Institutions of Capitalism*. New York: Free Press.

10

PERSPECTIVES ON GLOBALIZATIONAL AND ECONOMIC COORDINATION

Wyn Grant

In the opening chapter of this book, Hollingsworth and Boyer suggest that "we must be sensitive to how economic coordination is linked to all spatial-territorial areas – the level of regions within countries, the level of the nation-state, and levels beyond the nation-state." The process of globalization discussed in this chapter creates a need for improved economic coordination at the transnational level, yet it is at that level that it is particularly poorly developed and difficult to achieve. The development of economic globalization has not been counterbalanced by the development of appropriate mechanisms of governance.

The 1980s have seen an accelerating process of economic globalization, but a relatively limited development of political structures that can regulate this process. Indeed, the best developed mechanisms of governance that exist at the supranational level are intra- and interfirm: coordination within the new "stateless firms" discussed in this paper, and between firms through such devices as joint ventures and cartels. The chief executives of stateless firms claim with some justification that their enterprises "change relations *between* companies. We function as a lubricant for worldwide economic integration" (Taylor, 1991: 105). However, firms are not well placed to act as agents of international governance, particularly if the insertion of public policy objectives in the decision-making process is thought to be desirable. International firms create the need for improved international governance, but they do not and cannot provide it.

PROBLEMS OF DEFINITION

For the purposes of this paper, economic globalization is defined as a process in which transactions across the borders of nation-states increase in importance relative to those within nation-states; and whereby national boundaries cease to be a significant impediment to the movement of goods and services. Satisfaction of the first condition would be compatible with developments in conventional international trade; the second condition needs to be fulfilled before the economic globalization process is complete.

The concept of governance is central to the analysis being presented. It has a kind of reassuring vagueness which makes it an attractive word to deploy, but a more difficult word to define. Its application is particularly difficult at the international level as "The international system is without government. It is, moreover, notorious for its lack of hierarchy, for the absence of a system sovereign or sovereigns" (Finkelstein, 1991: 2-3). As a working definition, international governance may be referred to as "governing without sovereign authority relationships which transcend national frontiers." (Finkelstein, 1991: 10). As Finkelstein explains, the actual range of functions performed within a governance framework may vary from information creation and exchange, through the adoption of codes and regulations to the allocation of resources (Finkelstein, 1991: 14).

The concept has certainly evolved beyond a discussion of what international organizations do (or fail to do), so that while institution building may form part of the debate, it is no longer a central focus. Kratochwil and Ruggie (1986) argue that the concept has come to be associated with that of international regimes which encompasses formal institutional rules but is not limited to them. International regimes may be seen as a form of middle-level control among states which provide a framework for global economic transactions.

THE DEVELOPMENT AND LIMITS OF GLOBALIZATION

In his novel *Small World,* David Lodge explores the phenomenon of globalization by following his hero through a world changed by the jet plane, the direct dial international telephone, and the xerox machine. In the short period since that novel was written, one would need to add the fax machine, e-mail, and the Internet. In Western Europe and Japan there was a tenfold increase in the number of telefax subscribers in the second half of the 1980s to 1.2 million and 0.4 million respectively, while there were 2.5 million subscribers in the United States by the end of the decade (GATT, 1990: 38). The cost of telecommunications services has fallen, and their value has significantly increased. One indicator of increasing globalization is the marked increased in the number of international telephone calls.

More indicators could be provided, but it is necessary to caution against an increasingly prevalent form of global hype which argues that all boundaries between national markets have broken down and that the national state is an increasing irrelevance between the realities of the community and the shrinking world. It is too early to proclaim a *Borderless World,* the title of a book by Kenichi Ohmae. Ohmae informs us that "During 1988 nearly 90 percent of all Japanese honeymooners went abroad. Facts of these kinds are hard to ignore" (Ohmae, 1990: 19). Some of us might feel that it is possible to ignore them, or at least pause to ask questions about their significance. But Ohmae is not a man lacking in vision, one of a world in which "duty-free shops are the precursor to what life will be like in a genuinely borderless environment" (Ohmae, 1990: 27).

What is noticeable is that national differences in performance persist and that nations that perform well in some sectors, perform less than well in others. There is no better example than Japan. As Porter reminds us, "there are large portions of the Japanese economy that not only fail to measure up to the standards of the best worldwide competitors but fall far behind them" (Porter, 1990: 394). We are all too familiar with Japanese successes; we tend to forget about Japanese failures. These failures are not "accidental," but are related to national characteristics. Japan's lack of its own energy supplies has inhibited its progress in industries such as petrochemicals and aluminium smelting. In food processing, "Home market demand in the food sector (with heavy dependence on rice, fresh fish, and other distinctive dishes) is sufficiently out of synch with most important nations as to disadvantage Japanese firms abroad (but keep out foreign firms except in fast food, where American chains are popular)" (Porter, 1990: 405). Even in markets where products are less differentiated, the lesson that has been learned by Honda is that "For us, the priority is not to globalise our business, but to localise it" (*Financial Times,* December 5, 1990).

Overstating the impact of globalization is a danger, but so is understating it. Porter makes a distinction between global industries and those in which "The international industry is a collection of essentially domestic industries, hence the term multidomestic" (1990: 53). We can all think of service industries that are necessarily locally provided: Haircuts are likely to remain a distinctive cultural experience for some time to come. Even so, there is a clear overall trend. "Competition in many industries has internationalized, not only in manufacturing industries but increasingly in services" (Porter, 1990: 14). No country can stand aside from the impact of globalization.

This chapter does not seek to explain why globalization has occurred. An OECD symposium emphasized two factors, technological changes and economic liberalization (OECD, 1994). Arguments about the high cost of technological development leading to new products being marketed in many countries to recoup investment could apply to conventional forms of multinational business activity throughout the postwar period and indeed before then. There is rather more in the argument that improved communications and transportation technologies make it easier for firms to manage their operations on an international scale. Improvements in communications have also facilitated the globalization of financial markets, a phenomenon which has been both a driving force and a symptom of globalization. A politically mediated change, economic liberalization, has facilitated globalization by reducing restrictions on foreign investment, trade, and capital movements and generally creating a regulatory climate which is more conducive to operations on a global scale.

This chapter focuses on what is seen as an interesting and important aspect of the phenomenon of globalization: the emergence of the "stateless firm." It also considers the survival of the cartel as a generally illegal form of business cooperation, which is nevertheless attractive to its participants, and the development of a complex web of joint venture arrangements between major international firms. International firms are powerful actors in their own right, but also often have better developed coordination arrangements with other firms than exist between nation-states.

MULTINATIONALS AND THE EMERGENCE OF THE STATELESS FIRM

There is a vast literature on multinational firms and on foreign direct investment. The latter topic has received a recent stimulus from American concerns about increasing inward investment in that country, although it could be argued that all that is really happening is that the United States is moving to a position more similar to that of other advanced industrial countries in terms of the level of inward investment (Graham and Kurgman, 1989).

Global foreign direct investment has been growing faster than world trade and national economies. "While world trade volumes grew at a compound annual rate of 5% between 1983 and 1988, global FDI increased by over 20% in real terms over that period" (Julius, 1990: 14). FDI in the OECD economies has been growing four times as fast as GNP in the 1980s compared with twice as fast in the 1960s (Julius, 1990: 6). The United States has become a net inward investor, while Japan has become a significant source of outward investment flows.

The increase in the volume of foreign direct investment, along with shifts in the relative importance of different players and destinations, is by itself a significant aspect of economic globalization. An even more interesting development is the changing character of the companies involved in foreign direct investment. It must be stressed that what is being referred to here is an emergent rather than an established phenomenon, but one that may be significant if the pace of globalization is maintained.

The "traditional" model of a multinational company is of an organization whose base remains firmly located in its home state. Plants are opened overseas to circumvent protectionist barriers, to more easily serve local markets, or to exploit a technological lead. However, activities such as finance and research and development remain located in the home country. The directors and the shareholders are in the home country, and managers are sent out to manage a plant elsewhere as part of their career development. One consequence of this pattern of activity is the well-known "branch plants" syndrome, with local factories being vulnerable to downturns in the home state economy. The only significant exceptions to this general pattern have been Anglo-Dutch companies such as Unilever and Shell.

A recent development is the emergence of the "stateless company." The ownership of the company in terms of shareholdings is internationalized, a development reflected in the composition of the board of directors. The company no longer sees itself as being based in one country, but as operating globally. ICI is a good example of a company that has followed a deliberate strategy of internationalization. As a former chairman has commented, "we are undoubtedly the most international of all the big chemical companies" (quoted in Heller, 1987: 68). It is quoted on the New York and Tokyo stock exchanges, and has deliberately sought non-British members of its board of directors. Forty percent of its top 170 executives are not British.

Another example is ABB, formed from a merger of Sweden's ASEA with Switzerland's Brown Boveri. The headquarters were moved from Stockholm to Zurich to put the firm at the geographical center of the European markets. The managers are Swedish, Swiss, and German, business is done in English, and the books are kept in dollars (*Business Week,* May 14, 1990). ABB describes its "international organization as 'multi-domestic.' This means that we strive to be a local company everywhere and that we have many 'home countries'" (ABB, 1990: 7). The company's chief executive claims, "We have global coordination, but we have no national bias. The 100 professionals who happen to sit in Zurich could just as easily sit in Chicago or Frankfurt" (quoted in Taylor, 1991: 105).

One must be careful of overstating this trend. Hu warns that "stateless operations do not necessarily mean stateless corporations" and argues that "For a company to be stateless in the sense of being indifferent between nations, a necessary condition is that its operations should be distributed equally among nations" (Hu, 1992: 108–9). This is too stringent a criterion. First, the absence of a national bias does not mean that a company is indifferent between nations as sites for production or research and development operations, as sources of investment, or as markets. Second, no profit-maximizing company would distribute its operations equally among nations, but would concentrate on those countries which offered the best prospects for production, sales, and profits.

Given his definition, it is not surprising that Hu comes to the conclusion that "apart from the binational companies, there are no multinational, transnational or global enterprises, only national firms with international operations" (1992: 122). He uses as indicators the distribution of a company's assets and employees which would indeed be adequate for looking at conventional multinational operations. The crucial variable is not sales outside or assets outside the home country, phenomena which fit into the traditional picture of a multinational company, but rather shares held outside the home country. A *Business Week* analysis which ranks companies according to sales outside the home country looks less impressive when it is reconstituted according to shares held outside the home country (Table 10-1). Nestlé tops the table for sales (98 percent) and assets (95 percent) outside Switzerland, but its shares are overwhelmingly Swiss-held. The world of the stateless company has not yet arrived, but it is an incipient phenomenon which is worth attention.

It is worth noting that almost all the most internationalized companies are European. The Japanese company with the largest shareholding outside its home country is Canon (14 percent). Sony is the only major Japanese manufacturer with foreigners on its board, and most Japanese companies reserve senior management positions for Japanese nationals. Even given the expansion of Japanese foreign direct investment, less than 10 percent of Japanese companies' production is forecast to take place outside Japan by the mid-1990s compared with the seventeen percent for American firms. (Julius, 1990: 35). Globalization is still a phenomenon that affects countries in varying ways and to differing extents.

An important issue that arises in relation to stateless companies is whether they contribute to global convergence or divergence. A conven-

Table 10-1. Ranking of Multinational Companies by Shares Held Outside Home Country (20% or more of shares so held)

Company	Home country	Shares held outside home country (%)
ABB	Sweden	50
Bayer	Germany	48
Philips	Netherlands	46
Smithkline-Beecham	UK	46
Siemens	Germany	44
Hoescht	Germany	42
Unilever	Anglo-Dutch	27
Daimler Benz	Germany	25
Du Pont	US	24
SKF	Sweden	20
Electrolux	Sweden	20

Source: Business Week, May 14, 1990.

tional analysis might imply that companies want divergent conditions so that, for example, they can manufacture where labor and environmental production costs are low, and sell their products in markets where customers can afford to pay a price that gives them a good return. Global companies may also be able to take advantage of different taxation regimes. On the other hand, divergent conditions may give advantages to rivals already producing in a particular location. For example, the German chemical companies have favored uniform environmental standards in the European Community so that they are not disadvantaged by more stringent regulations in Germany.

Global companies recognize that there are still major divergences in national markets that have to be taken into account in their production and marketing strategies. The chief executive of ABB has stressed that his global managers "respect how different countries do things, and they have the imagination to appreciate why they do them that way" (Taylor, 1991: 94). But they also "push the limit of the culture ... They sort through the debris of cultural excuses and find opportunities to innovate" (Taylor, 1991: 94). One of ABB's biggest problems is a lack of global managers; "it is a crucial bottleneck for us" (Taylor, 1991: 94). Celebrations of the "growing cadre of global managers" (Reich, 1991: 77) may lead to a neglect of the fact that their relatively small numbers constitute a major constraint on the process of globalization, not least within global firms.

GLOBALIZATION AND ECONOMIC GOVERNANCE

It must first be made clear what this part of the chapter is not about. It is not yet another rehearsal of the role and limitations of international economic organizations. Some reference will be made later to the informal arrangements that were developed to coordinate the world economy in the wake of the severe shocks of the early and mid-1970s – economic summitry (Merlini, 1984), and the roles of G-2, G-3, G-5, and G-7 in managing the international monetary system through the Plaza and Louvre agreements (Funabashi, 1988).

A central theme of the argument is that it is important to consider how firms structure their relationships with one another in the international economy. Firms will seek out relationships with one another that enable them to achieve their goals. It is assumed that, in practice, these will often be satisficing rather than optimizing goals, and that firms will be ready to collude rather than compete to achieve a suboptimal but acceptable outcome. Global coordination can, of course, take place within a firm (Porter, 1990: 58–9), but building alliances with other firms may produce greater gains.

Facing the international firm is not, of course, an international state, but a series of nation-states which:

- Come together in international organizations to try to set a general framework for economic activity,
- Form coalitions within those organizations to pursue shared (or apparently shared) goals, e.g. the Cairns Group within GATT,
- Sometimes go as far as forming confederal quasistates to pursue common ends, e.g., the European Union.

However, even if there are limits to the extent to which authoritative decision making has been globalized, it can be argued that there is an emergence of an international political agenda which leads to the relatively rapid diffusion of policy problems and supposed solutions. Examples are (British led) privatization and (American led) deregulation, but the example that will be considered here is the emergence of an international regulatory agenda.

One point that should be made is that business associations do not generally function at a global level. They may confederate regionally (e.g., within the European Union or between the United States and Canada), and leading national associations may have regular meetings, although these may simply serve to expose the differences that exist between them on trade related questions. If one assumes that (the special case of employers' organizations concerned with collective bargaining aside) business associations are formed in response to the existence of an authoritative state, their absence at the global level is not surprising. Similarly, their emergence at the EU level (although usually as associations of associations) confirms the acquisition of some statelike properties by the EU.

CARTELS

Cartels are a recurrent but relatively understudied aspect of business activity. (For a general study see Mirow and Maurer, 1982). Because of their very nature, they are particularly difficult to research, and often only come to light as a result of investigations by fair trading authorities.

Although business enterprises have a general incentive to collude as a means of maintaining market share and driving up prices, whether they are able to do so depends on the existence of conditions that help to overcome the risk of one or more participant in the cartel breaking ranks and driving down prices. Certain industries are more prone to cartelization than others. The construction industry is particularly prone to cartelization because contracts are often allocated by tender. Hence, firms can collude over the tendering process in the expectation that each firm will have its turn. Any firm that breaks ranks can be easily identified. The procedures followed by governments for securing major overseas contracts for their national firms often have the effect of reinforcing cartelization practices by selecting one bidder for each contract.

Construction has certain special features as a sector, such as the way in which work is allocated through contracts. However, certain general characteristics of an industry appear to encourage cartelization such as a high entry price resulting from, for example, the capital intensive character of the industry, a stable population of firms, and a relatively undifferentiated set of products. These conditions are fulfilled in industries such as chemicals ("c is for chemicals is for cartels"), aluminium smelting, and steel. They are not fulfilled in industries such as consumer electronics. In the United Kingdom, all but two of the television manufacturers in business in 1987 were not in existence in 1972 (Cawson et al., 1990: 234).

The chemical industry has been characterized by cartelization from the prewar carving up of global markets by ICI, Du Pont, and IG Farben, to the succession of elaborate cartels exposed in the 1980s by the European Community which, in one case, even controlled the price of truck loads to individual customers. Even allowing for the postwar expansion of oil companies into the industry, the population of firms in the chemical industry has shown a remarkable stability. Industrial chemical products are relatively undifferentiated: PVC is PVC regardless of the firm that manufactures it.

Particular historical features can, of course, influence the pattern of cartelization in an industry. In aluminium smelting, "the development of cartels within the industry was to a large extent predetermined by the licence agreements of the original patents" (Graham, 1982: 18). In the late 1960s, a number of new producers emerged in the industry, some in bauxite producing countries, others in countries with cheap energy supplies. Faced with this new challenge and with increasing militancy on the part of the bauxite producers in the 1970s, "the leading aluminium companies closed ranks to coordinate member's investments, control prices and avoid over-production" (Graham, 1982: 257). Mikdashi argues that the cooperative strategies adopted by the aluminium companies "could only have appeared in a highly concentrated and international industry in which the component parts were deeply aware of their interdependence" (Mikdashi, 1974: 189).

The ability to cartelize can be undermined by technological changes that reduce entry costs. In the international telecommunications industry, the development of fiber optics and satellite communication are forcing change in combination with a move in some countries towards more liberalized telecommunications regimes. Such liberalization can, for example, permit cable companies to offer telephone services as well as television, so that old sectoral boundaries break down. The very size of the profits being made also attracts new entrants.

In the steel industry, entry costs are lower for the minimills which – making use of scrap metal as a raw material, electric arc furnaces, and new casting technologies – are able to produce steel more cheaply than their larger competitors. However, in the European Community, the EC's "manifest crisis" regime of the 1980s may well have served to protect the market share of the large integrated producers. The existence of cartels can be tolerated as a result of government inaction, or even reinforced, whether intentionally or not, by government policies.

JOINT VENTURES

Even in industries such as chemicals which have long experience of cartelization, cartels may fail to achieve the desired result in terms of a higher price or a protected market share. They may be disrupted by one or more members' breaking ranks. They may be broken up by national or international competition authorities, leading to fines or bad publicity. Moreover, the range of objectives that can be achieved through cartels is limited. They may help a firm to protect what it has, and to extract as high as possible a return from its existing assets, but they do not provide a means of opening up new markets, or developing new products, or of gaining access to new technologies.

In this area, joint ventures are more useful. They provide many of the advantages of a merger without many of its disadvantages. A company does not lose its identity or its control of its assets, but it is able to benefit from pooling those assets with others. It is possible to be involved in a large number of joint ventures simultaneously covering different markets and products. Such special-purpose arrangements can help manufacturers to fill gaps in their market coverage and seek manufacturing cost efficiencies. The OECD symposium of government officials and corporate managers reported that "the profusion of collaborative alliances and relationships among firms ... was regarded by some participants as one of the most distinctive features of globalization and as a new and prominent trait in corporate strategies of several industries" (OECD, 1994: 192).

The steel industry, which traditionally was based on (often state-owned) companies serving their own national markets, has seen an increasing number of cross-border joint ventures and minority shareholdings. For example, all the big U.S. integrated steelmakers except Bethlehem have forged alliances with the five main Japanese integrated steelmakers. The Japanese companies gain greater access to the U.S. market, particularly to Japanese car transplants, and the U.S. companies, which cannot afford to sustain an adequate level of research and development, gain access to Japanese technology. In Europe, there has been a series of cross-border joint ventures focused on finishing capacity. For example, Sollac of France has pooled its merchant bar and electrical sheet operations with Cockerill-Sambre of Belgium, its sheet piling and rail products with Arbed of Luxembourg, and its reinforcing activities with Riva, the Italian private sector producer.

However, the industry that has the most extensive and complex web of joint ventures is motor vehicles. As a former chairman of Rover, Sir Graham Day, has commented, "The motor industry is a global village with a spider's web of collaborative agreements" (*Financial Times,* September 13, 1991). One important factor in encouraging such joint ventures is the emergence of Japan as a leading car producer. A major car company official has commented, "This has irreversibly shifted the 'balance of power,' and joint ventures between competitors that were unthinkable a decade ago are expanding yearly."

All three leading American companies have links with at least one Japanese company (Ford with Mazda; General Motors with Isuzu, Suzuki and Toyota; Chrysler with Mitsubishi Motors). Such links may have provided a means for the American industry to learn at first hand about Japanese production methods and management techniques. The production philosophy at the Saturn plant of General Motors was learned to a large extent from its joint venture with Toyota in California. Joint ventures with Korean firms may be seen as a way of getting into the low-cost segment of the market.

The United States–Japan joint venture and minority shareholding links are the strongest in the world auto industry. United States companies have been involved in Europe through wholly-owned subsidiaries (note how Ford eventually got rid of the minority shareholding in Ford United Kingdom), although Chrysler may reenter the European market through joint ventures and collaboration. Links between Europe and Japan are still developing. Volkswagen produces a Toyota-designed truck in Hanover, while in Japan it has a cooperation arrangement with Nissan for local car assembly. In 1991 Mitsubishi Motors completed a deal with Volvo of Sweden and the Dutch government to create a joint venture in Netherlands with the aim of producing 200,000 cars a year in the second half of the 1990s.

Such arrangements are a rational response by companies as a means of combining assets and technological knowledge, sharing costs, and entering new markets as cheaply as possible. However, they can also inhibit competition and restrict access to technology and markets. Participants in the OECD symposium "pointed to the danger of global oligopolies and the lack of competition laws at the international level to regulate these cross-border alliances and ventures" (OECD, 1994: 192).

A GLOBAL REGULATORY AGENDA

The 1980s have often been celebrated as a decade of deregulation. In practice, however, the achievements of deregulation have often been more limited than has been claimed, while environmental pressures have led to the growth of new forms of regulation. Runge draws attention to the phenomenon of "ecoprotectionism" which "involves the internationalization of issues related to food, health and safety" (1990: 187). The globalization of financial markets creates a need for reregulation rather than deregulation.

It is certainly possible to discern something that might be recognized as an international regulatory agenda. National regulatory authorities are aware of steps taken by their counterparts elsewhere, and harmonization of measures may be necessary to prevent disruption to international trade. Brickman, Jasanoff, and Ilgen (1985: 300) note that "the United States undeniably plays a leadership role in the cross-national alignment and evolution of chemical control policies." However, they also emphasize the limits of international policy convergence. "There is still far more policy making and regulatory initiative taken in response to purely domestic circumstances than there is either formal intergovernmental agreement or spontaneous co-ordination." (Brickman, Jasanoff, and Ilgen, 1985: 298).

In international financial markets, global enterprises face national regulatory authorities with large variations in their supervision arrangements. The BCCI affair illustrates how difficult it is for international supervisory authorities to agree on common action when faced with a bank with a highly complex structure and no clear home base. National authorities can, of course, improve their stock of information by informal and ad hoc exchanges with their counterparts elsewhere, although these can be inhibited by confidentiality requirements and legal impediments. The first formal meeting between senior regulators from Japan, the United States, and the United Kingdom that was aimed at greater cooperation over securities markets regulation took place in September 1990. It was seen as reflecting "growing concern about the dangers of contagion spreading between national securities markets, and the increasingly cross-border nature of securities frauds" (*Financial Times,* September 11, 1990). It may be that an enhanced role will develop for the International Organization of Securities Commissions. Underhill (1991: 221) argues:

> In general, there is closer cooperation among the major industrialised economies on the management of the world's money and on the serious financial imbalances which have evolved among states ... Banks and financial markets are calling for a better-defined state role in structuring the process of marketisation, the better to take advantage of it without too many attendant risks.

However, relatively light or absent regulation can be a competitive advantage, and in countries with less stringent regulatory regimes, traders are likely to resist any move towards harmonization that would lead to the imposition of more stringent regulatory standards. Equally, national regulations can provide a useful barrier to the entry of foreign competitors into the national financial services market.

More generally, it is apparent that "The development of international business regulation has not taken place within an orderly framework of international organization providing an international political basis for the rational coordination of national state regulation" (Picciotto, 1989: 15). Various forms of international coordination have developed which have influenced changes in national regulations. "However, due to its narrow political base, international coordination has remained a technical and specialist matter" (Picciotto, 1989: 15). However, the issues can be redefined so that they become a matter of "high" politics (Hancher and Moran, 1989: 284).

Much of the recent work on regulation emphasizes the central role of the large, multinational firm, a theme emphasized earlier in the chapter. Such an enterprise serves as "a locus of power, a reservoir of expertise, a bearer of economic change, and an agent of enforcement in the implementation process" (Hancher and Moran, 1989: 272). Growing internationalization can limit the ability of a national government to regulate a firm. In extreme cases, the outcome is "regulation of government by the firm" (Cawson et al., 1989: 130). What all this suggests is that in the area of regulation – where one might expect government (whether a national government, the EC, or an international organization) to be the key actor – it is often the firm that emerges as the vital decision maker. If the power of the international firms is to be balanced by a mechanism or entity with a broader range of concerns, it is unrealistic to expect this to be done effectively at the national level.

CONCLUSIONS

The emergence of the stateless firm and the development of more complex forms of cross-national cooperation between firms provide a new set of imperatives and challenges for international economic cooperation between political decision makers. Of course, stateless firms may themselves see some benefits in the development of such cooperation. For example, in the longer run, conditions of exchange rate stability are helpful to their expansion plans. More generally, strategic planning by stateless firms is not assisted by a "climate of uncertainty" (ABB, 1990: 4) which a measure of international cooperation may help to reduce.

International forms of governance therefore need to incorporate the firm as a central and accepted actor. Stopford and Strange (1991: 22) argue that "The growth of global competition can be seen as moving the world towards a position where events are conditioned more by an emerging managerial technocracy than by traditional notions of state power." It may be that a dual response that combines both acceptance and challenge is the appropriate response to these developments. Leading stateless firms should be treated as legitimate actors in their own right in the international system, but there should also be a continuing development of supranational bodies that are in some ultimate sense politically accountable to democratically elected entities or individuals. A completely uncontrolled, largely oligopolistic world market could devour itself. Political regimes thus perform both a supporting and a controlling function.

One mechanism of international cooperation that has evolved in the 1970s and 1980s is that of the economic summit and the G-7 process. This has increasingly developed in practice into a G-3 process with the main leadership roles being performed by the United States (consulting with Canada), Germany (consulting with the other EC states in the G-7), and Japan. In particular G-7 played an important role in the restoration of greater exchange rate stability in the late 1980s.

There are, of course, severe limits to this process. Funabashi notes that "Although the Plaza strategy has given impetus to regime building, in essence the exercise remains an ad hoc process of adjustment" (1988: 242). Linkages with domestic policy remain weak, e.g., the problem of the United States budget deficit. An underlying problem is that the countries are not single actors. Recurrent tensions between finance ministries and central banks are a central inhibiting feature of the G-7 process, as is the large turnover of senior participants. Moreover, "transnational coalition building to facilitate the policy coordination process is still minimal" (Funabashi, 1988: 248).

More fundamental criticisms are offered by free market economists who see the economic summit process as essentially harmful. They dispute the claim that the informal links developed through the G-7 process assisted official cooperation after the 1987 stock market crash, arguing that attempts at coordination contributed to the crash. Even those better disposed to the G-7 process often argue that the early summits were the most productive. The summits have become something of a media circus, but the attention given to them may reinforce one of their most useful functions, that of energizing the policy process, "allowing central executives to overcome bureaucratic and political obstacles that would be obdurate under more normal circumstances" (Putnam, 1984: 75). Moreover, much of the important work is done by meetings of officials between, or in preparation for, the summits.

Dobson (1991) has sought to identify ways in which the G-7 process could be improved. Her suggestions include involving central bankers more closely, creating an institutional memory and support mechanism, in the form of a secretariat and strengthening implementation, in part through changes in national decision structures. Most controversially, she suggests that "After stage II of EMU is reached, the G-7 should be rationalized into a G-3" (Dobson, 1991: 150). The difficulty with this solution is that, by advancing an apparently realistic solution to the problem of international coordination, it creates a set of rules of the game which might well turn out to be skewed in favor of a small group of hegemon powers. A better alternative might be to widen the scope of G-7 to include major emerging economies such as India and China.

G-7 has reached a point at which it has to be either substantially revitalized or abandoned. G-7 has itself been looking at the need to rationalize the institutions of global cooperation. The difficulty of creating more effective international bodies is illustrated by the obstacles encountered in the transformation of GATT into a World Trade Organization (WTO). A fundamental problem is that the new organizational framework faces the same problems as its predecessor (e.g., a United States propensity to take unilateral action, United States–Japan and United States–European Union tensions) and little more in the way of authority or effective decision-making power to deal with them. Sectoral politics (e.g., agriculture, textiles) remain deeply embedded in the new organization, frustrating solutions that do not meet with the approval of key sectoral actors. While some analysts see the presence of regional trading blocs as compatible with multilateralism, the existence and likely growth of NAFTA and the European Union sits somewhat uncomfortably with the ostensibly global concerns of the World Trade Organization (WTO).

A more general concern is that stateless global firms may face new political formations operating at a purely regional level, which therefore cannot match the reach of the firms. One does not have to wish to indulge in utopian dreams about world government to recognize that the economic realities of the twenty-first century are going to require more effective regime formation at an international level. New institutional arrangements might have to come to terms with stateless firms as political actors in their own right, a prospect that raises difficult issues for democracy and political legitimacy. Democratically-formulated political goals might, however, better be served by coopting large firms into a political bargaining process that influences their behavior rather than treating them as exogenous actors whose actions can be effectively controlled by nation-states or even by regional confederations.

REFERENCES

ABB. 1990. *Annual Report.* Zurich: Asea Brown Boveri.
Brickman, R., S. Jasanoff, and T. Ilgen. 1985. *Controlling Chemicals: The Politics of Regulation in Europe and the United States.* Ithaca: Cornell University Press.
Cawson, A., G. Shepherd, and D. Webber. 1989. "Governments, Markets and Regulation in the West European Consumer Electronics Industry." In L.

Hancher and M. Moran, eds. *Capitalism, Culture and Economic Regulation.* Oxford: Clarendon Press. Pp. 109–33.

Cawson, A., K. Morgan, D. Webber, P. Holmes, and A. Stevens. 1990. *Hostile Brothers: Competition and Closure in the European Electronics Industry.* Oxford: Clarendon Press.

Dobson, W. 1991. *Economic Policy Coordination: Requiem or Prologue?* Washington, D.C.: Institute for International Economics. *Financial Times,* Sept. 13, 1991.

Finkelstein, L. S. 1991. "What is International Governance?" Annual Meeting of the International Studies Association, Vancouver.

Funabashi, Y. 1988. *Managing the Dollar: From the Plaza to the Louvre.* Washington: Institute for International Economics.

GATT. 1990. *International Trade 89-90: Volume 1.* Geneva: General Agreement on Tariffs and Trade.

Graham, E. M. and P. R. Krugman. 1989. *Foreign Direct Investment in the United States.* Washington: Institute for International Economics.

Graham, R. 1982. *The Aluminium Industry and the Third World.* London: Zed Books.

Hancher, L. and M. Moran. 1989. "Organizing Regulatory Space." In L. Hancher and M. Moran, eds. *Capitalism, Culture and Economic Regulation.* Oxford: Clarendon Press. Pp. 271–99.

Heller, R. 1987. *The State of Industry.* London: Sphere Books.

Hu, Y-S. 1992. "Global or Stateless Corporations are National Firms with International Operations." *California Management Review.* 34 (2): 107–26.

Julius, De Anne. 1990. *Global Companies and Public Policy.* London: The Royal Institute of International Affairs/Pinter Publishers.

Keohane, R. O. "The Study of International Regimes and the Classical Tradition in International Relations." Paper delivered at the 1986 annual meeting of the American Political Science Association, Washington, D.C.

Kratochwil, F. and J. Ruggie. 1986. "International Organization: A State of the Art on the Art of the State." *International Organization.* 40 (4).

Lodge, D. 1984. *Small World.* New York: Warner Books.

Merlini, C., ed. 1984. *Economic Summits and Western Decision-Making.* London: Croom Helm.

Mikdashi, Z. 1974. "Aluminium." In R. Vernon, ed. *Big Business and the State.* London: Macmillan. Pp. 170–94.

Mirow, K. R. and Maurer, H. 1982. *Webs of Power: International Cartels and the World Economy.* Boston: Houghton Mifflin.

OECD. 1994. *Industrial Policy in OECD Countries: Annual Review 1994.* Paris: Organization for Economic Cooperation and Development.

Ohmae, K. 1990. *The Borderless World: Power and Strategy in the Interlinked Economy.* London: Collins.

Picciotto, S. 1989. "Slicing a Shadow: Business Taxation in an International Framework." In L. Hancher and M. Moran, eds. *Capitalism, Culture and Economic Regulation.* Oxford: Clarendon Press. Pp. 12–47.

Porter, M. 1990. *The Competitive Advantage of Nations.* London: Macmillan.

Putnam, R. 1984. "The Western Economic Summits: a Political Interpretation." In C. Merlini, ed. *Economic Summits and Western Decision-Making.* London: Croom Helm. Pp. 43–88.

Reich, R. 1991. "Who is Them?" *Harvard Business Review.* March–April, 77–88.

Runge, C. F. 1990. "Prospects for the Uruguay Round in Agriculture." In H. J. Michaelman et al., eds. *The Political Economy of Agricultural Trade and Policy.* Boulder: Westview. Pp. 175–93.

Stopford, J. and S. Strange with J. S. Henley. 1991. *Rival States, Rival Firms.* Cambridge: Cambridge University Press.

Taylor, W. 1991. "The Logic of Global Business: an Interview with ABB's Percy Barnevik." *Harvard Business Review.* March–April 1991, 91–105.

Underhill, G. R. D. 1991. "Markets Beyond Politics? The State and the Internationalisation of Financial Markets." *European Journal of Political Research.* 19: 197–225.

11

GLOBALIZATION IN QUESTION: INTERNATIONAL ECONOMIC RELATIONS AND FORMS OF PUBLIC GOVERNANCE

Paul Hirst and Grahame Thompson

INTRODUCTION

"Globalization" has become an increasingly fashionable concept in the social sciences. It is widely supposed that the process of economic "globalization" has taken place or is taking place, leading to a situation in which most economic activities have been internationalized and the nation-state has lost its capacity as a locus of economic governance. A truly "global" economy would thus be a new stage in economic relationships, qualitatively different from previous structures of the international economy. This paper asks whether there is such a thing as a globalized economy. It further asks, if not, then how are we to characterize the present state of the world economy?

In the first place, we set out to examine whether such a process of globalization can be specified with some degree of rigor and assessed against the available evidence of international economic trends, thus enabling us to determine whether this phenomenon is taking place or not. To do this we have constructed two contrasting economic types: a fully globalized economy and an open international economy that is still fundamentally determined by processes occurring at the level of national economies. These types enable us to clarify the issues, and conceptually to specify the difference between a potentially new global economy and merely extensive and intensive international economic relations. Too often evidence of the latter is used to substantiate the former.

Second, having specified the ideal types, we go on to consider the main trends in the international economy and how they fit with the ideal type of globalization. Third, we examine both the constraints on, and the remaining forms of effectiveness of national economic management, given the current conjuncture in the international economy. In assessing the possibilities of governance at the international level we then examine supranational trading blocs and the possibilities of coordination through cooperation on the part of the major players.

A GLOBALIZED ECONOMY: WHAT WOULD IT LOOK LIKE?

A WORLD-WIDE INTERNATIONAL ECONOMY

The *world-wide international economy* is one in which the principal entities are nation states, and involves the process of the growing interconnection between national economies. It involves the increasing integration of more and more nations and economic actors into market relationships. Trade relations, as a result, take on the form of national specialization and the division of labor. The importance of trade is, however, progressively replaced by the centrality of investment relations between nations, which increasingly acts as the organizing principle of the system. The form of interdependence between nations remains, however, of the "strategic" kind. That is, it implies the continued relative separation of the domestic and the international frameworks for policy making and the management of economic affairs, and also a relative separation in terms of economic effects. Interactions are conceived as the "billiard ball" type; international events do not directly penetrate or permeate the domestic economy but are refracted through national policies and processes. The international and the domestic policy fields either remain separated as distinct levels of governance or they work "automatically." In the latter case, adjustments are not thought to be the subject of policy by public bodies or authorities, but are consequences of "unorganized" or "spontaneous" market forces.

Perhaps the classic case of such an "automatic" adjustment mechanism remains the gold standard (GS), which operated at the height of the *Pax Britannica* system from midcentury to 1914. Automatic is put in quotes here to signal the fact that this is a popular caricature. The actual system of adjustment took place very much in terms of overt domestic policy interventions. The flexibility in wages and prices that the GS system demanded (the international value of currencies could not be adjusted since these were fixed in terms of gold) had to be engineered by governments through domestic expenditure-reducing policies to influence the current account and interest rate policy to influence the capital account.

It is important to recognize that the GS and the *Pax Britannica* system was merely one of the structures of the international economy in this century. World War I wrecked the British hegemony, accelerating a process that would have occurred far more slowly merely as a consequence of British industrial decline. It resulted in a period of protectionism and national autarkic competition in the 1930s, followed by the establishment of American hegemony after World War II and the reopened international economy of the Bretton-Woods system. This indicates the danger of assuming that current major changes in the international economy are unprecedented and that they are inevitable or irreversible. The lifetime of a prevailing system of international economic relations in this century has been no more than 30 to 40 years. Such systems have been transformed by major changes in the politicoeconomic balance of power and the conjunctures that have effected these shifts have been large-scale conflicts between the major powers. In that sense, the worldwide international economy has been determined in its structure and the distribution of power within it by the major nation-states.

The period of this worldwide international economic system is also typified by the rise and maturity of the multinational corporation (MNC). The important aspect of these MNCs is that they retain a clear national home base; they are subject to the national regulations of the mother country, and by and large they are effectively policed by that home country.

A GLOBALIZED INTERNATIONAL ECONOMY

A *globalized international economy* is a distinct ideal-type from that of the worldwide economy and can be developed by contrast with it. In such a global system, distinct national economies are subsumed and rearticulated into the system by international processes and transactions. The worldwide economy, on the contrary, is one in which processes that are determined at the level of national economies still dominate and international phenomena are outcomes that emerge from the distinct and differential performance of the national economies. The worldwide economy is an aggregate of nationally located functions. Thus while there are in such an economy a wide and increasing range of international economic interactions (financial markets and trade in manufactured goods, for example), these tend to function as opportunities or constraints for nationally located economic actors and their public regulators.

The global economy raises these nationally-based interactions to a new power. The international system becomes autonomized, as markets and production become truly global. Domestic policy makers, whether private corporations or public regulators, now have routinely to take account of the predominately international determinants of their activities. As systemic interdependence grows, the national level is permeated by and transformed by the international. In such a globalized economy the problem this poses for public authorities is how to construct policies that coordinate and integrate their regulatory efforts in order to cope with the systematic interdependence between their economic actors.

The first major consequence of a globalized economy would thus be the fundamental problematicity of its governance. Global markets are difficult to regulate, even supposing effective cooperation by the regulators and a coincidence of their interests. The difficulty is to construct both effective and integrated patterns of public policy to cope with global market forces, since to work such policies would need to be coordinated from the level of international regulatory agencies down to key regional governments. The interdependence of states and markets would by no means necessarily result in a harmonious world integration in which world consumers benefit from truly independent allocative mechanisms. On the contrary, it is more than plausible that the populations of even successful and advanced states and regions would be at the mercy of autonomized and uncontrollable, because global, market forces. Interdependence would then readily promote *disintegration* – i.e., competition and conflict – between regulatory agencies at different levels. Such conflict would further weaken effective public governance at the global level. Enthusiasts for the efficiency of free markets and the superiority of corporate control to that of public agencies would see this as a rational world freed from the shackles of obsolete and ineffective national public interventions. Others, less sanguine but convinced that globalization *is* occurring, may see it as a world system in which there can be no generalized or sustained public reinsurance against the costs imposed by market distributions or market failures on localities.

Even if one does not endorse the concept of globalization, this ideal-type can help to highlight some of the importance of greater economic integration within the major regional trade blocs. Both the EU and NAFTA will soon be highly integrated markets of continental scale. Already in the case of the EU it is clear that there are fundamental problems of the integration and coordination of regulatory policies between the different public authorities at European Union, national, and regional levels.

It is also clear that this ideal-type highlights the problem of weak public governance for the major corporations. Even if such companies were truly global, they will not be able to operate in all markets equally effectively, and like governments will lack the capacity for reinsurance against unexpected shocks from their own resources alone. Governments would no longer be available to assist as they have been for "national champions." Firms would therefore seek to share risks and opportunities through intercorporate investments, partnerships, joint ventures, etc. Even in the current internationalized economy we can recognize such processes emerging.

A second major consequence of the notion of a globalizing international economy would be the transformation of MNCs into transnational corporations (TNCs) as the major players in the world economy. The TNC would be genuine footloose capital, without specific national identification and with an internationalized management, and at least potentially willing to locate and relocate anywhere in the globe to obtain either the most secure or the highest returns. In the financial sector this could be secured at the touch of a button and in a truly globalized economy would be wholly dictated by market forces, without reference to national monetary policies. In the case of primarily manufacturing companies they would source, produce, and market at the global level as strategy and opportunities dictated. The company would no longer be based on one predominant national location (as with the MNC) but would service global markets through global operations. Thus the TNC, unlike the MNC, could no longer be controlled or even constrained by the policies of particular national states. Rather it could escape all but the commonly agreed and enforced international regulatory standards. National governments could not thus effectively adopt particular regulatory policies that diverged from these standards to the detriment of TNCs operating within their borders. The TNC would be the main manifestation of a truly globalized economy.

Julius (1990) and Ohmae (1990) both consider this trend toward true TNCs to be well established. Ohmae argues that such "stateless" corporations are now the prime movers in an interlinked economy (ILE) centered in North America, Europe, and Japan. He contends that macroeconomic and industrial policy intervention by national governments can only distort and impede the rational process of resource allocation by corporate decisions and consumer choices on a global scale. Like Akio Morita of Sony, Ohmae argues that such corporations will pursue strategies of "global localization" in responding on a worldwide scale to specific regionalized markets and locating effectively to meet the varying demands of distinct localized groups of consumers. The assumption here is that TNC's will rely primarily on foreign direct investment and the full domestication of production to meet such specific market demands. This is in contrast to the strategy of flexibly specialized core production in the company's main location and the building of branch assembly plants where needed or dictated by national public policies. The later strategy is compatible with nationally based companies.

A third consequence of globalization would be the further decline in the political influence and economic bargaining power of labor. Globalized markets and TNCs would not be mirrored by an open world labor market. Thus while advanced companies might well continue to locate in the advanced countries, with all their advantages, rather than merely seek low wages, the trend of the global mobility of capital and the national fixity of labor would favor those advanced countries with the most tractable labor forces and the lowest social overheads relative to the benefits of labor competence and motivation. "Social democratic" strategies of enhancement of working conditions would thus be viable only if they assured the competitive advantage of the labor force, without constraining management prerogatives, and at no more overall cost in taxation than the average for the advanced world. Such strategies would clearly be a tall order and the tendency of globalization would be to favor management at the expense of even moderately organized labor, and therefore policies sympathetic to the former rather than the latter.

So far we have sought to clarify what would be involved in claiming either that we are firmly within a globalizing economy or that there are strong globalizing tendencies. Firmly to establish this is a rather difficult task. It is made doubly so, and the outcome quite uncertain, because of a number of changes in the international economy in the post–World War I period. Chief among these have been the change in hegemonic leadership during the interwar period and then the decline and possible collapse of the *Pax Americana* in the post-1970s period.

The *Pax Americana,* as it established and consolidated itself in the immediate post-1945 period, heralded the beginning of the liberal multilateral market system that supported the international economy during the long boom. But the American hegemony displayed a number of dimensions. Militarily it is arguable that the United States is still hegemonic. This was clearly the case in the context of the Gulf War. In addition, the United States still serves as the powerhouse of world demand, and acts as the guardian of the world open trading economy. But it no longer has monetary hegemony. No other power or combination of powers can yet challenge this residual hegemonic power that the United States displays. It may not be able to command the tight loyalty of the other western powers that it did during the period of the Cold War, but it retains considerable genuinely hegemonic strengths.

Both of these developments – the change and then the undermining of the hegemonic order, accompanied by the totally floating rate regime – provided the conditions in which the logic of the "worldwide economy" might be thought to have been undermined. These developments led to the abandonment of exchange controls, and the liberalization and then deregulation of international financial markets. But the floating exchange rate regime began to exhibit quite perverse "overshooting." It was accompanied by the supply side shock of the oil price hikes, with consequent massive increases of both the liquidity of the OPEC countries and the desire to borrow (given negative real interest rates) by the Third World countries to finance their current account deficits, leading to the so-called "Third World debt" problem. These features also initiated a serious recession in the international economy more generally, with a concomitant increase in government indebtedness. A chronic structural problem of the balance of payments between the United States and Japan in particular also emerged as the United States became a massive capital importer to finance its deteriorating trade balance.

The totally floating rate period did not last for long. In 1979, for instance, the EC set up the European Monetary System (EMS) to provide a zone of stability for the main European currencies (except the U.K. pound) against the vagaries of the U.S. dollar. In addition, the Louvre and Plaza accords between the Group of 7 (G-7) countries in the 1980s set in motion an attempt to monitor and "manage" fundamental disequilibrium in the exchange rates between its members. Explicit policy coordination at the world level was initiated in this case. This has not reversed the main trend which has been to further undermine the old postwar multilateral order. These events register the contingent nature of some of the phenomena that have been used to argue for a structured transformation in the international economy. Many of these trends could be reversed or interrupted as the international economy evolves. We should be cautious in ascribing too much significance to what might be temporary changes, dramatic though some of them have been.

The strong concept of a globalized economy acts as an ideal-type against which we can measure the actual trends within the international economy. This globalized economy has been contrasted to the notion of a worldwide economy in the preceding analysis in order to distinguish its particular and novel features. The opposition of these two types for conceptual clarity conceals a potential messy combination of the two in fact, which would make sifting the available evidence very difficult to determine trends. These two types of economies are not necessarily mutually exclusive; rather in certain conditions the globalized economy would *encompass and subsume* the world-wide economy; it transforms them as it reinforces them. There would thus be a complex combination of features of both types of economy present within the present conjuncture if this combined phenomenon were to occur. The problem in determining what is happening is to identify the dominant trends: that is, the growth of globalization or the continuation of the existing worldwide patterns. We now try to summarize and assess the main current trends.

THE PRESENT INTERNATIONAL ECONOMY

Here we examine the main trends in the international economy and comment on them in terms of how they fit with the globalization thesis. We identify five main trends that are discussed in turn.

1. Within the contemporary international economy the important relationships remain those between the more developed economies, the members of the Organization of Economic Cooperation and Development (OECD). Indeed, these economies have increased in their relative importance over recent years in terms of their share of world trade and investment. In 1989 over 80 percent of world trade was conducted between the OECD economies, and this rose to 85 percent if the ex-Eastern European and Soviet economies were included. The Group of 5 (G-5) main economies accounted for 75 percent of foreign direct investment. Thus for all practical intents and purposes it is the advanced industrial economies that constitute the membership of the "global" economy, if that entity can be said to exist. The LDCs (less developed countries), and even the NICs (newly industrializing countries), still constitute a very small part of the international economy. The primary producers are more or less totally dependent upon the MDCs (more developed countries) for markets and investment, which is a position that has not significantly changed for many decades. FDI (foreign direct investment) and trade flows thus remain distinctly "lumpy." Capital is not fleeing from the advanced countries; thus 14 percent of the world's population accounted for 75 percent of FDI in 1980–91 and for 70 percent of world trade in 1992 (Hirst and Thompson, 1994: 295–96).

2. There is little doubt that there has been a progressive internationalization of money and capital markets since the 1970s, and this was a marked change in relation to the post-1945 period. Many have seized upon this as a sign of the radical change towards a globalizing economy.

It has led to the argument that national economies are no longer governable because they have become increasingly penetrated by "international financial capital." This inability to control capital flows is claimed to undermine any remaining credibility of policies of national macroeconomic management.

But the implications of this internationalization of financial markets are not unambiguous. For instance Tomlinson (1988) presents data showing that the international financial penetration of the United Kingdom and other economies (in terms of openness to capital flows) was *greater* between 1905 and 1914 than it was between 1982 and 1986 (and similar results emerge for foreign trade as a percentage of GDP). Thus it is important to remember that the international economy was hardly less integrated between 1870 and 1914 than it is today.

We must be careful to elaborate the reasons for the admittedly phenomenal recent growth of international financial flows and liquidity. Here we need to emphasize:

- The floating of exchange rates.
- The oil price hike and consequent Third World debt problem.
- The unexpected emergence of vast and mobile OPEC funds.
- The international recession and the growth in government debt through the 1970s.
- The emergent structural imbalances in the balance of payments for a number of large economies.
- Finally, the liberalization and deregulation of financial markets by national governments.

All these features went to increase the extent of international capital flows. If we were to single out one central feature, it would surely be the floating of exchange rates. Many of the other features followed as a consequence of this (e.g., the integration of trading on currency and equity markets which *is* a new feature of the present period).

This demonstrates how many of these changes may be temporary. They are not irreversible. First, volatility on the international currency markets could diminish (indeed *has* diminished) as the EMS and the G-7 monitoring system was installed. All the major international currencies are now more or less "managed" currencies, which has seriously cut speculative activity (a factor that promoted volatility and exchange rate uncertainty). The continuing difficulties of the EMS do not necessarily contradict this statement, since the root cause is the divergent performance of economies in the EU and a *Bundesbank* policy that has put price stability in Germany above the maintenance of stability within the EMS. The problem is not speculators, but public policies that prompt speculation, by leading to uncertainty and anticipated changes in exchange rates. Secondly, after an initial enthusiastic embrace of market liberalization and deregulation, the authorities are recognizing that there are undesirable consequences of this and the trend now is for reregulation.

3. There has been an increasing volume of trade in semimanufactured and manufactured goods between the industrialized economies. Most markets for major industrial products are now international and major economies both import and export significant volumes of such goods, whereas before the 1960s home sourcing was dominant and export markets were more specialized. This has had an inevitable impact on the ability of individual economies to exercise national macromanagement strategies. We consider this point below, because domestic demand can be sourced from a wide range of foreign suppliers and strong national expansionary policies can be choked off by rapidly rising imports.

4. One of the main concomitants of the growth in interdependent trade relations is the progressive development of internationalized companies. The role of the TNCs in undermining national government's conduct of an independent economic policy has already been raised. But again the extent of these developments is questionable (Ostry, 1992). Most international companies still only operate in a small number of countries, or at most regionally. Typically most major manufacturing multinationals account for two-thirds of their sales within their home region; moreover, there seems to be no tendency for this ratio to diminish (Hirst and Thompson, 1996: Chapter 4). There are few true TNCs. The MNC form continues to dominate. The few exceptions to this do not yet make the rule. Thus the examples of transnational companies like ABB cited by Grant in Chapter 10 of this volume, while of interest, do not alter the aggregate statistical picture constructed from the best available data. In addition, most MNCs adapt passively to governmental policy rather than continually trying to undermine it. The real question to ask of MNCs is not why they are always threatening to up and leave a country if things seem to go badly for them there, but why the vast majority of them fail to leave and continue to stay put in their home base and major centers of investment? MNCs are very reluctant to uproot themselves because they get entrenched in specific national markets, and with local suppliers and dealers. This makes it both difficult and expensive to leave given national markets unless there are fundamental structural disincentives, rather than conjunctural difficulties or specific policy constraints imposed by national governments.

Nor is direct foreign investment as important as is often believed. Take
the case of Japan, for instance, which is often thought to be heralding a new
global assault on both the industrial and underdeveloped world with its investment strategies. A recent study tries to examine the character of Japanese direct foreign manufacturing investment (Williams et al. 1992); it is
fairly small-scale compared to the total volume of Japanese capital abroad,
and it is mainly aimed at providing transplants that have a high import content from Japan. In relation to Japanese trade growth, the aggregate growth
of direct investment is small. Moreover, it is no more efficient or profitable
than indigenous manufacturing. (Some of these conclusions might be altered, however, if a more disaggregated view were taken of Japanese FDI).
In general the most successful industrial nations (e.g., Germany and Japan)
have shown a great reluctance to develop core manufacturing activity
abroad; they keep the bulk of their value adding capacity at home. This is
for a variety of reasons, not all of which can be summed up in market efficiency or balance sheet terms. German and Japanese financial capital remains more "nationalistic," and is committed to its domestic manufacturing sector in a way Anglo-American capital is not. German and Japanese
firms still have a strong commitment to highly skilled and motivated national labor forces. A "deal" between labor and capital to sustain prosperity
was, in different ways, a core part of both their post-1945 national politicoeconomic settlements. In both countries there would be a massive political price to pay were a major part of manufacturing to be shipped abroad
and the prosperity of recent decades to falter.

5. Perhaps the most significant post-1970s development, and the most
enduring, is the formation of supranational trading and economic blocs.
One initial question, however, is exactly how to specify these blocs. Clearly
the EU and the NAFTA can be considered genuine blocs, or protoblocs,
without too much controversy. But are there any others? Japan is often seen
as the center of a protoblock encompassing much of the SE Asian Pacific rim
countries. But examination of trade and investment data show this to be
premature. Initially, therefore, it may be better to consider Japan as a single
country bloc. Lots of ad hoc combinations of countries that might form
(limited) trading and economic blocs around the Pacific Rim and in the rest
of Asia have been suggested, but at the present time these remain largely
speculative.

A more regionalized international economy would increase the possibility of protectionist attitudes and policies on the part of at least some of
the trading blocs. Such protectionism would weaken and even perhaps reverse some of the other trends towards economic internationalization previ-

ously identified, such as the growth in interdependence in world trade flows and the continuing integration of financial markets. The general issue to consider, however, is the likely form of the global economy as the liberal-multilateralist regime of the post-1945 period is replaced by other institutions. Will globalization – in the sense of open and unregulated world markets – replace the old regime of managed liberal multilateralism? Our suggestion is most likely not. The outcome is likely to be a messy mixture of liberal regulation (GATT) and the growing saliency of regional blocs, both being dominated by the triad of NAFTA, the EU, and Japan. The "G-3" will continue to dominate general international regimes and to bargain bilaterally between themselves and with lesser parties. The world economy will thus be governed, at least partially, and is unlikely to correspond to the ideal-type of an open global system.

CONSEQUENCES AND IMPLICATIONS: MANAGING THE NEW INTERNATIONAL ECONOMY?

In this section we look to the future in the light of the analysis presented so far. We are particularly interested in the prospects for the general management of the "regionalized" world economy previously indicated, and, on a more limited scale, the future for the EU as an entity capable of regional economic governance. What are the prospects for national state regulation in a rapidly internationalizing economy?

ECONOMIC MANAGEMENT, THE NATION-STATE, AND "GLOBALIZATION"

The upshot of internationalization and the accompanying volatility of markets has been to limit the effectiveness of the strategies of national economic management developed since the 1930s. Both the traditional Keynesian and newer national monetarist strategies that succeeded it in the late 1970s have become less and less effective. Traditional Keynesian policies of stabilizing economic activity by stimulating domestic demand in periods of downturn by means of fiscal and monetary policy have become severely constrained by the effects of such policies in producing inflation rates that diverge from those of dominant competitors, by the effect of sucking in foreign imports of manufactured goods when domestic demand has been stimulated, and by the consequent balance of payments constraint and exchange rate constraints generated by such boosting of domestic demand.

The policies of the French socialist government in the early 1980s and their subsequent abandonment have demonstrated the difficulties of "national Keynesianism." So too has the experience of the United States during the Reagan administration in following an expansionary policy, producing the current budget and trade deficits of the United States. International Keynesianism – involving coordinated policies on the part of a number of major states – is inherently unlikely, given the divergent interests of the major players in the international economy and the absence of a single hegemonic power able to underwrite the expansion of the international economy as the United States did between the end of World War II and 1972.

At the same time "national monetarist" policies have also failed. The rest of the advanced industrial countries are forced to follow the lead in monetary policy of the two most successful countries, Germany and Japan. The ERM (Exchange Rate Mechanism of the European Monetary System) before the crisis of 1992–93 limited the scope for monetary policy for all members of the EC, who were directly tied to the monetary regime of the *Bundesbank*. Controlling the money supply is inherently difficult given the internationalization of financial markets, the abolition of exchange controls, and the dominant role of credit money generated by the loans policy of financial institutions. The United Kingdom abandoned strict monetarism in the early 1980s. Its effects were severely deflationary. During the "Lawson boom" of the mid- to late 1980s, rapid expansion of domestic credit led both to high growth and to a substantial rise in imports of both consumer and capital goods, and thus to a worsening trade deficit. By the late 1980s the U.K. government had returned to a (rather traditional "quasi-Keynesian") tight interest rate policy in its attempt to control the money supply and inflation; interest rates affect the demand for money in the first instance, not its supply. This too was deflationary. Monetarism was intended as an *expansionary* policy, allied as it was with positive supply side measures. But these twin policy advances failed as an alternative to Keynesianism, because they have had severe deflationary rather than expansionary effects.

The result of this argument is that there is now no doctrinally grounded and technically effective regime of macroeconomic management that can produce sustained expansionary effects. It might appear that national macroeconomic management has ceased to provide a viable means of steering national economies in an internationalized system and that the nation-state has lost its salience in the face of "globalization" and supranational economic blocs.

This conclusion would be superficial. The mechanisms of national economic regulation have changed but governmental policies to sustain national economic performance retain much of their relevance, even if their nature, level, and function have changed. In the EU, for example, the (uncertain) prospect of monetary union and a single currency by the turn of the century, with the free movement of capital, labor, goods, and services under the single market policy that took full effect after 1992, along with a common regulatory framework imposed by Brussels, obviously have restricted or will further restrict some hitherto important areas of national management for most member states. But they make other areas of national policy more important – giving a new significance to nonmonetarist fiscal and supply side policies for instance (Hirst and Thompson, 1996d: Chapters 6 and 7).

While national governments may no longer be "sovereign" economic regulators in the traditional sense, they remain political communities with extensive powers to influence and sustain economic actors within their territories. Technical macroeconomic management is less effective, but the role of government as a facilitator and orchestrator of private economic actors remains strong. The *political* role of government is central in the new forms of economic management. Neither the financial markets nor the Brussels bureaucracy, to take the case of the most coherent trade bloc, can impose or secure the forms of social cohesion and the policies that follow from them that national governments can. National governments can still *compensate* for the effects of internationalization and for the continued volatility of the financial markets.

Before going into more detail on these key political orchestrational features let us look at the more overtly economic character of (nonmonetarist) fiscal policy. Fiscal policy has been in the shadow of monetary policy ever since the demise of Keynesianism, as already broadly sketched. During the late 1970s and 1980s, it became very difficult to argue for an "independent" fiscal policy, both nationally independent and also independent of monetary policy. However, things may now be about to change.

One thing the advent of a possible closer economic and monetary union with Europe (and more generally, the relative "cooling of the casino" internationally) could do is to help "disengage" fiscal from monetary policy once again. Take the case of the EU. The closer monetary union becomes, the more individual countries could engage in independent fiscal policies. This does not mean that they will be totally free to do as they wish on the fiscal front. The post-Maastricht guidelines for government fiscal balances are quite tight (around 3 percent of GDP). But these are only meant to be guidelines and in practice they may be quite flexible (more flexible than monetary guidelines for instance, which are to be under the direction of an "independent" European Central Bank). Thus, as decisions on monetary policy are increasingly taken elsewhere, i.e., centrally, individual governments will be able to decide their own fiscal policies relatively independently of monetary policy. This could enable some quite innovative fiscal responses as a result. Any new fiscal regime will also be operating in an environment of increasing financial and labor market integration, and this would need to be taken into account by policy makers.

Returning to the general role of the nation-state in regulating the economy, three key functions stem from its role as orchestrator of an economic consensus within a given community. States are not like markets; they are communities of fate which tie together actors who share certain common interests in the success or failure of their national economies. Markets may be international, but wealth and economic prosperity are national phenomena. They depend upon how well national economic actors can work together to secure key supply side outcomes. National policy provides certain key inputs that cannot be bought or traded on the market. The market is embedded in society, and governments remain a crucial element in the success of their societies – providing cohesion, solidarity, and certain crucial services that markets of themselves cannot.

The three key functions are:

1. The state, if it is to influence the economy, must construct a *distributional coalition,* that is, it wins the acceptance of key economic actors and the organized social interests representing them for a sustainable distribution of national income and expenditure which promotes competitive manufacturing performance (among other things). The major components of such a coalition are:
   —The balance of national income devoted respectively to consumption and investment.
   —A broad agreement on the level of taxation necessary to sustain state investment in infrastructure, training, and collective services for industry.
   —A framework for controlling wage settlements, the growth of credit, and levels of dividends such that inflation is kept within internationally tolerable limits (Hutton 1995).
2. Such a distributional coalition is only possible if the state performs another function, that is, the *orchestration of social consensus.* Such coalitions work only when they emerge from a collaborative political culture in which the major organized interests are accustomed to bargain over national economic goals, to make lasting commitments to determine policy by such bargaining, and to police their members' compliance with such bargains. Industry, organized labor, and the state achieve a successful balance between cooperation and competition; such a system is not devoid of conflict, nor are interests wholly coincident, but there are

mechanisms for resolving such differences. Such an overall consensus works only if it is also keyed in with the effective operation of more specific resource allocation mechanisms, such as the system of wage determination and the operation of capital markets. Such a national consensus may now be difficult to achieve through corporatist coordination through peak associations, but this difficulty does not alleviate the need for firms, public bodies, and labor interests to strike an ongoing and renegotiated balance between cooperating and competing. Consensus may have to be both more local and provisional, but it remains necessary to provide those inputs vital to an effective economy that markets of themselves cannot provide (Sabel, 1994, 1995).

3. The state achieves an adequate balance in the distribution of its fiscal resources and its regulatory activities between the national, regional, and municipal levels of government. The centralisation of EU policy is promoting the increasing importance of effective *regional* government. The regional provision of education and training, industrial finance, collective services for industry, and social services is gaining in importance. Regional governments are more able to assess the needs of industry because they possess more localized, and therefore accurate, information and because they are of a scale such that the key actors can interact successfully. Regional government cannot be seen as something inherently opposed to national economic management, but as a crucial component of it. It is the national state which determines the constitutional position, powers, and fiscal resources of lower tiers of government. Those national states that allow a considerable measure of autonomy to regional governments tend to have the best and most effective supply side regulation at the regional level. Germany and Italy offer obvious examples. The most prosperous *Länder*, like Baden-Württemburg and Bavaria, or most successful Italian regions like Emilia-Romagna, have achieved a high level of devolution of the tasks of economic management (Sabel, 1989).

The main problem about the way that nation-states continue to have a salience as a locus of economic management is that such activities now depend on social attitudes and institutions that are not equally available to all states. The new mechanisms of economic coordination and regulation give primacy to the high level of social cohesion and cooperation that the state can both call upon and develop. The new methods of national economic regulation in a more internationalized economy are not like Keynesianism, that is, a technique of macroeconomic management that was in principle available to every substantial and competently administered modern state if it

chose to adopt such a strategy. Rather the new methods rest on specific en-
sembles of social institutions, and these are more difficult to adopt or transfer by deliberate choice. States are thus in considerable measure trapped by
the legacies of social cohesion that they inherit. Countries like the United
States cannot just decide to adopt the more solidaristic and coordinative relations between industry, labor, and the state that have hitherto been characteristic of Germany and Japan. Into the early 1990s analysts have pressed
alternative national models on failing economies, claiming that if they
adopted certain institutions or practices, they could meet competitive pressures. "Learning from Japan" is commonplace, but so too are models like the
"Rhenish capitalism" of Albert (1993). Such models are increasingly seen to
be mirages, not least because *all* advanced economies are facing difficulties
and because the current tendencies favor more decentralized forms of coordination (Sabel, 1995).

This means that between blocs and within blocs there will be fundamental differences in the ability to respond to competitive pressures and
changing international conjunctures. Those societies that emphasize short-
term market performance, like the United Kingdom and the United States,
are threatened by the competitive pressures of societies that have concentrated on enhancing long term manufacturing competitiveness and have had
the social cohesion to achieve it, like Germany and Japan. The political
process and the interest group culture in societies like the United Kingdom
and the United States do not favor rapid adaptation in a more cooperative
direction; rather they emphasize competition and the dumping of social
costs on those who are both least organized or influential and least able to
bear them. This also pushes such societies away from effective international
or bloc cooperation.

The problem, then, is how far the more favorable conditions for effective national economic management are to be found either in the existing
national economies of the EU or as component parts of the evolving EU
supranational economic management structure itself. This issue we return
to in a moment. First we deal with the emergent management system, such
that it is, at the international level.

A REGULATED INTERNATIONAL
ECONOMIC ENVIRONMENT?

What are the prospects for a more regulated international economic environment if a more orderly pattern returns to the relationships between markets, countries, and blocs? As already indicated, there is still a great deal of
volatility here and increased uncertainty relative to the very stable position

before 1972, but nevertheless the indications are that not all the adverse trends giving rise to these uncertainties are set and robust. The inauguration of the EMS, and particularly its ERM component, in 1979 initially decreased the volatility of the members' exchange rates. In addition the G-5/G-7 summit system of policy coordination has seen some successes, particularly in its early days and in 1991 (Artis and Ostry, 1986; Putnam and Bayne, 1987; Thompson, 1990: Chapter 7).

These instances of policy coordination have only been of limited scope. They have involved monetary issues almost exclusively, though in recent years the monitoring of real variables like growth rates have been added to the agendas of such bodies. But "monitoring" is far from an active cooperation to change policy. By and large the G-5/G-7 countries have gone their own way on most domestic economic policy issues, and the divergence of basic philosophy and approach has been evident in the last ten to fifteen years. We should not dismiss outright the attempts at limited exchange rate and monetary coordination, nor should we exaggerate their importance or success.

The problem is the divergent interests that still characterize an international economy where, despite the claims of the "globalization" enthusiasts, the nation-state and increasingly trading blocs remain the dominant players. If nothing else the underlying economic conditions of the Japanese economy and the American economy should testify to a divergence of interests that will limit active and positive cooperation between them. Similar remarks can be made in the context of Germany and the rest of Europe.

This is not to suggest that complete noncooperation will ensue between the major players in the international economy, only that cooperation will be of a minimalist form, or that it will be cooperation by default as policies in the stronger economies dictate those in the weaker ones. Added to this are the very obvious differences in economic policy frameworks and outlooks that typify the main international trading countries that will inhibit coincidental agreements on more developed cooperative ventures. In many cases there are just not the domestic frameworks available to implement policies agreed within an international negotiating structure, even if they were more actively canvassed there. Fiscal policy initiatives are an obvious example. It is unlikely that a properly functioning fiscal federalism could be rapidly constructed within the EU, for instance.

But these caveats should not blind us to the way the international economy may have become so integrated that an outright return to overt protectionism between the blocs, while still a possibility, remains unlikely. The case of the financial balances between the major blocs illustrates this point (Thompson, 1992a: 147, Figure 2). These show that the EU has been in

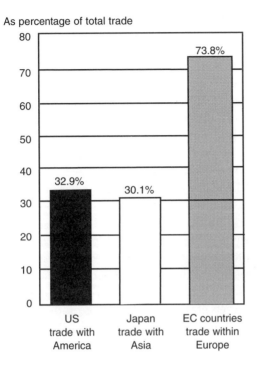

Figure 11-1. Intracontinental Trade 1990, i.e., Sum of Total Imports and Exports (SOURCE: OECD.)

rough balance on its savings and investments over the period between 1960 and 1990. Such was also the case for the United States and Japan until the early 1980s, but then the United States went into a dramatic international "deficit" as its savings collapsed while investment remained high (to finance its balance of payments/budget deficits). This twin deficit was financed by the Japanese, and to a lesser extent by the EU, in the mid-1980s. Thus despite some volatility in the overall trends, which show large swings in overall proportionate totals, the three main bloc powers appear to be locked together in a certain way. In particular, Japan could hardly continue to exist in its present form without the U.S. markets for its manufactured goods (although see below), while the United States needs Japan as a source of international finance.

These points are reinforced if we look at the structure of trade within the blocs. Figure 11-1 shows the percentage of total trade that each bloc leader conducted with its immediate client countries in 1990. Clearly the most integrated bloc on the trade front is the EU, with nearly 74 percent of its traded activity being conducted with other European countries. But the United States and Japan do not trade to such an extent with their natural "bloc associates." Indeed, at 33 and 30 percent, respectively, intrabloc trade is small. The United States and Japan must still look to the wider international environment for their trading partners. This should reinforce their mutual commitment to a more "open" trading environment. The United States may have much to fear from Japanese import penetration in its manufacturing sector, but it remains a major exporter of both manufactured goods and primary products, relying upon a liberal regime of world trade to do so. Japan may be a virtual trade policy captive of the United States, but the United States is still committed to free trade and will remain so, up to and until Japanese competition threatens a catastrophic collapse of its domestic manufacturing base.

Figure 11-2 gives an indication of the importance of trade to the three main economies/blocs between 1960 and 1991 (expressed as a percentage of GDP). What is remarkable is how the proportion of both exports and imports for all three sets of economies moved closer together in the late 1980s. This similarity in levels of trade to GDP ratios for the three main players as a whole indicates a symmetry that could once again lead to a rather more accommodating outlook. The most vulnerable economy remains the Japanese. This is signaled by the consistently greater importance of its exports to GDP ratio, and the recent rapid increase in its import penetration ratio. The Japanese economy still relies upon trade for its prosperity to a greater extent than do the other two main players, even though they all share a generally similar combined aggregated total of trade to GDP ratios (Thompson, 1992a: 146, Figure 1). Japanese export trade in particular is concentrated in a small number of sectors (motor vehicles and consumer electronics, for example), which make it very vulnerable to U.S. trade policy.

Finally, the three country groupings also display a growing similarity in the ratio of externally held assets – denominated in their respective "domestic" currency unit (the U.S. dollar, the Japanese yen, and the EU ECU) – to GNP. Between 1981 and 1988, the ratio of the share in currency portfolio of world financial wealth to GNP fell from 1.94 to 1.59 for the United States, while it rose from 0.21 to 0.34 and from 0.44 to 0.71 for Japan and the EC, respectively (Commission of the European Communities, 1990: 187, Table 7.5).

The point of this analysis is to indicate the emergence of three dominant players in the international economy. They are all roughly of the same economic size and standing. Thus *potentially* at least this encourages a better prospect for management of the international economy. It is easier to generate agreement among three players than the G-5/G-7, for instance.

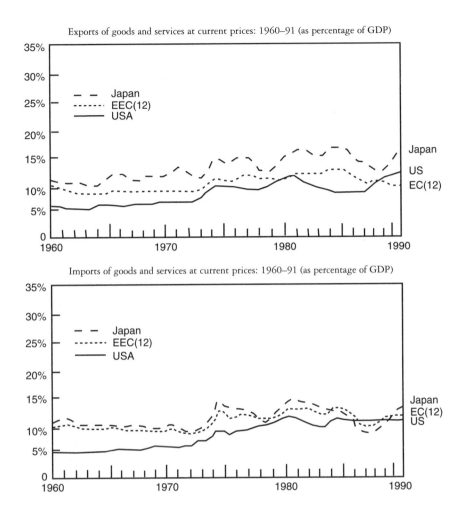

Figure 11-2. The Importance of Trade for Different Economies, 1960–91 (SOURCE: Compiled from *European Economy Annual Economic Review,* 29, 1986–7 [July 1986], updated 1991.)

But that does not mean new agreements will necessarily be easily forged. There are still significant policy differences on the form and style of economic management among the three main players, for instance, which could inhibit a more serious attempt at coordinating or cooperating on international economic management issues. In addition, a more active management style presumes that the blocs will form up into coherent managerial/regulatory entities themselves.

At this stage the analysis suggests that a modified multilateralism will prevail in the immediate future. It will be modified in the form of a dominant trilateralism among the three main players, but with additionally emergent bilateral negotiations among these three on important issues, and between them and other minor parties as well. Quite what the full consequences of this configuration for the management of international economic affairs might be remains an open question. But it does not seem that overt and widespread inward-looking protectionism is immediately likely. A minimal level of modified multilateral cooperation would seem enough to ensure the continued "openness" of the international economic system, even as it moves further away from the traditional postwar type of full liberal multilateralism.

CONCLUSION

We have tried to define the concept of a globalized economy and assess whether current trends in the international economy justify the use of this concept. The answer seems to be that globalization has not taken place and is unlikely to do so. The international economy is imperfectly governed through the limited cooperation of the major trade blocs and nation-states, but it is governed nonetheless and in a way that limits the power of the main financial markets. Nation-states can secure high levels of international economic activity and satisfactory external balances through appropriate mixtures of policy. Such policies increasingly tend to diverge from the Keynesian macroeconomic instruments of the 1945–73 period, and they depend on governments' capacities to coordinate and mobilize social actors. The result is that not all states are effective at meeting and mediating international competitive pressures through national policy resources. National success has depended on specific distributional contexts and on sources of social solidarity that are unevenly distributed among states, the United States and the United Kingdom lacking such capacities to a considerable degree and Japan and Germany continuing until recently to benefit from them. However, in both the latter cases, continued success in economic management depends on their developing their present forms of social cohesion into looser and more decentralized institutions. Should that capacity for cooperation established by their post-1945 settlements falter through the defection of firms, labor dissatisfaction, or other causes, then the capacity of Germany and Japan to manage their relation to the international economy to their own competitive advantage could decline.

Trade blocs are at an initial state of formation. Even the most advanced, the EU, is unlikely to become a superstate capable of exploiting the potential of a continental scale of economic organization. Whether blocs will come into conflict and radically weaken the current liberal regime of trade between the advanced industrial economies is still an open question, but that outcome seems unlikely. If the concept of "globalization" has had any merit, it is as a negative ideal-type that enables us to assess the shifting balance between international economic pressures and international governmental regulation and national and bloc-level economic management. We do not have a fully globalized economy; we do have an international economy and national and supranational policy responses to it.

REFERENCES

Albert, Michel. 1993. *Capitalism vs Capitalism.* London: Whurr.

Artis, Michael and Sylvia Ostry. 1986. *International Economic Policy Coordination.* Chatham House Papers No. 30. London: RIIA/Routledge.

Commission of the European Committee. 1990. *One Market, One Money.* European Economy No. 44, October. Brussels.

Hirst, Paul and Grahame Thompson. 1994. "Globalisation, Foreign Direct Investment, and International Governance." *Organisation.* 1 (2): October, 277–303.

——— 1996. *Globalisation in Question: The International Economy and Possibilities for Governance.* Cambridge: Polity Press.

Hutton, Will. 1995. *The State We're In.* London: Cape.

Julius, De Anne. 1990. *Global Companies and Public Policy.* London: RIIA/Pinter.

Ohmae, Kenichi. 1990. *The Borderless World.* London: Collins.

Ostry, Sylvia. 1992. "The Domestic Domain: The New International Policy Arena." *Transnational Corporations.* 1 (1): February, 7–26.

Putnam, Robert D. and Nicholas Bayne. 1987. *Hanging Together: Cooperation and Conflict in the Seven-Power Summits.* London: Sage.

Sabel, Charles F. 1989. "Flexible Specialisation and the Re-emergence of Regional Economies." In Paul Hirst and Jonathan Zeitlin, eds. *Reversing Industrial Decline?* Oxford: Berg. Pp. 17–70.

——— 1994. "Learning by Monitoring: The Institutions of Economic Development" In N. Smelser and R. Sinedberg, eds. *Handbook of Economic Sociology.* Princeton, N.J.: Princeton-Sage. Pp. 137–65.

——— 1995. "Bootstrapping Reform: Rebuilding Firms, the Welfare State and Unions." *Politics and Society.* 23 (1): March, 5–48.

Thompson, Grahame F. 1990. *The Political Economy of the New Right.* London: Pinter.

——— 1992a. "Economic Autonomy and the Advanced Industrial State." In Anthony G. McGrew and Paul G. Lewis et al. *Global Politics.* Cambridge: Polity Press. Chapter 10, Pp. 197–215.

1992b. "The Evolution of the Managed Economy in Europe." *Economy and Society.* 21 (2): May, 129–51.

Tomlinson, Jim. 1988. *Can Governments Manage the Economy?* London, Fabian Tract 524, January.

Williams, Karel, Colin Haslam, John Williams, Andy Adcroft, and Sukhdev Johal. 1992. *Factories as Warehouses: Japanese Manufacturing Foreign Direct Investment in Britain and the United States.* Occasional Papers on Business, Economy and Society No. 6, Polytechnic of East London.

12

CLUBS ARE TRUMP: THE FORMATION OF INTERNATIONAL REGIMES IN THE ABSENCE OF A HEGEMON

Lorraine Eden and Fen Osler Hampson

INTRODUCTION

Recent years have witnessed a growing debate among students of international relations as to why international regimes form.[1] The purpose of this chapter is to suggest that the formation of regimes is rooted in several types of international failure which prompt the development of governance structures either by states and/or by markets. Building on the recent work on international institutions and transactions cost economics by Yarbrough and Yarbrough, this chapter extends their argument of the study of international regimes (Yarbrough and Yarbrough, 1990).

We argue that state intervention represents one among many possible forms of organizing economic or political activity. Where structural failures exist at the domestic level some form of governance response, ei-

We would like to thank Max Cameron, Bruno Frey, Ernst Haas, Richard Higgott, Patrick James, Peter Katzenstein, James Keeley, Robert Keohane, Charles Kindleberger, Christopher Maule, Maureen Molot, Tony Porter, Carl Shoup, Susan Strange, Michael Webb, Oran Young, and Mark Zacher for helpful comments on the first draft, and David Hood for research assistance. The views expressed in this chapter and any remaining errors are the responsibility of the authors.

ther by firms (albeit as decentralized as the competitive market system) and/or by states may be required.[2]

Similarly, at the international level it may be necessary to devise institutions to facilitate cooperation in the presence of structural failures (Caporaso, 1993). Unlike some political economists who narrowly focus on transactions costs as if they were the only kind of market failure (Keohane, 1983, 1995), we identify four different types of structural failure that can contribute to the formation of international regimes: efficiency failures, distributional conflicts, macroeconomic instabilities, and security dilemmas.[3] As strategic rational actors, nation-states may respond to the presence of these structural failures by creating international regimes or some other kind of governance structure. In addition, we argue that, absent a hegemonic leader(s), coalitions of like-minded states, or *clubs,* may be the principal agent behind regime formation.[4]

REGIMES AS INTERNATIONAL GOVERNANCE STRUCTURES

Transactions costs have been used to explain both the formation of firms (Coase, 1937; Schnieberg and Hollingsworth, 1988; Williamson, 1975, 1985, 1986) and the formation of international regimes (Keohane, 1984, 1995). These two approaches treat governance structures as devices through which political and economic actors organize and manage their interdependencies. As a way of bridging these two approaches, we define *governance* as the set of practices whereby interdependent political and/or economic actors coordinate and/or hierarchically control their activities and interactions (Schnieberg and Hollingsworth, 1988; Williamson, 1975). *Governance structures* are therefore formal and informal institutional devices through which political and economic actors organize and manage their interdependencies. The purpose of such structures is to organize negotiation processes, set standards, perform allocative functions, monitor compliance, reduce conflict, and resolve disputes. These interdependencies can arise in firm-to-firm, firm-to-state, and state-to-state relations.

All governance structures are therefore formed in order to manage and stabilize the internal and external relations, both vertical and horizontal, of firm and/or state actors with other firms and/or states. We can think of a continuum of possible governance structures, either by firms and/or by states, and either at the domestic and/or international level. At the domestic level, state governance structures can vary from a low control form such as a nation of individual city states providing minimal public services (e.g., the city-states of early Greece) to a high control structure like a single tier command economy where the state produces most commodities (the USSR in the 1970s).

In terms of domestic governance by firms, the two polar cases are markets (perfectly competitive firms, the lowest control structure) and hierarchies (horizontally and vertically integrated firms, the highest control structure), with trade associations as an intermediate form between markets and hierarchies. Trade associations include alliances, such as cartels, peak associations, chambers of commerce, and employers' associations, that are designed to "promote and protect common interests by ordering, managing and stabilizing both the relations within the industry as well as the relations between industry members and those whose strategies and activities can decisively affect the industry's fortunes" (Schnieberg and Hollingsworth, 1988: 4).

The choice among domestic governance structures by firms is very much state driven; i.e., governments, through their constitutions and laws, determine the appropriate level and types of governance.[5] There is no inherent presumption that firm governance structures must be efficiency-improving. Firms are profit maximizers; hence they have incentives to reduce transactions costs (which is efficiency-enhancing), but they also have incentives to cartelize markets (efficiency-reducing).[6] Nor is there any presumption that firm governance structures can handle society's other goals (e.g., a fair distribution of income, stable macroeconomy, national security). As a result, assuming a given level of political failure, there is an inherent bias towards state governance to ensure efficiency, equity, stability, and security.

When structural failures go across national borders, they become international. Just as national failures create a demand for national governance structures, so too, it is argued here, do international failures create the need for international governance structures (IGSs). International failures create needs for international efficiency, stability, equity, and security. For example, social goods, transactions costs, and uncompetitive firm behavior all exist at the international level and therefore generate allocative failures. Global efficiency is not synonymous with an equitable distribution of world income and wealth. The global macroeconomy can be dysfunctional in the presence of financial panics (e.g., stock market crashes), unregulated money markets (e.g., the Eurocurrency market), or macroeconomic shocks (e.g., the oil shock). The security dilemmas posed by the proliferation of nuclear weapons, international terrorism, and ethnic conflicts all imply the need for international political order.

At the international level, these are perhaps more severe than at the domestic level. Domestic policy actions (e.g., beggar-thy-neighbor trade policies) can have negative spillover effects on trading partners; the larger and more open the economy, the larger the international spillovers (Cowhey, 1993a, 1993b). Trade wars and competitive devaluations can and have created global depressions (Gowa, 1994). Tax havens can siphon tax bases and revenues, wreaking havoc with the tax and expenditure policies of other countries. Too rapid monetary growth by large countries can spread inflation globally.

Given the potentially wide range of international failures, the likelihood that IGSs will form across a broad scope of international transactions is considerable. Possible types of firm IGSs can range from the lowest control structure, international transactions between unrelated firms, to high-control structure, hierarchies such as transnational corporations (TNCs) or cartelized TNC markets.[7] Middle-control governance structures would include international trade associations such as international cartels among unrelated firms.[8] Firm IGSs may be either welfare-improving (e.g., if global transactions costs are reduced) or -reducing (e.g., TNCs cartelize international markets). There is no presumption that firm IGSs are distributionally neutral or reduce security risks. Therefore there is a need for state IGSs, as regulatory devices either that prescribe and proscribe certain types of firm governance structures or that substitute state coordination and cooperative arrangements for firm IGSs.

State IGSs can also vary from low-control structures (i.e., competing nation-states and balance of power, the billiard ball analogy) to high-control structures (supranational governments, colonial empires). International regimes (or institutionalized norms and rules for cooperation) can be seen as middle-control state international governance structures, somewhat analogous to international trade associations among unrelated firms.[9] As such, regimes represent one set of governance options, but obviously not the only one, for coordinating and managing the vast array of relations among states.

We assume that, as strategic rational actors, states act so as to maximize their own objective functions given their constraints (history, place, resources, domestic politics) in the international system. As Snidal (1985: 594) argues, "[s]tates are better characterized by strategic rationality, which takes into account the likely reactions of other states as well as the pursuit of interests across a wide range of issues and through time." Governance structures are ways that nation-states can act so as to manage the global interdependencies generated by the politicoeconomic structures in which they find themselves.

However, this does *not* imply a presumption that all state IGSs must improve global welfare; they can be either global welfare-improving or -distorting. State IGSs, including regimes, may be used to offset interdependen-

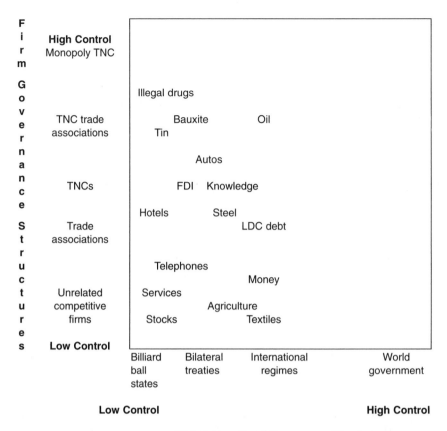

Figure 12-1. Governance Structures in International Markets

cies through ways that are welfare-reducing. For example, if a regime is set up to cartelize an international market or to shift the terms of trade in favor of members, global welfare may decline; cartelization and market rigging are not limited to firms. As Strange (1983: 345–6) notes, the focus on creating order in the international system ignores the questions of order for whom and whether greater order and managed interdependence are desirable.

In Figure 12-1 we make a preliminary attempt to categorize particular global markets in the 1990s in terms of their state and firm international governance structures. This figure characterizes (with a very broad brush!) only the international, not the domestic, governance structures. Firms may be state enterprises since the important issue here is not the ownership of the firm but the international relations between firms and between states, i.e., how much international regulation by states and how much international coordination among firms. We suggest that low-control IGSs include financial stock markets and business services where most international transactions are between unrelated firms and there is little international state governance. A high-control IGS, although clearly less so than in the 1960s, would be oil with three associations (OPEC, IEA, and the oil TNCs) managing international oil trade. It would appear from our figure that "mixed" government structures involving both states and firms are most common.

In summary, whether particular types of international politico-market failures tend to lead to the development of particular firm or state governance structures is a fascinating line of inquiry, but one that is not pursued in this chapter. Here we focus on one form of IGS, the international regime, a structure run by states in order to correct for various forms of international system failure. Why regimes form thus depends on the types of underlying structural failures to which we now turn.[10]

STRUCTURAL FAILURES: EFFICIENCY FAILURES

INTERNATIONAL SOCIAL GOODS

International social goods can be broken into four main categories depending on their jointness and nonexcludability characteristics. Private goods are one polar case (nonjoint and excludable); pure public goods the other polar case (joint and nonexcludable). Between the two extremes are joint goods (joint and excludable) and externalities (nonjoint and nonexcludable). Each of these three market failures (i.e., public goods, joint goods, externalities) has implications for international regimes.[11]

International Pure Public Goods.   While the two characteristics do not need to occur simultaneously, in the polar case – the pure public good – both jointness and nonexcludability coexist. Pure public goods are those whose benefits are consumed by all members of a community as soon as they are produced for, or by, any one member.

Relevant examples of the polar case of pure public goods are hard to find; one good example of a public good is knowledge, a public intermediate input into the production functions of all firms. Modern communications and information systems have made it relatively easy for firms to take technological innovations developed elsewhere and incorporate them into their own product lines. In the absence of patents or licensing laws, companies making use of these innovations have acted as free riders because they have been able to make use of those innovations at no extra cost to themselves and without having to compensate the original knowledge producers. In addition, many kinds of know-how are not patentable (e.g., management and processing trade secrets). In the absence of such protection, too little knowledge will be produced.

At the domestic level, the failure in the market for knowledge has led governments to establish patent and copyright legislation and laws to punish counterfeiting, to govern the provision and production of certain kinds of knowledge (e.g., in agriculture), to subsidize university research, and to encourage cooperative strategic partnering by firms. The most common firm governance structure to protect a "firm specific advantage" in knowledge is the hierarchy, i.e., horizontal and vertical integration. At the international level, governance structures include transnational corporations.[12] There is also an evolving intellectual property rights regime based on the extension of domestic patent legislation to cover foreign firms, bilateral treaties, and the World International Patent Organization (WIPO), set up to register patents and copyrights internationally.

Pure public goods represent one polar case of social goods. The other polar case is the private good, characterized by perfect nonjointness (or rivalry) and perfect excludability. Ignoring the other forms of market failure just listed, in the case of private goods no intervention is required to achieve efficiency. Figure 12-2 illustrates these two polar cases.[13] This figure shows a box with combinations of two characteristics: jointness and nonexcludability. Point A represents the polar case of private good, point C the polar case of a pure public good.

However, most social goods fall between the polar extremes. Normally either or both of the nonexcludability and jointness characteristics will be violated to some degree. For example, generally the marginal cost of extending provision to an additional consumer may be low, but not zero. As more and more consumers are added, it is likely that congestion costs will increase until in the limit the good becomes rival. In addition, jointness may be location-specific. Local public goods are public goods where the benefits are spatially limited to a particular area (Eden and McMillan, 1991). Thus one can speak of local, national, and international public goods depending on the area over which jointness exists. Similarly, the excludability characteristic depends on the costs of excluding relative to the demand for the service given the available techniques of exclusion, e.g., exclusion from a little-used bridge is feasible but costly, or scramblers can be used to exclude households from pay television.

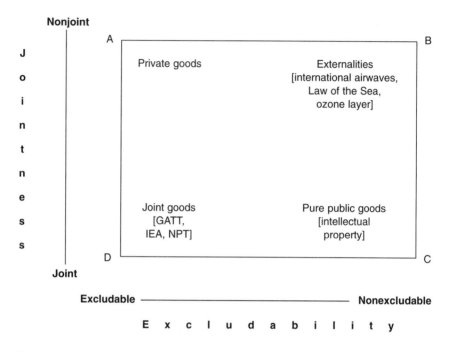

Figure 12-2. International Social Goods: Excludability and Jointness

International Joint Goods. Although mixed goods encompass a wide variety of these two characteristics, economists have focused on two particular mixed good cases, determined by their relative shares of the jointness and nonexcludability characteristics: externalities and joint goods. Joint goods are characterized by the jointness and excludability characteristics. Since the benefits from joint goods are excludable through the price mechanism, they can be provided through the private sector, e.g., cable and pay television, movie theatres, recreational facilities. Joint goods, by definition, can be extended or provided to somebody else without raising marginal costs.

When jointness extends to the international level but benefits remain excludable, the optimal club size is international.[14] Such international governance structures can be private (e.g., trade associations such as cartels) or state (e.g., international regimes). Many international economic regimes bear the hallmarks of joint goods. For example, the creation of the International Energy Agency (IEA) emergency oil sharing system in the mid-1970s was intended to dampen speculation in international oil markets in the event of sudden shortfall or disruption in oil supplies. The IEA is an oil consumer's club directed at mitigating the effects of a supply disruption among member oil-consuming, import-dependent states. While nonmembers may have benefitted from reduced oil price instabilities, the primary benefits from this insurance regime accrue to the members (Keohane, 1984: 217–40).

Likewise the GATT system, which has extended trade liberalization, facilitated multilateral consideration of commercial policy issues, and lowered tariff barriers among its members, also represents a kind of international club where the benefits are joint but excludable. GATT rules apply only to its members, and those who are not members are denied the key benefits of membership, e.g., the extension of most-favored-nation trading status. The formation of the GATT was driven by lessons from the 1930s tariff wars (Simmons, 1994); GATT has been called a peace treaty among warring states. Through international cooperation and restraints on noncooperative behavior, the GATT sought to prevent such instabilities from reoccurring (Goldstein, 1993).[15]

Similarly, the growing system of preferential trading areas represents the development of joint, but excludable, trade clubs in international political economy. These include the emerging North American free trade area, which is seeing the gradual removal of trade and tariff barriers among the United States, Canada, and Mexico, and Europe 1992, which has witnessed the effective removal of most border controls within the European Union. Even with the creation of a World Trade Organization (WTO) as a result of the successful completion of the Uruguay Round, we may still nevertheless expect to see the formation of "mini-GATTs" as small coalitions of like-minded nations, centered on North America, Europe, and Asia-Pacific, develop their own trade clubs.

The desire to establish clubs is not restricted to the field of international economics and trade relations. It can be argued that in international security certain arms control regimes have also established international joint, but excludable, clubs. The NPT (Nuclear Non-Proliferation Treaty) represents an international club in this sense. It is also a general club insofar as those states that have signed and ratified the treaty will not be denied access to nuclear technology and know-how provided it is put to peaceful purposes and they submit to the safeguard provisions of the IAEA (International Atomic Energy Agency).

International Externalities.   Externalities are unintended and uncompensated byproducts arising out of transactions among private agents, households, and/or firms, i.e., the so-called "third-party effects."[16] If private actions yield nonexcludable benefits to third parties for which the transactors cannot be compensated, we have a positive externality or an external economy. Similarly, if private actions create nonexcludable and uncompensated costs for third parties, we have a negative externality or an external diseconomy.

One example of an international aggregate external economy (or diseconomy, depending on one's views) is the spillover of cable television signals between countries. In the absence of bilateral or international agreements, consumers in the receiving country cannot be forced to pay for such spillovers. For example, Canadian cable television stations have retransmitted signals from American television stations to their Canadian customers without absorbing any of the U.S. programming costs.

Most international pollution problems are negative aggregate externalities or what might be termed "collective social bads."[17] This may represent one of the new and growing areas of demand for regimes. Ocean and air currents and river boundaries do not respect national borders and can carry harmful emissions from sources in one state into another. There are 214 river and lake basins globally that are shared by two or more states, and many of these represent some of the world's most important sources of fresh water, e.g., Great Lakes, Rhine, Amazon, Ganges, and Bramaphutra. At the same time they are used as general dumping grounds for the disposal of untreated sewage, industrial wastes, and agricultural runoffs (e.g., pesticides and fertilizers).

The externality problem is perhaps most severe in the case of common property resources: the "tragedy of the commons." An efficient property rights structure has four characteristics: universality (all resources are privately owned), exclusivity (no spillovers), transferability, and enforceability (Tietenberg, 1984). In the case of most externalities, the market failure is in the exclusivity characteristic. However, for common property resources the universality characteristic is also not met. As a result, these resources tend to be overexploited, their scarcity rent dissipated, and the net benefit from these resources to society competed down to zero.

The creation of the International Telegraph Union in 1932 by merging the International Telegraph Union and the International Radio Telegraph Convention was motivated, in part, by the problems of congestion and overcrowding in the use of the international airwaves (a global commons) (Cowhey, 1990; Krasner, 1991). The third Law of the Sea negotiations also have direct relevance in illustrating the tragedy of the international commons. The proposal for a new Law of the Sea was first made in 1967 by Dr. Arvid Pardo, the Maltese delegate to the United Nations. He urged that the seabed beyond the limits of national jurisdiction be declared "the common heritage of mankind." Ironically, however, much of the subsequent attention and effort in international negotiations had to do with the establishment of national property rights in the form of a 200-mile exclusive economic zone for coastal states while allowing provision for unimpeded transit through straits and archipelagos (Sebenius, 1984). The Vienna Convention for the Protection of the Ozone Layer (1985) and its related Montreal Protocols (1987) are illustrative of one such approach to an externalities problem that has global consequences.

International Transactions Costs. In a perfectly competitive, private goods world, characterized by perfect certainty, no efficiency failures would occur and therefore there would be no need for market regulation. However, the future is uncertain and perfect futures markets do not exist that allow traders to completely offset such uncertainties. As a result there are several obstacles to transactions-making that generate inefficiencies.

Casson (1982) provides a taxonomy of the various sequential obstacles to making a market: no buyer–seller contact, no knowledge of reciprocal wants, no agreement over price, no confidence that goods correspond to specification, difficulty in exchanging custody of goods, border taxes and regulations on trade, no confidence that restitution will be made for default. The costs incurred in attempts by traders to overcome these obstacles are called transactions costs. Thus transactions costs themselves are not a source of market failure, but reflect inherent structural failures of transactions-making in an uncertain world.

It was the recognition of these costs that led Williamson (1975, 1985, 1986) to propose the hierarchy as a governance method to economize on transactions costs and thus internalize uncertainty as a source of market failure. Teece (1981), Buckley and Casson (1976), Casson (1982), and Rugman (1986) have extended transactions cost economics to explain the existence of transnational corporations in what is now called the theory of internalization. These authors argue that transactions in an uncertain world are characterized by bounded rationality of the players, information impactedness of the goods, and asset specificity of the transactions. Buyers and sellers often have asymmetric information. Where numbers are small, players realize their interdependence and use opportunistic behavior to improve their terms of trade at the expense of their trading partners (Kydd and Snidal, 1995). Thus moral hazard and adverse selection problems are endemic to uncertain markets. By vertically and horizontally integrating, TNCs can reduce uncertainty and opportunistic behavior and thus improve global efficiency. Hierarchies are thus most likely to form where transactions are frequent, small numbers of players are involved, and high-cost fixed assets are involved.[18]

Similar arguments have been used to explain the formation of regimes. Keohane (1983) argues that regimes are useful when (a) a clear legal framework establishing liability is missing, (b) the market for information is imperfect, and (c) there are positive transactions costs. He goes on to discuss the issues raised in the previous paragraph and argues that regimes can be used to reduce international transactions costs. Such regimes are of two types: insurance regimes designed to reduce the effects of uncertainty, and control oriented regimes designed to create internal and environmental regularities, i.e., to reduce incentives for opportunistic behavior.

Our notion of transactions costs, based on Casson (1982), focuses on the costs involved in market making under uncertainty. Thus state international governance structures, such as regimes, can function as a way to improve market making. The international trade regime has a transactions cost reducing function. For example, the creation of international standards or harmonization of national standards through the GATT and bilateral treaties can reduce transactions costs. National tax and tariff policies can act as barriers to international trade. Harmonization or reduction of such barriers, increasing their transparency, and the substitution of rule making for managed trade through the GATT all act to reduce transactions costs. The movement to reduce border controls under Europe 1992 is an attempt to reduce interregional transactions costs. The private trade law regime is designed to reduce transactions costs incurred in commodity trade.

Another response to uncertainty is to reduce asymmetric information through the dissemination of information. One can argue that there are elements of an information-sharing regime through the activities of organizations like INTERPOL, UNEP, and UNESCO, which perform useful functions by encouraging the sharing of information globally.

International Noncompetitive Markets.   Most international markets are not competitive but rather dominated by small numbers of TNCs and/or state enterprises, e.g., oil, autos, telecommunications equipment, and semiconductors. Hymer (1976) was the first economist to explain the rise of TNCs by a monopoly power argument.[19] He argued that TNCs had firm-specific advantages that could be used to offset the higher costs of producing in foreign markets. These intangible, wholly-owned assets such as knowledge, brand names, and access to capital could be used to generate monopoly rents. Given that most TNCs operate in oligopolist markets, there would be either continual rivalry and strategic behavior, or attempts to cooperatively divide and cartelize the global market. Large TNCs thus can create international market imperfections through monopoly pricing, market segmentation, the erection of barriers to entry, the truncation of subsidiaries, and the exertion of bargaining power over small countries.

In addition, states in the 1980s exacerbated these conflicts through the use of strategic trade policies, the creation of national champions, and the competitive devaluations of domestic currencies. States have in the past formed international cartels, e.g., in uranium, oil, bauxite, and coffee, as methods of shifting the terms of trade in favor of domestic producers. The European Community has so heavily subsidized its agricultural sector that an industry which on comparative advantage grounds should be a net importer is now a large net exporter, as a result setting off a food subsidy war with the United States.

Thus noncompetitive international markets have both economic and political origins. International regimes can be used to reduce and/or control TNCs. For example, the foreign direct investment (FDI) regime includes bilateral FDI treaties designed to ensure national treatment and right of establishment for foreign firms. International tax treaties are designed to reduce TNC tax evasion through tax havens. In addition, there are TNC codes of conduct, albeit voluntary, such as the United Nations code.[20]

GATT can be seen as a way to control state attempts to use mercantilistic policies to increase their share of world exports. GATT may promote global efficiency by reducing the use of strategic trade policies and discouraging state cartelization of markets. For small countries, GATT has functioned to limit noncooperative behavior by larger members, effectively proscribing certain behaviors and forcing big states to play by the rules. However, derogations from the GATT have limited its effectiveness and induced other governance responses; e.g., the Cairns Group of small exporting nations was formed in response to the EC–U.S. food subsidies war allowed under GATT derogations in agriculture (Gilpin, 1987; Hampson with Hart, 1995; Jackson, 1989).

STRUCTURAL FAILURES: MACROECONOMIC INSTABILITIES

Even if all the conditions for efficient markets were met, there is still no assurance that markets will clear in an aggregate sense, i.e., there may be inherent tendencies in both capitalist and command economies towards systemic market failure. John Maynard Keynes was the first to argue that capitalistic economies could get stuck in an underemployment equilibrium, and since the 1940s most DMEs have made a formal commitment towards providing full employment, stable prices, and economic growth to their citizens. Domestic state governance structures are clearly necessary to achieve these internal domestic goals.[21]

However, domestic macroeconomic policies neither fully insulate economies from external shocks, nor protect neighboring economies from macroeconomic spillovers. The fully autonomous policies practiced in the 1930s, including competitive devaluations, bank panics, and insufficient money creation, were a prime cause of the Great Depression. The IMF and World Bank were formed as parts of the Bretton Woods monetary regime to cushion and control the effects of autonomous macroeconomic policies. As Ruggie argued, under the "compromise of embedded liberalism" inherent in Bretton Woods, nation-states were supposed to pursue Keynesian macroeconomic policies internally without disrupting international stability (Gilpin, 1987; Ruggie, 1983).

The collapse of Bretton Woods has been much studied; however, the international monetary regime that has emerged from it is less well charted. It consists of regional clubs (the EMS and the G-7), unregulated markets (the Eurodollar market), old international organizations (the IMF and World Bank), and the Bank for International Settlements (BIS) which acts as the central bankers' bank, particularly for European banks (Andrews, 1994; Goodman, 1992; Goodman and Pauly, 1993). International monetary coordination through central banks, particularly by the big G-7 members, Japan, West Germany, and the United States, has also played a role in dampening international macroeconomic instabilities (Helleiner, 1994).[22]

Whether or not international macroeconomic coordination is necessary is addressed by Cooper (1986). He argues that such coordination is useful because of time lags between the choice of a policy direction and its effects on the system, and the iterative nature of the policy process as it moves from one equilibrium to another. Given these problems, if disturbances continually disrupt the global economy, the time between equilibria will be lengthened and the amplitudes of the business cycle higher than necessary. As a result, international state coordination of macropolicies can reduce these time delay costs. However, Cooper argues that a macroeconomic stabilization regime built on policy cooperation does not exist and will probably be more difficult to form than other regimes. This is due to the lack of general consensual knowledge among academic and policy economists within and across countries.[23]

Recent cooperation in financial markets may be creating an international financial regime. Underhill (1990) has argued that states are making new international regulations and reregulating financial and credit markets. The European Union is introducing new banking, insurance, and credit regulations designed to harmonize domestic regulation of banking and financial services. The BIS has introduced capital adequacy requirements for its members that are designed to ensure national banks have sufficient equity capital to act as precautionary balances against bank panics. Underhill notes that part of these changes are designed to harmonize existing macroeconomic regulations; part are designed to reregulate previously unregulated financial markets. In each case the purpose is to reduce possible international macroeconomic instabilities and international transaction costs.

STRUCTURAL FAILURES: DISTRIBUTIONAL CONFLICTS

We argue that nation-states are rational actors with national interests. These interests are reflected in each state's social welfare function which records its goals and their rankings. Based on our previous analysis, states have a four-fold objective function: one that includes efficiency, equity, stability, and security. Even in an efficient and stable economy, states must be concerned with distributional conflicts, both internal (rich versus poor citizens) and between countries (DMEs [Developed Market Economies] versus LDCs [Less Developed Countries]). Different states will give varying weights to the variables in their preference functions, and these weights can change over time depending upon history, each nation-state's position in the global economy, and internal political structures (Cowhey, 1993a; Cowhey, 1993b).

It is legitimate to argue that states will be concerned with international income redistribution. Thus the international aid regime through, for example, foreign aid programs under the World Bank, LDC trade preferences in the GATT, and the Lomé conventions, can be seen as expressions of state concerns with income distribution. The LDC debt regime through the World Bank, the Paris Club, and the Baker and Brady plans can be seen as attempts to deal with LDC developmental needs, as well as managing the potential instabilities LDC defaults could generate.[24]

STRUCTURAL FAILURES: SECURITY DILEMMAS

The anarchic structure of the international system may also create a political demand for international regimes. This has typically been referred to by international relations scholars as the "security dilemma," rooted in the absence of a supranational authority in international politics and the fact that individual states are forced to provide for their own survival and welfare (Jervis, 1978, 1983).[25] Moreover, in the process of providing for their own security through various military measures, states may set in motion an escalatory dynamic as they seek not only to provide for their own security, but also to achieve a relative advantage over the military capabilities of other states (Solingen, 1994). This can lead to arms races and technological competition which can exacerbate political tensions and further heighten security problems (Downs et al., 1986).

A desire to curb this dilemma through the creation of arms control regimes and confidence-building measures represents one kind of international governance structural response to the security dilemmas of nation-states in an anarchical system. However, it is important to note that these regimes represent only one governance option in a variety of possible responses (Price, 1995). The escalatory dynamics of the security dilemma "can be checked by unilateral measures designed to reduce critical uncertainties for the other side regarding its own actions" (George, 1988: 671). Political concerts (e.g., Concert of Europe), balances of power, and proposals for world government represent other alternatives to the pathologies associated with the security dilemma (Jervis, 1983; Kupchan and Kupchan, 1991).

The security dilemma may also not be the only reason why arms control regimes emerge. The demand for these regimes may also be affected by a variety of contingent factors or constraints such as time urgency, fiscal constraints, presidential level leadership, etc., as noted by George (1988), but these represent second-level as opposed to first-level or structurally induced causes of a security regime. Arms agreements like SALT I and II, the INF Treaty, the Seabed Arms Treaty, the Nuclear Accidents Agreement, the Incidents at Sea Agreement, etc., can all be viewed as regime oriented, international governance responses to the political failures of an anarchical world.[26]

ISSUES AND IMPLICATIONS

In summary, the preceding discussion has developed a taxonomy of regimes as one form of state IGS designed to respond to four international politico-market failures: efficiency failures, distributional conflicts, macroeconomic instabilities, and security dilemmas. A number of important issues and implications follow from the preceding argument. These will be discussed in the following order:

- The role of hegemons versus clubs in the creation of international regimes.
- The role of search costs, uncertainty, and information in regime creation when N is large.

- The relationship between structural factors (or variables) and learning and cognition in regime formation.
- The treatment of contingent (or nonsystemic, nonstructural) factors in explanations about the origins of international regimes.

Before turning to these issues, two caveats are in order. First, in stressing the differential impact of markets and states as structural causes of international regimes, we do not wish to fall prey to a kind of economic determinism in drawing attention to the role of these factors in regime formation. As noted in the introduction, these represent first-level causal variables in regime formation. We argue the dynamics of the negotiation process and other proximate variables are of second-level order of importance. In the absence of these underlying structural conditions, it is hard to explain why regimes form; regimes are not "spontaneous" or "randomly generated" political orders (as suggested by some), but represent formal institutional responses to specific allocational, distributional, stabilization, and/or security problems in international relations. At the same time, it is important to realize that regimes represent only one kind of governance response to the kinds of market and political failures noted, and that regimes may not necessarily be optimal in terms of their efficiency, resource allocation, security, or distributional impacts.

Second, we wish to emphasize that the categories of politico-market failure as noted represent an idealized model of the structural conditions under which international regimes may form, as illustrated in Table 12-1. In reality, more than one of the preceding conditions may be reflected in the creation of a particular regime. Thus, typically, international regimes may be created to address a variety of political and market failures including social goods, transactions costs, distributional considerations, etc.

CLUBS ARE TRUMP: HEGEMONS VERSUS CLUBS IN REGIME CREATION

Keohane (1984) and Snidal (1985) have argued forcefully (and we believe correctly) that hegemons are not necessary to the maintenance and continuation of international regimes. They have challenged the theory of "hegemonic stability" on the ground that it fails to explain the lags between changes in power structures and changes in international regimes. They attribute the persistence of regimes in the presence of declining hegemons to the fact that regimes provide public goods and also lower transaction costs between their members. Thus it is in the rational self-interest of states to continue to abide by regimes even if there is no hegemon to enforce the rules.

Table 12-1. International Regimes and Structural Failures

Structural failures	Examples of international regimes
Efficiency Failures	
1. *Social Goods*	
a. Pure public goods	*Intellectual property regime* WIPO, bilateral patent treaties
b. Joint goods	*Trade regime:* GATT/WTO, preferred trading blocs, mini-GATTs
	Nuclear regime: NPT
c. Externalities	*Global commons regimes:* Law of the Sea, ozone layer, international airwaves
2. *Transactions costs*	*Trade regimes:* Europe 1992, GATT/WTO
	Standards regimes: private trade laws, GATT/WTO standards
	Information-sharing regimes: UNEP, UNESCO, INTERPOL
3. *Noncompetitive markets*	*Foreign investment regime:* bilateral investment treaties, TNC codes of conduct *Oil regime* Seven Sisters, OPEC, IEA
Macroeconomic Instabilities	*Monetary regime:* IMF, World Bank, BIS, G-7, EMS
Distributional Conflicts	*Trade regime:* UNCTAD, NIEO, GATT preferences to LDCs
	LDC debt regime: World Bank, IMF, Baker/Brady plans, Paris Club
Security Concerns	*Arms control regime* SALT I, SALT II, INF, NPT

Does the same argument apply to the creation of new regimes in the absence of a hegemon that is willing to provide international social goods? The question is of more than passing theoretical interest. Many analysts have pointed to the decline of the United States as the world's hegemonic leader. Although the exact magnitude of that decline is a matter of lively debate, most are in agreement that the 1950s and 1960s represented an exceptional period unlikely to be repeated in the near future (Kennedy, 1987, 1990; Nau, 1990; Nye, 1990).

Are hegemons necessary to the creation of international regimes? Our answer to this question is a qualified no. As the preceding discussion about the different sources of and responses to various kinds of politico-market failure suggests, if social preferences are sufficiently homogeneous among a group of actors (i.e., convergent), there may well be a shared desire or demand for regimes. But we argue that this demand usually goes beyond the desire to reduce uncertainty (which is ubiquitous) to include other disequilibria such as monopoly power, inequitable income distributions, macroinstabilities, etc. If small numbers exist, even in the absence of a hegemon, we argue that it is possible to develop governance structures that correct for international politico-market failures. This is true in the case of social goods and it is also likely to apply to other cases.

In any regime-building exercise – in any of our four categories of regimes – as the number of parties and interests increases (i.e., where N is large), the number of potential free riders also goes up and, in the absence of a hegemon, cooperation becomes increasingly difficult (Hardin, 1982: 38–49; Kahler, 1993). In addition to the free rider problem, rising N also raises the probability of increasingly divergent social preferences among the potential members of a new regime, thus posing an additional obstacle to international cooperation and negotiation, e.g., the difficulties of reaching agreement in the Uruguay Round of the GATT as noted. As N increases, the likelihood of different preference orderings among state actors grows, with some states favoring efficiency over equity considerations, others security over macroeconomic stability, etc.

Due to these sorts of structurally induced cleavages, cooperation in large numbers is difficult, and international regimes that are comprehensive or inclusive in terms of their membership will be difficult to form. Instead, the way to deal with diversity when faced with the problem of large numbers is through the club approach, i.e., through the coalition of small numbers of "like-minded" states, banding together to correct for structural politicomarket failures, share the benefits from exploiting economies of scale and the costs of providing social goods, and/or satisfy a taste for association with other like-minded states. To the extent that such benefits are fully or mostly excludable, clubs can capture the full benefits of such cooperation internally. Unlike Kahler who argues that minilateral leadership by great powers is the solution to achieving cooperation in large numbers, we argue that large groups have a natural tendency to break up into smaller groups as members enjoying similar social preference functions band together (Kahler, 1993). Such clubs provide rewards to their members in the form of direct benefits as well as enforceable penalties for noncompliant or recalcitrant behavior even though their membership may expand later on in response to political pressures from within and from without from nonmembers who wish to join the club. Clubs therefore should be viewed as dynamic institutions whose membership may well change over time.

As noted, there is some evidence that the club approach maybe the hallmark of the new international political economy, in addition to characterizing the approach increasingly being adopted to address external diseconomies in the areas of transboundary air and water pollution. The growing emergence of trading blocs in Europe, North America, and the Pacific is reflective of a club approach to the problems of coordinating divergent preferences and interests in international trade, investment, and even monetary relations (Sandholtz, 1993). The club approach has also been taken to address the problems of ozone depletion and acid rain, and may even come to characterize international approaches toward the complex problems of global warming (Hampson, 1989–90; Hampson, 1995). Similarly, in international security, regional (as distinct from global or transregional) approaches have been the hallmark of arms control and confidence-building regimes in spite of calls by some to expand regimes like the confidence-building regime in the OSCE (Organization for Security and Cooperation in Europe) to regions like the Pacific.

What may be a tendency in international relations to form coalitions of the "like-minded" is symptomatic of the structural difficulties associated with the formation of regimes which can effectively accommodate divergent state preferences toward regime goals. For example, bridging the acute imbalances in economic and political power between the world's poor and rich in international economic and environmental regimes may require distributional mechanisms and income reallocations that richer states are not prepared to accept.

Moreover, with small numbers, strategic behavior may make it difficult to form cooperative alliances since trust is a necessary input into such ventures. As Buckley and Casson (1988) have shown, all cooperative ventures are subject to strong and weak cheating pressures and ventures that start without trust and goodwill are likely to fail. Hence many international regimes may fail because the necessary consensus building and cooperative will are nonexistent. The failure to form an international debtors' club and the weakness of UNCTAD may also reflect such difficulties within LDCs where preferences and situations differ considerably. Given that there is an optimal club size, current groups such as the Group of 7 may be too large and disparate to act effectively (Mahler, 1984; Rothstein, 1984a, 1984b). In addition, inexpedient bargaining strategies, bad tactics, poor timing, and inadequate preparation may also frustrate regime formation.

Whether club approaches to international regime-building and cooperation are inherently good or bad is obviously a matter for debate and discussion, and one that we will not engage in here other than to point out that clubs are not necessarily bad things if the alternative is no cooperation at all (or, worse still, a growing spiral of mutual distrust, hostility, and conflict). As we have shown, international regimes are formed both for welfare-improving and welfare reducing reasons. Attempts to offset allocative failures such as international transactions costs and social goods are inherently welfare-improving; however, attempts to create order through cartelization and managed trade are global welfare reducing. For example, Europe 1992 has both effects: Border controls are reduced, but nonclub members may face more discrimination.

The "open club," which leaves room for the inclusion of additional members once resource allocation and distributional concerns are settled, may allow for some flexibility in addressing these sorts of conflicts. For example, the London agreement setting up a fund for developing countries to substitute ozone-friendly agents in industrial and consumer uses represents just such an approach in current efforts to get developing countries to sign on to the Montreal protocols of the Vienna Convention for the Protection of the Ozone Layer. Open clubs offer the advantage of allowing "voting with one's feet," i.e., a variety of international club regimes with varying memberships allow the possibility for states to choose regime clubs that best suit their interests and needs. As Tiebout (1956) first recognized some years ago, regional clubs may be more efficient and equitable than multilateral clubs. This has implications for the current debate over the relative merits of regional trading blocs as substitutes for the GATT.[27]

There is an obvious tension in any club agreement between the optimal size of the club and the marginal cost savings for existing members. Adding members may have other consequences too (e.g., inducing changes in distributional and allocative relations) which may be deemed undesirable by current members. Some of these tensions are evident in current concerns about the implications of a united Germany within the EU, particularly among the smaller states of the Community who worry openly about the political and economic clout of the new Germany and the diversion of investment funds away from the Community's poorer members (Spain, Portugal).

SEARCH COSTS, UNCERTAINTY, AND
INFORMATION-SHARING REGIMES

A second implication that follows from our discussion is that the creation of international information-sharing regimes, which allow parties to develop, share, and distribute new information in a timely manner, may be a necessary precondition for the subsequent creation and formation of regulatory or stabilization regimes. The reason for this is related to numbers in regime formation and issue complexity and density. As the number of parties involved in the negotiation and construction of new international regimes goes up, so too do search costs and uncertainty. This is because each party must have some understanding about the interests and concerns (or value preferences) of the other parties to the negotiation, which is complicated by large numbers.

Moreover, as noted by Putnam and others, international negotiations involve two-level games between a "domestic" and an "international" constituency. The creation of "win-win" sets (i.e., intersecting points on the contract curve) in international negotiation involves some understanding of each other actor's domestic constraints and freedom of maneuver, in addition to one's own (Putnam, 1988).

The large number of domestic and international actors involved either directly or indirectly in most international negotiations is further complicated by issue density and complexity. Whether the problem is one of ozone depletion or intellectual property, these are enormously complex problems not only in terms of their technical and scientific implications but also in the number of social and economic interests they affect.

The science of some issues has given rise to what Haas (1989) has called "epistemic communities," i.e., communities of technical specialists or experts who are conversant with the scientific or technical nature of the problem and who lobby their governments to take action on these issues. However, there are often major asymmetries in knowledge on any given issue, and state capabilities may vary substantially. Furthermore, experts in one country may not enjoy the same sort of access to political elites and policy makers that they do in another. In these circumstances there may be a greater need to share information and resources and to ensure that policy elites and diplomatic negotiators are on the same point on the learning curve (Young and Oshrenko, 1995).

A different kind of problem has to do with the reduction of scientific and technical uncertainties before deciding what is the relevant course of action on any given problem. Problems like global warming, toxic pollution, Arctic haze, etc., involve major uncertainties as to their causes, consequences, magnitude of effects, and social, economic, and biological impacts. These kinds of uncertainties will be reduced only through joint scientific research and cooperative undertakings involving experts from many countries. The creation of an international consensus among the experts as to the exact nature and magnitude of the problem may be a necessary precondition for subsequent policy intervention because policy makers will be reluctant to make tough policy choices when faced with high social, economic, and political costs of adjustment unless they are all convinced the problems are real and the costs of inaction outweigh the costs of action. This is akin to Cooper's notion about the requirements for "consensual knowledge" in macroeconomic policy coordination between states (Cooper, 1986).

These informational asymmetries across (and within) states, and the uncertainties associated with problems which are both complex and often nested within other problems (implying issue density), may require the establishment of institutionalized mechanisms at the international level for fostering research and sharing information prior to the formal creation of a regulatory regime. Likewise coordinated instruments for sharing information among parties who may not necessarily share interests may also be required. Thus much of the early efforts in regime building may be first directed at getting a handle on the problem. In this case information-sharing regimes can help reduce uncertainty in both the short run and the long run.[28]

STRUCTURES, COGNITION, AND LEARNING

The structural conditions just identified represent ideal types. Typically state actors will be in the position of determining whether or not they want to negotiate new international regimes. The possibilities will depend, *ceteris paribus,* on their preference functions and the manner in which they address the trade-offs between equity, efficiency, stability, and security. Each state is also likely to address these trade-offs somewhat differently because of domestic politics and other situational factors. We believe that the factors that determine how states define their regime goals is a rich area for future research and investigation. Although we only briefly sketch them here, among the relevant factors in any such examination are the following.

Positional Hierarchy. Positional hierarchy, i.e., how the political elites of any given country perceive their country's overall position in the global order, can influence willingness and ability to form international regimes. It may be the case that poor states are likely to judge membership in new regimes in terms of their distributional consequences; conversely, states that see themselves as being relatively well situated may be more concerned about efficiency and stabilization. While the prevailing view argues that hegemons are necessary to regime formation, in spite of their relative weak positioning, small states may be able to act as leaders and innovators in the formation of regimes.

Intrastate Coalitions and Bargaining. Newly created international regimes will typically have allocational and distributional consequences for affected domestic constituencies and interests within states (i.e., there are bound to be winners and losers). This point will not be lost on affected parties in the negotiation and bargaining processes associated with the establishment of new regimes. Domestic coalitions, intrastate bargaining processes, and interest group behavior will affect a state's negotiating position in international forums and the way it assesses efficiency-equity-stability-security trade-offs. As domestic coalitions shift over time, these trade-offs may well be assessed differently (Putnam, 1988).

Lessons of History and Learning. The roles of cognitive images and beliefs in decision making have been amply documented by students of foreign policy decision making, crisis management, and cognitive psychology (Jervis, 1983; Jervis et al., 1985; Larson, 1985; Neustadt and May, 1986). There are sound reasons for believing that many of these same factors will influence decision makers' values, beliefs, and attitudes towards new international regimes. Unfavorable experiences at the negotiating table or with the past performance of other regimes are likely to color preferences and predispositions in new exercises at regime creation. For example, it is argued by some that the perceived failure of the NIEO (new international economic order) in UNCTAD in the 1970s has made many LDCs skeptical about the first world's objectives in current efforts to combat the international drug trade, international terrorism, and environmental problems – the so-called "new" security agenda – through new regimes (Pratt, 1990; Runnalls, 1989).

Cognitive variables including ideas and perceptions based on historical experience are therefore likely to exert an important independent effect on new efforts at regime creation (Goldstein and Keohane, 1993). Although these factors do not clearly fall within the domain of "structural" conditions, they are clearly linked at the level of domestic politics and perceptions. The relationship between these two clusters of variables is obviously a dynamic one that merits close examination.

It is also important to address the issue of "learning" in the broader sense as discussed by Haas (1983, 1990). That is, how do certain problems come to be viewed as international problems that can no longer be ignored or simply dismissed? How do perceptions about market or politically induced failures form? What role do genetics, physics, etc. play in galvanizing public consciousness that there is a problem warranting political attention? Haas suggests that cybernetic principles can be used to discover these identity relationships and that the "organization, storage, and diffusion of information" may be crucial to the formation of particular mind sets. The ability of organizations to learn is also a fruitful area because, as Haas notes, "actor interests themselves may change in response to new knowledge; organizations may autonomously feed the process of change by the information and ideas they are able to mobilize" (1983: 57).

THE ROLE OF CONTINGENCY IN REGIME FORMATION

Some observers, notably Young (1989a: 107–90, 193–236), argue that certain factors like political leadership, the presence (or absence) of a crisis, and other aspects of the actual negotiating process may be important to the creation of international regimes. We would argue that these variables should be treated as stochastic or nonergodic elements insofar as their influence upon outcomes reflects the dominance of historically decisive, contingency dependent elements rather than systematic forces. David (1985) labels these "QWERTY factors" after the awkward layout of the typewriter keyboard that he points out was the product of a unique set of historical "happenings" rather than a socially optimal design.

Crises should also be treated as contingent events. Almost by definition they represent a class of noncontrollable events (if they were controllable then they could be prevented), but their specific role in regime formation obviously depends upon close scrutiny of the circumstances of the crisis itself and its subsequent consequences for the formation of a particular regime. We believe that the role of contingency in any theoretically-based, predictive model of regime causation should not be ignored and our preceding discussion about structural causes clearly represents only part of the story. Deductive, structurally-based explanations therefore must be complemented by inductive, historical analysis in order to understand fully why particular regimes have formed. However, path analysis and the uncovering of the historical sequence of events that led to a regime's creation requires more than just casual narrative.

In summary, we argue that structural causes are of first-level importance whereas contingency factors are only of second-level importance to the formation of international regimes. Since regimes are the results of willful human actions and not accidents of nature, their rise requires a close examination of underlying conditions (or perceived conditions) that make them necessary, even though proximate factors may first appear dominant.

CONCLUSIONS

The purpose of this chapter was to set out a taxonomy of underlying, structural factors that influence the formation of international regimes. We first developed a theory of state and/or firm governance structures in response to politico-market failures. We then extended this theory to the international level, and situated regimes as an intermediate form of state international governance structure, run by states in order to correct for various forms of international system failure. This chapter has outlined four structural failures: efficiency failures, distributional conflicts, macroeconomic instabilities, and security dilemmas.

In so constructing regimes as an intermediate form of state governance structure, we explicitly defined regimes as *state-run* governance structures: i.e., we argued that privately-run structures are not regimes. Second, we argued that international regimes are one of many governance responses to international politico-market failures, not necessarily the most likely to emerge. In some sense there are alternative substitutes for regimes – which may involve only firms and not states – and the choice of governance form depends on the underlying structural causes of system failure. Third, we argued that regimes do matter since international governance structures can affect outcomes. However, according to our taxonomy, regimes are not Groatian, i.e., they do not permeate international life, but are only one response among many to market failures. Last, we argued that governance structures, including regimes, in their management of interdependencies due to politico-market failures, may either enhance or reduce global welfare.

Our theory thus encompasses and clarifies many of the existing theories of international regimes found in the literature. In particular, it clarifies the distinction between the structural causes and the proximate factors that generate regimes. We have tried to relate the importance of these structural-functional variables within a broader, sequential understanding of regime formation. Our model has drawn from several different intellectual and theoretical traditions: public finance, transactions cost economics, international business, international relations theory, and regime theory. Although this construct may seem eclectic, we argue that there are systematic linkages that clearly argue in favor of a transtheoretic approach to the rise of regimes.

Lastly, we note that it may be necessary to redefine the term "regime" in the light of our analysis. We argue that regimes are more than principles, norms, rules, and procedures around which actors' expectations converge. Regimes generally take the form of international clubs whose members enjoy certain privileges as well as incurring specific rights and obligations. In international affairs clubs are trump!

ENDNOTES

1. Regimes are usually defined as "sets of principles, norms, rules, and decision-making procedures around which actors' expectations converge in a given area of international relations" (Krasner, 1983:2). On this debate, in addition to Krasner, see Haggard and Simons (1987), Keeley (1990), Strange (1988), and Young (1986, 1989a, 1989b).
2. The market failure approach to the functions of government was first developed by Musgrave (1959). It is now a recognized part of general public finance theory. Straightforward treatments of the various categories of market and political failures can be found in Boadway and Wildasin (1984), Brown and Jackson (1986), Musgrave, Musgrave, and Bird (1987), Rosen (1988), Stiglitz (1986). More advanced treatments of this subject can be found in Atkinson and Stiglitz (1980), Boadway and Bruce (1984), Cornes and Sandler (1986), Starrett (1988), and Tresch (1981). A useful compendium of readings on market failure is Cowan (1988).
3. This three-fold characterization of the functions of government was first developed by Musgrave (1959) in his multiple theory of the public household. See Chapters 1 through 3, pp. 3–57.
4. The strand of the international business literature which is necessary for our approach is the application of transactions cost economics to the theory of the multinational enterprise, i.e., the so-called "internalization theory." See Buckley and Casson (1976), Casson (1982), Rugman (1986), and Teece (1981).
5. Schneiberg and Hollingsworth (1988) argue that countries with strong antitrust laws, such as the United States, discourage the formation of trusts and cartels and thus tend to encourage their replacement with oligopolies and integrated firms. States can choose to substitute government production and provision (i.e., replace firm governance structures with state ones). Each country therefore chooses its governance structures as responses to domestic interdependencies among state and nonstate actors.
6. See Schneiberg and Hollingsworth (1988) for more detail on the anticompetitive use of trade associations as a governance structure. This is their major criticism of the Williamson transactions cost school, i.e., the implication that firm governance structures must be efficiency improving. Note the relation to one common criticism of regime theory.
7. Teece (1981) extended Williamson's transactions cost approach to analyze transnational corporations. This approach, now called the internalization approach, argues that TNCs are faced with transactions costs in intermediate

product, capital, and technology markets. By vertically and horizontally integrating, firms can internalize or arbitrage these transactions costs. Hence, this approach implies that TNCs are efficiency improving.

8. On the choice between TNCs and cartels, see Casson (1985).

9. Note that international regimes can vary considerably within themselves as an IGS in terms of their control characteristics. Keohane (1983) notes that regimes can be either for control or insurance purposes with insurance regimes focusing on coping with uncertainties rather than controlling members' behavior. Our definition of control has to do with control of the market through managing the interdependencies among state and/or nonstate actors that are vertically and horizontally interlinked. Control of members' behavior is one possible method of managing interdependencies; another is reduction of uncertainties. Hence our definition of control includes both of Keohane's regime types.

10. Most theories of regimes have focused on the public goods and/or transactions costs arguments. See Keohane (1984). Given that the definitions used in the literature have often been somewhat imprecise and confusing, in this next section we attempt to be explicit about the links between politico-market failures and the regimes they generate.

11. See endnote 2 for readings dealing with social goods.

12. On knowledge as a public good and the motivation for using hierarchies see Johnson (1970). See also Eden (1988).

13. This figure is based on one in Eden and McMillan (1991).

14. Club theory was developed by Buchanan (1965). A fuller treatment can be found in Buchanan (1968). A recent treatment is Cornes and Sandler (1986). A shorter review can be found in Boadway and Wildasin (1984).

15. The seminal chapter is Coase (1960). Good treatments of the externality literature can be found in Boadway and Wildasin (1984), Cornes and Sandler (1986), and Tresch (1981).

16. For good treatments of the literature on the economics of environmental externalities see Hartwick and Olewiler (1986) and Tietenberg (1984).

17. This analysis has been extended by Buckley and Casson (1988) to explain the rise of international equity joint ventures.

18. For a later, more radical view see Hymer (1975).

19. See the United Nations (1988) for a detailed discussion of the current regulations of foreign direct investment.

20. For a discussion of the stabilization function of government see Musgrave, Musgrave, and Bird (1987).

21. See Buiter and Marston (1986) on macroeconomic coordination.

22. See, however, Webb (1990). Webb argues that an international macroadjustment regime exists that consists of trade and capital controls, exchange rates, international financing for payments imbalances, and monetary and fiscal policies. This regime definition encompasses several of the regimes we have discussed above (i.e., the regimes are nested in a broader macroregime), but ignores the difficulties noted by Cooper in terms of the monetary regime. On the "nesting" of regimes within one another, see Keohane (1984: 90–91) and Aggarwal (1985).

23. See, for example, Crane (1984).

24. The responses of states to international anarchy are the subject of Oye (1986) and Axelrod and Keohane (1986).
25. For a discussion of partial security regimes see George, Farley, and Dallin (1988) and Carnesale and Haas (1987).
26. See Gilpin (1987), Chapter 5, for a review of the GATT and its problems. A detailed analysis can be found in Jackson (1989). Also see Finlayson and Zacher (1983).
27. It is interesting to note, for example, that much of the recent effort and energy within UNEP's (United Nations Environment Programme) Intergovernmental Panel on Climate Change has been directed at these two objectives; it has struck three panels involving a wide range of participants from member countries that are examining the science and modeling, social and economic impacts, and policy implications of global warming.
28. Higgott (1991) argues this with respect to the Cairns group in agricultural negotiations at the Uruguay Round.

REFERENCES

Aggarwal, Vinod K. 1985. *Liberal Protection: The International Politics of Organized Textile Trade.* Berkeley: University of California Press.

Andrews, David M. 1994. "Capital Mobility and State Autonomy: Toward a Structural Theory of International Monetary Relations." *International Studies Quarterly.* 38 (2): 193–218.

Atkinson, A. B. and J. E. Stiglitz. 1980. *Lectures on Public Economics.* London and New York: McGraw-Hill Book Company (UK) Limited.

Axelrod, Robert and Robert O. Keohane. 1986. "Achieving Cooperation under Anarchy: Strategies and Institutions." In Kenneth A. Oye, ed. *Cooperation Under Anarchy.* Princeton: Princeton University Press. Pp. 226–54.

Boadway, Robin W. and Neil Bruce. 1984. *Welfare Economics.* Oxford, U.K.: Basic Blackwell.

Boadway, Robin W. and David E. Wildasin. 1984. *Public Sector Economics,* 2nd ed. Boston and Toronto: Little, Brown and Company.

Brown, C. V. and P. M. Jackson. 1986. *Public Sector Economics,* 3rd ed. London: Basic Blackwell.

Buchanan, James. 1965. "An Economic Theory of Clubs." *Economica* 32 February, 1–14.

―――. 1968. *The Demand and Supply of Public Goods.* Chicago: Rand McNally.

Buckley, Peter and Mark Casson. 1976. *The Future of the Multinational Enterprise.* London: Macmillan.

―――. 1988. "A Theory of Cooperation in International Business." In Farok Contractor and Peter Lorange, eds. *Cooperative Strategies in International Business.* Lexington: Lexington Books. Pp. 31–53.

Buiter, Willem and Richard D. Marston, eds. 1986. *International Economic Policy Coordination.* Cambridge: Cambridge University Press.

Caporaso, James A. 1993. "International Relations Theory and Multilateralism: The Search for Foundations." In John Gerard Ruggie, ed. *Multilateralism*

Matters: The Theory and Praxis of an Institutional Form. New York: Columbia University Press. Pp. 51–90.

Carnesale, Albert and Richard N. Haass. 1987. *Superpower Arms Control: Setting the Record Straight.* Cambridge: Ballinger.

Casson, Mark. 1982. "Transaction Costs and the Theory of the Multinational Enterprise." In Alan Rugman, ed. *New Theories of the Multinational Enterprise.* London: Croom Helm. Pp. 24–43.

　　　1985. "Multinational Monopolies and International Cartels." In Peter Buckley and Mark Casson, eds. *The Economic Theory of the Multinational Enterprise: Selected Readings.* London: Macmillan. Pp. 60–97.

Coase, Ronald H. 1937. "The Nature of the Firm." *Economica (New Series)* 4 (November), 386–405.

　　　1960. "The Problem of Social Cost." *Journal of Law and Economics* 3: 1–44.

Cooper, Richard N. 1986. "The Prospects for International Economic Policy Coordination." In Willem Buiter and Richard D. Marston, eds. *International Economic Policy Coordination.* Cambridge: Cambridge University Press. Pp. 366–72.

Cornes, Richard and Todd Sandler. 1986. *The Theory of Externalities, Public Goods and Club Goods.* Cambridge: Cambridge University Press.

Cowan, Tyler, ed. 1988. *The Theory of Market Failure: A Critical Examination.* Fairfax, Va.: George Mason University Press.

Cowhey, Peter F. 1990. "The International Telecommunications Regime: The Political Economy of Regimes for High Technology." *International Organization.* 44 (2): 169–200.

　　　1993a. "Elect Locally – Order Globally: Domestic Politics and Multilateral Cooperation." In John Gerard Ruggie, ed. *Multilateralism Matters: The Theory and Praxis of an Institutional Form.* New York: Columbia University Press. Pp. 157–200.

　　　1993b. "Domestic Institutions and the Credibility of International Commitments: Japan and the United States." *International Organization.* 47 (2): 299–326.

Crane, Barbara. 1984. "Policy Coordination by Major Western Powers in Bargaining with the Third World: Debt Relief and the Common Fund." *International Organization.* 38 (3): 399–428.

David, Paul A. 1985. "Clio and the Economics of QWERTY." *The American Economic Review.* 75 (2): 332–37.

Downs, George W., David M. Rocke, and Randolph M. Siverson. 1986. "Arms Races and Cooperation." In Kenneth A. Oye, ed. *Cooperation Under Anarchy.* Princeton: Princeton University Press. Pp. 118–46.

Eden, Lorraine. 1988. "Pharmaceuticals in Canada: An Analysis of the Compulsory Licensing Debate." In Alan Rugman, ed. *International Business in Canada.* Toronto: Prentice-Hall. Pp. 245–67.

Eden, Lorraine and Melville McMillan. 1991. "Local Public Goods: Shoup Revisited." In Lorraine Eden, ed. *Retrospectives on Public Finance.* Durham, N.C.: Duke University Press. Pp. 177–202.

Finlayson, Jock A. and Mark W. Zacher. 1983. "The GATT and the Regulation of Trade Barriers: Regime Dynamics and Functions." In Stephen Krasner, ed. *International Regimes.* Ithaca: Cornell University Press. Pp. 273–314.

George, Alexander L. 1983. *Managing U.S.–Soviet Rivalry.* Boulder: Westview Press.

George, Alexander L., Philip J. Farley, and Alexander Dallin. 1988. *Soviet Security Cooperation: Achievements, Lessons, Failures.* New York: Oxford University Press.

Gilpin, Robert. 1987. *The Political Economy of International Relations.* Princeton: Princeton University Press.

Goodman, John. 1992. *Monetary Sovereignty: The Politics of Central Banking in Western Europe.* Ithaca: Cornell University Press.

Goodman, John and Louis Pauly. 1993. "The Obsolescence of Capital Controls? Economic Management in an Age of Capital Markets." *World Politics* 46 (1): 50–82.

Goldstein, Judith. 1993. "Creating the GATT Rules: Domestic Politics and Multilateral Cooperation." In John Gerard Ruggie, ed. *Multilateralism Matters: The Theory and Praxis of an Institutional Form.* New York: Columbia University Press. Pp. 201–32.

Goldstein, Judith and Robert O. Keohane, eds. 1993. *Ideas and Foreign Policy: Beliefs, Institutions, and Political Change.* Ithaca: Cornell University Press.

Gowa, Joanne. 1994. *Allies, Adversaries, and International Trade.* Princeton: Princeton University Press.

Haas, Ernest. 1983. "Words Can Hurt You; or, Who Said What to Whom about Regimes." In Stephen Krasner, ed. *International Regimes.* Ithaca: Cornell University Press. Pp. 23–60.

Haas, Ernest B. 1990. *When Knowledge Is Power: Three Models of Change in International Organizations.* Berkeley: University of California Press.

Haas, Peter. 1989. "Do Regimes Matter? Epistemic Communities and Mediterranean Pollution Control." *International Organization.* 43 (3): 377–404.

Haggard, Stephan and Beth Simmons. 1987. "Theories of International Regimes." *International Organization.* 41 (3): 491–517.

Hampson, Fen Osler. 1989–90. "Climate Change: Building International Coalitions of the Like-Minded." *International Journal* 65 (1): 61–7.

Hampson, Fen Osler with Michael Hart. 1995. *Multilateral Negotiations: Lessons from Arms Control, Trade, and the Environment.* Baltimore: Johns Hopkins University Press.

Hardin, Russell. 1982. *Collective Action.* Baltimore: John Hopkins University Press.

Hartwick, John M. and Nancy Olewiler. 1986. *The Economics of Natural Resource Use.* Cambridge: Harper & Row Publishers.

Helleiner, Eric. 1994. *States and the Reemergence of Global Finance: From Bretton Woods to the 1990s.* Ithaca: Cornell University Press.

Higgott, Richard. 1991. "Towards a Non-Hegemonic International Political Economy: An Antipodean Perspective." In Craig Murphy and Roger Tooze, eds. *The New International Political Economy,* International Political Economy Yearbook, Volume 5. New York: Lynne Rienner. Pp. 97–128.

Hymer, Stephen. 1975. "The Multinational Corporation and the Law of Uneven Development." In Hugo Radice, ed. *International Firms and Modern Imperialism.* London: Penguin. Pp. 89–104.

———. 1976. *The International Operations of National Firms: A Study of Foreign Direct Investment.* Cambridge: MIT Press.

Jackson, John H. 1989. *The World Trading System: Law and Policy of International Economic Relations.* Cambridge: MIT Press.

Jervis, Robert. 1978. "Cooperation Under the Security Dilemma." *World Politics* 30 (2): 167–214.

    1983. *Perception and Misperception in International Politics.* Princeton: Princeton University Press.

Jervis, Robert, Richard Ned Lebow and Janice Gross Stein. 1985. *Psychology and Deterrence.* Baltimore: John Hopkins University Press.

Johnson, Harry. 1970. "The Efficiency and Welfare Implications of the International Corporation." In Charles P. Kindleberger, ed. *The International Corporation.* Cambridge: MIT Press.

Kahler, Miles. 1993. "Multilateralism with Small and Large Numbers." In John Gerard Ruggie, ed. *Multilateralism Matters: The Theory and Praxis of an Institutional Form.* New York: Columbia University Press. Pp. 295–326.

Keeley, James F. 1990. "The Latest Wave: A Critical Review of the Regime Literature." In David G. Haglund and Michael K. Hawes, eds. *World Politics: Power, Interdependence, and Dependence.* Toronto: Harcourt, Brace, Jovanovich. Pp. 553–69.

Kennedy, Paul. 1987. *The Rise and Fall of the Great Powers: Economic Change and Military Conflict from 1500 to 2000.* New York: Random House.

    1990. "Fin-de-Siecle America." *The New York Review of Books* 38 (11): June 28, 31–40.

Keohane, Robert O. 1983. "The Demand for International Regimes." In Stephen Krasner, ed. *International Regimes.* Ithaca: Cornell University Press. Pp. 141–72.

    1984. *After Hegemony: Cooperation and Discord in the World Political Economy.* Princeton: Princeton University Press.

    1995. "The Analysis of International Regimes: Towards a European-American Research Program." In Volker Rittberger, ed. *Regime Theory and International Relations.* Oxford: Oxford University Press. Pp. 23–48.

Krasner, Stephen. 1983. "Structural Causes and Regime Consequences: Regimes as Intervening Variables." In Stephen Krasner, ed. *International Regimes.* Ithaca: Cornell University Press. Pp. 1–21.

    1991. "Global Communications and National Power." *World Politics* 47 (3): 226–366.

Kupchan, Charles A. and Clifford A. Kupchan. 1991. "Concerts, Collective Security, and the Future of Europe." *International Security.* 16 (1): 114–61.

Kydd, Andrew and Duncan Snydal. 1995. "Progress in Game Theoretical Analysis of International Regimes." In Volker Rittberger, ed. *Regime Theory and International Relations.* Oxford: Oxford University Press. Pp. 112–38.

Larson, Deborah Welch. 1985. *Origins of Containment: A Psychological Explanation.* Princeton: Princeton University Press.

Mahler, Vincent A. 1984. "The Political Economy of North-South Commodity Bargaining: The Case of the International Sugar Agreement." *International Organization.* 38 (4): 709–32.

Musgrave, Richard A. 1959. *The Theory of Public Finance: A Study in Political Economy.* New York: McGraw-Hill Book Company.

Musgrave, Richard A., Peggy B. Musgrave, and Richard M. Bird. 1987. *Public Finance in Theory and Practice,* first Canadian edition. Toronto: McGraw-Hill Ryerson Limited.

Nau, Henry R. 1990. *The Myth of America's Decline in the 1990s.* New York: Oxford University Press.

Neustadt, Richard E. and Ernest R. May. 1986. *Thinking in Time: The Uses of History for Decision Makers.* New York: Free Press.

Nye, Joseph S. 1990. *Bound to Lead: The Changing Nature of America's Power.* New York: Basic Books.

Oye, Kenneth A. 1986. "Explaining Cooperation under Anarchy." In Kenneth A. Oye, ed. *Cooperation Under Anarchy.* Princeton: Princeton University Press. Pp. 1–24.

Pigou, A. C. 1928. *A Study in Public Finance.* London: Macmillan.

Pratt, Cranford. 1990. *Middle Power Internationalism: The North-South Dimension.* Montreal: McGill-Queen's University Press.

Price, Richard. 1995. "A Genealogy of the Chemical Weapons Taboo." *International Organization.* 29 (1): 73–104.

Putnam, Robert D. 1988. "Diplomacy and Domestic Politics: The Logic of Two-Level Games." *International Organization.* 42 (3): 427–60.

Rittberger, Volker, ed. 1995. *Regime Theory and International Relations.* Oxford: Oxford University Press.

Rosen, Harvey S. 1988. *Public Finance,* 2nd ed. Homewood, Ill.: Irwin.

Rothstein, Robert L. 1984a. "Consensual Knowledge and International Collaboration: Some Lessons from the Commodity Negotiations." *International Organization.* 38 (4): 733–762.

1984b. "Regime Creation by a Coalition of the Weak: Lessons from the NIEO and the Integrated Program for Commodities." *International Studies Quarterly.* 28 (3): 307–28.

Ruggie, John Gerard. 1983. "International Regimes, Transactions, and Change: Embedded Liberalism in the Postwar Economic Order." In Stephen Krasner, ed. *International Regimes.* Ithaca: Cornell University Press. Pp. 423–88.

Rugman, Alan M. 1986. "New Theories of the Multinational Enterprise: An Assessment of Internalization Theory." *Bulletin of Economic Research* 38: 101–18.

Runnalls, David. 1989. "The Grand Bargain." *Peace and Security* 4 (3): 7–8.

Sandholtz, Wayne. 1993. "Choosing Monetary Union: Monetary Politics and Maastricht." *International Organization.* 47 (1): 1–39.

Schnieberg, Marc and J. Rogers Hollingsworth. 1988. "Can Transactions Cost Economics Explain Trade Associations?" Presented at the Swedish Colloquium for Advanced Study of the Social Science conference on "The Firm as a Nexus of Treaties." Uppsala, Sweden, June 6–8.

Sebenius, James K. 1984. *Negotiating the Law of the Sea.* Cambridge: Harvard University Press.

Simmons, Beth. 1994. *Who Adjusts? Domestic Sources of Foreign Economic Policy during the Interwar Years.* Princeton: Princeton University Press.

Snidal, Duncan. 1985. "The Limits of Hegemonic Stability Theory." *International Organization.* 39 (4): 579–615.

Solingen, Ethel. 1994. "The Domestic Sources of Regional Regimes: The Evolution of Nuclear Ambiguity." *International Studies Quarterly.* 38 (2): 305–38.

Starrett, David A. 1988. *Foundations of Public Economics.* Cambridge: Cambridge University Press.

Stiglitz, Joseph E. 1986. *Economics of the Public Sector.* New York: W. W. Norton and Company Limited.

Strange, Susan. 1983. "Cave! Hic Dragones: A Critique of Regime Analysis." In Stephen Krasner, ed. *International Regimes.* Ithaca: Cornell University Press. Pp. 337–54.

1988. *States and Markets.* New York: Basil Blackwell.

Teece, David J. 1981. "The Multinational Enterprise: Market Failure and Market Power Considerations." *Sloan Management Review.* 22 (3): 3–17.

Tiebout, Charles. 1956. "A Pure Theory of Local Expenditures." *Journal of Political Economy* 64 (October): 416–24.

Tietenberg, Tom. 1984. *Environmental and Natural Resource Economics.* Glenview, Illinois: Scott, Foresman and Company.

Tresch, Richard W. 1981. *Public Finance: A Normative Theory.* Georgetown, Ont.: Irwin-Dorsey Limited.

Underhill, Geoffrey R. D. 1990. "Markets Beyond Politics? The State and the Internationalization of Financial Markets." McMaster University, Department of Political Science, mimeo.

United Nations. 1988. *Transnational Corporations in World Development: Trends and Prospects.* United Nations UN/ST/CTC/89.

Webb, Michael. 1990. "Canada and the International Macroeconomic Adjustment Regime." Paper presented at the Conference on Canada and International Economic Regimes, Institute of International Relations, University of British Columbia, May 30–31.

Williamson, Oliver E. 1975. *Markets and Hierarchies: Analysis and Antitrust Implications.* New York: The Free Press.

1985. *The Economic Institutions of Capitalism.* New York: The Free Press.

1986. *Economic Organization.* Brighton: Wheatsheaf Books.

Yarbrough, Beth V. and Robert M. Yarbrough. 1990. "International Institutions and the New Economics of Organization." *International Organization* 44 (2): 235–59.

Young, Oran R. 1986. "International Regimes: Towards a New Theory of Institutions." *World Politics* 39 (1): 100–22.

1989a. *International Cooperation: Building Regimes for Natural Resources and the Environment.* Ithaca: Cornell University Press.

1989b. "Politics of International Regime Formation: Managing Natural Resources and the Environment." *International Organization 43 (3): 349–76.*

Young, Oran R. and Gail Oshrenko. 1995. "Testing Theories of Regime Formation: Findings from a Large Collaborative Research Project." In Volker Rittberger, ed. *Regime Theory and International Relations.* Oxford: Oxford University Press. Pp. 223–52.

13

THE EMERGING EUROPOLITY AND ITS IMPACT UPON NATIONAL SYSTEMS OF PRODUCTION

Philippe C. Schmitter

The Single European Act (SEA), as signed and quickly ratified by twelve sovereign national governments, and the Maastricht Accord (MAA), as signed and ratified with great difficulty by these same governments, have greatly accelerated European integration. There seems little doubt that they are going to change the pace and even the direction of that process, but what will be their joint impact upon the way in which capitalism is practiced in this part of the world?

The central theme of this chapter can be put quite simply – and dramatically: *Can the distinctive institutions that have long governed national capitalisms within Europe and that are currently being jeopardized by the rising tide of **global liberalization** and interdependence, be regrouped and revitalized at the **regional** level, i.e., at the level of the European Community (EC)?* As the SEA and the MAA are sequentially implemented over the next decade, will Europe enter the twenty-first century with a relatively unified ("convergent") set of norms and practices

This chapter was prepared while the author was a Fellow at the Center for Advanced Study in the Behavioral Sciences. I am grateful for financial support provided by National Science Foundation Grant #BNS-8700864 and by a Social Science Research Council (SSRC) Grant to the "Consortium for 1992." My colleagues in the Consortium have been generous with their time and criticism, for which I thank them – thereby, absolving them from responsibility for all remaining errors and misinterpretations. I have also benefited from the research assistance of James Kinzer and Matt Tupper.

regulating the production of goods and services and the exploitation of labor and capital? Or will its twelve or more members fail in this unprecedented endeavor – and either retreat to protecting their distinctive (if costly) institutions behind existing national boundaries, or resign themselves to playing a less distinctive (if still prosperous) role in an evolving global economy?

The answer to this question lies, first, in understanding the mix of governance mechanisms that have historically differentiated national capitalisms in Europe and, second, in projecting into the future the impact of the commitments that the twelve member states of the European Community have made with regard to each other.

MODES OF GOVERNANCE

The present chapter will contribute little to answering the first question. *Governing Capitalist Economies,*[1] as well as several essays in this volume,[2] has explored in considerable detail the variety of modes of sectoral governance and the configurations they have adopted in particular national settings. Elsewhere, I have also tried my hand at typologizing the range of possibilities and speculating about why one rather than another might be chosen.[3] Beneath the confusion of labels for the different modes and the profusion of factors alleged to explain their emergence or persistence, there seems to be widespread agreement on the following:

1. The efficiency or performance of a capitalist economy cannot be attributed to (or even modeled according to) the operation of a single type of exchange mechanism; i.e., it cannot be reduced to markets alone.
2. All these varied mechanisms or arrangements involve some degree to governance, i.e., some potential capability to coordinate the behavior of relevant actors by generating rules or enforcing sanctions.
3. The prevalent dichotomy of market versus state or market versus hierarchy must be supplemented by the recognition of various "intermediary" forms of governance that are no more ephemeral or contingent than their better known rivals.
4. There is no *a priori* or *a fortiori* reason why any one of these mechanisms is more efficient (or desirable) that the others, since their performance depends so much on the specific spatial and functional contexts in which they operate.
5. No single factor, e.g., technology, consumer preference, or international competition, can explain the selection, persistence, or adaptation of a given type of governance mechanism.

6. Another way of saying this is that, once chosen in a complex historical process, governance mechanisms tend to institutionalize themselves and to persist even when their initial conditions have changed or disappeared altogether.
7. Supplementing this historicity in origins is the tendency for sovereign political units, i.e., nation-states, to practice spatial discrimination and to encourage the formation of relatively similar governance mechanisms across different sectors and professions by law, custom, diffusion, and/or the development of a national "policy style."

Beyond these generalizations, there is still a good deal of essentially contested terrain. Perhaps the most disputable conclusion that emerges from several of the essays in this book is that *Europe (or, more specifically, continental Western Europe) is characterized by the role of a particularly dense and resilient cluster of "intermediary," i.e., nonmarket and nonstate, mechanisms.* One can speculate *ad infinitum* about the reason for this: the persistence of "precapitalist," guild-like institutions; the weakness of liberal, individualist ideology; the impact of repeated, large-scale international warfare; the strength of organized labor and social democratic parties; the overriding importance of maintaining public order in societies polarized by class cleavages during industrialization. The fact remains, however, that *associations* of capital, labor, and the professions, *networks* between social groups, *alliances* among firms, and especially, *private interest governments* engaging both producers and authorities seem to occupy a much more significant place in descriptions of how "business" is conducted in Europe than in comparable accounts of other advanced industrial societies. For example, it is possible (even commonplace) for textbooks on "business–government relations" in the United States not to mention the existence of trade or employer associations (and to refer to labor unions only as annoyances or impediments), whereas no analogous treatment of Europe could avoid discussing their integral role in the system of production and distribution.

While the labels for these intermediary coordinating mechanisms vary across authors, there is a fair amount of agreement about what, generically speaking, these institutions can do:

1. They can organize and, when necessary, enforce stable cooperative behavior among their members – despite competitive pressures that motivate individuals and firms to defect from common norms and practices.
2. They can enter into and guarantee relatively long term-contracts with interlocutors, i.e., with nonmembers who furnish crucial factor inputs to production such as labor, raw materials, subcomponents, distributive facilities, marketing services, etc.

3. They can negotiate agreements with state authorities for the delegation of authority necessary to produce selected "categoric goods" that will benefit their members and serve specified "public purposes."

Not all intermediary governance mechanisms perform all of these functions. Indeed, in some national contexts, doing so would contradict antitrust regulations and rules of competition that prohibit "actions in restraint of trade." Even within Europe, where we have reason to suspect that such institutions are more deeply embedded than elsewhere,[4] there is a great deal of variation from country to country and sector to sector – resulting precisely in the sort of differences in competitiveness that the SEA's project to "complete the Internal Market" was designed to eliminate.

For, contrary to the orthodoxy that associates efficiency and superior performance with the absence of any form of collective intervention between producers and consumers, *Europe's competitive advantage in contemporary world markets is confidently attributed precisely to the role that these "meddling" intermediaries perform in generating and updating worker skills, in ensuring flexible use of resources, in diffusing information, in sharing research and development costs, in lengthening time horizons and, generally, in underwriting what Streeck has called "diversified quality production."*[5] The implication is clear: with their resource endowments, their cost structures, their industrial organization, and their delicate political compromises, the countries of (Western) Europe can compete effectively with the less regulated, less taxed, and less skilled economies of North America and the Third World only if they manage to sustain their rich and complex infrastructure of intermediary modes of governance.

And this is precisely where the Europe 1992 Project of completing the internal market and its further extension at Maastricht becomes problematic. For the SEA poses a special threat to a wide range of class, sectoral, and professional arrangements – in particular, to the operation of "private interest governments (PIGs)" – within the twelve member states of the Community. Its commitment to the *mutual recognition* of norms and standards threatens to unleash a process of competition between national regulatory systems that are grounded in discriminatory treatment by trade and professional associations and/or by state and local agencies. Only if it can be shown (and argued convincingly before the European Court of Justice) that these practices are needed to serve some higher public purpose, e.g., to prevent fiscal evasion, to promote public health or morality, to protect the environment, or to guarantee honest competition, *and* that they do not discriminate against products or services from other member states, would these semiprivate, "off-loaded" arrangements for governing economic transactions be safe from challenge. Otherwise, the inexorable verdict of the market (not to mention those of the Court that originally established this principle in the *Cassis de Dijon* case of 1979) should eliminate most of these practices and eventually compel all individuals and firms in all sectors and professions in the EC to converge toward operating under the same set of rules of competition – presumably the one that is least restrictive and most immediately cost-effective.

Now that the MAA has been ratified and if and when it is implemented, its commitment to monetary union and a single European currency should irrevocably deprive national authorities of one of the few weapons they still had for the defense of national capitalist practices, i.e., competitive devaluation. It might even place severe restrictions on their ability to engage in "idiosyncratic" budgeting, i.e., running deliberate imbalances for purposes of macroeconomic reflation.

Should these two successive treatments be applied as envisaged, the twelve member states could be deprived of some of their most venerable and distinctive socioeconomic institutions, many of which have contributed significantly to sustaining their respective national versions of a generically European style of "organized capitalism" and to underwriting their capability to compete effectively within the specialized *niches* of "diversified quality production."

Before a change of such magnitude can occur, however, a great deal of political and legal maneuvering will intervene. Not only are national governments likely to be increasingly inventive in discovering "higher public purposes" which justify retaining the quality controls, entry barriers, production quotas, market shares, working conditions, price levels, fee setting arrangements, and standards of training imposed by their most prized national economic institutions, but the authorities of the European Community will no doubt find reasons for arguing that such an abrupt and extensive deregulation of the newly completed Internal Market would only lead to massive deception, fraud, mismanagement, and other forms of "opportunistic" behavior, and that therefore they should be empowered to intervene in these vulnerable markets at the level of the Community as a whole. To the extent that these efforts of Eurocrats to expand their *compétences* coincide with the interests of certain, well-placed capitalists in protecting their enterprises from "unfair" competition and "anarchic" local restrictions, the whole 1992 Project could be diverted from its original intent and exploited to produce a substantial "reregulation" of market relations among the Twelve. Rather than becoming extinct, private interest governments could even be given a new lease on life – either by being used at the national and subnational level as *agents* for the implementation of EC directives, or by being transposed to the supranational level in the form of Europewide autonomous *agencies*.

In order to assess which of these scenarios is most likely to impose itself, it is necessary to *reculer pour mieux sauter,* i.e., first to make an effort to understand what kind of a polity may be emerging from the SEA and its recent successor, the MAA. Only then, once one has a clear idea of the probably level and scope of Community authority, should it become possible to evaluate the future of national and supranational mechanisms for economic coordination. For if we have learned anything from our previous sectoral studies of the subject, it is that their formation, operation, and viability are closely associated with state authority. To the extent that the European Community (EC) presently lacks and/or never manages to acquire this ultimate capacity for controlling the movement of goods, services, people, and capital over a given territory and for directly and legitimately exercising coercion to back it up, then, it will be limited in its role as a sponsor or protector of whatever governance arrangements it enlists to help it with these tasks.

INTERPRETING THE EMERGENT EUROPOLITY

The SEA's self-imposed deadline of December 31, 1992 has passed. Most of its anticipated 282 *directives* were drafted by the Commission and approved by the Council of Ministers. Admittedly, some of those remaining deal with controversial matters of major importance, e.g., fiscal harmonization, but the "Internal Market" can already be declared a formal success. At the level of *transposition,* or the conversion of EC directives into national law, progress has been much less rapid and more uneven, but no one can say that the "1992 Process" did not advance very far – perhaps farther than the signers of the Act in 1985 intended or believed possible.

The subsequent agreements reached at Maastricht in December 1991 represented a significant extension of EC activity and even authority in two broad domains: monetary union and political cooperation. They also help to clarify somewhat the rules of the game and institutional *compétences* of the emergent Europolity, and have even given the outcome a new name, the *European Union (EU),* although only time will tell if this label sticks.

The Single European Act came in with a whimper; the Maastricht Accord with a bang. When the former was initialed in 1985 and ratified in 1986, even quite knowledgeable observers discounted its importance. There was very little in the Act that did not just repeat obligations previously assumed in the Treaty of Rome (if not acted upon); moreover, the member states had a past history of signing sonorous agreements to "relaunch" the integration process that produced little effect. The national governments that signed the SEA seemed not to have been fully cognizant of the full implication of its provisions, nor could they have foreseen the unprecedented response they evoked with the business community and eventually the public at large.

The MAA of December 1992 was a much more scrutinized affair and member state participants took the elaboration of their respective national positions much more seriously. It was preceded by a very complex structure of bilateral encounters between heads of state and ministers, as well as a steady flow of "white papers" and draft proposals from the Commission and two Inter-Governmental Conferences (IGCs): one on Economic and Monetary Union, the other on Political Union, that had been meeting over the previous year.[6] Considering all the hoopla among specialized "attentive elites," it is perhaps surprising how very little discussion there was in the public at large. Admittedly, the SEA was destined to have a much greater and more immediate impact upon the daily lives of individuals, affecting everything "from boar-meat to banking" as the *Financial Times* put it. The MAA focused more on the reform of institutions than the movement of "goods, services, capital and persons" and hence will take more time to produce effects that can be registered by government agencies, interest groups, political parties, and social movements in the member countries. However much the MAA may contribute to defining the future Europolity in the long run, it has not done much for increasing the popularity of the EC/EU in the short run.

The major "functional" accomplishment of the MAA consists in its provisions with regard to monetary union. This is a *spillover* beyond what was originally envisaged in the Treaty of Rome, although significant intergovernmental cooperation on this issue has been going on since 1972 when the "snake" was created and especially since 1979 when eight of the then nine member states formed the European Monetary System (EMS). What is different about the evolving European Monetary Union (EMU) is not only that it establishes a clear set of deadlines for attaining a much more ambitious goal – nothing less than the creation of a common currency with a critical decision (by qualified majority vote!) to come in 1996 – but that it does so through the creation of new Community institutions: the European System of Central Banks (ESCB) and eventually the European Central Bank (ECB) with very substantial resources and competences, *and* it specifies in rather considerable detail the criteria that have to be met in order to bring about nothing less than the *convergence* of macroeconomic performance among the participating countries. Moreover, the MAA stipulates in quite strong language that the ECB will enjoy virtually complete autonomy from its member governments, in effect, creating a major instrument of private interest governance at the very heart of EC policy making. Should this precedent be set firmly enough and function well, it is conceivable that a similar formula might be applied in the establishment of a European Securities and Exchange Commission, a European Rail Authority, a European Energy Agency, or a European Air-Controllers' Network.

Even if confined to the monetary field, member states will have "pooled" some of their most sovereign rights by 2001: to issue their own money, to run budgetary deficits, to borrow as much as they please (or can), to set their own interest rates and targets for monetary growth, to alter their rates of foreign exchange – in effect, to pursue any macroeconomic policy independent of the other participating member states. There are, of course, "opt-out" and "ease-out" clauses that can be used either to refuse to join or to force a member to derogate. It remains to be seen whether individual countries will use the former to protect their distinctive national institutions, or whether a qualified majority will have the courage to apply the latter against those who persist in discriminating in favor of specific sectors or engaging in persistent deficit spending.

Once, however, some subset of EC member states is locked into Stage III of the EMU in 1996, it is difficult to imagine how any of them could go back to issuing its own currency or even to improving its competitive market position through effective and exclusive national macroeconomic policies. As already suggested, this "locking in" at the supranational macrolevel could have the indirect effect of shifting the burden of industrial adjustment and export promotion to the mesolevel where most of the sectorally specific, national governance mechanisms have long been operating.

The MAA also encourages the Council of Ministers to take initiatives by qualified majority voting in other issue arenas that have either not been dealt with in the past or that have long remained dormant: public health, education, consumer protection, the promotion of "trans-European networks" in telecommunications, transport and energy, and the development of small and medium-sized firms. It places a higher threshold, i.e., unanimity, on its getting involved with such items as environmental protection, industrial policy, energy planning, and taxation. Almost all of these policy arenas are subject to heavy regulation and explicit coordination at the national level. Depending on the voting criteria and the implementation requirements, the EC could make extensive indirect use of these existing arrangements if and when it expands its *compétences* in these domains.

In Table 13-1, I have sought to describe the dynamics of the expansion of EC authority across the full range of issue arenas. Using a measurement device invented by Lindberg and Scheingold (and the scores

Table 13-1. Issue Arenas and Levels of Authority in Europe: 1950–2001

I. Economic issue arenas	1950	1957	1968	1970[a]	1992[b]	2001[c]
1. Goods/services	1	2	4[d] (3)	4 (3)	4	4
2. Agriculture	1	1	4	4	4	4
3. Capital flows[e]	1	1	1	1	4	4
4. Persons/workers[f]	1	1	2	2	3	4
5. Transportation	1	2	2	3 (2)	2	3
6. Energy[g]	1	2	1	1	2	2
7. Communications	1	1	1	1	2	3
8. Environment[h]	1	2	2	2	3	3
9. Regional development[i]	1	1	1	1	3	3
10. Competition	1	2	3 (2)	3 (2)	3	3
11. Industry[j]	1	2	2	2	2	3
12. Money/credit	1	1	2	2	2	4
13. Foreign exchange/loans	1	1	3 (2)	4 (2)	2	4
14. Revenue/taxes	1	1	3 (2)	3 (2)	2	3
15. Macroeconomic[k]	1	1	2	3	2	4
II. Sociocultural issue arenas						
1. Work conditions	1	1	2	2	2	3
2. Health	1	1	1	1	2	2
3. Social welfare	1	2	2	3 (2)	2	2
4. Education and research	1	1	3 (2)	3 (2)	2	3
5. Labor–management relations	1	1	1	1	1	3

Table 13-1 *(cont.)*

III. Politicoconstitutional issues						
1. Justice and property rights[l]	1	1	1	2	3	4
2. Citizenship[m]	1	1	1	1	2	3
3. Participation	1	1	2 (1)	2 (1)	2	2
4. Police and public order[n]	1	1	2 (1)	2 (1)	1	2

IV. International relations/ external security issues						
1. Commercial negotiations	1	1	3	4	5	5
2. Ecomilitary assistance	1	1	1	1	2	4
3. Diplomacy and IGO membership	1	1	2 (1)	2 (1)	2	4
4. Defense and war	1	1	1	1	2	3

[a] Source for the estimates, 1950–1970: Leon Lindberg and Stuart Scheingold, *Europe's Would-Be Polity* (1970: 67–71). Their estimates for 1970 were "projections based on existing treaty obligations and on obligations undertaken as a result of subsequent policy decisions" (p. 70).

[b] Estimated outcome of the Single European Act based on projections from existing treaty obligations and obligations undertaken subsequently. Score indicated for this and successive column represents the mode of independently provided evaluations by members of the Consortium for 1992 present at the Center for Advanced Study in the Behavioral Sciences in March 1992: Geoffrey Garrett, Peter Lange, Gary Marks, Philippe C. Schmitter, and David Soskice.

[c] Estimated outcome of the Maastricht Accord based on assumed treaty obligations and presumed ratification by member states.

[d] Scores in parentheses ( ) represent ex post revaluations in March 1992 of the original scores in Lindberg and Scheingold by members of the Consortium for 1992.

[e] Category not in Lindberg and Scheingold. My estimates for 1950–1970.

[f] Category not in Lindberg and Scheingold. My estimates for 1950–1970.

[g] Category not in Lindberg and Scheingold. My estimates for 1950–1970.

[h] Defined as "Exploitation and protection of natural resources" in Lindberg and Scheingold.

[i] Category not in Lindberg and Scheingold. My estimates for 1950–1970.

[j] Called "Economic development and planning" in Lindberg and Scheingold.

[k] Called "Counter-cyclical policy" in Lindberg and Scheingold.

[l] Category not in Lindberg and Scheingold. My estimates for 1950–1970.

[m] Category not in Lindberg and Scheingold. My estimates for 1950–1970.

[n] Called "Public health, safety and maintenance of public order" in Lindberg and Scheingold.

they proposed for the "foundational period" from 1950 to 1970), I have added estimates of the impact likely to be produced by the SEA as of the end of 1992 and of the probably effect of the MAA by 2001 – if it is ratified by member states. The scores in Table 13-1 confirm that *there is not an issue area that was the exclusive domain of national policy in 1950 and that has not somehow and to some degree been incorporated within the purview of the EC/EU*. Needless to say, this is most evident in economic matters, but one finds "4s" (mostly policy decisions at the EC level) and even a "5" (all policy decisions at the EC level) in the allegedly more sensitive politicoconstitutional and international relations/external security areas by 1992–2001. There are, however, three noticeable disappointments at the core of the Common Market: transportation, energy, and communications. All would seem intrinsically promising from a neofunctional perspective; indeed, they collectively facilitate the interdependence between other substantive policy areas. And yet, according to the scores in Table 13-1 they had barely been touched by 1970, and were expected to raise to the status of "only some decisions at the EC Level" by 1992. Energy – an intersectoral and, one would think, interspatial commodity *par excellence* – was judged to remain essentially in national hands through 2001, along with such other laggards as health, social welfare, political participation, and police and public order!

The great leaps forward in the future is anticipated in the mobility of persons and workers (a product of the SEA), money and credit, foreign exchange and loans, macroeconomic policy making (all obviously as a result of EMU), and the coordination of economic-military assistance to foreign countries, diplomatic initiatives, membership in international organizations, and matters of external security (presumably based on an optimistic assessment of impact of the clauses of the MAA that refer to political cooperation and defense policy).

The estimates for 1992 and 2001 are based on the modal response from five independent evaluations by participants in the "Consortium for 1992." They therefore disguise some significant divergences. For example, the most marked one came with regard to competition policy. Most of us scored this a 3, policy decision about equally distributed at the national and supranational levels, but one scholar gave it a 5, i.e., assigned it exclusively to the EC/EU by 2001 and another a 2, i.e., saw it as remaining a predominantly national matter. The areas of person and worker mobility, managing labor relations, citizenship, law and public order, and defense and war also brought out persistent differences among us about where the locus of decision making would lie at the turn of the century. There was no divergence, however, about the general trend and very few instances of anticipated "spillback" to a more national level of authority.

But for someone seeking to peer over the horizon for the emerging Europolity, the most interesting aspects of the MAA cannot be glimpsed from the probable range of activities the Community or Union will be performing in 2001. Rather, they are hidden in its excruciatingly abstruse provisions about institutions and decision rules. In its first paragraph (Art. A), the MAA announces that it is establishing a new entity: the *European Union (EU),* never subsequently defined but somehow more ambitious and overarching since it will contain the European Community (EC) and be "supplemented by the policies and forms of cooperation established by this Treaty." Repeating the opening phrase of the Treaty of Rome, it commits its members to "an ever closer union among the peoples of Europe,"[7] and then adds the dependent clause: "where decisions are taken as closely as possible to the citizens." This is an indirect reference to the latest buzzword in Eurospeak: *subsidiarity.*[8] In other words, whatever its functions, the EU is to be a dispersed polity where most decisions will presumably be taken (and not just implemented) by other than central governmental authorities. It hints that such a system might have several levels and even that subnational, i.e., local, provincial, or regional, units might be favored over national states. In common parlance, such a system is often called "federalist," but apparently the United Kingdom vetoed any mention of this F-word in the MAA.

These common provisions for the EU went on, however, to hint at several other features which sound more "statelike." For example, they announce the creation of a new "citizenship of the Union," the intention to "assert its identity on the international scene," to strengthen "economic and social cohesion" and "to maintain in full the *acquis communautaire* and to build upon it" (Art. B).[9] They promise the creation of "a single institutional framework to ensure the consistency and continuity of ... actions" and specifically call attention to the EU's eventual "actions as a whole in the context of its external relations, security, economic and development policies" (Art. C). If one took these pretensions seriously and ignored the caveats,[10] one might be tempted to conclude – erroneously – that a supranational state was being founded.

What actually seems more likely to emerge from the multiple (and by no means coherent) provisions of the MAA is something quite novel – and perhaps unexpected. How ironic it would be if the Eurocrats – normally so attentive at identifying unintended consequences and so skillful at turning them into an expansion of their *compétences* – should discover that their preferred design for the Europolity would be the accidental victim of their own efforts! For the MAA opens the way for the institutionalization of diversity – for a multitude of relatively independent European arrangements with distinct statutes, functions, resources, and memberships, not coordinated by a single central organization and operating under different decision rules.

No doubt, the Commission will work harder to defend the *acquis commu-nautaire,* a *single track and synchronized process,* and its own *concentric role,* but this may not be an easy task given the changing external context within which the Europolity is emerging.

The MAA abounds in potentially partial and eccentric arrangements. For example, it calls for a "third stage" European Central Bank with very considerable independence, not only from national governments, but also from the EC/EU itself. The field of monetary policy has long pioneered in *variable geometry* when the EMS went ahead without the participation of several member states, including a major player, the United Kingdom, until 1990. At the present time, neither Greece, Portugal, Spain, or Italy participate fully in it, although they are all committed to doing so eventually. According to the MAA, it will be possible to move ahead to the ECB in Stage III by a qualified majority vote and with as few as seven members. Countries whose economic performance does not meet the exacting standards for convergence will be declared "in derogation" and prohibited from participating in the decision. The United Kingdom asked for a special dispensation and can decide to "opt out" during Stage II. Social policy is another arena in which the MAA found it necessary to improvise. Again, the problem stemmed from British intransigence. The Conservative government opposed substituting worker rights and welfare provisions through European measures that had been removed from its national practices by the "Thatcher Revolution." A last minute solution was cobbled together to allow the other eleven member states to "opt in" for policies that will be decided by qualified majority in a reduced quorum, i.e., without British participation, if they so choose. In a separate protocol, the signatories pledge to use "EC institutions, procedures and mechanisms," but it is not inconceivable that they might eventually decide to establish a separate European Social Regime, say, for the administration of common pension or unemployment funds. In any case, an unusual precedent has been created that could be applied in other issue arenas.

In the field of foreign policy, for example, the Accord calls for "systematic cooperation," but places it outside formal EC institutions and the Treaty of Rome. It even sets up a new permanent "Political Committee consisting of Political Directors," a sort of embryonic Foreign Office, in Bruxelles to which "the Commission shall be fully associated" (Art. J.8) – but not in control. In a parallel fashion, the member states resorted to working through the Western European Union, an organization existing since 1954 for debating defense issues. The WEU will be opened to new members (but none will be compelled to join) and eventually become the "defence component" of the EU, but its relation to existing EC institutions seems very loosely defined – and deliberately so.

One could go on with other potentialities for partiality and eccentricity in the MAA:

1. A new advisory Committee of Regions is created with representatives from (unspecified) subnational units (Art. 198a) which, when combined with the promise of a substantial increase in funds for *economic and social cohesion* (Annex I, Protocol 15), could develop into a circuit of influence bypassing the national level of aggregation.

2. The European Parliament is granted important new powers: to form Committees of Enquiry (Art. 137b), to request that the Commission take specific initiatives (Art. 137a), to receive petitions from individual European citizens and "legal persons" (Art. 137c), to appoint an independent Ombudsman (Art. 137d), and, most significantly, to enter into an exceedingly complex *codecision* procedure (Art. 189b) for a wide range of issues whereby, should the Eurodeputies persist by an absolute majority in rejecting a Council decision, even a unanimous one, they can effectively veto its passage.

3. The signatories "invite" the European Parliament and the member state national parliaments to form and meet as often as necessary in a new representative assembly, the Conference of the Parliaments or *les Assises*.

4. An EU-wide organization for police cooperation (Europol) is established, as well as an unnamed "Coordinating Committee" consisting of senior national government officials which is empowered to make recommendations for action in such highly sensitive areas as asylum rights, visa requirements, immigration policy, drug trafficking, commercial fraud, judicial cooperation in civil and criminal matters, and terrorism.

The next closest *direct* approximation in the MAA to private interest governance, i.e., other than indirect implications of the European Central Bank provisions, emerges from the eleven member, "opt-in" agreement on social policy. Having set as their objectives nothing less than: "the promotion of employment, improved living and working conditions, proper social protection, dialogue between management and labor, the development of human resources with a view to lasting high employment and the combating of exclusion," the cosignatories first agreed to implement only measures that "take account of the diverse forms of national practices, in particular in the field of contractual relations," but they also committed themselves to respect "the need to maintain the competitiveness of the Community economy" (Annex I, Protocol 14, Art. 1). Some of the measures that satisfy these potentially contradictory imperatives are subject to qualified majority voting; the more important ones will require unanimity (Arts. 2.2 and 2.3).

Then comes the first of two oblique references to intermediary forms of governance: "A Member State may entrust management and labour, at their joint request, with the implementation of directives ...," (and, if these social partners agree in time) "the Member State concerned (will be) required to take any necessary measure enabling it at any time to be in a position to guarantee the results imposed by that Directive" (Art. 2.4). In short, national governments are committed by treaty to backstop with their authority whatever specific implementation measures are negotiated between the associations representing capital and labor.[11] They are not, however, required to off-load their responsibilities in this fashion.

The second provision has an even more "neocorporatist" aura about it and could represent a major innovation in EC decision-making procedures. The Commission commits itself to promoting a *dialogue* between management and labor and to ensuring their *balanced support* in drafting social policy initiatives (Art. 3.1). To this end, it agrees to consult these social partners *before* submitting any proposal to the Council (Art. 3.2) and to offer to them the opportunity to preempt eventual Community action by coming to a collective private agreement among themselves (Art. 3.3).[12] If, within nine months, management and labor reach such an agreement, it can either be implemented through existing national practices in the Member States or, "at the joint request of the signatory parties," it can be converted by a decision of the Council into a binding Community directive. The MAA even has a strange footnote at this point (the only one in the whole treaty) in which "the eleven High Contracting Parties" seem to have realized the political implications of following the private route toward ratification. This reservation collectively denies any obligation on the part of national governments to apply such agreements directly, to transpose their obligations into eventual national legislation, or to amend laws in force to facilitate their implementation![13]

These items were not listed because they are all likely to make some major contribution to the "institutionality" of the EC/EU. Some are clearly slated for political oblivion; others may remain only as minor nuisances. The provisions noted opening the door ever so slightly for private governance and interest concertation depend very much on the willingness of European business interests to enter into negotiations at the class or sectoral level, and there is little indication of this. Moreover, when their peak association, UNICE, dared to strike an agreement with the European Trade Union Confederation (ETUC) on the issue of prior consultation and negotiation among the "social partners," several of its member associations immediately denounced the action and declared its provisions null and void at the national level.[14]

Together, however, these features of the MAA do amount to a substantial increase in the complexity of both the systems of representation surrounding the Europolity and the levels of decision making within it. A greater variety of nonstate actors are going to be drawn into some regular (if not always very potent) relation with the EC/EU, and it is going to take the coordination of more collectivities to produce EC/EU policies. Subgroups of member states will be able to threaten more plausibly than before to go ahead on their own, within or even outside the Community framework. Individual countries in unanimity situations and even minimal blocking coalitions in qualified majority ones may become more reluctant to insist on their "sovereign rights."

Together, these potentialities for partiality and eccentricity could circumscribe the role of member states well beyond the formal treaty prescriptions that still assign a preponderance to the European Council or the Council of Ministers simply because national government leaders and representatives will have to make concessions – side payments, if you will – to various entities that can obstruct the passage even of the measures they unanimously want or imperiously need. In some cases, the only power of these semiindependent bodies is to clog the channels with rival proposals or to delay in issuing their approval, but European Parliament's newly acquired capacity to veto (and not just hold up) directives could well be crucial in this regard, especially if the less powerful bodies can learn how to cooperate with it.

The MAA may have changed the trajectory of European political integration and opened up a range of possible (but not ineluctable) outcomes that were not previously apparent to or desired by either national or supranational actors. Instead of the coherent system of *checks and balances* long awaited by Eurofederalists, it could encourage the development of a hybrid arrangement for *presences and absences* in which member states, specific industrial sectors, subnational polities, and supranational organizations will be able initially to pick and choose the obligations they prefer and only later discover which are compatible with each other. It is as if "Europe" – having been previously invited by its nation-states to sit down to a light snack of regional cooperation and by its supranational civil servants to a heavy *prix fixe* dinner of centralized governance – suddenly found itself before a *repas à la carte* prepared by several cooks and tempting the invitees with diverse, but unequally appealing, arrangements for managing their common affairs!

INSERTING THE INTERVENING CONDITIONS

But the MAA is not a self-implementing document and a great deal can occur between now and 1996 when Europe has its next rendezvous with in-

stitutional reform. David Marsh of the *Financial Times* caught the impend-
ing dilemma especially well:

> The challenge for the Community during the rest of the 1990s will be to
> manage its own enlargement and meet the expectations vested in it from
> outside – without disrupting the finely-tuned balance of interests and op-
> portunities among its present 12 member states.[15]

For the sake of brevity, I propose to concentrate upon four factors – two endogenous and two exogenous – that I believe will contribute the most during the ensuing period to determining what type of Europolity will emerge:

1. Implementation
2. Politicization
3. Enlargement
4. External security

IMPLEMENTATION

The EEC/EC has long suffered from an "implementation deficit." Much less
touted than its "democracy deficit," this incapacity to elicit reliable compliance with supranational regulations and directives has placed an invisible, but nonetheless effective, limit on the scope and efficiency of Community action. The main reason for this is quite obvious, namely, its almost
exclusive reliance upon agencies of national and subnational governments
for the enforcement of supranational norms.[16] Not only has the number of
reported infractions (as measured by court cases) been increasing monotonically, but as the EC/EU widens its policy domain to include more sensitive
regulatory and distributive issues that directly involve individual firms and
communities, there is every reason to expect that the incentives for "selective defection" (read, "cheating on specific obligations") are going to increase exponentially. At some point, the breakdown in compliance could
threaten the legitimacy of the whole Community effort.

So far, member states seem to have stuck, by and large, to their obligation of *pacta sunt servanda*, but the same cannot be said of their local and regional authorities. In the coming years the Commission – faced with a rapid
expansion of its administrative tasks and strong resistance to augmenting its
budget and staff – will be tempted to rely ever more on these subnational
agents for the implementation of its policies: hence, the attractiveness of developing linkages of representation, subsidization, and accountability that
circumvent the national level of governance and make local and regional au-

thorities more willing participants in Community programs. Needless to say, member states will resist this and may even prefer that the Commission (or other relatively independent Eurocracies) acquire a greater capacity for directly monitoring performance and punishing offenders to prevent both cheating by competing countries and diminution of their respective monopolies on territorial representation and authority. Somehow, I suspect, from the resolution of these internecine struggles over implementation, the EC/EU will be pushed closer toward acquiring the properties of a supranational state and, in the process, be tempted to rely upon networks, alliances, associations, and private interest governments – either by asserting control over the behavior of existing national and subnational organizations, or by creating relatively autonomous, self-regulating European ones.

POLITICIZATION

As spillovers have occurred and raised the level of supranational authority, neofunctionalists have long expected an increase in the controversiality of the integration process. Wider and wider groups are being affected; more and more policy attention has centered on Brussels. Why haven't the relevant publics, especially those in political parties and social movements, expressed greater concern? How can it be that approximately 50 percent of all legislation now being passed by national parliaments involves the *transposition* of EC norms and so few seem to be aware of this fact?[17]

In the "benevolent" scenario, the timing and content of politicization would have been controlled by the Eurocrats and their interest group allies. Blocked in their aspirations by the resistance of national politicians to supranationality, they would appeal directly to the publics benefitting from expanded trade, lower transaction costs, cheaper consumer prices, greater personal mobility, regional subsidies, etc. and mobilize them to clamor for an even greater transfer of sovereignty or funds to the emerging center. In the present situation, post-MAA, the inverse seems to be occurring with quite unpredictable effects.

For the first time, the ratification of an EC treaty solemnly (if agonizingly) agreed upon by all twelve governments was placed in serious jeopardy. Political parties and social movements that had never focused on Community issues or always acquiesced to them raised objections and used their opposition to Maastricht to score points against domestic adversaries. Moreover, the MAA triggered an extraordinary diversity of negative responses: to the loss of a respected national currency in Germany; to the "threat" of social legislation in Britain; to abortion and the freedom to travel in Ireland; to rights granted to non-nationals to vote in local elections in France; to doubts about promises of regional aid in Spain; to general fear of an expanded European role in foreign and defense policy in Denmark.

Moreover, even now that the MAA has passed all twelve parliaments (and popular referenda in Denmark, Ireland, and France), politicization may not diminish for there is still the delicate matter of where the additional necessary funds are going to come from and how they are to be distributed among member states. According to Commission estimates, its budget would have to increase by about 30 percent just to have enough to cover the commitments made at Maastricht, and there are strong signals that the habitual net contributors, the Germans, are in no mood to continue in that role.[18]

Again, it is too soon to tell whether EC/EU issues have finally broken through the barrier of public indifference and begun to influence the course of political careers. Turnout for Euroelections is still much lower than for national ones – and declining. Few candidates seem to win or lose because of what they do or do not do for Europe. Only highly specialized groups participate ex ante in the abstruse negotiations of EC *comitologie;* broader publics are, at best, represented ex post in the deliberations of the European Council or the votes of their national governments in the Council or Ministers. The European Parliament has seen its power increased marginally in both the SEA and the MAA, but is a long way from providing a mechanism of political accountability or even of symbolic attachment for the citizenry as a whole.

If and when large-scale politicization does occur, its impact may not be what the neofunctionalists anticipated. Instead of providing the critical impetus for a definitive transfer of sovereignty to a supranational state, it could power a nationalist reaction against such an outcome. This could result in a more confederal solution (if not the breakdown of the whole effort) under which authorities would protect the autonomy of special arrangements existing in each country and undermine the full impact of market liberalization and deregulation. Or the increased salience and controversiality surrounding EC issues could fragment into a multitude of subnational and/or sectoral demands for distinctive treatment which could, in turn, lead to a dispersed array of European institutions, each with different *compétences* and memberships. These are outcomes I have elsewhere called a *condominio* or a *consortio* – depending on the mix of territorial and functional constituencies involved.[19]

ENLARGEMENT

The tendency for the EEC/EC/EU to incorporate new members has been one of the hallmarks of its success. Even when it was by all accounts a stagnant enterprise, it still managed to attract new members. Nevertheless, enlargement has rarely been treated theoretically as if it were an explicit part of the integration process. Despite the fact that each successive increase in numbers has brought qualitative changes in rules and policies, they continue to be regarded as essentially fortuitous occurrences. Moreover, since membership has heretofore meant the acceptance by the newcomer of all the accumulated Community obligations (the famous *acquis communautaire*), the price for getting in has risen considerably. The longer a given country hesitates about joining, the more it will have to obey policies that it had no voice in producing.

And yet the queue is getting longer. Having held up all deliberations about "widening" until the Community was sufficiently "deepened" by fulfilling the obligations of the SEA and taking on the new commitments of the MAA, there is no further excuse for prolonging the issue. The coming years are likely to be overshadowed by "bloc negotiations" – first with the adjacent EFTA countries (as well as the idiosyncratic cases of Turkey, Malta, and Cyprus) and later with the much more problematic candidacies of the former COMECON countries in Eastern Europe (not to mention the former republics of the USSR). The sheer number of prospective members – as many as 30 to 35, depending on how many pieces emerge from Yugoslavia and how many former republics of the Soviet Union manage to pass the Eurotest – threatens to overwhelm existing EC/EU institutions. Even if only a few get in as full members, their accession will almost certainly produce some changes in voting rules in the Council, in the number of Commissioners, Eurodeputies, and judges of the Court, and perhaps even in the mode of selecting the President of the Commission. Those in the first "round" will raise the average prosperity, contribute positively to Community coffers, and generally strengthen the "Northern or Germanic Bloc" of members with high levels of welfare spending, exposure to the world economy, monetary stability, and organized group influence over public policy. Those in the second and subsequent rounds, however, pose a very different set of problems. Even the most favored among them – Czechoslovakia, Hungary, and Poland – would greatly increase the heterogeneity of member interests and put a heavy strain on the Community's meager resources for *economic and social cohesion*. Their domestic politics are still far from being consolidated and democratic so that it is difficult to imagine how they will fit into the internal processes of the Community, but there is little question that they will make common cause with the existing Southern Bloc in demanding more derogations, dispensations, and subsidies.

Until Europe's borders become stabilized – until we know for sure the number, variety, and range of those admitted to membership in the EC/EU

– it will be difficult to predict what type of polity will govern this ambiguous part of the world. One thing, however, seems relatively clear: The pressure for enlargement will be great and the consequences for failing to cope with it will be considerable. The economic and political stability of Eastern Europe and the former Soviet Union could well hinge upon it as will the security of Western Europe from the potential hoards of displaced persons that could be triggered by failure. My hunch is that the most likely Community response will be the creation of new forms of "quasimembership" that will include the recently liberated states (and some newly created ones) within diverse, functionally-based, regional organizations dealing with specific economic, social, or environmental issues while according them only an intermediary status in the central institutions of political decision making. In short, enlargement seems to be pushing the EC/EU toward a *condominio* type outcome.

EXTERNAL SECURITY

Since its inception, the European integration process has been able to free-ride on the politicomilitary security provided by NATO. Already the decline in American hegemony and shifts in U.S. foreign policy during the Reagan administration had raised questions in Europe about the wisdom of its continued dependence on the Atlantic Alliance. The subsequent end of the Cold War, the disbanding of the Warsaw Pact, the reunification of Germany, and the collapse of the Soviet Union radically changed the international context. The short-run consensus has favored a continuation of NATO and a (reduced) presence of American troops in Europe; the long-run perspective, however, requires that the region develop its own security arrangement.

For understanding likely developments in this exogenous area, integration theory has virtually nothing to offer. Once the European Defence Treaty had been rejected in 1954, making it clear that the direct, politico-military route to European unity was barred, the issue disappeared. Whatever "integrative" effects were produced by NATO – in logistical systems, strategic planning, or joint weapons production – were ignored or discounted. Weapons procurement – indeed, all forms of public procurement – were exempted from the process of general trade liberalization. The admission of Ireland, a neutral state, only reconfirmed the widespread assumption that the EEC/EC had and would continue to have nothing do with security matters.[20]

This, despite the fact that the core of European stateness and national integration had historically been built around the development of an autonomous "sovereign" capacity for defense and the creation of each unit's own armed forces exclusively for that purpose. Taxation, conscription, definition of borders, control over the mobility of persons, promotion of science and technology, even policies of public education and health – all reflected this overriding priority. Is it conceivable that the EC could become an effective and legitimate supranational authority without its own armed forces, without even its own capacity to monitor compliance with its norms and to apply coercion when they were transgressed? The viability of either a *consortio* or a *condominio* rests on the assumption that diverse functional tasks can be collectively accomplished while relying almost exclusively on national and subnational agents of policy implementation, supervised by a supranational juridical system which itself depends on the willing compliance of national and subnational courts. Given its very dispersed decisional structure, it is hard to imagine how a confederal system could credibly control its own coercive apparatus. Such tasks would be left exclusively in the hands of its component states, although they might agree to act in alliance to resolve particular threats.

The implication seems clear: Now that European security can no longer be taken for granted, i.e., now that new threats are surfacing that cannot be contained by existing NATO or bilateral commitments, only the emergence of something approaching a supranational state will be able to accomplish the task. Even if a "pluralistic security community" is firmly established among EC/EU members, it does not extend beyond their borders. Here is where the other exogenous variable, enlargement, comes into the picture. Presumably, the demands placed upon the EC/EU in the defense area will vary with the members' perception of likely security threats, and this will largely be a function of what happens to the East. Should some combination of full and partial membership – plus substantial Western assistance – help to stabilize economic and political outcomes in the territory reaching from the Baltic to the Adriatic and Black Seas, the pressure for developing an integrated European military command with its attending state-building properties would diminish, and looser forms of collective security and political concertation, such as the CSCE, the Council of Europe, the WEU, and/or a revised NATO could fill the gap.

Alternatively, no amount of "tinkering" may be sufficient to cope with the disintegration of markets and polities in Eastern Europe and the ex-Soviet Union. Serious, presently unforeseen, security threats could always emerge "out of theater" – for example, in the Near East and North Africa. In either of these scenarios, the entire process of regional integration could be jeopardized. European states could revert to *sauve-qui-peut* strategies based exclusively on national interest calculations, and the recourse to force to resolve potential disputes would again become plausible, tempered only by the mechanisms of the balance of power or the hegemony of a single actor.

SPECULATING ABOUT THE FUTURE OF MODES OF GOVERNANCE IN EUROPE

Existing governance mechanisms, especially those resting on the privileged role of associations and on the borrowed authority of private interest governments, are definitely imperiled at the national level and only weakly empowered at the supranational level by the SEA and MAA. Some particularly egregious cases of the former, for example, the British Milk Marketing Board, have seen the handwriting on the wall and taken steps to change their statues and practices.[21] Less visible and more pervasive ones such as the German systems of *Berufsgenossenschaften, Innungen,* and *Handwerkskammern* may survive more or less intact, especially where their effect is confined to naturally sheltered, local markets.[22]

The impact of *mutual recognition* upon the professions where some of the most entrenched self-governance mechanisms are to be found is just beginning to emerge. By abandoning the previous attempt to integrate each profession through *harmonization,* the Community has in effect foregone the opportunity to create Eurolevel PIGs for the certification of lawyers, accountants, engineers, surveyors, physicians, etc. The Directive on a General System for the Recognition of Higher Education Diplomas passed in 1988 and effective in 1991 does not challenge the role of national licensing bodies, but only requires them to admit members from other EC countries – under certain conditions and with some major exceptions. In effect, the Community sets minimal general standards and leaves the actual granting of specific professional titles and rights to practice to national authorities, whether they are private associations or state agencies.

The most impressive experiment at the supranational level – indeed, the only bona fide example of a EuroPIG in the Community's previous history – seems headed for oblivion: the steel industry. In part, it is the beneficiary of more favorable market conditions, in part the victim of the liberalizing, deregulating thrust of the SEA. Faced with protracted overproduction in the industry, the Community first tried voluntary restrictions on output (1974–80). When this failed, a "manifest crisis" was declared by the Council of Ministers and the European Confederation of Iron and Steel Industries (EUROFER) was encouraged to become a "cartel of cartels" and to play a major role in the restructuring of the industry through fixed prices and mandatory quotas. Action at this level was facilitated both by the exceptional powers conferred upon the High Authority (later Commission) by the treaty establishing the ECSC and by the fact that firms in this sector were already well organized in national governance arrangements. Even so, it proved difficult to prevent governments from continuing to grant subsidies and firms from engaging in a good deal of "opportunistic behavior." The whole experience is not regarded as one of the EC's more successful ventures in market management, and no one seems anxious to prolong or repeat it.[23] When it came to an effort to govern the sector of artificial fiber production, a different modality involving a looser, network structure was adopted, both because the EC lacked special supranational *compétences* and because the firms themselves had not been previously well organized at the national level.[24]

The one broad area of private governance which has definitely been given a big boost by the SEA is *normalization* or the setting of technical standards. The Act encouraged a "new approach" to this problem. Instead of attempting to establish through lengthy negotiation among national experts and formal international agreement all the excruciating details involved in defining a given product, Community authorities would only promulgate regulations or directives with a limited set of "essential requirements" and shift the balance toward private activity. Much of this takes place in European-level committees composed by national associations. The Comité Européen de Normalisation (CEN) and the Comité Européen de Normalisation Électrotechnique (CENELEC) are the most visible and venerable of these and their activity has boomed in recent years. Alongside them, a number of new European standard-setting associations have been formed to deal with specific sectors and they have individual private firms or public enterprises as direct members. For example, the European Telecommunications Standards Institute (ESTIC) is a joint venture of national PTs, private users, and equipment manufacturers that has been working to make telecommunications networks compatible across Europe. The resultant standards may not all be legally compulsory – i.e., converted into binding national norms – but they can be practically indispensable since only by complying with them can producers be assured of secure access to the Internal Market. And only the Commission decides whether a given committee or association is to be granted the quasiauthority for issuing Euronorms.[25]

Majone may have been unique in arguing that, despite protestations to the contrary, "a greatly accelerated growth of regulation is to be expected with the completion of the Internal Market."[26] Even before the SEA and in the absence of any specific provisions in the Treaty of Rome, the EC had already produced some 200 regulations in the areas of environmental protection alone. A similar, if more contentious, effort has long been underway in generating Community norms that define the quality of food and beverages and protect the consumers of these products, as can be testified by the periodic disputes between member states over such things as "pure beef," "mad cows," "uncontrolled hormones," "irradiated food," botulism, salmonella, and so forth.[27] As we have seen, the MAA explicitly mandates the Commission and Council to take initiatives in monetary union, social policy, consumer protection, public health, education, environmental standards, and the promotion of trans-European networks of communications, transport, and energy. Most of these are issue arenas that involve a heavy commitment to public regulation within each member state, although not necessarily a heavy reliance upon private networks, alliances, associations, or interest governments. As the EC moves into them, it may be tempted to off-load its *compétences* to such bodies in order to reduce transaction costs, improve legitimacy, or ensure better compliance. What is becoming clearer with each successive directive coming out of the Commission and passing the Council, however, is the *bien-fondé* of Majone's paradox that *attaining a less regulated Internal Market will require a great deal of regulation!*

Majone's insight does not rest merely on a projection of national policy-making styles to the supranational level. He observes that the Eurocrats, with their limited financial and personnel resources, are likely to find that regulation offers a relatively cheap and painless way to expand the scope and level of their authority. The direct administrative costs are borne mainly by member governments and the indirect ones are shifted to firms and ultimately to consumers. He might be pleased to note that *la géométrie variable* and the "eccentricity" subsequently introduced by the MAA makes such a strategy even easier to take, and spreads its effect across a more dispersed set of institutions.

"But this is only part of the explanation. Another important element is the interest of multi-national, export-oriented industries in avoiding inconsistent and progressively more stringent regulations in various EC and non-EC countries. Community regulation can eliminate or at least reduce this risk."[28] Capitalists from large enterprises, in other words, may have their own incentives for allying with Eurocrats. With the shortening of product cycles and increasing costs of research and development, technical norms and compatibility specifications have become an important component of competitiveness, with significant advantages going to those firms and countries that control them. Only if Europe has a unified capacity to impose its own regulations can it expect to use them to discriminate against Japanese and American competitors – and not be victimized by their efforts to do the same.[29] Also, European producers can potentially save on transaction costs by obtaining "one stop" certification for their products so as to avoid being "whipsawed" by each national and subnational authority trying to impose its own norms. Through *comitologie,* they have long enjoyed privileged access to the Commission and have every reason to believe that its regulatory effort will be more "technical" and "apolitical" than what they can expect elsewhere, especially since the norms adopted will depend almost exclusively on information provided by them.[30] Small and medium-size firms operating strictly in internal markets will, no doubt, view the overriding of national and local protective regulations – and the decline in the authority of the networks and associations that monitor and implement them – with alarm, but they are not likely to have the political clout to prevent such an outcome.

CONCLUSION

It is tempting to interpret the EC's institutional future in terms of a contest between two competing organizational principles, each reflecting different modes of interest representation and policy making in society. Where the units of authority have grown larger in area and population, and more heterogenous in social and economic composition, rulers and ruled have relied increasingly on specialized intermediaries to communicate with each other and to implement collective decisions. *Grosso modo,* these mechanisms of indirect linkage between governments and citizens have been aggregated along either *territorial* or *functional* principles. Various intermediaries – parties, associations, movements, networks, clienteles, groups of notables, levels of government – identify with the constituencies formed by these principles and *re*present their interests vis-à-vis authorities. It is this mix of territorial and functional constituencies, along with their corresponding relations of authority and accountability, that has come to define different types of the modern polity.

And the emerging Europolity is no different. It began with a dual bias: (1) toward channeling the representation of territorial interests exclusively through the national governments of member states, and (2) toward privileging the development of functional representation through transnational, European-level interest associations. The neofunctionalist strategy adopted by Jean Monnet *et Cie.* conceded the former as an inescapable (if eventually mutable) feature of the international system and sought to build gradually and surreptitiously upon the latter. After some initial successes, this failed for a variety of reasons and the ensuing period of "intergovernmentalism" from the mid-1960s to the early 1980s saw even the functional interests being transmitted and transacted largely through national territorial channels.[31] Since then, the mix of functional and territorial constituencies/authorities at various levels has shifted significantly within the EC/EU, giving rise to the present uncertainty about the eventual outcome.

For the institutions of intermediary governance to thrive, even to survive, in the post-1992 Integrated Market, the functional principle must predominate in the form of a deep-rooted *sectoralization* of public policy. The basic administrative structure of the Commission with its 23 Directorates General, most of which consist of sectors and all of which operate in considerable autonomy from each other, certainly encourages this outcome.[32] Nevertheless, the previous efforts at sectoral crisis management such as EUROFER have not been particularly successful and there is little sign of enthusiasm for repeating the experience. Even the new, proactive style for promoting sectoral competitiveness as embodied in EUREKA-95 HDTV is showing its deficiencies. Within the Commission itself the major line of cleavage is reported to be between advocates of "vertical" versus "horizontal" policies. The former would use EC funds and regulations to improve competitiveness sector by designated sector; the latter insist that whatever support is given should consist of general incentives (and disincentives, viz competition policy) that do not target a specific industry or product.

Leaving aside the personalities of the Commissioners involved and the clout of their respective national governments (whose interests they are *not* supposed to reflect), the outcome of this intrabureaucratic (but also highly charged ideological) struggle may well hinge on two of the factors mentioned as intervening variables.[33] The first is the extent to which the direct *implementation* capacity of the Commission remains limited and hence its reliance on national agencies increases. Will these public regulatory bodies and/or private self-regulatory associations prove to be reliable interlocutors for the Eurocrats in the future, or will the Eurocrats turn increasingly towards direct transactions with prominent Eurofirms and alliances of firms? The second hinges on the context of *external security*. Any effort to improve competitiveness through concerted, Europewide industrial policies would certainly meet with strong resistance from the United States and Japan. To the extent that their protestations – in GATT or elsewhere – could endanger the global trade regime and even affect the political standing of the EC and its member states during a delicate moment when the "New World Order" is being put together, the risk might seem too great.

A contrary tendency in Europe's future would be toward a *regionalization* of Community policy. So far, the indicators for this are weak. The Social and Structural Funds were doubled under the SEA, and may be increased again in an indeterminate amount under the MAA, but they are still relatively insignificant. Moreover, the direct representational links between the Commission and subnational political units are still informal, although the inclusion of a provision in the MAA for a "Comité des Régions" hints at their expansion in the near future. *Enlargement* is bound to increase sensitivity to spatial inequalities within the EC/EU, if only because the prospective Eastern members will greatly enhance the range of variation in economic performance and almost certainly compete with the existing recipients of regional funds. The reaction of the Greeks, Portuguese, Spaniards, and Irish to these competing claims, as well as the diminished willingness of rich Northerners to finance such solidaristic transfers, will in turn have an impact on the major variable determining whether sectoralization or territorialization will predominate beyond 1992.

Politicization is another factor. As the controversiality of EC/EU decisions inevitably increases, it could mobilize class, sectoral, or professional categories across national and subnational lines demanding special exemptions, or inversely it could find its expression in those territorial constituencies that are systemically disadvantaged by the free flow of goods, services, capital, and labor. Needless to say, the most explosive situations could develop out of a combination of the two, i.e., where industries suffering dramatically from increased regional or global competition are concentrated in a very few municipalities, provinces, or regions.

Obviously, it is too soon to judge which of these major trends will predominate, even now that the MAA has finally been ratified. However, it should be noted that, even if sectoralization does reassert itself during the 1990s, this would provide no guarantees for the health and safety of existing national or supranational arrangements. As we have stressed, private interest governments are just one of several ways in which sectors can be governed – and by no means the easiest to establish and sustain.[34] Whether considered in terms of the potential savings in transaction costs or the potential return on policy influence, this mechanism for self-enforced regulation depends critically upon the prior existence of closed social networks as well as the promotive efforts of public authorities. Even if Community officials were to decide (and member governments to agree) that European-level PIGs were an attractive solution for the problems of specific sectors, they would still have to cope with considerable variation in how these interests were organized at the national level in member states. With few exceptions – for example, the dairy industry or the accountancy profession – the existing associational structures would have to undergo very substantial changes before they could participate symmetrically in a Communitywide arrangement. Faced with the sheer complexity of engineering such a change, and the deficiencies of relying on existing national PIGs with asymmetric capacities for governing the behavior of their members, my hunch is that the EC/EU would be more likely to rely upon direct implementation through an American-style regulatory commission rather than off-load its responsibility to self-governing associations.

These choices of agency are supposed to be determined in the future by the principle of *subsidiarity*. As noted in footnote 7, this provision formally inserted in MAA would assign to the EC/EU only those actions that cannot be "sufficiently achieved" by member states and that can be "better achieved" by reason of scale or effect at the level of the Community. Needless to say, the criteria for assessing sufficiency and for measuring the economies of scale and the extent of externalities are left to an undetermined political (and, in all likelihood, juridical) process, but it should be noted that this concept has been used in the past (especially in Germany, the Netherlands, Belgium, and Austria) to justify the establishment of national standards and subsidies and to assign responsibility for their implementation in specific cases to semipublic, local, or sectoral associations. Present usage, however, seems to imply a more decentralized and less uniform interpretation of the term – even one that corresponds to the liberal notion: "he who governs best, governs least." Subsidiarity has been shifted from an ideology that facilitated the pursuit of public purpose by devolving responsibility for policy implementation to designated agents closer to the eventual recipients, to an ideology that would facilitate the deregulation of state intervention and protect the maximum expression of national autonomy. Moreover, while the original Social Catholic version placed a great deal of emphasis on the role of functional intermediaries, the new secular version seems to focus exclusively on the territorially based division of political labor and to accord a primacy to the nation-state level of aggregation.[35] Needless to say, the ideological battle over the application of this fashionable term is far from over and it is still conceivable that its "ancient" meaning could be revived and exploited to justify a substantial devolution of public authority to private associations for the governance of sectoral and professional matters.

To the extent that the practice of integration remains confined to formal intergovernmental agreements such as the SEA and the MAA and to the extent that the substance of these agreements relies heavily upon *mutual recognition* and *internal market competition* to resolve differences and govern exchanges between national economies, intermediate arrangements for sectoral coordination and governance would seem to have a dim future in Europe. They should be eliminated by market pressures or the formation of ever more extensive hierarchies among private firms. Only those countries that elected not to join the EC/EU could confidently expect to preserve their quaint practices of informal collusion, associational concertation, and private interest governance.[36]

However, the neofunctionalist approach to the study of integration has always insisted that the process was more complex and less formal – involving not only exchanges between infranational interest groups and supranational bureaucrats, but also transformations in the very nature of national states and their subnational political units. The eventual outcome was seen more as the product of emergent properties and unintended consequences than of rational intentions and explicit agreements.

Another way of putting it is that the neofunctionalist approach-cum-strategy assumes the gradual and inexorable formation of a "European Civil Society." Its most profound (if not always explicitly stated) hunch is that only the eventual articulation of transversal cleavages following class, sectoral, and professional lines across present national boundaries and their transformation into common, informal practices within private associations, parties and movements, as well as within individual enterprises and firms, will be effective in linking economic to political integration in the long run – never intergovernmental bargaining or constitutional drafting alone.[37] And, given the historical peculiarities of European – at least, continental European – capitalism, there is every reason to expect that, whatever the formal rules and market pressures, intermediate forms of sectoral governance will continue to play a significant, if not always predominant, role within this evolving civil society and contribute to enhancing its competitive advantage over other countries and world regions.

ENDNOTES

1. See Hollingsworth, Schmitter, and Streeck (1994).
2. Hollingsworth, Schmitter, and Streeck (1994).
3. Schmitter (1990). For alternative typologies and approaches, see Hollingsworth and Lindberg (1985), Campbell and Lindberg (1991), and Kitschelt (1991).
4. If one were to assign paternity to this observation, it should go Shonfield (1965).
5. See Sorge and Streeck (1988) for the origin of the concept and Streeck (1989) for its further development. The much more widely diffused notion of "flexible specialization," as developed by Piore and Sabel (1984), places much less emphasis on the central role of governance mechanisms. For a corrective to this, see Trigilia (1986).
6. The MAA was also preceded very closely by an agreement with the EFTA countries – Austria, Finland, Iceland, Liechtenstein, Norway, Sweden, and

Switzerland – to establish the European Economic Area (EEA). Originally conceived as a way of postponing the issue of enlargement, it would extend most of the provisions of the SEA (and hence most EC rules) to all 19 members, while leaving some especially sensitive issues such as agriculture, fishing, energy, and industrial subsidies pending. Although widely hailed as a success after protracted negotiations, it does not seem to have had the intended effect of putting off the issue of full membership until further progress has been made on monetary and political union. Austria and Sweden have already posed their candidacies; Finland and Switzerland are making similar noises; Norway is in the midst of a national debate on the issue. Meanwhile, the EEA is bogged down in a dispute with the European Court of Justice and is still a long way from ratification by all 19 national parliaments.

7. The reference to "peoples" rather than "states" is unusual – and significant since it opens up novel possibilities for an eventual shift to constituencies other than those defined at the national level by existing states. Needless to say, none of the founding treaties or their amendments make an effort to define what "Europe" is.

8. Which is (more or less) defined elsewhere (Art. 3b) as follows: "In areas which do not fall in its exclusive jurisdiction, the Community shall take action, in accordance with the principle of subsidiarity, only if and insofar as the objectives of the proposed action cannot be sufficiently achieved by the Member State and can, therefore, by reason of the scale or effects of proposed action be better achieved by the Community." Who should determine what "sufficiently" means and what criteria would be applied to estimate the economies of scale or the extent of externalities is presumably left to an unspecified political process.

   For a particularly stimulating discussion of the ambiguities of subsidiarity, see Gretschmann (1991).

9. The *acquis communautaire* is one of the most sacred of EC, now EU, concepts. It refers to the sum total of obligations that have accumulated since the founding of the ECSC and are embedded in innumerable treaties and protocols. So far, any state that applies to the EC/EU is expected to accept as a matter of principle the responsibility for fulfilling all these obligations, although in the actual negotiations for entry it is possible to delay the application of some of them. It is expressed designed to prevent any prospective member from "shopping around" for its own mix of obligations.

10. For example, Article F states that "the Union shall respect the national identifies of its Member States, whose governments are founded on the principles of democracy" and "fundamental rights ... as they result from the constitutional traditions common to the Member States."

11. The following paragraph (Art. 2.5) also frees up policy space for private governance by allowing any Member State to maintain or to introduce "more stringent preventive measures compatible with the Treaty," i.e., that do not manifestly discriminate against other EC producers.

12. This practice of obligatory, prior consultation of interest associations by drafters of policy initiatives seems to have been invented and "constitutionalized" in Switzerland where it is called *"Vernehmlassung."*

13. There is another peculiar item of *"corporatist-type subsidiarity"* in the Declaration on Co-operation with Charitable Associations (Annex II, Protocol 22)

where the signatories stress the importance of working through these intermediaries when dealing with social policy.

14. The British CBI complained the loudest, fearing "the reestablishment of corporatist structures and an empowerment of unions that the government would not welcome." "CBI may withdraw from European Pact" (*Financial Times,* November 11, 1991).

15. "A bumpy ride on the roller-coaster" (*Financial Times,* December 18, 1991, Section III, p. 1).

16. Seidentopf and Ziller (1988), Azzi (1985). For the notion of an "implementation deficit," see Schaefer (1991).

17. Lodge (1989). When Jacques Delors predicted that within ten years, 80% of all legislation would emanate from the EC, he did provoke a horrified reaction from Margaret Thatcher (*Financial Times,* July 25, 1988).

18. For example, "Brussels faces united German opposition on budget increases" (*Financial Times,* February 22–23, 1992); "EC faces long war over budget" (*Financial Times,* March 3, 1992); "Germany and Italy express concern about Delors budget" (*Financial Times,* March 17, 1992); "Germany will resist EC revenue plans" (*Financial Times,* March 24, 1992).

19. For a more detailed explication of the range of possible outcomes, see my "Interests, Powers and Functions: Emergent Properties and Unintended Consequences in the European Polity."

20. Hence, the notion that the EC is on its way to becoming the world's first "Great Civilian Power," i.e., capable of acting as a unit in a variety of arenas of international politics, but not of backing up its actions with armed force. See Pinder (1991). The originator of this notion seems to have been Duchêne (1973).

   For the contrary view that the EC is likely to develop into an aggressive superpower imposing *Pax Bruxellana* on the world, see Galtung (1973).

21. Cf. "UK milk board submits plan to become co-op" (*Financial Times,* April 15, 1992). The article makes it clear that the shift to "a single voluntary co-operative with pooled prices" which took two years to put together will have to be discussed "with the dairy trade, MAFF (the Ministry) and the EC."

   The Milk Marketing Board for England and Wales, along with analogous arrangements in the Netherlands, Austria, and Switzerland, has emerged as a sort of "archetype" of private governance. Created in the 1930s in response to market failure, this semipublic intermediary association has exercised offloaded responsibility for governing the price and quantity of milk for over 50 years until its recent discomfiture. See Grant (1985). Also the chapters by Franz Traxler, Peter Farago, and Frans van Waarden in Streeck and Schmitter (1985).

22. Streeck (1989); Grote (forthcoming).

23. After having encouraged EUROFER's private governance of steel production and quietly tolerated the efforts of the "Z Club" to control the market in stainless steel during the 1980s, the Commission has more recently shifted to an attack on cartelization in this sector. It launched an inquiry into the Z Club in July 1990, and, in April 1991, its officials raided the offices of four major manufacturers of construction steel and two industry trade associations to gather evidence on bid rigging activities. "Inquiry signals change in Commission's steel policy" (*Financial Times,* April 15, 1991).

24. Kennis (1991, 1992).
25. What little I know about this murky world of Euronormalization I owe to Pelkmans (1992).
26. Majone (1989).
27. Vogel (1991).
28. Majone (1989).
29. For a case study in this "new" form of international competition, see Cawson (1992). Cawson argues that the Eureka-95 HDTV program – with a development and investment budget second only to that of the Channel Tunnel! – constitutes a new form of EC private governance based not on restructuring an existing industry through fixed prices, controlled investments, and quotas, but on defining an emergent technology through product standardization, public incentives, and regulated access to public goods. If successful – and Cawson notes some serious errors and deficiencies in the approach – it could serve as a prototype for Community efforts at improving Europe's competitiveness in other high-tech areas.
30. I have learned a great deal form a case study of the evolving interest of large firms in regulation at the European level by Darden (1991). Darden focuses on the Conseil Européen de la Fédération de l'Industrie Chimique (CEFIC) which is arguably the EC's most impressive sectoral trade association. He shows how CEFIC has responded to the challenge of environmentalist demands by increasing its organizational capacity, especially by drawing resources directly from its large multinational firms rather than its national member associations, and created ad hoc task forces to deal with specific issues as they come before the Commission. CEFIC was quick to seize the opportunity offered by the supremacy of Community law and hence of EC environmental regulations that could preclude (or preempt) more stringent national ones. It has proposed becoming a standard-setting body for the Community and offered to play a key role in implementing the policy of eliminating chlorofluorocarbon production in Europe. Darden concludes that, on balance, CEFIC acts more like a pluralist lobby or pressure group than a classic corporatist "peak association" that can control the behavior of its (involuntary) members. Nevertheless, in a few areas such as GATT negotiations and standard setting, it has been able to exploit its role as a monopolistic, officially recognized, and indispensable intermediary. Its ability to make its decisions *allgemeinverbindlich,* i.e., binding on all producers regardless of whether they are its members, is still limited by the absence of state capacity within the EC. Only through changes at that level is it conceivable that CEFIC could follow the pattern of its most famous member, the German *Verband Chemische Industrie* (VCI), an association long regarded as one of Europe's most impressive national sectoral PIGs. Also see Jacek (1991).
31. For a brief account of the failure of Eurocorporatism at the macrolevel, see Schmitter and Streeck (1991).
32. For an account of the Commission's administrative structure which emphasizes sectoralization, see Peters (1992).
33. Out of ignorance, I have ignored the situation in the Common Agricultural Policy (CAP), despite the fact that it represents most of the EC budget. Its system of setting intervention prices yearly by *comitology* would seem to have at

least some of the characteristics of private interest governance in that producer associations are closely involved in making these decisions and seem to bear some responsibility for their implementation. Unlike most PIGs, however, the CAP operates through the distributive rather than the regulatory mode. Should the CAP be reformed in the future and converted into a scheme of entitlements – a sort of welfare policy for farmers – then the whole system of interest politics surrounding the present arrangements would change drastically.

34. For a discussion of the demanding conditions for their success, see the chapters in Streeck and Schmitter (1985).

35. I am especially indebted to Wolfgang Streeck for these reflections on the changing meaning of subsidiarity.

36. The fact that first Austria, then Sweden, and just recently Finland and Switzerland have all announced their wish to become full members of the EC/EU could eventually deprive us of some of the richest native accumulations of governance mechanisms in existence. Even these countries' ratification of the European Economic Area (EEA) treaty could place their diverse fauna of clans, networks, alliances, associations, and PIGs on the endangered species list! Once again, it would have been demonstrated that we social scientists only manage to discover and label phenomena once they are on the way to disappearing.

37. William Wallace has recently suggested drawing a distinction between two parallel integration processes: "Informal integration consists of those intense patterns of interaction which develop without the impetus of deliberate political decisions, following the dynamics of markets, technology, communications networks, and social change. Formal integration consists of those changes in the framework of rules and regulations which encourage – or inhibit, or redirect – informal flows. Informal integration is a continuous process, a flow: it creeps unawares out of the myriad transactions of private individuals pursuing private interests. Formal integration is discontinuous: it proceeds decision by decision, bargain by bargain, treaty by treaty." See Wallace (1990).

REFERENCES

Azzi, C. ed. 1985. *L'Application du Droit Communautaire par les états membres.* Maastricht: European Institute of Public Administration.

Campbell, John L. and Leon Lindberg. 1991. "The Evolution of Governance Structures." In J. Campbell, J. Rogers Hollingsworth, and Leon Lindberg, eds. *Governance in the American Economy.* Cambridge: Cambridge University Press. P. 11.

Cawson, Alan. 1992. "Sectoral Governance and Innovation: Private Interest Government and the Eureka HDTV Project." Paper presented to the Conference on Private Governments, Public Choices, Universita di Trento, Trento, June 10–12.

Darden, Keith A. 1991. "Organized Capitalists in Disorganized Capitalism." Seminar paper, Stanford University, Department of Political Science, October 31.

Duchêne, François. 1973. "Europe's Role in World Peace." In R. Mayne, ed. *Europe Tomorrow.* London: Fontana/Collins.

Financial Times. July 25, 1988; April 15, 1991; November 11, 1991; December 18, 1991; February 22–23, 1992; March 3, 1992; March 17, 1992; March 24, 1992; April 15, 1992.

Galtung, Johan. 1973. *The European Community: A Superpower in the Making.* Oslo: Universitetsforlaget.

Grant, Wyn. 1985. "Private Organizations as Agents of Public Policy; The Case of Milk Marketing in Britain." In P. Schmitter and W. Streeck, eds. *Private Interest Governments.* London: Sage. Pp. 182–196.

Gretschmann, Klaus. 1991. "The Subsidiarity Principle: Who Is to Do What in an Integrated Europe? In *Subsidiarity: The Challenge of Change,* Proceedings of the Jacques Delors Colloquium, European Institute of Public Administration, Maastricht. Pp. 45–61.

Grote, Jürgen. Forthcoming. "Small Firms in the European Community: Modes of Production, Governance and Territorial Interest Representation in Italy and Germany." In J. Greenwood, J. R. Grote, and K. Romit, eds. *Organized Interests and the European Community.* London: Sage.

Hollingsworth, J. Rogers and Leon Lindberg. 1985. "The Governance of the American Economy: The Role of Markets, Clans, Hierarchies and Associative Behavior." In P. Schmitter and W. Streeck, eds. *Private Interest Governments.* London: Sage. Pp. 221–54.

Hollingsworth, J. Rogers, Philippe C. Schmitter, and Wolfgang Streeck. 1994. *Governing Capitalist Economies: Performance and Control of Economic Sectors* New York: Oxford University Press.

Jacek, Henry J. 1991. "The Functions of Associations as Agents of Public Policy." In A. Martinelli, ed. *International Markets and Global Firms: A Comparative Study of Organized Business in the Chemical Industry.* London: Sage. Pp. 145–88.

Kennis, Patrick. 1991. "Industrial Re-structuring: the Case of the Chemical Fiber Industry in Europe." *EUI Working Paper.* No. 86/91.

———. 1992. *Social Construction of Industries: A World of Chemical Fibres.* Frankfurt/Boulder: Campus/Westview.

Kitschelt, Herbert. 1991. "Industrial Governance Structures, Innovation Strategies, and the Case of Japan: Sectoral or Cross-National Comparative Analysis?" *International Organization.* 45: 453–93.

Lodge, Juliette. 1989. "The Political Implications of 1991." *Politics* 9: 38.

Majone, Giandomenico. 1989. "Regulating Europe: Problems and Prospects." *Jahrbuch zur Staats- und Verwaltungswissenschaft.* 3: 159.

Pelkmans, Jacques. 1992. "A Political Economy of EC Technical Regulation." Paper presented at the ECSA Workshop on "The EC After Maastricht." Chicago, March 26–27.

Peters. B. Guy. 1992. "Bureaucratic Politics and the Institutions of the European Community." In A. Spragia, ed. *Euro-Politics.* Washington: Brookings Institution. Pp. 75–122.

Pinder, John. 1991. *European Community. The Building of a Union.* Oxford: Oxford University Press.

Piore, Michael and Charles Sabel. 1984. *The Second Industrial Divide.* New York: Basic Books.

Schaefer, Guenther F. 1991. "The Rise and Fall of Subsidiarity." *Futures* 23: 685–86.

Schmitter, P. C. 1990. "Sectors in Modern Capitalism: Models of Governance and Variations in Performance." In R. Brunetta and C. Dell'Aringa, eds. *Labour Relations and Economic Performance.* London: Macmillan. Pp. 3–39.

Schmitter P. C. and Wolfgang Streeck. 1991. "Organized Interests and the Europe of 1992." In N. J. Ornstein and M. Perlman, eds. *Political Power and Social Change.* Washington: AEI Press. Pp. 46–67.

Seidentopf, C. H. and J. Ziller, eds. 1988. *Making European Policies Work: The Implementation of Community Legislation in the Member States.* London: Sage.

Shonfield, Andrew. 1965. *Modern Capitalism.* Oxford: Oxford University Press.

Sorge, Arndt and Wolfgang Streeck. 1988. "Industrial Relations and Technical Change: The Case for an Extended Perspective." In R. Hyman and W. Streeck, eds. *New Technology and Industrial Relations.* London: Basic Blackwell. Pp. 19–47.

Streeck, Wolfgang. 1989. "On the Social and Political Conditions of Diversified Quality Production." Paper presented at the conference on "No Way to Full Employment?" Wissenschaftszentrum-Berlin für Sozialforschung, July 5–7.

———. 1989. "The Territorial Organization of Interests and the Logics of Associative Action: the Case of *Handwerk* Organization in West Germany." In W. Coleman and Henry J. Jacek, eds. *Regionalism, Business Interests and Public Policy.* London: Sage. Pp. 59–94.

Streeck, Wolfgang and Philippe Schmitter, eds. 1985. *Private Interest Government: Beyond Market and State.* London and Beverly Hills: Sage.

Trigilia, Carlo. 1986. *Grande partiti e piccole imprese.* Bologna: Il Mulino.

Vogel, David. 1991. "Protective Regulation and Protectionism in the European Community: The Creation of a Common Market for Food and Beverages." Paper presented at the Biennial Conference of the ECSA, George Mason University, May.

PART IV

CONCLUSION

14

FROM NATIONAL EMBEDDEDNESS TO SPATIAL AND INSTITUTIONAL NESTEDNESS

Robert Boyer and J. Rogers Hollingsworth

CAPITALISM, HISTORY, AND THE RISE OF MARKET: STILL THE PARADOX OF POLANYI

For many social scientists, the capitalist system is defined primarily as a market economy. This assumes that the rise, diffusion, and maturation of market mechanisms are the key features in periodizing the history of modern economies (Attali, 1981; Braudel, 1979). Ideally, a complete marketization of economic and social life would fulfill the ideal of modernity.

The previous chapters cast severe doubts about the omnipotence and exclusivity of market mechanisms in capitalist systems. In fact, this vision is severely challenged by many recent advances in various areas of the social sciences. First, it is not true that those historical moments that have been the most market oriented have been the most successful ones in providing growth and stability in the history of capitalist societies (Sabel and Zeitlin, 1985). Second, some of the most competitive firms, regions, and nations are based on mechanisms of economic coordination that are totally different from pure market mechanisms (Gerlach, 1992; Hamilton and Biggart, 1988). Third, from a theoretical standpoint, markets are only one among various alternative and often complementary coordinating mechanisms: hierarchies, networks, associations, and states have frequently been important mechanisms for coordinating actors in capitalist societies when adequately designed and blended (Campbell, Hollingsworth, and Lindberg, 1991; Hollingsworth, Schmitter, and Streeck, 1994). Fourth, the transition to market economies in eastern European countries is beginning to provide clear insights about the necessary embeddedness of a market logic within a whole set of values, legal frameworks, and nonmarket institutions.

Therefore, the conventional neoclassical vision of markets has to be significantly reassessed. The neo-Austrian school of economics since Von Mises vigorously argues for the inner superiority of the market as a coordinating mechanism: Markets allow for flexibility, trials, and errors, even if they do not provide for overall optimum performance. But markets are not the only institutional arrangement for organizing social and economic life. For Hayek (1980, 1976–82), a constitutional order and conventional values at the local level are necessary in order to organize and govern any society. Nevertheless, for Hayekians, markets must be the selective device and the final calibrator of institutional forms within modern societies, which are too complex to be governed by ex ante design of a set of explicit and politically constructed rules (Hayek, 1976–82; Nozick, 1974).

In contrast, we argue that the Hayekian optimism about the efficiency of markets is misplaced. First, markets cannot create the various prerequisites that are necessary for their implementation: the existence of contracts, the institutions necessary for the enforcement of contracts, the physical and institutional organizations that are necessary for transactions to occur, the publicity of the information related to markets, the ex ante assessment of the quality of the products that are to be exchanged. Second, too much coordination by markets may trigger global instabilities: This is especially the case with financial markets, as the crashes of 1929 or 1987 clearly reveal. Moreover, major instabilities tend to permeate product and financial markets with the potential to feed a major structural crisis. There is a dilemma inherent in market mechanisms. On the one side, fast reactions to market disequilibria constantly proportionate supply and demand for a large variety of goods, therefore providing a good allocative efficiency of scarce resources among alternative uses. But on the other side, the very same process may trigger major macroeconomic imbalances in the use of labor and existing equipment. Adjustments that are too rapid may lead to a collapse of the economic system, with major financial instabilities and/or mass unemployment. The interwar period in the United States and Europe provides a striking example of the potentially destructive impact of an untamed pure market logic. This Keynesian and Polanyian argument has been rejuvenated and made more rigorous by contemporary modeling (Dumenil and Levy, 1989).

Some degree of market conformity might be good for societies, but too much of it may be very destructive for economic efficiency and social justice as well. A second and important argument relates to history: The unprecedented post–World War II growth took place by taming and regulating the market, but subsequently this has been challenged by the reemergence of speculation, "short-run termism," and opportunism.

THE MISUNDERSTOOD POST–WORLD WAR II MIRACLE

In retrospect, the interwar period and the post-1945 reconstruction are enlightening about the surprising economic boom that took place after World War II. For many contemporary observers, most of the troubles associated with the great depression derived from labor market rigidities, too much state intervention, and lack of competition in product markets (Rueff, 1932). By contrast, present-day economic historians tend to argue that price and wage formations were far more competitive during the twenties than the sixties and seventies. Indeed, the American and French economies were structurally unstable during the twenties due to an excessive reliance on market mechanisms (Aglietta, 1982; Boyer and Mistral, 1982). Relatively few observers were convinced that markets had to be disciplined by public interventions (Weir and Skocpol, 1985). In retrospect, it appears that Polanyi (1957) was right: An excess of markets leads to instability.

The advanced industrialized countries overcame the interwar economic collapse by controlling and regulating markets, but not by a blind obedience to a mythical market efficiency (Milward, 1979: Vatter, 1985). The primacy of politics after World War II provided for significant changes in monetary and credit control, industrial relations, public infrastructures, and education. Thus, the state brought about such a complete redesign of the basic institutional forms of modern economies that growth and cyclical patterns were altered: mild recessions replaced depressions. Chronic inflation did occur, though unprecedented productivity increases were translated into a continuous rise in standards of living. This was not a victory of pure market mechanisms, but on the contrary the success was due to the taming of the market by large corporations, unions, and, of course, numerous state agencies. A similar "miracle" is currently taking place in some Asian countries. This period of history demonstrates that markets are efficient not only when they are used and channeled according to clear political or social aims (Wade, 1990), but also when they are contained and tamed by a variety of social and political institutions.

THE DOUBLE EMBEDDEDNESS OF THE FORDIST SOCIAL SYSTEMS OF PRODUCTION

A common process of institutional change took place after World War II for most advanced capitalist countries. The disruptions associated with the end of the war promoted the implementation and diffusion of the following institutional forms:

- The United States had the might to implement a new international regime, which complemented their diplomatic, military, economic, and technological hegemony. Consequently, other countries were able to design and implement their own national regimes, given the basic stability provided by *Pax Americana* (Calleo, 1982; Gilpin, 1987; Kindleberger, 1978).

- After World War II, governments developed genuine institutional forms concerning the wage labor-nexus, oligopolistic competition under the supervision of the state, and welfare systems covering education, health, and retirement. Each country exhibited its own specific forms of regulation and coordination. Despite national variations, this form of regulation has been discussed as the politics of Fordism, with a host of regulatory institutions embedded at the central level of nation states.

- But any social system of production has a spatial configuration, or variations by regions, and thus regional components. In other words, a country's social system of production is not necessarily homogeneous in spatial terms. In some cases, there were distinctive regional forms of coordination following World War II which shaped the cohesiveness of industrial districts: This was especially the case for the Third Italy and the German Lander, but various Japanese regions too (Friedman, 1988; Herrigel, 1990; Pyke and Sengenberger, 1992; Pyke, Becattini, and Sengenberger, 1991; Sabel and Zeitlin, 1985; Storper and Harrison, 1991; Zeitlin, 1990). In other configurations, there was the projection of national institutional forms upon regions or towns: This was apparently the case for France and to some extent the United Kingdom (Zeitlin, 1994). Thus markets became embedded in the social and political institutions at both the national and regional levels of societies (Lazonick, 1991).

The diffusion of mass production and consumption from the United States to Europe and Japan generated a genuine hybridization of national political bargaining and regional legacies in terms of productive systems. In this respect, social systems of production are embedded both into specific national institutional forms and regional orbits of trust, at least when strong local traditions continue to exist (Herrigel, 1995; Whitley and Hollingsworth, 1996, forthcoming). This helps to explain across countries the large diversity of capital–labor relations (Boyer, 1990b), various forms of oligopolistic competition (Dumez and Jeunemaitre, 1991), and, of course, differing forms of state intervention (André and Delorme, 1980).

It is now clear that these three types of regulatory systems – at the global, the national, and the subnational regional levels – coalesced into a surprisingly coherent growth regime between the end of World War II and the mid-1960s. And it was the containment of market forces that played a positive role in the unprecedented increases in productivity and standards of living that occurred in advanced industrial societies. The French École de la Régulation has demonstrated that this process was far more important than a mere catching up following the quasi-stagnation of the interwar period (Boyer and Saillard, 1995).

FROM EROSION TO THE CRISIS OF PREVIOUS INSTITUTIONAL ARRANGEMENTS

The success of this regulation mode set into motion three destabilizing mechanisms, which have led in recent years to a surge of market mechanisms that in turn are dissolving many previous national and regional institutions in which market activity had been embedded.

1. Initially, *Pax Americana* solved the inherent instability of the interwar international regime. The Bretton Woods system was so efficient in rebuilding the European and Japanese industrial capabilities that the American trade surplus declined from being largely positive to significantly negative. Similarly, despite the diffusion of the politics of Fordism (Boyer, 1990a), emerging financial innovations in country after country increasingly undermined the legitimacy of strongly regulated national monetary and financial regimes. Until some threshold during the 1970s, various national economies entered into acute competition with one another, creating excess capacity and some likelihood for creeping protectionist wars. Thus, national systems of production which were first quite independent, and then complementary, became more and more competitive with one another at the international level.

2. Simultaneously, the growth regime of individual countries encountered increasing difficulties in coping with labor discipline, investment efficiency, accelerating inflation, recurrent external disequilibria, emerging financial instabilities, and in some cases a loss of efficiency in Keynesian

counter-cyclical policies, thus creating public deficits and a loss of confidence in the capability of national governments to monitor macroeconomic activity (Calleo, 1992; O'Connor, 1973). Therefore, many institutional forms of regulation inherited from the post–World War II period were challenged, eroded or circumvented: the strategy of multinationals, the losing strength of unions in many but not all countries, and the political shift from Keynesian orthodoxy toward neoclassical-inspired conservative policies increasingly challenged the idea that markets had to be tamed and contained.

3. Consequently, the spatial distribution of economic activity within national borders and across countries has increasingly changed. On the one hand, the crisis of highly capital intensive sectors has led to the economic declines of some regions with heavy specialization in automobiles, equipment goods, and mining. This is but one example of a crisis in the regional embeddedness of postwar regulatory order. But on the other hand, the transformation in the coordination of advanced capitalist economies has provided new opportunities for densely organized industrial districts, particularly those with a high degree of industrial manufacturing adaptability and, most importantly, flexibility. The disruption of the postwar international regime altered the spatial distribution of social systems of production (Pyke, Becattini, and Sengenberger, 1991; Pyke and Sengenberger, 1992).

Throughout the seventies and eighties, these forces were eroding the previous macroeconomic regularities and thus brought about interrelated destabilizing factors. The demise of the postwar regulatory international system led to an intensification of the competition among the various national systems of production, and triggered significant shifts in market share and ultimately employment within and across countries. Increasingly, governments could rely less and less on conventional Keynesian policies which basically assumed a relative national autonomy, both in terms of competition in existing national product markets and of fiscal and monetary interventions. A new neoclassical economic theory began to emerge and provided a rationale for either a Keynesian or anti-Keynesian policy, aiming primarily at monetary stability, external competitiveness, and profit restoration. Many economic theorists now argue that public spending has little economic impact, given the full rationality of private agents, and that any economy operates near a Walrasian equilibria (Lucas, 1988; Sargent, 1979). Thus, the erosion of post–World War II institutions has accelerated and addressed a key question: What other economic institutions should replace the configuration of postwar regulatory regimes and Keynesian strategies?

THE RETURN TO THE MARKET:
THE PARADOX OF THE EIGHTIES

A conservative counterrevolution has made popular a simple and apparently efficient solution: Governments should rely basically on market mechanisms and only exceptionally on public interventions. The seduction of such a proposal is derived from several sources. First, modern consumers tend to observe that competition is better than administrative controls, which usually create rationing and some welfare loss. Second, the internationalization of the world economy has brought a new era of competition, which has partially destabilized national oligopolies: Some firms have suffered intensely from such a process, but consumers have tended to benefit from relative price decreases. Third, the highly regulated financial markets of the sixties have been transformed in order to cope with a wave of financial innovations, a surge in foreign investment, and the transnationalization of production. Thus, frequent instabilities have brought about major macroeconomic adjustments. In turn, structural changes in competition, finance, and technology have revealed many "labor market rigidities" that were often "hidden" during the high and stable growth era. Finally, during the 1980s, the motto of most international organizations and governments was simple indeed: increase flexibility in the labor market and attain a reduction in unemployment (OECD, 1985). The slump of the 1990s has even accelerated this strategy (OECD, 1994).

The ideological victory of laissez faire economics has been reinforced by the failure of an alternative strategy. A Keynesian reflation in a single nation is no longer possible in a largely open world economy, as the 1982 French experience demonstrated (Daley, 1996). Social pacts between labor and capital are more and more difficult, given the economic slowdown in most countries and the high public deficits that exist. Increasingly, social democratic arrangements are vulnerable to the intensity of foreign competition and the diffusion of financial innovations, as the Swedish case dramatically demonstrates. Finally, the unexpected collapse of Soviet-type economies provides the decisive and last resort argument in favor of markets: Is not the failure of Gosplan a direct proof of the greater efficiency of markets over any alternative coordinating mechanism? Thus, even social democratic governments have embraced laissez faire strategies in order to cure structural problems they were unable to resolve by any other method.

No doubt the market, when correctly organized and monitored, is quite efficient in the allocation of scarce resources. This tends to be especially the case with commodities having standardized qualities and a large number of transacting economic actors (Baker, 1994; Smith, 1990; Williamson, 1985). But more recent research in microeconomic theory demonstrates that it would be erroneous to extend such thinking to the entire economic system (see Chapter 2). As present-day Russia demonstrates, if there exists no stable national currency, the efficiency of commodity markets can be severely restricted, especially if there is lax control by public authorities over the existence of effective competition. Similarly, modern technological innovations frequently exhibit increasing returns to scale – for example, network effects, positive externalities associated with education and training, or basic scientific discoveries (Hollingsworth, Schmitter, and Streeck, 1994: 270–300; Streeck, 1991). Under these circumstances, market mechanisms lead to inefficient outcomes, i.e., insufficient investments in promising technologies or skills. Modern research in microeconomic theory is full of examples pointing out such discrepancies between market allocations and Pareto optima solutions (Akerlof, 1984; Grossman and Stiglitz, 1980; Stiglitz, 1987). The new growth theory has pointed out that the discrepancies between private and social rates of return play a role in explaining why growth may be inhibited due to the insufficient supply by the market of such essential ingredients as research and development expenditures, education, and public infrastructures (Lucas, 1988; Romer, 1986, 1990).

Therefore, not surprisingly, societies that rely heavily on markets usually encounter severe problems in terms of social justice or fairness. Over the long run, as the intensity of a market mentality increases in a society, there is a decline in the degree of solidarity among its members. Societies having high degrees of market mentality and in the pursuit of individual self-interest but with little sensitivity to social obligations tend to be ones with considerable social disintegration, crime, and deviance. And many of the social pathologies of contemporary America must be understood in terms of what happens when a society's market activity is not embedded in political institutions promoting a minimum degree of solidarity (Hollingsworth, 1996, forthcoming).

Thus, the 1980s experienced two major paradoxes. On the one hand, governments relied more and more upon markets in order to solve the many difficult issues that they were confronting, at the very moment when theorists were discovering that the efficiency of markets was restricted to a very small set of products (Akerlof, 1984; Alter and Hage, 1993; Baker, 1994; White, 1991). For example, typical credit or labor markets do not clear in the same way as do stock markets. Thus, financial instability is a likely pathology of markets. After all, Keynesian economists are right: Speculation on typical product markets is stabilizing, but too much competitive speculation on financial markets is potentially disruptive (Kaldor, 1939). Today, the debate about the need for regulating markets for derivatives is expressing the same concern about the detrimental impact of the spreading of new financial instruments and markets. More generally, it is clear that the most conservative strategies in the United States and United Kingdom have not delivered the expected results. There is still widespread deindustrialization and poor external competitiveness (Zeitlin, 1995).

On the other hand, those societies in which the market mentality is highly pervasive are undergoing very dynamic social change. The economies in such societies generate many new innovations which in turn destabilize most social institutions – including the norms, rules, and trust upon which the health of a capitalist economy depend. The market is the invisible hand, permanently altering institutions and promoting technical change.

SOCIAL SCIENCES AND INSTITUTIONAL CHANGE: ALTERNATIVE CONCEPTIONS

One of the novelties of the contemporary world is the experiencing of considerable structural change in economies organized and institutionalized according to a network of interrelated arrangements and coordinating mechanisms. But do the social sciences provide any convenient interpretation or theory about the processes now taking place all around the world? Three main visions are competing in order to shape our understanding and guide economic policies. Market, tradition, and polity are the main factors put forward by the literature. But this book argues that the *polity is an essential ingredient in the transition from one institutional regime to another.*

IS THE MARKET A SELECTIVE DEVICE BY WHICH WE MIGHT ASSESS ALTERNATIVE INSTITUTIONAL ARRANGEMENTS?

Transaction costs economics (Williamson, 1985), as well as the new institutional economics based upon agency theory (Tirole, 1988), have launched a renewed interest in the study of economic institutions (also see Eggertsson, 1990; Furubotn and Richter, 1991; North, 1990). These perspectives are built upon two pillars: (1) The rationality principle governs the behavior of actors whatever the context and delivers predictable patterns; (2) Markets organize competition among alternative strategies. In this literature, rationality, by definition, delivers the best strategies, and markets will favor the most appropriate behavior and thus deliver a convergence towards the perceived "one best way" of doing things. But in the tradition of Simon (1983), suppose that, in real economies, the minds of firm managers, consumers, workers, and bankers are unable to cope with all of the complexity and uncertainty involved in all of their economic transactions. Under such circumstances, institutional arrangements other than market mechanisms must be involved in coordinating transactions among economic actors.

Neoclassical economists still maintain that a market system will select the most efficient solution to problems, whether it be the development of a new product, a technology, a type of contract, or even collective institutional arrangements. The argument is quite convincing for ordinary goods of a given quality, which are supplied and demanded by a large number of traders according to anonymous transactions. In contrast, many pitfalls tend to occur when the transactions concern labor, skills, or finance, in which the product involves very complex technology. Markets then are quite likely to provide inefficient outcomes with rationing, speculative bubbles, financial instability, social exclusion, and inequalities.

The selection of institutional arrangements by an intense market mentality tends to be myopic and inefficient (Polanyi, 1957). Given the indivisibilities inherent in any institution, inefficient arrangements can survive since they benefit from their previous implementation. An intrinsically superior institution may suffer from its association with inefficient arrangements and be ruled out by market mechanisms. In contrast with general equilibrium theory, the Austrian school of economics actually recognizes that the market as a solution to problems may head to deadends, which then result in the call for some type of state intervention (Hayek, 1976–82). Such a conclusion is infrequently emphasized, but is very important in the present context.

The theory of voluntaristic, rational self-building of institutions can be applied to the analysis of how social systems of production are constructed (see Figure 14-1). With this theoretical perspective, organizational innovations derive from the rational calculus of individuals and firms that compare alternative solutions. The model assumes that any radical uncertainty can be removed by adequate insurance contracts and that each individual innovation can be disentangled from all the others in order to allow for a series of independent optimizing solutions. The model also assumes that the expansion of firms will be guided by the competition for finance, labor, natural resources, or alternative organizational forms.

To be more specific, this kind of social system of production would combine free trade, consumer sovereignty, optimal labor contracts with a high degree of flexibility, technological alliances and networks in order to discover new technologies, a benevolent urban and regional environment, and finally a minimalist state, without interference with private rational

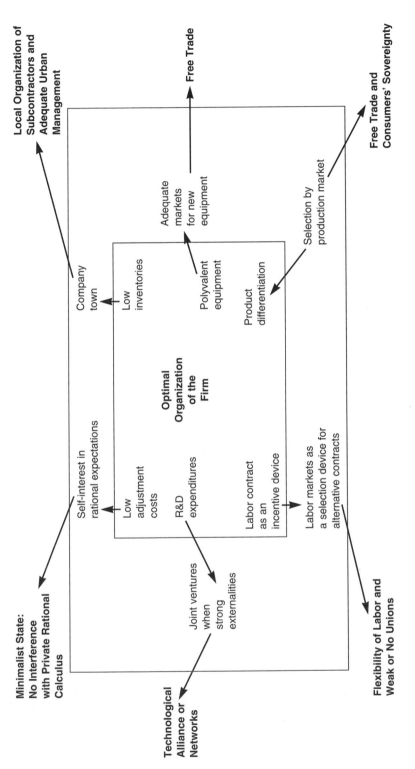

Figure 14-1. The "Self-Building" of Institutions and Social Systems of Production

calculus by firms. In this model, the managers who submit to market competition eventually obtain the best institutional arrangements, whereas civil servants and governments tend to make numerous mistakes.

This type of social system of production is quite idealized and does not fit with basic historical evidence. Given the strong complementarities among technologies, markets, and localization tendencies, any social system of production not only needs to be but is actually monitored by extramarket mechanisms: business ethics, rules of the game, business associations, and the state (Schneiberg and Hollingsworth, 1990). True, business histories provide many examples of a sectoral productive system built by the expansion of the strategy of a single or limited number of large firms, which attempt to internalize their strategies (Chandler, 1969, 1977, 1990). Nevertheless, at some threshold, external coordinating institutions are required: politicians to manage local political matters; an association of firms in order to establish industry standards, to foster product quality, and to set rules of fair competition; and a state in order to negotiate the opening of foreign markets but also to provide many of the same functions that business associations may be unable to establish (Campbell, Hollingsworth, and Lindberg, 1991; Hollingsworth and Lindberg, 1985; Schneiberg and Hollingsworth, 1990).

Similarly, a high wage, high skill economy cannot simply be implemented at will by a few entrepreneurs, however successful they might be in inventing new production methods. The Henry Ford experience of paying workers $5 a day is a wonderful example that clearly indicates the limits of purely private strategies in building a new economic and social configuration (Boyer and Orlean, 1991; Raff, 1988). Basically, the real world does not behave as the normative proposals of a voluntaristic, "rational" theory suggests for the construction of a social system of production. In short, capitalism does not operate in this way.

CONTRASTED REGIONAL TRAJECTORIES: STILL A STRONG SPATIAL EMBEDDEDNESS

The vision about the supremacy of the market as a coordinating institution is losing relevance and should be compared to alternative conceptions about the mechanisms that might monitor the transformation of institutional forms. The embeddedness hypothesis (Granovetter, 1985, 1992) argues that precapitalist logics are an essential ingredient for markets and capitalism to exist. For example, trust, reciprocity, and long-term strategies – prerequisites for a capitalist economy – require communities, associations, and/or networks for their existence. Totally rational individuals would recurrently break down previous institutional agreements if they were free to do so. Opportunistic behavior cannot be completely avoided by optimal contracts, either within or without vertical hierarchies (Williamson, 1985). Trust, reciprocity, and long-term relationships are sustained by families, community-like structures, and clans (Fukuyama, 1995; North, 1990; Polanyi, 1957; Polanyi-Levitt, 1990; Putnam, 1993).

This has a special relevance for social systems of production, since production systems relying on forms of flexible specialization or mass production require that firms be embedded in an institutional environment that will enhance a high degree of trust (Sabel, 1992). Products that embody a high degree of technological complexity, rapid and unpredictable innovations, and unexpected variations in demand cannot be produced in a world coordinated by pure market relations. Rather they can be produced only in a world that has institutional arrangements that provide trust, risk sharing, tacit knowledge, and strategic information. The social system of production portrayed in Figure 14-1 cannot provide the support for such products. However, Figure 14-2 portrays the kind of institutional environment within which firms must be embedded in order to have such prerequisites for complex technologies.

This type of embeddedness is especially important for productive systems that are an alternative to the mass production of standardized goods. The importance of quality, speed of delivery, and adaptability to demand shifts and new technological opportunities call for long-term relationships between managers and workers, large firms and their subcontractors, which cannot be totally formalized with explicit contracts (Hage and Jing, 1996, forthcoming). Minimal implicit agreements can only be reached by building upon trust relationships, which are not completely derived from a particular core economic activity. All the authors of Part II agree on the importance of rich localized interactions among economic actors if there are to be systems of flexible specialization. In this type of social system of production, the importance of regional economies is emphasized, and there is primary attention devoted to the institutional arrangements at the local level within which firms are embedded (Benko and Lipietz, 1989).

THE STATE MATTERS:
SOCIAL SYSTEMS OF PRODUCTION REVISITED

The resilience of coordination mechanisms other than markets is a prerequisite for the continuing dynamism of capitalism. At some threshold, the domination of the market rationale tends to challenge the viability of other institutional arrangements: the values of the community, the family, and

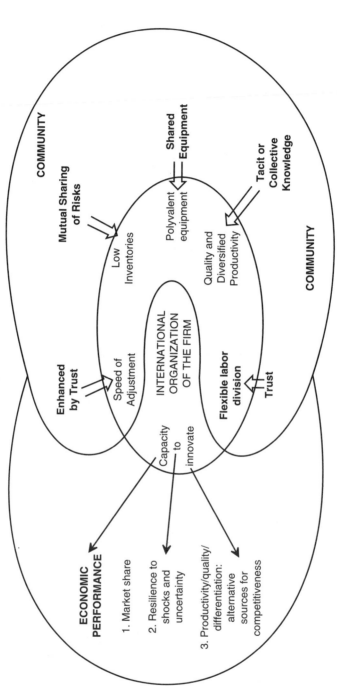

Figure 14-2. The Embeddedness of Social Systems of Production

other authority systems can be eroded under the pursuit of private interests by each individual. Thus we confront Polanyi's (1957, 1977) argument about the danger of the erosion of a society's cohesiveness when the market begins to dominate such fundamental social relations involving land, labor, and money (also see Gambetta, 1988; Polanyi-Levitt, 1990).

Capitalism, as we have previously suggested, is an extremely dynamic form of economy, and market activity – if not contained – will erode all kinds of traditional institutional arrangements. Yet many of these traditional institutional arrangements are necessary in order to provide the trust on which transactions among economic actors depend. Thus, institutional arrangements alternative to the market are needed in order *to contain* the explosive nature of the market. If traditional institutional arrangements are too strong in imposing social obligations on individual actors, the potential dynamism of markets will be stifled. But without these external constraints in sufficient force, the market will bring about its own destruction. Hence, it is necessary that the market and these countermarket forces be in a delicate balance (Hirsch, 1977; Hollingsworth, 1994; Kumar, 1983; Schumpeter, 1976). However, it is an extremely difficult task for social planners and societal elites to prepare "blueprints" for the institutional arrangements that will implement this type of delicate balance. Such a delicate balance, when in existence, is a product of the path dependent logic of the institutional history of a particular society.

This theme has been explored in more detail in Wolfgang Streeck's chapter: Some regulatory devices may challenge the conventional ways for organizing business activity and society and therefore enhance innovations in order finally to deliver a viable economic regime, which is closely shaped by each national regulatory style. Ex post, social values and dynamic economic efficiency can be reconciled, but ex ante it is quite difficult to make a correct assessment of the impact of any radical departure from past institutional arrangements.

This perspective has definite consequences fo the viability of social systems of production (Figure 14-3). The performance of a social system of production derives from the interaction of two contradictory forces. The logic of the firm induces an expansion from its inner organization toward the surrounding environment, and those are the dynamics contemplated by the conception of a self-building of institutions portrayed in Figure 14-1. But the state, in Figure 14-3, exerts a countervailing power in order to maintain the compatibility of firms with the social nexus upon which the related society is built. A conception of justice (embedded even into such things as a tax code and a welfare system), the structure of a society's industrial relations system, the organization of training for labor and management, the

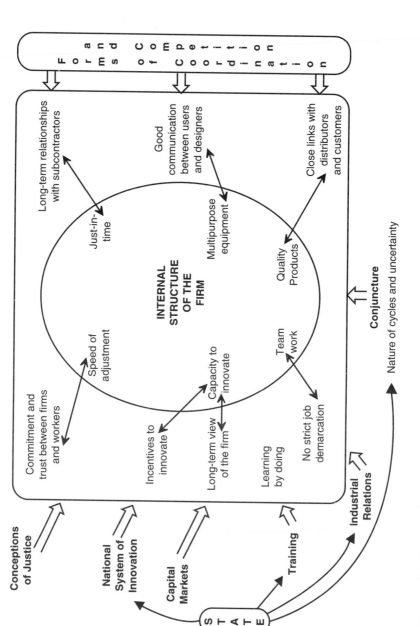

Figure 14-3. *Power and Polity Are Shaping Social Systems of Production and Partially the Internal Structure of the Firm*

monitoring by the capital markets, and the viability of a national system of innovation are the key forces that constrain pure profit maximizing. Initially, these regulatory mechanisms may hinder short-run efficiency, but over the longer run they facilitate innovative adaptations from firms, wage earners, and banks. And finally such regulatory mechanisms may deliver a genuine pattern of development.

Inherent in such an interpretation of social systems of production is a strong sense of historicity: Major political events and structural crises lead to the emergence of new laws, rules, and norms which place constraints on the behavior of firms and their performance. Thus, this vision is somehow eclectic between two extreme representations of state interventions: Governments are not totally powerless in intervening in economic activity, but at the same time they cannot unilaterally impose just any economic pattern on private actors. Between the extremes, state interventions may facilitate the emergence of social compromises and provide some collective prerogatives to associations and other intermediate bodies in charge of monitoring the behavior and strategies of groups of actors (Campbell and Lindberg, 1990; Schneiberg and Hollingsworth, 1990).

The timing of public interventions is important: When the economy collapses or is facing unprecedented challenges (wars, societal reconstruction, etc.), the radical uncertainty that paralyzes private agents can only be overcome by a clear statement about desirable and viable new institutional arrangements, legislation, or rules of the game. The compatibility of a complete nexus of institutional arrangements defines the condition for the efficacy of public interventions. In other words, the choice of new strategies is limited by the logic of institutional change of a particular society. And major new rules and institutional arrangements will in turn feed back and alter other institutional arrangements. Thus, the social and economic policies of Western countries have varied from country to country since World War II, for these have been constrained by the traditional rules and norms, social cleavages, and social structures of each society.

THE SOURCES OF INSTITUTIONAL CHANGE: THREE VISIONS AND A SYNTHESIS

This book proposes a syncretic approach to institutional building that combines three major interpretations, which in isolation cannot explain the shift of a social system of mass standardized production to one with a high capability of mass-producing differentiated quality goods. From a theoretical point of view, each interpretation has its strengths and weaknesses (see Figure 14-4).

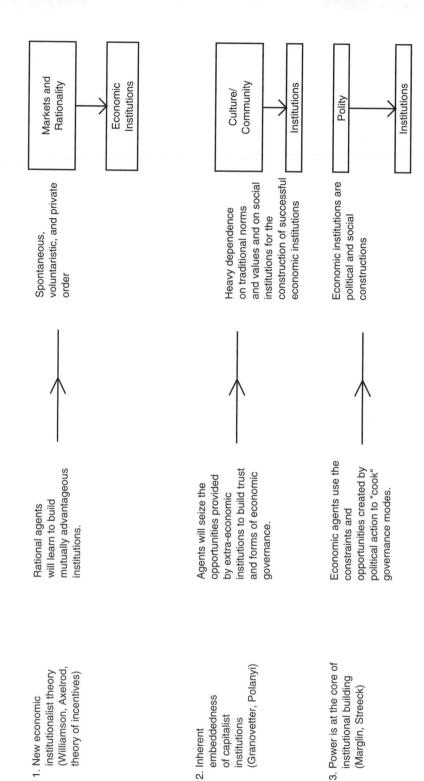

Figure 14-4. Three Visions of Institutional Change

The thinking of the new economic institutionalists (Williamson, 1985) is based upon a central hypothesis: Rational agents have self-interests in building efficient institutions in order to govern their strategic interactions. Consequently, mixing full rationality (i.e., the ability to compute the outcome of even highly complex strategic interactions) with market competition should deliver all of the optimal institutions that are needed in order to coordinate a complex capitalist economy, in the sense that the position of any actor cannot be improved without impairing the situation of another. Obviously, it is intuitively very appealing to believe that the principles of the invisible bond of the market can be transposed to all kinds of institutions and organizational forms. However, institutions involve complementarities among individual behaviors, and they are far more difficult to monitor than pure market relations among individual actors. Moreover, sunk costs invested in existing institutions provide them with a high degree of legitimacy. As a result, societies hardly ever have the liberty of renegotiating everything and rebuilding all new institutions. Even when there have been violent revolutions, many norms, rules, and institutional arrangements continue to persist. And even when actors may have a good sense of what a superior institutional arrangement may be at any one moment in time, it may be blocked by the habit and inertia of social interactions (Boyer and Orlean, 1992; David, 1988). Usually, some form of collective action is needed in order to overcome the hysteresis of inefficient institutions. In short, the world simply cannot continuously be reconstructed anew as the new economic institutionalists would have us believe.

The second approach argues that the social embeddedness of relationships in capitalist societies permits actors to circumvent the limits of pure rationality and the interactions of anonymous markets. For example, product and credit markets can exist because they are based on trust in the fulfillment of future transactions. But this form of trust is not easily manufactured. When economic activity is tightly connected with dense social relations based on family, religion, school ties, etc., tradition and trust can then be used to build useful and efficient economic institutions. Many observers have assumed that efficient institutions can exist only when traditional loyalties are abolished. However, a great deal of recent social science (Amsden, 1989; Granovetter, 1985, 1992, 1993; Hamilton, 1991; Hamilton and Biggart, 1988; Hamilton and Kao, 1991; Hamilton, Zeile, and Kim, 1990; Whitley, 1992a, 1992b) has demonstrated that many organizations – both public and private – operate effectively precisely because they have incorporated familial, feudal, and other traditional characteristics into their governance (Landes, 1951; Etzioni, 1988; Zelizer, 1988). This interpretation has a great deal to say about the relative ability of regions and countries to adopt the principles inherent in a social system of production. Nevertheless, we are still confronted with the mystery of how trust is manufactured in a modern economy: Why do individuals prefer to cooperate within a family, a group with strong school ties, etc., instead of being opportunistic? As Dore (1973, 1983, 1986) has suggested, today tradition is the unconscious outcome of yesterday's interactions and collective actions. Moreover, we are also faced with the problem of why market relations have not more seriously eroded the loyalty of Japanese workers or the trust one observes in Italian industrial districts (d'Iribarne, 1990; Pyke, Becattini, and Sengenberger, 1991; Pyke and Sengenberger, 1992). Of course, not any culture is ever invariant and static, but is continuously reactivated and reinvented, and the same is true in the Japanese and Italian cases.

What is missing in models one and two in Figure 14-4 is an emphasis on power. In model three, power is at the core of institution building. Individuals interact as economic agents through market competition, but simultaneously they fight for political power, e.g., to gain control over the rules of the game and to build asymmetries within the economic sphere (Marglin, 1991). Modern economic theory (Stiglitz, 1987; Stiglitz and Weiss, 1978) establishes the idea that some conflicting configurations call for collective interventions in economic activity, in order to restore better outcomes for all the participants. Moreover, considerable historical research exhibits an impressive series of economic interventions by the state, just to overcome deadends or to defend traditional societal values in an effort to promote effective economic institutions (Campbell and Lindberg, 1990; Gershenkron, 1962; North, 1981; Streeck, 1992). Given the coercive and persuasive power of modern states, this process provides a good bit of the explanation for the development of new institutional forms (North, 1981, 1990). If the process of trials and errors with the use of state power is sufficiently careful, a coherent "regulation" mode may emerge and deliver a superior configuration of institutions for almost any or all actors.

The polity is the sphere that allows for the recomposition of institutional forms, and this is why states and associations are so prevalent in modern economic activity (Campbell and Lindberg, 1990; Campbell, Hollingsworth, and Lindberg, 1991; Granovetter, 1993; Schneiberg and Hollingsworth, 1990). Sabel's concept of constitutional order in this volume provides another series of arguments of how political action enhances institutional transformation. First of all, any institutional form has to be organized according to a clear distinction between two levels: the definition of the rules of the game on one side and on the other the interaction of individuals and groups within a particular institutional setting (North, 1990). This is an interesting perspective with respect to the new economics of institutions (transaction costs economics, the theory of implicit contracts, principal/agent theory, theory of incentives, and noncooperative game theory). At any given moment in time, economic agents do not simultaneously play within and outside the game according to a joint strategy. Only in cases of total institutional breakdown does the tension among actors become so intense that they must fundamentally restructure most of the institutions of a society.

According to this interpretation, any institutional form exhibits a hierarchy involving a constitutional order and the way constituent members play the game. For example, within the state, a constitutional court usually deliberates about the compatibility of rulings among lower-level arbitration courts. Within large firms, a board is in charge of deciding among conflicting strategies proposed by competing plants or functional divisions. Markets are governed or monitored by regulatory agencies, charged with the responsibility of maintaining fair competition and/or impeding the emergence of monopoly power. Within associations, the same hierarchical phenomenon prevails. For example, the statutes of a political party, a union, or a business association organize the mutual responsibility and rights of constituents. Thus, all major coordinating mechanisms imply a constitutional order, i.e., a political process of institutionalization which is not left to the pure routine of everyday interactions. In other words, the polity is a necessary component in the institutionalization of all economic and social order.

There is a second reason for the importance of a constitutional order. Imagine, for example, that the very functioning of a given institutional form generates some learning that drastically alters the monitoring properties of the previous order. Alternatively, external shocks, depending on when the original constitutional order was constructed, may destabilize local systems. Under such circumstances, the players might be stuck with drastic choices of continued cooperation, exit, or voice. If they continue to interact within the old constitutional order, a rational decision might be to quit the game. By contrast, if they agree to deliberate about the ongoing problems, they might converge toward a redesign of the governance structure, possibly mutually advantageous for every member. The constitutional, political, and economic histories of modern societies provide large numbers of experiences leading to positive adaptations to new circumstances or issues (Hirschman, 1977; North, 1990).

The possibility of voice, in contrast with exit, opens large possibilities for social transformations. The ability to depart from a particular economic arena and to devise alternative rules of the game more suited to a new environment is clearly an important channel for economic reform, especially during crisis periods. Furthermore, an historical perspective suggests that this is the usual process for facilitating an increasing division of labor and greater specialization of organizations and individuals, and therefore for promoting a long-run trend towards product and process innovations. A constitutional order may well be the best instrument for converting one set of institutional arrangements into another, but it is a choice usually neglected within standard neoclassical theory.

Consequently, markets may be efficient in solving allocation problems when technological and economic changes are rapid, but other institutional arrangements also have a great deal of adaptability when the issue is about coordination and strategic interactions. It is erroneous to assume that simply because markets are flexible that all other institutions are inherently rigid. Everything depends on the nature of the problems to be solved (allocation/coordination) and the speed of change (moderate/fast). Let us now apply this perspective to contemporary changes in social systems of production.

CONVERGENCE, DIVERGENCE, OR COMPLEMENTARITY IN SOCIAL SYSTEMS OF PRODUCTION

NOT A SINGLE ONE BEST WAY

In order to attain desirable economic performance, the polity matters, especially during structural crises. Some political interventions have lasting influence on technical change and social values and contribute to the construction of various coordinating mechanisms. According to this vision, institutional arrangements can emerge historically from a great deal of trial and error and might be viable even in the long run. And the persistence of institutional arrangements limits the convergence of institutions across societies.

Thus, the conventional wisdom about the convergence of all societies belonging to the same borderless world is quite erroneous (Hollingsworth and Streeck, 1994; Kerr et al., 1960; Ohmae, 1991). Nor in our own day should we see the Japanization of most national industries as the future of industrial firms over the world, even though the Japanese in some sectors have a superior way of coordinating economic activity. Many German firms, Italian districts, and even Scandinavian firms have exhibited a longlasting competitiveness without any clear import of foreign principles, as they essentially build upon rich institutional and political environments that allow for either fast reactions to changing markets or for rapid product and process innovations.

Even if many products and equipment appear to be similar all over the world, they are not necessarily produced by organizations and coordinating mechanisms that are converging toward one best strategy. The dynamism inherent in the Japanese and German institutional configurations are quite dissimilar. Moreover, the French and American Fordist inertia do not have the same causes and consequences (Boyer, 1990a). One can observe diverging trajectories among the countries of Europe, and even more among the countries of North America and East Asia (Whitley, 1992a, 1992b). Furthermore, because of the lack of adequate political and social resources, an economy might be unable to import the institutional arrangements that would enhance its international competitiveness.

This inability to import major new institutional arrangements is often constrained by an existing institutional configuration with its own path dependent logic. Each institution is interdependent with other institutions, making it very difficult for a society to mimic the institutional arrangements of another country. Of course, institutions are fragile and are constantly changing, but the direction of the change is very much limited by the norms and rules and other institutional arrangements with which they are intricately linked at any moment in time (Denzau and North, 1994).

The incapacity of a society to alter its institutional configuration makes it vulnerable to absolute economic decline. And this kind of phenomenon is not without historical precedent. Indeed, this is the more common historical pattern (Mathias, 1969). In short, countries decline because they lack the capacity to mimic the most competitive institutional arrangements. Moreover, the way elites are socialized into the rules and norms of a society tends to blind them to the shortcomings of their own society's institutional makeup (Lazonick, 1991).

According to an alternative model of social evolution, societies might slowly become integrated into a larger system. For example, as various European countries become increasingly integrated into a larger European system, some argue that the distinctiveness of each society's social and political institutions could be eroded. And as this occurs, a society's social system of production may eventually be fundamentally transformed. But different systems evolving into a single larger system is a form of change somewhat different from distinct systems converging toward separate systems along some perceived best practice.

Is there a single method whereby social systems of production (SSP) can always be competitive? The answer is clearly no. This could only be the case if a system were always superior in all its components with respect to any alternative system. Such a system would always have lower costs at any volume of production, better quality for the same price, larger product differentiation for the same equipment and skills, and a capacity to make faster adjustments to evolving technologies without extra cost. In fact, the superiority of a SSP is shaped not only by its institutional arrangement but also by that of its competitors as well as the macroeconomic context within which it is embedded. A survey of the competitiveness of various conceptions of social systems of production expressed by the authors of this volume suggests four possible successors to the social system of mass standardized production (see Figure 14-5):

1. A social system of *customized production (CP)* which emphasizes the role of differentiation in modern societies and assumes both a reduction in the average size of production runs and a better concern for quality. If quality and differentiation were the major considerations that shape competition, then customized production might be the follower of Fordism. This is similar but not identical to flexible specialization (FS) and concerns the industries related to textiles, shoes – i.e., consumer products whereby concern with fashion plays an important role in shaping the behavior of economic actors (Piore and Sabel, 1984).

2. A social system of *diversified quality mass production (DQMP)* belongs to the Fordist legacy (high-volume components but not necessarily final products) and takes into account the changing nature of consumer preferences, but also with the same emphasis on quality and differentiation. A social system of diversified quality mass production will be superior to a social system of customized production if increasing returns to scale prevail, without extra costs for quality and product differentiation. The contemporary car industry is a good example of a social system of diversified quality mass production (Streeck, 1991).

3. *Flexible diversified quality mass production (FDQMP)* extends to the previous (DQMP) social system of production the adaptability to changing markets and rapidly evolving technologies, whatever the volume of production and the importance of quality. Thus, having the right organizational structures for making innovations and having ample funds for research and development are key elements in enhancing the possible superiority of FDQMP (Aoki, 1988). The electronic consumer goods industry tends to belong to this category, since technical change is more intensive than for the car industry.

4. A social system of *adaptive production (AP)* defines a fourth polar configuration of social systems of production. The idea is that competitiveness depends on the ability to deliver new products or new processes on a continuous basis. This model is superior to FDQMP only if technical change is fast. The speed of technical change is the key to

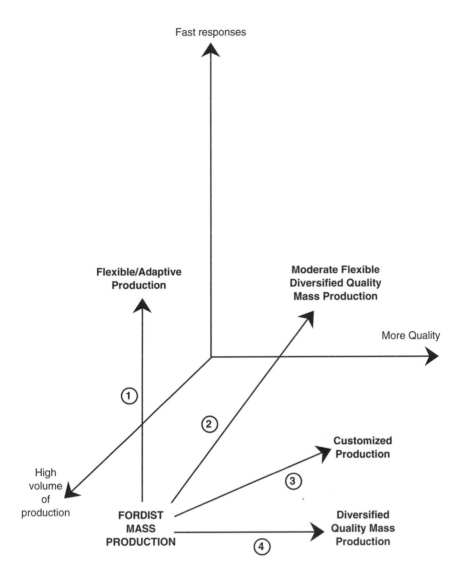

1. Sabel (1991, 1992); Hage and Jing (forthcoming)

2. Coriat (see Chapter 8 in this book)

3. Piore and Sabel (1984)

4. Streeck (1991); Hollingsworth, Schmitter, and Streeck (1994); Chapter 11

Figure 14-5. Four Visions of the Ongoing Transformations of Social Systems of Production

shaping the competitive position of any firm. Pharmaceuticals and the software industry are ideal-typical firms to be found in this configuration (Hage and Jing, 1996, forthcoming).

The absence of any single best way of organizing how a capitalist economy should be coordinated derives from two distinct considerations. First, each sector faces specific technological, economic, and institutional constraints which imply the adoption of one of the four social systems of production, without too much overlap among the various configurations. The previous examples suggest that these sectoral differences capture a large part of the reason for permanent variation in social systems of production. Alternatively, the general context within which a social system of production is located influences the degree of the competitiveness of each SSP, in such a manner that the superiority of any social system of production is context-dependent. If growth is stable, income levels rather low, and the rate of technological change is slow, Fordism might still be the most competitive social system of production. If on the contrary, consumers are far more selective, then customized production or diversified quality mass production may coexist. When technical change is especially rapid and/or markets are very uncertain, social systems of adaptive production might prevail. This is a means whereby we can tentatively reconcile alternative theoretical visions for social systems of production as expressed by the various authors in Part III. Of course, more discussion and empirical studies are still needed before we can reach firm conclusions on the subject.

VARIATION IN THE CAPACITY OF ALTERNATIVE INSTITUTIONAL FORMS TO MONITOR THE EMERGENCE OF ALTERNATIVE SOCIAL SYSTEMS OF PRODUCTION

When we scan the globe in spatial terms, we observe that there is considerable variation from one area to another in the mix of institutions that coordinate the behavior of economic actors. Systems of adaptive production, customized production, diversified quantity mass production, and flexible diversified quality mass production require a variable mix of markets, networks, associations, and hierarchies. And it is important to assess the relative effectiveness of the major coordinating mechanisms in fostering the implementation of each social system of production (see Table 14-1).

Adaptive productive systems require heavy investments in research and development expenditures, as well as well-developed systems of associations in order to provide information about rapidly changing markets and tech-

Table 14-1. What Institutional Arrangements Are Necessary to Sustain Alternative Social Systems of Production?

Nature of SSP	Production volume	Form of competition	Adaptability to environment	Markets	Networks	Associations	State
Adaptive Production (AP)	Low or high	Price or Quality	Strong	Quick responses	Built-in flexibility	Pooling information about markets and technologies	Clear rules of the game
Customized Production (CP)	Low	Quality	Moderate or high	Efficient for products, under control of labor	Allows learning by using	Helps to develop quality standards or norms	Role in education and training
Diversified Quality Mass Production (DQMP)	High	Quality	Moderate	Under strict control of high quality labor	Allows pooling of expertise	Important in providing training and skills	Enaction of technical norms
Flexible Diversified Quality Mass Production (FDQMP)	High	Quality	Strong	The tool for assessing competitiveness	Sharing risks in R&D	Reduce strategic uncertainty	Pro R&D policies

nologies. Moreover, the state must facilitate the development of research institutions (e.g., universities, research institutes, etc.) and enforce a set of rules and norms that are conducive to the development of venture capital markets. Indeed, without well-developed venture capital markets, capital is not likely to be available to small innovative firms with the capability to develop radically new technologies. But even then, firms must be tied into complex networks so that there is collective learning and risk sharing in the development of new technologies (Baker, 1994; Hollingsworth, 1991; Saxenian, 1994; Hage and Jing, forthcoming, 1996).

In social systems of customized production, the market is extremely important in coordinating economic activity, even though examples of industrial districts demonstrate that business associations are important for pooling information about markets and technologies (Pyke, Becattini, and Sengenberger, 1991; Pyke and Sengenberger, 1992; Sabel, 1988). Within customized production systems, firms tend to have workers with relatively broad and high levels of skills and high autonomy. Associations are important for establishing and enforcing standards for the production of goods, without which customers could not have high faith in the quality of products. The state tends to set the rules of the game and to organize the welfare and the credit facilities necessary for customized production.

Social systems of diversified quality mass production (DQMP) require excess or redundant investments in work skills which can be sustained over time if the firms making up such a system are engaged in highly developed collective forms of behavior with the capacity to impose obligations among each other. Firms may occasionally *voluntarily* invest in an excess of skills for their labor force under conditions conducive to social peace between management and labor. Within large firms, internal markets and a high stability of core workers may allow a significant investment in training and continuous skill upgrading in excess of current requisites for actual production. Conversely, if firms are not large enough and if labor mobility is very high, in the absence of public institutions, norms, or regulations, firms will generally underinvest: The United Kingdom and the United States are good examples, in contrast with the German system. In general, voluntary decisions tend to be less stable and less effective for the development of broad and high levels of skills and social peace than socially imposed or legally imposed arrangements. Firms in such a system tend to control markets in goods through oligopolistic pricing and quality differentiation, whereas the labor market tends to be organized in terms of the mobility of highly-trained workers who have met minimum certification standards, as in Germany, or by internal markets, as in large Japanese firms (Hollingsworth and Streeck, 1994; Streeck, 1991).

Flexible diversified quality mass production (FDQMP) requires coordinating mechanisms that can make the best use of technologies and information, features that require a high institutionalization of networks and associations. In short, this kind of system requires well-developed institutional arrangements which facilitate cooperation among competitors and long-term stable relationships with high levels of communication and trust among suppliers and customers.

The way local, regional, national, and transnational economies are coordinated is the result of complex configurations of forces that are deeply rooted in the histories of societies. Because the social processes that result in a particular social system of production are quite historically specific, the coordinating mechanisms (e.g., the state, associations, specific types of networks) that give support to such systems are not easily transferable from one country to another. This is the main reason there is no clear trend in the convergence of coordinating mechanisms and social systems of production.

SOME BASIC FALLACIES IN CONVERGENCE THEORY

The level of alternative governance modes is drastically changing relative to the two decades which followed World War II. After 1945, the implementation of a new international regime ironically helped nation-states to enhance their national autonomy. Until 1973, a slow process of internationalization in finance, trade, investment, and production complemented various national regulation modes without undermining the autonomy of national policies. During the last two decades, however, the intensity of international competition has interfered with the decisions of firms and the strategy of the unions and has somewhat undermined the autonomy of public authorities. A few scholars have developed the concept of globalization, assuming that national frontiers are rapidly blurring. Some analysts even assume that eventually nations and subnational regions will behave like small firms merged into an ocean of pure and perfect competition. This scenario tends to assume that the constraints associated with globalization would eventually lead to a convergence of a one best way for operating manufacturing firms, banks, unions, and even regional and national governments (see Ohmae, 1991).

This picture is more of a utopia than a relevant set of hypotheses for the next few decades. No international regime can be reduced to perfect market mechanisms, since this would combine emerging continental production and trading blocks on one side, and a global sectoral regime on the other, along with a whole spectrum of intermediate coordinating mechanisms. The nestedness of the various governance mechanisms that shape international relations is impressive and calls for a much richer analysis of the consequences of this new phase in internationalization. In spite of a creeping protectionism, the interdependence among nations has grown quite continuously in recent years, with only marginal and temporary slowdowns. But it is an inappropriate extrapolation to assume that the world economy now operates according to a single and unifying mechanism, i.e., market coordination.

This book challenges the relevance of the concept of globalization, for the evidence that the world is converging toward one global social system of production is simply not convincing. Even though the number of firms operating across borders is increasing, this does not mean that there is a convergence of socioeconomic systems or "regulation" modes (Ohmae, 1991). Such a fashionable interpretation is built on the assumptions that three major conditions exist: a complete globalization of factor markets (finance, natural resources, and highly skilled labor), the integration of product markets that can deliver anywhere a single price for the same good once exchange rates and transportation costs are taken into account, and finally the high mobility and transferability of modern technologies. Such an interpretation assumes that social systems of production would then converge toward the one best way and deliver equivalent productivity levels and standards of living.

However, the assumptions underlying such a globalization framework rest on weak foundations. First, it is true that financial markets are more integrated than ever. But since national structural competitiveness and macroeconomic policies continue to be different, nominal and real interest rates do not converge, even within the European Union. Thus, strong currency countries continue to benefit from lower interest payments, and this has facilitated the competitiveness of the Japanese and German social systems of production. Labor continues to be basically immobile, with the exception of those with low and high skills. For this reason, foreign investment is partially directed toward pools of skilled, disciplined, and/or low-paid labor in specific localities.

Second, production niches have not totally disappeared due to fierce international competition. The same goods continue to experience large price differentials across nations, according to the relative competitiveness of specific social systems of production and the products which they excel in producing (Hollingsworth, Schmitter, and Streeck, 1994: 270–300). The automobile industry is a good example of such a phenomenon. Even if large firms are transnational, their pricing policies are still oligopolistic. Furthermore, because of the large variability of exchange rates during the past two decades, the convergence of production costs (measured in a common currency) has not occurred.

Third, many modern technologies require knowledge based on learning by doing and/or learning by using. The blueprint of the recent Toyota factory, along with multiple visits of foreign managers and workers to Japan, have not formed a sufficient condition for Japanese quality standards and productivity levels to diffuse to other societies with different social systems of production. Similarly, information and knowledge can be borrowed and used profitably only if firms have a sufficient expertise in related scientific and technological fields. Thus, localization and history are important for implementing alternative social systems of production. The path dependence of specific institutional arrangements in each society places constraints on its capacity to mimic the social systems of production of other societies (Whitley and Hollingsworth, 1996, forthcoming).

From a theoretical standpoint, the coexistence of different social systems of production is more likely than their convergence. Obviously, it is quite logical for actors to provide different solutions to problems when they face different training systems, industrial relations systems, interest rates, real wages, public infrastructures, and tax and credit systems. But even if all these conditions were the same, different norms, rules, and value systems would still lead actors to provide different solutions to identical issues. For example, the training of workers is organized quite differently in Germany, Japan, and Sweden, but nevertheless these three economies benefit from a good skills portfolio. Differences in historical traditions lead to variability in norms and rules that produce different solutions to the same problems.

According to their social capabilities, the economies of different societies are more or less able to maintain different social systems of production and to sustain external competition. Thus a specialization process takes place across the globe, promoting relatively efficient social systems of production and sectors and reducing the share of less competitive sectors (Hollingsworth, Schmitter, and Streeck, 1994; Chapter 11). The international economy is likely to have far into the future the coexistence of quasi-specialization among societies, sustained by diverse social systems of production. This is a second reason for a diverging rather than a converging pattern of social systems of production at the global level. The process by which a social system of production evolves in a society is usually quite slow and does not display laser precision: Low wages and interest rates may compensate for obsolete technologies, and inefficient public infrastructures may hinder private competitiveness. Such examples are indeed quite numerous. North (1990) even argues that most institutions are inefficient. This is not a surprise since institutions have to define the mutual relationships among agents, a much more important role than achieving pure economic performance. The mechanisms for selecting institutions by competition are slow and partial, and such processes cannot effectively make choices among highly complementary institutional arrangements. Thus institutional convergence, broadly defined, either is false or only takes place over very long periods of history. But in the short term, regional and national institutions are extremely important and delineate very different socioeconomic equilibria.

A DOUBLE SHIFT IN REGULATION MODES

The diffusion of a market ideology across the globe, the intensification of foreign competition, the increasing sophistication of financial markets, and the loss of autonomy of nation-states constitute a threat for many national institutional arrangements. In other words, some trends toward the internationalization of the economy of individual countries suggest the emergence of transnational rules of the game (GATT, NAFTA, Maastricht Treaty, etc.), thus removing the space for maneuver by nation-states. On the other hand, the evolution toward new social systems of production has prompted the call for more localized institutional arrangements – at least for some manufacturing sectors (Sabel, 1988; Zeitlin, 1995). Thus, the subject of subnational regional economies is very much part of our consciousness. These two opposite movements suggest a double shift from the nation-state to supernational institutional arrangements on the one side and on the other to reemerging subnational regional economies. This double shift suggests a much more complex outlook than the simplistic vision of omniscient market mechanisms. Several examples illustrate the complexity of global trends during the 1980s and 1990s. See Table 14-2.

The management of money continues to be an important function of the nation-state, but the degree of state capacity to carry out this activity has been restricted primarily due to the surge of financial innovations and short run movements across national borders. The stabilization of exchange rates within the European Monetary System has reduced the ability of member states to use interest rates and exchange rates to solve internal problems. If a single European currency were to be instituted in the future, each national economy would then experience a loss of national autonomy with regard to monetary seigniorage. Similarly, the idea of a single European market assumes that the rules of competition will be monitored at a continental level. This also assumes a shift in the form of competition toward supranationality. Moreover, when alliances and partnerships take place among multinationals operating in different countries, cooperation and competition among firms is transferred to the global level. Indeed, as a result of the General Agreement on Tariffs and Trade (GATT) and the World Trade Organization,

Table 14-2. The Correspondence Between Alternative Institutional Arrangements and Level of Coordination

	Institutional arrangements			
Level of coordination	Markets	Networks	Associations	State
1. Local district	*	** Third Italy Silicon Valley	** Guilds, craft unions, business associations	R&D** Education and training***
2. Regions	*	** South Germany	* Business associations	R&D** Education and training***
3. Nations	** (During Fordist era)	* Promotional networks in U.S. (1950–70)	** Labor unions Business associations	Defense** Taxes*
4. Continental zones	** Financial services	*** Joint ventures, licensing agreements, sales and distributional ties	Formally existing but not very effective	Interest and exchange rates**
5. World	** Financial services	*** Joint ventures, licensing agreements, sales and distributional ties	Very weak when existing	Trade regulations** Interest and exchange rates**

   * Coordination weak to moderately effective
  ** Coordination moderately effective
*** Coordination very effective

trade regulations increasingly prevail at the international level and interfere more or less significantly with laws and industrial policies designed by particular states in order to enhance their society's competitiveness.

At the same time, some public interventions are easier to implement at a regional rather than at a national level. Research and development policies, training and education programs, public infrastructures, international marketing strategies, and subsidies and tax reductions increasingly appear to be more efficient when designed by concertation among local business associations, local or regional banks, unions, civil servants, and local governments. Indeed, one observes that the more competitive manufacturing sectors in Germany, Italy, Denmark, and Japan have usually benefited from strong and rather coherent institutional configurations of a regional nature (Hollingsworth, Schmitter, and Streeck, 1994; Pyke, Becattini, and Sengenberger, 1991; Sabel, 1988; Streeck, 1991). When trust, solidarity, and exact delivery are required, local economies experience many advantages. Thus even the most centralized countries such as France have been trying to organize the revival of small and medium-sized firms as well as regional and local districts in order to enhance competitiveness (Hage, 1995, forthcoming; Vickery, 1986).

Consequently, the national state is subjected to a double weakening by supranationalization on one side and regionalization on the other. What is left to the nation-state? Certainly, there remains a sense of national solidarity among citizens. Moreover, tax and welfare systems will long remain within the orbit of the state. Nevertheless, the intellectual and practical challenges associated with the double shift in regulatory modes is very much a fact in the political life of advanced industrial societies. Whereas a century-long legacy has progressively shaped sophisticated political institutions at the nation-state level, the drastic transformations observed during the last two decades have created a double gap between the new economic requirements and the existing political order.

At the supranational level, it has been quite difficult to develop a set of institutional arrangements equivalent to the national state (Hall, 1994). Just to take a single example, the European Community institutions have not compensated for the erosion of each constituent national state brought about by the internationalization of trade, production, and finance. One observes only partial or shaky international arrangements, whether at the sectoral level (microelectronics, car industry) or at the continental level (NAFTA, Maastricht treaty) (Boyer and Drache, 1996).

Concerning the subnational shift, it has been very difficult for highly centralized states to organize the decentralization of political and economic decisions at an appropriate level, whether regional or local (industrial districts, large cities, etc.). Therefore, in the 1990s, the nations that exhibit the more efficient social systems of production tend to benefit from densely organized regional economies: Germany, Japan, and Italy. If this diagnosis is correct, the double shift, which erodes the adequacy of the previous nation-state configurations, simultaneously alters the competitiveness of industrialized and industrializing countries. Similarly, the scope of various coordination mechanisms is altered by this two-sided movement away from the centrality of the nation-state.

Markets, networks, associations, and states have unequal abilities to cope efficiently with transnationalization and regionalization. From an historical perspective, markets appear to be the most pervasive coordinating mechanism, having the capacity to be extended from the local marketplace to fully integrated financial markets operating continuously, 24 hours a day throughout the world. Consequently, economic policies designed by the state are very much influenced by financial traders, who continuously reassess the viability of public and external deficits, unemployment rates, the size of political majorities, and so on.

Thus far, the history of European integration demonstrates that constructing the components of a supranational state is not an easy task and will require several decades to implement just the minimalist state-led regulations or principles at the level of the European Union. Meantime, the power of subnational regional states is still problematic by comparison with the power and omnipresence of the globalizing tendencies of financial markets – especially in the United States and the United Kingdom where industrial districts are weakly developed (Zeitlin, 1995).

By contrast, networks can be extended at the international level, provided that the number of the constituents is restricted and if the common interest is clear enough. Strategic alliances between two or more multinational firms have become increasingly common. Some are short-term in nature, while others appear to be long-lasting. Of course, strategic alliances at the global level are not a new phenomenon. But historically, they were aimed primarily at reducing the capital investment required by individual firms and at lowering the risks related to the entry into new markets. But in the contemporary world, strategic alliances at the global level are also increasingly associated with the rising speed of technological change. Partners increasingly participate in strategic alliances in order to diversify the risks involved in developing new technologies and to take advantage of other actors' developmental skills. However, there are many varieties of strategic alliances. Some involve technical exchange and cross-licensing, sales and distribution ties, while others involve joint development of products (Contractor and Lorange, 1988; Ohmae, 1985; Perlmutter and Heenan, 1986; Pucik, 1988).

Meantime, some types of networks are more easily developed at the regional or local than at the international level. In some areas, the network of firms is so dense that they take on the character of industrial districts. But for these to exist, there must be a configuration of regulatory institutions for the provision of common services and the resolution of internal conflicts. In short, firms must be embedded in a dense institutional environment with the capability of providing collective goods for training, research, and development and the resolution of conflicts between labor and capital (Pyke and Sengenberger, 1992; Zeitlin, 1995).

Finally, business associations are quite difficult to build at a transnational level. Most business associations remain local or national and their Europeanization is indeed limited, unless they already existed at a sectoral level in order to monitor competition. The organizational dilemma at the international level is even more severe for labor unions, which are usually divided along political or religious lines and national frontiers. Thus, as the double shift in regulation occurs, trade unions and business associations may well weaken at the level of the nation-state and remain extremely weak at the global and transnational level, while their strength at the subnational regional level is more variable both within and across countries. All of this discussion suggests that regulatory modes at the level of the nation-state – whether the polity, unions, or associations – could in the future experience further decline in their efficacy.

CONCLUSION

FROM NATIONAL EMBEDDEDNESS TO A COMPLEX NESTED STRUCTURE OF INSTITUTIONAL ARRANGEMENTS

These observations raise the issue of the recombination of economic institutions at various spatial levels (e.g., subnational region, nation-state, global). The 1990s are far from the 1960s, when the basic institutional arrangements were embedded mainly, if not totally, at the level of the nation-state (see Figure 14-6).

During the sixties, an international regulatory regime provided predictability and permitted ambitious national strategies, at least in OECD member countries. High growth dividends brought about an increase in welfare and tended to consolidate national compromises between labor and capital. True, regional economies experienced uneven growth, but due to redistributive mechanisms, undesirable consequences of such imbalances were minimized. With the passage of time, however, the embeddedness of economic institutions at the level of the nation-state has been progressively eroded. Because the search for increasing returns to scale has made the domestic market too small, firms increasingly must compete in the international economy if they are to survive, but the international economy has become an arena of fierce competition. Moreover, financial innovations have permeated and vigorously asserted themselves at the international level. The economic interactions among nations have increased, with rising interde-

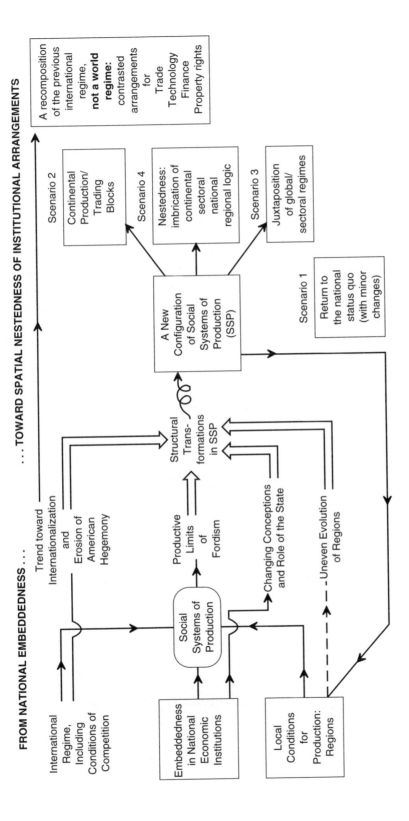

Figure 14-6. The Change in Basic Institutional Arrangements

pendence among nations. The American economy is no longer shielded from other major economic competitors. National economies are now nested into a set of interdependent flows involving trade, finance, and technology, and this has created new problems for nation-states.

It is useful to contrast the post–World War II period of *embeddedness* of national institutions with the present *nestedness* of major institutions which is a complex intertwining of institutions at all levels of the world, from the global arena to the regional level, also including nation-states and such continental entities as NAFTA and the European Union. The concept of nestedness implies several distinct but currently interacting features:

First, the institutional arrangements from the Fordist era that tended to operate mainly at the national level, but with few constraints from the supernational or subnational levels, are now dependent on a variety of international trends as well as on the capability of subregional entities. This is the first and basic meaning of nestedness. Simultaneously, market-type activities tend to escape domestic boundaries, and they increasingly exercise more and more influence on regions and nations all over the world.

Second, nestedness implies that multifaceted causality runs in virtually all directions among the various levels of society: nations, sectors, free trade zones, international regimes, supernational regions, large cities, and even small but well-specialized localities interact according to unprecedented configurations. This is a novelty with respect to most, if not all, past economic regimes. It is neither a bottom-up approach, from purely local competitiveness toward an anonymous world market, as pure economic theory might imply, nor is it a top-down mechanism. In Figure 14-7 we can observe how the various levels are interacting as an entire system.

The third feature of nestedness is that no single authority, let it be supernational, continental, national, or local, has the power to monitor and to regulate such a complex system. If, for example, a national government wishes to curb the negative influences of highly speculative financial markets operating at the world level, its strategy might end with consequences worse than taking no action – possibly substantial currency depreciation, higher interest rates, and/or foreign capital flight. Such a system is very different from the consequences that would have followed from similar regulations in the 1960s. Today, the emerging international forces are generally not able to complete a redefinition of national institutions. International trade agreements, for example, are concerned with the nature of products and public subsidies, but hardly at all with the type of organizations, policies, and resources necessary for the delivery of social welfare services within a particular country. Hence competitive wars tend to take place among countries, based on arguments of social dumping, and with very serious consequences. There is one more reason why coherence in economic coordination is becoming increasingly difficult: All the institutional arrangements for implementing the various functions of society do not occur at the same level. For example, finance and money tend to be highly internationalized, whereas welfare remains strictly limited to the national boundaries. Hence, possible conflicts between contradictory forces operate at different levels: Business may prefer market freedom and may operate at the subnational, nation-state, and global level, while the overall population may look to the nation-state to protect them at the subnational level from the adverse effects of market logic.

Nestedness makes economic policy and institutional change more difficult than ever, since no supranational central authority is effectively able to monitor effectively a series of innovations. Some developments appear initially to be highly innovative but then turn counterproductive when inserted into the whole system. For example, financial deregulation in the late 1970s was initially assumed to promote more efficiency in capital allocation across countries and sectors. Fifteen years later, however, the "short-termism" of financial markets increasingly permeated most areas of economic, social, and political life, thus introducing major and new sources of instability in economic expectations. Thus, the global effectiveness of financial deregulation may be mitigated. Some experts argue that the effects of financial deregulations have been negative, and they propose to tax "short-run" capital movements. But no single country has an interest in doing so alone. Thus, no country takes action to confront the problems. This is a prisoner dilemma type of configuration that is an indirect consequence of the nestedness of national and international institutions.

This perspective about the diffusion of power leads to the speculation that the evolution of capitalist institutions will produce a series of governance modes at various levels of society. This is exhibited by scenario four in Figure 14-7 (alternative scenarios will be discussed later). Competition might be coordinated partially at a *continental level* by free trade agreements, under the supervision of general rules of the game established worldwide. This however, would not exclude some specific *sectoral arrangements* between two countries concerning the auto and textile industries, movies, or agriculture. Individual societies at the level of the nation-state may regulate the way health care and welfare benefits are distributed according to long-run *national legacies*. But, again, the most localized interactions are plugged into the world international system, as demonstrated by the problems of pollution, ozone layer, biological diversity, and many other issues dealt with by the Rio world summit in the early 1990s. Acute conflicts of interest among industrialized and industrializing as well as poor and rich countries have made compromise especially difficult to achieve.

Given the structural character of such a shift from national embeddedness of economic institutions to their nestedness within a multilevel system, the national sources of competitiveness have been altered and have become much more complex. The quality of national systems of innovation, the nature of industrial relations systems, the level of skills, and the ability of economic actors to respond quickly to economic fluctuations and uncertainties mean that the nature of interactions among firms, between employees and employers, and between private business and public authorities have become crucial for the performance of national economies. But increasingly, the complexity and dynamism of these economies must be expressed at the subnational, regional, or local level. Nevertheless, the nature of the linkages between national and regional institutions plays an important role in shaping the ability of societies to evolve into different social systems of production. And some of the previous chapters provide examples of how economic dynamism is influenced by the linkages between local and national institutions. For example, the high quality of differentiated production in Germany results, in large part, from the combination of a decentralized system organized at the level of the länder which is intricately linked with a national system of codetermination (Herrigel, 1995). But in Britain these tight linkages between regional and national institutions are not so well established. As a result, there are weakly developed industrial districts and a weakly performing national economy (Zeitlin, 1995). Like Germany, Japan is a good example of complementarity between dense localized networks (Nagoya City as a company town) and strong national institutions (major banks, spring offensives, development agencies, etc.). In the contemporary world, regional, national, and international institutions must be nested together. The British case suggests how weakly developed regional structures may erode the vitality of previously quite successful institutional arrangements at the level of the nation-state (Zeitlin, 1995).

In more analytical terms, the institutional arrangements that at one time were congruent at the national levels are now more dispersed at multiple spatial levels (see Figure 14-7). Impressive economic performance now requires that economic actors be well coordinated at all spatial areas simultaneously. In short, actors must be nested in institutional arrangements that will be linked at all levels of reality. At the international level, for example, a trade regime is regulated by international agreements and tends to be much more multilateral than bilateral in nature: Rules are increasingly more of a constraint than a choice made by an individual nation-state. Increasingly, manufacturing and service firms are engaged in international competition. Moreover, the monetary systems are becoming more transnational in nature. For example, currency adjustments are no longer a safety

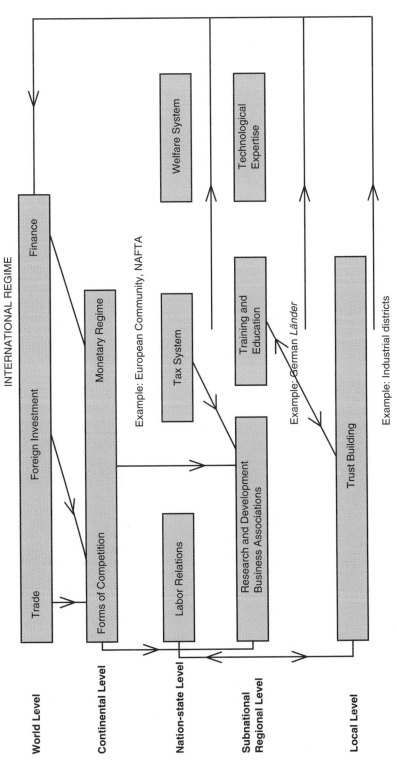

INTERNATIONAL REGIME

| World Level | Trade | Foreign Investment | Finance |
| Continental Level | Forms of Competition | Monetary Regime |

Example: European Community, NAFTA

| Nation-state Level | Labor Relations | Tax System | Welfare System |

| Subnational Regional Level | Research and Development Business Associations | Training and Education | Technological Expertise |

Example: German *Länder*

| Local Level | Trust Building |

Example: Industrial districts

Figure 14-7. The Nestedness of Institutional Arrangements

valve to be manipulated in response to extra competitiveness or inferior performance at the level of the nation-state. Indeed, nation-states have lost much of their capacity to control interest and exchange rates (Hall, 1994, 1996). Declining autonomy over these issues diminishes the capacity of states to regulate social policy and many other policy areas.

Conversely, the constitutional order that allocates power and resources differently between central and local authorities increasingly plays a role in shaping the ability of firms in a particular country to compete in the international arena. Thus, the parts of each system have become far more interdependent than during the 1960s, and the increasingly complex distribution of power and resources across geographical levels is further evidence of how economic institutions have become nested in a multiple world of reality.

Nevertheless, coordination of economic actors at the level of the nation-state has not completely disappeared and will probably not vanish, since it remains the level at which some social solidarity is still embedded and channeled into labor laws, a national tax system, and many welfare services. However, the future of many national institutional arrangements is extremely uncertain. So many contradictory forces are operating that it is difficult to imagine that the institutional environment into which firms were embedded in the 1960s will survive another generation. Irreversible forces have developed forms of social systems of production that are transnational, have shifted the division of labor among regions, and have transformed the relations between the state and the economy. As a result of these changes, one can imagine four different scenarios (see right side of Figure 14-6):

- *Scenario One:* If the contradictions inherent in the internationalization of the economy become too acute (mass and persisting unemployment, rising inequality, major regional imbalances, xenophobist movements, etc.), some governments may attempt to return to a so-called "Golden Age" by becoming increasingly nationalistic and by erecting barriers to finance, trade, and migration of persons. Given the extreme division of labor and interdependencies that now operate at the international level, such nationalistic policies for any particular country would lead to a substantial reduction in productivity and standards of living. Should this occur, any state implementing such policies would be acting contrary to its society's general economic welfare. Indeed, such a state would suffer such a major loss in legitimacy that such policies could not long be sustained.
- *Scenario Two:* Considering the emergence of the European Union, the North American Free Trade Area, and the further development of an

Asian trading block, one can easily imagine that increased international economic uncertainty will foster the development of monetary and economic zones designed to minimize the discrepancies in interest and exchange rates originating from the two other zones of the triad. In varying degrees, this scenario has been operating for more than a decade, and further developments along these lines are expected. Nevertheless, conflicting national interests within particular trading blocs might collide and provoke states to flirt with the first scenario, i.e., the effort to seek more autonomy at the level of individual nation-states. One could clearly observe this type of tension operating among Britain, Southern Europe, and the European Community during the period between 1990 and 1996.

- *Scenario Three:* This assumes that the juxtaposition of numerous conflicting sectoral and/or global regulatory regimes will nevertheless be sufficient to bring compatibility among conflicting interests, unequal competitiveness, and diverging trajectories among nations. For example, a GATT agreement on agricultural trade; the replacement of GATT by the WTO in order to remove bilateral self-restraint accords in the car, electronic, textile, and other industries; international regulation of banking and finance; a minimal social charter under the aegis of ILO; the development and implementation of an ecological tax for industrialized and industrializing countries; a codification of patents and intellectual rights; and a powerful group of seven to ten nation-states attempting to regulate interest and exchange rates – all of these things could eventually become a relatively coherent system of coordination, without any explicit design to do so. This would be a self-building of institutions at the international level, in accordance with an Austrian vision "à la Hayek." However, the likelihood of such a pluralistic system of coordination without a powerful state or a single hegemon to orchestrate such behavior and to act as an enforcer appears to be problematic.

- *Scenario Four:* The nestedness of a complex system of regional, national, continental, and world institutional arrangements into a legacy of national intervention, complemented by sectoral agreements, has been emerging for at least a decade. Nestedness means that subnational regimes, sectoral, national, and international logics are intertwined – with none being dominant – in a two-sided type of causality. For example, decisions in Brussels about economic regulations for the European Union have an increasing impact on the competitiveness of single nation-states, subnational regional dynamics, and the capacity of nation-states to shape their own economic and social policies. At the same time the cohesiveness of national and subnational regional interests of member states plays a role in shaping the regulations designed in Brussels. Another example of nestedness refers to the links among product, credit, and labor markets at multiple spatial levels. In the 1960s, wage formation was embedded in a variety of national compromises between capital and labor, and monetary and exchange rate policies were designed to reflect the specificity of national political and economic institutions (Hall, 1986). In the 1990s, however, the intense international competition of product markets and the strong flows of money across countries have undermined the strength of national systems of industrial relations and labor contracts. In some advanced industrial societies, low wages are threatening to become a basic ingredient in shaping national competitiveness and the capacity of a society to attract foreign capital. All of this is intertwined at the subnational regional, national, continental, and global levels and feeds back and influences the degree of stability and instability of the economy of any nation state (Mueller and Loveridge, 1995).

Thus in the 1960s, the way that institutions were embedded at the level of the nation-state influenced not only behavior and economic performance at the level of subnational regions but also the coordination of the international economy. But in the 1990s, the world trade regime and continental trade zones influence national policies and the structure and behavior of subnational regional groups. The flexibility and nature of national labor markets are subject to a double squeeze: from the outside by the international financial regime and from the inside by the ability of subnational regional groups to manufacture cooperation and trust among themselves.

How all of this fourth scenario will play out is uncertain, even though this scenario presently has considerable dynamism to it. Where is the theory that allows us to understand and guide such a process? Will public opinion accept such a complex set of institutional arrangements, especially in weaker countries that are more adversely affected by the ongoing transnationalization? What is the capacity of public authorities to build barriers to the process of transnationalization in order to preserve distinctive national institutions, macroeconomic performance, and high employment? Will the "satanic mills" created by the market that Karl Polanyi had discussed during the 1940s undermine the potential for social solidarity? Will nation-states have the capacity to respond to economic, social, and political innovations sufficiently quickly in order to prevent economic crises – even the repetition of a great depression?

The future is very much open, but a perspective on long-term historical trends suggests that taming the market has always been more rewarding over the longer term than myopically following it. Moreover, modern economic theory is slowly converging toward such a vision: Only short-run and marginal choices can be left to the market, whereas imaginative collective forms of coordination are addressing many of the more important social and political issues of our time. The most competitive firms, regions, or nations are not mimicking the market but on the contrary, they are struggling to manufacture consensus, trust, collective forms of governance, and long-term vision. The core message of this book suggests unconventional conclusions about economic policies for the future. As neo-Polanyians, we must move away from the rhetoric of what free marketers promise and attempt to convince our societies to build more livable communities and to construct new forms of a mixed economy. But as our institutions are increasingly nested in a world of subnational regions, nation-states, and continental and global regimes, do we have the capacity to govern ourselves democratically? Clearly one of the major challenges of our time is to create a new theory of democracy for governing institutions nested in a world of unprecedented complexity, one in which subnational regions, nation-states, and continental and global regimes are all intricately linked.

REFERENCES

Adams, William James. 1989. *Restructuring the French Economy: Government and the Rise of Market Competition Since World War II*. Washington: Brookings Institution.

Aglietta, Michel. 1982. *Regulation and Crisis of Capitalism*. New York: Monthly Review Press.

Akerlof, Georges A. 1984. *Economic Theorist's Book of Tales*. Cambridge: Cambridge University Press.

Alter, Catherine and Jerald Hage. 1993. *Organizations Working Together: Coordination in Interorganizational Networks*. Newbury Park, Cal.: Sage.

Amsden, Alice. 1989. *Asia's Next Giant: South Korea and Late Industrialization*. New York: Oxford University Press.

André, Christine and Robert Delorme. 1980. "Matériaux pour une comparaison internationale des dépenses publiques en longue période. Le cas de six pays industrialisés." *Statistiques et Etudes Financieres*. Paris: Ministère de l'Economie, des Finances et du Budget. No. ISSN 0015-9654.

Aoki, Masahiko. 1988. *Information, Incentives and Bargaining in the Japanese Economy*. Cambridge: Cambridge University Press.

Attali, Jacques. 1981. *Les trois mondes. Pour une théorie de l'après-crise*. Paris: Fayard

Baker, Wayne. 1994. *Networking Smart*. New York: McGraw-Hill.

Benko, Georges and Alain Lipietz, eds. 1989. *Les régions qui gagnent! Districts et réseaux: les nouveaux paradigmes de la géo-politique*. Paris: PUF, Economie en Liberté.

Boyer, Robert. 1979. "Wage Formation in Historical Perspective: The French Experience." *Cambridge Journal of Economics*. 3: 99–118.

———. 1987. "Régulation." In John Eatwell, Murray Milgate, and Peter Newman, eds. *The New Palgrave? A Dictionary of Economics*, 3 vol. London: Macmillan Press. Pp. 126–28.

———. 1990a. *The Regulation School. A Critical Introduction*. New York: Columbia University Press.

———. 1991. "Capital Labor Relation and Wage Formation: Continuities and Changes of National Trajectories Among OECD Countries." In Toshiyuki Mizogushi, ed. *Making Economies More Efficient and Equitable: Factors Determining Income Distribution*. Tokyo: Kinokuniya Company Ltd. and Oxford: Oxford University Press. Pp. 297–340.

———. 1993. "D'une série de National Labour Standards à un European Monetary Standard?" *Recherches Economiques de Louvain*. 59 (1–2): 119–53.

———. 1995. *The Capital Labor Relations in OECD Countries: From the Fordist "Golden Age" to Contrasted National Trajectories*. Document de travail CEPREMAP, 9020. September.

Boyer, Robert and Daniel Drache. 1996. *The Future of Nations and the Limits of Markets*. London: Routledge.

Boyer, Robert and Jacques Mistral. 1982. *Accumulation, Inflation, Crises*, 2nd ed. Paris: Presses Universitaires de France.

Boyer, Robert and André Orléan. 1991. Les transformations des conventions salariales entre theorie et histoire: d'Henry Ford au fordisme. *Revue Economique*. 42 (March): 233–72.

———. 1992. "How Do Conventions Evolve?" *Journal of Evolutionary Economics*. 2: 165–77.

Boyer, Robert and Yves Saillard, eds. 1995. *La theorie de la regulation: Etat des savoirs*. Paris: La decouverte.

Braudel, Fernand. 1979. *Civilisation matérielle, économie et capitalisme XV-XVIIIe siècles*, 3 vols. Paris: Armand Colin.

Calleo, David. 1982. *The Imperious Economy*. Cambridge: Harvard University Press.

———. 1992. *The Bankrupting of America: How the Federal Budget is Impoverishing the Nation*. New York: William Morrow and Co.

Campbell, John, J. Rogers Hollingsworth, and Leon Lindberg, eds. 1991. *The Governance of the American Economy*. Cambridge and New York: Cambridge University Press.

Campbell, John and Leon Lindberg. 1990. "Property Rights and the Organization of Economic Activity by the State." *American Sociological Review*. 55.

Chandler, Alfred D. 1969. *Strategy and Structure: Chapters in the History of the American Industrial Enterprise*. Cambridge: MIT Press.

———. 1977. *The Visible Hand: The Managerial Revolution in American Business*. Cambridge: Harvard University Press.

———. 1990. *Scale and Scope: The Dynamics of Industrial Capitalism*. Cambridge: Harvard University Press.

Contractor, F. and P. Lorange, eds. 1988. *Cooperative Strategies in International Business*. Lexington, Mass.: Lexington Books.

Daley, Anthony, ed. 1996. *The Mitterrand Era*. London: Macmillan.

David, Paul. 1988. "Path-Dependence: Putting the Past in the Future of Economics." *IMSS Technical Report.* No. 533 Stanford University.

Denzau, Arthur T. and Douglass North. 1994. "Shared Mental Models: Ideologies and Institutions," *Kyklos.* 47 (1): 3–31.

d'Iribarne, Ph. 1990. *Le chômage paradoxal.* Paris: PUF, Economie en Liberté.

Dore, Ronald. 1973. *British Factory, Japanese Factory: The Origins of Diversity in Industrial Relations.* Berkeley: University of California Press.

1983. "Goodwill and the Spirit of Market Capitalism." *The British Journal of Sociology.* 34: 459–82.

1986. *Flexible Rigidities: Industrial Policy and Structural Adjustment in the Japanese Economy, 1970–1980.* Stanford: Stanford University Press.

Dumenil, Gérard and Dominque Lévy. 1989. "Micro Adjustment Behavior and Macro Stability." *Seoul Journal of Economics.* 2 (1): 1–37.

Dumez, H. and A. Jeunemaitre. 1991. *La concurrence en Europe.* Paris: Seuil.

Eggertsson, Thrainn. 1990. *Economic Behavior and Institutions.* Cambridge: Cambridge University Press.

Etzioni, Amitai. 1988. *The Moral Dimension: Towards a New Economics.* New York: Free Press.

Friedland, Roger and A. F. Robertson, eds. 1990. *Beyond the Market Place: Rethinking Economy and Society.* New York: Aldine de Gruyter.

Friedman, David. 1988. *The Misunderstood Miracle: Industrial Development and Political Change in Japan.* Ithaca: Cornell University Press.

Fukuyama, Francis. 1995. *Trust: Social Virtues and the Creation of Prosperity.* New York: Free Press.

Furubotn, E. and Rudolf Richter, eds. 1991. *The New Institutional Economics.* Tübingen: J. C. B. Mohr.

Gambetta, D., ed. 1988. *Trust.* Oxford: Basil Blackwell.

Gerlach, Michael. 1992. *Alliance Capitalism: The Social Organization of Japanese Business.* Berkeley: University of California Press.

Gerschenkron, Alexander. 1962. *Economic Backwardness in Historical Perspective.* Cambridge: Harvard University Press.

Gilpin, Robert. 1987. *The Political Economy of International Relations.* Princeton: Princeton University Press.

Granovetter, Mark. 1984. "Small Is Beautiful: Labor Markets and Establishment Size." *American Sociological Review.* 49: 323–34.

1985. "Economic Action and Social Structures: The Problem of Embeddedness." *American Journal of Sociology.* 91: 481–510.

1992. "Economic Institutions as Social Constructions: A Framework of Analysis." *Acta Sociologica.* 35: 3–12.

1993. "Coase Revisited: Business Groups in the Modern Economy." Paper presented for ASSI Conference on Hierarchies, Markets, Power in the Economy: Theories and Lessons from History. December 15–17. Milan, Italy.

Grossman, S. and Joseph Stiglitz. 1980. "On the Impossibility of Informationally Efficient Markets." *American Economic Review.* 70: 393–408.

Hage, Jerald. 1996, forthcoming. "The Social System of Production in France." In J. Rogers Hollingsworth, Richard Whitely, and Jerald Hage, eds. *Firms, Markets, and Production Systems in Comparative Perspective.*

Hage, Jerald and Zhongren Jing. 1996, forthcoming. "Adaptive Costs: A New Paradigm for the Choice of Organization Form." In J. Rogers Hollingsworth, ed. *Social Actors and the Embeddedness of Institutions.* New York: M. E. Sharpe.

Hall, Peter A. 1986. *Governing the Economy.* New York: Oxford University Press.

    1994. "Central Bank Independence and Coordinated Wage Bargaining: Their Interaction in Germany and Europe." *German Politics and Society.* 31: 1–23.

    1996. "From One Modernization Strategy to Another: The Character and Consequences of Recent Economic Policy in France." (Paper Presented to Conference of Europeanists, Chicago, Illinois, March 15, 1996).

Hamilton, Gary, ed. 1991. *Business Networks and Economic Development in East and Southeast Asia.* Hong Kong: Centre of Asian Studies, Occasional Papers and Monographs, No. 99. University of Hong Kong.

Hamilton, Gary and Nicole Biggart. 1988. "Markets, Culture, and Authority: A Comparative Analysis of Management and Organization in the Far East." *American Journal of Sociology* (Supplement). 94: S52–S94.

Hamilton, Gary and Cheng-Shu Kao. 1991. "The Institutional Foundations of Chinese Business: The Family Firm in Taiwan." In Craig Calhoun, ed. *Comparative Social Research (Vol. 12): Business Institutions.* Greenwich, Conn.: JAI Press. Pp. 135–151.

Hamilton, Gary, Marco Orrù, and Nicole Biggart. 1987. "Enterprise Groups in East Asia: An Organizational Analysis. *Shoken Keizai* (Financial Economic Review). September.

Hamilton, Gary, William Zeile, and Wan-Jin-Kim. 1990. "The Network Structures of East Asian Economies." In S. R. Clegg and S. G. Redding, *Capitalism in Contrasting Cultures.* Berlin: de Gruyter. Pp. 105–129.

Hayek, Friedrich A. 1980. *Individualism and Economic Order.* Chicago and London: University of Chicago Press.

    1976–82. *Law, Legislation and Liberty,* 3 vols. Chicago: University of Chicago Press.

Hechter, Michael. 1987. *Principles of Group Solidarity.* Berkeley and London: University of California Press.

Herrigel, Gary. 1995. *Industrial Constructions: The Sources of German Industrial Power.* New York: Cambridge University Press.

Hirsch, Fred. 1977. *Social Limits to Growth.* London: Routledge and Kegan Paul.

Hirschmann, Albert O. 1977. *The Passions and the Interests: Political Arguments for Capitalism Before Its Triumph.* Princeton: Princeton University Press.

Hollingsworth, J. Rogers 1991. "The Logic of Coordinating American Manufacturing Sectors." In John C. Campbell, J. Rogers Hollingsworth, and Leon Lindberg, eds. *Governance of the American Economy.* New York: Cambridge Press. Pp. 3–34.

    1994. "Rethinking the Theory of the Liberal State: Towards a Conception of Collective Responsibility, Permanent Mobilization, and Citizenship." Paper presented before American Sociological Association, August 7, 1994, Los Angeles, California.

    1996, forthcoming. "The Social System of Production in the United States." In J. Rogers Hollingsworth, Richard Whitley, and Jerald Hage, eds. *Firms, Markets, and Production Systems in Comparative Perspective.*

Hollingsworth, J. Rogers and Leon Lindberg. 1985. "The Role of Markets, Clans, Hierarchies, and Associative Behavior." In Wolfgang Streeck and Philippe Schmitter, eds. *Private Interest Government: Beyond Market and State.* London and Beverly Hills: Sage. Pp. 221–54.

Hollingsworth, J. Rogers, Philippe C. Schmitter, and Wolfgang Streeck, eds. 1994. *Governing Capitalist Economies.* New York: Oxford University Press.

Hollingsworth, J. Rogers and Wolfgang Streeck. 1994. "Countries and Sectors: Performance, Convergence, and Competitiveness." In J. Rogers Hollingsworth, Philippe C. Schmitter, and Wolfgang Streeck, eds. *Governing Capitalist Economies.* New York: Oxford University Press. Pp. 270–300.

Kaldor, Nicholas. 1939. "Speculation and Economic Stability." *Review of Economics Studies.* (October). Reprinted in *Essays on Stability and Growth.* New York: Holmes and Meier. Second edition 1960. Pp. 17–58.

Kenney, Martin and Richard Florida. 1988. "Beyond Mass Production and the Labor Process in Japan." *Politics and Society.* 16: 121–58.

Kerr, Clark, John T. Dunlap, Frederick Harbison, and C. A. Myers. 1960. *Industrialism and Industrial Man.* Cambridge: Harvard University Press.

Kindleberger, Charles P. 1978. *Manias, Panics, and Crashes: A History of Financial Crises.* New York: Basic Books.

Kumar, Krishan. 1983. "Pre-Capitalist and Non-Capitalist Factors in the Development of Capitalism: Fred Hirsch and Joseph Schumpeter." In Adrian Ellis and Krishan Kumar, eds. *Dilemmas of Liberal Democracy.* London and New York: Tavistock Publications. Pp. 148–73.

Landes, David. 1951. "French Business and the Businessman: A Social and Cultural Analysis." In Hugh Aitken, ed. *Explorations in Enterprise.* Cambridge: Harvard University Press. Pp. 184–200.

Lazonick, William. 1991. *Business Organization and the Myth of the Market Economy.* Cambridge and New York: Cambridge University Press.

Lucas, Robert. 1988. "On the Mechanisms of Economic Development." *Journal of Monetary Economics.* 72: 3–42 (July).

1993. "Making miracles." *Econometrica.* 61 (March): 251–72.

Luhmann, Niklas. 1979. *Trust and Power.* Chichester: Wiley and Sons.

Marglin, Stephen A. 1991. "Understanding Capitalism: Control Versus Efficiency." In Bo Gustafsson, ed. *Power and Economic Institutions.* Aldershot, Hants, England: Edward Elgar. Pp. 225–52.

Mathias. 1969. *The First Industrial Nation.* London: Macmillan.

Milward, Alan S. 1979. *War, Economy and Society: 1939–1945.* Berkeley and Los Angeles: University of California.

Mowery, David. 1988. *International Collaborative Venture in U.S. Manufacturing.* Cambridge: Ballinger.

Mueller, Frank and Ray Loveridge. 1995. "The 'Second Industrial Divide'? The Role of the Large Firm in the Baden-Württemberg Model." *Industrial and Corporate Change.* 4: 555–82.

North, Douglass C. 1981. *Structure and Change in Economic History.* New York: Norton.

1990. *Institutions, Institutional Change and Economic Performance.* Cambridge and New York: Cambridge University Press.

Nozick, Robert. 1974. *Anarchy, State and Utopia.* New York: Basic Books.

O'Connor, James. 1973. *The Fiscal Crisis of the State.* New York: St. Martin's Press.

OECD. 1985 *Employment Outlook.* Paris. OECD.

____. 1994. *The OECD Jobs Study: Facts, Analysis, Strategies.* Paris: OECD.

Ohmae, K. 1985. *Triad Power. The Coming Shape of Global Competition.* New York: Free Press.

____. 1991. *The Borderless World.* London: Fontana.

Perlmutter, H. V. and D. A. Heenan. 1986. "Cooperate to Compete Globally." *Harvard Business Review.* 64: 136–52.

Piore, Michael and Charles Sabel. 1984. *The Second Industrial Divide.* New York: Basic Books.

Poggi, Gianfranco. 1993. *Money and the Modern Mind: George Simmel's Philosophy of Money.* Stanford: Stanford University Press.

Polanyi, Karl. 1957. *The Great Transformation: The Political and Economic Origins of Our Time.* Boston: Beacon Press (originally published in 1944).

____. 1977. *The Livelihood of Man.* Ed. by Harry Y. Pearson. New York: Academic Press.

Polanyi-Levitt, Kari, ed. 1990. *The Life and Work of Karl Polanyi: A Celebration.* Montreal: Black Rose Books.

Powell, Walter W. 1991. "Expanding the Scope of Institutional Analysis." In Walter W. Powell and Paul J. DiMaggio, eds. *The New Institutionalism in Organizational Analysis.* Chicago and London: University of Chicago Press. Pp. 183–203.

Pucik, Vladimir. 1988. "Strategic Alliances, Organizational Learning, and Competitive Advantage." *Human Resource Management.* 27: 77–93.

Putnam, Robert D. 1993. *Making Democracy Work.* Princeton: Princeton University Press.

Pyke, F. and W. Sengenberger, eds. 1992. *Industrial Districts and Local Regeneration.* Geneva: International Institute of Labour Studies.

Pyke, Fl, G. Becattini, and W. Sengenberger. 1991. *Industrial Districts and Inter-firm Co-operation in Italy.* Geneva: International Institute for Labour Studies.

Raff, D. M. G. 1988. "Wage Determination Theory and the Five-Dollar Day at Ford." *The Journal of Economic History.* XLVIII (June): 387–99.

Romer, P. 1986. "Increasing Returns and Long-run Growth." *Journal of Political Economy.* 94: 1002–37.

____. 1990. "Endogenous Technological Change." *Journal of Political Economy.* 98 (5) pt. 2: S71–S102.

Rueff, Jacques. 1932. "Pourquoi, malgré tout, je reste libéral." In *X-Crise De la récurrence des crises économique.* Paris: Economica. Pp. 63–71.

Sabel, Charles F. 1988. "The Re-emergence of Regional Economies." In Paul Hirst and Jonathan Zeitlin, eds. *Reversing Industrial Decline.* Oxford: Berg.

____. 1991. "Moebius-Strip Organizations and Open Labor Markets: Some Consequences of the Reintegration of Conception and Education in a Volatile Economy." In Pierre Bourdieu and James S. Coleman, eds. *Social Theory for a Changing Society.* Boulder: Westview Press. Pp. 23–63.

____. 1992. "Studied Trust: Building New Forms of Cooperative in a Volatile Economy." In Frank Pyke and Werner Sengenberger, eds. *Industrial Districts and Local Economic Regeneration.* Geneva: International Institute for Labour Studies. Pp. 215–50.

Sabel, Charles F. and Jonathan Zeitlin. 1985. "Historical Alternatives to Mass Production: Politics, Markets, and Technology in Nineteenth Century Industrialization." *Past and Present.* 108 (August): 133–76.

Sargent, T. J. 1979. *Macroeconomic Theory.* New York: Academic Press.

Saxenian, Annalee. 1994. *Regional Advantage: Culture and Competition in Silicon Valley and Route 128.* Cambridge: Harvard University Press.

Schneiberg, Marc and J. Rogers Hollingsworth. 1990. "Can Transaction Cost Economics Explain Trade Associations?" In Masahiko Aoki, Bo Gustafsson, and Oliver E. Williamson, eds. *The Firm as a Nexus of Treaties.* London: Sage Publications. Pp. 320–46.

Schumpeter, Joseph A. 1976. *Capitalism, Socialism, and Democracy.* 5th ed. London: Allen and Unwin.

Simon, Herbert. 1983. *Reason in Human Affairs.* Stanford: Stanford University Press.

Smith, Charles. 1990. *Auctions: The Social Construction of Value.* Berkeley: University of California Press.

Stiglitz, Joseph. 1987. "Dependence of Quality on Price." *Journal of Economic Literature* 25: 1–48.

Stiglitz, J. and A. Weiss. 1978. "Credit Rationing in Markets with Imperfect Competition." *American Economic Review* 71: 393–410.

Storper, Michael and Bennett Harrison. 1991. "Flexibility, Hierarchy, and Regional Development: The Changing Structure of Industrial Production Systems and Their Forms of Governance in the 1990s." *Research Policy.* 20: 407–22.

Stråth, Bo. 1996, forthcoming. "Sweden's Social System of Production." In Rogers Hollingsworth, Richard Whitley, and Jerald Hage, eds. *Firms, Markets, and Production Systems in Comparative Perspective.*

Streeck, Wolfgang. 1991. "On the Institutional Conditions of Diversified Quality Production." In Egon Matzner and Wolfgang Streeck, eds. *Beyond Keynesianism: The Socio-Economics of Production and Full Employment.* Aldershot, Hants, England: Edward Elgar. Pp. 21–61.

____ 1992. *Social Institutions and Economic Performance.* Newbury Park, Cal.: Sage.

Streeck, Wolfgang and Philippe C. Schmitter. 1985. "Community, Market, State – And Associations? The Prospective Contribution of Interest Governance to Social Order." In Wolfgang Streeck and Philippe C. Schmitter, eds. *Private Interest Government: Beyond Market and State.* Beverly Hills: Sage.

Tirole, Jean. 1988. *The Theory of Industrial Organization.* Cambridge: MIT Press.

Vatter, Harold. 1985. *The US Economy in World War II.* New York: Columbia University Press.

Vickery, Lister. 1986. "France." In Paul Burns and Him Dewhurst, eds. *Small Business in Europe.* London: Macmillan. Chapter 2.

Wade, R. 1990. *Governing the Market.* Princeton: Princeton University Press.

Weir, Margaret and Theda Skocpol. 1985. "State Structures and the Possibilities for 'Keynesian' Responses to the Great Depression in Sweden, Britain, and the United States." In Peter B. Evans, Dietrich Tueschemeyer, and Theda

Skocpol, eds. *Bringing the State Back in.* Cambridge: Cambridge University Press. Pp. 107–63.

White, Harrison, 1991. *Identity and Control: A Structural Theory of Social Action.* Princeton: Princeton University Press.

Whitley, Richard. 1992a. *Business Systems in East Asia: Firms, Markets, and Societies.* London and Newbury Park: Sage.

Whitley, Richard, ed. 1992b. *European Business Systems: Firms and Markets in Their National Contexts.* London: Sage.

Whitley, Richard and J. Rogers Hollingsworth. 1996, forthcoming. "The Industrial Structuring of Market Economies." In J. Rogers Hollingsworth, Richard Whitely, and Jerald Hage, eds. *Firms, Markets, and Production Systems in Comparative Perspective.*

Williamson, Oliver. 1985. *The Economic Institutions of Capitalism.* New York: Free Press.

Zeitlin, Jonathan. 1990. *Industrial Districts and Local Economic Regeneration: Models, Institutions and Policies.* Geneva: International Institute for Labour Studies.

1995. "Why Are There No Industrial Districts in the United Kingdom?" In Arnaldo Bagnasco and Charles Sabel, ed. *Small and Medium-Sized Enterprises.* London: Francis Pinter. Pp. 98–114.

Zelizer, Viviana. 1988. "Beyond the Polemics on the Market: Establishing a Theoretical and Empirical Agenda." *Sociological Forum.* 5: 614–34.

1989. "The Social Meaning of Money: 'Special Monies.'" *American Journal of Sociology.* 95: 342–77.

INDEX

growth of, 96
hierarchical structures versus, 96
human capital, 111, 164-5
innovation and, 101-4
joint ventures, 298
organization versus, 99
particularism and, 107-8
productivity and, 104
promotional, 11, 13, 94-121
strategic alliances, 298
transnational, 467
United States, 292
New Zealand, 315
Newly industrializing countries (NIC), 344
North, Douglass, 101, 267
North Atlantic Treaty Organization (NATO), 415-6

Obligational linkages, defined, 94
Ohmae, Kenichi, 321, 341
OPEC, 343, 345
Opportunism. *See* Trust
Organization of Economic Cooperation and Development (OECD) 1994 Symposium, 329-30
Ostrom, Elinor, 164, 180-81

Paradigm shifts, 171, 181
Path-dependence, 267
Pax Americana, 342, 436, 437
Pax Britannica, 338-9
Peugeot, 250, 254, 260
Plaza Strategy, 333
Pluralism, political, 208-9
Piore, Michael, 192
Polanyi, Karl, 207, 208, 216, 434, 435, 450, 447, 477. *See also* Embeddedness hypothesis
fictitious commodities and, 63
global interdependencies, 313-14
Polanyi effect, 208. *See also* Cultural contradiction of capitalism
Policy Approach, definition of, 134
Porter, Michael, 283
Post-Fordist mass production systems, definition of, 220-1, 260
Post-World War II economic miracle, 435-8
Private interest governments (PIGs), 397-8, 422
as a governance mechanism, 417
Maastrict Accord, 401-2, 408
Production technology. *See* Technology of production
Production, social systems of. *See* Social systems of production
Pro-market argument and critique, 6-8, 14, 19, 83, 87, 127, 131-2, 213-17, 314, 439-41

Promotional network, 11-12, 111-12
Property of reactivity, 246
Public goods, 52, 73, 378
as rationale for regimes, 377-9
international, 366-9
international social goods, 368
local public goods, 367
markets and, 79
pure public goods, 366-7
regions and, 25-6

Quality assurance, 250
definition of, 251
five stages of protocol, 251-2

Rationality 8-9
bounded 441-2
critique of economic, 197-217
instrumental, 205-6, 273, 276
Reactive-distributive approach to policy making
definition, 135, 137
dynamic efficiency and, 58
evolutionary selection and, 59, 155-6
information and, 58
Recor method, 256
static efficiency and, 57-8, 71-2
Redundant capacity, 205-6, 273, 276-7
Reflexivity, 160-62, 181, 191, 204
Regimes,
international regulatory, 32, 38, 366, 386-7. *See also* Global coordination
clubs, 362
origins of, 31-32, 362, 376-83
structural failures and, 378
of quality, 247-8
of supply, 247
of synchronous Production, 255
of variety, 245-249, 253, 256, 259-60
characteristics of, 256-7
definition of, 261
of virtual production, 246
of virtual variety, 248
of zero industry, 246
origins and formation, 361-62, 366, 371, 377-82, 385
Region
as unit of analysis versus nation-state, 312-13
definition, 25
economic development, 165-67, 312-13
Maastrict Accord committee of, 408, 422
Regional coordination, 25-26, 436, 438, 465-6, 467-8, 473
Regional government, 352